Everyday Finance: Economics, Personal Money Management, and Entrepreneurship

Everyday Finance: Economics, Personal Money Management, and Entrepreneurship

VOLUME 2

GALE
CENGAGE Learning

Detroit • New York • San Francisco • New Haven, Conn • Waterville, Maine • London

GALE
CENGAGE Learning

Everyday Finance: Economics, Personal
Money Management, and
Entrepreneurship
Thomas Riggs, Editor

Product Manager: Carol Nagel

Project Editor: Mary Rose Bonk

Rights Acquisition and Management:
Margaret Chamberlain-Gaston,
Jacqueline Key, and Kelly A. Quin

Composition: Evi Abou-El-Seoud

Manufacturing: Rita Wimberley

Imaging: Lezlie Light

Product Design: Jennifer Wahi

For product information and technology assistance, contact us at
Gale Customer Support, 1-800-877-4253.
For permission to use material from this text or product,
submit all requests online at **www.cengage.com/permissions.**
Further permissions questions can be emailed to
permissionrequest@cengage.com

While every effort has been made to ensure the reliability of the information presented in this publication, Gale, a part of Cengage Learning, does not guarantee the accuracy of the data contained herein. Gale accepts no payment for listing; and inclusion in the publication of any organization, agency, institution, publication, service, or individual does not imply endorsement of the editors or publisher. Errors brought to the attention of the publisher and verified to the satisfaction of the publisher will be corrected in future editions.

Library of Congress Cataloging-in-Publication Data

Everyday finance : economics, personal money management, and entrepreneurship / editor, Thomas Riggs; project editor, Mary Rose Bonk.
    p. cm.
    Includes bibliographical references and index.
    ISBN 978-1-4144-1049-4 (set) – ISBN 978-1-4144-1123-1 (vol. 1) – ISBN 978-1-4144-1124-8 (vol. 2)
    1. Economics. 2. Finance, Personal. 3. Entrepreneurship. 4. Riggs, Thomas, 1963- 5. Bonk, Mary, 1960-

HB171.E86 2008
332.024–dc22   2007035070

Gale
27500 Drake Rd.
Farmington Hills, MI, 48331-3535

ISBN-13: 978-1-4144-1049-4 (set)   ISBN-10: 1-4144-1049-2 (set)
ISBN-13: 978-1-4144-1123-1 (vol. 1)   ISBN-10: 1-4144-1123-5 (vol. 1)
ISBN-13: 978-1-4144-1124-8 (vol. 2)   ISBN-10: 1-4144-1124-3 (vol. 2)

This title is also available as an e-book.
ISBN-13: 978-1-4144-2929-8 ISBN-10: 1-4144-2929-0
Contact your Gale sales representative for ordering information.

Printed in the United States of America
2 3 4 5 6 7 11 10 09

Contents

What Is Money?

The Economy in Action

How the Economy Is Measured

Supply and Demand: The Relationship between Businesses and Consumers

Competition between Businesses

What Motivates Businesses

Labor: The People Working in the Economy

How Governments Raise Money

Who Oversees the Economy: Government Organizations

VOLUME 2

Personal Money Management: Buying, Borrowing, Saving, and Insuring

Entrepreneurship: The World of Business

Reader's Guide

Economics has suffered a dismal and dry reputation. Supply and demand, production possibility curve, marginal utility, income and substitution effects. These are not the most alluring terms, which is unfortunate, because they describe a curious and important topic: how people behave in a world of possibilities. As such, economics helps to explain a significant part of our lives, how we make choices and manage our daily affairs with the aid of two everyday notions, money and prices.

The purpose of this book—*Everyday Finance: Economics, Personal Money Management, and Entrepreneurship*—is to introduce the field of economics, as well as its related topics personal money management and entrepreneurship, in a simple, meaningful way. It is to show that even obscure topics are based on easy-to-understand ideas and that economics, personal money management, and entrepreneurship are related to our ordinary, everyday lives. It is for this reason we chose the title *Everyday Finance*. The word *finance*, which has several meanings, is used here to describe anything related to money and the economy. *Everyday Finance* was motivated by the growing awareness in the United States that economic literacy is essential for functioning in the modern world.

To explain the world of money, *Everyday Finance* features 300 articles, organized by subject into three major sections. The first, How the Economy Works, contains essays within several broad areas: macroeconomics, describing the economy as a whole; microeconomics, focusing on individual parts or forces in the economy; international trade, or buying and selling between countries; and the government's role in the economy. Some essays relate to more than one area and were placed where they would be most useful to a person not familiar with economics.

After the first section introduces the basic ideas of economics, the second and third sections explain how people are personally involved in the economy, either as consumers or business owners. The second section, Personal Money Management, is broken down into four typical consumer roles: buying, borrowing, saving, and insuring. The third section, Entrepreneurship, discusses running a business, attracting customers, managing money, working with employees, and business ethics and the law.

Every essay in *Everyday Finance* has five parts:

1. **What It Means,** introducing the essay topic and defining any unfamiliar terms.

2. **When Did It Begin,** giving historical information helpful in understanding the subject and its significance.

3. **More Detailed Information,** explaining the topic more fully and discussing related issues.

4. **Recent Trends,** providing a glimpse into the role of the subject in the present-day economy.

5. Sidebar box, often illustrating the topic with an example or anecdote.

Everyday Finance also includes biographies on seven influential economists throughout history. The book has over 220 images, as well as nearly 50 tables, charts, and graphs; a glossary of financial terms; a further reading section; and a subject index, listing all the topics featured in the book.

Acknowledgments

This project was a collaboration between the editorial staff, writers experienced in producing educational materials, and professionals involved in teaching economics and in the development of economics curriculum. The essays topics were selected with the help of our three distinguished advisers: Robert F. Duvall, president and chief executive officer, National Council on Economic Education; Peter F. Bell, executive director, New York State Council on Economic Education; and Sue Weaver, mentor teacher, Foundation for Teaching Economics. We are grateful for their advice and support. We would also like to express our appreciation to Jeff Bookwalter, professor of economics, University of Montana, for his suggestions on the book's organization, for reviewing the essays for accuracy, and for answering our many questions big and small.

Essential to the project were the essay writers: Mark Lane, Joseph Campana, Erin Brown, Stephen Meyer, Jonathan Kolstad, and Martha Sutro. Experienced teachers and writers of educational text, they deserve praise for their hard work in accomplishing the project's main goal: presenting abstract subjects in simple, accessible prose. The editing of the text was overseen by Anne Healey; assisting her in the editing were Lee Esbenshade, Laura Gabler, Chuck Cegielski, and Catherine Okelman-Anderson. Mariko Fujinaka was involved from the very beginning of the project, working with the advisers and organizing day-to-day tasks. Anne Healey, Lee Esbenshade, and Mariko Fujinaka also contributed text. Erin Brown, as well as Stephen Meyer and Anne Healey, helped with the auxiliary parts of the book, such as the photo selection, the captions, sources for further reading, and the glossary. Martin White wrote the index.

Finally, many thanks must be given to Mary Bonk, the in-house editor at Gale, who oversaw the book's production and kept the project on schedule; Carol Nagel, involved in the development of the book's idea; and Ellen McGeagh, who was responsible for other in-house tasks.

Thomas Riggs
Editor

Comments

Although great effort has gone into this project, we would appreciate any suggestions for future editions of *Everyday Finance*. Please send comments to the following address.

Editor, *Everyday Finance: Economics, Personal Money Management, and Entrepreneurship*
Cengage Gale
27500 Drake Road
Farmington Hills, Michigan 48331

Glossary

This glossary provides brief definitions of terms commonly used in economics, personal money management, and entrepreneurship.

A

ABSOLUTE ADVANTAGE. A term used in economics to describe the ability of one country to produce a specific good more efficiently than a second country can.

ACCOUNTANT. A person whose job is to manage the financial records of an organization and to prepare various kinds of financial reports.

ACCOUNTING. The recording and disclosure of a company's financial dealings.

ACQUISITION. The process of one company overtaking or absorbing another company.

ADVERTISING. All the methods that organizations use to communicate a message to potential customers. In most cases the message informs people about an organization's product or service and urges those people to purchase it.

AGGREGATE BEHAVIOR. The total results of individual actions in an economy.

AGGREGATE DEMAND. The amount of final products that all buyers in an economy demand (are willing and able to buy) at a given average price.

AGGREGATE EXPENDITURES. The total amount spent on goods and services in a nation's economy.

AGGREGATE SUPPLY. The total quantity of all final products an economy's sellers are willing to supply at a given price level.

AMERICAN STOCK EXCHANGE (AMEX). The third-largest U.S. stock exchange; it is located in New York City.

AMERICANS WITH DISABILITIES ACT. A U.S. federal law that prohibits workplace discrimination against people with disabilities.

AMEX. *see* American Stock Exchange.

ANNUAL PERCENTAGE RATE (APR). The interest rate on a loan, expressed as the percentage charged by the lender each year on the amount of a loan.

ANNUAL REPORT. A report issued by a company and covering the company's activities for the entire year, including financial statements and other documents.

ANTITRUST LEGISLATION. A set of laws that protect consumers and society by ensuring that businesses do not unfairly dominate their individual industries (a trust is a group of companies that attempts to do this).

APPRECIATION. An increase in value.

APR. *see* annual percentage rate.

ASSETS. All items of value (including investments) owned by a person or organization.

ATM. Automated teller machine; an electronic machine at which a bank customer can withdraw cash and make deposits by inserting a plastic card.

B

BACK TAXES. Taxes from a past taxation period that have not been paid.

BAIT AND SWITCH. A deceptive marketing tactic in which a retail business advertises a bargain to lure a customer into its store and then attempts to convince the customer to buy a more expensive product instead.

BALANCE. An amount of money remaining in a checking account; or an outstanding amount owed on a bill.

BALANCE OF PAYMENTS (BOP). A financial statement that summarizes a country's international economic purchases and sales. It shows all of the international money movements, called flows, in and out of the country in a certain time period.

BALANCE OF TRADE. The difference in value, over a period of time, between a country's imports and exports.

BALANCE SHEET. A document that details a company's assets (possessions) and liabilities (debts).

BANK. An institution that holds people's money for safekeeping and lends money to individuals and businesses for a variety of reasons.

BANK RESERVES. The money that a bank keeps on hand, either in its own vaults or in an account with a central bank.

BANKRUPT. The state of being unable to pay debts, which can lead to the seizure of property and other valuable resources.

BANKRUPTCY. A process by which a debtor who is deemed unable to pay off all his or her debts seeks legal protection from his or her creditors.

BARRIERS TO ENTRY. The obstacles that discourage and sometimes prevent new companies from entering an area of business.

BARTER. To exchange goods and services directly for other goods and services.

BBB. *see* Better Business Bureau.

BEA. *see* Bureau of Economic Analysis.

BEAR MARKET. A period during which stock prices generally decrease.

BENEFICIARY. A person or entity who receives benefits under the terms of a contract (such as an insurance policy or a will).

BENEFIT PACKAGE. The terms of an employment contract, including insurance coverage and other benefits.

BENEFITS. *see* employee benefits.

BETTER BUSINESS BUREAU (BBB). A national organization that protects consumers from unethical business practices.

BILL. A printed request for money that is owed for a particular product or service.

BLACK MARKET. The illegal buying and selling of goods and services.

BLACKLIST. To add someone to a list of people whom employers agree not to hire.

BLS. *see* Bureau of Labor Statistics.

BLUE CHIP. A stock that is expensive because it represents ownership in the world's largest and most stable corporations; also, a term used to refer to such companies; so named because of the color of high-value poker chips.

BLUE-COLLAR WORKERS. People who perform manual or physical labor, often for an hourly wage.

BOARD OF DIRECTORS. A group of people who the shareholders of a public company have elected to represent them in decisions regarding the operation of the company.

BOND. A type of investment that represents money loaned to a government or corporation, in exchange for which the borrowing government or company makes periodic payments of interest to the bond holder.

BOUNCED CHECK. A check that the recipient cannot cash because the person who wrote the check does not have sufficient funds in his or her bank account.

BRAND. A symbol (such as an image, a logo, or a name) that represents a product or service and that distinguishes the product or service from others in the marketplace.

BRAND RECOGNITION. The extent to which consumers recognize a company's brand among its competitors.

BROKER. A person who is authorized to make trades on a given stock exchange.

BROKERAGE FIRM. A company that facilitates trades between buyers and sellers on the stock market.

BUBBLE. A period of unsustainable economic growth (usually in the stock market or in real estate) fueled by excess optimism on the part of companies and investors.

BUDGET DEFICIT. The imbalance created when a country spends more money than it takes in.

BUDGETING. The practice of identifying income and desired expenditures and then creating a plan for spending.

BULL MARKET. A period of sustained stock-price increases during which investors make money rapidly.

BUREAU OF COMPETITION (BOC). The antitrust division of the Federal Trade Commission; its mission is to protect healthy competition in the marketplace.

BUREAU OF CONSUMER PROTECTION (BCP). A division of the Federal Trade Commission dedicated to protecting consumers against unfair or deceptive business practices.

BUREAU OF ECONOMIC ANALYSIS (BEA). A division of the U.S. Department of Commerce that collects, analyzes, and publishes statistics about the American economy.

BUREAU OF LABOR STATISTICS (BLS). A division of the U.S. Department of Labor that collects and analyzes information about the American workforce and economy.

BUSINESS CONTRACT. Written agreements concerning specific aspects of a commercial transaction.

BUSINESS CYCLE. A cyclical pattern, common to all capitalist economies, of periods of economic expansion followed by periods of economic contraction.

BUSINESS ETHICS. The application of moral considerations to business practices.

BUSINESS FINANCING. The activity of funding the many aspects of a business, including starting a business, running it, or expanding it.

BUSINESS PLAN. A document that describes what a business is, what strategies it will use to accomplish its financial goals, and how it expects to do business as it grows, usually planning for several years into the future.

BUSINESS TAX. A tax that the government requires a business to pay.

C

CORPORATION. A traditional for-profit corporation, so called because it is taxed under Subchapter C of the United States tax code. The corporation, as a single entity, pays taxes on its profits, and then its individual stockholders are taxed on the dividends (portions of profit) they receive.

CAPITAL. Money, buildings, equipment, and other items needed to start, maintain, or expand a business.

CAPITAL ACCOUNT. *see* financial account.

CAPITAL ASSETS. A financial term that refers to everything a person owns for both personal use and investment, such as homes, cars, jewelry, computers, household furnishings, and stocks and bonds (investments).

CAPITAL GAIN. A term used in the filing of income taxes, referring to the profit made when the value of a capital asset increases from its original purchase price; such gains are taxed at a different rate from regular income.

CAPITAL LOSS. A term used in assessing income taxes that refers to the amount of money lost when the value of a capital asset decreases from its original purchase price.

CAPITALISM. An economic system in which businesses are owned by private individuals who are allowed to compete freely in the pursuit of profits.

CAR INSURANCE. A contract between an insurance company and the owner of a vehicle that protects the vehicle's owner (or the person who leases the vehicle) from financial losses that result from car accidents.

CARTEL. An association of companies or nations that collaborate to control the market for a product by fixing prices, setting production quotas, and regulating market share.

CASH. The banknotes (bills) and coins used as money and accepted as legal tender (currency) in a society.

CASH A CHECK. To receive the funds specified on a check.

CASH COST. An amount of money that a business pays out to someone.

CASH FLOW. The movement of ready money, or cash, into and out of a company over a specified period of time.

CASHIER'S CHECK. A type of prepaid check issued by a bank that a customer may purchase in a specific amount in order to make a payment to a third party. Also referred to as a bank check, bank draft, or treasurer's check.

CD. *see* certificate of deposit.

CENTRAL BANK. A government entity responsible for setting a country's monetary policy.

CERTIFICATE OF DEPOSIT (CD). An investment offered by banks, savings and loan associations, and credit unions. The customer deposits money with the institution and agrees not to make any withdrawals on the money for a fixed amount of time; in exchange the customer earns interest on the deposit, called the maturity period.

CERTIFIED PUBLIC ACCOUNTANT (CPA). A public accountant (that is, one who provides information to members of the public rather than working within a single company) licensed by a U.S. state to practice there.

CETERIS PARIBUS. A Latin phrase that translates as "all other things being equal"; economists often use it to indicate that their analysis of a certain situation is based on the assumption that all other things besides the factors under consideration will remain constant.

CHANNEL OF DISTRIBUTION. The path a product takes as it moves from producer to end user (the consumer).

CHAPTER 11. A type of bankruptcy defined by the U.S. Bankruptcy Code; it allows a company to remain in business while the court decides how best to reorganize its debts.

CHARACTER LOAN. A loan based on the personal reputation, as well as credit rating, of the borrower.

CHARGE CARD. A kind of electronic-payment card that enables its holder to make purchases on short-term credit granted by the issuer of the card. Unlike a credit card, a charge card offers nonrevolving credit, meaning that the balance must be paid off in full each month.

CHARITY. An organization or fund that is established with the sole purpose of providing help or relief to people in need.

CHARTER. In business, a formal document legally establishing a company or organization as a corporation. Also called articles of incorporation.

CHECK. A paper form used to transfer money out of a bank account.

CHECK-CASHING ORGANIZATION. *see* check-cashing store.

CHECK-CASHING STORE. A business that cashes personal, payroll, and government checks for a fee. Also called a check-cashing organization.

CHECKING ACCOUNT. An account that an individual establishes at a financial institution that enables him or her to use forms called checks to transfer a specified amount of money to designated individuals or organizations.

CIRCULAR FLOW OF ECONOMIC ACTIVITY. An economic model illustrating the interaction between businesses and households in an economy, showing money and products moving in a circular fashion between the two.

CLAIM. A customer's formal request for reimbursement from an insurance company.

CLASS-ACTION LAWSUIT. A lawsuit that represents a large number of plaintiffs.

CLASSICAL ECONOMICS. The ideas of the first wave of modern economists, whose work spanned the late eighteenth century and much of the nineteenth century.

CLOSING COSTS. Fees for the various transactions that occur when a person buying a house has the property legally transferred to his or her name.

COBRA (CONSOLIDATED OMNIBUS BUDGET RECONCILIATION ACT). A U.S. federal law requiring group health-insurance plans sponsored by employers with 20 or more employees to offer continued health-insurance coverage to workers after they leave their jobs.

COLA. *see* Cost-of-Living Adjustment.

COLLATERAL. Any item or items of value that someone offers as proof of his ability to repay a loan, with the understanding that it will be forfeited to the lender if the loan cannot be repaid.

COLLECTION AGENCY. A business that specializes in collecting money owed to other companies.

COLLECTIVE BARGAINING AGREEMENT. An official agreement between a labor union and management regarding the specific terms of employment.

COLLISION INSURANCE. A form of car insurance that covers the policyholder's vehicle in the event of an accident in which he or she is determined to be at fault.

COLONIALISM. The practice by which nations create settlements, or colonies, in poorer countries for the purpose of exploiting their natural resources and labor force.

COMMAND ECONOMY. *see* planned economy.

COMMERCIAL BANK. A type of bank that has traditionally focused on short-term accounts and issuing business loans; can also mean a normal bank (as opposed to an investment bank).

COMMODITIES. Large amounts of bulk goods, such as crude oil, metals, sugar, coffee, and wheat, that investors buy and sell through agencies such as the New York Mercantile Exchange.

COMMON STOCK. The most common form of ownership in a company; its holders have the right to vote directly on matters related to the functioning of the company and receive dividends (shares in the company's profits) after the holders of preferred stock are paid.

COMMUNISM. A system in which the government controls the economy.

COMPARATIVE ADVANTAGE. An economic theory stating that two countries will maximize their profits by specializing and trading with each other, even if one has the ability to produce all goods more efficiently than the other.

COMPLEMENTARY GOOD. A product that is often bought in combination with, or consumed at the same time as, another good.

COMPREHENSIVE INSURANCE. A type of car insurance that covers damages to the policyholder's vehicle caused by incidents that are not considered to be collisions.

CONSOLIDATE. To combine a number of debts into one larger loan.

CONSUMER BILL OF RIGHTS. A set of U.S. regulations that protect consumers from hazards in the products they purchase and from misleading information about products. These regulations also provide support for consumers in instances when a product fails, breaks, or is faulty.

CONSUMER CREDIT PROTECTION ACT (CCPA). A consumer-protection law in the United States aimed at regulating the consumer credit industry.

CONSUMER PRICE INDEX (CPI). An index compiled by the Bureau of Labor Statistics that tracks the changing price of basic goods and services in the United States.

CONSUMER PRODUCT SAFETY COMMISSION (CPSC). An independent agency of the U.S. government whose mission is to protect the American public from unreasonable or significant risks of injury or death associated with consumer products.

CONSUMER SOVEREIGNTY. A term used by economists who argue that consumers dictate what goods and services are available in the market because producers respond to consumer buying patterns.

CONSUMER SURPLUS. The amount of money left over when a consumer is charged less for a good than he or she is willing to pay.

CONSUMPTION. In economics, a term that refers to how much money all consumers are spending on goods and services.

CO-PAYMENT. A portion of each medical or dental expense for which an insured patient is responsible.

COPYRIGHT. The legal right of an artist or writer to control the reproduction, distribution, display, performance, or circulation of his or her work.

CORE COMPETENCE. The centering of a business around the strengths that could give it an advantage over its competitors.

CORPORATE TAX REPORTING. The process by which corporations report their financial information to state and federal tax agencies.

CORPORATION. A kind of company that sells stocks (certificates that represent shares of ownership in the business) and that has a legal identity independent from the people who own or manage it.

COST OF LIVING. The amount of money required to maintain a certain basic level of material comfort from one year to the next.

COST-BENEFIT ANALYSIS. A method of comparing the positive and negative effects of a project, a decision, or another business venture that an organization is considering.

COST-OF-LIVING ADJUSTMENT (COLA). An annual adjustment of wage contracts, retirement benefits, and other payments; it is intended to offset increases in the cost of living.

COSTS OF PRODUCTION. The expenses to which a company is subject as it goes through the process of generating, selling, and delivering goods and services to consumers.

COUPON. The detachable portion of a bond (a type of investment) that the bond holder presents to receive the interest payment; can also mean a bond's interest rate.

CPA. *see* certified public accountant.

CPI. *see* Consumer Price Index.

CPSC. *see* Consumer Product Safety Commission.

CREDIT. In general terms, the capacity to borrow money; also, the maximum amount of money a lender is willing to lend to a customer.

CREDIT BUREAU. A for-profit company that evaluates and ranks the credit, or financial reputation, of individuals. Also called a credit-reporting agency.

CREDIT CARD. An electronic-payment card that allows the cardholder to make purchases on credit and pay for them at a later date.

CREDIT COUNSELING. A process in which a credit-counseling agency helps a debtor (a person in debt) make payments to his creditors (institutions, such as credit card companies and banks, to which a debtor owes money). Credit counseling is aimed at helping people avoid bankruptcy.

CREDIT HISTORY. A person's past borrowing and repayment behavior.

CREDIT INSURANCE. Protects businesses against loss when customers fail to pay the amounts they owe.

CREDIT LIMIT. The maximum amount a cardholder is allowed to charge to his or her card.

CREDIT REPORT. A detailed outline of a person's credit history (produced by a credit bureau) that lenders review to assess how financially responsible he or she is.

CREDIT SCORE. A numerical figure, calculated by a credit bureau based on a person's credit history, that is used to predict the likelihood that the individual will not adhere to the terms of a loan agreement.

CREDIT UNION. A nonprofit, member-owned financial institution that provides some of the same financial services as a bank.

CREDIT-COUNSELING AGENCY. An agency that helps people who owe money make a plan to pay off their debts.

CREDITOR. A person or institution to whom borrowed money is owed.

CREDIT-REPAIR COMPANY. A company that helps consumers get out of debt and restore their financial reputations.

CURRENCY. Bills and coins issued by a government.

CURRENCY EXCHANGE. The conversion of one country's currency to another's.

CURRENT ACCOUNT. The section of a balance-of-payments account that shows the financial transactions of imported and exported goods and services.

CUSTOMER SATISFACTION. A measure of how well a customer's expectations have been met by the product or service provided by a particular company.

CUSTOMER SERVICE. The term for building a relationship with customers and making this relationship a high priority for the business.

D

DAY TRADING. The buying and selling of high-risk stock in the same day.

DEBIT CARD. An electronic-payment card that withdraws funds directly from a personal bank account.

DEBT. Money owed by one person, company, or institution to another person, company, or institution.

DEBT CONSOLIDATION LOAN. One big loan that a borrower takes out in order to pay off a number of smaller debts.

DEBTOR. Anyone who borrows money and agrees to pay it back.

DEBT-TO-INCOME RATIO. The percentage of a consumer's monthly income that goes toward paying off credit card debt, student loans, and other debts.

DEDUCTIBLE. An agreed-upon amount of money that an insured person has to pay before the insurance company makes its contribution.

DEDUCTION. A sum that is deducted from a taxpayer's total, or gross, annual income, thereby reducing the amount of their income that can be taxed.

DEEDS OF PROPERTY. Documents showing proof of ownership of property.

DEFAULT. To fail to repay a loan or to keep to the terms of the loan agreement.

DEFICIT. The amount by which a government or business's expenditures exceed its income.

DEFICIT SPENDING. Government spending using borrowed money.

DEFLATION. A general fall in the prices of goods and services in an economy over an extended period of time; the opposite of inflation.

DEMAND. The amount of a particular good or service that buyers are willing or able to buy over a range of prices.

DENTAL INSURANCE. A plan designed to make dental care more affordable.

DEPARTMENT OF COMMERCE. *see* United States Department of Commerce.

DEPARTMENT OF LABOR. *see* United States Department of Labor.

DEPENDENT. A spouse, children, elderly parent, or other person whom a taxpayer financially supports.

DEPRECIATION. The decline in value of an asset over time.

DEPRECIATION TAX LAWS. Provisions that allow a business to count the depreciation of its aging assets (usually equipment) as a business loss. It subtracts from its taxable income certain amounts that represent the decrease in the value of its equipment, or assets.

DEPRESSION. A particularly long and severe recession (economic crisis).

DEPRESSION. *see* Great Depression.

DEREGULATION. The removal of government restrictions.

DERIVATIVE. A financial product whose value is based on (derived from) the performance of other financial products (one example would be a contract to buy a certain number of shares of a particular stock at a specific future date).

DEVELOPED COUNTRY. A fully modernized country with a high average income per citizen, high quality of life, and skilled labor force. Also referred to as an industrialized country or a First World country.

DEVELOPING COUNTRY. A country characterized by low per capita income, widespread poverty, and an undeveloped economic infrastructure; it typically has an economy based not on industry but on agriculture or extracting natural resources such as metals or coal. Sometimes referred to as a Third World country.

DIRECT DEPOSIT. A method of payment by which an employer deposits paychecks into employees' bank accounts electronically.

DIRECT MAILING. Marketing messages sent directly to consumers via the mail system.

DIRECT MARKETING. A specialized form of marketing in which promotional messages are delivered to a target population of people who have been identified as potential customers.

DISABILITY INSURANCE. An insurance plan that replaces a portion of a person's income when he or she cannot work because of an accident or illness.

DISCOUNT RATE. The interest rate that the Federal Reserve charges member banks to borrow money.

DISINFLATION. A slowdown in the rate of inflation.

DISPOSABLE INCOME. The amount of a person's income remaining after the deduction of taxes.

DISTRIBUTION. The movement of products from manufacturers to sales outlets to customers.

DISTRIBUTION OF INCOME. The way all the money earned in a nation is divided among people of various income levels.

DIVIDENDS. Portions of a company's profit that are distributed to its stockholders on a regular basis; the size of the dividend is calculated by taking the accumulated earnings the company chooses to distribute and dividing that amount by the number of shares held by the shareholder.

DIVISION OF LABOR. A method of producing goods or providing services whereby a job is split into separate, distinct tasks or roles, each of which is performed by one person or group of people. Also called specialization.

DOMESTIC. Based in the home country.

DOT-COM. A business that sells goods and services exclusively on the Internet.

DOUBLE-ENTRY ACCOUNTING. An accounting method in which each transaction is shown as a transfer from a source account (as a debit) to a destination account (as a credit).

DOW JONES INDUSTRIAL AVERAGE. A statistic that conveys the combined stock prices of the 30 top companies in the country; it is the figure most frequently used to measure the performance of the U.S. stock market.

DOWN PAYMENT. A portion of a product's price that is paid at the time of purchase, with the rest to be paid later.

DOWNSIZING. A strategy by which a company reduces its workforce and simplifies its business model in order to run its business more efficiently.

DUOPOLY. A situation in which two companies control a market for a particular good or service.

DURABLE GOODS. Goods that may be used repeatedly for a year or more (for example, wood products and computers).

DUTY. A tax on imports.

E

EARNED INCOME TAX CREDIT (EITC). A tax provision that reduces and in some cases eliminates the income taxes that the working poor pay in the United States, allowing people with low incomes to keep more of their earnings.

E-COMMERCE. The buying and selling of goods over the Internet.

ECONOMIC CONTRACTION. A period during which the economy slows down and fewer goods and services are sold.

ECONOMIC DEVELOPMENT. The transformation of a simple, stagnant national economy into a complex, dynamic one.

ECONOMIC GROWTH. An increase in the total value of goods and services produced by a country's economic system.

ECONOMIC INDICATOR. A statistic that reflects the health of the economy.

ECONOMIC INPUTS. The resources, such as land, raw materials, equipment, and labor, that are used to produce goods and services.

ECONOMIC LEGISLATION. Laws that regulate the affairs of private businesses with the intent of protecting consumers, small businesses, and the overall health of the economy.

ECONOMIC RENT. In modern economics, a term referring to the income generated by an asset over and above its "next best use."

ECONOMIC SHORTAGE. A situation in which sellers do not make enough of a product to satisfy those who want to buy it at a given price.

ECONOMIC SURPLUS. A general term for the monetary gain enjoyed by both producers and consumers in an economic transaction. For producers a surplus occurs when a product is sold for more than the cost of producing it; for consumers a surplus exists when they are able to purchase a product for less money than they would have been willing to pay for it.

ECONOMIES OF SCALE. An economic principle stating that when a company increases its output, its cost per unit will decrease.

EFFICIENCY. In economics, the ratio of the value of the output (goods produced or services performed) to the input (costs of production). A business is considered to be operating at optimal efficiency if it produces the greatest number of goods possible at the lowest possible cost.

ELASTICITY OF DEMAND. The degree to which price changes affect consumers' demand for a particular product; when the consumer reaction is strong, the demand for the product is said to be elastic (flexible), and when it is small, the demand is said to be inelastic (fixed).

ELECTRONIC BANKING. A form of banking in which funds are transferred through an exchange of electronic signals rather than through an exchange of cash, checks, or other types of paper documents.

ELECTRONIC BENEFIT TRANSFER (EBT) CARD. An electronic-payment card used in place of traditional paper food stamps.

ELECTRONIC FUNDS TRANSFER (EFT). Any financial transaction that originates from a telephone, electronic terminal, computer, or magnetic tape.

EMPLOYEE BENEFITS. The compensation an employee receives in addition to an hourly wage or annual salary. Common benefits include health insurance and vacation pay. Also called fringe benefits.

EMPLOYEE TURNOVER. The rate at which workers leave a company and are replaced.

EMPLOYMENT. In economics, the number of people in a country who are employed versus the country's entire labor force.

EMPLOYMENT AGENCY. A company that helps employers find employees in exchange for a fee.

ENTREPRENEUR. An individual who founds, owns, and manages his or her own businesses.

ENTREPRENEURSHIP. The practice of forming a new business or commercial enterprise, often in an industry or sector of the economy with a large capacity for growth.

EQUAL CREDIT OPPORTUNITY ACT. A U.S. law that prohibits credit lenders from discriminating against applicants on the basis of sex, race, age, marital status, religion, or national origin.

EQUAL EMPLOYMENT OPPORTUNITY COMMISSION (EEOC). The U.S. federal agency that investigates situations in which individuals claim they have been subject to discriminatory treatment in matters of employment.

EQUAL OPPORTUNITY. Providing every citizen with an equal chance of obtaining an education and a job and of being treated fairly on the job and in life generally. Most commonly used to refer to a company or organization's hiring and business practices.

EQUITY. The value of a mortgaged property minus the outstanding balance, or what the borrower still owes on the loan.

ERGONOMICS. The science of designing tools, machines, and work environments that allow people to perform tasks comfortably, safely, productively, and efficiently.

ESCROW. Money or property that will be transferred from one party to another but is held by a third party until the conditions of the transfer have been met.

ESTATE. The assets in a person's possession at the time of his or her death.

ESTATE TAX. In the United States, a tax on the right to transfer a deceased person's property to descendents. It is charged as a percentage of the total value of all the property owned by the deceased person.

EXCESS RESERVES. Any money in a bank beyond the amount that it is legally required to have on hand; this money can be used to make loans.

EXCHANGE RATE. The value of one country's currency expressed in terms of another country's currency.

EXCISE TAX. A fee charged by the government on specific goods or services that are purchased by some, but not all, consumers.

EXECUTIVE OFFICERS. The individuals who oversee the operational management of a company.

EXECUTOR. The person assigned the duty of carrying out the instructions contained in a will.

EXPECTED FAMILY CONTRIBUTION (EFC). The dollar amount the government determines that a family can contribute toward its child's expenses for college that year.

EXPENDITURE. An amount of money spent.

EXPENSE ACCOUNT. An allowance of funds allotted to an employee for business-related travel, dining, and entertainment.

EXPENSES. The money that a company spends in the course of doing business.

EXPLICIT COST. A measurement of the money sacrificed through actual payments for a particular economic choice. Compare with implicit cost.

EXPORTS. Goods and services that are produced or manufactured in one country and sent legally across borders for sale in another country.

EXTENDED WARRANTY. A plan that continues the manufacturer's warranty for a longer time period.

EXTERNALITY. A side effect of any market activity (an activity related to the buying and selling of goods and services) that either harms or benefits a third party not involved in that particular activity.

F

FACTORS OF PRODUCTION. In economics, all the resources required to produce goods and services. The three primary factors of production are land (including physical land and any natural resources such as oil or lumber needed in their operations), labor, and capital (money and equipment).

FAFSA. *see* Free Application for Federal Student Aid.

FAIR AND ACCURATE CREDIT TRANSACTIONS ACT. A U.S. law aimed at protecting consumers against identity theft; it stipulates that individuals must be able to obtain a free copy of their credit report from each of the major credit bureaus annually. The act also makes it possible for an individual to place a fraud alert on his or her credit history if he or she suspects that someone has stolen his or her identity.

FAIR CREDIT REPORTING ACT. A U.S. law that ensures the accuracy, privacy, and fairness of consumer credit files by imposing regulations on the credit-reporting industry.

FAIR DEBT COLLECTION PRACTICES ACT. A U.S. law that prohibits abusive, deceptive, and unfair debt-collection tactics.

FDA. *see* Food and Drug Administration.

FDIC. *see* Federal Deposit Insurance Corporation.

FEDERAL DEPOSIT INSURANCE CORPORATION (FDIC). An independent agency of the U.S. government whose mission is to maintain and strengthen public confidence in the American financial system. It does this by insuring (guaranteeing) deposits in banks and thrift institutions (which include savings banks, savings and loan associations, and credit unions) for up to $100,000 per depositor.

FEDERAL FUNDS RATE. The interest rate (fee expressed as a percentage of the loan amount) that banks charge one another to borrow money.

FEDERAL INSURANCE CONTRIBUTIONS ACT (FICA) TAX. *see* Social Security tax.

FEDERAL OPEN MARKET COMMITTEE (FOMC). A committee within the Federal Reserve System that is responsible for deciding whether the U.S. money supply should be increased, decreased, or kept constant, depending on economic conditions at the time.

FEDERAL RESERVE BOARD. The seven-member committee that oversees the Federal Reserve, the central banking system of the United States.

FEDERAL RESERVE SYSTEM. The central bank of the United States, an independent agency of the U.S. government. Often called "the Fed."

FEDERAL TRADE COMMISSION (FTC). An independent agency of the U.S. government that guards against business practices that interfere with competition in the marketplace and that protects American consumers from various kinds of fraud and deception.

FICA TAX. *see* Social Security tax.

FICO. The most widely used credit-scoring system, named after the company that developed the score, the Fair Isaac Corporation.

FINAL PRODUCTS. Products sold to their final buyer, rather than products sold in raw or intermediate forms and made into other products.

FINANCE CHARGE. The amount a customer is charged for the use of credit (interest fees plus any additional fees).

FINANCE COMPANY. An organization that makes loans to individuals and businesses. Unlike a bank, it does not receive cash deposits from clients, nor does it provide some other services common to banks, such as checking accounts.

FINANCIAL ACCOUNT. In balance-of-payment accounting, the financial account shows the transactions involving the purchase or sale of assets (including investments, loans, and currencies). Also called a capital account.

FINANCIAL AID. Monetary assistance for students pursuing a higher education; it includes loans, scholarships, and grants.

FINANCIAL MARKETS. Places, some real and some computerized, where people can buy and sell stocks (shares of ownership in a company) and bonds (shares of governmental and other types of debt).

FINANCIAL STATEMENTS. Documents that provide details about a company's performance and well-being over a given period of time.

FISCAL POLICY. The government strategy of influencing the nation's economy through alterations to tax rates and spending programs.

FIXED ASSETS. Tangible pieces of property, such as buildings or equipment, that a business keeps for long-term use. Also known as long-term assets.

FIXED COST. A production cost that does not change as the level of production activity varies. Examples include rent paid for office or factory space and the costs paid for insurance.

FIXED INCOME. Income payments that are set at a certain amount.

FOMC. *see* Federal Open Market Committee.

FOOD AND DRUG ADMINISTRATION (FDA). An agency within the U.S. Department of Health and Human Services that is responsible for protecting public health by guaranteeing the safety and effectiveness of foods, drugs, biological products (such as vaccines), cosmetics, and products that emit radiation.

FOOD STAMP. A coupon, issued by the U.S. government to low-income families, that can be redeemed for food.

FORECLOSURE. A legal process by which a bank takes possession of a property because the buyer of the property is no longer able to make payments on the loan he or she took out to purchase it.

FOREIGN AID. Money and other assistance that one nation gives to another.

FOREIGN DIRECT INVESTMENT (FDI). A company's investment of money or other resources in business activities outside its home country.

FOREIGN EXCHANGE. The exchange of one nation's currency for the currency of another nation.

FOREIGN EXCHANGE MARKET. A financial market for the buying and selling of currency, consisting of a worldwide network of brokers (agents who arrange purchases and sales) and banks. Also called the FX market.

FOREIGN WORKER. A person who travels to another country looking for work, usually in agriculture, and returns home or moves on to another country or region when the job is done. Also known as a migrant worker.

FRACTIONAL-RESERVE BANKING. A system in which banks keep cash on hand equal to only a fraction of the deposits they take in.

FRANCHISE. A license allowing one party, the franchisee, to use the brand name and business processes already developed by a parent company, the franchisor.

FREE APPLICATION FOR FEDERAL STUDENT AID (FAFSA). An application that a college student (or incoming student) in the United States uses to request financial aid from the federal government.

FREE MARKET. An economic system in which goods and services are bought and sold, with competition determining the prices.

FREE TRADE. The reduction or elimination of restrictions on goods traded across national borders or countries.

FREE TRADE ZONE. An area of a country where goods from foreign nations are not subject to normal export and import laws. Products may be shipped to free trade zones in a country without being subject to tariffs, quotas, or other restrictions. Products may be assembled, repackaged, refinished, or even manufactured there but not sold to consumers.

FREE-RIDER. A person who chooses not to contribute to or pay for a public good because he will benefit from that product or service whether or not he pays for it.

FRINGE BENEFITS. *see* employee benefits.

FTC. *see* Federal Trade Commission.

FULL-TIME EMPLOYEES. Those employees who work at least a standard number of hours per week (usually 40).

G

G8. *see* Group of Eight.

GAME THEORY. A branch of mathematics used to study real-world situations (especially economic decisions) in which two or more people make choices that affect one another. In such situations, each participant must take the other participant's potential decisions into account in order to make his or her own decisions.

GDP. *see* gross domestic product.

GENERAL PARTNERSHIP. A business partnership in which all the owners (partners) share in the financial profits and losses and share the liability for all debts.

GIFT CARD. A plastic, electronic version of the old paper gift certificate. It contains a computer microchip that stores a set value according to how much the giver spent to purchase the card.

GIFT CERTIFICATE. A voucher worth a certain amount of money that can be spent on products or services at the commercial establishment that issued it.

GLOBALIZATION. A process involving the merging of economies, governmental policies, political movements, and cultures around the world.

GNP. *see* gross national product.

GOVERNMENT FAILURE. A term used by economists to describe a situation in which a government's interventions in an economy make the economy less efficient or create new problems.

GOVERNMENT-GRANTED MONOPOLY. A legal form of monopoly in which the government grants one individual or corporation the right to be the sole provider of a good or service.

GRANT. Sum of money given for a specific purpose with no requirement that it be repaid.

GREAT DEPRESSION. A period of severe financial decline in North America and Europe that began in 1929 and lasted until about 1939.

GROSS DOMESTIC PRODUCT (GDP). The total value of all finished goods and services produced in a country in a given time period. More simply, it is a measure of the total size of an economy.

GROSS INCOME. The amount of a person's income before taxes are calculated.

GROSS NATIONAL PRODUCT (GNP). The total value of all the goods and services produced in a country during a specific period of time. GNP is similar to gross domestic product (GDP), except that it includes income the country's citizens make from foreign investments.

GROUP OF EIGHT (G8). An alliance of eight of the world's largest industrialized democratic nations that is dedicated to discussing major political and economic issues.

GUARANTOR. A person who agrees to assume responsibility for someone else's debts in the event that he or she fails to repay them.

GUILD. An association of workers involved with the same trade.

H

HEALTH INSURANCE. *see* medical insurance.

HEALTH MAINTENANCE ORGANIZATION. *see* HMO.

HEDGE FUND. A business that pools money together, typically from very wealthy people with experience in the financial world, and invests it in a wider variety of ways than more traditional investment firms do.

HEIR. A person who inherits property from a deceased person.

HMO (HEALTH MAINTENANCE ORGANIZATION). An organization in the United States that provides a specialized form of health insurance for a prepaid monthly fee. To receive reimbursement, subscribers to such plans must use doctors, hospitals, clinics, and other facilities and providers affiliated with the HMO.

HOME EQUITY LOAN. A form of loan in which the borrower uses his or her house as collateral to secure the loan. Also referred to as a second mortgage.

HOME INSURANCE. A contract between an insurance company and a homeowner that protects the homeowner from financial losses that can result from damages to his dwelling and to the possessions stored in it.

HOME LOAN. A loan that a person receives from a financial institution (such as a bank) to buy a house or apartment, with the house serving as security in the event that the homeowner fails to repay the loan. Often referred to as a mortgage.

HUMAN RESOURCES. The department in a company that is responsible for hiring and managing employees.

HYPERINFLATION. A drastic rise in prices across an economy.

I

IDENTITY THEFT. The act of stealing a person's identifying information and carrying out financial transactions in the victim's name.

IMF. *see* International Monetary Fund.

IMPLICIT COST. The value of anything (other than direct payment, which is the explicit cost) that is sacrificed in making an economic decision.

IMPORT QUOTA. A government-imposed limit on the quantity of a particular good or services that may be imported over a specified period of time.

IMPORTS. Foreign-manufactured goods and services that are brought into a country for sale.

INCOME. The money that an individual or businesses takes in during a given period as a result of work or investments.

INCOME EFFECT. An economic principle, used in the study of consumer behavior, stating that if a person has more money to spend, that person will purchase more goods.

INCOME STATEMENT. A report detailing a company's earnings and expenses.

INCOME TAXES. Taxes levied on the earnings that individuals and businesses make each year.

INCORPORATION. The process of forming a legal corporation.

INDEPENDENT CONTRACTOR. A person or company that works for another person or company without being a regular employee.

INDEX FUND. A bundle of investments composed of the same list of companies that make up a major stock market index (such as the S&P 500) and that will therefore mirror the financial performance of that index.

INDEX OF LEADING ECONOMIC INDICATORS. A system of evaluating the strength of the economy by monitoring statistics about the performance levels of 10 sectors of the economy and then combining the statistics into a single composite figure, or index, which is announced monthly.

INDIVIDUAL RETIREMENT ACCOUNT (IRA). An investment savings account that allows an individual to set aside money each year until he or she retires, when the individual can begin withdrawing money from the account. The account's gains are not taxed until that time.

INDUSTRIAL. Related to large-scale manufacturing.

INDUSTRIALIZED COUNTRY. *see* developed country.

INDUSTRIALIZED ECONOMY. An economy based on technology and manufacturing.

INELASTIC. Less sensitive to price changes; when a price change of a product does not have a strong effect on the demand for it, the demand is said to be inelastic (fixed).

INFLATION. The rising of prices across the economy, which can cause currency to lose value.

INFLATION RATE. The average percentage increase in the price of all goods and services in the economy.

INHERITANCE TAX. A tax on the portion of an estate an individual receives from a deceased person. It is calculated as a percentage of the amount that the heir receives.

INITIAL PUBLIC OFFERING (IPO). A process by which the public is given its first opportunity to purchase ownership in a previously private company.

INPUT. Any resource used to make a good or service.

INSIDER TRADING. The purchase or sale of a company's stocks, bonds, or mutual funds by a company insider; it is illegal if the insider is using information unavailable to the general public.

INSOLVENT. Unable to pay debts.

INSURANCE. An agreement that guarantees an individual, company, or other entity against the loss of money; it is provided to customers by an insurance company in exchange for regular payments.

INTELLECTUAL PROPERTY. Ideas or creative works that can be legally protected by copyrights, patents, or trademarks so that only the creator of the idea or work has the right to profit from it.

INTEREST. Fees paid to a lender by a borrower; its rate is usually a percentage of the loan amount.

INTEREST INCOME. Money earned on savings accounts.

INTERNAL REVENUE SERVICE (IRS). A bureau within the U.S. Department of the Treasury that is responsible for assessing and collecting most types of taxes owed by individual citizens and businesses.

INTERNATIONAL BANK FOR RECONSTRUCTION AND DEVELOPMENT (IBRD). The agency of the World Bank that offers loans to middle-income countries that have the means to repay such loans.

INTERNATIONAL DEVELOPMENT ASSOCIATION (IDA). The agency of the World Bank that is responsible for providing economic assistance and supervision to the world's poorest countries, which would not otherwise qualify for loans.

INTERNATIONAL LABOR ISSUES. A term used to refer to violations of workers' rights that recur consistently throughout the world.

INTERNATIONAL LABOR ORGANIZATION (ILO). The agency within the United Nations that seeks to secure rights for all workers.

INTERNATIONAL MONETARY FUND (IMF). A specialized agency of the United Nations that helps shape economic policies related to international trade, debt, and the exchange of money among participating countries.

INTERNATIONAL TRADE. Any legal exchange of goods and services between countries.

INTRA-INDUSTRY TRADE. The exchange of goods within the same industry.

INTRASTATE COMMERCE. Business transactions that occur between two or more U.S. states.

INVENTORY CONTROL. The tasks and activities related to the maintenance of a company's inventory (raw materials, unfinished products, and finished products that it still has on hand).

INVESTMENT. The spending of money by individuals, companies, and governments in order to make an economy grow.

INVESTMENT BANK. A bank that focuses on the buying and selling of stocks, bonds, and other securities in the financial markets.

INVESTMENT MANAGEMENT. The activity of overseeing and making decisions regarding the investments of an individual, company, or other institution.

IPO. *see* initial public offering.

IRA. *see* Individual Retirement Account.

IRS. *see* Internal Revenue Service.

ITEMIZE DEDUCTIONS. To list on a tax return (a report of one's annual income) each expense that will be exempt from taxation.

J

JOB APPLICATION. A questionnaire provided by an employer to every applicant for a given position; it creates a basic profile of a job candidate, including his or her contact information, level of education, previous employment history, and relevant skills.

JUMBO CD. *see* negotiable CD.

JUNK BOND. A bond issued by an unproven company or a company experiencing financial problems. In exchange for accepting the high risk of not being paid, purchasers of junk bonds are offered high interest rates. Also called a high-yield bond.

K

KEYNESIAN ECONOMICS. A school of thought based on the ideas of the twentieth-century British economist John Maynard Keynes. It emphasizes a balance between the private sector's freedom to conduct business and the government's role as a stabilizing force in the economy.

L

LABOR. In terms of the factors of production, labor refers to the supply of workers needed to produce goods and services as well as the abilities and skills that they are required to have.

LABOR FORCE. All the people in a country who are economically active during a given time period.

LABOR LAWS. Laws regulating employer-employee relationships.

LABOR MANAGEMENT. The process of planning which workers will take on which tasks, how workers will be organized, and who will supervise and direct them.

LABOR THEORY OF VALUE. The idea, upheld by the classical economists of the eighteenth and nineteenth centuries, that the value of a good or service results from the sum of the labor that went into producing it.

LABOR UNION. A group of workers who have joined together to negotiate with employers in order to bargain for better wages, benefits, and working conditions.

LAISSEZ-FAIRE ECONOMICS. The idea that society is best served when government has only minimal involvement in the economy.

LAW OF DEMAND. An economic principle holding that, all other factors being constant, buyers will purchase less and less of a particular product as prices for that product rise.

LAW OF DIMINISHING RETURNS. An economic idea that when one input in the production process is increased while the others are held steady, there will eventually be a point at which the increases in output per worker will begin to diminish.

LAW OF SUPPLY. An economic principle stating that, all other factors being constant, sellers will be willing to sell more and more of a particular product as prices for that product rise.

LEASE. A contract that grants someone the right to use a certain piece of property for a specific duration in exchange for a regular fee.

LEASING A CAR. A process by which a consumer pays for the right to drive a new car for a set length of time without actually purchasing it.

LEGAL TENDER. The currency (units of exchange) that by law cannot be refused in the settlement of a debt.

LEVY. To charge or collect a tax.

LIABILITIES. Debts that a company takes on as it conducts business.

LIABILITY. The responsibility that a company takes for damage or harm caused by its product.

LIABILITY INSURANCE. A type of insurance that covers bodily injury to others and damages to other people's property.

LIFE INSURANCE. A legal agreement between an insurance agency and the policyholder, according to which the agency agrees to pay a predetermined amount of money to a person or to a group of people, such as the insured's family, upon the death of the policyholder.

LIMITED LIABILITY COMPANY (LLC). A category of company that combines aspects of partnerships and corporations. As with a partnership, the owners have the freedom to choose how to split their profits among themselves. Unlike a partnership, however, an LLC is a legally separate entity, meaning its owners cannot be held personally liable (responsible) for the company's debts.

LIMITED PARTNERSHIP. A business partnership in which one or more of the owners (called the general partners) run the business and have unlimited liability, or are held entirely responsible for the business's debts. The limited partners, by contrast, invest in the business and have only limited personal liability for the debts.

LINE OF CREDIT. A form of loan, according to which a bank or other financial institution grants a consumer permission to spend up to a preapproved limit of money, with the understanding that he or she will pay it back over time.

LIQUID. Able to be converted into cash easily.

LIQUIDATE. To convert assets into cash.

LLC. *see* limited liability company.

LOAN. A sum of money borrowed by a corporation, individual consumer, or other entity.

LOBBY. To try to influence politicians to support, oppose, or modify certain legislation, according to the interests of the lobbying party (such as a particular industry or an organization).

LONG-TERM CAPITAL ASSETS. Assets that an investor has owned for more than a year (a distinction made in calculating capital-gains tax in the United States; gains on long-term assets are taxed at a lower rate than regular income).

M

M1. One of a variety of definitions of the U.S. money supply. It is the narrowest definition, including only those forms of money that can be used to purchase goods and services immediately without any substantial restrictions: currency (bills and coins issued by the government), traveler's checks, and checking-account balances.

M2. A definition of the U.S. money supply that includes M1 plus the money in most savings accounts, money market accounts, and CDs (certificates of deposit, a form of interest-bearing account that has time restrictions regarding when it can be cashed in) worth less than $100,000.

M3. One of a variety of ways to define the U.S. money supply. M3 is the broadest definition, including all the forms of money measured in M2 as well as some larger forms of assets and CDs valued at more than $100,000.

MACROECONOMICS. The branch of economics that examines the economy as a whole, concerning itself with the aggregate behavior (the total result of individual actions) of consumers and producers in various parts of the economy.

MANUAL LABOR. Work that involves a person's physical exertion.

MARGINAL UTILITY. The amount of satisfaction (or utility) a consumer receives from each additional unit of a good that he or she acquires.

MARKET. In economics, a place or system that allows buyers and sellers of goods and services to interact with one another.

MARKET ECONOMY. A system in which people voluntarily exchange goods and services for a price. Businesses and consumers, not the government, decide how much of a good or service is produced and purchased and how much it will cost.

MARKET FAILURE. A term used by economists to describe situations in which markets fail to serve, or are incapable of serving, the best interests of society.

MARKET FORCES. The interaction of supply and demand that drives a market economy.

MARKET RESEARCH. The gathering and analyzing of data about the best ways to advertise, sell, or distribute a particular product or service.

MARKET SHARE. The percentage of the total sales of a product that is sold by one company.

MARKETING. The process of promoting, selling, and distributing a product or service.

MARKETING STRATEGY. A plan describing how a company intends to build consumer awareness about its product or service.

MARXIST ECONOMICS. A branch of economic study based on the writings of the nineteenth-century German philosopher Karl Marx, who is best known for providing the intellectual foundation for the various socialist ideologies (beliefs in redistributing wealth and property so that individuals share the fruits of the economy more equally than under other political systems) that rose to prominence in Russia, China, and Eastern Europe in the early twentieth century.

MASS MARKETING. A form of marketing that attempts to create the largest possible market for a good or service. It includes print, radio, and television advertising; mail-order catalogs; catchy slogans and songs; and flyers.

MASS PRODUCTION. The manufacture, usually by machines, of products in large quantities.

MATURITY. The agreed-upon length of time that an investor will hold a security.

MECHANIZED LABOR. Work that is carried out by machines rather than people.

MEDICAID. A government-assistance program in the United States that provides health-care benefits to individuals and families with low income and limited resources.

MEDICAL INSURANCE. A contract under which a private medical insurance company or a government agency promises to pay for or provide health-care services to an individual or family. Also called health insurance.

MEDICARE. A national health-insurance program for Americans age 65 and older and disabled people.

MERGER. The joining of two separate companies into one larger company.

MICROECONOMICS. An approach to the study of economics that focuses on the decisions of individuals or groups and that involves attempts to understand particular sectors of an economy.

MICROLENDING. The practice of extending small loans to poor entrepreneurs who live in developing countries.

MIGRANT WORKER. *see* foreign worker.

MINIMUM WAGE. The lowest amount of money that employers are legally permitted to pay their workers per hour.

MIXED ECONOMIC SYSTEM. An economy that combines some amount of government planning with elements of a free-market economy.

MNC. *see* multinational corporation.

MONETARISM. *see* monetarist theory.

MONETARIST THEORY. An approach to economics that centers on the belief that the size of the money supply is more important than any other factor affecting the economy. Also called monetarism.

MONETARY POLICY. The government practice of adjusting the money supply in order to bring about a change in the economy.

MONEY. Anything to which people assign value in order to make it easier to exchange goods and services.

MONEY MARKET. The buying and selling of short-term, low-risk securities.

MONEY MARKET ACCOUNT. A type of savings account that usually requires larger minimum balances and places other restrictions on withdrawal of money in exchange for a higher interest rate (a fee paid to the customer for the use of his or her borrowed money) than standard savings accounts offer.

MONEY ORDER. A prepaid voucher for a specific amount of money that is used in lieu of cash or personal checks to make payments; it may be purchased at a bank, post office, and other qualified institution.

MONEY SUPPLY. The amount of money in circulation in an economy at any given time, including not just coins and bills but also bank-account balances.

MONOPOLISTIC COMPETITION. A market structure that combines the features of two opposing concepts, monopoly and perfect competition. In such a market numerous relatively small businesses sell similar but not identical products. Each firm has some amount of control over prices and market conditions even though there is a high level of competition among them.

MONOPOLY. A situation in which a single company or group of companies enjoys complete control over a certain business sector.

MORTGAGE. *see* home loan.

MORTGAGE BROKER. A person working at a bank or mortgage company who arranges home loans.

MORTGAGE PAYMENT. A monthly fee that goes toward paying off a loan used to buy a home.

MULTINATIONAL CORPORATION (MNC). Any business that has bases of activity in more than one country.

MULTIPLIER EFFECT. The idea that government spending has the power to promote further spending by businesses and consumers, thereby helping an economy grow.

MUNICIPAL BOND. A bond (a type of investment) issued by a government or a government agency below the state level.

MUTUAL FUND. A bundle of investments (including stocks, bonds, and other securities) that is managed for clients by an investment company.

N

NASDAQ. The largest electronic (meaning that all trading is done by computer) stock exchange in the United States.

NATIONAL CREDIT UNION ADMINISTRATION. An independent U.S. government agency that insures the deposits of its member credit unions.

NATIONAL DEBT. The amount of borrowed money a country's government owes.

NATURAL MONOPOLY. A situation in which a single company can produce a good more efficiently than two or more competing firms would be able to produce it.

NCD. *see* negotiable certificate of deposit.

NEGOTIABLE CERTIFICATE OF DEPOSIT (NCD). A CD with a face value of at least $100,000 that may be sold in secondary markets (from one investor to another). They are usually purchased by insurance companies, corporations, or other institutional investors.

NEGOTIABLE INSTRUMENT. A written order to pay an amount of money (such as a security) that can be sold by one party to another.

NEOCLASSICAL ECONOMICS. A school of economic thought, developed in the late nineteenth century, that accepts and builds upon the basic tenets of classical economics. Its basic principle is that the interaction of supply and demand is the most important element of a market economy. It is the dominant theoretical framework in modern economics.

NET EARNINGS. The amount of personal income an employee keeps after paying income taxes.

NET EXPORTS. The value of a country's exports minus the value of its total imports.

NET INCOME. The profit or loss that a company shows after all its costs, taxes, and other expenses are subtracted from the total receipts, or revenue.

NEW YORK STOCK EXCHANGE (NYSE). A stock exchange specializing in the stock of large companies. Located in New York City, it is the largest stock exchange in the world, in terms of the value of stocks that are bought and sold there.

NEWLY INDUSTRIALIZED COUNTRIES (NICS). Nations that have not quite attained the status of a developed country but are experiencing rapid economic and technological growth and are shifting from an agricultural economy into an industrialized economy (one based on technology and manufacturing).

NICHE MARKETING. Marketing that is focused entirely on one small segment of the population.

NO-FAULT INSURANCE. A type of car insurance policy that covers the insured person regardless of who is at fault in an accident.

NONDURABLE GOODS. Goods that cannot be reused or that are not expected to retain their value for more than a year (for example, food, clothing, and gas).

NONPROFIT ORGANIZATION. A business whose goal is to support an issue of public or private concern rather than achieve financial gain.

NORTH AMERICAN FREE TRADE AGREEMENT (NAFTA). A treaty between Canada, the United States, and Mexico that eased regulations for doing business across the borders of these three countries.

NYSE. *see* New York Stock Exchange.

O

OCCUPATIONAL SAFETY AND HEALTH ADMINISTRATION (OSHA). A division of the U.S. Department of Labor that regulates issues of safety and health in the workplace.

OFFSHORING. The practice of relocating businesses to parts of the world where production costs are lower.

OLIGOPOLY. A situation in which a small number of companies dominate the market for a particular good or service.

OPEN-MARKET OPERATIONS. A technique used in implementing monetary policy whereby the country's central bank (the Fed in the United States) buys and sells securities on the open market in order to make the nation's money supply larger or smaller (when it buys, it injects money into circulation, and when it sells, it takes money out of general circulation).

OPERATING COSTS. Expenses associated with running a business.

OPPORTUNITY COST. The cost of an economic decision expressed in terms of the next-best opportunity that is given up.

OUTPUT. The quantity of goods and services produced by an economy; also, in the context of production, the goods or services that a business produces.

OUTSOURCING. One business firm's hiring of another business firm to perform one or more jobs on its behalf.

OVERDRAFT. A situation in which a bank account holder does not have sufficient funds to cover checks and other withdrawals from the account.

OVERTIME. Time spent working above the agreed-upon number of hours per day, week, or month; also, the payment for overtime hours worked, usually calculated at an increased hourly rate.

P

PARTNERSHIP. A company in which two or more people, or partners, manage a business together and are personally responsible for the company's debts.

PATENT. The governmentally granted right to be the exclusive manufacturer or seller of an invention.

PAWNBROKER. A business that issues small, short-term loans in exchange for some piece of valuable property, which is held as collateral.

PAY STUB. The portion of a paycheck that includes information about an employee's earnings, which an employee keeps for his or her records.

PAYDAY. A specified date on which an employee receives his or her paycheck.

PAYDAY LOAN. A small, short-term loan that is intended to be repaid after the borrower's next payday.

PAYROLL. The record a company uses to keep track of the money it pays to its employees over a specific period of time; also, the total amount of money a company pays out to its employees during a given period.

PENSION. Regular payments an employee receives after he or she retires.

PER CAPITA INCOME. The average income per person in a country.

PERFECT COMPETITION. A theoretical concept describing a market composed of numerous sellers all offering an identical product, so that none of the sellers has the ability to control prices.

PERSONAL LOAN. Money lent by a financial institution to an individual for personal rather than commercial purposes.

PHILANTHROPIC INSTITUTION. An organization dedicated to helping people instead of making money.

PLANNED ECONOMY. An economic system in which government planners make all or most important economic decisions. Also referred to as a command economy.

POLICY. An insurance contract.

PORTFOLIO. The collection of investments held by an investor.

POSTDATE. To label something, usually a check, with a future date when it can be cashed.

POVERTY LEVEL. The level of household income beneath which an individual is determined to be living in poverty. The level is based on the amount of income that the government says is required to purchase the most basic necessities.

PPI. *see* Producer Price Index.

PPO (PREFERRED PROVIDER ORGANIZATION). A network of health-care providers that contracts with an insurer (usually an insurance company) to offer medical care at discounted rates in exchange for an increased volume of patients.

PREFERRED PROVIDER ORGANIZATION. *see* PPO.

PREFERRED STOCK. Stock that guarantees the shareholder the first right to receive a dividend. Unlike holders of common stock, preferred stockholders cannot vote on company matters.

PREMIUM. The fee for insurance coverage.

PRICE CEILING. A government-imposed maximum price that the seller of a particular good or service may charge.

PRICE FIXING. An illegal activity in which two or more competing businesses make agreements to keep their prices at levels that will ensure profitability.

PRICE FLOOR. A government-imposed minimum price that can be charged for a good or service.

PRICE GOUGING. The practice of setting unfairly high prices during a supply shortage.

PRICING. The process of determining and applying prices to goods and services.

PRIMARY CARE PHYSICIAN. A doctor who manages the health care of a patient with HMO insurance, referring the patient to specialists and authorizing procedures.

PRIME RATE. The standard interest rate set by major banks. It serves as a baseline to which individual banks add percentage points.

PRINCIPAL. The amount of a loan, not including interest (the fee for borrowing money).

PRIVATE SECTOR. That part of the economy that is not controlled by the government and that is run for profit.

PRIVATIZATION. Putting formerly state-run businesses into the hands of individuals and corporations.

PRODUCER PRICE INDEX (PPI). An index published monthly by the Bureau of Labor Statistics that measures the change in cost of materials used to make the products Americans consume.

PRODUCER SURPLUS. The difference between the minimum amount a producer can charge for a good or service without losing money and the price that the producer actually charges.

PRODUCT DEVELOPMENT. The process of bringing a new good or service to market. It includes generating ideas for a new product, gathering information about the needs and wants of the target market, and designing, engineering, and testing the product.

PRODUCT LIABILITY. The notion that anyone involved in the manufacturing or sale of a defective product may be held legally responsible for paying damages to anyone injured because of that product.

PRODUCTION COSTS. The money required to make and distribute a product.

PRODUCTION POSSIBILITIES CURVE. A graph used to show the different quantities of two goods that an economy can produce while using resources most efficiently. Also called the production possibilities frontier.

PRODUCTION POSSIBILITIES FRONTIER. *see* production possibilities curve.

PRODUCTIVITY. The ratio of output (goods created or services performed) to input (all costs of production, including workers' wages and costs required to run business equipment).

PROFIT. The money left over from a business's sales after all costs of production have been paid.

PROFIT SHARING. A plan that provides employees of a company with a percentage of the company's profits.

PROFIT-AND-LOSS STATEMENT. *see* income statement.

PROGRESSIVE TAX. A type of tax that imposes a larger percentage of tax on high-income earners than it does on low-income earners.

PROMISSORY NOTE. A written document that represents a debt and promises repayment at a later date.

PROMOTION. An employee's elevation to a more prestigious position, typically accompanied by a raise and additional responsibility.

PROPERTY. In financial terms, anything that can be owned; it can be tangible (for instance, land, a house, or shoes) or intangible (for instance, a bank-account balance or the patent on an invention).

PROPERTY TAX. A fee charged by the government on the value of privately owned property such as land, houses and other buildings, and machinery.

PROPORTIONAL TAX. A tax that takes the same percentage of income from everyone, regardless of how much or how little an individual earns. Sometimes known as a flat tax or flat-rate tax.

PROTECTIONISM. Any action taken by a government to protect domestic (its own country's) industries from foreign competition.

PUBLIC COMPANY. A company owned by investors or stockholders (people who have purchased shares in the company's ownership).

PUBLIC RELATIONS. The practice of building and maintaining an organization or individual's relationship with the public.

PUBLIC SECTOR. The part of a nation's economy that is controlled by the government.

PURCHASING POWER. The value of money measured by the items it can buy.

PYRAMID SCHEME. A fraudulent business practice that involves building a network, or "pyramid," of investors who pay money into the scheme with the hope of earning a high return on their investment. An investor pays to participate in the scheme and then recruits other investors, who subsequently pay money to the investor who recruited them.

Q

QUALITY CONTROL. A system by which products or services are inspected and evaluated to determine whether they meet expected levels of overall quality.

QUARTER. A period of three months, a unit of time commonly used in financial activity.

R

RAISE. An increase in a person's salary or wages.

RATE OF INFLATION. The percentage by which prices in general have gone up.

RATE OF RETURN. The gain or loss generated by an investment over a specific time period.

RATION. To place limits on the amount of a good that any individual can buy, usually in order to ensure that basic goods in short supply are distributed fairly.

RATIONAL EXPECTATION THEORY. An idea in economics that says that people use rationality, past experiences, and all available information to guide their financial decision-making. When considered as a factor in the overall economy, rational expectation theory leads to the conclusion that people's current expectations about the economy will influence the future course of the economy.

RECALL. A public request for consumers to return a product that has been found to be contaminated, defective, or otherwise unsafe.

RECESSION. A period of slow economic growth typically accompanied by increased unemployment.

REDISTRIBUTION OF WEALTH. The process of taxing the wealthy and using that money to pay for social benefits that will improve the living conditions of poorer people.

REFINANCE. To pay off a loan using another loan that has better terms (such as lower interest rates).

REGRESSIVE TAX. A type of tax that does not take income levels into account and in effect requires people with lower incomes to pay a larger proportion of their income than people with higher incomes.

REINSURANCE. Insurance for insurance companies.

REINVEST. To put a company's profits back into the company to help it grow.

RENT. The monthly fee paid by a person or business leasing an apartment, building, or other property.

RENTER'S INSURANCE. A form of property insurance for people who rent, rather than own, their homes; it covers the contents of the home in the case of theft or damage.

RENT-TO-OWN STORE. A business that allows customers to rent consumer goods, such as furniture and appliances, and that gives the customer the option of taking ownership of the item after a certain number of payments have been made.

RESERVE REQUIREMENT. The amount of money that the federal government requires banks to keep on hand (usually defined as a percentage of the amount of money that the bank takes in through customer deposits).

RESOURCES. The ingredients of production (including land and natural resources, the size and characteristics of the labor force, and the amount and variety of equipment available for production).

RÉSUMÉ. A document providing a detailed description of a person's previous work experience, educational background, and relevant job skills.

RETAIL BANK. A type of bank whose main business is handling the deposits and loans of individual consumers and businesses.

RETAIL PRICE. The price charged to a consumer.

RETAILING. The activity of selling goods directly to consumers who will use or consume the products (not resell them).

RETIREMENT PLAN. A financial arrangement that provides a person with income when he or she retires.

REVENUE. The total quantity of money that a business or organization brings in during a set period of time.

REVOLVING CREDIT. A credit agreement that allows a cardholder to carry a running balance on his or her credit card and requires that regular payments be made.

RIDER. A feature added to an insurance policy that offers a substantial benefit to customers for a small to moderate increase in price.

RISK MANAGEMENT. The process of identifying and analyzing risks (the possibility of loss, injury, disadvantage, or destruction) and creating plans to reduce the losses that an organization faces as it conducts business.

RISK PYRAMID. A diagram used to demonstrate the relationship between risk and reward in investing; the safest investments are located at the base of the pyramid, and the riskiest are grouped at the top. Both risks and rewards increase with each ascending tier.

RISK-BASED ASSETS. Investments that have value or generate money, or both, but that are not as secure as money in hand.

S

S CORPORATION. A type of corporation that is taxed under Subchapter S of the U.S. tax code. An S Corporation is taxed as if it were a partnership; all profit is passed directly to each of the company's owners, who in turn pays taxes as an individual.

S&P 500. An index used to gauge the performance of the U.S. stock market. It tracks the fluctuating stock values of 500 representative companies and combines them into one numerical figure. In full, Standard and Poor's 500.

SAFE-DEPOSIT BOX. A private, locked box inside a bank vault that an individual can rent to store valuables.

SALARY. An employee's pay, calculated on an annual basis.

SALES TAX. A fee charged by the government on the sale of a good or service and paid by the customer at the time of the sale.

SAVINGS ACCOUNT. A kind of bank account that pays the customer interest on the balance of the account.

SAVINGS AND LOAN ASSOCIATION. A type of financial institution that is member-owned and focuses on providing home loans.

SAVINGS BOND. A type of security (interest-paying investment) sold by the U.S. Treasury to individual investors and registered to the original purchaser.

SAY'S LAW. An economic theory developed in 1803 by French journalist, businessman, and economist Jean-Baptiste Say. It states that supply creates its own demand (and thus, an economic crisis will never be caused by supply outpacing demand). Also known as Say's Law of Markets.

SCARCITY. In economics, an imbalance between people's virtually unlimited desires and the limited resources available to satisfy those desires.

SCRIP. Any substitute for money or currency; it carries a monetary value without being legal tender.

SEC. *see* Securities and Exchange Commission.

SECOND MORTGAGE. *see* home equity loan.

SECURED LOAN. A loan in which the borrower is required to offer some form of collateral to the lender; if the borrower fails to repay the loan or to keep to the terms of the loan agreement, then the lender is legally entitled to take possession of the collateral.

SECURITIES AND EXCHANGE COMMISSION (SEC). A U.S. government agency that protects investors and maintains fair, orderly, and efficient financial markets.

SECURITY. A document, such as a stock certificate or a bond, that can be assigned value and bought and sold among investors.

SERVICE. The providing of intangible products such as health care, legal assistance, and insurance.

SERVICE INDUSTRIES. Forms of business activity dealing with human services rather than physical goods.

SEZ. *see* Special Economic Zone.

SHARE DRAFT ACCOUNT. A checking account at a credit union.

SHAREHOLDERS. People who own shares (portions) of a company.

SHORT-TERM CAPITAL ASSETS. Assets that an investor has held for less than a year; in the United States gains on such assets are taxed as ordinary income.

SMALL BUSINESS ADMINISTRATION (SBA). An independent agency of the U.S. government devoted to advancing the interests of American small businesses.

SMALL BUSINESS INVESTMENT COMPANY (SBIC). A government-sponsored private firm in the United States that assists entrepreneurs with the financing and management of their emerging companies. SBICs are licensed and financed by the Small Business Administration.

SOCIAL SECURITY. A U.S. government program that provides monthly financial benefits to senior citizens, veterans, the disabled, and surviving family members of deceased breadwinners; it is funded by a tax paid by all individuals who earn income.

SOCIAL SECURITY TAX. A tax paid by all working citizens to fund Social Security. Also known as the Federal Insurance Contributions Act tax (or FICA tax).

SOLE PROPRIETORSHIP. A business with a single owner (proprietor).

SOLVENT. Having enough money to pay back debts.

SPECIAL ECONOMIC ZONE (SEZ). A geographically separate area of a country that has fewer economic regulations than the rest of the country; its main purpose is to attract foreign investors.

SPECIAL SUPPLEMENTAL NUTRITION PROGRAM FOR WOMEN, INFANTS, AND CHILDREN. A government program in the United States whose mission is to improve the nutrition of low-income women, infants, and children under the age of five who are deemed to be at nutritional risk. Often referred to as the WIC Program.

SPECIALIZATION. *see* division of labor.

STAGFLATION. A term coined in the 1960s to describe the unusual economic phenomenon of inflation (the general rising of prices, usually a sign of economic growth) and economic stagnation occurring simultaneously.

STANDARD OF LIVING. The level of material comfort, or quality of life, enjoyed by an individual or group; in economics it is usually used to evaluate a nation's population.

START-UP COSTS. The money required to open a business.

STOCK. Portions of company ownership that can be bought and sold and that gain or lose value as the company prospers or struggles.

STOCK EXCHANGE. *see* stock market.

STOCK MARKET. A place where buyers and sellers of stocks come together to make trades. The term is also used to refer collectively to all the places in the world, some of which are real buildings and some of which exist mainly in computer networks, where stocks are bought and sold.

STOCK MARKET CRASH. A dramatic drop in the overall value of stocks on a stock exchange, causing widespread financial distress.

STOCK OPTIONS. Agreements providing employees of a company with the right to purchase shares in the company at a discounted price.

STOCKBROKER. A person who negotiates and executes the purchase and sale of stocks for clients.

STRESS MANAGEMENT. A set of strategies or responses used in the workplace to reduce the causes and effects of stress on workers and the organization.

STRIKE. A collective refusal of employees to report for work until their demands are met.

STUDENT AID REPORT (SAR). A report that the federal government issues after a college student (or incoming college student) applies for federal financial aid; the schools and state agencies use the report to determine the student's eligibility for additional aid.

STUDENT LOAN. A sum of money lent to a student who is pursuing higher education, such as college or university study.

SUBSIDIARY. A company that is controlled by a larger company.

SUBSIDY. Money that the government grants a company or organization to help it cover its operating expenses.

SUBSISTENCE FARMERS. Farmers who grow only enough to feed their own families.

SUBSTITUTE GOODS. Goods that can be used in place of other goods, in the way that margarine can be used in place of butter.

SUBSTITUTION EFFECT. An economic principle used in the study of consumer buying patterns, stating that if the price of the product a consumer usually buys goes up while the price of a similar item remains the same, the consumer will be more likely to substitute the second item for the first.

SUNK COST. A cost of production that has been incurred by a company in the past, that does not affect future costs, and that cannot be changed by any current or future actions or decisions.

SUPPLY. The amount of any good or service that a seller is willing or able to sell at a given price.

SUPPLY CHAIN. All of the elements in a process of providing a good or service to a customer, beginning with the raw material and ending with the sale of a finished product or service.

SUPPLY SIDE THEORY. An approach to economics based on the idea that the best way to make the economy grow is to encourage businesses to supply more goods and services for purchase.

SURPLUS. A situation in which there is more supply of a good than demand for it.

SUSTAINABLE DEVELOPMENT. Economic growth that minimizes pollution and the depletion of natural resources.

T

TARGET MARKET. The segment of consumers to whom a product is intended to appeal.

TARIFF. A tax on goods imported from other countries.

TAX. A fee that a government imposes on a type of economic activity.

TAX ASSESSOR. A public official who establishes the value of property for the purpose of determining the amount of tax the owner must pay.

TAX BRACKET. In the payment of U.S. income taxes, the category that determines what percentage of a person's income that he or she must pay as tax; the percentage increases as income increases.

TAX CREDIT. An amount of money that is subtracted from a person or business's total income-tax payment.

TAX EVASION. Hiding or failing to disclose earnings in order to avoid paying taxes on it.

TAX HAVEN. A country or other politically independent area with low or no income tax that attracts foreign businesses and individuals who want to avoid paying income taxes in their home country.

TAX LIABILITY. The amount of tax owed by an individual or business.

TAX REFUND. The money that the government returns to a person when he or she has overpaid on his or her income taxes.

TAX RETURN. A set of forms that individuals and businesses use to report the details of their earnings when paying income taxes to the federal and state governments.

TAX REVENUES. The amounts of money collected by the government through taxation.

TAX SHELTER. Any one of various tactics for reducing one's tax liability.

T-BILL. *see* Treasury bill.

TEMPORARY ASSISTANCE TO NEEDY FAMILIES (TANF). A government program administered by the Office of Family Assistance (a division of the U.S. Department of Health and Human Services) designed to create employment opportunities for needy families with dependent children.

TIME VALUE OF MONEY. An economic principle stating that cash received now is worth more than the same amount of cash received at a later date because money has the capacity to earn interest (fees paid to those who loan money).

TIPS. *see* Treasury Inflation-Protected Securities.

TITLE. A document showing proof of ownership of a piece of property.

TOTAL QUALITY MANAGEMENT (TQM). A philosophy of business management that seeks excellence and maximum efficiency in all areas of the production of goods and services.

TRADE. To buy and sell.

TRADE BARRIERS. Fees or limits on the goods and services that can move across borders.

TRADE BLOC. A group of nations that has reached a set of agreements regarding their economic relationships with each other. The agreements generally focus on the relaxation or elimination of trade barriers.

TRADE CREDIT. A contractual agreement in which one business receives goods or services from another business without having to pay immediately for those goods and services. The business that has received the goods or services will pay the lending business at a later date, which is specified in the agreement.

TRADE DEFICIT. The difference between the value of a country's imports and its exports, when the country imports more than it exports.

TRADE SURPLUS. The difference between the value of a country's imports and its exports, when the country exports more than it imports.

TRADEMARK. A legally registered name or symbol used to identify a brand or organization in the marketplace; registration gives the organization the right to be the sole user of the trademark.

TRANSFER PAYMENT. Money or other aid that a government gives to an individual or organization with no expectation that a good or service will be provided in return.

TRANSITION ECONOMY. An economy that is in the process of shifting from a planned-economy model to a free-market model.

TRANSNATIONAL COMPANY. A company that operates and invests in many countries around the world.

TRAVELER'S CHECK. A kind of check, typically used by people traveling in foreign countries, that may be purchased from a bank or other financial institution or at a travel service office in preset denominations ($10, $20, $50, $100, and higher). Unlike cash, they are protected against loss or theft.

TREASURY BILL. A government security that guarantees the investor a fixed return (usually about 3 percent of the invested amount) after a short period of time. Also called a T-bill.

TREASURY BOND. A long-term security sold by the U.S. Treasury that matures in 10 to 30 years and pays the investor interest every six months. Also called a T-bond.

TREASURY INFLATION-PROTECTED SECURITY. A type of security sold by the U.S. Treasury that takes inflation (the general rising of prices) into account; the face value of the security increases with inflation and decreases with deflation (a general decline in prices). Abbreviated as TIPS.

TREASURY NOTE. A security sold by the U.S. Treasury that has a maturity of 2, 3, 5, or 10 years and pays the investor interest every six months. Also called a T-note.

TREASURY SECURITIES. Investments offered by the U.S. government (specifically the Treasury) to individuals, institutions (both inside and outside of the United States), and foreign governments; in effect, these investors are loaning money to the government, and in exchange, they receive interest payments.

TRUST. A combination of companies, the intent of which is to reduce competition and control prices; also, property or money held by one party (the trustee) for the benefit of another (the beneficiary).

TRUTH IN LENDING ACT (TILA). A U.S. federal law requiring all lending institutions to state fully, in writing and in plain language, the terms of the loans they offer to customers.

TUITION. The basic cost of attending school, not including supplies and room and board.

U

UN. *see* United Nations.

UNEMPLOYMENT. The state of being unemployed; can also mean the rate of unemployment (the percentage of a nation's workforce that cannot find jobs).

UNEMPLOYMENT INSURANCE. A government system by which regular payments are made to qualified unemployed individuals (usually those who have been laid off).

UNION. *see* labor union.

UNION DUES. A portion of a worker's wages that pays for costs associated with the organization and governing of the labor union.

UNITED NATIONS (UN). An international organization dedicated to fostering legal, political, and economic cooperation among various nations.

UNITED STATES DEPARTMENT OF AGRICULTURE (USDA). The department of the federal government that develops policies regarding agriculture and food.

UNITED STATES DEPARTMENT OF COMMERCE. The department of the federal government that deals with issues of economic growth.

UNITED STATES DEPARTMENT OF LABOR. The federal agency responsible for regulating issues pertaining to the U.S. workforce, including occupational safety, wage and work-hours standards, and unemployment-insurance benefits.

UNITED STATES DEPARTMENT OF THE TREASURY. The department of the federal government that manages the country's revenue.

UNIVERSAL HEALTH CARE. A national system in which all residents have access to health care regardless of their ability to pay or their medical condition.

UNLIMITED LIABILITY. A situation in which those obligated to pay a debt have unlimited responsibility to do so.

UNSECURED LOAN. A type of loan that does not require the borrower to put up collateral.

USDA. *see* United States Department of Agriculture.

USURY. The practice of charging a borrower more interest than the law allows.

UTILITIES. Everyday services that are typically purchased by homeowners, such as electricity, gas, water, and waste disposal.

UTILITY. In economics, the amount of satisfaction consumers receive from the goods and services they purchase.

V

VALUE-ADDED TAX. A type of sales tax charged to businesses based on the value, or price, the business adds to the product it makes.

VARIABLE COSTS. The costs of production that vary according to the number of units of a product made or with the scale of the company's operation. Examples include the cost of raw materials and the wages paid to workers who are hired specifically for the production of that good.

VELOCITY OF MONEY. The speed with which the average dollar changes hands.

VENTURE CAPITAL. Money that serves as financial backing for new, generally unproven business enterprises, typically known as start-ups.

VENTURE CAPITALIST. An individual or group that provides start-up funding to new businesses.

VOLATILITY. The frequency and amount of price fluctuation of an investment.

W

WAGES. The payment that a worker or employee receives for his or her labor, usually paid for a specified quantity of labor, which most often is measured as a unit of time.

WARRANTY. A guarantee offered by the seller or manufacturer of a product, promising repair if the product breaks within a certain time after purchase.

WEB MANAGEMENT. All of the activities included in the process of posting and maintaining a website.

WELFARE. Government programs that provide aid to the poor.

WHITE-COLLAR WORKERS. Employees whose jobs do not involve manual labor and who generally receive a salary rather than an hourly wage.

WHOLESALE. The selling of goods that are intended to be resold (as when a distributor sells to a retailer), typically in large quantities and at lower prices than an individual customer would be charged.

WIC PROGRAM. *see* Special Supplemental Nutrition Program for Women, Infants, and Children.

WIRE TRANSFER. The electronic transfer of funds across a network controlled and maintained by hundreds of banks around the world, allowing people in different geographic locations to transfer money easily.

WORKER'S COMPENSATION. A type of insurance that employers must have to provide monetary compensation to employees who experience work-related illnesses or injuries.

WORK-STUDY. A program in which college students are paid to do a job at the school.

WORLD BANK. An international organization (consisting of member nations) that helps poor and developing countries build their economies by making loans to these countries and providing them with financial assistance and supervision.

WORLD TRADE ORGANIZATION (WTO). An institution composed of more than 150 countries, the purpose of which is to monitor international trade and promote increasingly free (unregulated) trade between countries.

WTO. *see* World Trade Organization.

Z

ZERO-COUPON BOND. A form of bond that does not conform to the basic model of paying a face value and then collecting interest until maturity. Instead of paying interest, it is sold at a discount off its face value; when it matures, the investor is paid the bond's face value. They allow people to make long-term investments at a low initial cost.

Personal Money Management

Buying, Borrowing, Saving, and Insuring

Introduction: Personal Money Management

Buying: The Consumer's Role in the Economy

Borrowing: When You Need More Money Than You Have

Saving and Investing: Planning for the Future

Protecting Yourself from Risk

Introduction: Personal Money Management

$ What It Means

Personal Money Management refers to the process of balancing one's individual wealth and income with financial needs, desires, and goals. Though some of us may survive without sophisticated money management strategies, none of us can escape financial pressures entirely. Most of us hold jobs during the most productive adult years of our lives, and the income we bring in must be managed effectively if we are to satisfy our basic needs and lead fulfilling lives. The decisions we make regarding our personal finances can be complicated, and they change as we pass through the various stages of life. While we may start our adult lives simply depositing our paychecks in bank accounts and spending most or all of that income using cash, checks, and credit cards, as we age we may find ourselves drawn more deeply into the worlds of borrowing, saving and investing, and insurance.

$ When Did It Begin

Personal money management is not new. Since the rise of capitalism (the economic system characterized by private ownership of property and the ability to pursue profit with relative freedom) in the 1600s, the survival of individual households has frequently depended on their ability to allocate income effectively. Likewise, financial success has since that time been at least theoretically possible through saving and investing any excess income.

Personal money management in the United States plays a much larger role in the financial success or failure of families today than it did in earlier eras, however, and it was a much more widely discussed topic at the beginning of the twenty-first century than it had ever been before. This was the result of a change in the structure of the U.S. economy that occurred between the middle and the end of the twentieth century.

In the mid-twentieth century many American workers could count on companies or unions (organized groups of workers who had the bargaining power to negotiate with employers) to solve many of their financial problems and help them prepare for the future. For example, if you got a job with a major corporation in the 1940s or 1950s, you could expect to be employed by that company for your entire career. During that time the company would likely pay not only for your health insurance but would also guarantee you a pension to live on after retirement. Many workers not entitled to such company benefits could get them by joining a union, which used its bargaining power to extract better treatment from company management and which provided members with many other financial benefits. This meant that personal money management, for many households, primarily meant nothing beyond the balancing of income and daily expenses.

By the beginning of the twenty-first century, however, workers were expected to fend for themselves. Companies constantly restructured themselves to adapt to changing conditions, cutting jobs in response to larger economic trends and reducing or eliminating employee benefits regardless of the effect this would have on households. During the late twentieth century, additionally, unions lost not only much of their influence but also many of their members, as the blue-collar industries that were most heavily unionized (such as the steel and automotive industries) fell on hard times. Pension plans for most U.S. workers were largely eliminated, and the rising cost of health care made it increasingly likely that this employee benefit, too, might become a thing of the past in the near future. Collectively, these changes shifted the responsibility for a household's financial well-being away from employers and onto employees. This made the need for effective personal money management much more important.

$ More Detailed Information

Personal money management at its most basic level concerns the purchases you must make to satisfy your everyday needs and desires. This means keeping track of your checking and other bank accounts, as well as the purchases you make using credit cards, to ensure that your monthly expenses do not exceed your income.

No matter who you are, you will almost certainly pay several basic expenses each month. First, you must pay for housing. You may pay rent to live in an apartment or house owned by someone else, or you may make a monthly mortgage payment to the bank that loaned you the money to buy your own home. In either case this will probably be your biggest single expense each month, but it is hardly the only one you will have to account for in your budget. You must also budget for bills, such as electricity, phone service, and water, and you must budget for groceries and other basic purchases. Further, unless you live in a major city served by an efficient public transportation system, you will likely need a car to get to and from work and the grocery store, and this may, like the purchase of a home, require borrowing money from a bank or other financial institution. In this case, you must budget for a monthly car payment.

Ideally you should make enough money every month to pay for all of these needs and still have savings to set aside for the future. Money left over after paying

expenses and setting aside savings can be confidently spent on entertainment or other nonessential purchases, but making such purchases in lieu of saving money is usually a bad idea. Going into debt to make such purchases (for example, by accumulating a credit card balance that you cannot pay off), or to pay for basic expenses, is almost always a bad idea. If you cannot live normally without going into debt each month, you may well be headed for a financial crisis.

Not all debt is unwise, however. As mentioned above, most people would be unable to make large purchases, such as purchases of homes or cars, without borrowing money. Since cars are essential to the daily lives of many, borrowing money to purchase a car is often unavoidable, even if it is not as financially advantageous as buying a car using cash. Borrowing money to buy a house, on the other hand, is sometimes a sounder financial decision than paying cash, since houses generally appreciate (gain value) over time. Thus, even though you must pay interest on the amount of money you owe the bank, the rate at which your home appreciates may outweigh the money you lose to interest payments. Borrowing money to start or enhance a business is another financially sound form of debt. Assuming that your

The way that people manage their money—whether they spend it all at fancy restaurants, purchase a house, or invest in their retirement—is often referred to as personal money management. In this photo a man reviews his financial documents. © *Comstock/Corbis.*

business is successful, the profits you bring in should compensate for the interest payments you must make. Likewise, borrowing money to put yourself or your children through college may be a wise financial decision, since a college education enables one to earn enough money to compensate for the expense of the loan, at least over the long term.

If you ever hope to have any financial independence (that is, to escape the pressures of living paycheck to paycheck, in fear of any accident or change that may interrupt your income), you will probably need to save around 10 percent of your income every month. Saving will allow you to reach both short-term and long-term financial goals. A common short-term goal may be the building of an emergency fund. Most financial experts suggest that you should have enough money in reserve to support yourself and your family for three to six months in case of accident, injury, or some other emergency. Other short-term goals might be saving enough for a vacation or the purchase of a new washer and dryer. Common long-term financial goals are saving enough money to make a down payment on a house (when borrowing money to buy a house, most people are required to pay a percentage of the sales price called a down payment, which typically ranges from 5 to 20 percent) and saving enough money to pay for your children to go to college. It is also necessary to save money for retirement. No matter how young you are, you cannot afford to ignore the fact that one day you will be unable or unwilling to work. Government sources of retirement funding, such as Social Security, generally only supplement the living expenses of the elderly, and the future of such programs in the United States is far from certain.

To reach your savings goals, it may be necessary to invest the money you set aside. Keeping money in a checking account usually amounts to losing money, since prices in the economy are always rising. One dollar today will always purchase more than one dollar next year; keeping money in a checking account that pays little or no interest means that your savings will lose value over time. Even savings accounts, which often pay a higher rate of interest in exchange for offering you less frequent access to your money, pay so little interest sometimes as to fall behind the rate at which prices rise.

Investing in financial markets, such as the stock and bond markets, is generally considered a good idea for anyone with a significant amount of accumulated savings. How and where you invest your money will depend on your own personal knowledge of the financial world, your tolerance of financial risk, your investing time frame, and your monetary requirements. The stock market, in which buyers and sellers come together to purchase shares of company ownership whose value fluctuates as companies flourish or struggle, generally offers the greatest potential for multiplying your savings, but it also offers greater risk than other forms of investment. Purchasing bonds is

PERSONAL FINANCIAL PLANNERS

Personal money management—managing your income not only so that it satisfies your present needs but also so that it prepares you for future goals—can be complicated, and the stakes can be high. Mismanaging your money could mean, for example, that you do not save enough money to put your children through college or to pay your living expenses in old age. Because of the complexity and risk involved, many households today turn all or part of their personal money management over to professionals. These professionals are generally called personal financial planners. Whereas the typical individual has never overseen the finances of any household but his own, a good personal financial planner brings a wealth of planning experience to the task of managing his or her clients' money. Good planners bring to the professional relationship the knowledge of how different areas of personal money management affect one another and of what challenges lay ahead at various stages of life, and they can help craft individualized, focused strategies for reaching financial goals.

usually a safer but less lucrative form of investing. A bond is a share of government or company debt; in exchange for lending money to a government entity or a corporation, the bondholder can count on regular payments of interest. As long as the government or company is stable, the bondholder can expect to receive these payments until the bond matures, at which point the initial loan amount will be returned. There are many other forms of investments, ranging from those that cater to people without specialized knowledge to those that cater to experts and institutions.

Saving and investing money will certainly go a long way toward preparing you for the future, but it can also be wise to purchase a variety of insurance policies to protect yourself further. To purchase insurance, an individual or family generally pays a monthly premium, or fee, that varies according to risk factors. Health insurance, which helps pay for medical care, is essential in today's world, given the often extremely high price of doctors' fees, tests, and surgical procedures. In general, the more likely a policy-holder is to need medical care (due to age, medical history, and other factors), the higher the premium will be. Homeowners' insurance is, likewise, generally a necessity for those who want to purchase a home today. This form of insurance pays for damage inflicted upon a home through no fault of the homeowner. If, for example, your home and possessions were demolished by a fire, your homeowners' insurance would pay to have the house rebuilt and would reimburse you for the value of the home's contents. Without homeowners' insurance, not only would you not be reimbursed for your losses, you would also still be required to pay back the money you borrowed from the bank to purchase your house. To ensure that they do not lose money in situations like this, most financial institutions require home buyers to purchase insurance. Again, the individual premium would be related to the risk of mishap that one's house represents: an old, wooden house with outdated wiring and plumbing would probably cost more to insure than a new, brick house.

Other forms of insurance can be just as crucial to a family's survival, even though they are less universal. If, for example, you are the main breadwinner for your household, you may want to purchase life or disability insurance. Life insurance guarantees that those who depend on your income will be provided for in the event of your untimely death, and disability insurance guarantees your household an income if you become unable to work because of illness or injury.

In short, it is impossible to live in the modern world without paying attention to money. To avoid inconvenience and hardship, you must be able to make sensible financial decisions. This requires, first of all, being knowledgeable about spending, borrowing, and saving money, and about insuring yourself and your property. With this knowledge in hand, you can set financial goals and craft plans for reaching them.

$ Recent Trends

Though personal money management represented a new burden for many individuals in the late twentieth and early twenty-first centuries, technological advances had the ability to lighten that burden significantly. Most financial information could, by this time, be accessed using the Internet at any time, so that individuals no longer had to wait for monthly banking or investment statements to confirm the results of their own record-keeping. This made it possible to have a more accurate idea of one's actual financial standing at any given moment and in turn to plan more effectively. Additionally, the Internet offered an ease of access to various consumer, banking, investment, and insurance opportunities that had never existed before. Whereas consumers in previous eras were restricted, in their financial decision-making, to the options available in their local area, the Internet in many cases eliminated these restrictions, allowing consumers to shop around not only for such goods as books, electronics, furniture, and even automobiles but also to choose among numerous competing insurance policies or mortgage companies. This frequently resulted in monetary savings for those consumers willing to undertake the task of researching their options online.

Buying: The Consumer's Role in the Economy

$ Overview: Personal Decision-Making and Shopping

What It Means

Individuals make hundreds, if not thousands, of personal economic decisions over the course of a year, including whether to buy generic or brand-name groceries, whether to splurge on a Hawaiian vacation or take an inexpensive camping trip, whether to send children to private or public school, whether to spend a tax refund (the money returned to a person when she has overpaid on her income taxes) on a new television or save it for an emergency (such as a car repair), and countless others.

In all of these decisions, two basic economic principles apply: scarcity and opportunity cost. They underpin the decisions of multimillion-dollar corporations, subsistence farmers (those who grow only enough to feed their own families), governments—indeed, every economic entity you can think of.

Scarcity has to do with the fact that resources are limited: no one has an infinite amount of money, or time, or land, or water, or energy. Choices—our decisions to buy or do one thing and not another—are necessary because we cannot have everything at once. If we have a week of vacation time to spend, we cannot fly to Hawaii and also drive to the state park in Oregon. If we do choose to treat ourselves to the Hawaiian vacation, then we probably should not spend that tax refund to treat ourselves to a new TV. Every time we make a choice, we say "yes" to one thing and "no" to another (or several others). It is not that we do not also want all of those things we say "no" to; it is just that we cannot have it all, and we decide that the thing we say "yes" to is the best choice.

In economics, the things we say "no" to are called opportunity costs. More precisely, the opportunity cost of a given choice is the value of the next-best alternative, which we sacrifice, or say "no" to. So, for example, if you choose to spend the weekend with friends, the opportunity cost is that you do not get to spend the weekend alone (cleaning the house, or catching up on e-mails, or studying for a test).

The choices we make about how to spend our resources (time, money, and energy) involve costs and benefits, or trade-offs. The benefit of spending the weekend with friends is that you will likely have fun and be rejuvenated by human contact; but the cost of this choice might be facing Monday with a dirty house and an in-box full of unanswered e-mails, or it might be that you are not fully prepared for an important biology test. In addition to weighing the various costs and benefits associated with our decisions, we must also try to anticipate possible consequences. The consequence of living another week in a dirty house is fairly insignificant; but what if the consequence of doing poorly on the biology test is that you do not qualify for that summer internship? And what if that summer internship could make or break your chances of getting into your first-choice university? These potential consequences probably outweigh the amount of fun you could have in a single weekend.

Understanding the principles of scarcity and opportunity cost are critical to our ability to make good decisions about how to spend our time, money, and energy. As consumers in a society where the allure of goods and services can exert a powerful pull on our psyches, it is particularly important to be able to weigh the costs and benefits of how we spend (or choose not to spend) our money, because for most of us, the more money we choose to spend, the more time and energy we must devote (or sacrifice) to the project of earning money.

When Did It Begin

Scarcity and opportunity costs were a fact of human existence long before they were articulated as central concepts of economic theory.

Adam Smith (1723–90), David Ricardo (1772–1823), and other economists of the so-called classical school (which emerged in the eighteenth century) were primarily concerned with high-level economic workings

People are constantly making economic decisions in their lives. In the 1995 movie *Clueless* Alicia Silverstone, pictured here, plays a character who must decide whether to continue living her materialistic lifestyle or pursue emotional and intellectual growth. *Paramount/The Kobal Collection/The Picture Desk, Inc.*

such as the rise of commercial industry, price dynamics, and the benefits of trade. The next wave of economic theory (which emerged in the late nineteenth century and became known as the neoclassical school) began to focus more attention on the value of goods and services to individual consumers.

The German statistician Ernst Engel (1821–96) and the French sociologist and economist Pierre Guillaume Frédéric Le Play (1806–82) both produced important studies relating to family budgets, and the turn of the twentieth century in the United States saw a proliferation of popular literature concerning economic advice for individuals and families, with titles such as *How to Get Ahead, Thrift and Success,* and *A.B.C. of Home Saving.*

In spite of such prudent-sounding titles, however, at the start of the twentieth century there was the beginning of a societal move away from the age-old moral edict to work hard, be thrifty, and save, save, save. With the rise of advertising came a new kind of consumer culture in which people desired material goods and services as never before. As consumerism has continued to grow and flourish, it has had a profound impact on the way individuals make economic decisions.

More Detailed Information

Making good personal economic decisions requires planning, levelheadedness, and the ability to weigh the costs and benefits of one's various options.

Every person needs to figure out how to make the money he or she earns pay for housing, transportation, food, and clothing. Most people also need to pay for health care, education, and a few haircuts per year and would like to have something left over for entertainment, such as movies, concerts, cable television, and miniature golf. And we know that we are supposed to be saving a little bit every month, too. In economics, the process of dividing up your paycheck to cover your monthly expenses is called resource allocation: the money you have earned is the resource, and you must portion it out as best you can to cover your needs and wants. A budget is a kind of map, or plan for how to do this. It helps you establish your financial priorities and make your spending habits predictable.

Making a list before you go shopping is also a good way to plan. It is a way of reminding yourself what your purpose is in going to a given store, so that you do not come home with an armload of things you never intended to buy. These spur-of-the-moment purchases are called "impulse buys," because people buy them impulsively, without thinking their way through the cost-benefit scenario. Say, for example, you have budgeted $125 for clothing this month and you plan to spend it on a pair of jeans and a pair of sneakers. At the mall you go to the shoe store first and find the sneakers you want for $60. You plan to spend the remaining $65 on jeans, but when you get to the cash register at the shoe store, there is a whole rack of socks that are 50 percent off. You actually have enough socks, but these are a great bargain. Before you know it, you have spent $15 on socks. (How could you pass them up for $3 per pair?) At the time, it did not occur to you that part of the cost of buying the socks would be not having enough for the jeans. Now you only have $50 left over for jeans, but when you get to the jeans store, the pair you want is $70. Of course, you could forego the jeans and resolve to buy them next month, but if you are like most American consumers, you will buy them anyway, vowing to borrow that extra $20 from somewhere else in your budget. One or two impulse buys may not seem like a big deal, but if you are not careful they can turn your budget into a real juggling act.

Unfortunately for modern consumers, the forces of advertising and marketing are constantly appealing to our impulses and emotions, beckoning us to throw our best-laid plans and our rational thinking out the window for the instant gratification of an irresistible purchase.

Another major pitfall for budgeters everywhere is the availability of consumer credit. Consumer credit is a form of loan extended by banks and other financial institutions that enables consumers to "buy now and pay later" with an electronic-payment card called a credit card. The consumer receives a statement (or bill) at the end of the month, at which time he or she can pay off the entire balance of his or her purchases or make a small minimum payment and allow the balance to carry over to the next month. If the consumer carries a balance on the card, the money owed (also called the debt) is subject to interest charges (a percentage of the balance, which may be thought of as a fee for owing the money).

Consumer credit seems to alleviate the problem of scarcity: instead of having to choose between this or that purchase, we are suddenly able to have both. This makes it easy for millions of individuals and families to live beyond their means (that is, to spend more than they earn). Many of them gradually build up thousands of dollars worth of debt that can take years, or even a lifetime, to pay off. Indeed, while credit cards grant us the temporary illusion that we can have it all, in fact they may carry one of the heftiest opportunity costs of all, because if we constantly avoid making hard choices at the cash register, allowing ourselves to slip into debt, the thing we are saying "no" to, or sacrificing, is our financial freedom.

WHAT THINGS COST

As modern consumers, we are conditioned to think about how much things cost by looking at a price tag. Suppose, for instance, that Jacob wants to buy a digital camcorder so that he can start making videos with his friends. The camcorder he wants has a price tag of $299. If Jacob babysits every weekend and saves everything he earns, he could have enough for the camcorder in about a month. For most of us, the question of whether or not to buy the camcorder basically comes down to "How can I come up with $299?"

But although the price of the camcorder is $299, its cost to Jacob is actually higher. In order to evaluate the true cost of the camcorder, he needs to factor in all of the things he will be giving up in order to get it. For example, if he babysits every Friday and Saturday night for a month, part of the cost of the camcorder is the sacrifice of time with friends; if he saves all his money for a month, another part of the cost of the camcorder is a month of not spending money on movies, magazines, music, or clothes. Is the camcorder still worth it? In order to make this determination, Jacob must weigh these costs against the benefits he expects to get from buying the camcorder. For example, the camcorder will bring him hours of entertainment with friends; it will be an outlet for his creativity; it will enable him to document his life, and he plans to post the videos on the Internet so that his best friend, who moved to Brazil, can see what he is up to. The process of weighing these costs and benefits is called cost-benefit analysis. It may sound like a technical term, but in fact it is the basic building block of economic decision-making and the only way we can determine if something is really "worth it."

Recent Trends

During the 1990s and through the first five years of the twenty-first century, the most alarming financial trend among American consumers was the skyrocketing level of credit card debt. In 2006 Clear Point Financial Solutions, a credit-repair company (which helps consumers get out of debt and restore their financial reputations) presented some staggering statistics:

- The average American spends $1.22 for every dollar earned.

- The average American carries more than $11,000 in credit card debt.

- Americans owe a combined total of $2 trillion in credit card debt.

- Americans owe more in credit card debt than they do for education loans.

- In 2000 American undergraduate students carried an average credit card balance of $2,748; graduate students carried an average balance of $4,776.

In light of these troubling trends, many educators were placing new emphasis on teaching high school students basic economic concepts and skills for making responsible personal economic decisions.

COMMON CONCERNS

$ Budgeting

What It Means

Budgeting is a form of fiscal planning that enables individuals or other entities to make informed financial decisions. Budgeting focuses on two principal aspects of a financial situation: income or revenue (in other words the amount of money that is earned over a set period of time) and expenditures (the amount of money that is spent). Through budgeting individuals keep track of how much money they spend on certain aspects of their lives and try to figure out ways to cut their regular expenses to free up

money for other expenditures they might like to make. The actual financial plan created by the process of budgeting is called a budget.

There are many types of budgets. Governments create budgets to ensure that they take in enough revenue (generally through the collection of taxes) to pay for social programs, such as schools, police and fire departments, public parks, financial assistance programs for low-income families, and various other projects having to do with the effective management of a community. Corporations use budgets to calculate methods of minimizing overhead (expenditures relating to running a company, such as purchasing supplies, paying employees, renting office space, and so on) in order to maximize profits.

Individuals and families also use budgets, as a means of managing their personal finances. In creating a personal budget an individual or a family must consider a number of factors, relating to both their financial resources and their financial goals. In certain respects the first step to creating a budget involves establishing

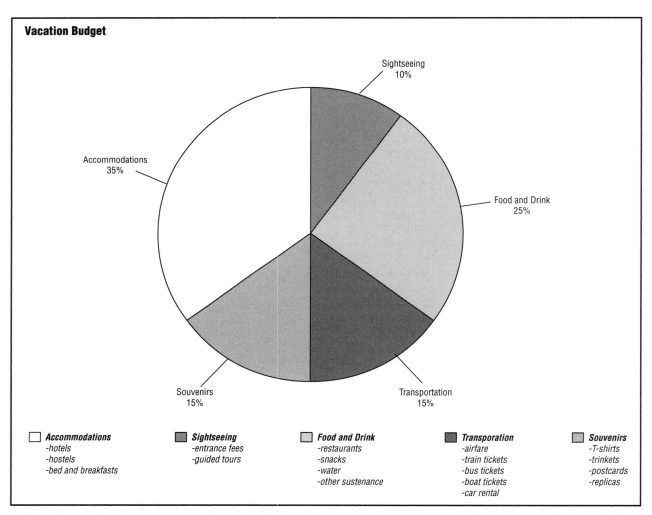

Vacation Budget

- Accommodations 35%
- Sightseeing 10%
- Food and Drink 25%
- Transportation 15%
- Souvenirs 15%

Accommodations	Sightseeing	Food and Drink	Transporation	Souvenirs
-hotels	-entrance fees	-restaurants	-airfare	-T-shirts
-hostels	-guided tours	-snacks	-train tickets	-trinkets
-bed and breakfasts		-water	-bus tickets	-postcards
		-other sustenance	-boat tickets	-replicas
			-car rental	

Budgeting is a good way to organize your finances and to make sure you do not spend more money than you have. This pie graph shows how the funds available for a typical vacation might be divided up. *Illustration by GGS Information Services. Cengage Learning, Gale.*

priorities concerning how money is spent. All families have a certain number of expenses, relating to food, shelter, rent or a home mortgage, clothing, and utilities (everyday services, such as electricity, water, sewer, and waste disposal), that are essential to maintaining a healthy and safe existence. For some families, particularly those with low incomes and/or a large number of children, these necessary expenditures account for most if not all of their monthly earnings. In these instances a budget might prove vital to making certain that these necessary payments are made in a timely way, thereby ensuring the family's continued financial security.

For families or individuals with larger incomes, a budget can help maximize financial resources to increase overall quality of life. Having additional income above and beyond the payment of necessary expenses gives an individual or a family a wider range of choices regarding how much money to spend on particular aspects of their lives. The amount of money that an individual or a family sets aside for a specific purpose will generally depend on what activities or consumer products they regard as important to their happiness. A young man in his 20s, for example, with few financial responsibilities beyond paying rent and utilities, putting gas in the car, and eating, might create a budget that allows him to set aside money for recreational pursuits, such as taking exotic vacations or purchasing a motorcycle. As people grow older and start families, their financial priorities often change, both because their personal interests evolve over time and because their financial responsibilities increase as they assume responsibility for the care and upbringing of children. For these families a budget might enable them to save money for their children's education or to begin investing a certain portion of their monthly income in an individual retirement account, or IRA (an investment savings account that individuals set aside to use as income in the future, after they retire from their jobs).

When Did It Begin

Some form of budgeting has undoubtedly played a central role in financial management since approximately 3100 BC, when people in ancient Mesopotamia (a region roughly consisting of what is now Iraq) first began keeping written records of crop production on clay tablets. In English usage the word *budget* traces its origins to the fifteenth century. Originally a term designating a leather wallet or pouch, it eventually came to refer to the contents of such a pouch; by the first half of the eighteenth century, the term *budget* had come to refer to the English government's statement of annual expenditures. In nineteenth-century America the increased practice of household budgeting roughly corresponded to the emergence of home economics (the science of running or managing a household) as an educational discipline. In the twentieth century the concept of household budgeting became a subject of economic study. In his land-

mark books *Human Capital* (1964) and *A Treatise on the Family* (1981), Nobel prize-winning economist Gary S. Becker (b. 1930) analyzed the importance of budgeting in determining how modern families function.

More Detailed Information

According to many experts one of the keys to creating a workable budget is simplicity. For most people income is the most predictable aspect of their financial lives; their paycheck comes from a single source and remains constant from pay period to pay period, whether it is calculated by the week, month, or year. When it comes to expenses, however, a person's financial picture becomes more complicated. Some expenses, such as housing, cable television, and car payments, remain fixed from month to month and are therefore easy to anticipate when drawing up a budget. Other monthly expenses, on the other hand, are variable: heating costs rise and fall depending on the season, gasoline prices fluctuate constantly, phone bills are typically calculated according to the calls that are made, and so on. At the same time, irregular expenses (for example, paying to get a computer repaired or purchasing a new couch) arise constantly and often cannot be predicted. Thus to try to create a budget that accounts for all expenditures would be extremely complicated if not outright impossible.

By dividing a budget into broad categories, however, a person can allow for more flexibility in monitoring expenditures. Typical budget categories might include housing (rent or mortgage payments), food (including meals that are prepared at home, snacks purchased from a vending machine or corner store, and so on), car (such as monthly car loan payments, auto insurance, gas, and minor maintenance), basic utilities (including phone, Internet, and cable television), clothing, entertainment (movies, going out to restaurants, buying beer or wine, visiting a museum, and the like), and general household items, ranging from laundry detergent to toothpaste.

In essence budgeting is a means of controlling monthly expenses. Monthly spending habits vary widely, depending on the life situation of the person. For example, the expenses of a single young man will typically be less complicated than those of a large family. Say a young man earns a net income (the amount of personal income remaining after taxes) of $2,800 a month working as a computer programmer in a major city. His obligatory monthly expenses include rent ($1,200), utilities ($150 on average), clothing ($50 on average), public transportation ($100), laundry ($25), and groceries ($275). Theoretically at the end of the month he will have an additional $1,000 of his monthly earnings, a considerable surplus.

In all likelihood, however, the young man's monthly spending will greatly exceed these necessary expenses. For example, he might stop by a local pub every Friday after work to drink pitchers of beer and shoot pool with his

ENVELOPE ACCOUNTING

Effective budgeting (the practice of creating a financial plan designed to manage one's income more efficiently) requires discipline. Over the years people have invented various methods of regulating their monthly spending. One popular method of budgeting is known as envelope accounting. With envelope accounting consumers set aside a certain amount of cash each month (for groceries, gasoline, and so on), which they place in envelopes designated for these specific purchases. When the money in one spending envelope runs out, the consumer must cease spending in that category for the rest of the month; if the expense proves essential (for example, groceries) the consumer can move money from another envelope, with the understanding that expenditures in that particular category will have to be sacrificed. In this way consumers keep their spending within specific predetermined limits. Psychologically paying cash for most basic expenditures can make it easier for individuals to stick to a budget. Consumers sometimes do not grasp the repercussions of what they are spending in the moment when they use a debit card (a plastic card used to make purchases, which deducts funds from an individual's bank account electronically); because they are not technically handing over money they can easily lose track of how much they spend.

friends ($200 a month), go to the movies once a week ($50 a month, with popcorn), purchase various magazines at the corner newsstand ($30), purchase a latte each morning at the coffee shop ($100 a month), rent videos a couple evenings a week ($40 a month), eat some form of takeout three nights a week ($180 a month), and download 50 to 100 songs off the Internet ($49.50 to $99). In addition he might buy pizza slices on his way home from the pub ($25), buy candy bars or other snacks whenever the mood strikes him ($25), and purchase at least two expensive items a month, such as running sneakers, stereo equipment, or a handheld gaming device ($200).

After all these additional expenses the young man might find himself with somewhere between $50 and $100 remaining each month. When other, irregular expenses occur (for example, flights home to visit family twice a year, $1,000; taxis home from the pub when it is too cold to walk, $100 each winter; a visit to the dentist, $150; laptop repair, $250) the young man might find that he does not have enough money to cover them and must charge some of the expenses to his credit card. Rather than having a sizable surplus at the end of the year (money that could have gone toward taking a trip to Europe, investing in an IRA, or putting a down payment on a home), the young man has a gradually increasing debt.

This situation could easily be avoided if the young man were to draw up and follow a basic monthly budget,

allowing him to regulate his expenses to ensure that he lives within his means. In creating a budget the young man would start by keeping track of everything he spends over the course of a single month. The initial totals might look like the following: $1,200 for rent, $150 for utilities, $50 for clothing, $100 for subway cards, $25 for laundry, $275 for groceries, $475 for entertainment (including pub night, movies, and takeout), $300 for "large" purchases (sneakers, song downloads, and so on), and $150 on miscellaneous items (such as magazines and coffee). After adding up all his expenses the young man will see that he spends roughly $2,725 of his $2,800 salary every month, leaving him only $75 left over for additional expenses. As the young man begins to consider his future and develop long-term financial goals for himself, some of these expenditures might seem frivolous. He might find ways to reduce his spending, some of which might be easy for him to do; he might decide that he can make his own coffee in the morning ($30, as opposed to $100), read magazines at the public library (free, instead of $30), or start going to movies only once a month ($12, rather than $50). Others (such as giving up the sneakers and the electronic games and cutting back on his Friday nights at the pub) might seem more difficult to sacrifice. Still, even if the young man can cut his unnecessary expenditures by 50 percent, he will find himself with an extra $500 a month, or $6,000 a year.

Recent Trends

Traditionally many people have written budgets by hand on pieces of paper, which they subsequently keep stored in folders or file cabinets. With the advent of the personal computer, budgeting has become a far more simple process for most consumers. A number of products allow individuals to use electronic spreadsheets (an accounting method that organizes different categories of income and expenditures into individual columns), and money management software is available for people to keep track of their financial activities. Many of these software programs generate monthly reports, allowing consumers to identify general trends in their spending habits.

$ Bills

What It Means

In the most basic sense a bill is a printed request for money that is owed for a particular product or service. Bills are used to collect payments in a wide range of business transactions, from monthly telephone charges to automobile repairs. In some cases (for example, a document listing the costs involved with a housepainting job or a statement listing the items in a shipment of office equipment) a bill can also be called an invoice. Upon completing a meal at a restaurant, a person receives a final bill, which is typically referred to as a check or, in informal usage, a tab.

Paying bills is a regular and unavoidable ritual of modern life. There are two basic types of bills. Some bills (for example, the invoice an electrician presents a customer after rewiring his kitchen or the bill an accountant presents a client after preparing her taxes) require a one-time payment and are generally due within a certain number of days after the customer receives the bill. Other goods and services, such as utilities (services—including electricity, water, and natural gas—involved with the day-to-day operation of a home or an office), garbage disposal, and telephone charges, are continually recurring and must be paid on a regular basis, usually every month. These monthly bills are often generally referred to as "the bills," as in, "We need to pay the bills before we even think about taking a vacation."

In standard economic terms the person or party who owes money on a bill is known as a debtor, while the party to whom the money is owed is known as a creditor. The money a customer owes toward all his or her bills is sometimes referred to, collectively, as debt. Almost all bills must be paid in full within a certain amount of time, usually a month. One notable exception to this rule involves credit cards (plastic cards used to purchase goods

or services in advance of actually paying for them). With credit card bills customers must make a minimum monthly payment, usually consisting of the interest (a percentage of the amount owed that is charged by the credit card company as a fee for using the card) on the balance due, as well as a small portion of the principal (the amount of money owed, not including the interest). In some cases involving one-time bills, a creditor will come to an agreement with a debtor that allows him or her to pay a bill in installments. These arrangements generally apply to large bills, such as for a hospital stay or a major home repair, and require a level of trust between the customer and the person providing the service or item. After paying a bill the customer will often receive a receipt, a document that provides evidence of the bill's payment.

When a bill goes unpaid for a long period of time, it will usually be sent to a collection agency, a company that attempts to collect payment for the unpaid bill on behalf of the company or individual to which the money is owed. When trying to collect money on an unpaid bill, collection agencies will often use aggressive tactics, such as making repeated phone calls to the debtor's residence or sending a series of threatening letters. If a collection agency is unable to collect payment for an unpaid bill, it will often report the customer's name to credit bureaus (companies that evaluate and rank the credit, or financial reputation, of individuals).

When Did It Begin

Some form of bill has likely existed for as long as human beings have engaged in commercial activities. Historians have uncovered evidence of various invoices and bills that were used in the ancient world. The oldest bills were inscribed on clay tablets and were typically used to document the exchange of material goods. Archaeologists have discovered evidence of business transactions in Assyria (an ancient kingdom in Asia in what is now Iraq), in the form of invoices showing lists of material items relating to a sale of goods, along with their equivalent values in silver.

Evidence of the use of bills in ancient civilization also appears in the Code of Hammurabi, a legal code dating to about 1760 BC. The code was created by Hammurabi (c. 1810 BC–1750 BC), the sixth king of Babylon (an ancient holy city located in Mesopotamia, a region in what would become the modern Middle East), and is widely regarded to be among the oldest existing sets of laws in the world. It contains specific laws regarding transactions between merchants, requiring one merchant to provide an itemized list of goods being sold and the other to provide documentation showing that money has been paid.

More Detailed Information

There are many types of bills, which are roughly divided into two categories: recurring (or monthly) and one-time

A bill is a request for payment from an individual or company who has provided a good or service. Although bills are often still issued as paper documents, the advent of electronic banking services has made it possible to pay bills through the Internet. *AP Images.*

FAMOUS UNPAID BILLS

A bill is a printed statement requesting money for a specific product or service. Generally the person who receives the bill is obligated to pay the amount due within a short amount of time after the bill is issued. On occasion, however, a bill never gets paid, because the person who owes the money either disappears or dies before settling the account (paying off the account in full). There are numerous instances of famous individuals who left behind unpaid bills. Upon his death Irish author Oscar Wilde (1854–1900) left behind an unpaid bill for more than 2,600 French francs (a currency used in France until the early twenty-first century) at a Parisian hotel named, simply, L'Htel. T.E. Lawrence (1888–1935), the British soldier better known as Lawrence of Arabia, left behind an unpaid bar bill at the Baron Hotel in Aleppo, Syria. In both cases the hotels framed the unpaid bills and put them on display in tribute to their famous customers.

bills. Typical recurring bills include phone bills, cable-television bills, power bills (generally involving charges for electricity and natural gas, which are used to run appliances in addition to heating and cooling a home), water bills, sewer bills, and so on. Usually these bills arrive in the mail once a month and are due within two to three weeks from the time they are mailed to the customer. While all bills include a deadline for payment, most monthly bills include a grace period (a length of time extending past the deadline, during which a payment can still be made without resulting in penalty charges or cancellation of service). The length of the grace period varies from company to company and is sometimes determined by the customer's past payments; customers with a record of making late payments or who have poor credit histories are generally given a shorter grace period to pay their bills. In most cases when a customer is unable to pay a bill by the due date, he or she can call the company to try to work out a more flexible payment schedule. Many companies will allow customers to pay bills late, as long as they commit to making the payment by a specific date, agreed upon by both the company and the customer.

Printed bills vary in content and format, depending on the service or product. Still almost all bills contain the same basic information. A customer will find, at the top of most bills, his or her name, address, and account number. The top of the invoice will also typically include the date of the bill and in some cases the payment due date.

In many cases the top of the bill will provide contact information for the company's customer service department, usually a toll-free phone number and an e-mail address. A customer will usually find, directly below the date, several lines of information relating to the service, along with a breakdown of previous charges, payments received, and current charges and a due date. This section is generally referred to as the account summary. For some services this section is relatively straightforward; for example, a cable-television bill will probably list a single amount due, along with, in most cases, any relevant taxes. Other bills, however, can be more complicated. In some areas certain utilities are billed together. A power bill, for instance, may include a breakdown of specific charges for electricity and natural gas, along with the total amount due. Power bill charges may be further broken down into regulated (rates dictated by the government) and deregulated or market (rates determined by the level of competition between companies providing the same service). In addition to this basic outline of charges, power bills also include a second, more extensive breakdown of customer usage, rates, and charges. This breakdown often appears on the back of the bill and contains detailed information concerning the transmission or delivery of the power, storage of the power, supply of the power, and so on. Because this information is highly technical, most customers simply ignore this portion of the bill.

A payment stub, also known as a return portion, usually makes up the bottom portion of a printed bill. This section repeats the same basic information concerning the account information, the charges due, and the due date; it also includes a place where the customer can write the amount enclosed. This section is generally perforated at the top, so that the customer can remove it from the upper portion of the bill and send it, along with a personal check (a piece of paper that facilitates the transfer of money from the customer's bank account), in a payment envelope provided by the company. These payment envelopes usually have a small window between the middle and the right side of the front; the name and address of the company appear on the return portion of the bill, positioned to be visible through the envelope window once the stub is in the envelope.

One-time bills, such as an invoice for car repairs or for an order of photocopies, look slightly different than recurring bills. Much of the same basic information (the customer's account data, the bill date, the due date, and the amount due) is more or less the same. These invoices differ mainly in the way they list the products or services that the customer has received. For example, a bill from a photocopy store might include a column itemizing the products or services provided, along with the individual charges for each. Such a bill might list separate charges for the photocopies, for stapling, and for any other products or services that have been rendered. These amounts will subsequently be tallied as the amount due. The bottom of the invoice might also include several past-due boxes. These boxes provide the past and current charges, along with the number of days the amount has been due. Past-due boxes might appear in the following order: 1–30 days past due, 31–60 days past due, 61–90 days past due, and more than 90 days past due.

Recent Trends

Traditionally people pay their bills by mailing checks to the companies to which they owe money. With the rise of the Internet in the 1990s, however, banks began offering online bill-pay services for their customers, and more and more consumers began to pay their bills electronically. For a small monthly fee customers are now able to use bill-pay services to send money to their creditors. To use bill pay customers create a list of creditors on a personal account page on the bank's website. Each listing includes a column for the amount of money that the customer wants to pay and a column for the date the customer wants the payment to be sent. Electronic bill pay offers several advantages. For one, money travels more quickly electronically than it does by regular mail, thereby providing customers with additional assurance that their payment will arrive on time. Bill pay also spares consumers the postage costs involved with mailing payments to all their creditors each month, while also cutting down on the number of personal checks they write.

$ Buying a Car

What It Means

For most people buying a car (especially a new car) is the second most expensive type of purchase they will make in their lives (buying a house is usually the most expensive). Going about buying a car involves some big decisions, decisions that buyers should be informed about before they take the plunge. Even if you are buying a used car, which will likely cost significantly less, familiarizing yourself with the process will help you get the most for your money and avoid being taken advantage of by the seller.

There are many factors to consider in deciding what kind of car you will buy. First, how much can you afford to spend? If you are planning to pay for the car outright, how much of your savings can you spare? If you are planning to get financing (a loan that you will pay off in monthly installments, along with interest payments, or fees the lender charges for the loan), how much of your income can you put toward car payments each month?

Once you have figured out your financial limits, research various makes and models of cars and consider what features the car you buy must have (as well as which ones are on your wish list). What are the respective safety ratings of various models? Which ones can accommodate your lifestyle (number of family members or friends, space for dogs or gear, and so forth)? Which ones come with a sunroof? Information about new and older models is available through consumer reporting agencies, auto magazines, buying guides, and vehicle reviews on the Internet.

DEALERSHIP SCAMS

There are many ways in which car dealerships take advantage of inexperienced or uninformed customers to bump up the price of a car. One common tactic involves the dealer's extended warranty for the vehicle (a plan that continues the manufacturer's warranty, a guarantee from the manufacturer that promises to pay for repairs to the car within a certain time frame after it is purchased, for a longer time period). A car salesperson may claim that the bank that is financing the buyer's car loan requires the customer to purchase such an extended warranty. This claim is false: the only contingency or requirement a bank makes in relation to a car loan is that the car be insured. Also, the extended warranty the dealer is offering is likely to be incomplete and overpriced. One way to call the salesperson's bluff is to ask him or her to write the extended warranty contingency information on paper. Usually the salesperson will begin backpedaling and come up with a reason to waive the extended warranty "requirement." Note that it might be advantageous to buy an extended warranty, but you will likely find better coverage at a lower price elsewhere.

Keep in mind that in addition to the sale price, there are other major factors that will affect how economical a car is for you in the long run: What kind of gas mileage does the car get? What is the repair record for that model or for a car of that age? How much will it cost to insure? Remember too that you might want to resell or trade in the vehicle someday and that some cars retain their value better than others over time.

The more prepared you are when you step into a car dealership (or even into the driveway of an independent seller), the less likely you will be to make a hasty or unwise decision.

When Did It Begin

Early prototypes of automobiles may be traced back to European inventors in the late seventeenth century. In the United States the first patent for an automobile was granted to Oliver Evans (1755–1819) in 1789. But while automotive technology continued to advance in Europe and America throughout the nineteenth century, the automobile remained more of a novelty than a necessity of life for the average family. In the late nineteenth and early twentieth centuries, however, inventors (most notably Henry Ford) figured out how to mass-produce the automobile, thereby greatly lessening the cost of each vehicle. In the United States 1905 was the first year that automobile sales to average users surpassed sales to hobbyists. By the 1920s it had become standard for most middle-class and even some working-class families to own their own car. Car ownership in America reached new heights in the post–World War II era as suburban housing sprang up outside metropolitan areas, highway infrastructure was vastly expanded, and more and more people became dependent upon the automobile for daily transportation.

More Detailed Information

Buying a New Car When you have decided on a couple of models you are interested in, shop around to find the best price by comparing the listings in newspaper ads, at dealerships, and on the Internet.

If you are planning to get financing for your car, obtain a copy of your credit report (a detailed summary of your credit history that lenders will review to assess how financially responsible you are) from one of the national credit bureaus (Equifax, Experian, and TransUnion) to make sure there are no issues that will prevent you from getting a good interest rate. Also, inquire about financing options at your bank and other lending agencies: often they will offer you a better rate than the car dealership. When you are setting up your financing, remember that the lowest monthly payment is not necessarily the best deal. The total amount you will pay for the car in the end will be determined by the price you settle on with the dealer, the interest rate, and the duration of the loan (how many months it will take you to pay it off).

When you go to the car dealership, plan to negotiate on the price of the car. Most dealers have a certain amount of flexibility in how much they need to profit on any individual car, usually between 10 and 20 percent of the price. Following are some key terms you will want to be familiar with before you enter into the bargaining process.

Invoice price is the initial amount the car manufacturer charges the dealer for the car. The final cost to the dealer is usually lower than this because dealers receive various discounts, rebates (a return of part of a payment), and incentive awards (cost reductions offered by the manufacturer to encourage the dealer to sell more of certain models).

Base price is the cost of the car without options (options are extras, such as air conditioning, alloy wheels, leather upholstery, a CD changer, and so forth). The base price only includes the car's standard equipment and the factory warranty (a guarantee from the manufacturer that promises to pay for repairs to the car within a certain time frame after it is purchased).

Monroney sticker price is the manufacturer's suggested retail price (MSRP). It includes the

People must weigh several factors when buying a car, including how much money to spend and how to pay for it. In order to attract customers, a car dealer will frequently offer a range of financial incentives, including cash rebates. © *Kim Kulish/Corbis.*

base price, the options already installed by the manufacturer, and the manufacturer's transportation charge (the charge for shipping the car from the factory to the dealership). Federal law requires that the sticker price be displayed in the car window and only be removed by the buyer. The sticker also shows the vehicle's fuel economy (or gas mileage).

Dealer sticker price, usually displayed on a secondary sticker on the window, indicates the MSRP plus the suggested retail price of dealer-installed options, additional dealer markup (ADM) or additional dealer profit (ADP), and dealer add-ons, such as interior and exterior protectants for the vehicle or an upgraded alarm system. Be advised that dealer add-ons are exorbitantly overpriced and that the same services can be purchased elsewhere for a fraction of the cost. In general beware of the dealer sticker price! It is just a tactic used by the dealer to start the negotiations at a higher price so that the salesperson can seem to come down on the price without losing any actual profit.

When you have settled on a fair price with the salesperson, be sure to read the contract carefully before you sign it, and do not drive off the lot without a copy of it in hand.

Buying a Used Car Used cars are available from a variety of sources, including dealerships, rental-car companies, and private sellers. Whether you are buying a used car from a dealer, your coworker, or a stranger who advertised in the classified ads (advertisements in the classified section of the newspaper), make sure you check the car out thoroughly before you commit to buying it. Obtain an inspection checklist from a used-car buying guide, and look over the car yourself. Test-drive the vehicle under a variety of road conditions, such as in stop-and-go traffic, on the highway, and on hills. Ask the seller for records of the car's maintenance history (if the seller does not have records, ask him or her to get them from a mechanic who has worked on the car over time). Most importantly, get an official inspection from an independent mechanic you choose yourself. When the mechanic has completed the inspection, make sure to get a report in writing that itemizes any problems the car has and that estimates the cost of necessary repairs. This report can be an important tool for negotiating the price of the car.

Recent Trends

During the 1990s the American automotive landscape was overrun by gas-guzzling sport-utility vehicles (SUVs), some of them averaging just 16 miles to the gallon. There seemed to be no end in sight to the consumer love affair with these vehicles. In the early 2000s, however, as gas prices soared as high as three dollars per

gallon and the dangers of global warming received unprecedented media attention, the need to reduce our dependence on fossil fuels (such as oil) suddenly became an urgent national issue.

Correspondingly the auto industry saw a sharp increase in consumer demand for fuel-efficient vehicles and vehicles that could run on alternative fuels, such as ethanol, electricity, and biodiesel. Whereas SUVs had been the most fashionable cars of the previous decade, high-profile Hollywood celebrities like Cameron Diaz, Leonardo DiCaprio, Will Ferrell, and others promoted the cause (and the glamour) of fuel efficiency by driving hybrid cars. Among the most sought-after green cars (those that preserved environmental quality) were the Ford Escape Hybrid, which got 33 miles to the gallon, and the Honda Civic Hybrid, which averaged 50 miles per gallon. Across the auto industry major manufacturers announced plans to broaden their offerings of clean, fuel-efficient models.

$ Leasing a Car

What It Means

Leasing a car is a process in which a consumer pays for the right to drive a new car for a set length of time without actually purchasing it. A lease is a contract that grants an individual the right to use a certain piece of property for a specific duration in exchange for a regular fee. The individual or entity that owns the property is known as a lessor, while the person paying for the right to borrow the property is the lessee. New-car leases require monthly payments, and they typically span a period of 24 to 48 months. In some cases, a consumer has the right to purchase the vehicle outright at the end of the lease agreement.

A monthly car lease payment is made up of two main parts: the depreciation cost and the finance charge. Depreciation refers to the value the car loses over time. All cars, whether owned, leased, or rented for a short period, are subject to depreciation. In the case of a leased car, the dollar value of the depreciation is the difference between the new car's initial value, or price tag, and its projected value at the time the lease expires, also known as the residual value. The amount of the monthly payments, therefore, is based on the estimated depreciation of the car over the duration of the contract. For example, a consumer wishes to lease a car valued at $20,000 for a period of 48 months. Both parties (the lessor and lessee) agree that, at the end of the period, the car's value will have decreased to $11,600. The depreciation value of the car will be $8,400. Therefore, over the 48-month period of the lease agreement, the consumer will make monthly depreciation payments of $175 ($8,400 divided by 48 months). In essence, the consumer is paying only for the amount of value he or she is using, rather than the car's full value.

The second part of the lease payment, the finance charge, is an additional fee a lessee pays for the right to drive the car. It is calculated as a percentage of the money that the lessor has invested in the car while the lessee drives it and is similar to the interest paid on a loan. The finance charge on an automobile lease is also known as the lease factor or money factor.

When Did It Begin

Automobile leasing first gained popularity in the 1960s. Faced with increasing new-car prices and rising car-loan interest rates, many American consumers of the period began to explore other ways of acquiring a new vehicle without taking on a hefty down payment (the amount of money a consumer pays up front when purchasing a car) and the hassle involved with selling their old car when they wanted to upgrade to a newer model. Since most car-leasing agreements also included a service contract, consumers were spared additional costs of maintenance and repairs. Between 1965 and 1975, the number of annual automobile leases in the United States nearly doubled, from 270,000 to 500,000.

More Detailed Information

A consumer needs to consider a number of factors when leasing a car. The primary consideration is the car's initial value. Generally, the initial value for a leased vehicle is determined by the manufacturer's suggested retail price (MSRP or SRP); this is the same as the full price a consumer might have to pay if the car was purchased. The initial value is not always firm, however, and consumers can frequently negotiate a lower price before taking on the lease.

In addition to the depreciation and interest payments, several other costs are involved in leasing a car. The first payment a lessee makes is the drive-off fee. This fee includes an acquisition fee (an administrative cost related to the creation of the lease agreement), vehicle registration fees (fees relating to the registration of the vehicle under state law), and a destination charge (the cost of transporting the vehicle from the manufacturer to the pick-up site). The drive-off fee can also include a cap reduction fee (similar to, though smaller than, a down payment), which is applied toward the depreciation cost. In most states, a lessee must also pay a monthly sales tax.

By leasing a car, a consumer pays for the right to drive a particular vehicle without taking ownership of it. General Motors made this electric car available for leasing in the late 1990s and early 2000s. *AP Images.*

The sales tax applies only to the depreciation value of the car rather than to the full value, so it is significantly less than the sales tax on new-car purchases.

Car leases also require security deposits. The security deposit is a one-time payment the lessee makes as a guarantee that the car will be returned in compliance with the terms of the lease agreement. If the lessee returns the car in a manner that violates the terms of the lease, for example, the car is damaged, or the car is returned late, then the security deposit may be forfeited. In some cases the lessee may have the option of paying a larger security deposit in exchange for a lower interest rate. Although this method requires a larger cash payment at the start of the lease, lowering the interest rate results in a smaller monthly payment.

Automobile leases specify a set of basic restrictions related to the use, maintenance, and overall care of the car being leased. A lease agreement will generally include a clause related to the car's condition at the end of the lease period, often referred to as the "wear and tear" clause. Because the overall condition of a car invariably deteriorates over time, car lease agreements typically allow for some depreciation. In cases in which a lessee has let the vehicle deteriorate beyond the allowable amount, for example, by permitting the family dog to chew the upholstery, or by driving the vehicle over a curb and damaging the undercarriage, then the lessee will be held liable for the excessive damage. Automobile leases also include a mileage clause, which specifies the number of miles (usually stated as an annual amount) the lessee is entitled to drive the car without extra charges.

Recent Trends

The automobile leasing industry experienced a rapid rise throughout the 1990s. Car leases in 1990 accounted for 13.5 percent of all new-car sales in the United States; by 1996 this figure had risen to 30 percent. According to many economic analysts one of the major factors behind the increase was a change in the United States tax laws. Prior to 1990, car owners could claim on their annual tax returns the interest from car loan payments as a deduction (a sum that is deducted from a taxpayer's total, or gross, annual income, thereby reducing the amount of their income that can be taxed). The new tax code of 1990, however, eliminated this deduction. As a result, the option of leasing a car became attractive to more consumers. Another factor in the rise of auto leasing was the trend in the 1990s toward corporate downsizing (a strategy by which a company reduces its work force and simplifies its business model in order to run its business more efficiently). As demand for company vehicles among major corporations declined, automakers and leasing companies began to target the growing small business market. Auto leasing proved to be an attractive option for many small business owners, because the lower monthly payments

---

LEASING THE ELECTRIC CAR

In the late 1990s public demand increased for environmentally friendly automobiles (cars that emit little or no pollutants). In response, the American automaker General Motors (GM) developed the EV1, an electric car that derived all of its power from a lead-acid battery (a form of rechargeable battery). At the beginning of GM's program in 1997, the company produced 650 EV1s. These vehicles could not be purchased; they were available to consumers only on a two-year lease (in other words, consumers could drive the car for 24 months in exchange for a monthly payment). In 1999 GM built an additional 465 EV1s, which were also lease-only.

The EV1s proved extremely popular with their lessees (the consumers who leased the cars), and several consumers renewed their leases. Many of the lessees even expressed interest in purchasing their vehicles outright. GM refused, however, citing issues of potential liability (the responsibility that a company takes for damage or harm caused by their product). Even after some customers offered to waive the company's liability for the EV1, GM refused to sell them. GM discontinued the EV1 program in 2003. By mid-2005 all of the leased EV1s had been recalled, and, with the exception of a few that were donated to university science departments, the cars were destroyed.

---

allowed them to retain more cash for other business expenses.

$ Buying a Home

What It Means

For most people the biggest purchase they will make in their lifetime is that of a home. Owning a home has many benefits: it is great to be able to call a place your own, to put down roots in a community, and to personalize your living space however you like. Buying a home also makes a lot of financial sense: instead of paying rent to a landlord, you pay off part of your mortgage (home loan) every month and come closer and closer to owning the place outright; meanwhile you can deduct the interest you pay on the loan from your taxes. As you build equity (the value of the property minus the outstanding balance, or what you still owe, on the loan) on the home, you increase your financial security.

But owning a home is also a huge responsibility: on top of paying the mortgage each month, you must pay property taxes, sewer bills, and various other costs. You will also spend time and money on maintenance and repairs; everything from pruning the trees to fixing the furnace is up to you. You cannot afford to neglect this upkeep, for if you do, you will lose value on your investment in the long run. Another potential drawback of

Buying a home is usually the most important financial decision a consumer will ever have to make. In this photo prospective home buyers discuss features of a house with their real estate agent. © *Shelley Gazin/Corbis.*

owning a home is that it is more difficult to move on short notice. Depending on the real-estate market where you live, it may take time to sell the house, and in the meantime your money is tied up in the property. Remember too that while owning a home is generally considered to be one of the safer investments you can make, it is not risk free: the value of the house can decline for a variety of reasons, including a downturn in the economy, the closure of a school in your neighborhood, or damage caused by a natural disaster.

Because buying a home is such a major commitment, it is important to inform yourself and consider many factors carefully before you take the leap.

When Did It Begin

The history of land ownership varies from country to country. In the United States, where owning one's own home has long been thought of as a fundamental part of the American Dream, it was Thomas Jefferson (1743–1862) who established the notion that every citizen has the right to own land. "Nothing is ours, which another may deprive us of," Jefferson said in 1786.

After the Civil War (1861–65) and the onset of the Industrial Revolution (the rapid, major change from an economy based on manual labour to one dominated by industry and the manufacture of machinery that spread from England to the United States in the early nineteenth century), the concept of the American home shifted away from the independent farmstead, where the family cooperated in both economic and domestic work, to a

headquarters for the wife and mother and a place of comfort and refuge to which the children and husband returned after long days at work and school. In the late nineteenth century this notion of home was available only to the privileged few, while the working classes lived in crowded apartments. By the end of World War I (1914–18), however, there was a movement afoot to make home ownership available to a broader segment of the American public.

Still, the most significant rise in single family homeownership came in the aftermath of World War II (1939–45). We trace modern notions of the American Dream to this postwar period, when a generation of young adults, eager to put the sacrifices and communal necessities of the Great Depression (1929 to about 1939) and the war behind them, sought privacy, security, and space in home ownership. Fueled by this demand, the housing industry experienced a massive boom in the construction of affordable single-family homes within driving distance of urban centers of employment. This was the beginning of American suburbia as we know it today.

More Detailed Information

The first step in buying a house is to assess what you can afford. A number of factors, including your income, your monthly expenses, the amount you have saved for the down payment, and the interest rate on your home loan, will determine this figure. Financial advisers recommend using the same ratio of income to payment as when you rent an apartment: your mortgage payment should be equal to or less than 25 percent of your monthly income.

Once you have a rough idea of your price range, it is time to shop for a loan. There are several different types of home loans, but the safest ones are fixed-rate loans: the interest rate and the monthly mortgage payment stay the same over the entire term of the loan (usually 30 years). In order to calculate the specifics of your loan, a mortgage broker (a person working at a bank or mortgage company who arranges home loans) will need to see many of your financial records, including tax returns, recent pay stubs from your job, credit card statements, bank account statements, and so forth. The broker will also obtain a copy of your credit report (a detailed record of your credit history compiled by a national credit-reporting agency). The higher your credit score (a measure of how financially responsible you are) and the lower your debt-to-income ratio (the percentage of your monthly income that goes toward paying off credit card debt, student loans, and other debts), the better the interest rate and the higher the loan amount the broker will offer you.

It is a good idea to prequalify for a loan before you begin house hunting. Being prequalified means that a bank or mortgage company has promised to give you a loan for a certain amount, and the paperwork just needs to be finalized. Shopping for a home with a loan in place puts you in a good position to negotiate when you find a house you like, because the seller can be assured that you can get the financing.

The best way to begin your house hunt is by listing your personal criteria: How many bedrooms? A garage? A basement? A garden? Make separate lists of your wants and needs, and try to find a balance between the two. It is also a good idea to narrow down your search to a couple of neighborhoods that meet your location priorities (for example, where the school districts are good or where your commute to work will be short). Especially if you are a first-time home buyer, it is a good idea to work with a realtor (or buying agent), as he or she will have access to more listings than you and will be able to represent you in the negotiating process.

When you find a house in your price range that you want to buy, the next step is to make an offer. The seller has already listed a sale price, but the amount of your offer will likely be lower unless the real-estate market is extremely competitive. Your realtor will be able to advise you in making an offer that is realistic and fair. He or she will also do the work of drawing up a formal offer in writing. The seller may make a counteroffer, and eventually both parties will agree on a price. Before the deal is closed, however, it is wise to get a professional home inspection. An inspector will alert you to any problems with the condition of the house that might cost you serious money, or even health problems, down the road. Usually there is a contingency in the offer you submit stating that if the inspection uncovers major problems, you can walk away from the deal or renegotiate the price.

Other important steps before you can finalize your loan include buying a homeowner's insurance policy (the lender will not sign off on the loan until the property is insured) and paying closing costs (a long list of fees and payments associated with transferring the property into your name). Finally, after all the requirements are met and the documents are signed, the keys to the home are yours.

Condominiums   For those who wish to own their own home without taking on the full burden of caring for a single-family house, condominiums offer an excellent alternative. A condominium can be a unit of a larger building, like an apartment, or it can be a freestanding structure, like a townhouse. In either case the condominium belongs to a group of similar units, where maintenance of the entire complex (including the lawns, lobby, laundry room, and any other spaces that are common to all the residents) is centralized. This means that a management company takes care of the work, and all of the condominium owners share in the cost. The sale price of a condominium is also more affordable, in general, than that of a detached single-family house, so a condominium can be a great option for people who want to reap the financial benefits of property ownership, such

A HOMEOWNER CANNOT BE A COMMUNIST

William Levitt (1907–94) was a savvy real-estate developer who anticipated the demand for affordable housing for homecoming GIs (U.S. military personnel) after World War II. His pioneering Long Island building project, Levittown, earned him widespread credit as the founder of modern American suburbia. Completed in 1947, Levittown was a planned community of mass-produced houses, each featuring two bedrooms and modern appliances, which sold for between $8,000 and $12,000 each.

The success of Levitt's concept was phenomenal, and he went on to build subsequent Levittowns in Pennsylvania and New Jersey. Other builders rushed to copy the Levittown model, and the face of American housing was changed forever.

An ally of Joseph McCarthy (1907–57), the Wisconsin senator who became the representative of virulent anticommunist sentiment during the 1950s, Levitt once famously quipped, "No man who owns his own house and lot can be a Communist. He has too much to do."

Criticized by some for the boring uniformity of the houses he built, Levitt also came under attack for his racially discriminatory policies. Although he sold his business for a fortune in 1967, his subsequent business ventures failed, and he died on the verge of bankruptcy.

as tax credits and investment value, but are not ready to be solely responsible for a house.

Recent Trends

In the early 2000s interest rates on home loans reached historic lows in the United States. Whereas in the late 1970s and early 1980s the typical 30-year mortgage carried an interest rate near 20 percent, a buyer could get a 30-year mortgage in 2003 for around 5 percent. These low interest rates contributed significantly to a major real-estate market boom. First-time homebuyers entered the market in record numbers, and many people approached home-buying as the best investment they could make. In 2004, while the stock market experienced a downturn, more than 8 million homes were sold in the United States, many of them to buyers purchasing second, third, and even fourth homes as investments. These buyers planned to rent out the additional houses while the property values continued their steep increase and then sell the houses a few years later at a substantial profit. Indeed, in desirable metropolitan areas in Nevada, California, Washington D.C., and Florida, property values went up an astonishing 30 percent during 2004; it was not uncommon for sellers in these markets to receive multiple offers on a home and often to see competitive bidding drive the sale price well above the original asking price. By 2006, however, although interest rates remained favorable, many regions of the country were experiencing significant slowing in real-estate markets, and investors were rushing to unload their properties while they could still expect to make a profit.

$ Renting an Apartment

What It Means

An apartment is a room or suite of rooms designed to function as an independent living space (or residence). The term *unit* is often used to refer to an apartment, which is usually just one portion of a building that accommodates multiple households. Renting an apartment means entering into a legal arrangement with a landlord (the owner of the property) to live in the space for an agreed-upon fee. This fee, which is usually paid on a monthly basis, is called rent. The renter who occupies the apartment is also known as the tenant.

In essence renting is a form of borrowing. Just as you rent a video from the video store with the intention of watching it and returning it, you rent an apartment with the understanding that you will live there for a period of time and eventually return the property to its owner. You rent a video so you can watch the movie without buying it; you rent an apartment so you can live in a particular place without taking on the legal and financial responsibilities of owning it.

The legal agreement between landlord and tenant is represented by a contract called a lease. All of the legal terms of the rental agreement are contained in the lease, so it is important to read it carefully and understand what is expected of you and what you may expect from the landlord. You should also keep a copy of the lease for your records, so that you may refer to it if you need to.

Renting an apartment is not an investment that gains value over time, the way owning a house does. The rent you pay is simply the price of having a roof over your head. Still, there are benefits to renting, such as the freedom to move more easily and the convenience of knowing that someone else is responsible for repairs, property taxes, and other potential headaches and costs.

When you rent an apartment or a house, you do not have any long-term legal and financial obligations to worry about. Another benefit of renting is that the property owner is responsible for repairs. *Photograph by Kelly A. Quin. Cengage Learning, Gale.*

When Did It Begin

Apartment is an American term that came into use in the late nineteenth century in association with an emerging trend in urban housing in New York City. Apartment-style living, with multiple households in the same building, had become popular in Europe decades earlier with the advent of the Industrial Revolution (the rapid, major change in the late eighteenth and early nineteenth centuries from an economy based on manual labor to one dominated by industry and the manufacture of machinery), but in Europe an apartment was and still is more commonly referred to as a flat.

The trend was slower to catch on in the United States, where multiunit housing carried the negative image of tenements: overcrowded, often squalid buildings occupied by immigrants and the working classes. After the Civil War (1861–65), however, as urban real estate became increasingly scarce and expensive, builders began to promote apartment living as a convenient, affordable, even fashionable option for the middle and upper classes. New apartment buildings were modeled after those in Paris, and the units were advertised as "French flats" to ensure that they would not be confused with tenements.

Designed by the Paris-trained American architect Richard Morris Hunt (1828–95) and built by Rutherford Stuyvesant (1842–unknown) in 1869, the Stuyvesant Apartments on East 18th Street in Manhattan was the first apartment building designed in accordance with this new concept. Within 10 years the construction of apartment buildings was booming in New York and elsewhere. By the 1900s, more than 75 percent of American city-dwellers were living in apartments.

More Detailed Information

There are a number of ways of finding an apartment. First, ask around: friends, coworkers, and other local contacts might know of someone who is moving out of a great place that has not yet been put on the market. In addition to using the word-of-mouth approach, many people hunt for an apartment by reading through the classified ads (advertisements in the classified section of the newspaper). In cities where apartments are hard to find, it may be worthwhile to pay for the help of an apartment-finding service. This may mean buying a $50 subscription to a database containing listings that are not available to the general public, or it may mean hiring your own private agent whose fee is as much as one month's rent.

There are many factors to consider when choosing an apartment. Probably first and foremost is the price. As a rule of thumb most money experts suggest that your rent should be no more than 25 percent of your total income. So, for example, if you bring home $3,000 per month, you can afford to pay a maximum of $750 a month in rent. Another important consideration is the location of the apartment: Is it close to public transpor-

tation? Are there amenities nearby, like a grocery store, a bank, and a post office? Is the neighborhood safe? Can you park on the street? All of these factors will make an impact on your daily life.

When you have found an apartment you want to rent, you will likely be asked to fill out an application providing information about your financial situation and your rental history, and you will be asked for a list of references the landlord may contact to confirm that you will be a reliable tenant. While the landlord verifies information about you, you in turn may want to inspect the apartment to make sure it is safe and in good repair. Do the appliances work properly? Are smoke detectors provided? Are the locks secure? Is anything broken or damaged? Identify any problems before you sign the lease, and make sure the landlord agrees either to fix them or at least not to hold you responsible for them.

Once landlord and prospective tenant have satisfied their concerns, the next step is signing the lease. A binding legal contract, the lease stipulates the amount of rent to be paid, as well as the amount of the security deposit. The security deposit (often as much as one month's rent) is paid to the landlord before you move in (usually along with the first and last months' rent) and returned to you when you move out, provided the apartment is in good condition. If anything has been broken or damaged during the time your tenancy, the landlord will deduct the cost of the repair from your deposit.

The lease also outlines a variety of other rules and aspects of the agreement, such as the length of time the tenant will occupy the apartment (the term of a lease may vary from one month to one year); what day of the month the rent is due (usually on or before the fifth); whether utilities, such as electricity and water, are included in or must be paid separately from the rent; whether the tenant may keep a pet, smoke cigarettes, or have a waterbed in the apartment; and many other details. Importantly, too, the lease spells out what happens if you have to break the lease. Say, for example, that you are in the middle of a one-year lease when you get a great new job in another city or when a family member becomes ill and you have to move home. In some cases the landlord may charge a penalty for breaking the lease; in others you may be required to continue paying rent, even after you have moved out, until a new tenant is found.

The fine points of landlord/tenant rights and regulations vary from state to state in the United States, but many of the provisions are common to all states. For example, all states stipulate that both parties must obey health codes and safety rules, that the tenant must not damage the landlord's property or disturb neighbors, and that the landlord is required to give adequate notice (usually 24 hours) before he or she may enter a tenant's apartment. Also, the landlord may not shut off utilities, remove a tenant's belongings from his or her apartment,

RENTING VS. BUYING

According to conventional wisdom renting an apartment is the same as throwing your money away: why would you give $500 to $1000 to a landlord each month when you could put the same money toward paying down the mortgage (paying back the loan) on your own home and build equity (the value of the property minus the outstanding balance, or what you still owe, on the loan) over time? While it is true that owning a home is a desirable long-term investment for many people, the question of whether to rent or buy is not as simple as it seems. Following are some of the pros and cons of each.

The Benefits of Renting Instead of Buying

1. The cost of renting an apartment is more or less fixed for the term of the lease (the rental agreement). By contrast the costs of buying and owning a home are variable and are often hard to predict.
2. You do not need much money up front to rent an apartment, whereas saving for a down payment on a home may take years.
3. When you rent your home, you do not gain equity, but you do not risk losing it either. Owning your home can be more risky. Equity may go up, go down, or stay the same. You have no control over changes in the real-estate market.

4. Someone else (the landlord or rental company) is responsible for most maintenance and repairs on a rental property. Maintenance and repairs on your own home take time and money.
5. When your lease ends on a rented apartment, you are free to move. If you own a home, however, you usually have to go through the arduous process of selling the house in order to move.

The Benefits of Buying Instead of Renting

1. Over time the amount a homeowner owes on the mortgage, or home loan, goes down and equity goes up, even if the value of the home stays the same. When you rent you never build equity or receive any return on the rent money you pay.
2. You are free to paint, remodel, and personalize the home you own however you like. With most rentals, however, you have little ability to change or customize the apartment to fit your needs.
3. If you own your home, the interest you pay on your mortgage is tax deductible. Renters receive no tax advantages related to their residence.

---

or lock a tenant out of his or her apartment in order to collect the rent.

If the tenant fails to pay rent, breaks the rules of the lease, or refuses to move out when the term of the lease is over, the landlord may file a lawsuit to evict (or remove) the tenant. If a judge determines that the eviction request is valid, the tenant may be physically removed from the apartment by a law enforcement officer. Eviction is a serious matter that reflects badly on your rental history and may make future landlords less likely to rent to you. If you need help negotiating a dispute with your landlord, there are state rental and housing agencies that can advise you.

Recent Trends

It has long been assumed that owning your own home is a cornerstone of the American Dream and that the only people who do not graduate from renting an apartment to buying a home are those who lack the financial means to do so. In the early 2000s, however, these assumptions were changing. According to studies done by the Fannie Mae Foundation (an organization that works to help low-, moderate-, and middle-income families buy homes) and the National Multi-Housing Council, an increasing number of high-income Americans were renting apartments as a lifestyle choice. This trend was especially prevalent in high-density urban areas among young adults, singles, and married couples without children (or whose children were grown). For these households the benefits of renting included financial flexibility (because

their investment money was not tied up in a house); the ability to live in desirable urban locations near restaurants, entertainment, and shopping and to do away with long commutes from the suburbs; and liberation from home improvements, yard work, and other such responsibilities. In response to (or perhaps fueling) this change of attitude, developers introduced a new model of high-end apartment building that offers customized interior design, on-site fitness centers, high-speed Internet access, and movie-screening rooms. Some of these cutting-edge buildings even feature an on-site concierge (a staff person who attends the front desk) to facilitate housekeeping, babysitting, grocery delivery, pet care, show tickets, and other arrangements.

HOW TO PAY FOR EVERYDAY PURCHASES

$ Cash

What It Means

Cash refers to the banknotes, or bills, and coins used as money and accepted as legal tender in a society. Legal tender is the currency (units of exchange) that by law cannot be refused in the settlement of a debt in the same currency. Paying for a good or a service with cash is different than paying for a good or a service with a check, a

Cash refers to paper and coin currency issued by a country or group of countries. Paying with cash completes a sales transaction immediately, while other forms of payment, such as a credit card, require clearance from a bank before the transaction is finished. *AP Images.*

credit card, or a debit card, none of which, strictly speaking, are legal tender. In other words, if a person goes to a restaurant in the United States and receives a bill at the end of the meal for $15, then the restaurant must accept payment if the person offers $15 in U.S. cash. The restaurant probably does not accept money in a foreign currency, and it could have a policy against accepting checks, credit cards, or debit cards. The establishment is not required by law to accept these alternative forms of payment. By paying cash, the patron settles his debt with the restaurant immediately. Checks, credit cards, and debit cards, on the other hand, defer payment. If the restaurant accepts payment by check, credit card, or debit card, then they are accepting a promise that they will receive the $15 from a financial institution at a later date.

In the United States cash includes seven units of paper currency and six units of coins. The units of paper cash are the one-dollar bill ($1), the two-dollar bill ($2), the five-dollar bill ($5), the ten-dollar bill ($10), the twenty-dollar bill ($20), the fifty-dollar bill ($50), and the one-hundred-dollar bill ($100). The coins are the penny ($.01), the nickel ($.05), the dime ($.10), the quarter ($.25), the half dollar or fifty-cent piece ($.50), and the silver dollar ($1.00). Of the paper currency, the most frequently used units of cash in the United States are one-, five-, ten-, and twenty-dollar bills. The most frequently used coins are the penny, the nickel, the dime, and the quarter.

When Did It Begin

European explorers of southern India in the sixteenth century encountered the Tamil people, who used a coin called the *kasu* as their currency. The English began referring to this coin as "cass," but this word soon merged with the existing English word *cash*, which meant a box or a chest. The English began calling the Tamil coin "cash." As English exploration of the world continued, the original sense of the word *cash* became obsolete, and the word came to signify money.

Throughout the seventeenth century the English traded with China. At the time, the Chinese called their currency the *wen*, which were coins made of brass, iron, or copper. The English called the *wen* cash. Although most *wen* coins were round with a square hole in the middle, some were shaped like knives, hoes, or shields. No matter the shape, each coin had a round or square hole, which the Chinese used to string the coins together to make larger denominations of money. The *wen* was the Chinese currency from the sixth century BC until AD 1889.

MARY PECK BUTTERWORTH

Mary Peck Butterworth (1686–1775) was one of America's earliest counterfeiters. She made phony cash in colonial Rhode Island from 1716 to 1723. According to those who testified against her, Butterworth used a hot iron to transfer the pattern of colonial legal tender onto phony paper bills. She then used a quill pen and ink to color in the design. At the height of her operation, Butterworth employed most of her extended family in her counterfeiting industry and was reportedly selling her bills for half of their face value. There were so many phony bills in circulation that the Rhode Island economy was in danger of crumbling. Butterworth and her husband were arrested by colonial authorities shortly after purchasing a new home. Two relatives testified against the counterfeiters, but authorities ultimately dropped the case because of a lack of hard evidence. Butterworth is said to have given up counterfeiting after the trial.

More Detailed Information

In most currencies throughout the world, coins are used for the lower-valued cash units and banknotes (bills) are used for the higher-valued cash units. Before banknotes were created, people carried precious metals, such as gold and silver, if they wished to purchase expensive items. However, carrying gold and silver is heavy as well as dangerous. The first people to substitute paper currency for precious metals were the Chinese during the Sui dynasty in the seventh century AD. Aggravated by the weight of the *wen* they carried on strings, these people began leaving their coins with a person who in return gave them a slip of paper indicating how much money he was storing for them. The person could retrieve his coins by presenting the note back to the holder. Gradually this paper currency came to be circulated among merchants and consumers throughout small villages and townships of China. A note could be given as a promise to pay the recipient a specified amount of precious metal that was stored somewhere. In a sense, the early bank notes were IOUs, or promissory notes. At first, these notes could be used only in certain areas and were valid for only a short period of time. By AD 960, however, banknotes were printed by the government of the Sung dynasty and were valid throughout the kingdom of China.

In the United States the U.S. dollar was established as the nation's official currency by a body known as the Congress of the Confederation of the United States on July 6, 1785. Since 1861 U.S. banknotes have been printed by the Bureau of Engraving and Printing (BEP), an official government agency. Money is printed at the BEP facilities in Washington, D.C., and Fort Worth, Texas. These notes are then transported to the Federal Reserve, the central banking system in the country, which puts the money into circulation. In 1995 there were more than $380 billion U.S. dollars in circulation. Two-thirds of these dollars were outside the country's borders. Within a decade that figure had doubled to nearly $760 billion, with about the same fraction in circulation outside the country. Today there is no note larger than the $100 bill, though this was not always the case. Until 1945 the BEP printed $500, $1,000, $5,000, and $10,000 bills.

Most banknotes are printed on a heavy paper that is mixed with linen and cotton. This product is more durable than ordinary paper, so that the money will not rip easily or disintegrate after it has changed hands numerous times. Throughout history, however, banknotes have been issued on some interesting materials. In French Canada in 1865, emergency paper money was printed on playing cards. In the Netherlands in the sixteenth century, banknotes were issued on leather, and once, in a crisis, people used the covers of church hymnals to make paper currency. Between World War I and World War II, some German towns printed bills on silk. During the Boer War in 1902 in South Africa money was printed on khaki fabric.

U.S. coins are produced at the U.S. Mint, which was founded in 1792 with the passage of the Coinage Act. The first office of the U.S. Mint was established in Philadelphia, Pennsylvania, which in the 1790s was the nation's capital. The main office is still in Philadelphia, and branch offices are located in Denver, Colorado; San Francisco, California; and West Point, New York. The U.S. Mint sells the coins it produces to the Federal Reserve, which puts them into circulation.

Recent Trends

Most Americans pay for goods and services with a debit card or a credit card rather than with cash. According to some estimates, U.S. shoppers were making one-third of their purchases with a debit card as of July 2006. Since 2000 the use of debit cards has increased by 50 percent in the United States. Rather than going to the bank to withdraw money, shoppers frequently use their debit cards to retrieve cash from their bank accounts when they purchase items in a store. Before concluding most debit-card transactions, the store cashier will ask a customer if he or she wishes to have any additional "cash back." The customer has the option to withdraw a certain amount of cash from his or her bank account. If the customer chooses $20 cash back, for example, then $20 will be added to the bill for the goods purchased, and the cashier will give the customer $20 in cash.

Many Americans prefer using credit cards to cash. Since 1990 credit-card debt in the United States has soared. In 1990 some 82 million Americans had credit cards. By 2003 that number had grown to 144 million. During that period the amount that Americans charged rose from $338 billion to $1.5 trillion. As of 2006 research indicated that Americans owed more than $800 billion in credit-card debt. The average balance (the amount owed) on an American's credit card is $9,300.

$ Checking Account

What It Means

A checking account is an account that an individual establishes at a financial institution in order to pay monthly expenses and to purchase goods and services. When a person opens a checking account, he or she receives a checkbook and a ledger to record the funds released from and deposited into the account and the amount of money remaining in the account. A checkbook contains a series of checks, or small rectangular pieces of paper, printed on which are the account holder's name, address, and account number; the banking institution's name; and a series of blank lines. The account holder writes instructions on these lines authorizing the financial institution to release from the checking account a specified amount of money to designated individuals, businesses, or other organizations.

For example, a person who is charged $92 for a furnace repair by a repair person may pay the bill with a check rather than with cash. To pay with a check, the person removes a check from the checkbook and writes the following information on it: the day's date; the name of the institution or individual authorized to receive the funds from the account; the amount in dollars and cents that the institution or individual may receive from the account; and his signature as the account holder, which verifies that he releases the funds to the designated institution or individual. The repair person will then have the option of taking the check to his banking institution, to the customer's banking institution, or possibly to a third party to cash the check (receive the funds specified on the check). When the repair person cashes the check, the money will be withdrawn, or subtracted, from the customer's checking account.

When Did It Begin

The first paper money issued by the Chinese in the seventh century AD functioned in much the same way that a check does today. Back then, Chinese currency consisted of brass, iron, and copper coins with holes in the middle. The Chinese would run a string through the holes to make larger denominations of money, but carrying these weighty metals became inconvenient and dangerous. To eliminate the burden of carrying these coins, the Chinese

With a checking account, a person can use checks to pay bills and purchase everyday goods and services. The amount of the checks can be recorded in a check register, or ledger, such as the one shown here. *Photograph by Kelly A. Quin. Cengage Learning, Gale.*

FRANK WILLIAM ABAGNALE, JR.

Born on April 27, 1948, in Westchester County, New York, Frank William Abagnale, Jr., operates a financial fraud consultancy firm known as Abagnale and Associates. Abagnale is an expert on the subject of financial fraud, having written fraudulent checks totaling over $2.5 million for five years during the 1960s. During this time Abagnale maintained at least eight aliases (false names) and wrote bad checks in 26 countries. Among his many identities Abignale assumed the name of Frank Williams and posed as a pilot for the commercial airline Pan Am. He used his fake employment status to obtain free flights from the airline. He also pretended to be a physician named Frank Connors and supervised interns for 11 months at a medical facility in Georgia. Abganale was finally arrested in France in 1969. He served six months in a French prison, another six months in a Swedish prison, and then five years of a 12-year sentence for forging checks under an assumed name in the United States. After being released, Abagnale attempted to pay back everyone he had swindled. A major Hollywood movie called *Catch Me If You Can* was based on Abagnale's life.

began storing their money with a trusted individual in exchange for a note stating how many coins were held in storage. Gradually, people began to purchase goods and services with these notes instead of offering coins at the point of sale. If a person bought an item with a note, the seller could then take the note to the place where the coins were stored and retrieve the coins. If the seller did not wish to carry the coins on his person, he could request that the coins now be stored on his behalf, rather than on behalf of the previous owner of the coins. Or, if he chose, the seller could take the coins and store them with another trusted individual. The individuals who stored money for merchants and consumers were performing a service similar to modern banks. The notes used as a means of exchange resembled modern checks because a person could cash or redeem these notes the way people today cash checks.

More Detailed Information

There are two important differences between a checking account and a savings account. The first difference is the purpose of each type of account. In most cases, a person opens a savings account to hold or accumulate funds he or she intends to store for a period of time, rather than spend. People may establish a savings account in order to one day purchase a large item, such as a car or a house. Some people store money in a savings account in case they lose their job or source of income. If such an event were to occur, a person could immediately withdraw the money or transfer it into his or her checking account without paying the bank a fee. (Other forms of invest-

ment, such as mutual funds and retirement funds, charge significant penalties if funds are withdrawn before a pre-arranged date.) The purpose of a checking account, on the other hand, is not to store and accumulate funds, but rather to pay for regular expenses, such as phone bills and car payments.

The second difference between a checking and a savings account is that savings accounts pay interest and most checking accounts do not. The interest on a savings account is a small fee that the bank pays an individual for storing his or her money in that institution. For example, if a savings account pays 3 percent interest, this means that at certain specified times of the year, the bank will add 3 percent to the sum, or balance, in the client's account. Interest allows the balance in the savings account to grow even if the customer does not deposit additional funds. Until the 1930s it was illegal in the United States for a bank to pay interest on checking accounts. Now some checking accounts pay small amounts of interest, but they require an individual to maintain a specified minimum balance. For example, a bank may have a type of checking account called a "preferred checking account" or an "advantage checking account" that pays 0.5 percent interest if the client maintains a minimum balance of $1,500. According to this agreement, if the client is to receive the interest, then the account must have at least $1,500 on the date that the bank is scheduled to pay the interest.

Anyone who has a checking account must be careful to track the funds that are deposited into the account and withdrawn from it. This is called balancing the account, or balancing the checkbook. A person balances an account in a ledger or transaction register by adding all deposits to the total sum in the account and subtracting the value of each check from the total in the account. For example, if there is $200 in an account and a check is written for $95, then the account holder should subtract $95 from $200 and note that $105 remains in the account. Maintaining accurate records will prevent an overdraft, or writing a check for an amount greater than the balance of the account. For example, if the person with $105 in his account wrote another check for $150, then the $150 check is an overdraft. The account holder would receive a notification from his bank informing him that the check could not be cashed because there were insufficient funds in the account. The account holder would have to pay a penalty for "bouncing" the check. To prevent this, some people have checking accounts with overdraft protection. If a person with overdraft protection overdraws his or her checking account, the bank will automatically draw the insufficient funds either from the person's savings account or charge those funds to his credit card.

Recent Trends

Since the turn of the millennium more people have begun using new technology to purchase goods and services and to pay their bills. Rather than write a check or pay cash, many people purchase goods with a debit card, which is a plastic card that resembles a credit card but operates like a check. In order to conduct a transaction with a debit card, either the merchant or the customer swipes the card through a computer terminal. The computer then reads the banking information encoded in a strip on the card and verifies with the customer's financial institution that the customer has enough money in his or her account to pay for the merchandise. If the account has sufficient funds, then the customer is asked to verify the purchase price for the goods. Depending on the merchant's computer system, the customer is asked to verify the transaction in one of two ways: either by entering his personal four-digit code number (known as a PIN, or personal identification number) or by signing a sales receipt. According to some estimates, U.S. shoppers made approximately one-third of their purchases in 2006 with a debit card.

Instead of writing checks to pay monthly bills, many Americans make arrangements to have funds automatically withdrawn from their checking accounts each month. For example, a person can give permission to the energy company to withdraw funds from his or her account to pay for the monthly heating bill. Similar arrangements can be made for the phone bill, the cable-television bill, and mortgage and car payments. Instead of writing these withdrawals in a traditional checkbook, the individual can verify the status of his or her account by visiting the bank's website and logging in to his or her account with a username and password.

$ Credit Card

What It Means

A credit card is an electronic-payment card that enables the cardholder to make purchases against a line of credit. (A line of credit is a form of loan, according to which a bank or other financial institution grants a consumer permission to spend up to a preapproved limit of money, with the understanding that he or she will pay it back over time.) Other forms of electronic-payment cards include debit cards, which take the funds for a purchase directly from the cardholder's checking account; and charge cards, which require the cardholder to pay off the entire balance of his or her purchases at the end of each billing cycle (usually monthly).

Unlike a debit card or a charge card, a credit card permits the cardholder to maintain a running balance (debt) from one billing cycle to the next, as long as he or she makes a small minimum payment each month. This form of credit is called "revolving credit" because it continues to roll over at the end of each billing cycle; there is no set number of installments for paying off the balance, as is the case with a home loan, or a car loan. The amount of credit available on the account (figured as the difference between the credit limit and the balance at any

---

THE MINIMUM-PAYMENT TRAP

Credit cards are electronic-payment cards that offer consumers a convenient way to "buy now and pay later." The bank that issues the credit card extends a line of credit, meaning that the cardholder can make purchases up to a preset spending limit and pay them off over time (along with a fee called interest). The option to gradually pay off a purchase appeals to many people.

Credit card debt can quickly spiral out of control, however. Part of the problem is that the bank only requires the cardholder to make a minimum monthly payment that is a small percentage of what he or she owes. Consider this: you have a credit card with a $5,000 credit limit. Over the course of two years, you buy a new TV, a couple of plane tickets, some new clothes, and a few restaurant meals on special occasions. Suddenly the balance on your card is $3,800.

Suppose the annual interest rate (APR) is 17.24 percent (a common rate for young, less financially established cardholders) and your minimum monthly payments are $76 (or 2 percent of your balance). If you only pay the minimum each month, it will take more than 30 years to pay off the card. In the end, that $3,800 in purchases will have cost you more than $12,000.

---

given time) is continually expanding and shrinking according to how much the cardholder spends using the card and how much he or she pays off each month. The balance that remains on the account from one month to the next is called revolving debt. This debt is subject to interest charges, which typically range from 5 percent to 25 percent a year.

The two biggest brands of credit card in the world are MasterCard and Visa. It is important to note, however, that Visa, MasterCard, and other brands (such as American Express and Discover) do not issue cards to people. Rather, they license their brand to individual member banks, and the banks issue the cards and extend credit to account holders. Further, each issuing bank is responsible for setting the specific terms of its customers' credit card accounts (such as the interest rate), which means that not all Visa cards, for example, are alike.

When Did It Begin

Visa and MasterCard trace their origins to 1958 and 1966, respectively. Visa's predecessor was Bank-Americard, the product of California-based Bank of America. In 1966 Bank of America began to offer other U.S. banks licenses for the right to issue the Bank-Americard, and in the early 1970s it started expanding internationally. MasterCard's predecessor, introduced in 1966 to compete with BankAmericard, was "Master Charge: The Interbank Card." It was created by the Interbank Card Association (ICA), an association of banks.

Credit cards enable people to make purchases on a "buy now, pay later" basis. Banks, department stores, and other retail establishments that issue credit cards offer revolving credit, meaning that the cardholder can carry a balance from one month to the next and pay it off in small installments. *Photograph by Kelly A. Quin. Cengage Learning, Gale.*

Master Charge, too, expanded rapidly: two years after launching the card, the ICA had begun to partner with foreign banks.

In the early years of credit cards, merchants had to obtain authorization for each purchase their customers made by calling the issuing bank on the telephone. This process was revolutionized in the early 1970s, however, when issuing banks and merchants became linked through a centralized computer network, which enabled authorizations to be transmitted electronically. Another major technological advancement of this period was the introduction of the magnetic stripe on the back of the card, which increased the efficiency of authorization and helped to prevent fraud (such as illegal use of the card). The magnetic stripe contains encrypted data that, when swiped through a reading device at the point of sale (or cash register), identifies the account and the cardholder.

More Detailed Information

Each bank sets its own terms for the credit cards it issues. Further, a given bank may set different terms for different cardholders, according to their income and credit history (a financial report card of sorts that shows how much money a person owes to his various creditors and how reliable he is about paying his bills on time). If a person has a low income and a poor credit history, the bank must assume that extending credit to him is risky, and it will likely charge him a high interest rate in order to offset this risk (or it might deny his application altogether). On the other hand, if someone has a fairly high income and an exemplary credit history, the bank will rank him as a safe person to extend credit to and will likely offer a lower interest rate.

Annual Percentage Rate (APR) Annual percentage rate (APR) is one of the most important variables to consider when using a credit card. The APR on the card is the amount of interest, such as 15 percent, the bank will charge the cardholder per year on her revolving account balance. The higher the credit card's APR, the more it costs to carry a balance on that card.

Credit cards usually specify one APR for purchases and another, higher APR for cash advances. With a cash advance the cardholder withdraws money against his credit limit. To do so, he can make the transaction with a bank teller, or he can insert his credit card into an ATM (automated teller machine), enter his PIN (personal identification number), and withdraw cash. Usually only a portion of the card's total credit limit is available for cash advances. In addition, many card-issuing banks charge a cash-advance fee, typically calculated as 2 to 3 percent of the total amount of the advance.

Minimum Payments Credit card holders receive a monthly statement, or bill, which summarizes the activity (purchases and payments) on the card for that month. The statement also specifies the minimum payment the cardholder must make for that billing period in order to keep the account in good standing. The minimum payment tends to be just a tiny amount (such as 2 to 4 percent) of the total balance; often it is only slightly more than the interest charged on the balance for the same period. Thus, if the cardholder only pays the minimum each month while the balance continues to accrue interest, it can take him years, even decades, to pay off the debt.

Late Fees A credit card statement stipulates the date by which the payment must be received by the issuing bank. If the payment is late, the issuing bank will charge the cardholder a late fee. Late payments can also result in other penalties, such as an increase in the card's APR and a blemish on the cardholder's credit rating.

Over-Limit Penalties If the cardholder's account balance exceeds his or her preset credit limit, the bank may charge an over-limit penalty for that billing cycle. In many cases, when someone tries to make a purchase that will put his or her account over the limit, the card will be denied at the point of sale; but if the purchase is only a few dollars over the limit, the transaction will sometimes go through. Also, sometimes it is interest charges that put the balance over the limit.

Recent Trends

In the 1990s many banks that issued credit cards launched aggressive marketing campaigns aimed at college students. Whereas it was once unheard of for someone without a steady income to receive a credit card, by 2004 about 75 percent of college students had a least one credit card, and 40 percent had at least four. Young, free from parental supervision, and financially inexperienced, students could fill out a credit card application in about five minutes and receive a card with a $2,000 spending limit within a couple of weeks. Over the course of four years of college, they could rack up debt that would burden them for years to come. According to Nellie Mae, a student-loan provider, in 2004 college seniors carried an average of nearly $3,000 in credit card debt.

MASTERCARD

What It Means

MasterCard is the second-largest brand of electronic-payment card in the United States after Visa. A Mas-

SECURITY BREACH

At the start of the twenty-first century, increasing numbers of people began to conduct their financial transactions (including basic banking, paying bills, and trading stocks) over the Internet. Thus, the ability of companies to ensure the security and privacy of electronically transmitted financial information became paramount. In 2005 MasterCard (one of the world's leading credit card companies) and a number of other credit card companies suffered a public-relations disaster when it was revealed that a massive security breach had occurred at CardSystems Solutions, Inc., a third-party processor of payment-card data in Tucson, Arizona. The breach, which was described as one of the largest of its kind in history, exposed an estimated 40 million credit card accounts (13.9 million of which belonged to MasterCard customers) to potential fraud. Although MasterCard acted swiftly to identify and correct the problem, the incident highlighted the extreme difficulty of providing total information security in the electronic age.

terCard (like a Visa card) can be either of the two major types of electronic-payment cards: a credit card or a debit card. A credit card works according to a "pay later" system, whereby its holder makes purchases on a line of credit (a type of loan) issued by a bank or other financial institution and repays the amount of those purchases to the bank in monthly installments. A debit card (also known as a check card) works according to a "pay now" system, allowing its holder to access existing cash funds in his or her checking account electronically instead of paying with cash or a check (a paper form used to transfer money out of a bank account).

MasterCard is the brand name of MasterCard Worldwide, an international membership organization that is jointly owned by nearly 25,000 banks and other financial institutions. MasterCard itself does not issue credit to cardholders; the member banks issue cards under their own names. As such, MasterCard is also not involved in setting annual fees or determining interest rates (interest is a fee charged as a percentage of the outstanding balance) associated with the card.

When Did It Begin

MasterCard traces its origins to 1966, when a group of banks formed the member-owned Interbank Card Association (ICA) to compete with California-based Bank of America, which had begun issuing the BankAmericard (now Visa card) in 1958. The ICA's answer to the BankAmericard was "Master Charge: The Interbank Card." Within two years ICA had begun to expand into international markets, partnering with banks in Mexico, Europe, and Japan. In 1979 ICA renamed Master Charge as MasterCard.

MasterCard is one of the two most recognized brands of credit card in the world. With the launch of its award-winning "Priceless" ad campaign in 1997, the company made measurable gains in its ongoing effort to compete with its number one rival, Visa. *The Advertising Archive Ltd.*

At first, bank authorizations for credit card purchases were issued over the telephone. In the early 1970s, however, ICA revolutionized its authorization process, establishing in 1973 a centralized computer network that linked merchants (anyone receiving a credit card payment) with the financial institutions that issued the cards, and introducing in 1974 a magnetic strip on the back of its cards. The latter made authorizations more efficient while also reducing the possibility of fraud.

More Detailed Information

In the 1980s MasterCard began to expand its range of products and services, most notably by entering the automated teller machine (ATM) market. With the purchase of Cirrus, the world's largest ATM network, in 1988, and the subsequent launch of the MasterCard/CIRRUS ATM Network, MasterCard delivered fast and easy cash access to its cardholders at more than 50,000 locations worldwide.

In 1991 MasterCard partnered with Europay International (a leading financial-services provider in Europe) to introduce Maestro, a global online point-of-sale debit network, which enabled cardholders to substitute MasterCard for cash and checks anywhere the MasterCard logo was displayed. This innovation greatly increased the use of MasterCard for ordinary retail transactions such as buying groceries or gas.

By the start of the twenty-first century, MasterCard's services were available in more than 210 countries and territories, and its cards were accepted at more than 24 million locations worldwide. The three largest shareholders (thus the three most prominent banks issuing MasterCard credit cards) were JPMorgan Chase, Citigroup, and Bank of America. In addition to Visa, MasterCard's main competitors were American Express and Discover.

MasterCard's business model is three-tiered. First and foremost, the company is a franchisor, which means that it licenses its name and trademark (its franchise) to the financial institutions that wish to issue its cards. On this tier, the company's primary activities include developing marketing strategies to enhance the strength of its brand name and setting terms of use with, and collecting fees from, its members, or franchisees.

On the second tier of its business model, MasterCard is concerned with processing the billions of transactions that occur with its cards around the world every day. The company must maintain its transaction-authorization network (the global electronic system that processes purchases) and keep pace with technological advances that will increase the speed and efficiency of the system.

On the third tier, MasterCard offers professional advisory services to its members. Introduced in 2001, MasterCard Advisors is a global consultancy program that tracks consumer behavior patterns and buying trends and provides other strategic solutions to help its members expand their businesses.

Recent Trends

In the 1990s, in spite of continued innovations and advances, MasterCard continued to trail behind its number one competitor, Visa, in terms of brand recognition and credit card billings worldwide. Perhaps MasterCard's greatest strategic initiative at the turn of the century was the launch of its award-winning "Priceless" advertising campaign in 1997. The ads presented a list of goods and services with their accompanying price tags, followed by some intangible aspect of living well, such as reading bedtime stories to one's child, which was acknowledged as "priceless." Using the tagline "There are some things money can't buy. For everything else, there's MasterCard," MasterCard successfully positioned itself as a friendly, down-to-earth credit card company that simply wanted to make buying things easier so that people could get on with the truly important things in life. The campaign, which ran in some 210 countries and 49 languages, dramatically increased MasterCard's brand recognition and contributed to significant growth for the company.

In 2006 the company changed its name from MasterCard International to MasterCard Worldwide in order to place more emphasis on the global scale of its operations.

VISA CARD

What It Means

Visa is the world's leading brand of electronic-payment card. There are more than one billion Visa cards in circulation.

The two main forms of electronic-payment card are credit cards and debit cards. A credit card enables its holder to make purchases on a line of credit (a kind of loan) issued by a financial institution, usually a bank. A debit card (also known as a check card) simply allows its holder to access existing cash funds in his or her checking account. Whereas a credit card allows the cardholder to repay the amount of the purchase to the bank in monthly installments, debit cards require that the purchase be paid for in full at the time of the sale.

Visa is the brand name of Visa International Service Association, a company owned by some 20,000 member banks that are licensed to issue Visa cards under their own names (for example, Bank of America Visa or Wells Fargo Visa). Visa International itself does not issue cards or provide credit to cardholders. Rather, each member bank issues the cards, setting its own terms of agreement (such as the annual fee for using the card, the interest rate that will be charged on outstanding credit balances, and late-payment penalties) with cardholders. Member banks are

---

RADICAL THINKER

The founder and original CEO of Visa, the world's leading credit card company, was banker Dee W. Hock (b. 1929), a self-taught financial visionary who believed that the key to his company's success was a blend of chaos and order. According to the company's business model, "chaos" refers to the fact that the banks that issue Visa cards must compete with each other for cardholders, and "order" refers to the necessity that competing banks cooperate to make the Visa system work. Hock coined the term chaordic to describe this inherent tension within the company. In 1991 he was inducted into the U.S. Business Hall of Fame.

---

also responsible for contacting merchants with requests that they accept Visa cards and for providing the necessary technical support for these merchants to handle Visa purchase transactions. The banks that issue Visa cards compete with one another for cardholders, yet they are all bound together by the need to cooperate so that participating merchants can take a Visa card issued by any bank.

Visa International's central role is to serve as a hub between cardholders and merchants. It does this by maintaining the massive, around-the-clock electronic-payment network through which purchases are processed. Visa International is also responsible for enhancing its brand name through marketing, sponsorship agreements, and other activities. In turn, Visa makes most of its money by charging its member banks fees.

When Did It Begin

The Visa brand traces its origins to 1958, when California-based Bank of America began issuing BankAmericard, the first electronic-payment card of its kind. In 1966 Bank of America began licensing other U.S. banks to issue the BankAmericard. In 1970 the bank agreed to sell the BankAmericard credit card program to NBI (National BankAmericard, Inc.), a newly formed corporation in which all of the banks that issued BankAmericard had equal ownership. The creation of NBI was spearheaded by Dee W. Hock (b. 1929), a banker at National Bank in Seattle, one of the licensee banks.

In the early 1970s BankAmericard began a process of international expansion. Through agreements with foreign banks, the card was issued under many different names, including Barclaycard in the United Kingdom, Chargex in Canada, Sumitomo Card in Japan, and Bancomer in Mexico. Finally, in 1976 BankAmericard and affiliated cards were rebranded as "Visa," a name that could be instantly recognized (and pronounced the same way) all over the world.

More Detailed Information

Since the name Visa was introduced to the world more than three decades ago, the company has achieved phenomenal growth and capitalized on emerging technologies to increase the efficiency, convenience, and reliability of its services. Throughout most its history, Visa surpassed its main competitors, including MasterCard, American Express, and Discover, in terms of brand recognition and worldwide billings.

One of Visa's greatest successes in promoting its brand name came in 1986, when the company became the official credit card sponsor of the Olympic Games. According to the agreement, Visa would pay a significant sponsorship fee in exchange for being the only credit or debit card accepted for purchases of tickets, souvenir merchandise, and all other items sold at Olympic events. Visa would also be the only card accepted by automated teller machines (ATMs) in the Olympic complex and other official Olympic venues. Further, Visa would be the only credit card company entitled to advertise or display its logo at the games. This exclusive agreement, which was planned to continue through the 2012 Olympics, proved enormously successful in raising international public awareness of the Visa brand.

Also during the 1980s Visa greatly expanded its services by providing cardholders with immediate access to cash through a partnership with Plus System, Inc., one of the largest ATM networks in the United States. In the late 1980s, through an agreement with Interlink, the largest network in the United States for accepting debit cards in restaurants and retail stores, Visa became the leading brand for debit cards nationwide. By enabling its cardholders to use a debit card to pay for everyday purchases such as groceries and gas, Visa opened up a vast new frontier of payment convenience for its cardholders. In the 1990s, with the advent of Internet commerce and the rapid increase in demand for debit card use, Visa was focused on implementing new technologies to improve the speed, capacity, and security of its payment-processing network.

Recent Trends

In the early twenty-first century, as more and more people began to rely on the Internet for shopping, banking, paying bills, and other financial activities, securing electronic information against fraud became crucial in the credit card industry. Credit card fraud is a form of stealing in which someone purchases goods or services with a credit card number that does not belong to them. Often the thief makes thousands of dollars in purchases before either the cardholder or the bank realize the card is being misused. Among other initiatives, in 2002 Visa launched "Verified by Visa," a program designed to enhance the security of online purchasing by requiring a password (chosen by the cardholder and registered with the bank that issued the Visa card) before the completion of any purchase.

In 2005, however, both Visa and MasterCard were implicated in a high-profile security breach at CardSystems Solutions, a small, third-party payment processor in Tucson, Arizona, which left the accounts of some 40 million cardholders (most of them Visa and MasterCard) exposed to fraud. The breach drew significant attention to the difficulty of safeguarding electronic information. Shortly thereafter, in an effort to restore consumer confidence in the electronic-payment system, the rival companies joined forces to create the PCI (Payment Card Industry) Security Standards Council, an independent body that would establish and enforce security standards throughout the industry.

$ Charge Card

What It Means

A charge card is a kind of electronic-payment card that enables its holder to make purchases on short-term credit granted by the issuer of the card. The two other most common forms of electronic-payment card are the credit card and the debit card.

Although the terms *charge card* and *credit card* are often used interchangeably, they are not the same. With a charge card the cardholder is required to pay off the full amount of the balance on the card at the end of each billing cycle (usually one month). By contrast, a credit card allows the cardholder to carry a running balance on the card from one billing cycle to the next, because he or she is only required to make a nominal minimum payment (for example, if a credit card balance is $500, the minimum monthly payment might only be $15). Credit cards offer what is called revolving credit; the running balance on the card is called revolving debt.

A charge card is also different from a debit card. With charge card purchases the card issuer (American Express, for instance) pays the merchant and then bills the cardholder at the end of the month, but debit card purchases are withdrawn directly from the cardholder's bank account. If adequate funds are not present in the account at the time of the purchase, then the transaction will not be approved.

When Did It Begin

The Western Union Telegraph Company introduced the first consumer charge card in 1914, enabling its customers to charge Western Union purchases to an account and pay later. Department stores and other retail businesses soon followed suit, offering charge cards exclusively for use in their own establishments.

The first multiuse charge card was introduced in 1950, when businessman Frank McNamara (1917–57) and two of his associates founded the Diner's Club. That year, with an original membership of just 200 cardholders

Purchases made with a charge card must be paid off in full at the end of each billing cycle. The American Express card, the most prominent brand of charge card in the world, has long been a mark of prestige for individual consumers and businesses. *Photograph by Kelly A. Quin. Cengage Learning, Gale.*

(mostly businessmen who needed to dine out with clients), the Diner's Club card was accepted by about two dozen restaurants in New York City. The card quickly became a desirable sign of status and buying power, and the Diner's Club saw exponential growth in the number of its cardholders and participating merchants.

More than half a century later, Diner's Club remains one of the leading issuers of charge cards in the world, along with American Express (which started providing charge cards in 1958).

More Detailed Information

The difference between a charge card (nonrevolving credit) and a credit card (revolving credit) is significant. By requiring cardholders to pay off the full amount of their balances each month, charge cards essentially force these consumers to live within their means. A cardholder who fails to pay off the full balance at the end of the billing cycle may jeopardize the standing of her account and will likely incur a penalty fee of up to 5 percent of his or her remaining balance. While these terms are rigorous, the great benefit of the charge card is that, because the cardholder pays the balance in full each month, there are no interest charges (fees figured as a percentage rate of the amount owed) and no spending limit imposed on the card.

With a credit card, on the other hand, the cardholder has the option to make purchases far above what he or she can pay off in the course of a single billing period. Meanwhile, the balance he or she carries on the card is subject to interest charges. If the interest rate is high and the cardholder's minimum monthly payments are low, the interest charges will make the balance continuously increase, and a credit card user can easily become buried under a mountain of debt that will take years to pay off. In 2006 the U.S. Government Accountability Office (the investigative arm of Congress) estimated that the credit card industry was receiving about 70 percent of its revenue from interest on revolving debt and from late-payment penalties.

Credit cards are popular, but for various reasons some people prefer charge cards. Over the decades Diner's Club and American Express have successfully marketed their cards as symbols of affluence, worldliness, and social influence. Indeed, one of American Express's best-known advertising slogans is "Membership has its privileges." In addition to individuals seeking such prestige, government agencies and companies (from small

THE FIRST SUPPER

The Diner's Club card was the first multiuse charge card (a payment card that can be used to make purchases at numerous business establishments instead of just one). According to legend, the inspiration for the card came in 1949, when businessman Frank McNamara was out to dinner with a client at a New York City restaurant called Major's Cabin Grill. When the bill came, McNamara was embarrassed to discover that he had left his wallet in the pocket of another suit. Although he did not have to work off the tab by washing dishes (his wife was able to bail him out), McNamara did not soon forget the experience. Certain that a businessman should be able to spend what he could afford, rather than being limited to the amount of cash he had on hand, McNamara got together with his lawyer and hammered out an idea, wherein certain restaurants would agree to allow financially responsible individuals to sign for their meals and pay the bill later. In February 1950 he returned to the same restaurant, and when the bill came, he presented the first Diner's Club card (it was made of cardboard), asking the waiter to "charge it." In the payment-card industry that meal is still referred to as "The First Supper" (a tongue-in-cheek reference to the biblical story of Christ's Last Supper).

businesses to major international corporations) have also adopted charge cards as a tool of choice for managing expenses and extending spending privileges to employees.

Even though charge card companies do not collect interest payments from cardholders, they still make money. First, most companies charge individual cardholders a hefty annual fee (from $100 to $300) for the privilege of using their cards. More importantly, though, they charge merchants who sell to the cardholders a flat per-transaction fee (about 30 cents) and a "discount fee" (measured as a percentage of the total sale). Credit card companies also charge discount fees, but historically their rates have been significantly lower (about 2 percent for Visa and MasterCard, compared to 4 percent for American Express). Charge card companies justify their higher rates to merchants by pointing out that they deliver more upscale cardholders who make larger purchases.

Recent Trends

At the beginning of the twenty-first century, competition for customers in the electronic-payment industry was fierce. Credit card companies flooded the market with card offers, while more and more consumers became comfortable with carrying a substantial load of revolving debt. Those consumers who did not want to carry debt had the option of paying for purchases immediately with a debit card, which draws money from the consumer's checking account.

Faced with the challenge of how to remain relevant in this atmosphere, charge card companies maintained their time-tested strategies: rather than trying to be all things to all people, they continued to focus on providing prestige and unparalleled benefits packages to the niche markets they had always served. A niche market is a narrow segment of the population with specialized needs (for example, business travelers).

Benefits packages, also called rewards programs, included premium sky miles (points that a person earns by making purchases on his or her card; these points are redeemable toward the price of an airline ticket), access to restricted airport lounges, guaranteed hotel reservations, and even cash rebates (refunds based on a percentage of the amount a person spends with a particular card).

In addition to competing with each other, electronic-payment cards were also trying to convert consumers to using cards in situations where they normally paid with cash or checks. Thus Diner's Club sought to broker deals with fast-food merchants, while American Express teamed up with luxury apartment buildings in New York to enable tenants to pay rent with their cards.

$ Debit Card

What It Means

A debit card is a plastic electronic-payment card that draws funds for purchases directly from the cardholder's bank account (to debit means to withdraw or spend). It can also be used to withdraw cash from a checking account at ATMs (automated teller machines). Debit cards are issued by banks to their account holders. When used to make purchases, the debit card is a convenient and secure alternative to cash that works like an electronic, or "paperless," check. Indeed, because debit cards usually draw funds from checking accounts, they are often referred to as "check cards."

And yet, in its physical appearance and technology, a debit card is more like a credit card than a check. Like credit cards, debit cards bear the logo of a major credit card company (especially MasterCard and Visa), and on the back they have a magnetic stripe that contains the information needed to process a transaction. At the time of purchase (commonly known as the point of sale, or POS), the merchant swipes the debit card through a card-reader machine. In order to complete the transaction the customer must either enter a PIN (personal identification number) or sign for the purchase (as is done with a credit card). The details of the purchase are processed electronically through a central computer network run by MasterCard, Visa, or whichever credit card company is affiliated with the card, and then transmitted to the cardholder's bank, where funds are withdrawn.

The source of the funds is the major difference between debit cards and credit cards. With a credit card, the cardholder makes purchases on a line of credit, a

A debit card is a plastic card that enables individual to make purchases or receive cash by withdrawing funds from a bank account electronically. Almost all retail stores contain electronic scanners, shown here, which "read" the bank account information contained on a consumer's debit card in order to perform a transaction. *Photograph by Kelly A. Quin. Cengage Learning, Gale.*

maximum purchasing amount that is based on the cardholder's potential to pay, rather than the amount of money he or she has available in the bank. In other words, the credit card user is allowed to "pay later"; the bank that issued the card pays for the purchase and expects the cardholder to repay the bank in the future. With a debit card, on the other hand, the cardholder is required to "pay now," meaning that she can only make purchases up to the amount of funds that she has in the bank. If she tries to make a purchase that exceeds the amount of these funds, the card will be declined. Although the withdrawal of funds appears to happen immediately, there is in fact a lag time during which the transaction is complete but the funds have not yet left the cardholder's account.

When Did It Begin

Introduced in the early 1980s, the first debit cards were called "ATM cards" because their sole function was to enable bank customers to withdraw cash from their bank accounts using ATMs. The original ATM cards could not be used to make retail purchases.

By the mid-1980s many merchants had begun to use computerized point-of-sale (POS) systems, which enabled customers to swipe their ATM cards at cash registers, enter a PIN, and pay for their purchases through an electronic transfer of funds from their bank account to the merchant. POS systems were primarily available at grocery stores, gas stations, and other businesses that processed a high volume of customers making relatively inexpensive purchases.

The watershed moment for debit cards came in the early 1990s, when the cards were enhanced with the Visa or MasterCard logos, meaning that they could be used to make purchases anywhere that Visa or MasterCard credit cards were accepted. This innovation vastly expanded the use of debit cards.

More Detailed Information

When a debit card is swiped through a reader at the time of a purchase, the merchant asks the cardholder, "Debit or credit?" If the customer chooses "debit," it will be an online transaction. He or she must enter a PIN for electronic authorization. Once the card is verified, the

PAY WITH YOUR DRIVER'S LICENSE?

A debit card is an electronic-payment card with a magnetic stripe on the back that takes funds for purchases directly out of the cardholder's bank account. Debit cards bear the logos of major credit card companies, such as Visa and MasterCard, and are processed through the same electronic infrastructure as credit cards. For the convenience of using the electronic-payment system, merchants pay a per-transaction fee to the bank that issues the debit card. Although the fee is generally no more than 2 percent of the amount of the sale, these fees add up, and some people claim that merchants pass the fee on to the customer in the form of higher prices.

In 2007 a fledgling company called National Payment Card (NPC) launched a radical new plan to reduce these processing fees by turning driver's licenses into payment cards. A driver's license has a magnetic stripe on the back, NPC reasoned; why not simply link that stripe to a person's bank account? Originally introduced at gas stations in Texas during an era of skyrocketing gasoline prices, the NPC program promised retailers a flat fee of just 15 cents per transaction and customers a 10-cents-per-gallon reduction in the price of gas. Although the potential for the driver's license payment card seemed strong, it remained to be seen whether the idea would catch on.

PIN is authorized, and the system has confirmed that there are sufficient funds in the customer's account, the purchase is complete. No signature from the customer is needed. Usually the bank puts an immediate hold on the funds to cover the purchase (meaning that the amount of the purchase is subtracted from what is called the "available funds" in the account), and the transaction is cleared through a regional network at the end of the day.

If the customer chooses "credit," it will be an off-line transaction. The card is still swiped through a reader, but no PIN is required. Instead, when the system has verified the card and confirmed that there are sufficient funds in the customer's account, the customer signs a receipt (as he or she would if using a credit card), and the purchase is complete. With off-line transactions, however, the process of clearing the transactions happens in stages: although the bank may place an immediate hold on the funds to cover the transaction, the funds may not actually leave the cardholder's account for a couple of days.

As with credit cards, merchants who accept debit cards pay a per-transaction processing fee known as an "interchange fee" for the convenience of using the card system. Typically an online transaction carries a set fee of 7.5 to 10 cents, whereas the fee for an off-line is calculated as a percentage (usually about 2 percent) of the total sale. The bulk of the fee goes to the bank that issued the

card, and a fraction of the fee is given to the credit card company. Thus, the merchant prefers customers to choose online PIN transactions, while the bank prefers them to choose off-line signature transactions.

For consumers the most significant drawback of a debit card arises in the unfortunate event that the card is lost or stolen. Debit cards carry a greater liability risk than credit cards, meaning that if the card falls into the wrong hands and that person begins making unauthorized purchases, the cardholder may be held responsible for the transactions. With a credit card the cardholder is not liable for more than $50 of fraudulent card use. But with a debit card, if the cardholder waits more than two business days to notify the bank about the missing card, he or she may be liable for up to $500 of fraudulent spending.

There are other ways that a missing debit card can be more problematic than a missing credit card. With a credit card, the only issue to resolve with the credit card company is whether or not the cardholder owes money for fraudulent purchases. In contrast, the holder of a lost or stolen debit card must persuade the bank to restore illegally spend funds to his or her bank account. Further, if the bank account has been depleted, the cardholder may face an overdraft situation (in which he or she does not have sufficient funds to cover checks, automatic payments, and other withdrawals from the account).

Recent Trends

In the mid-1990s the use of debit cards began growing at an exponential rate. In 2003 the number of electronic-payment transactions (debit cards and credit cards together) surpassed the number of paper check transactions in the United States for the first time. With an estimated annual growth rate of 23.5 percent (twice the growth rate of credit card usage), debit cards were the fastest-growing type of electronic payment, and it was projected that debit card transactions would surpass both paper check transactions and credit card transactions within a few years.

With growing awareness about the overwhelming burden of consumer debt and high interest payments (in 2005 the average U.S. household carried $9,200 in credit card debt), many Americans began to favor their debit cards over their credit cards as a way of improving their personal financial discipline. Some consumers prefer to use their debit cards knowing that they have a built-in spending cap based on the amount of funds available in their accounts. Some use their debit card instead of cash to facilitate money management; the fact that all transactions are printed on the cardholder's bank statement can make it easier to keep track of purchases.

Debit card issuers also sought to increase their competitive edge against credit cards by introducing the same kinds of rewards programs that credit cards had been offering their cardholders for years, such as points toward air travel, sweepstakes entries, and cash rebates (or refunds).

$ Electronic Banking

What It Means

Electronic banking is a form of banking in which funds are transferred through an exchange of electronic signals rather than through an exchange of cash, checks, or other types of paper documents. Transfers of funds occur between financial institutions such as banks and credit unions. They also occur between financial institutions and commercial institutions such as stores. Whenever someone withdraws cash from an automated teller machine (ATM) or pays for groceries using a debit card (which draws the amount owed to the store from a savings or checking account), the funds are transferred via electronic banking.

Electronic banking relies on intricate computer systems that communicate using telephone lines. These computer systems record transfers and ownership of funds, and they control the methods customers and commercial institutions use to access funds. A common method of access (or identification) is by access code, such as a personal identification number (PIN) that one might use to withdraw cash from an ATM machine.

There are various electronic banking systems, and they range in size. An example of a small system is an ATM network, a set of interconnected automated teller machines that are linked to a centralized financial institution and its computer system. An example of a large electronic banking system is the Federal Reserve Wire Network, called Fedwire. This system allows participants to handle large, time-sensitive payments, such as those required to settle real estate transactions.

When Did It Begin

For decades financial institutions have used powerful computer networks to automate millions of daily transactions. In the 1950s the Bank of America was one of the first institutions to develop the idea that electronic

Electronic banking allows people to transfer funds, pay bills, and conduct other financial transactions electronically. For some people the most common mode of electronic banking is the automated teller machine, or ATM. *AP Images.*

TELEPHONE BANKING

Some financial institutions provide a service called telephone banking, which enables customers to make banking transactions over the phone. This service relies on technology known as interactive voice response (IVR), an automated telephone information system that can speak to the person placing the call as well as access secure financial data from computer databases. Although customers cannot make cash withdrawals or deposits, they can obtain information about the balances of their checking or savings accounts as well as records of their most recent transactions and transfers.

computers could take over the banking tasks of handling checks and balancing accounts, which was, at that time, extremely labor-intensive. Other institutions gradually joined the effort and progressed away from using paper checks and toward all-electronic banking. Data-processing machines, robotic document sorting, and the invention of optical character recognition (a computer application that translates handwritten or typewritten words into text that can be machine-edited) were a few of the developments which allowed this evolution.

The first electronic banking machines were able to keep records of deposits and withdrawals from each client, make account balance information available instantaneously, monitor overdrafts, stop payments, and hold funds. The machines responsible for this work today are as exact and reliable as the banking industry requires them to be.

More Detailed Information

Electronic banking laid the groundwork for speed and convenience in individual and commercial (business) banking. The spread of personal computer use has added another layer of convenience and speed to the process. Electronic banking allows customers of most banks to do their banking at any hour of the day, regardless of the bank's operating hours. If customers choose to do such things as transfer funds or pay bills, they can usually do so from anywhere Internet access is available.

Online banking typically offers bank statements, electronic bill payment, funds transfers between a customer's checking and savings accounts (or to another customer's account), loan applications and transactions, and purchasing or sales of investments, all of which allow customers to maintain their accounts without making a trip to the bank itself.

When funds are transferred between accounts by electronic means, it is called an electronic funds transfer (EFT). The Electronic Fund Transfer Act, passed by the federal government in 1978, established that an elec-

tronic funds transfer is any financial transaction that originates from a telephone, electronic terminal, computer, or magnetic tape (storage tape of the sort used in video or audio cassettes).

A wire transfer is the electronic transfer of funds across a network controlled and maintained by hundreds of banks around the world. Usually wire transfers are reserved for moving large sums of money. Wire transfers allow people in different geographic locations to transfer money easily. The wire transfer payment system called Fedwire (Federal Reserve Wire Network) links the offices of the Federal Reserve (the central bank of the U.S. government), the U.S. Treasury (the department of the federal government that manages the country's revenue), and other government agencies and institutions.

One of the largest companies that provide electronic money services is Western Union. The company started out in 1851 as a transmitter of telegraphs, messages sent through wires as coded electronic pulses. As the telegraph became an obsolete form of communicating information in the mid-twentieth century, Western Union redefined itself as a provider of electronic financial transactions. Now named Western Union Financial Services, Inc., the company specializes in electronic money transfers and business communications services.

Another prominent provider of electronic financial transactions is PayPal, a service founded in 1999. It is used to process payments when people buy or sell things on the Internet. The service first gained popularity among people who used the auction website eBay. Most of the sellers on the site were not professional merchants and so were not equipped to accept credit cards; PayPal enabled them to receive electronic payments while also giving buyers an alternative to mailing paper checks or money orders. In 2002 eBay acquired PayPal.

Recent Trends

As online banking has become more sophisticated, banks have been formed that operate exclusively as electronic banks and have no physical storefront for customers to use. Without the costs of purchasing and maintaining physical "bricks-and-mortar" structures like traditional banks do, online banks are able to offer higher interest rates on savings accounts (interest payments are fees that customers collect for keeping their money in the bank). Customers at online banks can use the Internet to conduct all the standard banking transactions (including paying bills online, viewing images of cancelled checks, and transferring money to accounts at other banks and brokerages).

Many of these customers have their employer automatically deposit their paychecks into their bank accounts electronically (a method called direct deposit, which is also very commonly used by clients of traditional banks). Some employers, however, do not offer direct deposit. If a customer of an online bank receives a paper check, he or she cannot walk into their bank and cash it. He or she must mail the check to their bank or deposit it in an ATM that accepts deposits for their bank. Some customers view this inconvenience as a drawback of using an online bank.

$ Money Order

What It Means

A money order is a means of payment for a prearranged amount of money. It is much like a certified check (for a fee, a bank can certify that the funds exist in a depositor's checking account in order to assure the person receiving payment that the check will clear; the bank sets aside the funds for that particular check written on that account), except that the money for a money order is prepaid. A money order can be made out to a specific individual or institution, and the institution issuing the money order charges a fee for its services. People who do not have personal checking accounts often use money orders to pay bills and make purchases. Money orders may be purchased in specific amounts at banks, post offices, and other qualified institutions (many independent companies, such as Western Union, sell money orders through supermarkets, convenience stores, and other retail outlets).

A money order is a fast, reliable, and convenient way of transferring a small sum of money (most institutions sell money orders for up to $1,000) between payor (the person making the payment) and payee (the person receiving the payment). It is particularly useful for sending money through the mail because it can only be redeemed, or cashed, by the designated payee, with valid identification (such as a driver's license or passport). Money orders are also considered more secure for the payee than personal checks because the order is prepaid by the payor and the payee is actually receiving his or her payment from the bank, postal service, or other institution. According to the Federal Reserve (the central banking system of the United States), 889 million money orders were purchased in the United States in 2005; the gross value of these transactions (including processing fees) was $145 billion.

When Did It Begin

The U.S. Postal Service (USPS) introduced money orders in 1864, at a time when Civil War soldiers in the field were having difficulty sending money to and receiving money from their homes. (Bank checks were almost unheard of then, and an envelope containing cash was likely to arrive with a slit in the side and the money gone.) Originally sold almost exclusively in army camps, money

To transfer money using any phone, call toll free 1-877-984-0473
(Para transerir dinero usando cualquier teléfono llame al, número gratuito 1-877-984-0473)
Please write down the information from the Western Union customer service representative
(Por favor anote la información proporcionada por el representante de Servicios al Cliente)

Customer Transaction Number:
(Número de las transaccion del cliente:)

☐ send *(enviar)*
☐ receive *(recibir)*

Amount Sent:
(Cantidad enviada:) $

Fee:
(Tarifa:) $

TTPDIRCOB 09/04

This service protected by Patent No. 6,488,203

A money order offers a quick, easy, and reliable way of making a payment or sending money through the mail. Western Union, which is one of the most recognized brands of money order, sells money orders in post offices, supermarkets, convenience stores, and other locations. *Photograph by Kelly A. Quin. Cengage Learning, Gale.*

UNCLAIMED MONEY ORDERS

The U.S Postal Service charges a nominal fee for issuing money orders (a prepaid certificate for a specific amount of money that is used to make payments in lieu of cash or personal checks), but its real profits from this service come from all of the money orders that go unclaimed. Every year more than $25 million in postal service money orders remain forgotten or lost and uncashed.

Name and address records are not kept for domestic money order purchases, and the USPS will not contact you if a money order you purchase remains uncashed by its recipient. The best way to confirm that a money order you've sent has been received and redeemed is to request a photocopy of the redeemed money order (which will show the recipient's signature endorsement) at the time of your original purchase.

orders were soon in demand across the country because they were the most expedient and secure way of sending money through the mail. In 1869 the USPS expanded its service to include foreign money orders, which were extremely popular with immigrants.

In 1882 the American Express Company introduced a money order of its own, which rivaled the postal service money order because it was more secure (postal money orders were more vulnerable to being altered) and could be bought and cashed at a wider number of locations.

More Detailed Information

Here is an example of how a money order works. Linda needs to pay her utility bill in the amount of $215.63, but she does not have a checking account. Linda, the payor (the person who wishes to use the money order to make some kind of payment) goes to the post office and requests a money order in the amount of $215.63. Linda must pay the post office $215.63 plus a small service fee based on the amount of the money order. In 2007 the U.S. Postal Service charged $.95 for money orders under $500 and $1.30 for money orders between $500.01 and $1,000.

Linda's money order is printed by a machine in the specified amount. Some issuers require that the name of the payee be printed on the money order at the time of purchase, but others allow the payor to fill in this information later. Linda receives the money order, which she must complete and sign before mailing or delivering it to the power company. Note that a completed money order cannot be changed or altered. Along with the money order Linda receives a receipt for her records, and a third copy is kept by the issuer. Linda may also request that a photocopy of the redeemed money order with the payee's signature endorsement be sent to her for her records. When the power company receives the money order, they

will deposit it into a bank account. A payee may also choose to redeem a money order for cash at the post office or other issuing location.

A money order has no expiration date. Each money order has a unique serial number that may be traced in case of loss or theft. If the payor keeps his or her receipt as proof of purchase, a record of the serial number, or both, he or she can request a refund for the money order if it is not redeemed.

Like cash, money orders contain various security features so that they may not be counterfeited. Postal money orders (PMOs) issued by the USPS in particular are considered among the most difficult financial documents to counterfeit. Security features of a PMO include watermarks (images of Ben Franklin that can be detected when the document is held up to the light), a dark security thread that runs alongside the watermark with the tiny letters "USPS" facing backward and forward, and a rainbow of inked patterns and tones. If any of these features is not present when the document is held up to the light, it may be counterfeit.

Recent Trends

Between 2004 and 2006 there was a significant surge in fraud schemes involving fake PMOs, in spite of the highly touted difficulty of counterfeiting them. FBI (Federal Bureau of Investigation) and postal inspectors reported that much of the counterfeiting seemed to originate in Nigeria, Ghana, and Eastern Europe. Most of the schemes did not involve attempts by swindlers to redeem the bogus money orders themselves; rather, the worthless money orders were used to pay for merchandise being sold over the Internet. In a typical scam the merchandise seller receives a counterfeit PMO in the mail that is printed for a value greater than the price of the item being purchased. The seller is asked to deposit the money order, keep the cost of the item, and send the excess balance back in cash along with the merchandise.

In April 2005 law enforcement officials estimated that the postal service had intercepted millions of dollars worth of counterfeit PMOs being sent through the mail.

$ Cashier's Check

What It Means

A cashier's check is purchased by a customer at a bank as a means of making a payment to a third party. Sometimes referred to as a bank check, a bank draft, or a treasurer's check, a cashier's check is written by the bank against its own funds and signed by a bank teller. A cashier's check is similar to a money order (another form of prepaid check) except that unlike a money order (which can be purchased at the post office and various retail outlets), a cashier's check can only be issued by a bank; and unlike a money order, for which the maximum amount is usually $1000, a cashier's check can be written for any amount.

A cashier's check is issued directly from a bank, not from a person's account. Because it is guaranteed by the bank's funds, a cashier's check is considered to be more trustworthy than a standard personal check. *Erik Isakson/Rubberball Productions/Getty Images.*

A cashier's check is considered more secure than a personal check because it is backed by the bank's funds rather than those of an individual. In other words a cashier's check is guaranteed not to bounce. (A check is said to bounce when, upon being deposited, it turns out that there are insufficient funds to cover the amount of the check in the account against which it was written.)

A cashier's check is a fast, convenient, and reliable way of making a payment. When the payee (the party to whom the check is written) receives the check, he or she can cash the check instantly; there is usually no delay time to confirm that the check will clear. Thus, because it is practically the equivalent of cash, a cashier's check is often preferred as the quickest way to close a sale: once the check has been received by the seller, the transaction is effectively complete.

When Did It Begin

No one knows exactly when the first check was written. Some scholars believe that checks were used in ancient banking systems (in Persia and China, for example) as a convenience for traders who wanted to avoid both the hassle and the risk of transporting large amounts of currency (especially gold) across great distances to do business. No documentary evidence of these practices has been found, however.

The use of checks in modern banking is most reliably traced to early sixteenth-century Holland, when Amsterdam was a major hub of international trade. Not wanting to hold onto large stores of cash, businesspeople began depositing their money with "cashiers," who agreed to keep the money safe for a fee. When the depositor needed to pay someone, he or she could request that the cashier issue a written order (also known as a bill of exchange) for payment of a specified amount to a specified payee (the person the depositor wanted to pay), who could then exchange the written order for cash.

By the late eighteenth century the use of checks as a method of arranging payments had spread to England and other places in Europe. Check-writing practices

BE ON THE LOOKOUT FOR CASHIER'S CHECK SCAMS

With the increased quality of laser printers and the proliferation of online auctions and other Internet businesses, scam artists have more tools and more opportunities than ever for making money illegally with counterfeit cashier's checks (checks issued by a bank that a customer may purchase in a specific amount in order to make a payment to a third party). Here are a few indications that a cashier's check you received might be part of a scam:

- The check is in payment for a major ticket item that you sold on eBay or another online auction site, it is written for significantly more than the agreed selling price, and the person who sent the check is asking you to return the additional money to him or her.
- The check is for winnings in a lottery that you never entered.
- The person who gave you the check contacted you by e-mail or in an online chatroom.

If you have any reason to suspect that a cashier's check you received is not legitimate, have it verified by a financial institution (such as a bank) before you attempt to deposit or cash it.

evolved during this period, and specialized forms of checks, such as the cashier's check (then known as bankers' checks), were introduced.

More Detailed Information

Here is how a cashier's check works. Felix wishes to purchase a chandelier from an antique dealer, Sally. The price of the chandelier is $2,450. Felix has the funds available in his checking account, but Sally will not accept a personal check at her antique store for that amount. Felix does not wish to withdraw the money in cash, because he is not comfortable carrying such a large amount of money in his wallet. Instead, Felix decides to purchase a cashier's check.

At the bank Felix pays the teller (or asks the teller to withdraw from his account) $2,450 plus the small service fee (usually not more than $5) that is charged by the bank. Felix gives his own name and the name of the antique dealer. The teller prints out a cashier's check that shows the name of the payee (Sally), the name of the remitter (Felix), and the amount ($2,450). The check is signed by the bank teller or another bank official. Felix also receives a receipt for the transaction. When Felix presents the cashier's check to Sally, he should be able to take home the chandelier right away, because the check is guaranteed by the bank that issued it. Then Sally may either deposit the check into her own bank account or she

may cash the check. In either case, she must endorse the check with her signature. If she wishes to cash it, she must also show proper identification (such as a business license, driver's license, or passport) to prove that she is indeed the party to whom the check was issued.

A cashier's check has a number of official features to show that it is legitimate. The name of the issuing bank is usually displayed prominently on the check, as well as words designating that it as a cashier's check. A cashier's check also has security features to prevent it from being easily counterfeited: these include special ink patterns, watermarks, security threads, and the special bond paper on which it is printed.

If a cashier's check is lost or stolen, either the remitter or the payee (whoever was in possession of the check at the time) may file a claim with the bank that issued the check. The bank will not act on the claim (the claim does not become effective) for 90 days, however, during which time the check is vulnerable to being cashed. (To cash it would be difficult, given the need to provide the signature and identification of the payee, but not impossible.) Note that it is not possible to place a stop-payment order on a cashier's check. If after 90 days the check is still missing and has not been cashed, the bank will reissue it.

Recent Trends

The years 2005 and 2006 saw a dramatic rise in the use of counterfeit cashier's checks by scam artists. In one typical scenario the scam artist sends a cashier's check as payment for an item he has agreed to purchase or has won in an auction over the Internet. Strangely, however, the cashier's check is made out for significantly more than the price of the item. The "buyer" asks the seller to ship the item along with the extra money from the cashed cashier's check. With the latest sophisticated printing techniques, the bank often cannot tell that the check is a fake, and it is deposited into the seller's account. It may be weeks or even months before the check is recognized as a counterfeit, but when it is, the seller who deposited the check is held responsible for it.

In a similar scenario an unsuspecting victim receives a cashier's check for a lottery she never entered, along with a message explaining that she will only need to pay the taxes on the winnings after the check is cashed. The scam artist receives the "tax money" from the victim, and the victim is held responsible by the bank for the counterfeit check that represents her "winnings."

$ Traveler's Check

What It Means

A traveler's check (sometimes spelled "cheque") is a specialized kind of check (a written order to pay) that may be purchased from a bank or other financial institution, at an AAA (American Automobile Association) office, or at other travel service offices in preset denominations ($10, $20, $50, $100, and higher). Purchasers can then spend the checks elsewhere (they are often bought for use internationally) as cash. Traveler's checks can be used to pay for hotels, restaurants, train tickets, souvenirs, and other purchases. They can also be exchanged for the currency of the country you are in at banks and money-changing bureaus, although there is usually a small commission fee for this service.

The primary benefit of traveler's checks is that they are protected against loss or theft. At the time you purchase your traveler's checks, each one should be inscribed with your signature on the specified line. Later, when you use the check to pay for something, you must countersign the check on a different line to endorse it, and the signatures must match. Usually you are also required to

show your passport or other photo identification bearing the same signature. Thus, if the checks are lost or stolen, they cannot be spent by someone else. Furthermore, each check is identified by a serial number; as long as you can produce a record of those serial numbers (you should keep this record separate from the checks themselves), the lost or stolen checks can be replaced.

Traveler's checks have long been favored as the most convenient and reliable way of carrying money when traveling in foreign countries, although the rapid growth of electronic banking has dramatically diminished their use since the mid-1990s.

When Did It Begin

Prior to the invention of traveler's checks in the late eighteenth century, travelers often avoided the risk of

Traveler's Checks (continued)

Sample A

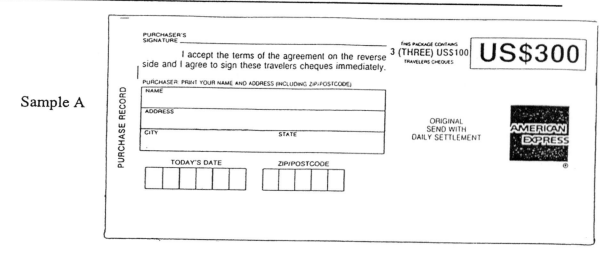

Sample B

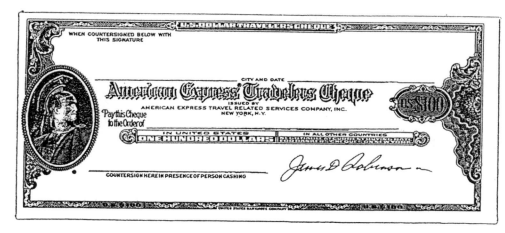

Traveler's checks have long been considered one of the safest ways of carrying money while traveling. The purchase record, shown here above the traveler's check itself, is a receipt that enables a customer to replace lost or stolen checks. *Photograph by Kelly A. Quin. Cengage Learning, Gale.*

STILL THE SAFEST WAY TO CARRY MONEY ABROAD

Traveler's checks (prepaid vouchers in set denominations that can be used to make purchases while traveling) have come to seem a bit antiquated since the mid-1990s, when electronic banking made it possible to withdraw cash from your home bank account at ATMs (automated teller machines) around the world. Many people argue, however, that traveler's checks remain the safest and most reliable way to carry money in foreign countries. First, traveler's checks are designed to be loss- and theft-proof: they cannot be used by anyone but the original purchaser. Also, as long as the original purchaser keeps a record of the checks' serial numbers, lost or stolen checks can be replaced. Another benefit of traveler's checks is that, unlike various electronic banking options, they function independently of computer systems and phone lines, so there is never a problem of networks being down or other electronic malfunctions.

carrying large amounts of cash by carrying a letter of credit from their bank. A letter of credit guarantees that its holder has the funds to pay for his or her purchases. By presenting a letter of credit, the traveler assured merchants that they could submit bills to the traveler's bank and depend on receiving payment for goods that were sold. A traveler might also present the letter for credit at a foreign bank in order to obtain cash (and the foreign bank could expect to be reimbursed by the traveler's bank.) Letters of credit were not universally accepted, however, especially outside of major cities.

Robert Harries of the London Exchange Banking Company in England is credited with devising the earliest prototype of the traveler's check to replace the traditional letter of credit in 1792. Originally introduced as "circular notes," these checks were issued in set denominations and guaranteed against loss and theft; they were accepted in about 90 cities around the world. In another, later effort to transcend the limitations of letters of credit, the modern traveler's check (which requires a countersignature) was invented by Marcellus Flemming Berry for the American Express Company in 1891.

More Detailed Information

American Express remains the largest provider of traveler's checks in the world. American Express traveler's checks may be purchased at American Express offices or at many banks. Another major provider of traveler's checks is Thomas Cook, a British banking and tourism company. Visa and MasterCard (the two most prominent brands of electronic payment card, which include credit and debit cards) also issue traveler's checks. Some com-

panies now offer dual-signature traveler's checks so that the same checks may be used by two companions traveling together.

Traveler's checks are available in a number of currencies, including American dollars, Australian dollars, Euros, British pounds, and Japanese yen. If a check is used to make a purchase that costs less than the denomination of the check, the traveler can expect to receive his or her change in the currency of the country he or she is in. The merchant, exchange bureau, or other payee who receives a traveler's check may redeem the check by depositing it into his or her bank account. The check is then settled, or cleared, with the traveler's check issuer, much in the same way as other checks are cleared. Traveler's checks do not expire, so unused checks may be held by the purchaser indefinitely until he or she has occasion to spend them.

For the bank or other issuing institution, traveler's checks amount to an interest-free loan: the purchaser of the traveler's checks has given cash to the bank and will not spend the checks for days, weeks, or even months in the future. Because of this benefit, many banks will issue traveler's checks to their account holders without any additional commission charges. When a commission fee is charged, it is usually between 1 and 4 percent of the total value of checks purchased.

Recent Trends

With the rapid expansion and advancement of electronic banking since the mid-1990s, the use of traveler's checks has declined significantly. Now travelers can get cash on demand almost anywhere in the world simply by putting a bank card into an ATM (automated teller machine), entering a PIN (personal identification number), and selecting the amount of local currency they desire. Travelers can also make many purchases directly using a debit card (an electronic payment card that withdraws funds directly from a personal bank account).

To compensate for the diminished popularity of traveler's checks, some companies (including American Express and Travelex Worldwide) now also sell traveler's check cards. These are reloadable prepaid plastic payment cards that function much like a debit card, within certain limits. American Express, for example, charges a one-time issuance fee of $14.95, requires an initial minimum deposit of $300, and allows a maximum prepaid balance of $2,750 on their traveler's check cards. The primary benefit of these cards over regular debit cards is an added level of security: they are not linked with your bank account and can be replaced if lost or stolen.

$ Gift Certificate

What It Means

A gift certificate is a paper voucher worth a certain amount of money that can be redeemed by the recipient for an equal value of merchandise at the commercial establishment that issued the certificate. Gift certificates are sold by an endless variety of businesses, including bookstores, music stores, toy stores, clothing stores, and restaurants. A person typically purchases a gift certificate when he or she wishes to give someone a gift but is unsure what specifically that person would like. Gift certificates have the dual benefit of seeming like a more personal and more tasteful gesture than a gift of cash or a check, while averting the awkwardness of purchasing a gift that the recipient does not like, which will either go unused or need to be exchanged.

In financial terms, a gift certificate is a form of scrip. Scrip is any substitute for money or currency; it carries a monetary value without being legal tender. Other forms of scrip include subway tokens and carnival or arcade tickets. One significant restriction associated with scrip (and this applies to gift certificates) is that, while scrip is purchased with currency and carries the value of that currency, it can almost never be converted back into real money; for example, the recipient of a gift certificate cannot take it to the store where the certificate was purchased and redeem it for cash.

When Did It Begin

The use of scrip in the United States may be traced to the mining and logging camps of the early 1800s. Stationed in remote places far from regular towns, the camps functioned in many ways as self-contained economies. The mining and logging companies that ran the camps often paid their workers wholly or partially in "company scrip," which could be spent on food, supplies, and miscellaneous items at the company store.

The use of paper gift certificates in the United States dates back at least to the 1930s, as evidenced by references to them in various magazine advertisements.

A gift certificate is a coupon, typically worth a designated amount, that can be used to buy goods and services at specified businesses. A standard gift certificate includes several pieces of information, including the recipient's name, the expiration date, and the amount available to spend. © *BurkeTriolo Productions/Brand X/Corbis.*

More Detailed Information

Both the giver and the receiver of a gift certificate benefit from this choice of gift in a number of ways. For the giver, purchasing a gift certificate takes much of the guesswork out of giving a present. It is convenient to purchase, easy to mail (if necessary), and carries a high probability that the recipient will be able to use it to buy something he or she really wants or needs. Also, a gift certificate conveys some sense that the giver has put thought into the gift. Say, for example, that Uncle George wants to buy gifts for his niece Penny and his nephew Bernard, whom he sees only once a year. He knows that Penny loves to paint and Bernard loves geology, so he buys Penny a gift certificate for O'Shea's Fine Art Supplies and Bernard a gift certificate for Lou's Rock Shop. The gift certificates show that Uncle George remembers something about the kids. Meanwhile Penny and Bernard can use their certificates to buy something they have been wanting.

In economic terms, a gift certificate might be described as a highly efficient gift, because little or no value is lost in the transaction (whereas the gift of a tie that is never worn, or a birdfeeder that is never used, is highly inefficient because the value of the gift to the recipient is much lower than its cost for the giver). By this measure, the most efficient present a person can give is cash; but under many circumstances, cash gifts are considered crass or socially unacceptable.

For the consumer one of the drawbacks of a gift certificate is that it can be lost, stolen, or destroyed. This is also a potential for lost economic efficiency. Although paper gift certificates usually carry a serial number, which enables the merchant to keep track of gift-certificate sales, often the merchant stipulates that it takes no responsibility for and will not replace lost, stolen, or destroyed gift certificates. Furthermore, some gift certificates carry expiration dates, after which their value is void. A gift certificate that sits in a sock drawer until it expires is an economically inefficient gift.

Gift certificates also carry a number of benefits for the merchants that sell them. When a store sells a gift certificate, it receives money up front for a certain value of merchandise that may or may not be claimed in the future. In 2006 the financial-services research firm TowerGroup estimated that roughly 10 percent of the value of gift certificates is never redeemed. This value amounts to something like free money for the merchant. Gift certificates are also beneficial to the merchant because they bring new customers into the store, and often the recipient of a gift certificate spends more than the value of the certificate during that shopping trip.

Recent Trends

Gift certificates have been around for decades, but they were never a booming industry unto themselves. This changed in the mid-1990s with the introduction of the

GIFT CARDS FOR FUNDRAISING

A plastic, electronic gift card is the modern equivalent of a paper gift certificate (that is, a voucher worth a certain amount of money that can be spent on merchandise at the commercial establishment that issued the card). Many nonprofit organizations (businesses whose main objectives are not profit-oriented), especially private schools, have discovered that the gift card can be used to raise money. Here is how it works: St. Joseph's School purchases 200 gift cards valued at $50 each from the Value Village supermarket chain. Because the school buys such a high volume of cards, Value Village agrees to sell them at a 9 percent discount; so instead of paying $10,000 for the cards, St. Joseph's only pays $9,100. The school then sells each card to the parents of its students for $50, the card's full value. The parents are able to redeem the cards for $50 worth of groceries, and in the process St. Joseph's earns $900, which it can put toward books, field trips, and other expenses of running the school. Value Village sacrifices $900 in sales, but it gains a reputation for investing in the community, which benefits overall sales in the long run.

electronic gift card, a plastic card the size of a credit card. It contains a microchip that records the value ascribed to the card when it is purchased. With their sleek, high-tech design and attractive packaging, gift cards became a runaway hit with the American public, achieving exponential growth over the course of a decade. Gift cards were introduced in 1995, and over the course of that first year they accounted for $1 billion in sales in the United States. In 2006 gift-card sales were $70 billion.

$ Gift Card

What It Means

A gift card is a plastic, electronic version of the old paper gift certificate (a paper voucher that can be spent at a specific store). The card contains a computer microchip that stores a set value according to how much the giver spends at the time he or she purchases the card. In industry terms, this kind of card is described as a "prepaid" or "stored-value" payment device. A balance of funds is stored on the card until it is spent by the person who received it as a gift.

Some gift cards are sold by specific retailers (such as Gap, Barnes & Noble, and Target) and can only be redeemed at those retail establishments; these are called "closed-system" cards. Others are sold by credit card companies (such as Visa, MasterCard, and American Express) and can be spent anywhere those cards are accepted; these gift cards are called "open-system" cards.

Since their introduction in the mid-1990s, gift cards have been an increasingly popular solution to the age-old dilemma of what to buy for family and friends on birthdays and holidays, when you have no clue what they would like. As an alternative to giving an envelope of cash (which many people find to be crass or impersonal) or taking a gamble on a sweater that will probably be returned or pushed to the back of the closet, a gift card has become a fashionable way to show you care by allowing someone to pick out something that he or she really likes.

When Did It Begin

Gift cards came into use in the American marketplace in the mid-1990s, but the origin of "prepaid" cards can be traced to the early 1970s, when transit cards were first issued as a convenient way to prepay for a block of subway or bus rides. At about the same time, colleges and universities began offering prepaid cards that students could use to make purchases on campus. Closed-system cards found another application in the late 1980s with the advent of prepaid phone cards.

The video-store chain Blockbuster is credited with introducing, in 1995, the first closed-system prepaid gift card. The idea caught on immediately, and 10 years later just about every major retailer in the United States offered a closed-system gift card for purchases at their locations.

The first open-system cards were made available in the early 1990s, when the federal government began replacing paper-based food stamps (vouchers issued as public assistance to low-income families) with Electronic Benefit Transfer (EBT) cards, which could be used to buy food at grocery stores. In the mid-1990s Visa and a London-based company called Mondex International introduced prepaid open-system cards that could be used anywhere as a form of electronic cash. Although these and other open-system cards were slower to catch on, in 2005 industry analysts stated that prepaid or stored-value cards had great potential for other uses.

More Detailed Information

Advantages and Disadvantages of Gift Cards for the Consumer In the United States gift cards accounted for $19 billion in sales during the 2005 Christmas holiday season and $25 billion during the same season the following year. Analysts agreed that the tremendous popularity of gift cards was attributable to their convenience (in terms of both purchasing and mailing) and apparent respectability. Gift cards somehow managed to convey a certain amount of thoughtfulness on the part of the giver, unlike a check or an envelope of cash.

Still, however, gift cards carried certain drawbacks for the consumer. In 2006 many cards still carried a range of restrictions, including expiration dates, dormancy charges (for instance, the value of a card might diminish by $2 if it was not used for six months), and the inability to combine the balance on the card with another payment form

For holidays, birthdays, and other occasions, people sometimes find it convenient to give gift cards, a computerized card that allows the recipient to make purchases at a particular retail outlet or restaurant. Gift cards are issued by a wide range of businesses. *AP Images.*

(say, for example, you have a $30 gift card and want to use it as partial payment for a $50 set of towels; in some cases the card is rejected for "insufficient funds," so you can only use it for a purchase of $30 or under).

Advantages and Disadvantages for the Retailer

However popular gift cards may be with consumers, retailers love the cards even more. Retailers benefit from selling gift cards in several ways. First, they receive money up front for the purchase; if the gift card is lost, destroyed, or for any reason goes unredeemed, the retailer has effectively received "free money" for the original purchase of the card. Second, the gift card draws new customers (the card recipients) into their stores. Third, the person redeeming the gift card often spends more than the amount of the card. Lastly, it often happens that when the gift card is redeemed, a small balance remains unspent on the card. If this balance is not spent at a later date, the retailer makes

an extra profit. In 2006 J.C. Williams Group, a global retail-consulting firm, estimated that about 10 percent of the prepaid value of gift cards is never spent.

The main disadvantage for retailers is that gift cards are relatively expensive to manufacture. Depending on the volume of cards a retailer orders, the cards can cost up to $3 each. The retailer also must pay fees to the outside firm that handles the electronic network used to process the cards.

Recent Trends

Nearly a decade after they were introduced, gift cards were still growing in popularity at a remarkable rate of about 20 percent per year. The gift-card trend experienced a major explosion during the 2005 Christmas holiday season, when a new crop of merchants began to offer the cards. Whereas gift cards had previously been

STARBUCKS GIFT CARDS

As of 2006 one of the most successful gift cards in North America was the one offered by Starbucks. The specialty-coffee powerhouse began offering gift cards in 2001. Five years later it had sold about 96 million Starbucks Cards, and the cards had been reloaded (had more money added to them) some 38 million times. Indeed, the company estimated that as much as 10 percent of all the coffee drinks it sold in North America were paid for with gift cards. Also, Starbucks was the only company that allowed you to use your gift card to buy a gift card for someone else.

offered mainly by department stores, specialty stores, and other mall-type retailers, suddenly supermarkets, drug stores, fast-food restaurants, convenience stores, and even gas stations were jumping on the bandwagon. Part of the tremendous appeal of these practical gift cards was that they could be purchased on the way home from work, while filling up the gas tank or buying a quart of milk at the supermarket; suddenly there was a new way to accomplish that notoriously stressful holiday shopping without breaking the bank or setting foot in a crowded mall. But department-store gift cards were still the most popular kind of gift card during the 2006 holiday season, accounting for 37.9 percent of all gift cards sold to American consumers.

Borrowing: When You Need More Money Than You Have

$ Overview: Why People Go into Debt

What It Means

The term *debt* refers to something (whether it is money, a piece of property, or a service) that an individual owes to another individual or an entity. In most cases people owe a debt because they have borrowed something from someone else. Debts arise frequently in everyday life, in a variety of contexts. In cases involving people who know each other, debts may take the form of informal understandings and are primarily a way for people to repay favors. For example, a person might owe (or feel that he owes) his neighbor a ride to the airport because that neighbor took care of his dog while he was on vacation. In another instance a friend might owe another friend lunch because that friend helped her move into a new apartment. In these cases the debt is rarely called a debt and is generally considered nonbinding; that is to say there is no real obligation, outside of a sense of personal responsibility, to repay the person who performed the favor.

In modern economic terms debt refers almost exclusively to financial debt (in other words money). When people borrow money they do so with the understanding that they will pay the money back at a later date; the money that a person owes is referred to as debt. In some cases a person borrows a specific amount of money, which they receive all at once, in what is called a lump sum. This type of borrowed money is typically referred to as a loan. In other cases a person applies for credit. Typically credit refers to an amount of money that is made available for a person to borrow, usually with a specified maximum amount that can be borrowed, known as a credit limit. Credit is available in various forms; the most common type of credit among American consumers is the credit card. A credit card is a plastic card that a person (in this case known as a cardholder) can use to make purchases, receive cash (known as a cash advance), or pay off other debts, up to the credit limit specified in the card agreement. The more a person spends (or charges) with a credit card, the more debt he or she accrues.

In most cases people borrow money or receive credit from established financial institutions, such as a bank, a lending company, or a credit card company. When a person borrows money from a financial institution, that money is subject to an interest charge. In basic terms interest represents the fee a financial institution charges a person when he or she borrows money. Interest is reflected as a percentage of the amount of money borrowed and is generally calculated on an annual basis. When people borrow money the total amount of their debt is not limited to the amount of money borrowed; their debt also includes the interest that accumulates on the borrowed money over time. The longer a person remains in debt, the greater the amount of interest he or she will ultimately pay. People who owe debts are commonly known as debtors, while the people to whom they owe the money are called creditors.

When Did It Begin

Debt has existed since the earliest human civilizations. Ancient societies often imposed severe penalties on people who failed to repay their debts in a timely manner. In Babylonia (a kingdom that existed between roughly 2000 and 540 BC, in a region covering what is now Iraq) debtors who were unable to pay their creditors were frequently imprisoned. The Code of Hammurabi, a legal code devised in the eighteenth century BC by the Babylonian king Hammurabi, allowed a debtor to offer his creditor a piece of property, in the event he had no money to repay his debt. In certain cases a debtor in Babylonia might be forced to sell one of his family members into temporary slavery (for a period not exceeding three years) to satisfy his debt.

Ancient Hebrew law (the law of the early Jewish race, written around 1000 BC) contained numerous rules and stipulations relating to unpaid debts. In some cases a

CHARLES DICKENS AND THE DEBTORS PRISON

Debt is money that one person owes to another. Before the nineteenth century people who were unable to pay their debts were put into debtors prisons. Over time debtors prisons gained a reputation for being overcrowded and unsanitary. During the eighteenth and nineteenth centuries a number of prominent figures began to speak out against the inhumane nature of debtors prisons. One of the most famous authors to write about the squalid conditions of debtors prisons was the English novelist Charles Dickens (1812–70). He included lengthy descriptions of debtors prisons in several of his works, including *Oliver Twist* (1837–39), *Hard Times* (1854), and *A Tale of Two Cities* (1859). Indeed for Dickens the issue of debtors prisons was personal. His father, John Dickens, spent several months in the Marshalsea Prison, a notorious penitentiary in London, England, after amassing too much debt.

man who borrowed money gave his creditor one of his possessions to hold as a guarantee that he would repay the debt (in modern terminology this possession is known as collateral, while the type of debt is often referred to as a secured debt, in that the piece of property acts as security that the debt will be paid). In order to protect debtors who were poor, Hebrew law required a creditor to return the piece of property to the debtor before nightfall; references to this rule appear in the Old Testament of the Bible, in the books of Exodus (22:26–27) and Deuteronomy (24:11–13). As in ancient Babylonia, Hebrew law also allowed slavery as a means of resolving unpaid debt, although in this case the debtor himself was the one who was enslaved. Similar laws permitting the enslavement of debtors also existed in ancient Greek and Roman civilizations.

Throughout medieval Europe (a period of European history also known as the Middle Ages that roughly spanned the fifth through the fifteenth century AD) and well into the nineteenth century, debtors were frequently thrown into debtors prisons for failing to repay debts. Debtors prisons were notorious for their unhealthy, crowded conditions, and many debtors died before being released. Debtors prisons were also established in the United States during the colonial period. By the eighteenth century people began to speak out against the inhumane treatment suffered by inmates of debtors prisons. English author Samuel Johnson (1709–84) was an outspoken critic of the institution; one of his close friends, the poet Richard Savage (1697–1743), died in debtors prison. Johnson declared that "the confinement of any man in the sloth and darkness of a prison, is a loss to the nation, and no gain to the creditor." Debtors prisons were finally outlawed in the United

States in 1833; England followed suit in 1869, with passage of the Debtors Act.

In early nineteenth-century America people often fled to the frontier to elude creditors; indeed, if someone was said to have "gone to Texas," it was understood that he had become insolvent (in other words he was unable to pay his debts; this is also known as being bankrupt).

More Detailed Information

People go into debt for a variety of reasons. In many cases people take on debt because they want to make a major purchase (such as buying a car or a home) that they cannot afford to pay for in cash. In most instances these purchases can be described as necessary; people need to live somewhere, and most people need some form of reliable transportation to get to work. If people tried to save up the money necessary to buy a house with cash, they would likely have to wait several years, if not decades, before they had enough money to purchase the house. Furthermore they would be spending a good deal of their monthly income on rent, which would further delay their home purchase. By going into debt to purchase a home, on the other hand, a person could inhabit the home right away. His or her monthly loan payment (also known as a mortgage) would be roughly comparable to the amount of money he or she would spend on rent each month. Technically the person would not own the home outright; the lending institution would own it until the person had paid for the house in its entirety. Still the person would be paying toward full ownership of the house, while also building equity (the share a person has of a house's monetary value) in the meantime.

In this sense taking out a loan in order to purchase a home is often referred to as good debt, in that it offers a substantial reward (ownership of the house) after the debt is paid off. Several other forms of debt can be considered good debt. For example, taking out a loan to pay for a college education (commonly known as a student loan) is generally regarded to be a form of good debt, because the reward of receiving a college degree typically translates into a higher income in the future. By having put himself or herself in a position to obtain a high-paying job after graduation, a college graduate not only will earn the money to pay off student loans in a relatively short period of time but also will have a greater range of financial choices in general, in large part as a result of his or her education. Buying a car could also be considered good debt, in that a person paying a monthly car loan is paying toward full ownership of the car (as a person paying a monthly home mortgage does toward a house). Granted a car does not build equity the way a house does; cars tend to lose value, or depreciate, over time, while in almost all cases houses gain value, or appreciate. Still, if a person takes good care of a car, that car will prove to have been a good investment after it has been fully paid for.

Some debts, on the other hand, do not qualify as necessary and contain little to no future value for the debtor. This debt could be categorized as bad debt. In general credit card debt (also known as consumer debt) qualifies as bad debt. Many people use credit cards to make purchases that have no lasting value, such as dining out at a restaurant, purchasing groceries, or buying clothes. All people need to eat and wear clothing, so these purchases are in one sense necessary. But these are not the sorts of purchases that justify going into debt. People who work a job earn a certain amount of money every month for living expenses, which includes food and clothing. If a person's income allows for $400 a month to be spent on food and clothing, then it is reasonable for that person to limit that spending to $400. Many people fall into debt, however, when they use a credit card to buy more consumer goods than they can afford to pay for each month. If a person routinely spends $500 a month on food and clothing and can only reasonably afford $400, he or she will have accrued $1,200 in debt in a year's time. When one factors in interest charges, that debt will expand substantially. If this pattern were to continue for several years, that person would develop a significant debt problem.

Some forms of debt are unavoidable. For example, if a person becomes seriously injured in a car crash and does not have health insurance, he or she might be forced to take on debt to receive proper medical care. Often this debt will be very expensive (health-care costs have risen dramatically in the United States since the 1990s), but to most people it will prove far preferable to living with permanent health problems.

Recent Trends

In the United States the total amount of personal debt rose considerably between the early 1990s and the first decade of the twenty-first century. In 1994 consumer debt in the United States amounted to roughly a trillion dollars; by 2004 this total had risen to $2.14 trillion. Mortgage debts also rose substantially over these years, from roughly $3.2 trillion in 1994 to $7.6 trillion in 2004.

TYPES OF LOANS

$ Loan

What It Means

A loan refers to a sum of money borrowed by a corporation, an individual consumer, or another entity. Generally speaking people use loans to pay for goods or services that they are unable to pay for in full at the time of purchase. The cost of a loan to the consumer typically takes the form of interest (a percentage of the loan amount that must be repaid in addition to the original

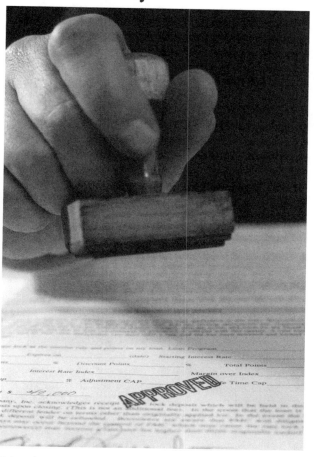

A loan is a sum of money borrowed to pay for expensive goods, such as cars and homes; to finance new business ventures; and to cover such unexpected costs as a hospital bill. Here a lender stamps his approval on a loan application. © *Duncan Smith/Corbis.*

amount of the loan, which is known as the principal). Interest is usually calculated on an annual basis. The two types of interest rates are fixed and adjustable. A fixed rate is an annual percentage rate that never changes, while an adjustable rate fluctuates regularly. The amount of money owed by the borrower for the duration of the loan is often referred to as debt.

There are two principal parties to a loan. One is the individual or entity providing the loan, also known as the lender. Lenders are usually financial institutions, such as banks, credit card companies, or other commercial entities, that are authorized by law to loan money to businesses or consumers at established interest rates. The other party to the loan is the person or group that is receiving the loan, also known as the borrower. Many lending situations also involve a third party, known as a broker. The broker is an agent who acts as an intermediary in creating the loan and who receives a commission, or fee, for overseeing specific aspects of the lending process.

The two basic types of loans are secured and unsecured. With a secured loan the lender assumes certain rights of ownership over the item being purchased by the borrower. Typical examples of secured loans are home loans, also known as mortgages, and car loans. In the case of home loans the lending institution has the right to sell the borrower's house or property in the event the borrower fails to repay the loan according to the requirements of the loan agreement. This right is known as a lien. To fail to repay the borrowed amount is to default on a loan. Unsecured loans include credit card loans, personal loans, or bonds (notes issued by the borrower to the lender pledging repayment of a loan).

Credit refers to the trust placed by a lender in the borrower's ability to repay a certain amount of money in an agreed-upon manner. The more faith a lender has in the ability of the borrower to repay a loan, the greater the amount of money the lender will offer to that borrower. A borrower's credit rating is determined by such factors as income, employment status, current level of debt, family responsibilities, total assets (items of value owned by the borrower, such as an automobile or a piece of property), and past credit history. These factors also play a key role in determining the interest rate of the loan. A borrower with an excellent credit rating will generally receive a favorable interest rate on a loan, because the risk of defaulting on the loan is relatively low. On the other hand high-risk borrowers, such as consumers who have bad credit histories or who hold low-paying jobs, will usually only receive a loan if they agree to repay the money at a substantially higher interest rate.

When Did It Begin

Some form of lending likely existed in the earliest civilizations. Historical sources indicate that loans served an important role in the commercial activities of the ancient Greeks and Romans, and numerous allusions to lending practices appear in the Bible. The Bible makes repeated references to the practice of usury, or the charging of interest on loans. Originally usury could refer to any form of interest, regardless of the percentage rate, although over time it came to mean interest charged at an excessive or unfair rate. Various passages in the Old Testament contain explicit rules concerning interest. For example, Exodus 25:25 expressly forbids charging interest on loans to the poor, and Deuteronomy 23:19–20 prohibits Jewish people from lending at interest to other Jews, while allowing them to charge interest to people of other faiths. Because usury and debt were regarded as immoral by early Christians, the lending of money at interest was officially prohibited by Pope Leo I in the fifth century AD.

Because of these bans on the charging of interest, most loans in medieval Europe involved collateral, which is a piece of property or another object of value given by the borrower to the lender as an assurance of intention to repay a loan. Such lenders, also known as pawnbrokers,

retained the collateral for a set amount of time and then sold it back to the borrower, collecting an agreed-upon fee in the process. In the Middle Ages the most powerful money lenders in Europe were Jews, the Lombards of northern Italy, and the Cahorsins of southern France. Because these groups amassed a great deal of wealth through the collection of fees on loans, they were generally despised and frequently persecuted.

As economies expanded toward the end of the Middle Ages (c. 500–c. 1500), usury laws began to be viewed as a hindrance to commercial growth, and laws against charging interest relaxed considerably. By the early sixteenth century the modern practice of charging interest on loans had gained widespread acceptance throughout Europe.

More Detailed Information

All loans are governed by the terms stated in a contract established between the lender and the borrower. This contract, also known as a loan agreement, outlines the various terms relating to the loan and its repayment. These terms include the amount of the loan, the interest rate (a finance charge), the amount of time the borrower will have to repay the loan, and, in most cases, a payment schedule specifying the amount of money the borrower must pay each month until the loan is completely paid. In the United States the rules governing the issuance and administration of commercial loans fall under the Uniform Commission Code, a system of laws created in the 1950s to ensure that business transactions are conducted in a fair and standardized manner from state to state.

Most loans are categorized as installment loans, which are loans that require the borrower to make periodic payments, with interest, until the loan is repaid. Most installment loans require the borrower to make a minimum payment each month. Typical installment loans include automobile loans, home mortgages, and student loans. The duration of an installment loan varies widely and is generally determined by the amount of the monthly payment. In the case of most home mortgages, the duration of the loan repayment schedule can be 15, 25, or 30 years, depending on how much money the borrower is able or willing to repay each month. In the case of automobile loans, the duration is much shorter, and the monthly payments are considerably less. Installment loans are sometimes referred to as closed-end loans.

Other common types of loans include time loans, term loans, and demand loans. Time loans are short-term loans that the borrower is obligated to repay in full after an agreed-upon length of time. The duration of time loans is frequently measured in months. The repayment date of the loan is often referred to as the point at which the loan reaches its maturity. In most cases the interest on a time loan is paid at the time of the loan's initiation, as a deduction from the total amount borrowed. Term loans are similar to time loans, in that they are repaid after the loan reaches its maturity, except that term loans have longer durations, generally between one and 15 years. Term loans also require the borrower to make regular interest payments, typically every month, quarter, half year, or year, before the principal is repaid in full. Like term loans, demand loans require the borrower to pay regular interest, in advance of repaying the full principal of the loan. Unlike term and time loans, however, demand loans have no set duration and therefore have no maturity date. In other words a demand loan is a loan for which a lender may demand repayment at any time.

In some cases a financial institution will offer credit to a consumer or a business, enabling them to borrow sums of money at their discretion. A credit card, or electronic payment card, is a plastic card that enables customers to purchase goods or receive cash by borrowing money from the financial institution from which they received the card. A credit card has a line of credit, or credit limit, given as a set dollar amount that the customer is entitled to borrow. Consumers repay credit cards, with interest, on a monthly basis. In some cases a bank will offer a consumer or business a line of credit without issuing a card; this is known simply as a line of credit. Lines of credit are also subject to interest rates. One typical example of a line of credit is the home equity line of credit, which allows a home owner to borrow funds against the value of his or her house. In some cases involving the purchase of goods and services, a seller might extend credit to a buyer without charging the buyer interest. For example, a store might allow a customer to acquire goods without paying for them right away; the store then issues a bill, typically at the end of the month, itemizing the amount owed, which the customer is obligated to pay within an agreed-upon amount of time.

Recent Trends

The 1990s witnessed a precipitous and dramatic increase in the number of loans being offered to borrowers with poor credit ratings. These loans typically offer relatively small lines of credit, usually have high interest rates, and often include additional fees, because of the higher likelihood of default on the part of the borrower. Because the interest rates on these loans were often significantly higher than the prime rate (the lowest or most favorable interest rate available), they became known as subprime loans. In the early twenty-first century subprime loans began to play a significant role in the home mortgage industry. Between 1996 and 2004 subprime mortgages accounted for only 9 percent of all mortgages in the United States; by 2006 this ratio had risen to 21 percent and accounted for $600 billion in home loans. The situation reached a breaking point in 2006, when a large number of subprime borrowers, faced with declining home prices and financial problems, suddenly defaulted on loans, forcing several of the nation's leading sublenders to declare bankruptcy. The crisis spread to the worldwide

PRIME RATE

All consumer or commercial loans are subject to interest rates. The term *interest rate* refers to a percentage, generally calculated annually, which the borrower must pay on the loan, in addition to repaying the original amount of the loan (also known as the principal). Interest rates vary widely and are determined by the credit rating (the factors determining the borrower's ability to repay a loan) of the borrower. A borrower with a good credit rating will usually receive a favorable, or low, interest rate, while a borrower with a bad credit rating will receive an unfavorable, or high, interest rate.

Prime rate refers to the most favorable interest rate offered to borrowers. The prime rate is influenced by decisions of the Federal Reserve, the government organization responsible for overseeing and regulating the U.S. economy, and is used by large banks as a means of determining interest rates on loans to their preferred customers. Recipients of loans at the prime rate are generally large, highly profitable companies. The prime rate also plays a role in establishing the interest rates on loans offered to less-preferred borrowers. For example, if a large multinational corporation receives a loan at the prime rate of 5.4 percent, a smaller, less-established company might receive a loan at "prime plus two" (in other words at 7.4 percent).

financial markets, as banks in many countries had invested in packaged home loans from the United States.

$ Line of Credit

What It Means

A line of credit (often referred to as an LOC) is a form of loan in which a bank or other financial institution (the lender) grants an individual (the borrower) the right to spend up to a certain preset amount of money (called a credit limit). Unlike an installment loan, where the borrower takes out the entire loan amount up front, a line of credit means that those funds are available to the borrower but that she is only accountable for the amount that she uses. For example, if Gwen takes out a $3,000 line of credit but ends up spending just $1,750, then she only needs to make payments and pay interest (a fee that is charged for borrowing money) on the $1,750, and the additional $1,250 remains available for her to use if she needs it in the future. Both kinds of loan charge interest, a fee that is calculated as a percentage of the amount of borrowed money.

Because it continues to turn over (or renew itself) from one billing cycle to the next, a line of credit is defined as "revolving credit." Whereas an installment loan (such as a home loan or a car loan) is paid off in a set number of equal installments, the amount a person owes on a line of credit continually fluctuates depending on the

THE DIFFERENCE BETWEEN A LINE OF CREDIT AND A LOAN

A line of credit and an installment loan both involve borrowing money from a financial institution such as a bank. The two are not the same, however.

- With a line of credit you have a spending limit, and you can spend a little of it at a time, as expenses arise. A loan offers you a lump sum of money all at once, which you may use for a big purchase, such as a car or cosmetic surgery.

- A line of credit is "revolving"; the credit is continually available from one billing period to the next, and the amount you are required to pay back each billing period increases and decreases according to the balance on your account. A loan is "non-revolving"; you receive the money once and then begin to pay it back in set installments over a fixed number of months.

- Interest is a fee for borrowing money, typically calculated as a percentage of the amount owed. The interest rate on a line of credit is variable; that is, the percentage fluctuates according to changes in the economy. The interest rate on a loan is fixed, meaning that the percentage stays the same from the day you take out the loan until the day it is paid off.

amount he spends versus the size of the payments he makes. Meanwhile, as he pays his balance down, the size of his required monthly payment also decreases. The balance that remains on the account from one month to the next is called revolving debt.

A line of credit offers more flexibility than a traditional installment loan, but it also carries some risk. An installment loan has an interest rate (the percentage used to calculate the interest fee) that is locked in, meaning it will not change over the lifetime of the loan. In contrast, the interest rate on a line of credit is variable, meaning that it will fluctuate according to changes in the economy. This can be advantageous for the borrower if interest rates are falling, but disadvantageous if they are rising.

When Did It Begin

Instances of people taking on obligations of debt can be traced to ancient civilizations, but consumer credit did not become a fact of life until the mid-twentieth century. In the nineteenth century many merchants allowed some customers to pay for furniture and other household goods on installment plans. Still, however, then and in the early twentieth century, it was almost unheard of for a financial institution (such as a bank) to extend consumer credit. This was in part because of the difficulty of assessing the average individual borrower's financial de-

pendability, and also because managing such loans required too much money and effort.

The advent of consumer credit as we know it today coincided with the mass production of consumer goods and the increasing urbanization of American society, trends that became particularly strong in the era after World War II (which ended in 1945). The initial rise in consumers' use of credit after the war was related to people taking out loans to buy homes, but after credit cards were introduced in the 1960s, the number of American families carrying revolving debt increased steadily. Whereas in 1970 only 16 percent of American families held a general-purpose, bank-issued credit card, by 2006 that number had risen to 71 percent.

More Detailed Information

A line of credit may be secured or unsecured. A secured line of credit is one in which the borrower puts up some form of collateral (property of value that will be forfeited to the lender if the loan cannot be repaid), such as a building, car, or business. Although the borrower risks losing his property when he takes out a secured line of credit, the benefit is that he can usually obtain a significantly higher credit line at significantly lower interest than with an unsecured line of credit. This is because the lender's risk of losing money is greatly reduced by the collateral. A secured line of credit can be a useful financial tool, especially for small business owners who may need extra funds to buy new equipment, cover payroll, launch new marketing initiatives, or simply maintain steady cash flow (the balance between incoming and outgoing money) through ups and downs in sales.

A home equity line of credit is also secured, with the collateral being the house the borrower owns. With this line of credit, the limit is determined by the amount of equity the person has in his or her home. Equity is the difference between the market value of the home (how much it could be sold for) and the outstanding balance (amount still owed) on the original home loan. Many people take out a home equity line of credit in order to finance home repairs, improvements, and remodeling. Still, however, there are no restrictions on what this line of credit can be used for, and many people also use it to pay for college tuition, medical expenses, or even a vacation splurge. Another significant advantage of a business or home equity line of credit is that the interest the borrower pays on the debt is often tax deductible. That is, when it comes time to pay annual income tax, he can subtract the interest payments from his earnings, thereby reducing the amount of income tax he has to pay.

An unsecured line of credit is one in which the lender extends credit without the borrower putting up any collateral. A credit card (an electronic-payment card) is an example of an unsecured line of credit. In the absence of collateral, the lender must judge how reliable the borrower is (and therefore how much credit to extend and

A line of credit is a type of loan that enables borrowers to spend some or all of a preset sum of money. Many retailers make lines of credit available in order to encourage customers to purchase products. *AP Images.*

how much interest to charge) based solely on his or her proof of income and credit score (a kind of financial report card that details a person's payment history with creditors, landlords, utility companies, and others). Because the borrower does not put his or her property directly at risk—indeed, the borrower does not even need to own any property—he or she can expect the lender to offer a more conservative amount of credit and charge a higher interest rate.

Recent Trends

Banks that issue credit cards have been in the business of extending unsecured lines of credit to consumers since the 1960s. These cards may be used to make purchases anywhere that the particular card brand (such as Visa and MasterCard) is accepted. Individual retail chains (including Target, Home Depot, Best Buy, Macy's, and Sears) also extend their own unsecured credit lines to customers for exclusive use in their stores. In the 1990s many retailers, realizing that there were profits to be made from offering credit cards, began to promote such cards more aggressively.

Here is how it works: Alfred goes to the checkout at Target, ready to pay for his purchases with a Visa card, or perhaps with cash. The cashier tells him that he can get a

15 percent discount on these purchases if he applies for a Target Card (line of credit). The application process is simple; he can be approved for at least a small line of credit on the spot, and as long as he opts to pay for the purchases with his new Target Card, he can save 15 percent. The problem with these exclusive merchant lines of credit is that they often carry much higher interest rates than regular credit cards. Therefore, if Alfred carries a balance on this card, the interest charges will quickly make him lose his 15 percent savings.

$ Personal Loan

What It Means

Generally speaking a personal loan refers to money that is borrowed from a financial institution, known in these situations as the lender, for personal (as opposed to business) use. Personal loans tend to be for relatively small amounts, especially when compared to larger, long-term loans, such as home loans (also known as mortgages). While personal loans are typically used to pay for one-time expenses (such as medical bills, home repairs, or a significant purchase), a borrower (the individual receiving the loan) is usually not required to disclose the specific purpose for the loan. Indeed many borrowers seek personal loans simply to have a large sum of cash, which they can spend at their discretion.

Most personal loans fall under the category of unsecured loans. The two basic types of loans are secured and unsecured. With secured loans the borrower is required to offer some form of collateral to the lender in exchange for the loan. The term *collateral* refers to a piece of property or another asset belonging to the borrower, such as a car or a home, which is offered as a guarantee that the borrower will repay the loan. If the borrower goes into default (in other words fails to repay the loan or to keep to the terms of the loan agreement) then the lender is legally entitled to take possession of the collateral. Unsecured loans, on the other hand, do not require the borrower to put up collateral.

Because most personal loans are unsecured, they are often accompanied by a higher interest rate (a percentage of the money borrowed, calculated on an annual basis, which accrues over the life of the loan) than with secured loans. All loan payments consist of two parts: the interest and the principal (the amount of money borrowed, not including interest). As a guarantee that he or she will repay a personal loan, a borrower will often sign a document, known as a promissory note, pledging to repay the loan. For this reason personal loans are sometimes referred to as signature loans. Other common terms for personal loans are *character loans* (because they are based on the personal reputation, as well as credit rating, of the borrower) and *good-faith loans.*

THE MORRIS PLAN

A personal loan (money that is lent to an individual for personal rather than commercial purposes) is one of the most common forms of consumer loans. One of the distinctive features of personal loans is that they are unsecured. In other words a personal loan does not require the borrower to provide the bank with collateral (property, such as a home, a car, or another item of value) as a guarantee that he or she will repay the loan. Because personal loans do not require collateral, they are based on a degree of trust between the lender (the financial institution or another entity lending the money) and the borrower (the person borrowing the money).

Prior to the twentieth century American banks rarely offered unsecured loans to their customers. In the early 1900s a Virginia lawyer named Arthur J. Morris (1881–1973) set out to change this practice. In 1910 Morris founded the Morris Plan Bank, one of the first financial institutions in the United States dedicated to offering personal loans to the working poor. Morris believed it was fundamentally unfair to deny the majority of a country's citizens the right to borrow money to improve their standard of living (a way of measuring an individual's economic well-being that is based on the quantity and quality of consumer goods available to that individual). While largely motivated by his concern for the financial struggles of working-class Americans, Morris also believed that extending unsecured loans to a larger percentage of the population would help stimulate the economy in general. By increasing consumer spending on manufactured goods, personal loans would help increase manufacturing, thus leading to more jobs. Morris's economic philosophy, known as the Morris Plan, helped lay the foundation for modern lending practices in the United States.

When Did It Begin

Personal loans have probably existed since the earliest commercial transactions. In ancient civilizations in Greece, Rome, and the Middle East, lending at interest was a common practice. Lenders frequently set up tables in a central marketplace, where they offered loans to qualified customers at a set interest rate.

In the United States during the nineteenth and early twentieth centuries, unsecured loans were generally difficult for the average consumer to obtain. Traditionally banks only issued personal loans to select customers, who had a proven record of paying their debts. For the majority of individuals, however, these loans were unavailable. Most people seeking personal loans were forced to go to loan sharks. Loan sharks lend money to unproven customers at extremely high (and often illegal) interest rates.

In the early 1900s lending practices in the United States began to change dramatically. One of the pioneers of the modern personal loan industry was a Virginia lawyer named Arthur J. Morris (1881–1973), who founded his first bank in 1910 with the aim of extending credit to lower- and middle-income consumers. Known as the Morris Plan Bank, the bank was originally funded with $20,000, most of which was contributed by Morris himself. The bank's earliest loans were designed to help the working poor purchase items that would improve their quality of life, such as homes or cars, or that would provide them with financial security in the event of an emergency.

By the early 1920s other banks throughout the United States began to implement the lending practices of the Morris Plan Bank. In 1920 a bank in Bridgeport, Connecticut, became the first financial institution to advertise personal loan products to lower income consumers. According to history professor Lendol G. Calder, author of *Financing the American Dream: A Cultural History of Consumer Credit* (Princeton University Press, 1999), only six banks in 1923 offered unsecured loans in the United States; by 1929 the number of banks offering personal loans had increased to 208. By 1931 Morris Plan banks had been established in more than 100 cities and were lending approximately $220 million annually in unsecured personal loans.

More Detailed Information

Applying for a personal loan is a relatively straightforward process. Applicants begin by completing a loan application. In filling out the application, prospective borrowers provide basic information about themselves, including name, Social Security number, date of birth, and contact information (generally street address, home phone number, work phone number, and e-mail address). Applicants will also be asked to provide employment information, such as the name and address of his or her employer and his or her job title and gross income (total amount of money earned before taxes). The loan application will also include a line for the desired loan amount. In some cases there might be a line where the applicant will be asked to describe the purpose of the loan (for example, the applicant might write "home repairs" or "consolidate debt"). Debt consolidation refers to the practice by which consumers use one form of credit (such as a personal loan or a credit card) to pay off several other existing debts, thereby consolidating several monthly payments into a single monthly payment. Debt consolidation is a common reason that borrowers apply for personal loans.

The bank or lending institution employee responsible for considering loan applications is known as a loan officer. In determining whether an applicant qualifies for a loan, a loan officer will consider several factors relating to the applicant's overall financial situation. In addition to considering the applicant's income, the loan officer will typically request a credit report (a detailed outline of the applicant's credit history) from a credit bureau (an

Many personal loans are taken for large, one-time expenses, such as home repairs and medical bills. Once a borrower has completed the application process and been approved for the personal loan, his or her signature on the loan contract serves as a legal promise to repay the money. *Photograph by Kelly A. Quin. Cengage Learning, Gale.*

organization that sells consumer credit reports to lending institutions). Credit reports typically provide specific information concerning an individual's current debts and credit history. A prospective borrower with a history of making debt payments on time will have a much greater chance of receiving a loan than a customer who has a history of late payments. One other important factor for loan officers considering a loan application is the applicant's debt-to-income ratio (the amount of income a consumer uses to pay off debt every month). Debt-to-income ratios are calculated as a percentage. For example, if an individual earns $4,000 a month and makes annual payments of $800 a month on credit card debts, their debt-to-income ratio would be calculated at 20 percent. In general lenders will only offer an unsecured loan to an individual with a debt-to-income ratio of 35 percent or lower.

Interest rates for unsecured loans tend to be considerably higher (often double the percentage rate) than rates on secured loans. Personal loans usually are for smaller amounts and have maximum repayment schedules of between 48 and 60 months. The repayment schedule is generally determined according to the amount borrowed. For example, while a borrower might have 48 months to repay a $5,000 loan, he or she might only have 12 months to pay off a $500 loan.

Recent Trends

With the rise of the Internet in the late 1990s, more and more potential borrowers have applied online for personal loans. Applicants can generally complete and submit their loan applications electronically and will often receive a response from a lending institution the same day. Many banks and other financial institutions have even created websites that allow existing customers to submit loan applications online, thereby saving them the trouble of visiting the bank to fill out an application.

$ Student Loan

What It Means

A student loan is a sum of money made available to a student who is pursuing higher education, such as college or university study. Because higher education costs tend to be expensive, and because few students are able to work a full-time job while going to school, student loans provide a valuable form of financial assistance. Student loans are designed to help students pay for such expenses as tuition (the basic cost of attending school), student fees (book purchases, library fees, and athletic charges, for example), and room and board (housing and meals). In general, student loans cater to those students who are in need of financial assistance, though many student loans are available to any student who applies for them, regardless of his or her financial situation. Student loans fall under the general category of financial aid, along with scholarships and grants. Scholarships and grants are typically made available to students based on academic or athletic achievement or financial need. Unlike these forms of financial assistance, student loans must be repaid.

Almost all loans require the person borrowing the money (the borrower) to pay interest on the loan. Interest is a percentage of the loan amount that the borrower must pay in addition to repaying the loan. Student loans also require the borrower to pay interest on the money he or she borrows, though the interest rates on student loans tend to be lower than interest rates on other loans. Students who receive a student loan are not required to repay the loan until they have either finished their education or are no longer enrolled as a full-time student. In most cases, student loans allow students a grace period (a period during which a person is not required to meet an obligation) after they leave school, during which time they are not required to make payments on the loan. Grace periods on student loans generally span from 6 to 12 months.

When Did It Begin

In the United States student loans originated out of the federal government's desire to provide higher-education opportunities to a broader portion of the population. The earliest form of government assistance for higher education was created by the Morrill Land Grant Act of 1862. Under this law, the government gave federal land to individual states. The states then sold the land and used the proceeds to form colleges. These colleges were primarily designed to promote the study of agriculture and engineering.

The first student loan programs were created in 1958 with the passage of the National Defense Education Act (NDEA). Congress passed the NDEA in response to the

Student loans help students cover the costs of college, graduate school, and other forms of higher education. In the early twenty-first century more than 25 percent of undergraduates in the United States received student loans. © *Mango Productions/Corbis.*

October 4, 1957, launch of the Sputnik space satellite by the Soviet Union (a confederation of socialist nations also known as the Union of Soviet Socialist Republics, or USSR). Because the Soviet Union was believed to pose a military threat to the United States, Congress believed that creating educational opportunities, specifically in the fields of mathematics and science, was vital to national security. To help make higher education financially feasible for more students, the law included a provision for the establishment of the National Defense Student Loan Program. These early student loans were designated solely for highly qualified students and were intended exclusively for the study of science, math, and foreign languages. This program later became known as the Federal Perkins Student Loan Program. With the passage of the Higher Education Act of 1965, student loans became available to a wider range of students, and loans were offered in all fields of study. By the early twenty-first century, more than 600,000 students in the United States were receiving federally guaranteed student loans each year.

More Detailed Information

Student loans come in two basic types: subsidized and unsubsidized. In the case of subsidized student loans, the federal government will pay the interest on the loan while the student is still enrolled in school. For example, say an undergraduate college student takes out a student loan of $8,000 over a four-year period. If the loan accrues $2,000 in interest over the course of four years, the student will only owe $8,000 when he or she graduates. However, as soon as the student begins to pay off the loan (generally within six months of leaving school), he or she will begin paying interest on the loan. Subsidized loans are designed to offset the financial difficulties involved in pursuing a higher education. In the case of unsubsidized loans, the student is responsible for both the total loan amount and the interest accrued during his or her years in school. For example, if a student takes out a loan for $8,000 and $2,000 in interest accrues over the course of his or her years in school, then the student will owe $10,000 at the time he or she begins to pay off the loan. This practice of adding the interest to the amount of the loan is known as capitalization. Furthermore, as the student pays off the $10,000, additional interest will accrue on whatever amount is remaining on the loan until the loan is paid off completely.

A large number of student loans are guaranteed by the federal government. This means that the government subsidizes the loan while the student is in school, pays any expenses involved with managing the loan, and takes responsibility for repaying the loan in the event that the student defaults (fails to repay the loan). There are two principal types of federal student loans, each catering to a specific type of student. Perkins Loans cater to students with the greatest level of financial need; these loans are subsidized, have low interest rates, and have grace periods of nine months. The repayment schedule for Perkins Loans generally lasts 10 years. Stafford Loans, on the other hand, are available to all students and are the most popular form of federal student loan. Like Perkins Loans, Stafford Loans offer low interest rates (though slightly higher than rates on Perkins Loans) and are often subsidized. The repayment terms of Stafford Loans, however, tend to be longer; in some cases a graduate might take up to 30 years to repay a Stafford Loan completely.

In addition to federally guaranteed loans, there are many private lenders who provide student loans. Private student loans are unsubsidized, have a higher interest rate than federal student loans, and often require the student to pay an origination fee on the loan (a one-time charge for receiving the loan, which is deducted from the loan amount the student receives). The main advantage of private student loans is that they generally offer a higher maximum loan amount than that of federal loans.

Some students have difficulty repaying their student loans after they leave school. In many cases, these students can request that they be allowed to defer the repayment of the loan temporarily by applying for hardship forbearance. Hardship forbearance provides former students with the opportunity to skip student loan payments in times of financial difficulty, often for periods of six months. In some cases, students may reapply for hardship forbearance in extreme circumstances; for example, if they are unemployed or injured and unable to work. While all federal loans provide borrowers with the option to defer payment of the loan, some private loans do not.

In some cases, students can have their loans decreased, or even cancelled, if they agree to enter a certain line of work after they leave school. This option is usually available to students who perform volunteer work (for example, helping build houses for the poor), who serve in the military, or who take teaching jobs in low-income communities. This practice of waiving loan payments is known as loan forgiveness.

Recent Trends

In the 1990s the number of lenders offering federally guaranteed student loans rose dramatically. As competition for the student-loan market increased, lenders began to offer incentives to financial-aid administrators (officials who are responsible for providing students with information about financial aid options) so that administrators would recommend lenders' loan products to students. These incentives took the form of gifts, stock (shares in

FINANCIAL AID PAYS OFF

Financial aid is monetary assistance designated for students pursuing a higher education. A student loan is a form of financial aid. When a student leaves school, he or she is obligated to repay the student loan. In addition to loans, students can also apply for other types of financial aid, including scholarships and grants, which do not have to be repaid.

The cost of higher education increases dramatically each year. Tuition rates rise between five and eight percent annually, and financial aid is crucial to the majority of Americans seeking a higher education. Although higher education is an expensive investment, it usually pays off for the student. According to the United States Census Bureau (a government organization that collects data on U.S. citizens), an individual with an undergraduate college degree earns, on average, double the amount of income over the course of his or her lifetime than an individual without a college degree earns.

the lending company), and sometimes cash payments. As lawmakers learned about these practices, they began to demand tighter restrictions on the way that student loan companies offered their products to students. In June 2007 the U.S. Department of Education implemented new rules concerning the $85-billion-a-year student loan industry. For example, admission officials were required to list the names of three possible lenders when offering financial aid information to students, and many gifts and incentives were outlawed.

$ Car Loan

What It Means

A car loan (also known as an automobile loan, or auto loan) is a sum of money a consumer borrows in order to purchase a car. Generally speaking a loan is an amount of money that is lent to an individual, a business, or another entity. The party that lends the money is known as the lender, while the party borrowing the money is called the borrower. When taking out a loan a borrower agrees to pay back the full loan amount, as well as any interest (a percentage of the loan amount, usually calculated on an annual basis), by a certain date, typically by making monthly payments.

Car loans follow most of the same rules and procedures that apply to other loans. In most cases when purchasing a car, a borrower will specifically apply for a car loan; however, a consumer can also use a personal loan (a loan obtained by an individual to use at his or her discretion) for the same purpose. All car loans are for specific lengths of time, generally anywhere between 24 and 60 months, although some car loans can be for longer periods. This type of loan is also known as

A car loan is money borrowed to finance the purchase of a new car or truck. Borrowers can typically take possession of a new vehicle upon completing the loan process. © *Comstock/Corbis.*

financing. Car loans generally include a variety of fees and taxes, which are added to the total loan amount.

Many consumers apply for car loans at their local bank. When applying for a car loan a borrower will usually begin by specifying how much money he or she wants to borrow. The borrower will then provide information about his or her financial situation, beginning with income (the amount of money he or she earns by working). Most lenders will require the borrower to provide some proof of employment, usually in the form of a pay stub (the portion of a paycheck that includes information about an employee's earnings, which an employee keeps for his or her records) or a copy of a tax return (the form submitted by individuals when paying taxes). The lender will also check the borrower's credit report. A credit report is a detailed record of an individual's past credit (in short, borrowing) activities, whether in the form of loans or other debts (money owed). If the prospective borrower has a bad credit history, he or she may be ineligible for a car loan.

Often a bank or financial institution will preapprove certain customers for car loans. In these situations a consumer has a certain number of days (often 30, sometimes 45) to decide whether to seek full approval for

a car loan. Because most borrowers secure a car loan before actually shopping for a car, when an application for a car loan is approved, a lender will generally give the borrower a maximum amount he or she will be able to borrow. The borrower is then free to use this money to purchase the car of his or her choosing; however, the borrower is not required to spend the full amount offered by the lender. For example, while a bank might approve a car loan of $50,000 for a long-term customer, that customer has the right to spend only a fraction of that amount.

When Did It Begin

The car loan officially originated in 1919, when the General Motors Corporation (an automobile manufacturer founded in 1908 in Flint, Michigan) established the General Motors Acceptance Corporation, or GMAC. GMAC arose in response to the growing demand for automobiles among American consumers after World War I. In 1919 GMAC established offices in five North American cities; a year later it opened its first office in Great Britain. As the car loan business expanded, other automobile manufacturers began to develop their own financing divisions. One of the most prominent was the

Ford Motor Credit Company, founded in 1923. Although car loans were available most American consumers during the first half of the twentieth century paid cash for their automobiles.

More Detailed Information

When a borrower takes out a loan on a car, he or she is agreeing to buy the car. Upon entering into the loan agreement the borrower gains the right to drive the car, while also taking possession of the car's title (a document showing proof of ownership of a piece of property). Technically speaking, however, the borrower does not yet own the car; the lender owns the car until the borrower has finished paying off the loan.

Each car payment consists of two parts: the principal (the original amount of the loan) and the interest. Interest on car loans depends primarily on three main factors: the credit rating of the car buyer, whether the car is new or used, and the price of the car. As a rule interest rates on new cars tend to be lower than interest rates on used cars. Also, as the price of a car goes up, the interest rate will usually go down. For example, if a consumer wants to purchase a used truck listed for $2,500, the loan interest rate might be 6.49 percent; if that same consumer wants to purchase a new $40,000 Lexus, the interest rate might only be 5.49 percent.

The bulk of a monthly car payment goes toward the principal, so that the total amount of the loan decreases steadily with each payment. As a borrower pays off more of the principal of the loan, he or she moves closer to full ownership of the car. The amount of money the borrower has paid toward full ownership is known as equity; in other words with each loan payment the borrower earns additional equity in the car. At the same time, the value of the car steadily decreases over the course of the loan, meaning that the car will never be worth the amount of the original loan. For example, say a borrower takes out a $10,000 loan to pay for a car. At the time of purchase the car is worth about $10,000 (minus fees and taxes). Four years later, when the borrower has paid off the loan, the car may be worth only $2,000. If the borrower has neglected to take good care of the car, it might be worth substantially less. This process by which the car loses its value over time is known as depreciation.

Traditionally car loans were for short periods, generally about 24 months and no longer than 36 months. In the 1980s, however, standard car loan periods began to get longer. There were two key reasons for this change. For one, in the early 1980s more and more consumers began to lease their cars (they paid a monthly fee in exchange for the right to drive a particular car) rather than purchase cars outright. Car leases were primarily attractive because they did not require a down payment, and they tended to require lower monthly payments than traditional car loans. In order to compete with the car leasing industry, a number of lenders began to offer car

UPSIDE-DOWN CAR LOANS

Car loans are loans used to purchase cars. Traditionally car loans were for a period of 24 to 36 months. Beginning in the 1990s, however, consumers began to extend the financing period for their car loans, sometimes for as long as 72 months. As a result consumers were able to make lower monthly payments on their cars, because they were spread out over a longer period. One problem with these extended car loan periods, however, is that the value of the car often decreases at a faster rate than the loan amount. For example, after three years of payments a person might have $5,000 remaining on the car loan, but the car itself might be worth only $3,000. This predicament is commonly referred to as being upside down with a car loan. As long as the car owner makes regular payments and takes care of the vehicle, upside-down loans will not necessarily pose a problem. But if that person totals the car (wrecks it so badly that the cost of repairing it exceeds the value of the car) and the auto insurance will only pay $3,000 for it, then he or she will still owe an additional $2,000 toward the car, even though the car can no longer be driven. To remedy this problem many car loan companies now offer gap insurance, which covers the difference between the loan amount and the value of the car in the event the car is totaled.

loans for longer terms. As a result loan periods of 48, 60, and 72 months became standard. In some cases borrowers were able to receive even longer periods over which to repay their loans. For example, when a borrower purchases a luxury vehicle (a car, a truck, or another vehicle that is more expensive than average cars and generally includes additional features designed to increase car performance or comfort), he or she will sometimes have as long as 84 months to repay the loan. In the early twenty-first century a luxury car was generally defined as a vehicle costing in excess of $30,000. From the early 1990s to the middle of the following decade, the proportion of Americans who owned luxury cars rose from 10 to 30 percent. This overall rise in the price of motor vehicles was the second significant reason that standard car loans became longer in duration.

Recent Trends

As with a number of other types of loans, car loans have become increasingly available over the Internet since the late 1990s. There are many advantages involved with shopping for car loans online. For one, shopping for loans online allows consumers to compare interest rates from a wide range of lenders, in a relatively short amount of time, therefore giving them a better chance of securing the best deal. Also, because online car loan companies require little cost overhead (the expenses involved with running a business, including renting an office, paying employees, buying office supplies, and so on), they can often offer consumers lower interest rates than those offered by traditional banks.

$ Home Loan

What It Means

A home is usually the single most expensive purchase that a person will ever make. Few people, however, have enough money to pay for a home in its entirety up-front. Instead, most choose to take out a home loan, which is also called a mortgage. This entails borrowing money from a financial institution (such as a bank) to buy the house and then spreading out the repayment of the loan over a long period of time. That period is often 30 years. The lender also charges the borrower a fee called interest, which is a certain percentage of the amount of the loan.

A borrower repays a home loan on a monthly basis. Usually the payment is the same amount each month for the life of the loan. The amount of the payment is de-

A home loan is a sum of money borrowed by an individual in order to purchase a house. Buying a home is an expensive, complicated process, typically requiring the assistance of a real estate agent, such as the one in this photo. © *Chuck Savage/Corbis.*

termined by several factors: the amount of the loan, the term (time span) of the loan, and the annual percentage rate (APR; the percentage charged by the lender each year on the amount of the loan).

For example, imagine you need to borrow $160,000 to buy a house, and you want to pay back the loan over 30 years (which would be 360 monthly payments). For that service the bank would charge you a fee—for example, 8 percent each year on the amount of the loan. In order to pay off both the original loan amount plus the 8 percent annual fee, you would need to make 360 payments of $1,174.02. This process of gradually paying back a loan over a long period of time is called amortization.

When Did It Begin

It was not until the creation of the Federal Housing Administration (FHA) in 1934 that long-term loans became widely used as a means of purchasing homes in the United States. Prior to the creation of the FHA, most loans had short terms of one to three years and only covered 30 to 50 percent of the price of the property. This was in part because few individual investors or small local banks could afford to loan such large sums of money for very long; the risk of it not being paid back was too great. People usually refinanced (took out new loans for) their homes every few years, which put them at risk of not finding a new loan to replace the old and therefore losing ownership of the house.

The FHA offered a mortgage-insurance system backed by the Federal Reserve, the central bank of the United States. This system made home loans less risky for lenders because the loans were backed up with money held by the federal government; if a borrower defaulted on (failed to pay back) one of these insured mortgages, the lender would still be repaid. As a result, banks started to offer longer-term loans for a much larger portion of the purchase price. Soon 30-year loans for 80 percent of the purchase price became commonplace, allowing more people than ever before to afford to buy their own homes.

More Detailed Information

A home loan is usually obtained from a bank but can be received from any institution willing to loan the money. Lenders normally require an initial payment from the borrower, typically 20 percent of the purchase price of the house; this is called a down payment. If the house is selling for $200,000, for example, the borrower must make a down payment of $40,000 and can then take out a $160,000 loan to cover the rest. Lenders require a down payment as a way to ensure that they can recover the money they have loaned in case the borrower defaults on it (that is, fails to repay it). In the case of default, the lender has the right to repossess the property and sell it to pay off the loan. The process of a lender taking possession of a property as a result of a defaulted loan is called foreclosure.

Lenders evaluate potential borrowers to make sure they are reliable enough to pay back the loan. Among the factors they review are the borrower's income and ability to make the down payment. The U.S. government provides various forms of assistance to people who would not normally qualify for home loans. For instance, the Federal Housing Administration insures loans for low-income citizens in order to encourage banks to lend to them. It also runs programs that offer grants (money that does not have to be repaid) to cover down payments. One such program is the American Dream Down Payment Initiative. The Department of Veterans Affairs provides similar assistance for people who have served in the U.S. military.

The calculation banks use to determine monthly loan payments is complicated and often not understood by borrowers. Banks charge an annual percentage rate (APR) on the loan amount, or principal, in order to be compensated for the service of lending money (as well as to pay for their own expenses, such as hiring employees and maintaining buildings). Although the interest rate is quoted as an annual rate, in actuality the interest on a home loan is usually charged monthly. For example, if the APR were 8 percent, the monthly interest rate would be 0.6667 percent (8 percent divided by 12 months). The interest also compounds monthly, meaning that each month the interest fee is added to the original loan amount, and this sum is used as the basis for the next month's interest. The borrower ends up paying interest on the accumulated interest as well as on the original loan amount.

To understand how this works, imagine that you had to pay an 8 percent annual fee on $100. The first month you would pay an interest fee of roughly 0.6667 percent of $100, or a little more than 66 cents, raising the total amount due to just over $100.66. The second month you would pay 0.6667 percent on the new loan amount ($100.66), or 67 cents, bringing the total due to almost $101.34. After 12 months of applying a compounding monthly interest rate of 0.6667, the total amount owed would be $108.30, or 8 percent more than the original loan amount plus 30 cents, the amount of interest that accumulated through compounding.

Mortgage payments are even more complicated because two things happen each month: in the example of an 8 percent APR, a fee of 0.6667 percent is charged to the total amount of the loan, but the total amount of the loan is reduced because the borrower has made a payment. Because the payment by the borrower is more than the fee of the monthly interest rate, the total amount owed gradually goes down.

This method of calculation requires that borrowers pay more in interest each month at the beginning of the loan than at the end. This can be seen in the example of a $160,000 loan paid over a 30-year period with an APR of 8 percent. After the first month of the loan, the bank charges a monthly interest rate of 0.6667 percent (really two-thirds of a percent, which would be a 0 with an infinite number of 6s after the decimal point, but it is rounded up at the fourth decimal point) on the $160,000 loan amount, for a fee of $1,066.67. At the same time, the borrower sends the bank a mortgage payment of $1,174.02; of this amount, $1,066.67 goes toward paying off the interest charge, and the remainder, $107.35, is subtracted from the $160,000 loan, bring the total amount due down to $159,892.65. The next month the bank charges the same monthly interest rate of 0.6667 on this new amount, $159,892.65, resulting in an interest charge of $1,065.95, just slightly less than the month before. When the borrower sends in his $1,174.02 payment, $1,065.95 goes toward paying off the new interest charge and the rest, $108.07, is subtracted from the loan amount ($159,892.65-$108.07), with the resulting total amount due being $159,784.58.

Over the course of 30 years, three things happen: the total amount due on the loan gradually goes down; the interest charge also slowly reduces (because it is a fixed percent, 0.6667, of a gradually reducing loan amount); and an increasing amount of the payment begins to go to the loan amount, not the interest (because the interest charge gradually goes down while the borrower's payment, $1,174.02, remains the same). After 270 months, or three-fourths of the way through the loan, $532.72 of the monthly payment goes toward interest and $641.30 is subtracted from the loan amount. By the end of the loan, the borrower would have paid $160,000 in principal and $262,652.18 in interest.

Purchasing a home involves paying what are called "closing costs" to cover the various transactions that must occur. Fees are charged by the broker or agent who arranges the home loan, the people who inspect the property to make sure it is sound, the title insurance company (which researches the legal ownership of the property to make sure the seller is really the owner and insures that the transfer of ownership goes smoothly). Additionally, there are various local and state taxes and fees to be paid, and there may be a partial payment due at the time of the mortgage's inception. These charges are usually paid by the buyer at the very end of the lending process (hence the term *closing costs*).

In order to protect themselves and the home buyer from financial loss, lenders require that the property be covered by a homeowner's insurance policy that insures the property against loss from fire (and in certain cases flood or earthquake) damage. To guarantee that the borrower makes his or her insurance payments, mortgage lenders set up what is called an escrow account and require that the borrower deposit a monthly payment into it to cover the cost of the insurance. When the annual insurance bill comes due, the mortgage company uses the

REVERSE MORTGAGES

Whereas a regular home mortgage is a lump-sum loan that is used to buy a house and then repaid over a period of many years, a reverse mortgage is an arrangement in which a home owner puts his or her home up as collateral in order to borrow money from a bank. This loan is often divided into small monthly amounts, the repayment of which is deferred until the owner moves out of the house or dies. When the house is sold, the loan is expected to be paid back. In other words, a traditional mortgage is a means to purchase a house; a reverse mortgage uses a house as a means to generate income. A reverse mortgage generally appeals to older people who may have need of additional income but whose greatest single asset is their house. In the United States a reverse mortgage is only available to those age 62 and older.

money in the escrow account to pay it on behalf of the borrower.

Additionally, most real estate is subject to property tax, which is used to fund public schools and other local government programs. Because a failure to pay these taxes can lead to the seizure and sale of the property, the lender wants to make sure that these taxes are paid and hence requires the buyer to pay another monthly amount into the escrow account.

Despite the large amount of interest paid, there are many benefits to having a home loan. They allow people to buy homes that they would otherwise be unable to afford. In addition, once someone has a fixed-rate mortgage, the monthly payment never goes up. Rents, however, almost always rise over time. A homeowner also builds up equity in the house over the years. Equity is the difference between the current value of the property and the loans against it. In the above example of the $200,000 house, the owner immediately has $40,000 in equity because of the down payment; as the owner gradually pays back the loan, his or her equity increases. Furthermore, it is likely that 10 years later the house itself will have increased in value. If the house is, for example, worth $260,000 by then, the owner will have gained an additional $60,000 in equity. An owner can turn the equity in a house into cash by selling the house and pocketing the profits, possibly with the intention of buying another house, taking a long vacation, or having extra money for retirement. Finally, interest is usually deducted from a person's taxable income, meaning that person will owe less in taxes.

Recent Trends

For many decades the only type of mortgage an average person could get was a fixed-rate 15- or 30-year loan. In the late 1970s interest rates in the United States rose

sharply. Because the interest rate for a home loan has a direct impact on the size of the mortgage payment (higher interest rates mean higher monthly payments), fewer people could afford to buy homes or qualify for mortgages. This situation was made more difficult by a high rate of inflation (the general rising of prices), which lowered the value of any money that people had saved up. To encourage borrowing, lenders responded by offering new types of mortgages with lower monthly payments or artificially low interest rates. Among these were adjustable-rate mortgages whose interest rate (and therefore monthly payments) changed over time and interest-only mortgages whose monthly payments included only the interest on the loan and no repayment of principal.

Over time these new types of home loans contributed to a surge in lending and a nationwide increase in housing prices beginning in the late 1990s. This trend helped stimulate economic growth by generating income for those who invested in existing properties and for those involved in building new ones. The banking industry got a boost from people taking out second or third mortgages on their homes in order to take advantage of historically low interest rates. All this changed in 2006, when home prices throughout the United States, seen by many as overinflated, began to decline, and large numbers of people started to default on their loans. The resulting crisis destabilized both the U.S. housing market and financial institutions worldwide that had invested in packaged home loans from the United States.

$ Home Equity Loan

What It Means

A home equity loan is a loan that is available to homeowners. In the most basic sense a loan is a sum of money that is borrowed by a person or company and then repaid, with interest (a percentage of the loan amount, usually calculated on an annual basis), over a set period of time. Two principal parties are involved in loan transactions: a borrower (the party borrowing the money) and a lender (the party lending the money). The two basic types of loans are secured and unsecured. In obtaining a secured loan the borrower presents the lender with some piece of property (for example, an automobile), of which the lender can claim ownership in the event the borrower fails to repay the loan (also known as defaulting on a loan). This property is known as collateral. Unsecured loans, on the other hand, do not require the borrower to have collateral. A home equity loan is a form of secured loan, in that the borrower uses his or her house as collateral to secure the loan. People take out home equity loans for various purposes, such as undertaking home improvements or paying off debt (something—for example, money, a piece of property, or a service—that an individual owes to another individual or an entity).

In a home equity loan, a person borrows money and backs up the loan with the value of his or her home. Many homeowners take out home equity loans in order to remodel or do other improvements to their homes. © *2007/Jupiterimages.*

In almost all cases a home equity loan will represent the second loan a borrower secures using his or her house as collateral. Because houses are very expensive, most homebuyers must first take out a loan to purchase a house. These home loans (commonly known as mortgages) are for large amounts of money and are repaid in monthly installments over a long period of time, typically 30 years. As time passes the value of the home will usually increase (a process known as appreciation), while the total of the mortgage that remains to be paid gradually decreases. The difference between the value of the house and the amount remaining on the mortgage is known as equity. Put another way equity represents the amount of money a homeowner is able to retain after he or she sells the home and pays off the remainder of the mortgage. For example, say a couple purchases a home for $200,000. They pay $20,000 up front (known as a down payment) and then take out a loan for the remaining $180,000. On the day they complete the purchase of the house (also known as the closing), the couple has $20,000 in equity (in other words the original down payment). Two years later their house is valued at $220,000, and the amount remaining on their mortgage is $176,000. In this scenario the couple would have

$44,000 in equity on their home. With home equity loans the amount of money a homeowner can borrow depends on the amount of equity he or she has in the house. Traditionally this type of home loan is referred to as a second mortgage.

When Did It Begin

In certain respects the modern home equity loan dates to the Great Depression. The Great Depression, or simply Depression, was a period of severe worldwide economic hardship dating from 1929 to about 1939. In the early years of the Depression, a large number of American property owners, many of them farmers, were in danger of losing their properties because they were unable to keep up with their monthly mortgage payments. In order to provide property owners relief from the burden of their mortgage payments, lenders began to offer them additional loans, or second mortgages. As with the original mortgage these additional property loans were secured loans, using the borrower's house or farm as collateral. While these loans did provide temporary financial relief to some property owners, in most cases they merely plunged the borrower deeper in debt; unable to pay off their debts, many American homeowners and farmers lost their

THE TAX REFORM ACT AND THE RISE OF MORTGAGE DEBT

In 1986 the U.S. Congress passed the Tax Reform Act, which brought sweeping changes to existing tax laws. Under the Tax Reform Act taxpayers with consumer loans (borrowed money) were no longer entitled to deduct the interest (a percentage of the loan amount that the person borrowing the money must repay, along with the loan amount) from these loans on their taxes. One type of loan that was exempt from the new tax law, however, was the home equity loan (a loan a homeowner can get by borrowing against the value of his or her house). In the wake of the new law, more borrowers began to favor home equity loans rather than standard consumer loans.

properties, which were subsequently sold by the lender (a process known as foreclosure). Because second mortgages were usually associated with poverty, they were often considered a source of social stigma for much of the twentieth century.

Home equity loans became more common during the 1980s, following the passage of the Tax Reform Act of 1986. Under the Tax Reform Act interest on standard consumer loans was no longer tax deductible. In other words consumers could no longer deduct their interest payments from their taxable income, meaning their tax payments were higher. Home loans, on the other hand, were considered exempt from these new restrictions. This exemption included second mortgages. As more borrowers began to recognize the economic advantages of securing a home equity loan, rather than a loan that was not tax deductible, the home equity loan business began to thrive. In many cases consumers used home equity loans to pay off their existing, nondeductible loans, a process known as debt consolidation.

More Detailed Information

The two basic types of home equity loans are closed end and open end. A closed-end home equity loan involves a fixed amount of money; the borrower receives the entire amount of the loan (known as a lump sum) upon completing the loan agreement process (or closing). Closed-end home equity loans usually have fixed interest rates (in other words the interest rate remains the same for the life of the loan). Typically the amount of the loan will depend on the amount of equity the borrower has in his or her house; the loan amount might also depend to some degree on the borrower's credit rating (in other words whether he or she has a proven record of paying off debts in a timely manner). In most cases a borrower is able to borrow up to 100 percent of the equity he or she has in a

house. When economists talk about second mortgages they are typically referring to closed-end home equity loans.

With open-end home equity loans, on the other hand, the borrower does not take the lump sum of the loan amount all at once. Instead the borrower receives the loan as credit (that is, as a maximum amount of money he or she can borrow), which the borrower can use as desired. This type of home equity loan is commonly referred to as a home equity line of credit (HELOC). The borrower can take money out of a HELOC at any time and is only required to pay back the amount he or she actually uses. A HELOC is subject to what is known as a draw period, during which the borrower is entitled to borrow money, up to the total amount of the loan, whenever he or she wants. In this way open-end home equity loans give the borrower a greater amount of flexibility. Most open-end home equity loans have variable, or adjustable, interest rates. These rates tend to change over the life of the loan.

Recent Trends

Through the late 1990s most people seeking home equity loans took out closed-end loans, or second mortgages, rather than open-end loans. In the early years of the twenty-first century, however, this trend changed dramatically, as more people began to use their equity to take out HELOCs. For example, in the year 2000, American banks generated more than $163 billion in traditional closed-end home equity loans versus just over $133 billion in HELOCs. During the first half of 2004 the total amount of closed-end loans generated by banks was $88 billion, reflecting a moderate rise; during the same period banks generated more than $356 billion in HELOCs, more than a 250 percent increase compared to the year 2000.

$ Payday Loan

What It Means

A payday loan is a small cash loan, usually between $100 and $1000, that is extended to a customer over a short time period, typically one to two weeks. The term *payday loan* suggests that the borrower will be able to repay the loan upon receiving his or her next paycheck.

Payday lenders in the United States generally operate out of either small independent storefronts or franchises (licenses granted to market a company's goods or services in a certain territory) that belong to multistate chains; some also market loans via toll-free phone numbers and over the Internet. The typical payday loan customer is a low-income earner with little or no means of borrowing money elsewhere.

Also known as a payday advance or a deferred-deposit loan, a payday loan is much quicker and easier to obtain than a traditional bank loan. The borrower simply writes a post-dated personal check (a check dated with a later date that cannot be cashed until that date) to the lender for the amount of money he or she wants to borrow, plus the fee, or finance charge, for the loan. The finance charge typically ranges from $15 to $30 for each $100 borrowed.

When the loan is due to be repaid, the balance and fee(s) must be paid in full. The borrower may pay the money back by replacing the check with cash or by allowing the check to be deposited (so that funds will be withdrawn from his or her checking account). If the borrower cannot repay the loan at the time it is due, he or she may elect to pay only the finance charge and roll over (or renew) the loan for another pay period (at which point another finance charge will be applied).

In spite of its apparent convenience, a payday loan is extremely expensive: the fee associated with borrowing the money is many times higher than the amount a traditional lender would charge in interest. There is much debate about whether payday lending offers a beneficial resource to its customers or whether it preys upon and worsens the circumstances of those who are already financially vulnerable.

When Did It Begin

The practice of borrowing money against a post-dated check dates back at least to the Great Depression (the most significant banking-industry failure in U.S. history, lasting from 1929 to about 1939), when most Americans were struggling to make ends meet, but the astronomical rise of payday lending in the United States occurred only in the early 1990s. The stage was set for this boom in the late 1980s when the federal government relaxed restrictions on how much interest a lending institution could legally charge. Also during this period the banking industry underwent a radical transformation that resulted in a dramatic decrease in the number of banks in the United States; in particular it reduced the small-loan services available to poor, inner-city customers. In the aftermath of these changes, payday loan stores filled the void in lending services available to this segment of the population.

In 1992 payday lending locations were scarce, if not unheard of, in the United States. By 2004 payday lending had become a $40-billion-per-year business (in terms of how much money was loaned out), with more payday loan store locations in the United States than McDonald's restaurant franchises (according to the Community Financial Services Association of America, there were over 22,000 payday loan stores compared to 13,600 McDonald's locations).

More Detailed Information

For many people who need fast cash, the convenience of a payday loan is hard to resist. Unlike with most traditional loans, borrowers are not required to provide information about their credit history (a record of other financial dealings). All they need is a verifiable source of income, a checking account, and some valid identification, such as a driver's license or passport.

Compared to the cost of a typical bank loan or even of a cash advance from a credit card company, however, the cost of borrowing from a payday lender is exorbitant. The APR (or annual percentage rate charged in interest) on a personal bank loan, even for someone with a poor credit history, might be somewhere between 9 and 13 percent; for a cash advance on a credit card, it might be as high as 50 percent. Compare this to a payday loan, for which the average APR is 470 percent!

Here is how it works: say you borrow $100 from a payday lender for a term of 14 days. The finance charge for the loan is $15. This finance charge is equivalent to an APR of 390 percent, which means that if it took you a full year to pay back the $100, you would pay $390 in interest. While it might seem unlikely that it would take anyone an entire year to pay back a mere $100, data shows that most payday loan borrowers roll over their loan multiple times. This means they pay $15 every two weeks (it is not unusual for a borrower to end up paying $60 in finance charges on a $100 loan) just to avoid having to pay back the original $100. In cases where a lender allows only a limited number of rollovers, the borrower often takes out another payday loan from a different lender in order to pay off the first loan. Many working poor people become trapped in this cycle of borrowing and paying huge sums in finance charges over the course of a year. Although the payday loan industry maintains that its loans are only intended to cover the occasional emergency, national data shows that the average payday loan customer takes out between 8 and 13 loans per year, usually to cover such routine expenses as rent, utilities, and food.

Defenders of payday lending claim that the service represents the democratization of credit, meaning that it makes credit (or loans) available as a financial resource for people who are otherwise unable to obtain a credit card or borrow money when they need it. Further, they argue, it is only reasonable that lenders protect themselves by charging high interest rates, because they are dealing with high-risk borrowers who would never receive a loan from the average bank. Critics of payday lending, on the other hand, claim that these businesses prey on people who are financially insecure and uninformed about other options they might have for making ends meet.

Recent Trends

Controversy over payday lending practices continued to grow between 2003 and 2007, especially as numerous studies conducted by the Center for Responsible Lending, the Consumers Union, the National Consumer Law Center, and other groups revealed that payday lending

ALTERNATIVES TO PAYDAY LOANS

In an effort to help millions of Americans avoid the debt trap of payday loans (short-term, high-interest cash loans secured by a check dated in the future), consumer protection groups are seeking to educate the public about the various alternatives to payday loans that are likely to be cheaper and easier to repay. Instead of a payday loan, they urge, consider one of the following:

- Establishing a payment plan with your creditor (the person to whom you owe money)
- Asking for an advance on your wages from your employer
- Consulting a credit counselor
- Inquiring about emergency assistance programs
- Enrolling in an overdraft protection program (a system that temporarily covers you if you withdraw more than the balance of your account) at your bank or credit union
- Applying for a credit union loan
- Taking out a cash advance on your credit card
- Borrowing from friends or family

stores were disproportionately concentrated in African-American neighborhoods and near military bases.

The laws governing the payday lending industry in the United States vary from state to state. In some states, such as Georgia and New York, payday lending is effectively banned by consumer loan laws that cap interest rates in the double digits. In response to public outcry and pressure from numerous consumer protection groups, many other states sought to impose restrictions on the payday lending industry, including limits on the amount of a loan based on the customer's income, limits on how many loans a borrower could take out at a time, and limits on how many times a borrower could roll over the same loan.

Still, the payday lending industry proved difficult to reform. One strategy lenders used to circumvent (or get around) state laws was to form alliances with banks in less-restrictive states and borrow their charters (which are like licenses) to operate as usual in the state where reforms were imposed. This was referred to as the rent-a-bank tactic.

$ Debt Consolidation Loan

What It Means

A debt consolidation loan is one big loan that a borrower takes out in order to pay off a number of smaller debts. It may also be referred to as refinancing one's debt. There are three main reasons for taking out a debt consolidation loan: to lower the fee, or interest rate, of the loan; to make a person's debt more manageable; and to reduce the size of the required monthly loan payment.

One reason people consolidate their debts under a new loan is to secure a lower interest rate (the interest rate on a loan is the percentage of extra money a borrower pays per year on top of the balance of money owed; it can be thought of as the cost of borrowing the money) or even simply to secure a fixed interest rate. Unlike a variable interest rate, which fluctuates according to changes in the economy, a fixed interest rate remains the same until the entire balance of the debt is paid off.

Some people take out debt consolidation loans in order to make their debts easier to manage. Rather than keeping track of several different payments to different creditors (or lenders), which may all be due at different times during the month, a debt consolidation loan enables the borrower to make one easy payment per month. With only one due date to remember, the borrower greatly reduces the risk of missing a payment and incurring costly late-payment penalties.

A third reason for a debt consolidation loan is that the minimum payment on such a loan is often less than the sum of several minimum payments on smaller debts. If the borrower uses less of his or her monthly income to pay off debt, it should be easier for him or her to handle basic monthly expenses for housing, food, utilities, and such. Some financial advisers say that if the borrower can live more comfortably within his means, he will be less likely to continue to build more debt.

When Did It Begin

Before the middle of the twentieth century, consumer debt was relatively unheard-of. Financial institutions (such as banks) rarely extended credit to individuals because it was difficult to assess their financial reliability, and because managing such loans was expensive and time-consuming. The concept of debt consolidation applied exclusively to matters of public (government) debt. In 1886, for example, Japan passed the drastic Consolidation of the Public Loan Act to convert the various loans that made up the national debt to a lower interest rate and a single set of terms.

The period after World War II (which ended in 1945), however, was marked by a number of economic developments in the United States, including the mass production of consumer goods, the increasing urbanization of American society, and the advent of consumer credit. By the 1960s more and more Americans were taking on consumer debt, and there was a dramatic rise in the number of personal bankruptcies. (Bankruptcy is a declaration of financial insolvency, or inability to pay off one's debts.) Alongside these trends, independent lending companies began to offer debt consolidation loans to households in financial crisis. Many of them charged exorbitant interest rates. The practice of taking advantage of people in financial trouble by lending them money at very high interest rates or charging high fees to initiate the loan is called predatory lending.

More Detailed Information

Usually a consolidation loan is used to pay off unsecured, revolving debts, especially credit card balances. Unsecured debt is any debt that is not backed up by collateral (something, such as a house or a car, that the lender can assume ownership of if the borrower becomes unable to pay back the debt). "Revolving" means that the debt is open-ended; unlike an installment loan (as for a car), where the borrower borrows a finite sum of money and then pays it back in set installments over a fixed period of months, the balance of revolving debt continues to rise and fall (within an allowed credit limit) according to how much the borrower spends and how much he or she pays off each month. Unsecured, revolving debt is considered a more dangerous kind of debt to carry, because it is easy for consumers to get in over their heads.

If you own your home, the best way to consolidate your debt is usually with a home equity loan (also called a second mortgage). With this kind of loan, you borrow against the amount of equity you have in the home. Equity is the difference between the market value of the home (the amount you could sell it for) and the outstanding balance on your original home loan. So, for example, if your house is worth $240,000 and you owe $195,000 on your mortgage, then you may be able to borrow up to $45,000 (the difference between the two numbers) with a home equity loan. Because a home equity loan is secured (the home is your collateral), the lender regards it as a lesser risk than an unsecured loan and will usually offer you a more favorable interest rate. Also, the interest you pay on a home equity loan (as with a regular home loan) is often tax deductible, meaning it can help reduce the amount of annual income tax you have to pay.

If a person does not own a home or other property that he or she can use to take out a secured loan, it is possible to obtain an unsecured debt consolidation loan. The Federal Trade Commission (a U.S. government agency) and other consumer-protection groups caution consumers to choose carefully among the private companies that offer these loans. Many do not fully disclose the fees and other terms associated with their loans, and they may make inflated or false promises about their ability to alleviate debt.

In general, many critics warn that debt consolidation loans are not the cure-all that many people think they are. The problem with debt consolidation, they say, is that it makes you feel as though you have taken care of your debt problem, when in fact you have only rearranged the problem. Debt consolidation may get you a lower interest rate and a lower monthly payment, but it does not make the debt go away. Also, many people do not realize that a lower monthly payment often just means that the term of

For this woman and many like her, trying to keep up with multiple payments on individual, high-interest debts can be stressful and discouraging. A debt consolidation loan, which loan folds various separate debts into one large debt, often at a lower overall interest rate, can make paying off debt feel a lot more manageable. *Photograph by Kelly A. Quin. Cengage Learning, Gale.*

the loan is extended; thus, even with a lower interest rate, stretching the loan out over a longer period may ultimately cause the borrower to pay more interest.

Moreover, a debt consolidation loan does nothing to help someone change the spending habits that got him or her into debt in the first place. Indeed, according to one study, more than three-quarters of the people who consolidate their debt and clear their credit cards gradually build balances back up on those empty cards.

Recent Trends

By the end of 2003, U.S. consumer debt had topped $2 trillion. This unprecedented figure demonstrated that the level of debt carried by the average American household was escalating rapidly. Indeed, American consumer debt was far higher than that of any other country, and the $2 trillion figure represented a doubling of this debt in less than a decade.

As Americans with heavy debt loads have become increasingly anxious about their vulnerability to financial ruin, the debt consolidation industry has boomed. The Internet and television have become flooded with ads for "get-out-of-debt-quick" plans that promise financial miracles and peace of mind. Many honest loan companies do offer legitimate debt consolidation loans that can greatly facilitate the process of getting out of debt; but there are also many companies that make false claims and can potentially cause consumers more financial harm.

STUDENT LOAN CONSOLIDATION

A debt consolidation loan enables a person to combine a number of different debts into one larger but ultimately more manageable debt. In the past couple of decades, as the cost of a college education has become higher than ever, many college graduates have been entering the workforce burdened by tens of thousands of dollars in student loans. One way to relieve some of the stress associated with these debts is to consolidate them into a single loan. The benefits of doing so include locking in the lowest-possible interest rate, lowering monthly payments by as much as 60 percent, and making it easier for a borrower to keep track of his or her loans. Whereas obtaining a consolidation loan to alleviate credit card debt has its pros and cons, most financial advisers agree that consolidating student loans is always a good idea.

One way to shop for a reputable loan company is through the Better Business Bureau (BBB), an independent consumer-protection organization that publishes "Reliability Reports" about all kinds of U.S. businesses.

WHO LENDS MONEY

$ Bank

What It Means

A bank, at its most basic level, is an institution that holds people's money for safekeeping and lends money to individuals and businesses for a variety of reasons. The money people put, or deposit, in a bank is not separate from the money the bank loans out: banks take in money from people (referred to as depositors) precisely so they can lend it out and charge interest (a fee people must pay to borrow money). Banks also pay interest to depositors, depending on what type of account they open. A bank makes profits by taking in more money in interest payments on loans than it spends paying interest to its depositors and servicing their accounts.

The deposit-taking and lending activities of banks affect far more than the individual goals of consumers and businesses, however; these activities are central to the functioning of a modern capitalist economy (one in which businesses are largely owned by private individuals, not the government). When banks receive deposits, they typically lend as much of that money out as possible, so they can charge interest and maximize their profits. The law usually requires them to set aside (reserve) only a small portion of the deposits, allowing the bank to loan much more money than it keeps in its reserves. This is called fractional reserve banking. The money is simulta-neously recorded as being in the depositors' accounts and as on loan to someone else; in this way the bank has created more money than physically exists in the form of bills and coins. Banks actually create much of the money that is circulating in the economy at any given time.

Some institutions that engage in a similar process of taking deposits and making loans are not, strictly speaking, banks. Savings and loan associations and credit unions are among the most prominent examples of what are called thrift institutions. Thrifts were originally associated with community-building and the encouraging of personal savings, and because of this history they are subject to different legal standards than banks, even though they have come to function much as banks do.

These days many banks count on noninterest fees, those charged to account-holders and customers for various kinds of financial services and products, for a growing amount of their profits. Also, banks use the money depositors bring in to invest in financial markets (places, some real and some computerized, where people can buy and sell stocks, or shares of ownership in a company, and bonds, or shares of governmental and other types of debt), as well as to make loans. Those banks that focus on the deposits and loans of individual consumers and businesses are called retail banks, and those that focus on the buying and selling of stocks, bonds, and other securities in the financial markets are called investment banks. Today many companies combine retail and investment banking.

All banks and banklike institutions in a modern economy are subject to the regulation and policies of a central bank, which ensures the banking system's reliability and oversees the money supply (the amount of money circulating in the economy) with the goal of encouraging overall economic health. The central bank in the United States is called the Federal Reserve System.

When Did It Begin

Banking is thought to have grown naturally out of the invention of money. Once any culture had agreed to use a given symbol (gold, discs of stone, cows, shells) to indicate value, the people in that culture had to think about how to store those items safely. Historical evidence of people storing and loaning money has been found as far back as the eighteenth century BC in ancient Babylon (located in present-day Iraq) and also in ancient Greece, among other early civilizations. Banking became more regulated and efficient in ancient Rome.

The modern banking system has its roots in Europe of the Middle Ages (a period that lasted from about 500–1500 AD), where gold was the most common form of money. Because gold is heavy and cumbersome, it was difficult to carry in large quantities and to store safely, so people began depositing their money with goldsmiths, men who worked with gold and therefore had sufficient storage facilities and knowledge of the metal's purity.

A bank is a financial institution where people can deposit money into savings and checking accounts and take out loans. Pictured here is a vault, where a bank stores some of its money.   *Photograph by Spencer Grant. Photo Researchers, Inc. Reproduced by permission.*

When an individual deposited gold for safekeeping with a goldsmith, the goldsmith examined the gold to judge its purity and then issued a receipt. Goldsmiths charged a fee for storing gold, just as banks today charge a fee for maintaining checking and savings accounts.

Before long, whole societies began recognizing the value of a goldsmith's receipt, and the receipts were used as money, which made retrieving and exchanging actual gold unnecessary. After some time the goldsmiths perceived that, as people were using the receipts to buy most of what they needed, it was very unlikely that a majority of depositors would demand their gold all at once. Because it was only necessary to keep a fraction of that gold on hand at any given time, goldsmiths saw that they could make loans in the form of paper money and that they could loan out far more than they had in reserve. Thus was born the concept of fractional-reserve banking, which has led to the huge significance of banks in modern economies.

More Detailed Information

Banks literally create money in today's world. Only about one-third of the money supply in the United States, for instance, consists of government-issued bills and coins.

Most of the rest of the money supply is made up of checkable deposits (the money that people have in various kinds of bank accounts).

To understand how banks create money, imagine that you are the first person to deposit money in Bank A, which has just opened for business. You take a stack of $1-, $5-, $10-, $20-, $50-, and $100-bills out from under your mattress, and you open an account at Bank A. Bank A gives you a receipt stating that your stack of money added up to $1,000, which you still possess even though you are no longer keeping the money at your house. You go home, confident that the bank will take care of your money.

After you leave, Bank A will lend out as much of that $1,000 as the law allows. Say that the government currently requires Bank A to set aside 10 percent, or $100, of your deposit, and that Jane Smith walks into the bank asking for a $900 loan. If the bank approves Jane's loan application, it will give her a checkbook with a balance of $900. Jane now has $900, and you have $1,000, where before only $1,000 existed. The bank has created money out of thin air, by adding numbers to its balance sheet.

But the potential for money creation does not stop there. When Jane writes checks on her account, the

BANKS IN TRANSITION

Banks have traditionally depended on the interest (fees paid to borrow money) they charge on their loans to consumers and businesses for the vast majority of their profits. Increasingly, however, banks count on other fees (those charged to maintain people's accounts; to help people buy and sell stock, or shares of ownership in companies; and to provide other financial services) for their earnings. Large international banks in particular tend to make sure that they have numerous ways of making a profit. For instance, in 2005 JPMorgan Chase & Co., one of the world's largest banks, made more than 60 percent of its income in noninterest fees, and CitiGroup, the world's largest bank by many measures, acquired close to half of its profits from these fees. When the gap shrinks between the interest rates banks pay their depositors and the interest rates banks earn from borrowers, those banks that depend on fees remain profitable while the more traditionally structured banks struggle.

checks will be deposited into other banks, and those banks will use the increased size of their deposit balances to finance more loans.

What happens if you go back and demand your $1,000 (or go to the ATM—automated teller machine—and take it out the day after Bank A has made loans based on your deposit)? As long as Bank A is a soundly run bank, you will be able to get the full balance of your account in cash, and there will be no problem. But what happens if, a year down the road, all of Bank A's customers show up demanding cash? What if every customer at every bank in the country wanted their entire account balances in cash? This would be an enormous problem. There would not be enough hard currency to repay everyone. This situation is called a banking run, and it is catastrophic for the economy.

Banking runs are increasingly uncommon in developed economies. They have always occurred as a result of financial panic, when people lose faith in the banking system's ability to keep their money secure. For instance, the Great Depression (1929-39) resulted in a run on U.S. banks. There were numerous bank runs before that, especially in the early decades of the twentieth century. In response to these events, the U.S. banking system was centralized to increase its reliability. The resulting central bank, created in 1913, the Federal Reserve System (or the Fed), is an independent agency of the U.S. government.

The Fed is essentially a bank for banks. Bank A can borrow money from the Fed to pay depositors or to build up its reserves so that it can make more loans, and it can store its reserves with the Fed. The Fed also serves as a bank for the U.S. government. When you get a tax refund, an unemployment check, or any other payment from the federal government, it comes in the form of a check drawn on the Federal Reserve System. Most importantly, the Fed is responsible for overseeing the money supply. Because banks have the ability to create money, and because the size of the money supply is one of the most important factors in the economy's health, the Fed attempts to control the amount of money deposited in and loaned out by banks. The Fed can increase or decrease the money supply to sustain favorable economic conditions. It does this in various ways, all of which have one aim: to affect the amount of money that banks have in reserve. The larger banks' reserves are, the more money they create, and vice versa. The Fed's goal in regulating the money supply is the long-term health of the economy.

Recent Trends

In the early years of the twenty-first century, interest rates were at historic lows. This meant that people who wanted to borrow money from banks could do so much more cheaply than in past decades. For example, in much of 1981 the prime interest rate (the interest rate that banks usually use as a basic guideline for establishing other rates, such as those for home loans) was near 20 percent, and in some months it was more than 20 percent. By 2003 the prime interest rate hovered at around 4 percent. On a purchase as large as a home, which costs hundreds of thousands of dollars, a 16 percent variation in the interest rate makes an enormous difference to the consumer. A $200,000 home purchased at an interest rate of 20 percent would result in a monthly mortgage payment (for a 30-year loan, the most common type of home loan) of around $3,350. Over the 30 years of the loan's life, the purchaser would end up paying more than $1 million in interest. The same $200,000 loan at a 4 percent interest rate would result in a monthly payment of under $1000 and total interest payments of around $144,000 over the loan's 30-year life.

It would seem, then, that banks would prefer the interest-rate climate of 1981 to that of 2003, because the former would allow them to make $1 million instead of $144,000 in profit on a $200,000 home loan. The catch, however, is that low interest rates encourage a much larger number of borrowers to apply for loans. Indeed, the years 2001–2005 saw Americans become homeowners at record rates. This meant that banks were making more loans than ever before. Though their profits on an individual loan were smaller, they were making so many loans, both to homeowners and to businesses, that banks boomed during those years even while many other sectors of the U.S. economy struggled. Consumers, meanwhile, were not necessarily running away with homes at bargain prices. Though the price consumers paid to borrow money was low by historic standards, real estate prices grew enormously as sellers took advantage of the competition among buyers.

$ Credit Union

What It Means

A credit union, like a bank, is an institution that offers financial services to its customers. Among these services are checking and savings accounts, credit cards, and loans. A credit union, however, is different from a bank because it is cooperative (it is owned and managed by its customers, also known as members) and nonprofit (banks, on the other hand, offer their services to make a profit). Because of its nonprofit status, a credit union is required by law to operate with its members' financial benefit in mind. Therefore, interest rates (which measure the cost of borrowing money) are often more favorable to costumers at a credit union than at a bank, where making money from its services is a top priority.

Credit union membership can be restrictive and have eligibility requirements. Some credit unions, for instance, are open only to particular segments of the population, such as those in certain labor unions, employees of specific companies, or residents of a particular neighborhood. In other words, members must share a common bond. Once you are a member of a credit union, you can usually remain so for life; you will probably not lose your membership if your circumstances change and you no longer meet the membership criteria. For example, if you belong to your neighborhood credit union but later move to another state, you can still keep your membership at your old credit union.

When Did It Begin

The first credit unions as they exist today were organized in Germany by economist Hermann Schulze-Delitzsch (1808-83) in 1852 and Mayor Friedrich Wilhelm Raiffeisen (1818-88) of Heddesdorf (now Neuwied) in 1864. These credit unions were owned and governed by their members, which elected volunteer boards of directors. Schulze-Delitzsch's credit union arose from the need for food during a time of famine. The cooperative baked and sold bread to its members and then began to provide credit, thus becoming known as the "people's bank." Raiffeisen's credit union, on the other hand, offered credit to the farming community so farmers could buy equipment and animals.

In 1900 Alphonse Desjardins (1854-1920), a stenographer in the Canadian Parliament, established the first credit union in North America. His goal was to provide low-interest credit to working-class people, who previously had access only to loans with exceedingly high interest rates. This credit union, Caisses Populaires

A credit union is a financial institution, similar to a bank, that operates on a cooperative, nonprofit basis. Because in the past they often served low-income customers, credit unions used to be referred to as "poor man's banks." *AP Images.*

WORLD'S LARGEST CREDIT UNION

Navy Federal Credit Union, based in Merrifield, Virginia, is the world's largest credit union, both in terms of membership and assets. It began with just seven members, each providing $10, in 1933. The goal of these seven civilian Navy personnel was to provide each other with emergency loans. By 2006 Navy Federal had grown to more than 2.8 million members and had $27 billion in assets. Membership was open to anyone in the Department of the Navy, including both the U.S. Navy and the U.S. Marine Corps; contractors working for the Department of the Navy; those in officer candidate programs, such as the U.S. Coast Guard Academy and the U.S. Merchant Marine Academy; and family members.

Desjardins, opened in Lévis, Québec, Canada. Desjardins was also responsible for helping launch the first credit union in the United States, St. Mary's Cooperative Credit Association in Manchester, New Hampshire, in 1909.

That same year the Massachusetts Credit Union Act was established. The act served as the foundation for many credit union laws to come. Boston merchant Edward Filene (1860-1937) was a key figure in establishing the act, and he was a strong influence in many subsequent credit union developments. In 1934 he helped organize the Credit Union National Extension Bureau, the predecessor to the Credit Union National Association, which provides services, such as industry information and public relations, to credit unions in the United States.

The Federal Credit Union Act, which allowed for the formation of credit unions anywhere in the United States, became law in 1934. The act set up dual chartering, which meant credit unions could be chartered (given the right to do business) by either the federal government or a state government. Those chartered by the federal government fell under the jurisdiction of the National Credit Union Administration, while state-chartered credit unions were ruled by the state.

Credit unions continued to grow in number. There were 8,683 credit unions in the United States in 1945, rising to 23,876 in 1969. In the 1970s new laws allowed U.S. credit unions to offer more services to their members, such as home loans. By 2005 the number of credit unions worldwide had surpassed 40,000, representing more than 120 million people in 84 countries. Canada was the country with the highest percentage of its population serviced by credit unions.

More Detailed Information

Though owned by its members, a credit union is controlled by a volunteer board of directors, which the members elect. All federal credit unions in the United States are also overseen by the National Credit Union Administration (NCUA), an independent government agency. As part of its mission, the NCUA insures savings of up to $100,000 in all federal and most state credit unions. If a credit union were to fail and close down, any savings account of $100,000 or less would be protected by the NCUA.

There are both philosophical and financial differences between traditional banks and credit unions. Credit unions are seen as democratic, with each member being an equal owner. All deposits are grouped together so that loans can be made to fellow members in need. This breeds a sense of community. Banks, on the other hand, are governed by shareholders (people who own stock in the bank), and bank customers, unless they happen to be shareholders, have no power over how the bank is managed. The goal of banks is to make a profit, and profits are distributed to the shareholders. Banks must pay federal income taxes; credit unions are nonprofit institutions and thus do not pay federal taxes.

Because they are nonprofit and do not pay taxes, credit unions often provide better interest rates than banks do on savings accounts and loans. Although rates change on a daily basis, the following examples from the United States in November 2006 reflect this trend: for a regular savings account (in which a customer received interest, or payment, for money placed in an account), credit unions offered an average interest rate of .93 percent, compared with .72 percent at banks (the higher number reflecting more money for the customer); for a two-year, new car loan (in which a customer borrowed money and was charged interest), the average rate was 6.19 percent at a credit union and 7.58 at a bank (the lower number indicating a smaller payment for the loan). For home loans there was little difference: an average of 6.38 percent at credit unions versus 6.34 percent at banks for a 30-year, "fixed rate" loan.

Credit unions offer many of the basic services that banks do. These include savings accounts (known as "share" accounts in credit unions to emphasize member ownership), checking accounts (called share draft accounts), money market accounts, credit cards and cash cards, and various loans, including car, home, and home equity. Banks, however, offer a wider range of loans and services, especially for businesses. In addition, large banks often have more branches and ATMs (automated teller machines for withdrawing cash and making deposits), which can be convenient for customers.

Recent Trends

Because of their history of serving low-income customers, credit unions were known as poor man's banks. Someone with little money could apply for a loan at a credit union and have some hope of receiving it, whereas at a traditional bank such a customer would likely be turned away.

Credit union membership was also restricted to specific work groups or communities. As a result, credit unions provided little competition to traditional banks.

Times have changed, however, and modern-day credit unions offer many services and attractive rates, and restrictions regarding membership have loosened. In the United States banks have launched attacks against credit unions, namely in the form of lobbying Congress to change the tax-free structure of credit unions. Banks feel it is unfair that credit unions are not required to pay taxes and believe credit unions have grown larger and more "bank-like" than Congress first intended when it passed the Federal Credit Union Act in 1934. Credit unions argue that they earned tax-free status because they were nonprofit, cooperative institutions, a status that has not changed. In addition, large credit unions claim they still adhere to the same principles and fundamental structure as small credit unions.

$ Savings and Loan Association

What It Means

Savings and loan associations are institutions that were originally established to allow ordinary people to deposit their savings and take out loans, primarily for the purpose of buying homes. They are similar to banks but are more limited in their functions; banks use the deposits of account holders to finance a wider range of loans and other investments. Another characteristic of most savings and loan associations is that they are owned and operated by their members (the people who deposit money in them) and for their members' benefit.

In the 1980s, for a complex set of reasons, large numbers of savings and loan associations became insolvent (they could no longer meet their expenses and were going bankrupt), and bungled government attempts to deal with this developing crisis worsened its ultimate outcome. The savings and loan industry collapsed, and the eventual government cost of repairing the financial damage caused by the collapse was more than $150 billion, most of which was shouldered by taxpayers. The savings and loan crisis was the most significant banking-industry failure since the Great Depression (1929-39).

When Did It Begin

Businesses called building societies established in England in the early 1800s enabled communities to pool their money to finance the building of homes. The first savings and loan association in the United States, a direct descendent of these building societies, was the Oxford Provident Building Association of Frankfort, Pennsylvania, established in 1831. Meant to serve as an intermediary between people who wanted to save money and people who wanted to borrow money, Oxford Provident accepted regular payments from its members, with the eventual goal of enabling all the members, through loans,

A savings and loan association is a type of financial institution in the United States that allows people to deposit their savings and take out loans, particularly to buy homes. In 1989, as a result of a financial scandal, a number of savings and loans went bankrupt, causing thousands of investors to lose their life savings and leading to the conviction of this lawyer and banker, Charles Keating Jr. *AP Images.*

to build or purchase their own homes. Though the terminology and operational details of savings and loan associations changed over time, this remained the basic model and purpose for the institutions, which spread all over the United States in the years after the Civil War (1861–65).

The savings and loan industry flourished during the post-World War II housing boom in America (this occurred primarily in the 1950s and 1960s), when savings and loan associations had a reputation for being community-building tools for ordinary citizens. From their beginnings and until the latter part of the twentieth century, most savings and loan associations only gave loans to members buying houses within strict geographical boundaries (often only residential real estate located within 50 miles of the association's office qualified for a loan).

More Detailed Information

The savings and loan association business model ran into serious trouble in the 1970s, and it reached crisis stage in

S&LS AND JUNK BONDS

The savings and loan (S&L) crisis of the 1980s is often thought of in combination with junk bonds. Junk bonds are essentially high-risk investments (ventures that promise to pay investors back at a high rate if they succeed but that are more likely to fail than safer investments). Though most mainstream investors today, using different investment strategies than in the past, put some of their money in investments that could be classified as junk bonds, this was less common in the 1980s.

Savings and loan associations were established to allow ordinary people to deposit their savings and take out loans, primarily for the purpose of buying homes. But when the S&L industry found itself in trouble in the 1980s, the U.S. government changed the restrictions that had previously limited the savings and loan associations to making housing loans, now permitting them to invest depositors' money widely. One result of this change was that it created a large market for junk bonds. The struggling savings and loan industry needed to make money fast and was suddenly allowed to make high-risk investments; hence, many savings and loan associations bought junk bonds.

While corruption and shady deals played a part in the savings and loan crisis, these were probably symptoms rather than causes of the larger problem: the industry could no longer sustain itself, and the government was hoping to bail the industry out through deregulation (removing regulations and restrictions). Deregulation was not the answer for the savings and loan industry, but it did create the conditions that allowed junk-bond dealers to prosper. Many people fault the junk-bond dealers themselves, while other people argue that the government, and not junk bonds, was to blame for the industry's collapse.

the 1980s. Many factors contributed to the difficulties the industry faced, but most of these factors were tied to one glaring issue: rising interest rates.

Like banks, savings and loans are able to make loans in proportion to the amount of money they take in through deposits. If you open an account at a savings and loan association, the money you deposit will be used to finance home loans for other people. The association makes money by charging borrowers interest (a fee paid to borrow money) on these loans. Because the depositors are essentially loaning the association money, they are paid interest as well. To remain profitable, a savings and loan association has to maintain a balance between the interest it takes in from borrowers and the interest it pays to depositors. This can be a delicate balance to maintain, however, because savings deposits are short-term loans, with an interest rate that fluctuates daily; whereas mortgages are long-term loans (usually 30 years), and the home owner usually pays an interest rate that does not change (called a fixed rate). Normally these two interest rates are not that far apart, but if interest rates rise dra-

matically, a business whose profits depend on making more on mortgage-loan interest than it pays out in savings-account interest cannot remain profitable.

To understand how this situation played out in the savings and loan industry, consider that in 1965 a savings and loan association member might have received interest at a rate of around 2 percent on a savings account and might have been able to get a 30-year fixed-rate mortgage loan at an interest rate of around 6 percent. Once that loan went into effect, the interest rate was fixed, or locked in; the member could never be required to make payments based on a higher interest rate, no matter what happened to interest rates in the wider economy over time. In the late 1970s, though, interest rates climbed to double-digit numbers before peaking at more than 20 percent. During this time the savings and loan association member with the 1965 loan would still be paying interest at the 6 percent rate even though the depositors were being paid interest at current rates. A business that brings in money at a rate of 6 percent while paying money out at nearly 20 percent is clearly in a vulnerable financial position. Because the savings and loan industry's profits depended almost entirely on long-term home loans, it had no way of breaking this stranglehold imposed on it by rising interest rates. The fact that savings and loan associations' business prospects were limited to strict geographical areas made it even harder for the industry to find options for coping with these financial difficulties.

Recent Trends

Government attempts to bail out the savings and loan industry were ineffectual, partly because economists underestimated the severity of the problem and partly because politicians did not want to take responsibility for such an overwhelming problem. The U.S. government pinned its hopes on deregulation (the removal of government restrictions): savings and loan associations were allowed to invest the money of their depositors more broadly, and they were permitted to fudge the rules of general accounting.

The accounting tricks the industry was authorized to use essentially made it appear that savings and loan associations were profitable when they were not, thus relieving the federal government of any immediate responsibility to take over numerous failing associations. Additionally, the riskier investments the associations began making were essentially subsidized (financially supported) by the U.S. government, which insured association deposits (promising to pay back the depositors in case of loss) but did not charge the associations higher insurance rates for riskier investments, as a for-profit insurance company would have done. The savings and loan associations, desperate for money, could (and did) gamble on risky ventures, knowing their losses would be paid for by the government. Even though interest rates dropped in the mid-1980s and there seemed to be hope of recovery, changes in the economy affecting the housing market hurt the savings and loan industry further.

When President George H. W. Bush (b. 1924) took office in 1989, he immediately took action to repair the problems, reorganizing the government offices that regulated the industry and imposing tougher financial and accounting standards, but large numbers of savings and loan associations could not meet these standards. With hundreds of associations bankrupt and the U.S. government responsible for repaying depositors (who were all repaid), roughly 80 percent of the total bill (estimated at around $150 billion) was eventually passed on to the taxpayers.

$ Finance Company

What It Means

A finance company is an organization that makes loans to individuals and businesses. Unlike a bank, a finance company does not receive cash deposits from clients, nor does it provide some other services common to banks, such as checking accounts. Finance companies make a profit from the interest rates (the fees charged for the use of borrowed money) they charge on their loans, which are normally higher than the interest rates that banks charge their clients.

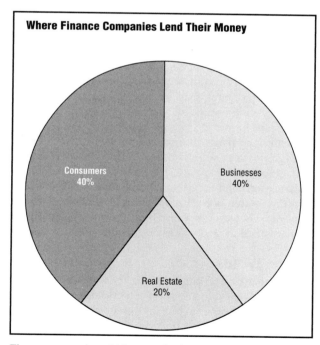

Where Finance Companies Lend Their Money

Consumers 40%

Businesses 40%

Real Estate 20%

Finance companies, which generally charge higher fees than banks, are more likely to give loans to people with a poor history of repaying debts. This chart shows what percentage of money lent by finance companies is given to consumers, businesses, and real estate buyers. *Illustration by GGS Information Services. Cengage Learning, Gale.*

Many finance companies lend to clients who cannot obtain loans from banks because of a poor credit history (the record of an individual's payments to the institutions who have loaned him money in the past). Such clients secure their loans with finance companies by offering collateral (by pledging to give the company a personal asset, or possession, of equal value to the loan if payment on the loan is not made). In other words if Bob borrowed $5,000 from a finance company to cover the costs of starting a house-painting business, the finance company might ask that he offer his pickup truck as collateral. If Bob were to default (fail to make payments) on the loan, the finance company would take possession of his pickup truck.

Some large companies own finance companies that provide clients with loans to purchase goods from the large company. Under this arrangement the large entity is called the parent company, and the smaller entity is called a subsidiary, or a captive finance company. Each of the leading American automotive manufacturers maintains an affiliation with a captive finance company that finances the loans on the sales of their vehicles. For example, many people who purchase vehicles from General Motors obtain their loans from General Motors Acceptance Corporation (GMAC). The Ford Motor Company owns Ford Motor Credit Company (FMCC), and Daimler Chrysler owns a finance company called Daimler Chrysler Financial Services.

When Did It Begin

General Motors was the first of the Big Three American auto manufacturers to open a captive finance company, establishing branches of GMAC in Detroit, Chicago, New York, San Francisco, and Toronto in 1919. The following year GMAC expanded to Great Britain, and by 1928 they had issued more than four million loans. In 1985 the company earned $1 billion in revenues. That same year GMAC began offering home loans and soon after branched out further by lending to large and small businesses and by selling insurance. After recording earnings of $1.8 billion in 2001, GMAC had financed more than $1 trillion in loans on more than 150 million vehicles since its inception. Ford Motor Credit Company began operations in 1959 and manages approximately $150 billion in loans in 35 countries. Daimler Chrysler Financial Services began operations in 2002.

Such finance companies as Allied Capital and the Money Store, which specialize in lending to small businesses, began operations as far back as the 1950s and 1960s, but these companies experienced major growth in the 1990s, when Americans started borrowing larger sums of money for both personal use and for their small businesses. As lending increased, more people defaulted on loans and filed for bankruptcy, which made banks reluctant to continue lending money, especially to small companies that were unlikely to remain in business. This

JOHN M. MCNAMARA

In 1994 John M. McNamara, a Buick Dealer operating on Long Island, was found guilty of securing more than $6 billion in fake loans from the GMAC finance company over a period of 11 years. McNamara borrowed money from GMAC, claiming that he needed funds to ship vans to the Middle East. None of the vans was ever built or shipped, however. McNamara used the money to make investments in real estate, gold mines, oil businesses, and a mortgage finance company. He also used the funds to bribe Long Island business partners in order to ensure that they remain quiet about his activities. At the time he was charged, McNamara owed GMAC $436 million. His bail, which he paid, was set at $300 million. After discovering the scandal, GMAC fired several of its top employees for not properly monitoring the loan, but no one affiliated with the finance company was charged of conspiring with McNamara.

created a large pool of loan candidates for finance companies. For example, in 1996, 37 percent of the small-business owners in America requested loans from banks, and 25 percent of these were rejected. Companies like Allied Financial began providing loans to these clients at high interest rates.

More Detailed Information

Most economists separate finance companies into three major categories. The first group, known as consumer finance companies, makes small loans to individuals, usually on terms that are unfavorable for the client. These businesses, which are also called direct-loan and payday loan companies, have been accused of taking advantage of people who are in desperate need of cash. A typical relationship between a direct-loan company and a client might go something like the following. The client needs $200 to cover the rest of his monthly expenses, but he has no money left in the bank and his next paycheck is two weeks away. The client goes to the consumer finance company with a personal check, proof of income (an old paycheck stub), and a recent bank statement. The finance company verifies the client's identity and check to make sure that he is currently employed. Before leaving with the $200 in cash, the client writes a check for $230 and postdates it by two weeks (writes a date on the check that is two weeks later than the date of the current transaction). This check will serve as collateral for the loan. If the customer does not show up to pay the $230 dollars for the $200 loan, the finance company will cash the check. Such a company may also ask for the title of the customer's car to ensure that the customer does not close his checking account and leave the direct loan company with no way of getting value back for the loan. Though the $30 fee for the loan may seem fair given that the client

needs the money, this charge amounts to 15 percent interest on a two-week loan, or 390 percent annually. Loans that are offered for interest rates higher than the market average are called subprime loans. Because some direct-loan companies demand even higher rates of interest, many states in the United States have established small-loan laws that cap interest rates on these subprime loans at or around 25 percent.

The second type of finance company is called a sales finance company, or an acceptance company. These agencies make loans to businesses to help those businesses cover short-term costs. Acceptance companies provide a service for businesses that is similar to the service direct-loan companies provide for individuals. There are some important differences, however. First, businesses that conduct transactions with (borrow money from) acceptance companies are large corporations with high credit ratings. Such corporations are not asked to secure their loans with collateral. Second, in these transactions the businesses usually receive interest rates that are the equivalent of, or slightly better than, rates they would receive from a bank. In many cases the terms of the loan stipulate how the business can allocate the borrowed funds (for example, to meet payroll or to purchase inventory). Businesses cannot use these funds to do such things as build a new plant or buy additional real estate. The sums involved in these loans are quite large, often in the millions of dollars.

Commercial finance companies, which are also called commercial credit companies, are the third type of finance company. They make loans to small and large businesses, often to help them cover costs for new equipment. Because they represent a greater risk for the commercial credit company, small businesses often pay higher interest rates than large businesses. The interest rates on these subprime loans tend to be between 0.1 and 0.6 percent higher than prime rate loans, which are the loans given by banks to more financially qualified clients. Though this may seem like a small difference, these percentage points often translate into thousands of extra dollars in revenue for the finance company. The finance companies often need this extra money from their paying customers, however, because they tend to have a greater number of delinquent clients than banks have.

Recent Trends

Though banking institutions remain the most popular source of business loans, many Americans seeking loans for small businesses have begun to prefer finance companies to banks because finance companies are less concerned with their prospective clients' credit history. This means that a finance company is more likely to approve a loan request than a bank and that a finance company will be apt to lend more money for longer periods of time than a bank. Small business owners generally request loans from finance companies to purchase inventory (the goods they sell) from wholesalers (the companies that sell goods to retail stores). In exchange for favorable terms on a loan, finance companies often require small business owners to make their assets available as collateral.

Commercial finance companies grew steadily throughout the 1990s, and by the end of the 1990s they were the second largest provider of business credit in the United States. During the 1990s the Money Store and AT&T Small Business Lending had emerged as the two largest finance companies in the United States. In 1997 the Money Store offered 1,784 loans to small businesses for a total of $784 million. AT&T Small Business Lending offered 1,254 loans for $480.5 million that year. Six U.S. finance companies loaned at least $100 million each to businesses in 1997, and nine more finance companies loaned at least $50 million each.

$ Pawnbroker

What It Means

Often referred to as the "poor man's bank," a pawnbroker is someone who offers monetary loans to borrowers in exchange for a pledge, or pawn, of personal property. Items that are commonly pawned include jewelry, guns, musical instruments, and electronic equipment. The pawned item serves as collateral (that is, a form of security, or a guarantee: the borrower must repay the loan in order to collect his or her property). The

pawnbroker (also known as a collateral lender) agrees to hold on to the property for a set period of time, usually a few months, and charges the borrower some rate of interest on the loan. Interest is a percentage added to the amount of the loan. For example, if Larry borrows $100 at 8 percent interest, then he must repay a total of $108 when the loan comes due.

If the borrower defaults on the loan (meaning he or she fails to repay it) during the agreed-upon period, then the pawnbroker takes ownership of the property and is free to sell it. A pawnbroker may also buy an item outright with the intention of reselling it at a profit. In this case, the original seller of the item receives cash with no repayment obligation. A pawnbroker typically operates out of a storefront known as a pawnshop.

Although there are some high-end pawnbrokers who deal with large sums of money, the average pawnbroker usually lends relatively small amounts of cash (often less than $100) to people who need immediate funds for a car repair, a medical bill, or some other unforeseen expense.

When Did It Begin

The practice of pawnbroking has existed throughout much of human history. In China the trade is 3,000 years old. In the ancient city of Babylon people used their crops, gold, silver, and other collateral to take out loans from merchants. Pawnbrokers were also known to have existed in ancient Greece and Rome, and regulations

A pawnbroker is type of moneylender who provides loans to individuals in exchange for a valuable piece of property, such as jewelry. A pawnbroker's place of business is known as a pawnshop. *Photograph by Kelly A. Quin. Cengage Learning, Gale.*

A ROYAL PAWN

Pawnbroking, the business of extending cash loans in exchange for a pledge of personal property, has a long history. Perhaps the greatest legend in the history of the business is that Queen Isabella I of Castile (in Spain) pawned her jewels in order to finance Christopher Columbus's first voyage to America in 1492. Some sources (including one of the most significant early studies of pawnbroking in the United States, published by Samuel Levine in 1911) have claimed that this actually happened, while others maintain that the queen only offered to pawn her jewels, and when lenders saw how serious she was about making the voyage possible, they accepted her royal word as collateral (security) for the loan. Ultimately, the tale has been widely dismissed as a myth that was begun by Bartolomé de Las Casas, a sixteenth-century Spanish historian.

established by those civilizations have served as the basis for the modern legal framework surrounding the trade.

During the Middle Ages (about 500 to about 1500) in Europe, the Catholic Church prohibited charging interest on loans, citing the Bible's dictum against usury (the practice of charging interest). Still, pawnbroking was practiced by people outside the religion. In fifteenth-century Rome the Franciscans (a religious order associated with St. Francis of Assisi) began to offer loans to the poor in exchange for some form of pledge (with minimal interest), in order to protect the poor from usury and other abuses by corrupt pawnbrokers. This kind of charitable pawnbroking institution was called a *monte di piet* (which literally means "mountain of pity"; later it became better known by the French term *mont-de-piété*).

The rise of pawnbroking in Europe during the Middle Ages may be traced to the wealthy Lombardy region of northern Italy; thus, pawnbroking is also known as "Lombard banking." The symbol of the pawnbroker, a configuration of three balls, or globes, suspended from an arcing bar, was originally used by the Lombards to identify their lending houses. Later the symbol became associated with the Medicis, a powerful banking (and pawnbroking) family in Florence, Italy, who adopted the three balls as part of their family crest.

In the United States pawnshops were certainly established by the early 1800s, if not earlier.

More Detailed Information

When a customer pawns an item, he or she receives a pawn ticket (a kind of receipt), on which the terms of the loan are printed. The ticket states the name of the customer, his or her contact information, a description of the item, the amount borrowed, the interest rate, the amount of any service charge associated with the loan, and the date of the repayment deadline.

It is important to note that when a borrower pledges an item of his or her property as collateral for a loan, the pawnbroker will only lend a percentage (usually 30 to 50 percent) of the resale value of the property. For example, if a customer needs a loan of $100 and the pawnbroker lends 50 percent, the customer must be able to pledge an item or items whose estimated resale value is at least $200. One of the benefits of the pawnbroking system is that a person cannot borrow more than he or she can pledge in property; therefore, he or she is unlikely to become seriously overextended in debt.

Another principal benefit of borrowing money from a pawnbroker is that a person can use his or her property to guarantee the loan, rather than relying upon his or her credit history. (Credit history is like a financial report card: it contains information about a person's borrowing and repaying habits for such things as credit cards, school loans, and home mortgages; it also itemizes "risk factors" associated with a potential borrower, such as late payments, evictions, and recent bankruptcy filings. Traditional lending facilities, such as banks, always check a person's credit history before agreeing to lend him or her money.) People who borrow from pawnbrokers often live without much financial security; they may have bad credit histories, or, if they have never had a credit card or taken out a bank loan, they may simply have no credit history at all. By providing immediate cash with minimal paperwork, the pawnbroker provides a valuable service for a significant segment of the population who may not have the option to borrow money through other institutions.

In most countries where pawnbroking is prevalent, there are legal limitations on the rate of interest that may be charged on a collateral loan. In the United States pawnbrokers must be licensed and follow various regulations at the federal, state, and local level. At the federal level, pawnbrokers are regulated by both the Federal Reserve Board (which oversees the U.S. banking system) and the Bureau of Alcohol, Tobacco, Firearms, and Explosives. Also, under the Patriot Act of 2001, U.S. pawnbrokers are required to check their customers against the Treasury Department's database of known terrorists.

There are also regulations to prevent thieves from selling stolen goods to pawnbrokers. These regulations include a waiting period (usually about 30 days) between the time a pawnbroker buys a piece of property and the time when he or she is free to resell it; this allows time for stolen items to be tracked down by the police. Most states in the United States also require the pawnbroker to file regular police reports listing the items that have been pawned in their shop and their customers' driver's license (or other state-issued ID card) numbers, Social Security numbers, and physical descriptions. In some states pawnbrokers are required to take a picture or thumbprint of every pawn customer. According to the National Pawnbroker's Association, less than 1 percent of items that come through pawnshops are stolen.

Recent Trends

During the 1980s and 1990s the pawnbroking industry in the United States grew rapidly. According to a study by economist John P. Caskey that was published in the *Journal of Money, Credit, and Banking* in 1991, there were an estimated 6,900 pawnshops in the United States in 1988 (which means there was about one pawnshop for every two commercial banks). A study conducted in 1998 by Robert W. Johnson and Dixie P. Johnson of the Credit Research Center at Georgetown University stated that the number had nearly doubled, to 13,000.

All of these researchers attributed the rapid proliferation of pawnshops in the United States at the end of the twentieth century to the ongoing rise in the number of people living in poverty. The Georgetown study demonstrated that low-income individuals are more likely not only to be ineligible for loans from traditional lending institutions (such as banks) but also to distrust these institutions, preferring to make purchases and pay bills with cash and money orders. Another reason for the growth in pawnbroking during these decades was the relaxation of laws regulating pawnshops. This allowed pawnbrokers to charge a higher rate of interest on their loans, and as a result pawnbroking became a more lucrative business.

$ Rent-to-Own Store

What It Means

A rent-to-own (RTO) store allows customers to rent consumer goods, such as furniture, appliances, home electronics, and computers, by paying regular rental rates. The customer has the option of taking ownership of the item after a certain number of payments have been made. In other words, each rental payment is applied toward the sale price of the goods. There are approximately 8,300 RTO stores in the United States, serving some 3 million customers per year.

The RTO industry caters to individuals and families who want to furnish their homes but are unable to pay for such purchases outright or cannot or do not want to obtain traditional credit financing. Credit financing is a loan to the consumer that allows him or her to purchase goods or services and then pay back the loan in monthly installments. The loan carries interest at an annual percentage rate (APR), meaning that a certain percentage of the outstanding balance is charged to the account annually. The interest charges add to the total cost of the item. For example, if a consumer buys a $600 sofa on credit at an APR of 10 percent and takes one year to pay off the loan, then the consumer will have paid a total of $660 for the sofa by the end of the year.

Defining itself as an alternative to the long-term financial obligation of credit financing, the RTO industry boasts that its customers can make payments toward owning goods without taking on debt (what is owed on a

At a rent-to-own store a customer can rent such goods as furniture, electronics products, and household appliances for a period of time while also having the right to purchase the product after making a certain number of payments. There are about 8,300 rent-to-own stores in the United States. *Donald Nausbaum/Getty Images.*

loan) and without paying interest. Also, customers are able to return the rented item and terminate the rental agreement at any time; there is no obligation to continue making rental payments until the consumer owns the item. RTO stores cite this no-obligation, no-debt policy as the foundation of their success. However, critics of the RTO industry insist that although RTO stores do not disclose an official APR, there is nevertheless an effective interest rate associated with their rental services. The fact is that a customer who pays off all of the installments in order to complete the purchase of an item ends up paying a significantly higher price than the retail value of the item.

When Did It Begin

The rent-to-own industry emerged in the late 1960s. An industry that leased furniture and appliances was already established by that time (a lease is a kind of rental contract). Extending credit to customers so that they could pay off their furniture and appliance purchases over time was also

FRINGE BANKING

The term *fringe banking* describes a number of alternative financial services that are provided to a segment of the population that is typically denied access to or chooses not to use traditional financial services. The fringe-banking industry includes

- payday lenders (businesses that extend short-term, high-interest loans to people who need extra money to cover expenses until their next paycheck);
- check-cashing stores (businesses that cash personal, payroll, and government checks for a fee);
- pawnbrokers (businesses that lend money in exchange for a piece of collateral, or material insurance, such as jewelry, guns, electronics, or other items of value);
- rent-to-own stores.

These businesses often cater to low-income individuals, the working poor, and the "unbanked," or people who do not have bank accounts. While the fringe-banking industry claims that it provides much needed services to people whose financial needs are not adequately met by traditional banks, many consumer-advocate groups argue that the industry preys on society's most financially vulnerable people by charging exorbitant fees for their services.

common practice. However, many people who wanted to own household furnishings did not qualify for credit. When a bank or other financial institution (the lender) extends credit to an individual (the borrower), the institution is taking a risk because there is a possibility that the borrower will not repay the loan. To protect itself, the lender reserves the right to deny credit to individuals who do not meet a certain income requirement, have a history of not paying their bills, or are otherwise deemed too much of a risk. The rent-to-own concept was the brainchild of an owner of a retail appliance store whose customers were being turned down for credit. The concept spread quickly, and in little more than three decades, RTO stores had grown into a thriving $6-billion-per-year industry.

More Detailed Information

An RTO transaction involves a short-term (weekly or monthly) rental contract that can be terminated or changed at any time. At the time the rental agreement is made, the RTO store specifies an outright cash price for the item if the customer were to purchase the item on the spot. In many cases, this price is already significantly higher than the retail market price (the "going rate") for the item. The RTO also discloses the total amount the customer will pay to own the item if he or she extends the contract over the full-payment period.

For example, at Lenny's Rent-to-Own, a customer can buy a dishwasher outright for $700 or can pay $18 per week for 78 weeks. In the latter case, the total cost of the dishwasher will be $1,404. If the customer chooses to make a fewer number of higher payments; that is, if he or she elects to buy the dishwasher more quickly, the total amount he or she pays to own the dishwasher will be less. Although the store does not refer to the cost of paying for the dishwasher over time, the effective APR of buying the dishwasher over 78 weeks would be 100 percent, which is much higher than the APR would be to buy the dishwasher with credit financing. RTO stores justify the high cost of buying items over time by saying that the cost of the service they provide is built into the cost of the item.

At the end of each rental agreement period, the customer has several options. He or she can

- terminate the agreement and return the rented item without any further obligation;
- renew the contract by making another rental payment;
- change the terms of the rental agreement by selecting a different payment amount;
- execute the early-purchase option to assume ownership of the product (this is another way of ending, or completing, the rental agreement).

If the customer chooses to renew the agreement for the full-payment period, the customer gains ownership of the item. Each time the agreement is renewed, the RTO store is required by law to restate the amount of time it will take the customer to pay for the item completely at the payment rate he or she has chosen and the total cost of the item by the time it has been paid for in full. If the customer terminates the agreement and returns the item, then the item is typically refurbished and reoffered for rent at a lower rate. According to a 2001 study by the Federal Trade Commission (FTC), a federal agency that seeks to ensure fair competition between businesses and protect consumers from various kinds of fraud and deception, about 70 percent of RTO customers ultimately took ownership of the items they had been renting.

Recent Trends

Consumer advocates began to criticize the RTO industry and call for government regulations to reform RTO practices in the early 1980s, but the issue did not gain widespread attention until 1993. In that year, an article in the *Wall Street Journal* alleged abuses by Rent-A-Center, the largest RTO business in the United States at that time. Since then, consumer advocates and the RTO industry have become involved in a protracted legal and public-relations battle (the term *public relations* has to do with a company's public image). Regulations that do exist for RTOs are enacted on a state-by-state basis. In 2006 Wisconsin and New Jersey carried the strictest regulations in the country for RTOs.

$ Check-Cashing Store

What It Means

Check-cashing organizations (CCOs), commonly known as check-cashing stores, are business outlets that cash checks for a fee. They cash a variety of checks, including payroll checks, personal checks, government checks (such as Social Security checks), income-tax refunds, insurance checks, money orders, and cashier's checks (the latter two are different kinds of prepaid vouchers that can be purchased in order to make a payment to a third party; both are commonly used in lieu of personal checks). Many check-cashing stores also offer various secondary services, including payday loans (small, short-term loans that are intended to be repaid on the borrower's next payday), money transfers, and bill paying (wherein a customer can pay his or her utility bill and other bills through the CCO). Some outlets also sell money orders, lottery tickets, bus passes, fax-transmission services, prepaid phone cards, and postage stamps.

In the United States the clientele at check-cashing stores are predominantly low-income and working-poor individuals, many of whom belong to minority ethnic groups. Most do not have accounts with traditional financial institutions such as banks. People who are either unwilling or unable to do business with banks are often described as "unbanked." In 2006 the Federal Reserve Board (a committee that oversees the Federal Reserve, the central banking system of the United States) estimated that nearly 13 percent of U.S. families did not hold a checking account. Substantial research has been conducted to understand why this population tends to avoid traditional financial institutions. Although there is still debate on the subject, some reasons include: a basic distrust of banks, the perception that bank fees are too high, and the failure of banks to provide financial services that cater to the needs of low-income people.

The check-cashing industry has grown tremendously since the mid-1980s. In the United States in 2006 there were approximately 13,000 check-cashing locations, which cashed more than $80 billion worth of checks per year. CCOs may be small, independently owned businesses or large regional or national chains. The most prominent CCOs in the United States are ACE Cash Express, Cash America International, and EZCorp.

CCOs have also been the subject of intense public and government scrutiny: while some people claim that check-cashing stores provide much-needed financial

Check cashing stores are businesses that cash payroll, government assistance, personal, and other kinds of checks for a fee. Often referred to as part of the "fringe banking" industry, they cater to people who do not have bank accounts *Photograph by Kelly A. Quin. Cengage Learning, Gale.*

WILL PAPER CHECKS BECOME OBSOLETE?

With the rapid growth of electronic banking services starting in the mid-1990s, the use of paper checks declined precipitously. Many employees now have their wages electronically transferred into their bank accounts. Millions of households pay their bills over the Internet. Also, consumers make a significant proportion of their purchases with plastic electronic-payment cards such as debit and credit cards (the former withdraws funds from the cardholder's bank account; the latter allows the cardholder to make purchases on credit, to be paid off at a later date).

For millions of "unbanked" Americans (those who do not hold traditional bank accounts), however, there was another form of electronic money that promised to revolutionize the way they received and spent money. This was the "prepaid" or "stored-value" card, a plastic card containing a microchip that can record (or store) some value of money. The explosion of gift cards (plastic cards that contain electronically stored funds to be spent at retail outlets) in the mid-1990s was one of the most successful early applications of the stored-value concept. Another application that was likely to erode the use of paper checks was the idea of transferring the value of a person's paycheck onto a stored-value card that he or she could then use to pay for purchases or insert into special ATMs (automated teller machines) called RPMs (rapid payment machines) in order to withdraw cash.

In the face of these technological advances, check-cashing organizations (businesses that cash checks for a fee) were forced to adapt and expand their services to remain useful to customers.

services to a segment of the population that is not adequately served elsewhere, others contend that the industry unfairly exploits the country's most financially vulnerable population by charging exorbitant fees.

When Did It Begin

Commercial check cashing emerged in the United States in the early 1930s as a niche business for processing payroll and public-assistance (government-aid) checks. In the aftermath of the sweeping bank failures of the late 1920s and early 1930s, many Americans were reluctant to deposit checks into banks, preferring instead to cash their checks at neighborhood bars and stores that charged a small fee for the service. With the establishment in 1934 of the FDIC (Federal Deposit Insurance Corporation, which guarantees individual bank deposits against bank failure), public confidence in banks was largely regained, and growth of the check-cashing industry remained modest for decades.

The industry received a major boost in 1980 with the advent of bank deregulation. By lifting certain government

restrictions on how banks, savings banks, and credit unions (member-owned financial institutions) could operate, deregulation led to increased competition between the various kinds of mainstream financial institutions. In the scramble for profit that ensued, many traditional banking facilities closed less-profitable branches in poor urban neighborhoods, introduced fees for check cashing and penalties for accounts that dipped below a certain balance, and stopped providing the types of services (such as small, short-term loans) that low-income households need.

Thus, deregulation created a void in which a large segment of the population did not have adequate access to basic banking services. This void was quickly filled by check-cashing stores and other "fringe-banking" services, such as payday loan centers and pawnshops (issuers of small, short-term loans in exchange for some piece of valuable property, which is held as security).

More Detailed Information

Probably the greatest appeal of a check-cashing store is the convenience it offers. Unlike banks, which generally observe regular business hours, most CCOs stay open late (some are open 24 hours), six or seven days a week. Also, many banks place a hold on a check (especially if it is written for a greater amount than the balance in the depositor's checking account) so that the depositor cannot access the funds until the check has cleared (been determined to be valid), which often takes a number of days. By contrast, a check-cashing store offers the check holder instant cash. Millions of Americans experience cash-flow shortages (meaning that the money from one paycheck barely lasts until, or even runs out before, the next paycheck is received). For these people the benefit of getting instant cash seems to outweigh the fee associated with the convenience. Indeed, according to Financial Service Centers of America (FiSCA), an industry trade group that represents CCOs and payday lenders, 30 million people cash 180 million checks at CCOs in the United States every year.

Check-cashing stores calculate the fee for cashing a check as a percentage of the amount of the check. The maximum percentages vary from state to state according to state laws, but it is usually between 2 and 3 percent for a payroll or government check. For example, if you cash a $500 paycheck at a check-cashing store that charges 2.5 percent, the fee will be $12.50. Fees for cashing personal checks are much higher and can even exceed 15 percent, because there is a greater chance that the check will not clear. While these fees might seem trivial compared to the benefit of gaining instant access to your funds, they add up: FiSCA has estimated annual check-cashing revenues in the United States to be more than $1.6 billion. Further, studies have suggested that the average unbanked American spends approximately 10 percent of his or her annual income on check cashing and other "fringe-banking" services.

The most significant secondary service offered by CCOs is payday loans. Alongside check cashing, payday loans became a booming business in the 1990s. For people who hold checking accounts, payday loans are intended to cover unexpected expenses and general cash-flow shortages and to help avoid bounced checks and overdraft charges. (When someone's bank account does not have enough funds to cover a check they have written, that check is said to "bounce" when the receiver tries to cash it.) A customer takes out a payday loan by writing the lender a postdated check (postdating means labeling it with a future date when it can be cashed) for a certain amount of money. The term of the loan is usually one to two weeks, according to when the borrower expects to receive his or her next paycheck. The fee for taking out the loan is usually between $15 and $30 for every $100 borrowed. Even though this fee amounts to a very high annual interest rate (anywhere between 300 and 900 percent), many people are willing to pay it in exchange for fast access to needed cash.

Recent Trends

The ability to offer a wide range of services became critical for CCOs in the mid-1990s, when the rapid growth of electronic banking (particularly direct deposit) presented a major challenge to the industry. Direct deposit is a system that enables employers and government agencies to send payments electronically to an employee or recipient's bank account. The funds transfer immediately, so there is no need for the bank to impose a hold on the payment, and there is no associated fee. The rise of paperless transactions threatened to take a major bite out of CCOs' main business, processing paper checks. It was in large part the advent of direct deposit that led many CCOs to expand their services to include sales of lottery tickets, bus passes, phone cards, and postage stamps. CCOs also responded by finding ways to participate in the direct-deposit process. For example, they partnered with banks to receive the deposits of a segment of customers (especially those without bank accounts) and charged those customers a flat monthly fee (usually under $10) to withdraw their funds.

These and other partnership arrangements led to an increasingly blurry distinction between CCOs and mainstream financial services in the first decade of the twenty-first century.

PROBLEMS WITH DEBT

$ Credit Counseling

What It Means

Credit counseling, referred to as debt counseling in many English-speaking countries, is a process in which a credit-counseling agency helps a debtor (a person in debt) make payments to his creditors (institutions, such as credit card

NATIONAL FOUNDATION FOR CREDIT COUNSELING

The National Foundation for Credit Counseling (NFCC) is a nonprofit organization that consists of more than 100 credit-counseling agencies (agencies that help people who owe money make a plan to pay off their debts) with a total of more than 900 offices throughout the United States. The NFCC is funded by creditors and provides counseling to clients at little or no cost. On average one million Americans seek credit counseling through one of the NFCC member organizations each year, and nearly one-third of these clients are able to manage their debt after completing counseling. All NFCC counselors must complete a comprehensive training program and pass an exam before receiving certification as an NFCC counselor. This certification process is overseen by the Council on Accreditation of Services for Families and Children, Inc., an international accrediting body that has licensed more than 1,400 social-service programs worldwide.

companies and banks, to which a debtor owes money). A person needs credit counseling when he or she can no longer afford to make the minimum monthly payments on his consumer debts. (Consumer debt is defined as all nonmortgaged loans, which means that it does not include house payments.) This often happens when a person acquires several credit cards and reaches the credit limit (the maximum dollar amount the person is allowed to charge to the card) on each of the cards.

Such a person is in danger of having to file for bankruptcy. Bankruptcy is a legal term meaning that the federal government has officially recognized that an individual can no longer pay his or her debts. A person who successfully files for bankruptcy is relieved of some debt and is put on a government-monitored payment plan to meet the rest of the debt. Credit counseling is aimed at helping people avoid bankruptcy.

When Did It Begin

In the United States credit counseling began in 1951, when the National Foundation for Credit Counseling (NFCC) was established by the nation's leading creditors. The organization's mission was to educate clients in matters of finance and to help individuals reduce debt and thereby avoid bankruptcy. Most early credit counseling occurred in face-to-face sessions. As more Americans accrued unmanageable debt, however, face-to-face counseling for all of the people in need of debt relief became impossible.

By the early 1990s there were approximately 200 credit-counseling firms, most of which worked under the auspices of the NFCC. The number of credit-counseling

Credit counseling is a professional service designed to help consumers repay their debts. Individuals frequently meet with a credit counselor to discuss ways of managing their finances more effectively. *Altrendo Images/Altrendo/Getty Images.*

agencies began to increase drastically in 1993, when the Association of Independent Consumer Credit Counseling Agencies, or AICCCA, was founded. This organization adopted a telephone-service model, and within a decade there were more than 1,000 credit-counseling organizations in the United States. Most of these new agencies did not work under the auspices of the NFCC.

More Detailed Information

Credit counseling has two components: education and debt management. First, counselors teach their clients how interest rates (the fees that lending institutions charge for their loans) affect monthly payments. Second, counselors put their clients on debt management plans (DMPs), which reorganize a client's payments to creditors. Most DMPs consolidate the debtor's loans. This means that the counseling agency combines all of the client's monthly payments on consumer debt (for example, car payments, student loans, and various credit card payments) into one monthly payment. The client makes this payment directly to the credit-counseling agency, and the agency distributes these funds to the various creditors. A DMP is structured to last a fixed period of time, usually three to six years, and during this time the debtor is not permitted to accrue new debts by, for instance, opening a new credit card account or taking out a loan for an automobile.

Typically the total amount of the debtor's single payment to the credit-counseling agency is less than the sum of the person's separate monthly payments on consumer debt. For instance, a person may have monthly payments of $500 on student loans and $300 on a car plus a minimum payment (the lowest permissible monthly payment on a larger debt to a credit card company) of $100 on a Visa credit card, a minimum of $200 on a MasterCard, and a minimum of $300 on a Discover credit card. In this example, the sum of the debtor's payments to creditors is $1,400 per month. These monthly payments to creditors do not include the individual's living costs, such as a mortgage (monthly payments on a house) or rent for an apartment, food, utilities (payments to water, power, telephone, and other companies that provide services to homes), and other financial responsibilities, such as the costs associated with raising children. If the debtor earns $2,000 per month at a job, he or she would probably not be able to make payments to all these creditors each month. A counseling agency would use a DMP to help the debtor establish a monthly budget that took into account the person's entire set of financial responsibilities. Instead of making a series of separate payments to each of the creditors totaling $1,400, the debtor might send one check of $1,000 each month to the credit-counseling agency.

People on DMPs usually end up paying less on their debts than they actually owe. This happens because creditors would rather acquire some portion of the money owed to them than nothing at all. In many cases creditors help fund credit-counseling agencies, which means that lending institutions, such as banks, contribute money to help operate these organizations. The counseling agencies also make what is called a Fair Share arrangement with creditors. According to these arrangements the counseling agency keeps a portion of the client's monthly payment, sometimes as much as 30 percent. In the example above the credit agency would keep $300 of the $1,000 paid on the debtor's DMP.

Recent Trends

Consumer debt began rising significantly in the 1980s as Americans began taking out larger mortgages on houses, leasing more expensive automobiles, and paying for more goods and services on credit cards. By 2005 Americans owed a total of nearly $750 billion to credit card companies alone. With this drastic rise in debt, the number of credit-counseling agencies in the United States also increased significantly. Unfortunately, many of these new organizations were corrupt, and there was a crisis in the credit-counseling industry in the early 2000s. Preying on Americans in need of debt relief, many fraudulent businesses advertised themselves as nonprofit organizations that would help consumers restructure payment plans. These organizations often charged a high initial fee (which the organization kept) and lied about how effective the debt management plan would be in reducing the client's outstanding loan payments. At the same time, credit card companies had begun to decrease the percentages of their Fair Share arrangements with many legitimate credit-counseling agencies, which reduced the number of people these legitimate agencies could serve. In 2005 the U.S. Congress passed a law that required individuals to seek credit counseling from a government-approved organization before filing for bankruptcy.

$ Credit Bureau

What It Means

A credit bureau is a for-profit business firm that gathers information about a person's or a business firm's financial stability and capacity to pay future debts. The credit bureau makes money by selling this information to interested parties. Credit bureaus that specialize in collecting and selling information about individuals are called consumer credit bureaus; commercial credit bureaus, meanwhile, handle the credit histories of business firms.

THE SCORE

Most banks and credit institutions rely heavily on credit scores, as well as the more detailed information supplied by a credit report, to determine whether or not and on what terms to lend money to a person or a business. Though credit scores are calculated in different ways, most of the widely used methods are based on the FICO scoring system (named after the Fair Isaac Corporation, the score's developer), which was established in 1989. Though the mathematical process used to arrive at FICO scores is not public knowledge, the basic function of these scores is widely known: they are meant to predict the likelihood that a person or business will default on a loan in the next 24 months. FICO scores usually range from 300 to 850, but the U.S. median is roughly 725. A person with a credit score of 660 or lower is probably at risk of being turned down for most loans. Everyone has three different scores, however, because there are three major consumer credit bureaus in the United States (Equifax, Experian, and TransUnion), each of which calculates a person's credit score individually.

If you walk into a bank and ask for a loan, the bank will go through a process to approve you for that loan. Naturally, the bank will want to know whether you are likely to pay them back. The bank could conduct its own lengthy examination of your past behavior in relation to borrowing money and paying it back, but this would not be very efficient. Instead, the bank will pay a credit bureau to supply this information.

Credit bureaus build files on the majority of consumers and businesses in the economy. If you are an adult in the United States, your entire loan and credit-card history (as well as your banking and employment records and some personal information) is likely on file with the three main consumer credit bureaus in the country: Equifax, Experian, and TransUnion. When you apply for a loan or a credit card or try to enter into any other type of credit agreement, the prospective creditor will request a summary of your credit history from one or more credit bureaus. The summary is called a credit report, and it includes a credit score, which is a numerical figure (usually ranging from 300 to 850) that represents the likelihood that you will repay a loan.

Though credit bureaus amass and distribute credit information, they do not ultimately decide whether or not a given consumer or business gets credit or a loan. Creditors set their own standards for acceptable credit ratings and histories.

When Did It Begin

Credit bureaus are a modern phenomenon. Some organized collectors of consumer credit information existed as early as the 1860s, but the economic expansion of the

24-Month Payment History

Date:	Aug 05	Sep 05	Oct 05	Nov 05	Dec 05	Jan 06	Feb 06	Mar 06	Apr 06	May 06	Jun 06	Jul 06	Aug 06	Sep 06	Oct 06	Nov 06	Dec 06	Jan 07	Feb 07	Mar 07	Apr 07	May 07	Jun 07	Jul 07
Experian:	OK	OK	OK	OK	OK	OK	OK	OK	OK	OK	OK	OK	OK	OK	OK	OK	OK	OK	OK	OK	OK	OK	OK	OK
Equifax:																								
TransUnion:																								
US DEP ED																								

	EXPERIAN	**EQUIFAX**	**TRANSUNION**
Account Name:	US DEPT OF EDUCATION		US DEP ED
Account Number:			
Acct Type:	Education Loan		Installment account
Acct Status:	Closed		Closed
Monthly Payment:			$50.00
Date Open:	8/1/1995		8/1/1995
Balance:			$0.00
Terms:	27 Months		27 Months
High Balance:			$6,193.00
Limit:			
Past Due:			$0.00
Payment Status:	Paid satisfactorily		Paid or paying as agreed
Comments:			Closed

Credit Bureaus, such as Experian, Equifax, and TransUnion, compile financial data on individuals and companies and issue reports indicating their past behavior in paying off debts. The credit report seen here shows a person's history of paying off a student loan over the course of 27 months. *Photograph by Kelly A. Quin. Cengage Learning, Gale.*

twentieth century brought with it the more comprehensive credit bureaus of today. When much of the U.S. population was agrarian and geographically stable, decisions about lending money or entering into credit agreements were based largely on personal knowledge of the borrower. As the U.S. population grew and became more mobile in the years after World War I, however, businesses needed access to more objective information about people's creditworthiness, and an interconnected network of credit bureaus grew up in response.

Changing attitudes about credit, too, gave rise to the need for more thorough information about creditworthiness. In nineteenth-century America it was very uncommon for people to buy nonessential items on credit. A farmer might borrow money to buy equipment or seed because these purchases were investments that would bring in more money at harvest time, but only the very wealthy regularly used credit to buy items not essential to their survival. Debt was considered dangerous and even immoral well into the twentieth century. As people became more comfortable with buying goods and services on credit, and as credit became easier to obtain, the need for credit bureaus grew.

More Detailed Information

In recent decades credit has become easier and easier to obtain. Credit cards, for instance, were once issued primarily to the wealthier classes in society and were used only occasionally. At the beginning of the twenty-first century, almost half of all Americans had at least one general-purpose credit card (that is, a Visa, MasterCard, American Express, or Discover card). The rise of credit as a common way to buy necessities, luxuries, and everything in between means that credit bureaus process more information and are a more vital part of the overall economy than ever before. Credit bureaus also keep track of and analyze the data derived from an ever-increasing number of loans for homes, cars, and other high-cost items.

Today's credit bureaus regularly gather information from creditors (banks; credit-card issuers; mortgage companies, which specialize in lending money to home buyers; and other businesses that extend credit to individuals and businesses) and assemble it into files on individual consumers and businesses, while updating their existing files. In addition to the data gleaned from creditors, credit files might also contain one's employment history, previous addresses, aliases, bankruptcy filings, and evictions. Information normally stays on a credit report for seven years before being removed.

Most of the local and regional consumer credit bureaus in the Untied States are owned by or are under contract to one of the three primary consumer credit-reporting services mentioned above. Each of these three companies gathers and distributes information separately, and credit scores and reports differ slightly from bureau to bureau. Each company maintains around 200 million individual consumer credit files. Often a lender will use an average of the credit ratings provided by the three different bureaus when deciding whether or not to make a loan.

The primary commercial credit bureau in the United States is Dun and Bradstreet. D and B has credit files on more than 23 million companies in North America and on more than 100 million businesses worldwide.

In addition to providing creditors with information necessary to determine a credit applicant's qualifications, credit bureaus make their data available for more controversial purposes. For instance, direct-mail marketers often buy information from credit bureaus in their search for potential customers. If you have ever received a letter telling you that you have been preapproved for a particular credit card at a specific annual percentage rate, it is true; the credit-card company already knows your credit rating and has indeed already approved you for the specified card. Prospective employers and landlords sometimes purchase credit histories, too.

Recent Trends

The first law establishing guidelines and consumer protections in the realm of credit reporting was the Fair Credit Reporting Act (FCRA) of 1970. The FCRA was passed by the U.S. Congress in response to growing concerns about inaccurate credit reports in the 1960s. Even after the law was passed, however, consumers typically had very little knowledge of what creditors were reporting about them, and credit bureaus kept individual credit ratings and the contents of credit reports secret.

Renewed worries about the reliability and privacy of credit reports has led to greater government regulation since the mid-1990s. Congress amended the FCRA in 1996 to deter creditors from making certain kinds of inquiries into a consumer's credit history and to allow consumers to remove their credit reports from the lists sold to marketers. The amendment also gave consumers more power to question the accuracy of their credit reports and tightened laws punishing creditors who report inaccurate information to credit bureaus.

In 2000 the credit bureaus allowed consumers to obtain to their credit scores for the first time, and another amendment to the FCRA in 2003 further increased public access to the credit-reporting process. Since 2005, as mandated by the amendment, U.S. consumers have been entitled to one free copy of their credit report annually from each of the three national credit bureaus. Additionally, anyone who has been turned down for a loan or other transaction due to credit reporting has the right, under the amended law, to see his or her entire credit file as kept by each of the three main agencies, an almost unthinkable liberty in previous decades. The

amendment also added further consumer protections to guard against identity theft, a new issue for credit bureaus in the early years of the twenty-first century.

$ Bankruptcy

What It Means

Bankruptcy is the legal process by which individuals or businesses declare their inability to pay their bills and are excused from paying all or part of what they owe. As such, bankruptcy offers relief from the burden of excessive debt. Filing bankruptcy paperwork with a court of law is often called filing for bankruptcy protection.

What is it that bankruptcy protects someone from? If a person falls behind in paying his or her bills, the people who are owed money are legally allowed to try to collect it. Often this involves sending letters demanding payment or calling on the phone to try aggressively to get the person to pay up. In the case of unpaid rent, a landlord can kick a tenant out; in the case of unpaid car payments the company that loaned the money to buy the car can forcibly take the car back. But in the case of personal loans or medical bills, there is nothing for the creditors to come and get. (Anyone who borrows money and agrees to pay it back is called a debtor; a person or institution to whom the money is owed is called a creditor.) The best the creditors can do is keep trying to get the debtor to pay, and legally they are allowed to do so for as long as the debt is owed. This is often the point at which a debtor turns to bankruptcy. If a judge grants the bankruptcy request, the court orders that the bills are no longer valid. Therefore, the person who filed for bankruptcy is protected from further collection efforts by the creditors and is not responsible for paying the debts.

When Did It Begin

Throughout history there have been various approaches to dealing with people who owed money but could not pay it back. In the Bible the prophet Moses described a "jubilee year" that occurred once every 50 years; during that year all debts were forgiven, and all slaves were set free. In Europe during the Middle Ages (a period that lasted from about 500 to 1500), a person who was unable to pay his or her debts could pledge service to a lord or nobleman and provide labor in exchange for wiping out the debt. At other times in history, debtors were considered criminals; in Great Britain and colonial America in the eighteenth century, those who could not pay their creditors were put into debtor's prisons.

Bankruptcy is specifically mentioned in Article 1, Section 8 of the U.S. Constitution, which gives Congress the right to establish federal bankruptcy laws. In 1800 Congress passed the first such law, which was replaced by various other laws throughout the following century. The first significant and permanent federal bankruptcy laws in the United States were established with the Bankruptcy

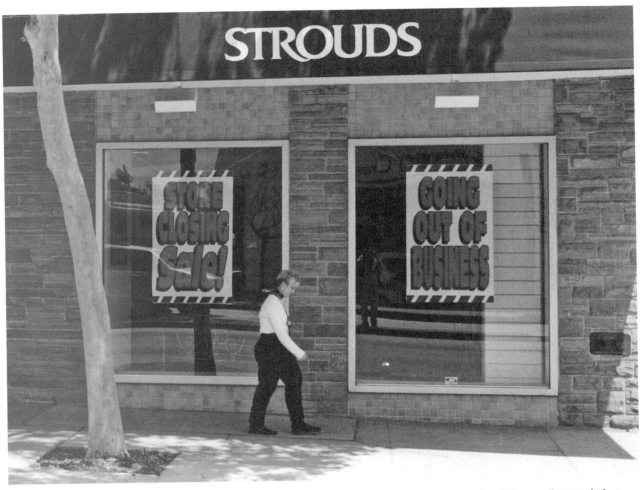

Individuals and companies file for bankruptcy protection when they are no longer able to pay their debts. When retail stores declare bankruptcy, they typically hold a "going out of business" sale. *AP Images.*

Act of 1898. Its measures included creating a system of special bankruptcy courts. This act provided the foundation for U.S. bankruptcy law for 80 years, until it was significantly amended by new laws in 1978 and 2005.

More Detailed Information

For both individuals and corporations the cause of bankruptcy is the same: not being able to pay back what they owe. For individuals this commonly arises from being too far in debt (as a result of unexpectedly high medical bills, charging too much on credit cards, or taking out too many personal loans) or from a sharp drop in income (because of the loss of a job or the death of a spouse, for instance). If a corporation is in debt, it is usually the result of borrowing money from a bank to finance the running or expansion of the business.

In the United States the process of declaring bankruptcy is similar for individuals and corporations. Bankruptcy procedures are fairly complicated, and debtors usually hire lawyers to handle the case. In its most basic form bankruptcy involves filing a formal petition with the United States Bankruptcy Court. This petition lists all of the filer's outstanding debts and the creditors to whom they are owed, and it also includes a list of the filer's major assets. Assets are the things a person or corporation owns that are of significant value. For an individual this might include a car, a house, and any money remaining in the bank. For a corporation assets can include anything owned by the business, such as buildings, unsold products, raw materials, vehicles, and office equipment. A judge examines the documents and decides whether or not to grant the bankruptcy request.

There are many types of bankruptcy, and in the United States the name for each is the chapter number under which it appears in the U.S. Bankruptcy Code. The most common forms of bankruptcy are Chapter 7, Chapter 11, and Chapter 13. A Chapter 7 bankruptcy provides a clean slate by wiping out all debts owed up until the time of filing. A Chapter 11 bankruptcy is primarily used by businesses. It allows a company to remain in business while the court decides how best to reorganize its debts. This may involve eliminating, consolidating (combining a number of debts into one larger loan), or reducing them. Chapter 13 is an alternate form of personal bankruptcy that neither eliminates debt nor requires selling the filer's assets; instead, the court arranges a three- to five-year payment plan with the filer's creditors, after which the remaining debt is cleared.

While filing for bankruptcy offers relief from extreme debt, it has long-term consequences. The bankruptcy stays on record for 10 years, so anyone who can check a person's credit history will know about the bankruptcy. This can be a problem because few banks will loan money or offer a credit card to someone who has gone bankrupt, and if they do, they will charge a high interest rate (interest is a fee for borrowing money). While bankruptcy offers protection from past debts, it can make life in its wake much more expensive; for this reason bankruptcy is almost always a choice of last resort.

Recent Trends

In 2005 the U.S. Congress passed the Bankruptcy Abuse Prevention and Consumer Protection Act, which changed the country's bankruptcy laws by making filing for bankruptcy more difficult. The greatest change was adding a required "means test," which evaluated filers' incomes to determine whether or not they could afford to pay off their debts. If the court determined that the filer had enough income to repay the debts, a Chapter 7 filing was denied, and Chapter 13 was granted instead. This made it harder to qualify for the traditional "fresh start" of a Chapter 7 bankruptcy.

Additional changes to the law involved making the paperwork associated with bankruptcy more extensive and complicated, increasing the filing fees, and requiring filers to take classes about responsible debt management. Because of the additional paperwork and court time required to file, lawyers' fees also increased, making filing for bankruptcy more expensive.

$ Garnished Wages

What It Means

Garnished wages (wages being the monetary compensation paid to an employee) are wages that are deducted from an employee's regular paycheck in order to pay off a debt (or in some cases debts) incurred by that employee. Debt refers to money that one party (such as an individual, a company, or another entity) owes to another party. To pay a debt is also referred to as satisfying a debt. The party that owes the money is known as the debtor, while the party to whom the money is owed is called a creditor. The practice of taking possession of a debtor's wages is commonly known as garnishment.

Situations involving the garnishment of a debtor's wages always involve three parties: the creditor, the

COLLECTION AGENCIES

A collection agency is a business that specializes in collecting money owed to other companies. A credit card company, for instance, might hire a collection agency to track down customers who have stopped paying their bills. The collection agency will then call or send letters to the customers in an attempt to get them to pay what they owe. If the debt is owed to another company, how does a collection agency make money? Either the agency receives a percentage of the money it collects on behalf of a client, or it buys the debt from the client for a small price and is then entitled to keep any of the money it manages to collect.

debtor, and the person or entity who has control over the debtor's wages (typically the debtor's employer), also known as the garnishee. Situations involving wage garnishment are usually the result of a legal action, in which the creditor (known within the context of the legal action as the plaintiff) files a lawsuit (an action taken in a court of law to resolve a dispute, in this case over the repayment of a debt) against the debtor (or defendant) to obtain the money that is owed. If a court decides in favor of the plaintiff, then it will order that the garnishee retain a portion of the defendant's wages, which is then paid to the creditor. The court's decision is known as the judgment, while the order is commonly referred to as a court order. The debtor never actually receives the wages that are garnished but rather a reduced paycheck that reflects the deduction of a percentage of his or her wages. Wage garnishment is typically the final recourse taken in situations involving the satisfaction of a debt, after the creditor has exhausted all other alternatives (for example, presenting the debtor with a bill for the debt or contacting the debtor to request repayment of the debt).

When Did It Begin

Wage garnishment traces its origins to the legal code of ancient Rome, which gave judges the power to order a debtor's employer to cooperate with creditors in ensuring that his or her debts were repaid. This method of debt collection became standard practice in Europe during the Middle Ages (a historical period roughly extending from the fifth century through the fifteenth century). Eventually wage garnishment procedures fell under the jurisdiction of English common law. Broadly speaking common law is a legal code based on custom, as opposed to a legal system based on the official passage of laws (also known as statutory law). Over time common law is reinforced through the standard practices of society and by the court rulings of judges. These court rulings, which play a significant role in determining future court rulings

When a person fails to pay a debt, such as taxes or child support, a court might order the person's employer to garnish, or take, a portion of each paycheck and send it to the individual or organization that is owed the money. Wages are garnished until the debt is paid back. *Getty Images.*

concerning the same legal issue, are also known as legal precedent.

In the United States wage garnishment procedures date to the colonial era (a historical period from the early seventeenth century into the mid-eighteenth century when England had colonial settlements in America) and were inherited directly from English common law. Following American independence (the Declaration of Independence was passed on July 4, 1776) individual states developed their own legal precedents concerning the garnishment of a debtor's wages. The laws derived from these precedents became increasingly particular over time and varied from state to state. During the nineteenth century, for example, the state of Missouri prohibited the garnishment of wages in cases where the debtor was the head of a household (in other words responsible for the care of dependent children, minors, or other individuals). The first federal law in the United States to specifically regulate wage garnishment was the Consumer Credit Protection Act, or CCPA. Passed on May 29, 1968, the CCPA instituted several legal restrictions designed to protect the debtor from undue hardship in the repayment of a debt through garnished wages. One significant provision of the CCPA established that a

maximum of 25 percent of a debtor's disposable income (income after the deduction of taxes) was subject to garnishment. Since then a number of state laws have set the percentage of income subject to garnishment at rates that are lower than the federal maximum. Other states have passed laws exempting certain necessary expenses (for example, medical costs) from being factored into a debtor's garnished wages. In Florida a parent who pays more than 50 percent of the money toward the support of a child is not subject to wage garnishment.

More Detailed Information

Wage garnishment is similar in principle to other methods of taking possession of a debtor's assets (in other words items of value owned by the debtor) to satisfy a debt. One of these other methods is known as a lien. A lien enables a creditor to seize a piece of property owned by the debtor in situations when the debtor fails to repay a debt. Another method, known as an attachment, allows the creditor to seize a debtor's property in anticipation of a favorable ruling in a legal action. An attachment is generally ordered by a court when it deems that the creditor has a strong case against the debtor. Wage garnishment differs from these forms of debt satisfaction in two significant respects. For one, wage garnishment always involves the debtor's income rather than a piece of material property (such as a car or a home). At the same time, wage garnishment gives a creditor a right to claim a debtor's future earnings until the entire debt is repaid.

A number of debt situations require the garnishment of an employee's wages. These include the payment of child support (money a divorced parent must pay toward the support of his or her children), tax debt (unpaid taxes), money due to a court in unpaid fines, and other debts deemed subject to wage garnishment by a court judgment. These other debts can range from money owed to an electrician for rewiring a house to unpaid credit card debts. In cases where a debtor owes more than one debt, federal law mandates that certain debts receive a higher priority than others. For example, the debt with the highest priority is unpaid federal tax; other taxes (for example, state or city) are the next highest priority, followed by other debts (such as credit card debts). Some states prohibit the garnishment of wages except for certain debts; for example, Pennsylvania law allows wage garnishment only in cases involving unpaid taxes, child support, federal student loans, and court fines and other forms of restitution related to a criminal act.

Recent Trends

In the United States the practice of garnishing employee wages became more widespread following the passage of the Bankruptcy Abuse and Consumer Protection Act of October 2005. Under this law debtors wishing to file for bankruptcy (a process by which a debtor who is deemed unable to pay off all his or her debts seeks legal protection from his or her creditors) became subject to stricter rules

GARNISHED WAGES AND DEADBEAT DADS

When a person owes money (in other words debt) he or she will sometimes be required to repay that debt with garnished wages. Garnished wages are wages that are withheld from an employee's paycheck so that they can be paid toward his or her debt; this process is known as wage garnishment. Many debts are subject to wage garnishment. One form of debt that began to cause a great deal of concern in the 1980s was child support (money a parent is required to pay toward the support of his or her child). This concern arose out of the increasing number of absent fathers who were not taking financial responsibility for their children. In media coverage of the problem these fathers became known as deadbeat dads. In order to address the public's growing concern, the federal government passed several laws designed to enforce the payment of child support through garnished wages, including the Personal Responsibility and Work Opportunity Reconciliation Act (PRWORA) of 1996. This law mandated that employers report all new employees to the federal government in a timely manner, thereby making it easier to locate deadbeat dads.

concerning the settlement of past debts. In the past most debtors filing for bankruptcy could escape all responsibility for repaying former debts; under the new law, however, debtors were compelled to agree to a strict five-year repayment program to satisfy as many outstanding debts as possible. As a result the number of debtors subject to wage garnishment rose significantly.

Saving and Investing: Planning for the Future

$ Overview: Saving and Investing Money

What It Means

Saving money and investing it wisely are crucial to long-term financial success. To save money one must first draft a sensible budget (a catalog of expenses and revenues) to be sure that monthly expenses do not exceed his or her monthly income. If after tallying all expenses one discovers that he or she is spending more money than he or she is making, it is crucial that the person cut back spending or earn more income rather than charging more purchases on a credit card. Maxing out credit cards (going as far into debt on the card as is permitted) and then opening lines of credit on new credit cards makes it nearly impossible for a person to allocate funds for future use.

After creating a budget a person would be wise to commit to storing some excess revenues in a savings account. Though the money in a savings account earns a small amount of interest (an annual fee paid by the financial institution to those who store money there), most people do not maintain these accounts because of the returns they provide. Rather, people maintain savings accounts so that they can have access to money needed for purchases and expenses beyond the scope of their monthly budgets. For example, the money in a savings account can be accessed if someone experiences a spell of bad health and accrues medical bills or if one becomes unemployed. Many financial advisers recommend that to see oneself through an unexpected financial crisis, a person should maintain enough money in a savings account to cover four months' worth of expenses.

Investing is spending money in an attempt to generate more revenue in the future. Purchasing a home is an investment because in most cases the value of a home increases with time. For example, suppose a person buys a home for $80,000, and the house rises in value to $110,000 over five years. If desired, the person can sell the home and draw a profit of $30,000 or can choose to live in the home for several more years, during which time the home will likely continue to appreciate in value. Unlike buying a home, purchasing a car, a computer, or a television is not an investment because these items tend to lose value over time. When people buy these things they do not expect that in the future they will be able to sell them for a profit. In addition to buying a home, one can invest money sensibly by purchasing stocks (shares of ownership in a company), bonds (loans to the government or a corporation that are paid back with interest), or mutual funds (a bundle of investments including stocks, bonds, and other securities that are managed by an investment company).

When Did It Begin

Many historians believe that the practice of saving commodities and currency in banks began in 3000 BC when people stored grains and precious metals in sealed areas of temples. These first banks were located in temples because these structures were well built, frequently occupied, and therefore difficult to rob. Furthermore temples were considered a safe place to store valuables because many people figured that the potential of inciting the wrath of the gods would deter criminals from stealing. Historical records charting the beginnings of investment are unclear. Some evidence indicates that Roman investors bought shares in groups of publicani (groups of publicans, people who in modern parlance would be called general contractors, or private contractors) who collected tolls at ports, recruited for the military, and oversaw building projects. Other findings suggest that by the eleventh century in Cairo, merchants and investors had established trade relationships that resembled, in a rudimentary way, the methods of buying and selling in a stock market.

Many contend that the first formal gatherings of investors took place in the thirteenth century among Flemish commodities traders in the house of a man named Van Der Beurse in the city of Bruges. Investors throughout the Netherlands followed suit, and soon

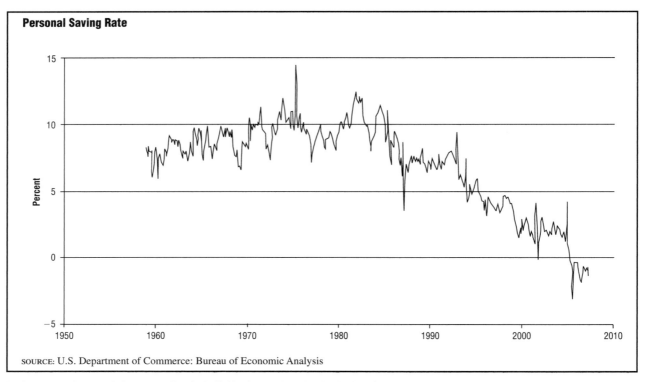

Personal Saving Rate

SOURCE: U.S. Department of Commerce: Bureau of Economic Analysis

Saving money is not only important for the individuals who do it, but it also benefits the economy as a whole. Many people were alarmed by the dramatic decline in personal savings that took place in the United States during the late twentieth and early twenty-first centuries. *Illustration by GGS Information Services. Cengage Learning, Gale.*

there were similar groups meeting in Amsterdam and Ghent. Elsewhere at this time, Venetian bankers were trading in government securities. The first company to issue stock was the Dutch East India Company. Shares in the company were first traded in 1602 at the Amsterdam Stock Exchange. Mutual funds were introduced much later. MFS Investment Management, formerly known as Massachusetts Financial Services, is believed to have invented the mutual fund in 1924. Sales of mutual funds curtailed during the Great Depression (1929 to about 1939) but picked up again in the 1940s. By the 1960s there were as many as 270 mutual funds, and by the middle of the first decade of the twenty-first century there were more than 8,000.

More Detailed Information

Rather than buying shares of stock in one company or putting all of their money into a single real estate venture, most investors compile an investment portfolio, which is a collection of different assets, such as stocks, bonds, mutual funds, real estate, and perhaps a collection of art or other rare memorabilia that tends to hold its value or appreciate over time. One could view a portfolio as a pie and each slice of the pie as a different type of asset. Maintaining a range of assets is called diversifying the investment portfolio. All investors are strongly urged to

diversify their portfolios because no one knows how any single type of asset will perform from year to year. The average investor is also advised to buy and hold or to keep his or her money invested for a long period of time. Though the value of a portfolio will fluctuate from year to year, over a sustained period of time (10 to 20 years or more), the overwhelming majority of diversified investment portfolios will earn considerable returns, or profits. Rashly deciding to buy and sell assets based on sudden fluctuations in the market is the worst investment strategy, especially for those who cannot afford to lose money.

Diversifying a portfolio can be a complicated yet interesting process because one has so many options when investing money. A wise investor will commit different sums of money for different periods of time, and he or she will manage risk, taking some chances on stocks that may either lose value or pay high returns and investing conservatively by purchasing stocks that tend to pay smaller returns but rarely lose their value. Money market accounts are short-term investments that pay relatively low returns but often guarantee profit. For example, a certificate of deposit, or CD, is a time deposit issued by banks that pays a fixed interest rate for a predefined term, usually six months or a year. The interest rate on a CD is higher than the interest rate for a savings account; however, the investor must pay a fee if he or she withdraws funds from a CD before the account matures, or expires. Treasury bills, or T-bills, are another money market instrument. These notes, which are issued by the federal government, usually mature in a year, at which time the government repays the principal of the loan plus a fixed rate of interest. When one "buys" T-bills, one is actually lending the government money that will be paid back with interest at a predetermined date in the future. As with CDs, T-bills pay modest returns in a short period of time. Both are considered to be risk-free investments.

Mutual funds carry more risk but can pay higher returns. Because a single mutual fund consists of a bundle of assets, the amount of risk one assumes when purchasing a mutual fund depends on the nature of the assets in the bundle. (Both mutual funds and portfolios are groupings of different assets, but there is a distinction. If the portfolio is the pie, one mutual fund would be a slice of the pie. That particular slice would be further subdivided into shares of stocks, bonds, money market investments, and other securities.) Mutual funds that invest in stocks that pay potential high returns are called growth funds. Such funds pose more risk than income or value funds, which tend to pay lower returns. Some mutual funds require investors to keep their money in the funds for a fixed period of time, usually between three and seven years.

Most investment portfolios have a retirement fund, normally called an individual retirement account, or IRA. Typically investors do not have access to the funds in an IRA until age 59. In exchange for committing their money for an extended period of time, investors usually see sizable returns in these funds, which many retired people use as income after they have left their careers. One of the most important things to consider when purchasing an IRA is the tax laws that apply to the account. In a traditional IRA an investor is not taxed on the money he or she puts into the account; however, one does pay income tax when withdrawing from the account in retirement. With a Roth IRA one invests after-tax income but later pays no taxes when withdrawing from the account in retirement.

Because investing is such a complex and risky process, many people come together in groups called investment clubs to increase their chances of maximizing their portfolios. In some investment clubs members pool their money together and compile a single portfolio. In other clubs people gather to learn more about investing and to exchange views on recent trends in the stock market and in the economy in general but maintain their own portfolios.

Recent Trends

Since 1990 household debt has grown more quickly than household income throughout the United States. On a monthly and yearly basis many families spend more money than they take in. However, in the overwhelming majority of cases, household net worth is still greater than

BETTERINVESTING

Founded in 1951, BetterInvesting, which is also known as the National Association of Investors Corporation (NAIC), is a non-profit organization that, as of the early twenty-first century, oversees some 13,000 local investment clubs that have an estimated total of about 120,000 individual members. Throughout its history BetterInvesting has helped more than 5 million investors arrange and manage profitable investment portfolios. The group sponsors local, regional, and national educational events, as well as providing stock-analysis tools, investment software, online tutorials, and access to experienced, savvy investors. The goal of BetterInvesting is to encourage members to be lifetime investors in the stock market and to help members formulate an investment strategy that helps them achieve financial independence.

The mentors at BetterInvesting operate according to four investment principles. First, members are strongly encouraged to invest regularly, despite market conditions. Long-established patterns indicate that the market takes a downturn one of every four years. Thus, there is no reason to panic or make drastic alterations to one's investment strategy when one of these downturns occurs. Second, investors should reinvest all earnings. This means that retrieving earnings from the market to spend in other areas depletes the strength of one's portfolio. The key to success is to keep one's money in the market for a long period of time. Third, BetterInvesting advises members to invest in growth stocks, or stocks that present some risk but also pay higher returns. Last, as most financial advisers urge their clients, BetterInvesting stresses the importance of diversifying one's investment portfolio.

household debt. In other words in most households the combined value of the equity in the home, the investment portfolio, material possessions, and earned income is greater than the combined value of all liabilities, such as credit card debt and the amount owed on the house, the car, and all other materials that have been financed. The increase in household net worth has been due largely to an increase in property values and the reliable performance of mutual funds. Many families are spending more and saving less because their assets are appreciating steadily. As long as these assets continue to appreciate, economists think that families will be able to sustain their debt. However, families that steadily acquire debt risk financial peril because real estate and securities markets require sustained investment in order to provide returns. If the majority of Americans continue to pay large sums to credit card companies and to banks, they will have less to invest in the stock market and real estate.

Membership in investment clubs, especially among males, rose in the 1980s and 1990s but has fallen since the turn of the century. Since that time membership among women has increased substantially. Most women prefer to belong to women-only investment clubs, with the typical member of such a club being a college-educated woman older than 50 who no longer is responsible for raising children. These women-only clubs tend to have a distinct approach to finance. Some emphasize motivational speaking and empowerment and use investing as a way to help women achieve independence. Others, with names like Girl Power and Chicks Laying Nest Eggs, deliberately mock gender stereotypes.

MOTIVATIONS FOR SAVING AND INVESTING

$ Time Value of Money

What It Means

The concept of the time value of money is the idea that cash received now is worth more than the same amount of cash received at a later date because money has the capacity to earn interest. A person who receives a sum of cash can put that money in a savings account and immediately begin to earn interest on that money. In this case interest refers to the fee the bank pays a client for depositing money.

To illustrate the principle of the time value of money, consider a scenario in which a person has the option of receiving $100 one year in the future or receiving $100 immediately and depositing the money in a bank account that pays a simple interest rate of 5 percent each year. Simple interest is calculated only on the initial sum of money. Thus, if the person chose to take the money immediately and deposit it into the account, he or she would have $105 at the end of a year. At the end of the second year, the person would have $110. A simple interest rate of 5 percent would add $5, or 5 percent of $100 (the original sum), each year. On the other hand, if that person waited a year to receive the money, he or she would only have $100.

In this example the benefit between taking the money immediately and waiting is small, but that is because the original sum is small. If the original sum were $1 million, the person would have $1,050,000 at the end of a year if the account paid a simple yearly interest rate of 5 percent. In this particular case the person has an extra $50,000 instead of only $5 after a year. This simple interest rate would add $50,000 to the original sum every year.

When Did It Begin

The practice of charging interest on loans, which dates back to ancient societies, indicates that moneylenders have long had an intuitive, if not explicitly stated, understanding of the time value of money. Records dating as far back as 5000 BC indicate that the Mesopotamians,

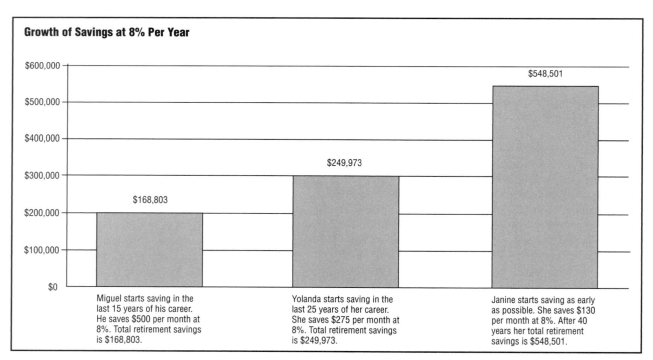

Growth of Savings at 8% Per Year

$548,501

$249,973

$168,803

Miguel starts saving in the last 15 years of his career. He saves $500 per month at 8%. Total retirement savings is $168,803.

Yolanda starts saving in the last 25 years of her career. She saves $275 per month at 8%. Total retirement savings is $249,973.

Janine starts saving as early as possible. She saves $130 per month at 8%. After 40 years her total retirement savings is $548,501.

It may seem silly to begin saving for retirement in your twenties until you consider the "time value of money"—that is, the way money gains value by earning interest over time. This bar graph shows the dramatic benefits of starting to save early. *Illustration by GGS Information Services. Cengage Learning, Gale.*

Hittites, Phoenicians, and Egyptians charged interest when they loaned such items as olives, dates, seeds, and animals. The time value of any loaned item was perhaps easiest to see with the loaning of seeds because any successfully planted seed would yield a plant that would produce more additional seeds. Thus, it was wise to get seeds in the ground, both to yield a healthy crop and to have more seeds for future plantings.

During the Middle Ages (from about 500 to about 1500) there is also evidence that people understood the time value of money. At trade fairs merchants and money changers in need of cash would often issue documents to others that could be redeemed at future trade fairs. If a person had accepted a document in exchange for a certain amount of cash, the merchant would often pay the person back with additional cash when he returned to redeem the document. Thus, both parties in the transaction understood that the original value of the loan would grow over time because the merchant was going to use the funds acquired in the loan to make more money.

More Detailed Information

The time value of $1 million from the earlier example increases more dramatically if, instead of being simple interest, the interest is compounded. With compound interest the interest is calculated not solely on the beginning principal but rather on that and then the new principal each time the interest is paid. Thus, with a compound interest rate of 5 percent, the person who received $1 million would still have $1,050,00 after the first year. However, in the second year, rather than adding another 5 percent of the original principal of $1 million, 5 percent of the new principal of $1,050,000 is added to the balance in the savings account. Thus, instead of having $1,100,000 at the end of the second year in an account bearing simple interest, the person has $1,102,500 if the money is in an account that pays compound interest. At the end of three years the person has $1,157,625 with compound interest and only $1,150,000 with the simple interest.

The value of the $1 million would increase even more dramatically if the account bearing compound interest paid that interest quarterly (four times a year) rather than annually (only once a year). In this case every three months the account would pay 1.25 percent (a quarter of the 5 percent annual rate), and at the end of a year the person would have $1,050,945 instead of $1,050,000. At the end of the second year, the person would have $1,104,486 instead of $1,102,500. The person who accepted the $1 million immediately and placed the cash into such an account would have $104,486 more than the person who waited one year to accept the $1 million.

When considering the time value of money, people generally want to know two things: the future value of cash invested today (how much more it would be worth

---

INFLATION

The time value of money—the idea that cash received now is worth more than the same amount of cash received at a later date—is sometimes discussed to encourage people to save and invest money. If you had two choices, either to receive $100 now and put it in a savings account (where in a year the value might increase to $105) or to receive the same $100 a year from now, it would be simple to decide what to do. The $100 now, because banks pay you interest, or a fee, on money in savings accounts, is worth more.

Over the course of a year, however, what happens to the value of $100 is more complicated. Usually prices of everything you want to buy, from gum to a new car, gets a little more expensive every year. This rising of prices is called inflation. As a result, although you might have $105 in your bank account after a year because of interest, the value of each dollar in the account is worth less than the year before. The real change in the value of your savings account money depends on two factors: how much it increased because of interest and how much it decreased because of inflation. In any case, it is always better to receive the $100 now and to earn interest than to receive the same amount of money a year from now.

---

in the future because of interest) and the present value of cash received at a later date (how much one would need to put into an account now to have, as a result of interest, a certain amount, say $1 million, at that later date). Although, in most real-world cases, determining these figures requires the use of more complex mathematical equations, the preceding examples provide a general idea. Say you wanted to know the present value of $100 that you were going to receive in a year. If the simple interest rate were 5 percent, you have to determine how much to put into an account now for that money to be worth $100 in a year. To do that you would divide $100 by 1.05 (which represents the 5 percent interest per year), which is about $95.24. Thus, given a simple interest rate of 5 percent, $100 received a year from now would be worth only $95.25 today. In the same manner, the present value of $1 million received a year from now is $952,380 today.

It is especially important to have a sense of the time value of money when considering annuities. An annuity is an equal, annual series of cash flows. Annuities may be equal annual payments of money or equal annual receipts of money. Thus, assuming there is fixed rate of interest a person's mortgage (the loan taken to pay for a home) is an annuity because the person pays the same amount to the finance company each time she makes a payment. A person thinking about buying a house might have second thoughts upon discovering that she will be required to pay $1,500 every month for 30 years in order to purchase

---

the home. However, according to the principle of the time value of money, that $1,500 is going to amount to a smaller sum of money each passing year because as time goes by that $1,500 will hold less value. More than likely what seems like a large monthly payment in the early years of the mortgage will feel like a less significant monthly outlay of cash over the course of the loan.

Recent Trends

Because real estate typically appreciates, or increases in value, one can see the time value of money when investing in a home. For young people coming out of school and entering the job market, it is usually wise to stop renting an apartment as soon as possible and buy a home, which over the course of a 30-year mortgage is very likely to increase in value. Increasingly adults in their early 20s have been doing that. According to the U.S. Census Bureau, homeownership among people under the age of 25 increased dramatically from 1994 to 2004. In 1994 only 14.9 percent of adults under 25 owned homes. Ten years later 25.2 percent of adults in this age group owned homes.

One of the reasons for this trend is the reduction of minimum down payments. In the past home buyers were often required to make a down payment for as much as 20 percent of the value of the home. For a $100,000 home, which is a modest dwelling in many communities, one would need $20,000 to spend on the home in order to secure a loan. Such requirements prevented young first-time buyers from purchasing homes. Many of these requirements have either vanished altogether or been greatly reduced. People can now purchase homes by putting zero to 5 percent down on the home. Such terms have allowed young people to enter the housing market, which in turn has allowed them to benefit from the time value of money—because of rising home prices, the $100,000 house they buy today will likely be worth much more in the future.

$ Risk versus Reward

What It Means

In economics, "risk" refers to the likelihood that a person will lose money on an investment. An investment is the purchase of an asset for the purpose of earning money. For example, an investor buys shares of stock (units of ownership in a company) with the hope that the company will make money and the value of the stock will rise. If the stock does rise, the investor is rewarded. Stock she purchased for, say, $100 a share is now selling at $120 a share, which means that the investor could, if she wished, sell that stock for a profit. There is no guarantee, however, that the company will make money and cause the value of the stock to rise. If the value of the stock were to dip to $90 per share and the investor were to sell her

shares at that point, she would have less money than when she made the investment.

It is generally true that the greater the risk a person takes, the greater the reward he or she will receive if the investment makes money. On the other hand, if an investor only takes a small risk, he or she is likely to earn a small reward. This principle is called the risk/reward trade-off. If a person buys stock in a company that has been stable for decades, such as Coca-Cola, that person assumes little risk. In other words, it is unlikely that the investor will lose money. It is also equally unlikely that the investor will make a lot of money immediately after buying the stock. If that person invests money in a less stable company, for example, a new technology firm, he or she assumes a great risk. The company could go out of business within months, in which case the investor would lose the entire value of his or her investment. The company could also make a great deal of money within a couple of months and one day develop into a major

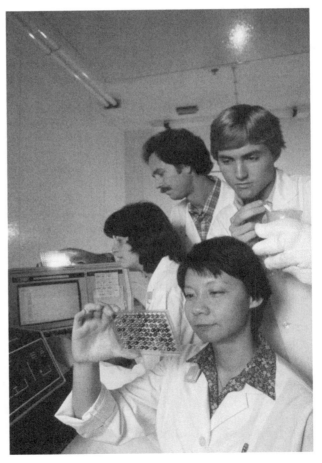

When making business decisions, individuals and companies often weigh possible risks against potential rewards. In the science and technology industries, companies often risk large amounts of capital to fund research facilities. © *Roger Ressmeyer/Corbis.*

corporation. If that were to happen, the investor could become exceptionally wealthy off a small investment.

It is important to note that individual investors are not the only ones who take financial risks. Banks and other financial institutions take risks when they loan money to individuals and businesses. Likewise, insurance companies take risks when they agree to reimburse their customers in the event of a future loss.

When Did It Begin

People have been taking financial risks since the beginning of commerce, which some anthropologists believe dates as far back as 150,000 years ago. Advanced, in-depth mathematical calculations of risk are relatively new. Two events, one seemingly minor and the other of major historical significance, transformed risk analysis into a complex science. The seemingly minor event was the 1944 publication of *Theory of Games and Economic Behavior* by mathematician John von Neumann (1903–57) and economist Oskar Morgenstern (1902–77). This book created a field of study called game theory, which is now considered one of the more important areas of research in contemporary economics. Game theory analyzes the complex process by which individuals, competing for scarce resources, attempt to maximize the benefits they receive and minimize the harm they experience. Scholars in this new science calculated risk and reward mathematically with a set of complex equations.

The other event that spurred the development of risk analysis was the Cold War, a 50-year period of tension—though never an open war—between the United States and the Soviet Union. Among many things, the era was characterized by espionage and a nuclear arms race, during which each nation prepared for war with the other. As the Cold War progressed, a process called scenario analysis developed and was employed by leaders of both nations to help them predict outcomes of their military and political decisions. In the 1970s insurance companies began using scenario analysis to calculate the premiums (prices the insured clients are charged) on policies for oil tankers.

More Detailed Information

Most economists and investment advisers use what is called the risk pyramid to demonstrate the relationship between risk and reward. Although renderings of the pyramid vary, the safest investments are always located at the base of the pyramid, and the riskiest investments are grouped at the top. In all drawings of risk pyramids, risks and rewards increase with each ascending tier. Most versions of the pyramid have four tiers, with the foundation consisting of the safest possible investments, which include savings accounts, money market accounts, and Treasury bills.

Money market accounts are savings accounts in which the individual receives a slightly higher rate of in-

terest than is typical in normal savings accounts (interest is the fee earned by keeping money in the account; it is calculated as a percentage of the total amount) in exchange for agreeing to maintain a higher minimum balance than is required by most savings accounts. Some money market accounts place a limit on the number of transactions an individual can perform. Many people do not consider savings and money market accounts to be true investments, even though both do pay interest and therefore make money for the people who hold them. The interest on these accounts is low, and there is virtually no risk of losing money. The benefit of maintaining such an account is that the person has immediate access to the funds in the account. Treasury bills (also called T-bills) are government securities that guarantee the investor a fixed return (usually about 3 percent of the invested amount) after a short period of time. Many economists regard T-bills as the safest form of investment.

The second tier of the risk pyramid consists of a series of relatively safe investment options, although compared to the bottom tier, the risks are greater and the returns are potentially higher. This tier includes conservative stock purchases and balanced mutual funds. An example of a conservative stock would be shares in a stable, long-standing corporation, such as General Electric. A mutual fund is an investment that combines the money of several investors and purchases a package of stocks, bonds, and other investment securities. There are many different mutual funds available to investors, each posing different degrees of risk. A balanced mutual fund spreads an investor's money among safe and slightly less conservative stocks. Investors who purchase these relatively low-risk stocks and mutual funds are advised to adopt a "buy and hold" strategy. This means that, after making the initial investment, the investor should expect gradual growth over a long period of time (about 20 or 30 years).

The third tier of the risk pyramid consists of growth funds. Investors at this level put their money into aggressive mutual funds, riskier stocks (such as shares in a start-up technology firm), and investment real estate. An example of investment real estate would be a rental property. Such investors may hold these investments for a long period of time, but they initiate these transactions with the understanding that they may have to sell quickly.

The top tier of the risk pyramid poses the greatest risks for the investor but often pays the highest, most immediate returns. People investing at this level engage in day trading (the buying and selling of high-risk stock in the same day) and purchase commodities (large amounts of bulk goods, such as crude oil, metals, sugar, coffee, and wheat, which are bought and sold through agencies such as the New York Mercantile Exchange). Trading at this level of the risk pyramid is called speculation.

No matter what type of investment an individual makes, there are always two factors to consider when evaluating risk and reward. The first factor is called the

FRANK HYNEMAN KNIGHT

Born in McLean County, Illinois, to devout Christian parents, Frank Hyneman Knight (1885–1972) failed to complete high school but nevertheless went on to become one of the most influential economists in U.S. history. In 1905, at age 20, Hyneman began his college studies in Tennessee, where over the course of eight years he spent time at three universities, earning two bachelor's degrees and a master's degree. In 1913 he moved to Ithaca, New York, completing a Ph.D. in economics in 1916. He spent the main part of his career as a professor at the University of Chicago, serving as head of the economics department from the 1920s through the late 1940s. Knight was infamous for provoking quarrels about economic principles with his colleagues in the department and with other leading economic thinkers when he reviewed their books in leading economics journals. Fellow economists referred to Knight as the "Grand Old Man," and although they did not always like him personally, they admired his hard work and respected his intelligence.

Knight's best-known book is *Risk, Uncertainty, and Profit* (1921). In it he makes an important distinction between risk, which he defines as randomness with measurable and probable outcomes, and uncertainty, which he defines as randomness with immeasurable and unknowable outcomes. Many CEOs and entrepreneurs still run their businesses according to the principles outlined in this book.

To combat this dangerous trend, the Federal Reserve (the central banking system of the United States) began scrutinizing the lending practices of all American financial institutions. Initial data on these supervisory reports indicated that lenders were issuing too many faulty loans. It was revealed that, in interviewing customers applying for loans, many lenders were willing to accept the customer's most optimistic economic forecasts as the likely future scenario. In other words, when these banks asked applicants to predict future earnings, they were willing to accept what were perhaps unsound calculations. As a result, large sums were lent to clients, and both clients and financial institutions assumed irresponsibly high risks. In 2006 the Federal Reserve urged all banks to minimize risks by returning to more sound lending practices.

$ Financial Planning

What It Means

Financial planning involves the setting of long-term goals for spending, saving, and investing. Expenses include money spent on groceries, clothing, child care, and other necessities, as well as monthly bills such as mortgage payments (the monthly fee paid by those who have purchased homes with money borrowed from a financial institution) or rent (the monthly fee paid by people who lease space in an apartment or house); utilities (gas, electric, water, sewage, and garbage disposal bills); telephone expenses (cell phone and landline); credit card payments; cable television and Internet bills; and payments on other outstanding loans (car payments and student loans, for example). Expenses also include dollars spent on pleasure, which can include an evening out at a restaurant or the movies or, possibly, a family vacation.

Savings usually refers to the amount of money one keeps in a savings account at a bank. Such accounts typically pay low interest (which means a savings account is, technically speaking, an investment), but people who maintain savings accounts are usually permitted to withdraw their money at any time without having to pay a penalty. When assembling a financial plan, it is a good idea to keep some money in a savings account in case an emergency expense (such as a costly repair to an automobile or the unexpected loss of employment) arises. Many professional financial planners suggest that, if possible, one should maintain a sum that equals four months worth of expenses in a savings account.

Investments refers to assets such as stocks, bonds, mutual funds, and life insurance policies that one purchases with the hope that the asset will appreciate in value or generate more income in the future. A good financial plan will include investments that will one day provide for the funding of one's children's college educations and for an individual's postretirement needs. Most safe long-term investments (those that are likely to pay moderate returns) require an individual to keep the invested money

time horizon of the investment, which refers to the amount of time the investor wishes to have his or her money tied up in the investment. Some investors prefer to make an original outlay of funds and than add to that outlay at regular intervals. Such investors tend to benefit the most at the second tier of the risk pyramid. The second factor is called the bankroll, which refers to the amount of money the investor can afford to lose. A wealthy investor with millions of dollars of holdings is best served by investing a portion of those holdings aggressively.

Recent Trends

The real estate market experienced a decline beginning in 2006, leading to a drastic increase in the number of foreclosures on both commercial and personal mortgage loans. (A foreclosure is a legal process by which a bank takes possession of a property because the buyer of the property is no longer able to make payments on the mortgage loan he took out to purchase it.) In December 2006 nearly 110,000 Americans were entering some sort of mortgage foreclosure procedure with their lender. According to some statistical accounts, foreclosure rates increased 42 percent between 2005 and 2006. By comparison, in the early 1950s lenders foreclosed on a mere 0.04 percent of the mortgages they authorized.

in an account for a predetermined amount of time. Funds in many retirement plans, for example, cannot be accessed without penalty until the investor is 59 years old.

When Did It Begin

In one sense financial planning could be said to have begun as far back as 9500 BC with the start of agriculture in the Fertile Crescent of Southwest Asia (what is today Iraq and Syria). Since people were subsisting on what they could harvest, any planning associated with rationing crops and storing them for later use or trading them with others could be considered financial planning. With regard to savings, it is believed that people began storing grains and precious metals in banks in 3000 BC. At the time, banks were housed in temples because these structures were well built and frequently occupied by priests and other worshipers. With regard to investing, people could purchase stock as far back as the Roman Empire. The first stock brokers (people who facilitate the trading of stocks among buyers and sellers) are believed to have appeared in twelfth-century France.

Through the centuries stock brokers have served as financial advisers, attempting to help clients conduct sensible and profitable transactions by discussing trends in the stock market and the direction of the economy. However, stock brokers do not necessarily discuss the individual client's specific financial situation and the person's long-range goals and needs. Personal financial planning of this sort began much more recently. In 1969 a group of financial service consultants (professionals who gave clients advice on how to invest their money) met in Chicago to discuss their dissatisfaction with the state of the financial services industry. This initial meeting led to the formation in 1970 of a trade union called the International Association of Financial Planners. In 1971 the group created the College of Financial Planning, which in turn introduced the Certified Financial Planner (CFP) designation for those who successfully completed study there. The institution graduated its first class in 1973. Members of the profession vow to give more comprehensive individual service to their clients.

More Detailed Information

Given the complexities of modern life, many people hire personal financial planners to help them devise and execute a financial plan that fits their lifestyle and earning patterns. Whether hiring a financial planner or developing his or her own strategy, a person should follow a series of steps to ensure long-term financial security. First it is necessary to set goals. It is never too early for a person to begin considering the type of house and the type of neighborhood he or she would like to live in. It is also necessary for a person to consider the job he or she would like to hold. If the salaries available along a certain career path are not likely to enable a person to live in the house and neighborhood of his or her choice, it then becomes

necessary to modify long-term goals. One either has to consider other lines of work or be satisfied in a more economical home. From the beginning it is crucial to understand that lifestyle choices must be consistent with earnings; otherwise a person risks going into unmanageable debt.

After stating his or her goals a person must gather relevant information and then carefully analyze that information to begin charting a course that will help him or her realize the established goals. For example, if two 30-year-old working parents with two kids hope to pay for their children's college tuition and to retire comfortably by age 62, they need to gather a substantial amount of information about college tuition and retirement funds. If their children are five and three, the couple has about 13 years to establish a college fund. To figure out how much money they should deposit in the fund, they must review tuition costs at the schools their children might one day attend and check the average annual rate of tuition increases at those schools. In this way the couple can decide how much to put into the account every year. Likewise, with their retirement fund, the couple needs to do research on the funds available, the tax laws associated with those funds, and the average returns on those funds.

After the information has been gathered and analyzed, it is time to build a plan. Most financial planners suggest that an individual reserve 20 percent of his or her pretax income for long-range investments. Second most financial planners suggest that people invest their money aggressively in the early stages of the investment process and conservatively in the later stages of the process. For example, the couple saving for their young children's college tuition might invest in some riskier mutual funds in the early going because these investments might yield high returns, and if they do not, there is still time to recoup losses. However, as their children enter high school and move closer to graduation, a financial planner will suggest that the couple invest in more conservative mutual funds. These funds may not yield high returns, but they are unlikely to lose money. Whatever long-range plan a person devises, it is important to make sure that this plan is consistent with the person's present lifestyle. Parents are not advised to budget for colleges that force them to compromise their present happiness because it is possible that their children will not share the parents' ambitions for college. Likewise, with retirement plans, investors are not advised to construct a plan that forces them to forgo too much of what they enjoy doing in the present.

Perhaps the hardest step in the process is abiding by the plan. For example, if a plan requires an investor to deposit $400 each month into a fund, the investor must be disciplined enough to stick with the plan. This often means that one cannot have the very latest technology, the most stylish clothes, or the most elegant car. Keeping with a plan requires discipline and sound decision-making.

MAXED OUT

Released to critical acclaim in 2006, *Maxed Out: Hard Times, Easy Credit, and the Era of Predatory Lenders* is a documentary film that examines the harmful practices in the credit card industry. Director James Scurlock claims that credit card companies make a concerted effort to provide credit cards and to extend large amounts of credit to people whom these companies know are likely to have difficulty paying their credit card bills. Among those likely to accrue large amounts of debt on credit cards are college students, poor people, and others who may not have a thorough understanding of the interest rates and finance charges associated with their balance (the amount owed) on the credit card. According to Scurlock, many of the people in America most in need of a sound financial plan never get an opportunity to make one because they listen to the dangerously bad advice of creditors looking to make some quick and easy money.

Maxed Out received mixed but largely positive reviews when it played at film festivals in the United States. Most critics praised the movie for exposing wrongdoing in the lending industry. Others, however, argued that the film oversimplified a complex issue.

Most financial planners suggest that a person arrange with his or her bank to have investment funds automatically drawn from his or her checking account each month. Left to themselves, most investors stray from their plans and neglect to make their monthly or quarterly investments. Often when they have strayed too far, they give up on their plans. The last step is to review the plan at scheduled intervals. This allows a person to make deliberate and prudent modifications to the plan rather than hasty changes.

Recent Trends

In the early years of the twenty-first century, it appeared that some Americans had not planned their finances well. For example, in 2006 banks filed 1.2 million foreclosure proceedings (processes by which a financial institution holding a mortgage repossesses a home) against homeowners. This represented a 42 percent increase from 2005. About this same time it was estimated that one in 73 households filed for bankruptcy and that the average American owed $8,000 in credit card debt. Statistics from 2006 indicated that credit card spending was at an all-time high, with data indicating that Americans put as much as 25 percent of their purchases on credit cards.

While the preceding statistics may paint a dire picture, other statistics suggested that Americans were seeing the wisdom in sound financial planning. For example, more American families were enlisting the services of personal financial planners each year, and as of 2003

personal financial planning was one of the fastest-growing career fields in the country. In 1993 only 40 percent of the Certified Public Accounting firms in the United States offered personal financial planning services. By 2003 more than 60 percent of the firms in the country offered those services. According to the Bureau of Labor Statistics (BLS), in 2004 there were over 158,000 personal financial advisers working in the United States, 40 percent of whom were self-employed. The BLS predicted that the field would grow at a rate of 18 to 26 percent each year until 2014. In 2004 the median salary for personal financial planers was $61,000. More important than the salary, surveys conducted among workers in the field indicated that personal financial planners found considerable satisfaction in their work, with the majority of respondents saying that they found their work exciting and worthwhile.

$ Saving for College

What It Means

Most financial planners advise parents to begin saving for their children's college educations as soon as possible. Some parents begin saving for college before their children are born, but many parents cannot afford to allocate funds for college until later in their children's lives. Whenever parents begin to save, adhering to a set of basic guidelines can maximize the funds students have for school and minimize the debt they incur while completing their studies.

First, the parents or guardians (and possibly the student as well) should review their present financial circumstances and create a sensible budget. Parents who are beginning to allocate funds when their children are very young can consult one of the many online college-cost calculators to determine how much a college education is projected to cost when their child is scheduled to attend. Such calculators project average fees for public, private, and Ivy League schools. They also estimate how much money parents should allocate per month based on how old their children are when they start the savings plan. For example, according to some 2007 estimates, parents of a newborn child who plan to send the child to a state college should invest $312 per month in order to be able to cover expenses fully by the time he or she starts school. Another projection calculated in 2007 was that parents who want to pay for an Ivy League school and begin their savings plan when their child is 8 will need to invest $1,385 a month.

After establishing a budget, the next step is to choose an investment plan that offers tax advantages and to contribute funds to the plan consistently. There are four major types of college-investment plans: 529 Plans (also known as Qualified Tuition Plans, or QTPs); Coverdell Education Savings Accounts (often called ESAs); and Uniform Gifts to Minors Act (UGMA) and Uniform

Transfers to Minors Act (UTMA) accounts, which allow donors to give assets such as stocks, bonds, and real estate to their children. Most people investing in one of these plans seek professional assistance to help them choose and manage the plan. The final step is to monitor the progress of the investment and to make changes to the investment strategy if necessary.

When Did It Begin

The UGMA is an act of federal legislation that took effect in 1956 with the approval of the New York Stock Exchange, the Association of Stock Exchange Firms, and the American Bar Association (an association of American lawyers). The act permits minors to receive gifts such as cash, stocks, bonds, and other securities that are managed by a custodian until the minor reaches the age of majority (18, 21, or 25, depending on the laws of the state in which the minor lives). Under the provisions of the law a parent may transfer as much as $11,000 per year ($22,000 per year for a couple) to a child's UGMA account without the funds being subject to a gift tax. When the child comes of age he may use the funds as he wishes. No one, not even the former custodian of the account, can dictate how the funds are allocated. Adopted in 1986, the UTMA extends the UGMA to include other types of gifts, such as real estate and art.

QTPs, or 529 Plans, were created under the Small Business Job Protection Act of 1996. These investment plans allow more significant contributions than UGMA and UTMA accounts (a parent can make a lump-sum investment of as much as $60,000 at one time), but all funds in the account must be used to pay for a college education. Coverdell Education Savings Accounts were created by the Economic Growth and Tax Relief Reconciliation Act of 2001. Parents may contribute up to $2,000 annually to Coverdell ESAs.

More Detailed Information

The investment plan most widely used by people saving money for their children's college education is the 529 Plan. The specific details of a 529 Plan are determined on a state-by-state basis. In general, there are two types of 529 Plans: prepaid plans and savings plans. As of 2007, all 50 states in the United States as well as the District of Columbia offered at least one of the two types of 529 Plans. According to a prepaid plan, a person pays current rates for tuition credits that will be used in the future by the student (referred to as the beneficiary). Thus, the initial investment in a prepaid 529 Plan increases at exactly the same rate as college tuition. Prepaid plans can be sponsored either by states or by individual institutions of higher education. For example, if someone purchases a prepaid plan under the auspices of New York State, the beneficiary of the plan will have tuition paid at a New York State school at some future date. If a person invests in a 529 Plan through a private institution, the beneficiary must attend that institution.

Savings-based 529 Plans are only sponsored by states. According to this type of plan, a person invests as much as he or she wishes (up to $60,000 in one lump sum) in mutual funds (a bundle of investments, including stocks, bonds, and other securities, that is managed by an investment company). The mutual funds available for 529 Plans are determined by the state sponsoring the plan. Whereas the investment in a prepaid plan is guaranteed to cover tuition at a later date, investments in savings-based 529 Plans are subject to market risk. These plans, however, typically pay greater returns (meaning the money invested grows more) and offer the beneficiary the option of using the returns for all fees associated with college, including room and board. Profits on a 529 Plan are not taxed over the life of the investment. Nor are they taxed when funds are withdrawn. If the beneficiary does not use the funds for education there is a significant financial penalty.

Investors in both types of accounts are allowed to change the beneficiary. They are also permitted to name themselves as the beneficiary of the account. Any beneficiary on a 529 must be related to the investor named on the account.

In addition to saving for college, it is crucial that students research and apply for some of the many scholarships that are available. Students interested in obtaining scholarships should begin their research by consulting with their guidance counselors to find out what scholarships are available within their local communities and at the universities the student would like to attend. Churches and chambers of commerce in many cities offer modest scholarships, as do community foundations, nonprofit organizations, and volunteer organizations. Labor unions (organizations of workers that are formed to protect workers' rights) frequently offer scholarships for members and their children. Upon first glance, the funds available from these organizations may appear to be small relative to the charges for tuition and dormitory expenses, but scholarships can help with payments for textbooks and school supplies.

Aside from scholarships, all students requiring financial assistance should fill out the Free Application for Federal Student Aid (FAFSA) forms that are available in the guidance or administrative offices of their school or online at the FAFSA website. Students seeking federal aid are required to submit a new form prior to each year for which they are seeking financial assistance. Based on the information submitted on this form, the government issues a Student Aid Report (SAR), which contains several figures, including the Expected Family Contribution (EFC; the dollar amount the government determines that the family can contribute toward the child's expenses for college that year) and the amount that the federal

COVERDELL EDUCATION SAVINGS ACCOUNT

The Coverdell Education Savings Account (often called Coverdell ESA) was named after Paul Douglas Coverdell (1939–2000), a Republican senator from Georgia who was the strongest advocate for the fund. Coverdell, who also served as the director of the Peace Corps from 1989 to 1991, died one year before the savings account was established. Parents maintaining a Coverdell ESA may contribute up to $2,000 each year toward their children's educations. These contributions are invested in mutual funds and are subject to all of the risks associated with this type of investment. The money from a Coverdell ESA must be withdrawn by the beneficiary by age 30 and used for education. Profits on these funds are not taxed. Coverdell accounts may also be withdrawn tax-free to pay for private elementary and high schools. In addition to paying for tuition, these monies can be used to pay for room and board, books, school uniforms, transportation, and daycare for the children of students attending college. Beneficiaries of Coverdell ESAs must be related to the donor investing in the fund. If the stated beneficiary chooses not to attend college, the donor may name another beneficiary under the age of 30.

government will contribute to the student's college education that semester.

Awards are granted in the form of Pell Grants, Federal and Supplemental Educational Opportunity Grants (FSEOGs), Academic Competitiveness Grants (ACGs), and Science and Mathematics Access to Retain Talent Grants (SMART Grants). Although these figures are subject to change, in 2007 the maximum FSEOG was $4,000 per year and the maximum Pell Grant was $4,310 per year. The maximum Pell Grant was scheduled to increase to $5,400 per year by 2012. ACGs offer a maximum of $750 and $1,300 for each of the first two years of study, respectively. Aimed at returning juniors and seniors, SMART Grants provide a maximum of $4,000 a year for the third and fourth years of study. All funds are awarded at the discretion of the university. In addition to these grants, students can also qualify for student loans and work-study (programs wherein students are paid to do a manageable job at the university, such as answering phones in one of the department offices or working in the athletic facility).

Recent Trends

According to reports from 2006, the average cost for private colleges and universities was more than $30,000 per year, while the average cost for public colleges and universities was under $6,000 for the 2006–07 academic year. This later figure includes two- and four-year state institutions. These costs do not include room and board,

which cost an average of $6,900 for state schools and $8,150 for private schools. Thus, at that time, going to college and living on campus for four years cost somewhere between $50,000 and $160,000.

Since 1995 the average cost of college has risen at nearly twice the rate of inflation (the general rising of prices in the economy). From 2002 to 2006 the rate of tuition growth for private colleges was about 6 percent a year, but most financial advisers were telling their clients to expect tuition to rise at 7 percent a year. From the 2004–05 academic year to the 2005–06 academic year, tuition at state schools increased by an average of 7.1 percent. That figure dropped to 6.3 percent the following academic year. At these rates, tuition and fees for state and private schools would nearly double in 10 years.

Increases in student aid lag behind the tuition increases. For example, from the 2004–05 academic year to the 2005–06 academic year, student aid increased by just 3.7 percent. Furthermore, student-aid packages often consist of loans, which must be paid back with interest, rather than grants, which are awards and do not need to be repaid. According to some reports, 51 percent of the money given in financial-aid packages comes in the form of loans. Only 44 percent of student financial aid comes from grants.

Data indicates, however, that the steep costs of college are worth the expense. As of 2005, women between the ages of 25 and 54 who held bachelor's degrees earned 70 percent more income than women who only held high school diplomas. For men in that age bracket the difference was 63 percent.

$ Retirement Plans

What It Means

A retirement plan is a financial arrangement that provides a person with income when they retire. Workers in the United States and many other developed countries typically retire from work at or around age 65. After they retire and no longer receive a salary, the retirement plans in which they are enrolled provide them with the money they need to maintain their standard of living.

Retirement plans are usually set up by the past employer of the person retiring, although insurance companies, government agencies, and trade unions may also set up plans. The money the retirement plan pays to the retiree comes out of a fund to which the retiree, when he or she was employed, regularly contributed. Usually the employer takes the contributed amount out of each paycheck an employee receives and puts it into an investment product such as stock. Whether the investment gains or loses money, it is saved in the retirement account until the time the employee stops working, and then it is paid out to the employee. The payments that the retirement plan owes the employee are called the benefits.

A retirement plan that guarantees a participating employee a specific monthly benefit at the time of retirement is called a defined benefit plan. These benefits typically continue until the former employee, and often the spouse, dies. This type of plan may provide a specified amount of money each month, which is usually dependent on the participant's salary level and how many years he or she has belonged to the plan. In general, the participant does not make decisions about how money is invested; the institution managing the retirement plan takes care of all investment decisions. With many plans the employer as well as the employee contributes money to the plan. Defined benefit plans are sometimes called fully funded pension plans.

A retirement plan that provides an individual account for each participant and bases the benefit on the amount of money contributed as well as on the performance of the investments is called a defined contribution plan. The amount of the benefit paid out is less predictable than it is in a defined retirement plan. Also, the employee, not the institution, takes on the investment risk. Some examples of defined contribution plans are 401(k) plans, 403(b) plans, employee stock-ownership plans, and profit-sharing plans.

Most retirement plans are either defined benefit plans or defined contribution plans, but some retirement plans, called hybrid plans, combine features of both defined benefit and defined contribution plans.

When Did It Begin

Up until the 1870s, most businesses in the United States were small, family-run enterprises that did not have formal plans for providing money to employees after they retired. Most Americans were still working as farmers, and it was more typical for older Americans to stay involved in work in old age, providing guidance to younger workers even if they did not have stamina or high rates of productivity. In 1875 the American Express Company established the first private pension plan in the United States.

Between 1875 and 1929 private-sector pension plans gradually grew more popular in the United States and Canada. Some of the major U.S. companies to establish plans in this period were Standard Oil of New Jersey, U.S. Steel Corporation, General Electric Co., American Telephone and Telegraph Co., Goodyear Tire and Rubber Co., and Eastman Kodak Co. By 1940, 4.1 million private-sector workers (15 percent of all private-sector workers) were covered by pension plans.

Retirement plans enable people to put aside money to cover living expenses after they stop working. In this photo a couple reviews their retirement portfolio. © *Fog City Productions/Brand X/Corbis.*

DIFFERENT TYPES OF INDIVIDUAL RETIREMENT ACCOUNTS

With the Roth IRA, which was established by the Taxpayer Relief Act of 1997, taxpayers are allowed to save for retirement while allowing the saved funds to grow without being taxed. Taxes are paid on contributions, but withdrawals are not taxed. The levels at which taxpayers may contribute are subject to certain income limits.

The SIMPLE IRA, which stands for Savings Incentive Match Plan for Employees, is a simplified employee pension plan. The employer is allowed to deduct certain taxes when they make contributions to the SIMPLE. The employer makes either matching or nonelective contributions to each eligible employee's SIMPLE IRA, and employees may make salary-deferral contributions to the plan.

The traditional IRA differs from both the Roth and the SIMPLE IRA. Individual taxpayers are allowed to contribute pretax earnings up to a maximum yearly allowance and to defer income taxes until they withdraw the money after retirement.

SEP IRA stands for a Simplified Employee Pension IRA. This type of plan allows an employer to make retirement plan contributions into a traditional IRA established in the employee's name instead of into a pension-fund account in the company's name. Usually SEP IRAs are formed by a small business or a self-employed person.

In 1935 President Roosevelt signed the Social Security Act, a federally sponsored social insurance program that provided benefits to retirees and the unemployed and a lump-sum benefit at death. The government raised money for this program by imposing a tax on workers' wages. Social Security did not guarantee financial security for retirees, and so the introduction of the program did not radically affect the trend of older workers putting off retirement until they could not physically manage work anymore. Even through the 1950s, the concept of retirement had not become widespread.

In the 1940s the large American automaker General Motors was chaired by Charles Erwin Wilson (1890–1961). Wilson designed GM's first modern pension fund, which was distinct from other pension plans because it allowed employed to choose to invest in all publicly traded stocks, not just GM stocks. By 1990, 39.5 million private-sector workers (43 percent of all such workers) were covered by a pension plan.

More Detailed Information

In the United States individuals who follow a common pattern of working until they reach their 60s or 70s usually retire and begin to live on income from their savings account, the government's Social Security program, or a retirement plan such as an IRA (or a combination of the three). There are many different types of retirement plans and a variety of different tax laws and regulations that apply to them.

A defined benefit plan provides employees with retirement benefits that are predetermined by such things as their salary, the number of years they have worked at an organization, and their age when they retire. This type of plan may be funded, meaning that the employer has also contributed to the investment fund. Most defined benefit plans are funded because the governments in many countries, including the United States, the United Kingdom, and Australia, encourage them by providing tax incentives if individuals and businesses contribute to them. A defined benefit plan may also be an unfunded plan, meaning that neither the employee nor the employer sets funds aside on a regular basis. The benefits for these plans come out of taxes and the contributions of current workers, as in the case of the Social Security system in the United States. The participant in a defined benefit plan does not need to demonstrate an ability to save money in order to receive the benefit of such a plan.

A defined contribution plan gives the employee the responsibility of choosing the types of investments to use, ranging from mutual funds to individual stocks to securities. Some of these plans give the employer the ability to contribute a matching dollar amount to the employee's contributions. These plans usually restrict the participant from taking funds out of the plan before they reach a certain age (typically 59.5 years old) without being charged a penalty.

Defined contribution plans that are commonly used include 401(k) plans, Individual Retirement Accounts (IRAs), Keogh Plans, and profit-sharing plans.

The 401(k) plan, sometimes called a salary-reduction plan, is a retirement plan that is provided to employees at most large companies and many small ones. Employees can contribute to the 401(k) plan by having a designated amount of pretax dollars deducted from their paychecks. The employee is usually allowed to select from a variety of investment choices. These choices consist of different mutual funds that emphasize stocks, bonds, and money market investments. Employers generally match part of the employee's contribution, giving employees an incentive to save more money for retirement. The employee pays no taxes until he or she begins to withdraw money, which he or she must do between the ages of 59.5 and 70.5.

An IRA is a retirement account that allows an individual to set aside money each year until withdrawals begin at age 59.5 or later. IRA plans are tax-deferred plans, meaning that payment of some or all of the taxes are deferred, or put off, until a future date, rather than in the year the investment creates income. In contrast to a

401(k) plan, an IRA is funded entirely by the individual taxpayer.

A Keogh Plan is a retirement plan similar to the 401(k) and IRA, but it is for workers who are either self-employed or employed by unincorporated businesses. The Keogh Plan is also known as HR 10, and as with the IRA, the earnings from its investments are tax-deferred until the capital is taken out of the plan by the retiree, which he or she must do between the ages of 59.5 and 70.5 or take a 10 percent penalty. Usually people who use Keogh Plans invest their money in combinations of stocks, bonds, money market funds, and mutual funds.

A profit-sharing plan is one that provides employees with a portion of the profits of the company. There is no requirement for the company to contribute to the plan; it can also decide what portion of the profit will be shared and may make profit-sharing contributions whether or not the business was profitable for a given year. When instituted, each employee receives a percentage of profits based on the company's earnings, an arrangement that commonly gives them a strong sense of ownership in the company.

A 403(b) plan, also called a tax-sheltered annuity plan, is similar to a 401(k) plan, but it is offered by nonprofit organizations, such as public schools, universities, and charitable organizations, rather than corporations. A 403(b) plan can take the form of an annuity contract, which is a program provided by an insurance company. It can also take the form of a custodial account, which invests the contributions into mutual funds. Finally, it can be a retirement-income account that is established for church employees. The contributions to the 403(b) plan are not taxed until the employee begins to withdraw from the plan, which usually happens after retirement.

Recent Trends

Defined benefit retirement plans became popular in the years following World War II (1939–45). By the late 1970s approximately 62 percent of all active workers in the United States were covered exclusively by defined benefit plans, according to the Employee Benefit Research Institute. After this peak, employer participation in these plans gradually declined, and by 1997 only 13 percent of employees had a pension plan as their sole retirement benefit. As defined benefit plans have waned in popularity, defined contribution plans have grown in popularity. The amount of active workers with a defined contribution plan and no pension was 16 percent in 1979, but by 2004 that figure had increased to 62 percent.

At the same time that more people have become covered by defined contribution plans, a series of bankruptcies in large corporate industries such as steel, airlines, and auto parts has had the effect of shifting the burden of retirement management to employees. Many of the baby boomers (people born between 1946 and 1964) have

witnessed a reduction in stable sources of retirement income in the late twentieth and early twenty-first centuries. At the same time, average life expectancy has increased steadily, which means retirees need to spread their retirement incomes out over more time, on average, than previous generations of retirees.

These factors, in addition to low participation rates in 401(k)s, pre-retirement 401(k) withdrawals, and low rates of savings in general, have meant that more than almost three-quarters of working-age households are at risk of seeing their standard of living decline in retirement, according to the Center for Retirement Research. Social Security only replaces approximately a third of pre-retirement income for the average earner retiring at age 62.

WHERE TO SAVE AND INVEST

$ Savings Account

What It Means

A person who wants to put aside money and keep it in a safe place will often deposit these funds in a savings

People use savings accounts to put aside money for some future purpose. In the late seventeenth-century King William III of England authorized the creation of a national savings bank as a means of raising money for his war against France. *Hulton Archive/Getty Images.*

THE MANY FLAVORS OF SAVINGS ACCOUNTS

When a person wants to save money, it is often a good idea to place it in a savings account at a financial institution. The money will be safe and will also gain interest (a percentage of the amount of money kept in the account and paid by the financial institution). In addition to basic savings accounts, there are a number of different types of savings accounts to appeal to customers' needs. An education savings account, for instance, stores funds that will eventually pay for a child's education, such as college tuition. Health savings accounts are a way to save money for medical expenses. Christmas savings accounts help individuals save money to pay for holiday gifts and expenses. Some of these savings accounts come with tax benefits, thus providing financial incentives to save.

account at a bank or other financial institution. In the United States savings accounts are available at a number of financial institutions, including commercial banks, credit unions, and savings and loan associations. These establishments are usually insured, which means the money they hold will be protected if the institution somehow fails.

Financial institutions pay customers a fee called interest on the money they keep in savings accounts, and in this way savings accounts grow. The interest is calculated as a percentage of the amount of money in the account. For example, a deposit of $100 into a savings account that pays an annual interest rate of 4 percent would grow into $104 after one year. There is often no minimum dollar amount required to open a savings account, which makes it a practical and appealing option to many. Most individuals who participate in banking have a savings account, and some financial institutions require customers to have savings accounts before they can open other types of accounts.

A savings account is not the only way to keep money at a bank. Other deposit accounts include checking accounts, money market accounts, and certificates of deposit (CDs). Each kind has different features. Checking accounts, for instance, often do not generate interest but are more convenient for everyday use. CDs and money market accounts generally earn more interest than savings accounts, but they are more restrictive in allowing customers to access their money.

When Did It Begin

Historical records show that the first time people were paid interest for putting their money in banks was when the Bank of England was founded in 1694. The English, however, did not invent the idea of paying interest. The concept existed in Italian banking and Dutch lending systems, both of which influenced the development of banking in England.

The British government's finances were in shambles in 1688, when King William III and Queen Mary II came into power in England. In addition, William was engaged in an expensive war with King Louis XIV of France. After William spent all of the money he had borrowed from merchants and goldsmiths, he asked his government, known as Parliament, to find a way to raise more money. Parliament passed a bill that allowed for the creation of a government-run institution called Governor and Company of the Bank of England. The bill allowed citizens of England to deposit their money in the newly formed bank, which then loaned this money to the English government (that is, King William). To reward citizens for loaning their money, the government offered the bank's customers an 8 percent payment every year the money was loaned. For example, if someone loaned £100 to the bank, after one year the bank would reward him with £8 (8 percent of £100).

At first the bank was restricted to loaning money to the English government, and it was intended to be closed after the loan was repaid. The government, however, never paid off the loan, and the bank still operates today, as the Bank of England.

More Detailed Information

A savings account is the most common type of bank account in the United States. It is also often the first financial account a person will have; parents tend to establish savings accounts for their children in order to teach them the value of saving money and to educate them about how banking works. Once a savings account is set up, the account holder is usually given a passbook, a small book in which to keep track of transactions, including deposits, withdrawals, interest payments, and any fees that the bank charges. The first entry in the passbook is the opening deposit. The financial institution also sends a monthly statement that lists all transactions, and the account holder is responsible for checking the statement for accuracy in comparison with the passbook or register. This is known as reconciling an account. More recently, transactions and balances are kept track of electronically.

Although savings accounts are relatively uncomplicated, they do come with some restrictions. U.S. regulations allow savings account holders to make up to six transfers or withdrawals from their savings accounts per month (or within the four-week cycle that appears on each statement). Only half of those six transfers or withdrawals can be made by check or debit card (a plastic card used to withdraw or electronically transfer funds from an account at the point of sale, such as at a supermarket checkout). The remaining three must be made in person at an automated teller machine (ATM) or bank branch. If a savings account holder does not follow this guideline, the bank may charge penalty fees, close the account, or reclassify it as a checking account.

Because of these regulations, most individuals in the United States have both savings and checking accounts. Checking accounts offer flexibility and accessibility of funds, and there are no restrictions on withdrawals or transfers. Many individuals thus use checking accounts for everyday purchases and paying bills and use savings accounts to save money and earn interest.

These federal guidelines were established to encourage U.S. citizens to save their money and to stabilize the money held by financial institutions. Although checking accounts are designed to fluctuate, banks prefer that savings accounts remain fairly predictable because they use the money in those accounts to make loans to other customers. For example, when a person borrows money from the bank to buy a house, the money loaned to that person often comes from other customers' savings accounts. If the balances in savings accounts were to fluctuate too greatly, banks would not have a clear picture of how much money was available for loans. Lending money is how banks make most of their profits. Even though a bank pays annual interest to customers' savings accounts, it will usually loan that money to other customers at a higher annual interest rate.

There is usually no minimum dollar amount required to open a savings account, but there may be various fees. For instance, once a savings account is opened, a bank may charge the customer a fee if the account balance falls under a certain amount. In some cases institutions will charge a fee just for having a savings account. Others may assess a fee for making certain kinds of withdrawals or for letting an account sit too long with no activity. In the United Kingdom and some other countries, a type of savings account known as a notice deposit account charges a fee if an account holder makes a withdrawal without providing a 90-day advance notice.

Putting money in a savings account is not the only way people can collect interest from a bank. They can also invest in CDs (certificates of deposit) and money market accounts. Traditional CDs offer higher interest rates than savings accounts, but after a CD is purchased, it cannot be cashed or have any funds withdrawn for a fixed period of time. Money market accounts are a type of savings account that have a higher minimum dollar requirement to open and often restrict access to funds.

Recent Trends

The Internet has changed the way people bank. Virtual banks, banks with no physical presence or a very limited one, offer online banking services to customers. Because such banks cost less to operate, they tend to offer higher interest rates than traditional banking institutions. In 2000, for example, an online bank called ING Direct, part of the Netherlands-based financial company ING Group, began offering customers savings accounts with attractive interest rates. ING Direct had fewer physical locations than traditional banks, so it was able to offer customers a higher interest rate on their savings accounts.

Although traditional savings accounts are probably not in danger of extinction, the onslaught of new types of accounts has given them increased competition. For instance, in the late twentieth century banks began offering checking accounts that paid interest at rates rivaling those of savings accounts. Many customers found this option appealing because their money was more accessible in a checking account.

$ Money Market Account

What It Means

A money market account, or money market deposit account (MMDA), is a form of bank account that imposes strict rules regarding balance size and the number of withdrawals that can be made each month. In exchange, banks pay money market account holders interest (a fee owed to those who lend money) at a higher rate than they do the holders of other account types.

Banks and other savings institutions, such as credit unions and savings and loan associations, take in money from account holders in the form of deposits, but they do not simply store this money in their vaults. They lend it to other borrowers or invest it with the intent of making profits for themselves. Thus, when you deposit money in a bank, you are lending the bank money. In return for this loan, the bank pays you interest. Different types of bank accounts pay interest at different rates. In general, you can expect to collect interest at higher rates the larger and more stable your bank balance is, since large, stable pools of money make it easier for a bank to invest profitably.

Basic checking accounts, which offer easy and instant access to deposited money, pay little or no interest and have few restrictions. If you open a basic checking account, you can generally keep your balance as high or as low as you like, and you can expect to withdraw money (for example, by writing checks, transferring funds online, or making withdrawals from automated teller machines, known as ATMs) as often as you like. The resulting instability of checking account balances restricts the kinds of investments banks can make using this source of funds. Savings accounts, on the other hand, are not meant to be used for ordinary transactions. Some limitations are usually placed on withdrawals made from savings accounts; therefore, these accounts provide banks with a more stable stream of money than checking accounts, and they pay higher interest rates.

A money market account is a form of savings account. If you open a money market account, you will probably be required to maintain a relatively high balance (usually ranging from $100 to $2,500) at all times, and you will probably be allowed to make only a small number of withdrawals per month (usually around six).

A money market account is a bank account that has certain restrictions—for example, a high minimum balance—in exchange for offering customers a better-than-average interest rate. In this photo a bank official discusses the features of a money market account with a customer. *Photograph by Kelly A. Quin. Cengage Learning, Gale.*

Because these rules result in higher and more stable account balances, they make it easier for banks to invest profitably. In exchange, banks pay higher rates of interest on money market accounts than they do on most other types of accounts.

When Did It Begin

Money market accounts came into being as a result of the Garn-St. Germain Depository Institutions Act of 1982. This act consisted of many provisions which worked together to deregulate the banking industry, primarily in the hope of helping the numerous struggling savings and loan associations across the United States. Savings and loan associations (or S&Ls) were failing in part due to government restrictions on the types of investments they could make. Garn-St. Germain removed some of the key restrictions on S&Ls and reformed other aspects of the banking industry.

Prior to the Garn-St. Germain Act, there had been limits on the amount of interest a savings institution could pay depositors. By allowing savings institutions to offer money market accounts, a form of savings account with no interest-rate ceiling, the Act made it easier for them to attract deposits. The Garn-St. Germain Act failed to save S&Ls from financial disaster, but money market accounts became a lasting feature of the banking industry.

More Detailed Information

Money market accounts offer a combination of financial gain (through interest payments) and liquidity (the ability to convert account balances into cash easily). This combination allows them to fill an important need in the financial life of individuals, families, and businesses.

At one end of the financial spectrum, a basic checking account offers little if any financial gain, since most such accounts do not pay interest, but this is offset by an extremely high level of liquidity. Checking accounts are ideal for storing the money that you need to pay your ordinary expenses, but it is not advisable to use checking accounts for saving money. If you have money left over after paying your expenses each month, there are better ways of saving and investing those excess funds than in a checking account.

At the other end of the financial spectrum, stocks (shares of company ownership), offer the possibility of large financial gain (as company owners, stockholders earn money when a company prospers) but a comparatively low level of liquidity. To invest effectively in the stock market, it is generally necessary to commit your money for a long period of time. Monthly and yearly fluctuations in stock value can be drastic, but over periods of five or ten years stock gains often outweigh losses and outpace the gains made by other types of investments. If you do not need access to your savings for five or more years, investing in stocks may be a good idea.

Money market accounts fall somewhere in the middle. If you do not need access to your money right away but expect to need it within a year or so, a money market account may be the ideal place to put your savings. If, for example, you are trying to save money to purchase a car or a house six months from now, a money market account might be the best place to put your money in the meantime. You will earn interest each month, but you will have easy access to your money when the time comes to make the purchase.

Financial advisers generally suggest, moreover, that individuals and families always have enough money available (that is, saved in a form that offers a high level of liquidity) to support themselves for three to six months in case of emergency. Money market accounts are among the most sensible places to keep such emergency funds, since they offer sufficient liquidity to deal with any financial demands caused by emergencies while paying interest on your savings until the money is needed.

Added to this balance of financial gain and liquidity is the safety that comes with saving money in a bank, as opposed to investing it in the stock market (or other financial markets), where there are no guarantees that you will not lose your money. The Federal Deposit Insurance Corporation (FDIC), a government agency responsible for guaranteeing the stability of banks nationwide, insures money market account balances up to $100,000. In other words, if you open a money market account with a bank that goes out of business, the FDIC will pay you the full value of your balance as long as it does not exceed $100,000.

Recent Trends

One of the chief attractions of money market accounts is that they pay higher interest rates than other kinds of bank accounts. During the late 1990s and the early years of the twenty-first century, however, all interest rates in the United States were at historically low levels. This was good in many ways. It became easier for many people to take out the loans that they needed to buy homes, and it made business owners more likely to expand their

---

CHOOSING A MONEY MARKET ACCOUNT

A money market account is a bank account that pays a higher rate of interest (a fee paid for the use of borrowed money) than most other types of accounts in exchange for requiring that you maintain a minimum balance and only make a limited number of withdrawals each month. Interest rates, minimum balances, and restrictions on withdrawals vary from bank to bank and sometimes within banks, as banks generally offer more than one variety of money market account. For example, a bank may offer a basic money market account that requires a minimum balance of $100 but pays relatively low interest. It might also offer a money market account with a minimum balance of $500 and an interest rate that increases as your balance rises. Finally, it might offer a money market account that is linked to your savings, checking, and other account types.

Depending on the amount of money you want to deposit and your plans for that money, there is probably a money market account that will meet your needs. It is necessary, however, to understand all of a bank's different offerings before choosing a money market account.

---

operations using borrowed money. Low interest rates, however, made bank accounts of all kinds less attractive forms of investment than they had traditionally been. In the mid-1980s, for example, a money market account may have paid interest at a rate of around 10 percent. In 2005, by contrast, the average interest rate paid by money market accounts was around 1 percent. Since prices across the economy were generally rising, in the late 1990s and the early years of the following decade, at a rate of around 3 percent a year, saving money in a bank meant losing money.

$ Certificate of Deposit

What It Means

A certificate of deposit (CD) is a short-to-medium-term investment offered by banks, savings and loan associations, and credit unions. As with savings accounts, the customer deposits money with the institution and in exchange receives a fee called interest, which is calculated as a percentage of the amount deposited (for instance, 3 percent interest on a $100 deposit is $3). Also known as a time deposit, a CD earns a higher interest rate than a regular savings account, because the investor agrees not to make any withdrawals on the money for a fixed amount of time, called the maturity period. In effect, purchasing a CD is like lending money to the bank in exchange for a favorable interest rate. When the CD matures (has been held for the agreed-upon length of

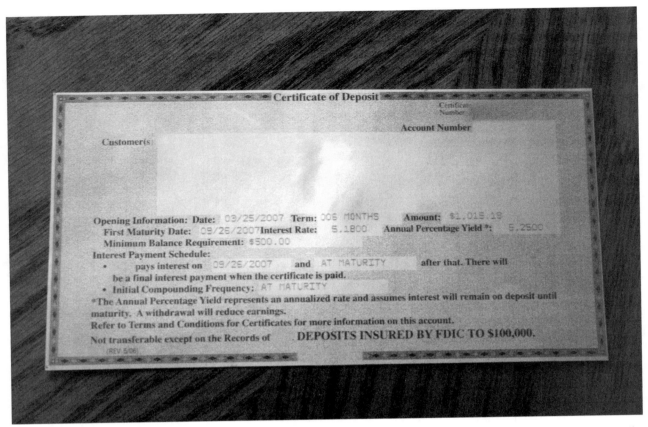

Certificates of deposit, or CDs, are short-to medium-term investments that provide higher interest rates than regular bank accounts. The certificate shown here represents the investor's receipt for his or her deposit. *Photograph by Kelly A. Quin. Cengage Learning, Gale.*

time), the investor may redeem it for the original amount of the investment plus any interest that has accrued (accumulated).

While it is possible for the investor to withdraw money from the CD before the maturity date is reached, there is a significant penalty for doing so; this is usually calculated by subtracting from the amount of interest earned. In the past the investor received a paper certificate as receipt for his or her investment (hence the term *certificate of deposit*), but this practice has become less common; it is now more likely that the CD will simply be represented as an item in the investor's monthly bank statement.

A certificate of deposit is generally considered to be one of the safest investments a person can make, because the deposit is backed by the FDIC (Federal Deposit Insurance Corporation) or the NCUA (National Credit Union Administration). Both the FDIC and the NCUA guarantee the stability of the U.S. financial system by insuring the deposits of their member institutions for up to $100,000 per depositor.

When Did It Begin

Certificates of deposit were introduced in the nineteenth century as a way for way for banks to borrow money from investors in order to fund their own investments and operations. Certificates of deposit increasingly enabled banks to compete with other institutions (such as the U.S. Treasury, which offers savings bonds; and finance companies, which offer a variety of investments) for the uninvested dollars of individuals and corporations.

Particularly useful because of its large denomination was the "negotiable certificate of deposit" (or NCD), a CD with a face value of at least $100,000. NCDs were introduced in 1961. Usually purchased by insurance companies, corporations, or other institutional investors, NCDs may be sold in secondary markets (from one investor to another) at a substantial profit, although they cannot be drawn upon before the maturity date.

More Detailed Information

Before purchasing a CD from one financial intuition or another, it is essential to understand the specific terms of the investment.

The Minimum Deposit Financial institutions typically require a minimum deposit of $500 to purchase a CD. Some institutions may stipulate higher minimums of $1,000, $2,500, $10,000, or more. CDs of less than $100,000 are considered "small CDs," while those over

$100,000 are called "large CDs," "jumbo CDs," or "negotiable CDs" (often referred to as NCDs).

The Maturity Period CDs are sold with maturity periods in increments of 31 days and 3, 6, 12, 18, 24, 36, 48, and 60 months. In many cases, investors time their CDs to reach maturity in advance of some anticipated expense, such as a tax payment, a child's college tuition, or a luxury vacation. At the time of maturity, the investor may cash out the CD, receiving back the amount of the principal along with the accrued interest. He or she may also elect to "roll it over," depositing the money into a new CD.

The Annual Percentage Rate of Interest (APR) CDs usually carry a fixed annual percentage rate (APR) by which interest is calculated. In most cases, the larger the deposit and the longer the maturity period, the higher the interest rate will be. In 2005 average APRs for CDs ranged from 2.29 percent (for a 3-month maturity) to 4.09 percent (for a 60-month maturity).

How Interest Accrues The interest on certificates of deposit is referred to as compounding interest. This means that the interest builds upon itself. For example, if Darrin buys a $500 CD with a three-year maturity at a 4 percent APR, then at the end the first year he will have earned $20 in interest; his investment will then be worth $520. If the interest compounds annually, then over the course of the second year he will earn $20.80 in interest, because the interest is calculated based on the $520 that is now in the account. Although the extra 80 cents may seem insignificant, continually increasing interest can add up. Interest may be set to compound daily, monthly, quarterly (every three months), or annually. The shorter the compounding period, the more quickly interest will accrue.

Most institutions allow the investor to choose how she wishes to receive interest. For example, she may elect to leave the interest in the CD (in which case it continues to compound), to receive a monthly or quarterly check for the interest accrued, or to have the interest credited to another checking or savings account in monthly or quarterly installments (the two latter choices would mean that interest would not compound).

Penalties for Early Withdrawal If the investor decides to draw on the funds in a CD before the maturity date is reached, he will incur a significant penalty. For example, the terms of a one-year CD may state that "the penalty is equal to 180 days' interest on the amount of principal withdrawn" and that "if the early-withdrawal penalty is greater than the interest earned, the difference will be deducted from principal." To apply those terms to a specific example, suppose that Gwen purchases a $1,000, one-year CD with a 3.6 percent APR. One month into the maturity period, however, she needs to cash out the CD because of a family emergency. At the end of one month, the CD has earned $3 in interest; but

---

JUMBO CDS

A CD (certificate of deposit) is a savings deposit that earns a higher interest rate than it would in a regular savings account because the depositor agrees not to draw on the funds for a set period of time. CDs of less than $100,000 (usually purchased by individual investors) are considered "small CDs," while those over $100,000 (usually purchased by corporations and other institutional investors) are called "large CDs," "negotiable CDs," or "jumbo CDs."

Jumbo CDs fall into four basic categories according to the type of issuer:

- Domestic CDs are issued by U.S. banks domestically (that is, within the United States).
- Eurodollar CDs or Euro CDs are dollar-denominated CDs issued by foreign banks abroad.
- Yankee CDs are issued by U.S. branches of foreign banks.
- Thrift CDs are issued by savings and loan associations. (A savings and loan is a type of financial institution that is member-owned and focuses on providing home loans).

The interest rates, risk, and popularity of the four types of jumbo CDs vary significantly.

---

the penalty for early withdrawal is the interest that she would have earned in 180 days (six months), or $18; therefore, when Gwen cashes out the CD, the total money she receives is $985 ($1,003 minus $18). Penalties provide a strong incentive for investors to leave their money in the bank until the maturity date. Still, however, an investor might be willing to accept the penalty if he or she has the opportunity to reallocate the money toward an investment that yields a greater return (such as one with a higher interest rate) or if he or she simply has an urgent need to access the funds right away.

Recent Trends

Introduced in 1994, the "callable CD" features an important variation on the traditional certificate of deposit. Like the traditional CD, the callable CD is issued by a bank, savings and loan, or credit union; is insured by the FDIC or NCUA up to $100,000; pays a specific interest rate; and carries a preset maturity period, at the end of which the investor is repaid the principal amount of the CD along with any interest earned.

Unlike the traditional CD (for which the maturity date does not exceed 5 years), however, the callable CD carries a typical maturity period of 10 to 15 years and contains a "call" feature. This entitles the bank to call (buy back) the CD at its discretion before the maturity date is reached, usually after 12, 18, or 24 months. In exchange for accepting a level of uncertainty about the CD, the investor benefits from a premium interest rate.

Usually a bank will exercise its option to call a CD if fluctuations in the economy lead to a drop in national interest rates, causing the interest rate on the CD to be higher than the going rate (meaning that the bank is paying the investor too much interest on the money it has borrowed). Conversely, a bank is likely to waive its call option and allow a CD to reach maturity if national interest rates rise above the fixed level on the CD (meaning that the bank is paying the investor less than the going rate on the money it has borrowed).

Because callable CDs are susceptible to fluctuations in market interest rates, they are not ideal for elderly investors and others who are looking for stable investments with predictable maturity periods.

$ Common Stock

What It Means

Common stock is the most prevalent form of ownership of a public company, which is a corporation that is owned by public investors. Anyone who gives money to the company in exchange for partial ownership of that company is a public investor. By contrast, a private company is owned by a small group of individuals who usually have a direct involvement in the company's operations. Ownership of a public corporation is apportioned into a set number of shares, each of which represents a fraction of ownership in the company. Stockholders, or shareholders, are those individuals who own stock in a particular company.

There are several basic characteristics of common stock that distinguish it from other forms of stock. For one, owners of common stock have the right to vote directly on matters related to the functioning of the company. Owners of preferred stock, which is a stock that guarantees the shareholder the first right to receive a dividend (a payment, usually distributed four times a year, that companies pay to shareholders, generally based on the overall performance of the company during that quarter), do not share the right to vote on company matters. Preferred stock is the second most typical form of ownership in a publicly owned company.

Capital stock generally refers to the total number of stock shares that a company is authorized to sell to investors. A company's capital stock is related to the amount of money the company is able to invest in its own growth. In other words if a company is confident in its potential for increased profitability (its capacity for earning more money), it will increase the number of shares it makes available to the public, thereby increasing its capital stock. Companies generally use additional money raised by increases in capital stock to invest in projects or equipment designed to expand their business. The term

When people buy stock, they receive partial ownership of a company and help it raise money for expansion. In this 2000 photo the president of Krispy Kreme Doughnuts presides over the initial sale of its stock to the public. *AP Images.*

capital stock is also used more broadly to refer to a company's full offering of both common and preferred stock.

Blue-chip stocks are the stocks of companies that have a reputation for continued high performance and profitability over a considerable period of time. Blue-chip stocks are considered a safe investment because they tend to pay consistent dividends, regardless of the overall state of the general economy. Because blue-chip companies tend to enjoy large earnings, blue-chip stocks tend to have a high price and to pay a more modest (but reliable) dividend. The name *blue-chip* is derived from the blue chips (generally those having the highest value) used in poker games. Blue-chip stocks are sometimes referred to as bellwether stocks.

When Did It Begin

The history of common stock remains a subject of debate among economists and scholars. In their article "The First Multinationals: Assyria circa 2000 BC," published in 1998 in *Management International Review* (a journal dedicated to the study of business management), economics professors Karl Moore and David Lewis argued that the practice of issuing common stock originated with the Assyrians in the year 2000 BC. The Assyrians inhabited Mesopotamia, a region in the Middle East that lies in present-day Iraq, Syria, and Turkey.

The first-known printed share or stock certificate, a document demonstrating legal proof of ownership of shares in a corporation, was issued in the year 1606. It was issued by the Dutch East India Company, a multinational corporation (a company that oversees business in more than one country) founded in the Netherlands in 1602. A few of these original Dutch East India Company share certificates still exist.

More Detailed Information

Shareholders who own common stock have the unique right to vote on issues relating to the company. Each share is worth one vote, so the number of votes held by individual shareholders is directly related to the number of shares of common stock they own. Shareholders owning common stock vote to elect the corporation's board of directors (the group responsible for making decisions regarding the operation of the company), to help determine the company's goals and objectives, and to approve stock splits. A stock split occurs when a company decides to divide each outstanding, or already owned, share of stock into two or more shares; it is accompanied by a proportional lowering of the value of each share. For example, if a company decides to split its stock in two, a shareholder who previously owned 100 shares of stock at $10 per share will now own 200 shares of stock worth $5 per share. A stock split does not alter the overall value of a shareholder's stake in the company. By splitting their stock and sub-

THE FIRST PRINTED SHARE CERTIFICATE

Owners of common stock (the most common form of ownership in a company) receive share certificates, which are engraved documents demonstrating proof of their share in the company's ownership. According to historians the oldest known share certificate was issued by the Dutch East India Company in 1606. Founded in 1602, the Dutch East India Company was the first multinational corporation (a company with corporate holdings in more than one nation) in history, and it quickly became a powerful force in overseas trade. A copy of an early Dutch East India Company share certificate currently resides at the Amsterdam Stock Exchange, a center for commercial trading activities in the Netherlands. By the eighteenth century the issuing of share certificates had become standard practice, and it is now required of all corporations when selling shares of common stock.

sequently lowering share prices, companies attempt to attract new shareholders.

There are several other distinctive features of common stock. One involves the issuing of a share certificate, which serves as proof of the shareholder's equity, or ownership, in the company. Secondly, shareholders who own common stock have the right to examine all documents relating to the operation of the company, including bookkeeping accounts, which maintain a record of all the company's financial transactions. Holders of common stock also have what is known as a preemptive right, which entitles them to purchase additional shares of common stock in proportion to the amount of stock they already own before any additional shares of the stock becomes available to the general public. Additionally, owners of common stock receive a pro rata, or proportional, share of corporate dividends. When a corporation goes out of business, however, owners of common stock are the last to be compensated. They must wait until the company's debts (monies owed) have been repaid and the owners of preferred stock have received compensation before they receive their share of whatever funds remain.

Recent Trends

One of the most important gauges of common stock levels is the Dow Jones Industrial Average (often called the Dow), an index measuring the performance of 30 leading American companies through an analysis of their stock value. While the Dow measures all forms of stock, it consists predominantly of common stock and is therefore a reliable indicator of the general performance of common stock at any given time. The Standard and Poor's 500 (S&P 500) index includes 500 large corporations and is often seen as a more reliable indicator of the performance of the stock market.

In mid-2006, after several months of low or moderate growth, common stock prices began to rise steadily at the same time that the price of oil, which had reached record high levels earlier in the year, began to decline. As oil prices went down, investors had more money to invest in the stock market, and the Dow Jones industrial average began to rise, exceeding 12,500 (in broad terms, the sum of the stock prices of the 30 companies that comprise the Dow) for the first time ever on December 27, 2006.

STOCK MARKET

What It Means

Stock market is a term referring to a place where buyers and sellers of stocks come together. It may also be used to refer collectively to all the places in the world, some of which are real buildings and some of which exist mainly in computer networks, where stocks are bought and sold.

A stock is a share of ownership in a company. If you buy one share of stock in Wal-Mart, you literally own one tiny portion of that enormous company. As a shareholder in Wal-Mart, you can expect to profit as the company profits, because your stock will most likely increase in value when the company performs well. But your stock also stands to lose value when Wal-Mart does not perform well. Based on your predictions about how Wal-Mart will perform in the future, you may want to buy more stock in Wal-Mart to make more money or sell your stock in Wal-Mart to avoid losing money. To buy or sell your Wal-Mart stock, you might contact a stockbroker (someone authorized to place orders for the purchase and sale of stocks) by phone, and the broker would then forward your order to someone who would carry out the transaction on the floor of the New York Stock Exchange (NYSE), located on Wall Street in New York City, where stock in the largest American companies is bought and sold.

There are numerous other regional stock exchanges in the United States, but the most prominent domestic stock exchange other than the NYSE is the NASDAQ, a virtual exchange (this means that all trading is done by computer) specializing in smaller U.S. companies. There are, additionally, stock exchanges in all developed countries and in many developing countries. In addition to the NYSE and the NASDAQ, the world's largest stock exchanges are in the United Kingdom, Japan, France, Germany, and India.

The stock market is where shares in publicly owned companies are bought and sold. Trading on the stock market can be extremely hectic, as shown in this image from the floor of the New York Stock Exchange. *AP Images.*

When Did It Begin

The first phenomena resembling stock markets probably arose in thirteenth–fifteenth century Italy, when leading citizens of city-states like Venice, Florence, and Genoa were forced to pay a portion of the debt incurred by local governments and the Catholic Church in their efforts to provide for defense and the maintenance of trade routes. These shares of debt collected interest (a fee paid to someone who loans money to someone else), and because of this, the owners of shares could expect to make a profit. Shares in the public debt therefore acquired value, and the governing authorities allowed people to buy and sell these shares. The government and Church were providing people with a way to make money at the same time that those people were paying the institutions' debts; thus, an effective way of financing large projects was discovered.

This model was later adopted by businesses who wanted to raise money for expansion and other pricey ventures. In 1602 the Dutch East India Company not only decided to sell stock in its company, it created for that purpose what is generally considered the world's first continuously operating stock market, the Amsterdam Stock Exchange. Once the value of stocks in the Dutch East India Company became widely recognized, stockholders could use their shares as collateral for loans. (Collateral is any item or items of value that you offer as proof of your ability to repay a loan.) This gave rise to many of the financial intricacies of present-day stock trading, such as options and derivatives, which are essentially complex ways of buying stock, and accordingly to the specialized investors that characterize developed stock markets.

The forerunner to the New York Stock Exchange was created in 1792, when 24 brokers agreed to deal only with one another in the buying and selling of the U.S. government's debt. The London Stock Exchange came into being in 1801 and became the world's largest and most important stock market. It was instrumental in raising the capital necessary for England to defeat Napoleon, the French leader who attempted to conquer much of Europe in the early nineteenth century, and many countries attempted to copy the London exchange's success. Stock markets appeared in most European capitals or other large cities. World War I (1914–17) brought about declines in the European stock markets, while the NYSE expanded in the following years. This growth slowed dramatically in 1929, when a stock market crash signaled the beginning of the Great Depression.

More Detailed Information

The need to raise money to pay for business ventures remains a principle reason for a company to sell stock, and the promise of large increases in the value of a stock is the primary reason for an individual or institution to buy stock. The stock market is a crucial factor in economic growth on a large scale, because it allows businesses to grow more rapidly than they could if they were funded privately, and because it allows investors to make larger amounts of money than they could by placing their money in bank accounts.

For a business to be listed (to have its stock made available for trading) on a stock exchange, it has to meet certain requirements. Each stock exchange establishes its own requirements, usually relating to a business's financial soundness and the amount of capital (money and other assets) that it has, and when a company meets these requirements, it can choose to go public on one of the world's stock exchanges. Going public refers to the transition that a business makes from being a privately owned organization to being a business owned by the public, or stockholders. When a company makes its stock available for purchase for the first time, this is called an initial public offering (IPO). Once it has sold all shares of its stock, a business has access to the money raised in this process. The leaders of the company are no longer answerable only to themselves at this point. They must answer to shareholders, the true owners of the company.

In the stock market prices fluctuate according to the law of supply and demand. As demand for a stock increases, its price increases, and vice versa. Demand is created or lessened for a stock, of course, when a company is known to be profitable or known to be struggling. Demand can additionally be affected based on any positive or negative news about a stock. Stock markets are thus vulnerable to human psychology. For instance, when large numbers of people get enthusiastic about a stock and decide to buy it, they can greatly inflate the stock price in a short period of time.

Sometimes the price of a stock rises so high that it loses its correlation to company earnings. This happened on a large scale in the late 1920s and also in the late 1990s. The 1929 stock market crash, like the lesser and more gradual crash that occurred in 2001–02, started when investors widely understood that the inflated value of stock prices could not last. Investors sold off stocks in large numbers, stock prices dropped across the market, and many people who had invested heavily in stocks lost a great deal of money.

While the stock market offers investors the potential to multiply their money more quickly than they might be able to do by other means, it is also inherently risky. Most financial professionals advise investors to resist the temptation to make quick profits. Those who invest with an eye toward long-term profit often balance investment in risky stocks (frequently these are stocks in untested companies, or companies specializing in new technologies) with investment in larger companies less subject to volatility. Since World War II the U.S. stock market has increased in value by an average of 10 percent a year, in spite of dramatic fluctuations from year to year and decade to decade.

WHAT IS WITH ALL THAT SCREAMING?

One of the most common images associated with the stock market in America is that of the floor of the New York Stock Exchange (NYSE), where the goings-on are dramatic and odd enough to have been featured in numerous Hollywood movies. On the floor, in both movies and real life, disorderly bunches of men and women scream and wave their hands at one another, barking out orders for the buying and selling of stocks. This is called an "open outcry" system of stock trading; the traders on the floor are carrying out orders that have been communicated to them through brokers, the people with whom most investors have traditionally dealt when they want to buy or sell stock. The open outcry system is more organized than it looks. Those members of the NYSE interested in buying or selling a particular stock gather at an appointed place on the floor, where their transactions are facilitated by a person called a specialist (who acts essentially like an auctioneer).

This form of trading, of course, relies heavily on the expert ability of the participants and is subject to human error. Although this used to be the only way to trade stocks, today the NYSE is one of the last stock exchanges that conducts a substantial part of its transactions in this way. An increasing amount of NYSE trades, like trades conducted on other stock exchanges inside and outside the United States, are made by computer. The proponents of computer trading argue that it is faster, more efficient, and less open to manipulation by brokers and other insiders.

People are still able to invest in government debt as well. They do so usually by buying items commonly called government bonds, which are traded not in the stock market but in the bond market. The bond market includes other types of bonds in addition to government bonds and works in a similar way to stock markets. One key difference between stocks and government bonds is that the value of government bonds is largely risk-free, meaning that as long as the issuing country itself continues to exist and is not in a severe financial crisis, the bondholder can expect repayment. Bonds can generally be expected to increase in value at a steady rate, but they are unable to match the explosive growth sometimes offered by stocks.

Recent Trends

A period of sustained stock-price increases is called a bull market. During bull markets, investors make money rapidly. Between 1991 and 2000, the United States experienced the longest and most vigorous bull market in its history.

The performance of the U.S. stock market is most frequently measured according to the Dow Jones In-dustrial Average, a statistic that conveys the combined stock prices of the 30 top companies in the country. In 1991 the Dow, as it is commonly called, reached the 3000-point mark for the first time in its history. By 1995 the Dow had passed 4000 points, and by 1998 it had surpassed the 9000-point mark. In 2000 the Dow peaked at more than 11,700 points, and many analysts seemed to think that, despite the unprecedented growth of the stock market over the decade, the bull market might go on forever.

However, a number of unforeseen factors, including irrational inflation of stocks in technology companies and unethical accounting practices that made some companies appear to be more profitable than they really were, triggered large-scale declines in the stock market beginning in 2000. The already vulnerable economy received another tremendous blow with the terrorist attacks of September 11, 2001, which forced the New York Stock Exchange to close for six days (the longest closure since the Great Depression) and which further undermined investor confidence in the stock market. These conditions created what is called a bear market, or a period during which stock prices generally decrease. By late 2002 the Dow had returned to pre–1998 levels, bottoming out at 7,286.27. It was not until 2006 that the Dow returned to the level it had reached at its peak in 2000.

NEW YORK STOCK EXCHANGE

What It Means

The New York Stock Exchange (NYSE) is the oldest stock exchange in the United States. It is also the largest stock exchange in the world, in terms of the value of stocks that are bought and sold there.

Stocks are shares of ownership in a company. By selling stocks, a company is able to amass money that it can use to expand its operations. If the company prospers, shares of its stock rise in value, and stockholders profit. If a company struggles, the value of its shares declines, and stockholders lose money. At a stock exchange, people buy and sell stocks, either through intermediaries known as stockbrokers or via computers, hoping to get rid of unprofitable stocks and acquire profitable ones. There are numerous stock exchanges in the United States, and there are large stock exchanges in most developed countries.

The NYSE is an exchange specializing in the stock of large companies. All stock exchanges have minimum requirements that companies must meet to be listed (to be allowed to sell stock on the exchange). A company must prove that its earnings rise above a certain level, that it can issue a certain amount of stock, that it has a certain amount of capital (money, equipment, property, and other resources for doing business), and that it is otherwise in good financial condition. As of 2007 there were more than 2,700 stocks listed on the NYSE.

The New York Stock Exchange, or NYSE, is a place where people buy and sell stocks in publicly owned companies. As the largest stock market in the world, the NYSE has a very busy trading floor. *AP Images.*

The NYSE is located at the corner of Wall and Broad streets in New York City. Most other prominent stock exchanges have been thoroughly computerized, but many NYSE trades still take place in person on the floor of the exchange. To trade at the NYSE, a person must be a member of the exchange (or the representative of a member). The number of memberships is limited to 1,366, but memberships can be bought and sold. The highest price ever paid for a membership, as of 2007, was $4 million.

When Did It Begin

After the Revolutionary War (1775–83) the U.S. government was in debt to those people who had financed the war. It needed to raise money to pay back these creditors. In 1790, as other governments before it had done, the U.S. government began selling shares of its debt in order to raise money. This meant that a person could loan the government money to cover a portion of the nation's debt, and in return for doing so, the government would pay him or her a fee, called interest, periodically for the length of the loan.

Instead of this being a simple loan (where the original borrower would have to be paid back), the purchaser of debt was buying what is called a security, a contract that is declared to have value and that can be traded. Because these securities collected interest, a person could gain money simply by holding them. People began to buy and sell government securities from each other, and this led to the development of a securities market. As with any market, the forces of supply and demand were at work (in this case, the quantity of shares for sale versus the number of people who wanted to buy them), causing the prices of securities to fluctuate. This arrangement allowed the government to raise the money it needed while also creating wealth-building opportunities that had not existed before.

By 1792 people in New York City could buy five different securities. Three of these were forms of government debt, and two were shares of stock in banks. It was in this year that 24 businessmen met on Wall Street in New York City, under a buttonwood tree, to discuss arrangements for the formal buying and selling of securities. They agreed to buy and sell securities with each other on a commission basis (people who wanted to buy and sell stocks would place orders with these men, who would charge a fee for their services). The so-called Buttonwood Agreement laid the foundations for what became known, in 1817, as the New York Stock and Exchange Board. In 1863 the organization changed its name to the New York Stock Exchange.

More Detailed Information

In the early stages of the New York exchange, its members carried out trades on behalf of investors at designated times. The exchange's president would read out a list of stocks that could be traded, one at a time, and traders would buy and sell stocks as they were called out. There was a morning trading session and an afternoon trading session. In 1871, however, to facilitate more efficient investment, the NYSE moved to a system of continuous trading. Under this system so-called specialists, who orchestrated sales of a particular stock, were posted at a specific spot on the floor of the stock exchange, and members who had orders to buy or sell that stock went to that spot at any point during trading hours to conduct their transaction. This form of continuous trading has remained standard practice at the NYSE ever since.

The buying and selling that occurs on the floor of the NYSE is only the last stage of the trading process. A trade begins with an individual's desire to buy or sell one or more stocks on the NYSE. This person may be anywhere in the world.

As an illustration of the stock-trading process, imagine an individual investor, Kate, who lives in Florida and wants to buy up to $1,000 worth of stock in the computer company IBM, which is traded on the NYSE. Kate has researched IBM's past performance and potential for

THE GROWTH OF THE NEW YORK STOCK EXCHANGE

During the first half of the nineteenth century, the New York Stock Exchange (called the New York Stock and Exchange Board at that time) grew as a result of brisk trading in railroad stock. New railroads were being built all over the United States, and the enormous amount of money involved in constructing a railroad could be raised only by selling stock (shares of ownership) in railroad companies. The exchange also played a key role in the industrial growth of the United States after the Civil War (1861–65). During this time the stock exchange mobilized money to help the economy grow extremely fast. Despite the rapid growth of the American economy, though, New York was still a financial center of only secondary importance. London was the world's financial capital and boasted the world's largest stock exchange.

World War I (1914–18), however, devastated Europe without severely damaging the U.S. economy. In fact, the American stock market boomed in the decade after the war, placing New York City and the New York Stock Exchange (NYSE) in a position of primary importance in world economics. Although the NYSE and the American economy were crippled by the Great Depression (a worldwide financial decline) in the 1930s, World War II (1939–45) and its aftermath brought boom times to the United States again, while Europe continued to suffer economically. In the postwar years the NYSE fully eclipsed other stock exchanges, and its premier status among stock markets has not been seriously contested since then.

future profits, and she believes that buying stock in the company today is a good idea. She calls her stockbroker, Joe, who also lives in Florida but is affiliated with Merrill Lynch, a financial-services firm that is a member of the NYSE and is therefore entitled to carry out trades on the exchange floor. Joe agrees with Kate's analysis that IBM is a good bet, and he tells her that the market price for IBM that day should be about $95 per share. Kate authorizes Joe to spend $950 to buy 100 shares on her behalf. Joe enters Kate's order into his computer, sending it to a Merrill Lynch broker on the floor of the NYSE.

Fred, a Merrill Lynch floor broker at the NYSE, receives the order (either as a computer printout or on a handheld computer), which informs him that he needs to buy 100 shares of IBM stock. He goes over to the spot on the trading floor that is reserved for the buying and selling of IBM stock. There he finds another floor broker, Roger, who is looking to sell IBM stock for his own client. Fred and Roger agree on a price, facilitated by Tina, the IBM specialist on the floor responsible for ensuring that trades are carried out fairly. Tina records the sale, and the terms of the sale are transmitted to Merrill Lynch as well as to Roger's brokerage firm.

At this point Kate's order is completed. She owns 100 shares of IBM stock, and she has the potential to profit or lose money as the value of IBM shares fluctuates. She has to pay the total value of her stock purchase, plus a commission that goes to the brokers, within three days.

Recent Trends

Today the NYSE is unique among the major world stock exchanges in its continued reliance on person-to-person trading on the floor of the stock exchange. On the other most prominent American stock exchange, the National Association of Securities Dealers Automated Quotations (NASDAQ), all trades occur entirely within computer systems. Most of the world's other large stock exchanges, such as the London Stock Exchange and the Tokyo Stock Exchange, operate almost exclusively through electronic trading.

The NYSE has increasingly integrated electronic trading with its traditional specialist-based trading on the floor. As of 2007 roughly 50 percent of stock trades on the NYSE were made electronically. The exchange did not plan, however, to abandon person-to-person trades completely. Instead, it intended to remain a hybrid exchange, where some transactions are computerized and others are conducted in person.

NASDAQ

What It Means

The NASDAQ stock market is the United States' largest electronic stock exchange. A stock is a portion of a company's ownership that can be purchased and sold. The value of a stock rises or falls depending on the company's performance. This means that people generally want to buy the stocks of companies that perform well and sell the stocks of companies that do not perform well.

Stock exchanges (also called stock markets) are places where the buyers and sellers of stocks come together to make trades. Some stock exchanges, such as the New York Stock Exchange (NYSE), provide physical locations where trading occurs. NASDAQ trades, on the other hand, are processed by computers.

The NASDAQ is commonly associated, in the minds of many, with technology stocks. While many older, more established companies list their stock (make their stock available for trading) on the NYSE, many of the top younger companies, such as Microsoft, Apple, and Google, have chosen to list their stock on the NASDAQ.

When Did It Begin

The NASDAQ stock market opened for trading on February 8, 1971. NASDAQ was originally an acronym for National Association of Securities Dealers Automated Quotations, but the exchange has over time severed its connection to the association of securities dealers that founded it. (A security is a contract that is assigned value

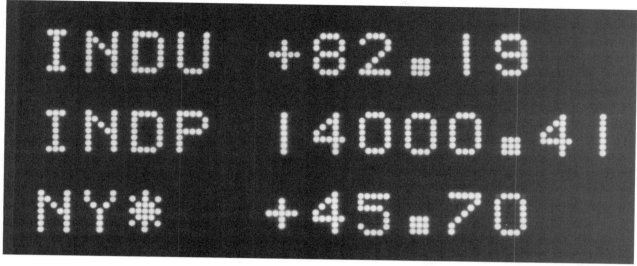

The NASDAQ, an electronic stock market where people purchase shares in various businesses, is commonly associated with newer companies in the technology industry. Shifts in the value of the NASDAQ and other stock markets are often displayed on an electronic board. *Mario Tama/Getty Images.*

so that it may be bought or sold. Stocks are a type of security, as are bonds, which typically represent money that citizens have loaned to the government.) NASDAQ was the world's first electronic stock exchange. Prior to its introduction, stock trades around the world had to be conducted at a physical location where brokers (people who are authorized to make trades on a given stock exchange) met to negotiate the orders of the buyers and sellers that they represented.

Although the NASDAQ's trades were always processed electronically, in the exchange's early years investors still had to use the telephone to place orders for trades. During a stock market crash in 1987 (a crash occurs when many stocks lose value at once, causing a stock exchange to lose a large amount of total value), the people who facilitated trades on the NASDAQ stopped accepting phone calls from small investors, preventing these individuals from trading stocks that were losing value quickly. In response to this breakdown of the NASDAQ system, the exchange established an electronic method for placing orders, allowing individual investors to trade stocks by computer.

More Detailed Information

The fact that the NASDAQ is an electronic stock exchange does not mean that there is no human involvement in the trading process. In fact, the terms of all trades are established by market makers, companies that pay for the right to buy and sell one particular stock on the NASDAQ. They are responsible, each day, for determining the buying and selling prices of that stock. They post a price at which they will be willing to buy the stock and a slightly higher price at which they will be willing to sell that same stock. The difference in the two prices, called the spread, allows them to make a profit.

Market makers enter the buy and sell prices for individual stocks into NASDAQ computers, and investors enter their orders to buy or sell stocks into NASDAQ computers. When investors list buying and selling prices that are in synch with the prices listed by market makers, computers process these orders.

In traditional stock trading, such as the trading that occurs at the NYSE, the people who function as market makers are called specialists. Specialists stand at a certain location on the floor of the exchange and personally process buying and selling orders. But trading using a NASDAQ market maker and trading using a NYSE specialist are different in another important way. The NASDAQ is what is called a dealer exchange, while the NYSE is what is called an auction exchange. On the NASDAQ, market makers are dealers of certain stocks. Investors buy stocks from market makers and sell them to market makers. On the NYSE, specialists function as auctioneers. They set prices so that buyers and sellers can make trades with one another.

Older, well-established, reliable companies, such as Ford Motor Company, General Electric, and IBM, typically list their stocks on the NYSE, whose history dates to 1792 and is closely linked to the rise of the American economy in the nineteenth and twentieth centuries. The NASDAQ, by contrast, typically attracts newer companies with smaller initial assets (the money used to start a business) but large potential for growth. Microsoft, Apple, and Google, all among the United States' most important corporations in the early twenty-first century, listed their stocks on the NASDAQ. Companies that go public (that allow investors to buy and sell their stock)

NO LONGER JUST A STOCK MARKET

In 2000 NASDAQ ceased being a private, nonprofit stock exchange and became a public, for-profit corporation called the NASDAQ Stock Market, Inc. Like any other business, NASDAQ provides products. The stock-trading service is its central product; others include a variety of index funds (which allow investors to purchase stock in numerous companies at once) and sets of data about stocks and companies. Investors may judge the value of those products and NASDAQ's future prospects and buy or sell the company's stock accordingly. (Incidentally, the New York Stock Exchange followed suit in 2006, becoming a public company whose stock can be bought and sold.) Where can investors buy and sell NASDAQ stock? On the NASDAQ stock market, of course.

therefore often consider how they want to be perceived (as stable and reliable or as daring and innovative) before deciding whether to list their stock on the NYSE or the NASDAQ.

Because of its concentration of newer and less stable companies, the NASDAQ is generally considered more volatile, as a whole, than the NYSE. As of 2007 the NASDAQ was listing the stock of more companies than the NYSE (roughly 3,200 versus roughly 2,700). The number of trades conducted on the NASDAQ each day is also usually larger than the number conducted on the NYSE, but the NYSE remains the world's largest stock market in terms of the value of the stock that is bought and sold there. Together these two stock exchanges are among the most important elements of the U.S. economy.

Recent Trends

For most of the 1990s, there was a bull market for stocks in the United States. A bull market is a period when the stock market as a whole is gaining value and investors are consistently making profits. The 1990s bull market was strongly tied to the rapid growth, starting in approximately 1995, of Internet-related businesses. The general public was becoming increasingly aware of how the Internet operated, and businesses rushed to capitalize on the possibilities for making profits online. This created an environment in which new companies were given huge amounts of financial backing to pursue Internet-related businesses (often called dot-coms).

Many of these companies listed their stock on the NASDAQ, and in some cases dot-com stock prices rose enormously in value even though the companies did little to justify the confidence in their future performance. More and more people rushed to capitalize on the huge increases in technology stock prices. These investors were

making unwise stock purchases, betting on stock price increases rather than on actual company performance. The result was what became known, in retrospect, as the dot-com bubble.

A bubble is a period of unsustainable stock-market growth fueled by excess optimism on the part of companies and investors. Stock-market bubbles burst when it becomes clear that the optimism was inaccurate. In the case of the dot-com bubble, this began to happen in the spring of 2000, when the total value of stocks traded on the NASDAQ peaked and began to decline. The NASDAQ perpetuated the dot-com bubble more than any other stock market, and it paid the heaviest price. As of 2007 the total value of the stocks traded on the NASDAQ remained less than half of what it had been before the bubble burst.

$ Bond

What It Means

A bond is a type of investment that represents money loaned to a government or corporation. Local, state, and national governments often need to borrow money to pay for the services and projects they oversee, such as road construction, public schools, and emergency assistance; and corporations often need to borrow money to expand their operations. Because these organizations and the sums of money they require are so large, they cannot simply ask a bank for a loan the way individuals or small businesses can. Instead, they raise money by issuing bonds, which are essentially IOUs. This allows them to draw from a wide pool of investors to finance their projects. To attract funds the bond-issuing organization (the borrower) agrees to pay interest (a fee for the use of borrowed money) to investors (the lenders). Bonds pay a fixed yearly interest rate (often called the bond's "coupon") for a set number of years. At the end of this period the bond matures, and the bond issuer returns the original amount paid by the investor (this amount is called the bond's "face value").

For example, say that a company or government issued 10-year bonds at a 10 percent interest rate and offered these bonds in units with a face value of $1,000 each. This would mean that an investor who paid $1,000 for one of these bonds could expect to collect $100 a year for 10 years. Once the 10-year-period was up, the bond-issuing organization would return the $1,000 face value of the bond to the investor.

When Did It Begin

Bonds date to at least thirteenth- to fifteenth-century Italy, when local governments and the Catholic Church sometimes raised money from, and paid interest to, prominent private citizens. The contracts representing the borrowers' debt obligations began to be seen as valuable in their own right, since they represented the potential to earn money in the future. Thus, markets (systems allowing buyers and sellers to come together) for these early forms of bonds developed. In other words, a person who lent money to a government or the Church could sell the contract entitling him to future interest payments to another person. This occurs in more complex form on the bond markets of today.

In 1693 King William III of England issued bonds to nobles in London. These are generally considered the first modern bonds, because they represent the first examples of bonds whose purchasers were guaranteed to be repaid. Previously bonds had been more akin to private loans in which an element of trust had to be present for a lender to feel confident in purchasing shares of debt. Because the British Parliament had gained enough power to sufficiently balance the king's power with that of private citizens, William III had a legal obligation to pay back the purchasers of those 1693 bonds.

More Detailed Information

Some people buy bonds directly from their issuers. This is called buying bonds on the primary market. On the pri-

A bond sold by an unstable company, called a junk bond, is a high-risk investment because it is uncertain whether the company will be able to pay it back. One of the biggest financial scandals in U.S. history occurred in 1989 when Michael Milken, the infamous "junk-bond king" of Wall Street, was indicted on 98 felony charges of investment fraud and other financial crimes. *AP Images.*

mary market, bonds sell for their face value. Some people buy bonds on the primary market, collect interest until those bonds mature, and then receive their original investment back. It is not necessary to do this, though. There is a secondary market for bonds allowing bond holders to sell their bonds at any time. The price of bonds in the secondary market does not necessarily match their face values. This is because the supply (the quantity of bonds sellers want to sell at a given price) or demand (the quantity of bonds buyers want to buy at a given price) for certain bonds changes depending on financial conditions.

One of the main reasons that the price of bonds fluctuates is that interest rates in the economy change. Basic interest rates are highly influenced by central banks such as the U.S. Federal Reserve System (often called the Fed). If, for example, a corporation issues 10-year bonds that pay 10 percent interest today, and then a few months down the road the Fed works to raise the basic interest rates in the economy so that corporations begin issuing bonds at 11 percent, then the value of those previously issued bonds will fall, since no one would choose to collect 10 percent interest when she could be collecting 11 percent interest. On the other hand, if the Fed lowered interest rates so that bonds began paying 9 percent, those bonds paying 10-percent interest would become very attractive to investors, and their price would rise.

It is important for investors to consider background information about the issuer of a bond before making a purchase. Bonds are generally classified according to their issuer and the level of risk that the issuer represents.

Bonds issued by the U.S. government, commonly called government bonds, are considered largely risk-free, since the government is not likely to collapse overnight, and it can always collect taxes to pay back bond holders. There are three basic kinds of government bonds: Treasury bills, which mature in less than one year; Treasury notes, which mature in one to 10 years; and Treasury bonds, which mature in more than 10 years. Because they mature in such a short time, Treasury bills are not technically considered bonds, but they are issued in the same way and have the same characteristics as bonds, aside from the length of their maturity. Bonds issued by other stable governments are also considered extremely safe investments. This is not the case with many poorer and undeveloped countries, since these countries are often politically and economically unstable. The possibility exists that such a country will be unable to pay bondholders.

Slightly more risky than U.S. bonds are municipal bonds, which are issued by governments and government agencies below the state level. In addition to state governments and government departments, cities, counties, school districts, and public airports are among the many entities that might issue bonds to pay for projects or services. One reason municipal bonds are attractive to investors is that, unlike other bonds, the earnings that

INVESTMENT AND AGING

Bonds, which are loans of money to a government or company that pay the purchaser a fixed rate of interest (a fee for the use of borrowed money), typically serve a different investment purpose than stocks, which are shares of company ownership that gain value when a company prospers and lose value when a company struggles. Stocks typically offer higher returns on a buyer's initial investment, especially if the investor can wait out the ups and downs of the market over the long term, whereas bonds pay a fixed amount of money regardless of wider economic conditions.

Most financial experts therefore recommend that investors focus on stocks while they are young and then devote an increasing portion of their investments to bonds as they age. The stock market is a good way to increase wealth, especially over the long term, but it cannot generally be counted on for a steady income from year to year. After accumulating wealth in the stock market during one's prime working years, an investor would ideally focus on bonds upon retirement, using that accumulated wealth to generate a consistent income from the interest rates on bonds.

come from most munis, as they are called, are exempt from both federal and state income taxes.

Companies are more likely to go bankrupt or become unable to pay bond holders than are national, state, or local governments, so corporate bonds carry a higher level of risk. They also offer the potential for higher returns, however, because of this risk. Corporate bonds can be categorized as short-term (these mature in less than five years), intermediate (five to 12 years), or long-term (over 12 years).

The risk level among corporate bonds varies depending on the issuing company, and in general, the riskier bonds pay the highest interest rates. There are three major companies in the United States (Moody's, Standard & Poor's, and Fitch) that rate corporate bonds according to the company's likelihood of defaulting on its debts. The highest-rated bonds are those issued by so-called "blue-chip" companies, the largest and most stable corporations in the world. Bonds issued by less-established companies are rated lower. In addition to detailed rankings, the three bond-rating firms place bonds in one of two categories: investment or junk grade. Junk bonds are bonds issued by unproven companies, or companies experiencing financial problems. People who purchase junk bonds accept the risk of not being paid in exchange for high interest rates they will be paid if the company is able to continue meeting its obligations to lenders.

There is also a form of bond that does not conform to the basic model of paying a face value and then collecting interest until maturity. These bonds are called zero-coupon bonds, meaning that they pay no interest. Instead, they are sold at a steep discount off their face value, they typically take a long time to mature, and they pay face value upon maturity. They allow people to make long-term investments (for college savings or retirement, for example) at a low initial cost. Zero-coupon bonds are issued by all levels of government and by companies.

Recent Trends

In the early twenty-first century, bonds had a much lower profile among the general public than did stocks. Whereas bonds are shares of government or company debt, stocks are shares of company ownership. Instead of paying a fixed rate of interest, as bonds do, stocks generally gain value when a company prospers and lose value when a company struggles. This tends to allow for more fluctuation in stock prices than in bond prices, and it gives stock holders the chance to make more money more quickly than bond holders. When investors can make big profits in the stock market, bonds are generally less attractive investments.

Bonds were particularly unattractive to many investors during the 1990s, when the U.S. stock market experienced its biggest boom in history. Though the stock market crashed in 2000 and lost 40 percent of its value over the next two years, most investors continued to be more interested in the stock market than in the bond market.

$ Mutual Fund

What It Means

A mutual fund is a form of investment that involves pooling the money of many people and using it to buy numerous stocks, bonds, or other securities. Stocks are shares of company ownership that generally gain value when the company prospers and lose value when the company struggles. Bonds are a way of lending money to the government or a company; the holder of a bond is paid interest (a fee for the use of borrowed money) by the government or company. Stocks and bonds are two among numerous kinds of securities. A security is any contract that can be assigned value, bought, and sold. Securities are traded on various financial markets, the places or computer systems that allow buyers and sellers to come together and make exchanges.

If you believe that Coca-Cola is going to experience great success in the next several years, you might take your money out of the bank and buy Coca-Cola stock through the New York Stock Exchange (the financial market where Coca-Cola stock is traded), hoping that your savings will grow as a result. If Coca-Cola stock does not increase in value, however, you lose money. Because even the most knowledgeable investors cannot perfectly predict the future, it is generally advisable to buy more than one form of security at a time to insure yourself

A mutual fund, which pools together money, makes it easier for investors to hold shares in more than one company at the same time, thereby increasing their chances of receiving a return on their investment. In this photo a mutual fund manager reviews economic data. © *Najlah Feanny/Corbis.*

against inevitable losses. For example, in addition to Coca-Cola, you might buy stock in Microsoft, Nike, and General Motors, hoping that if any of the stocks lose value, the other stocks will gain value and balance out your losses. You might additionally buy bonds from the U.S. government, since the government guarantees you regular payments of interest. Thus, you would have ways of earning money in the financial markets even if some of your investment decisions turned out to be bad ones. Ideally you would spread your money among dozens, hundreds, or even thousands of investments that work together to ensure you of profits while protecting you from losses. This is called diversifying your investments.

Mutual funds are an easy, effective way of diversifying. The average person interested in investing may lack the in-depth knowledge of the financial world that the most successful investors have, and he or she may be uncertain about choosing individual stocks, let alone figuring out how to choose and balance dozens of them in order to minimize risk while still making a sizable profit. In such a case mutual funds can be a sensible alternative. Mutual funds are managed by experts who have thorough knowledge of financial markets and who decide

how best to allocate their investors' pooled money. Rather than researching financial markets for years and spending hours, days, and weeks buying and selling individual stocks and bonds yourself, you can easily diversify your money by purchasing shares of a mutual fund. A share of a mutual fund gains or loses value in proportion to the gains or losses of all of the different securities that the fund owns.

When Did It Begin

The first mutual fund in the United States was the Massachusetts Investors Trust, founded in 1924 with a pool of $50,000. By the end of its first year of operation, the fund had approximately 200 shareholders and $392,000. But this promising start for the industry was derailed by the Great Depression, the severe economic crisis that gripped the world economy in the 1930s.

In response to the Depression, with the intent of preventing future economic crises, numerous new financial regulations were passed at the national level. Among these laws, the Securities Acts of 1933 and 1934 specified some of the basic guidelines that mutual funds would be required to follow, and the Investment Company Act of

MUTUAL FUND FAMILIES

Mutual funds are businesses that pool the money of many investors and buy numerous shares of stocks (shares of company ownership, which gain or lose value as the company prospers or struggles), bonds (shares of government or company debt, which collect interest, a fee paid to money lenders), and other securities (a security is any contract, such as a stock or bond, that can be assigned value, bought, and sold). In the United States many mutual funds are part of a larger group of funds called a fund family. A fund family is essentially a brand name. Some prominent fund families in the United States are Vanguard, American Funds, and Fidelity. These fund families offer numerous different funds, each of which has different investing goals and different strengths and weaknesses. There are several hundred fund families in the United States and more than 8,000 individual mutual funds.

1940 more fully established the ground rules for the industry. The mutual funds of today are still governed by those 1940 guidelines.

By the 1960s the mutual-fund industry, composed of around 270 funds, had become a vibrant part of the overall economy. The popularity of mutual funds grew greatly as a result of changes to the U.S. tax code implemented in 1975. The changes made it possible for people to make tax-free investments for their retirement, thereby encouraging millions of people to invest money in stocks, bonds, and other securities. Since mutual funds allow easy diversification and are accessible to ordinary people, they became one of the most popular ways of investing for retirement during this time. Retirement investing remains at the heart of the mutual-fund industry.

More Detailed Information

Though mutual funds simplify investing in some important ways, the process of choosing a mutual fund can be complicated. By 2006 there were more than 8,000 mutual funds in the United States (worldwide, there were more than 60,000). This means that there were roughly as many mutual funds as there were stocks available for purchase in the United States. Additionally, there are numerous different types of mutual funds, each of which has a distinct purpose and approach to investing.

Most mutual funds are focused on the stock market and consist of hundreds of different stocks. Stock funds, also called equity funds, can be classified in a number of ways. One way they can be classified is according to their strategy: as growth funds, value funds, or blend funds. Growth funds are mutual funds that own stock in companies expected to grow quickly and produce large gains in stock value. This is the riskiest class of mutual funds. Value funds invest in older, established companies, es-

pecially those whose value may not be fully reflected by their stock prices (in other words, those whose stock prices are lower than they should be, given the company's potential for future growth). Value funds are not as risky as growth funds, but they also do not offer the chance for the big profits that growth funds sometimes generate. Blend funds mix aspects of growth and value funds.

Mutual funds can also be classified according to the value of the companies on which they are focused. Large-cap funds invest in so-called "blue-chip" companies whose value (as measured by the number of stock shares in that company times the value of each share) is at the top range among all companies. Mid-cap funds allocate their money to the stock of companies valued in the middle range of all companies, and small-cap funds focus on newer, up-and-coming companies that have the potential for large growth.

Sector funds are another prominent form of mutual fund. Sector funds are stock funds that focus at least 25 percent of their investments on a particular sector of the economy. For example, there are sector funds that invest in technology companies, utility companies, food companies, and automotive companies, among many others.

Index funds, meanwhile, attempt to match one of the many prominent indices used to measure the performance of the stock market. The S&P 500, for example, is an index (a measure of the value of representative companies) that tracks the performance of 500 of the largest corporations in the world. There are dozens of indices that track American companies and hundreds of indices that track different groups of companies around the world. An index fund focuses on one such index and attempts to match its performance. Thus, an S&P 500 index fund would mirror the gains or losses of those 500 companies in the index.

There are also numerous international funds. Global funds are mutual funds that invest in the stock of U.S. companies as well as the stock of companies in other countries. Foreign funds focus on the stock of companies outside the United States. A country specific fund invests in one particular country. Emerging markets funds invest in countries that are only beginning to develop economically.

In addition to all of the above, which represent only some of the total variety of stock funds, investors can choose bond funds. Bond funds are safe investments that offer a consistent, but fairly low, level of growth. Among bond funds, there are municipal bond funds, which specialize in the bonds of state and local governments; U.S. government bond funds, which specialize in the bonds of the national government; corporate bond funds, which specialize in the bonds of corporations; and mortgage-backed securities funds, which specialize in securities that are related to the loans people take out to purchase homes.

Another mutual fund variety that is considered an extremely safe vehicle for investing is the money-market fund. Money-market funds invest in what are called short-term debt instruments: securities that represent shares of debt that must be repaid within 13 months. Examples of short-term debt instruments are Certificates of Deposit (CDs), a form of investment that gains value but can only be redeemed on a certain date, and repurchase agreements, a form of investment that involves the sale of securities with an agreement to repurchase them at a set price on a particular day. The least risky of all mutual funds, money market funds typically offer the most modest gains.

Recent Trends

As of 2006 U.S. mutual funds managed around $10 trillion, up from $135 billion in 1980. To understand the magnitude of this amount of money, consider that in 2006 the entire U.S. Gross Domestic Product (GDP), the total value of all goods and services produced in the country, was around $12 trillion. More than half of the $10 trillion invested in mutual funds was in stock funds at that time. All in all, the mutual-fund industry was an enormous force in U.S. financial markets.

Some investors, however, were beginning to turn away from mutual funds and toward a new form of investment fund called an exchange-traded fund (ETF). ETFs, first created in 1990, combine the diversifying aspect of mutual-fund investing with the characteristics of stocks: while they are composed of many different stock holdings, ETFs can be bought and sold on stock markets like ordinary stocks (mutual fund shares are purchased directly from the mutual-fund company; they are not bought and sold on financial markets, even though they are composed of securities that are bought and sold on financial markets). Because of the way ETFs were structured, they could be managed at a lower cost than mutual funds, and their presence on stock markets made them attractive both to the ordinary investors who often bought mutual-fund shares and to more sophisticated investors. In 2006 the number of ETFs grew from under 100 to more than 400, and some observers were beginning to wonder whether they might not eclipse mutual funds at some point in the future.

$ Treasury Securities

What It Means

The United States Department of the Treasury is the department in the U.S. federal government that manages the country's revenue (funds). The Treasury sells financial assets called securities to individuals, institutions (both inside and outside of the United States), and foreign governments. To be more precise, by selling Treasury securities to people or institutions, the government is borrowing money from them. This borrowed money, which is used to fund various government programs and services, is part of the country's national debt. In exchange for lending their money, purchasers of Treasury securities get to collect a fee (called interest) after a specified period of time.

In the world of investing, there are various kinds of securities (stocks, for instance); the kind that the U.S. Treasury sells are called bonds. Bonds require the issuer (in this case the federal government) to pay the holder of the bond the face value of the bond plus interest (an additional fee added to the loan) at a specific time in the future. The day the original amount must be repaid is referred to as the day the bond matures. There are five types of Treasury securities: Treasury bills (T-bills), Treasury notes (T-notes), Treasury bonds (T-bonds), Treasury Inflation-Protected Securities (TIPS), and savings bonds.

In effect, a person who buys a Treasury security is loaning the government money for a specific period of

One way the U.S. government raises money is by selling treasury securities, or bonds, which buyers are able to redeem at a higher price in the future. The government first sold treasury bonds during World War I and advertised them with posters. *The Library of Congress.*

TREASURYDIRECT

In 2002 the United States Treasury established a website (http://www.treasurydirect.gov) that allowed investors to purchase securities, a type of financial investment, directly from the United States Treasury. Through the website investors could withdraw money from U.S. Treasury accounts and move it into their own personal accounts. In addition, investors could set their online accounts to purchase new Treasury securities automatically when their currently held securities matured (that is, reached the end of their term). TreasuryDirect was the first and only website that let investors buy and redeem Treasury securities electronically. The site also offered information on the recent performance of all types of Treasury securities. This data was available to any investor who held a Web account with TreasuryDirect.

time and in exchange for a specific fee. For example, if an individual purchased a $970 T-bill that matured in six months, that person would be lending the federal government $970 for six months. Suppose that the agreed-upon interest rate for this bond was 3.09 percent. If the person bought it in January, the government would repay the investor $1,000 in June, when the bond matured. The additional $30 would be the interest (also called the coupon) on the loan (because 3.09 percent of $970 is $30).

When Did It Begin

During World War I (1914–18) the United States began loaning large sums of money to the Allied forces (Great Britain, France, and Russia) to help them fund the war. To raise money for the loans, the U.S. government borrowed money from U.S. citizens by issuing Liberty Bonds, which were the first Treasury securities. The country lost money on these bonds because after the war the European nations were either unable to repay the loans or could only repay them at drastically reduced rates of interest. Meanwhile, the Liberty Bonds were maturing, and U.S. citizens were owed money on the loans they had made to the government. The government repaid U.S. citizens at the initially promised rates of interest. Liberty Bonds were, however, discontinued after World War I.

The government made no similar offerings to the public until 1935, when it began selling "baby bonds," so called because they were issued in small denominations. From 1935 to 1941 the government issued $3.5 billion worth of these bonds at 2.9 percent interest. During World War II (1939–45) the Treasury Department took baby bonds off the market and started issuing Defense Savings Bonds at the same interest rates. After the Korean War (1950–53) these bonds were renamed "savings bonds."

More Detailed Information

Each of the different types of Treasury security is issued on different terms. The shortest-term securities are Treasury bills (T-bills). These are issued in denominations of $1,000 up to a maximum of $5 million and with maturity dates of 4 weeks (one month), 13 weeks (three months), or 26 weeks (six months). The Bureau of the Public Debt (an agency in the Department of the Treasury) holds weekly auctions for T-bills at more than 40,000 locations throughout the United States. There are two ways for an investor to bid on a T-bill: noncompetitive bids and competitive bids. In a noncompetitive bid the investor agrees to an interest rate established by the Bureau of Public Debt at the auction. Investors making noncompetitive bids are guaranteed to receive the bill they request (a T-bill in the desired amount that matures at the desired time). With a competitive bid the investor requests a higher interest rate. These bids may be accepted, rejected, or accepted in part (for less than the desired amount, less than the desired interest rate, or both). Noncompetitive bids can be made directly to the government or through a bank or broker. Competitive bids must be made through a bank or broker.

Although T-bills are issued in denominations of $1,000, the terms of the transaction are slightly more complicated. T-bills are actually issued at a discount, the amount of which is determined by the interest rate. For example, a 13-week $10,000 T-bill with an interest rate of 2.04 percent would be issued at the discount rate of $9,800. At the end of the 13 weeks, the investor receives $10,000; this is the original amount plus the interest fee, which is 2.04 percent of the original amount, or $200.

Treasury notes, or T-notes, are longer-term securities. Issued in denominations of $1,000 up to a maximum of $1 million, they have maturities of 2, 3, 5, or 10 years. The Treasury pays the investor interest on T-notes every six months. When the bond matures, the investor receives face value, meaning that if a two-year bond was issued for $10,000, the investor will be paid $10,000 at the end of two years. During this time the investor will have received four interest payments. T-notes are auctioned less frequently than T-bills (monthly or a few times a year, depending on the kind of note). As with T-bills, investors can make either competitive or noncompetitive bids for T-notes.

T-bonds are issued for even longer; they mature in 10 to 30 years, and, like T-notes, they pay interest every six months. T-bonds tend to have the highest interest rates, as a way to persuade people to loan their money for such a long time.

In 1997 the U.S. Treasury began issuing another kind of security, called Treasury Inflation-Protected Securities (TIPS). Inflation, the general rising of prices, decreases the value of the dollar, and many investors are worried about their money losing value this way. TIPS were designed to address this concern. These securities have 5-, 10-, and 25-year maturities and pay interest every six months. With TIPS the principal (the face value of the security) increases with inflation and decreases with deflation (a general decline in prices). This means that if an investor purchased a five-year TIPS for $10,000 (the principal), and the economy subsequently experienced significant inflation, the face value of the security would be adjusted (in this case increased) to reflect the general rise in prices.

Finally, savings bonds are Treasury securities for individual investors only. These securities must be held for at least one year and can be redeemed anytime thereafter. Unlike the other Treasury securities, savings bonds cannot be traded among investors, because they are registered to the original purchaser.

Recent Trends

The U.S. Treasury market is considered the safest market in the world. This means that investors are more likely to earn a profit on their investment if they purchase U.S. Treasury securities than if they invest in any other market. Because of this reliability, the central banks of other countries often buy U.S. Treasury securities. Starting in 2000 there was an increase in foreign demand for such securities; foreign investors wanted to make safe investments to balance out their more risky investments in developing nations (which are not industrialized and tend to have unstable economies). At the end of 2003, nearly 38 percent of the money the U.S. government owed on Treasury securities was owed to foreign investors.

While foreign investors in the international market at this time were financially cushioned by the modest profits they earned from Treasury securities, investors within the United States were not drawing as much profit from these securities as they had in the past. This was because, with so many international lenders eager to invest in the United States, the U.S. Treasury was able to charge more for its securities while offering lower interest rates.

$ Hedge Fund

What It Means

A hedge fund is a business that pools money together, typically from very wealthy people with experience in the financial world, and invests it in a wider variety of ways than more traditional investment firms do. A traditional investor or investment firm buys a number of different stocks (shares of company ownership) in the hope that, as those companies prosper, their stock shares will gain value; this is called taking a "long" position on those stocks. Such investors or firms might also buy bonds (a loan of money to a government or company, in exchange for which the borrowing government or company makes periodic payments of interest to the bond holder) in the hope that their gains in value will balance out any stock losses. But stock market gains are hard to predict, so a

long approach to stocks exposes an investor to losses, and bonds usually do not pay off at a high enough rate to compensate in the event of a drop in stock values.

Hedge funds were initially created to "hedge" the bets of investors by taking a "short" as well as a long approach to stocks, bonds, and other forms of securities (a security is any contract that can be assigned value and can then be bought and sold by investors). To "hedge" an investment simply means taking action to reduce the risk of losing money. The first hedge funds, launched in the United States in the middle of the twentieth century, bet on some stocks to win and others to lose, thereby minimizing the losses of investors during difficult economic times.

Today, the world of investing is more complex, and hedge funds are less uniform in their approach to investing. Hedge funds do generally go long on investments at the same time that they engage in "short selling." In simple terms, short selling, or "shorting," is the practice of borrowing stocks (typically from another broker), selling them, then buying the stocks back at a lower price, earning a profit on the difference. While hedge fund managers do engage in short selling, hedging against potential losses is not their main purpose anymore. Instead, hedge funds are loosely united by a few basic characteristics.

Because of the way they are set up, hedge funds are not subject to many government restrictions. Therefore, they can buy a wider variety of investments and take more risks than more heavily regulated investment firms can. They can also make more investments using borrowed money than other firms can, allowing them to invest far more money than they actually collect from individual investors. This flexibility allows them to take advantage of changing conditions in the financial markets that more traditional, slower-moving investors cannot. It also gives them the chance to outperform other investors. Because of the chance for high returns, hedge fund managers charge extremely high fees and make some of the highest salaries in the world.

When Did It Begin

Alfred Winslow Jones, trained as a sociologist, got his introduction to the world of big business while working as a writer for *Fortune* magazine during World War II. As he researched and wrote a technical piece for the magazine about stock-market forecasting (predicting the future gains and losses of various stocks), Jones came up with the idea that would serve as the foundation for the hedge-fund industry.

Jones did not believe that any forecaster, no matter the degree of his economic or mathematical skills, could reliably predict the future of the stock market. Instead, he began trying to figure out ways of protecting investors from stock-market fluctuations. The investing strategy Jones came up with involved a combination of two

HEDGE FUNDS, THE ECONOMY, AND REGULATION

Hedge funds are specialized investing companies that collect money from wealthy individuals and institutions and then invest it in a variety of creative, often risky ways. Hedge funds attract investors by offering the possibility for extremely high returns. The potential for an extreme level of profit exists in part because hedge funds are not subject to many government regulations. This allows them to react to changing economic conditions on a daily basis and, in general, to pursue all available means of making money. By contrast, more traditional investment companies are prevented by the government from making certain types of investments.

For much of the twentieth century, hedge funds accounted for only a small percentage of investment activity worldwide. Even in the early 1990s, hedge funds still numbered in the hundreds, and their risky strategies did not represent a substantial danger to the overall economy. Public perception of hedge funds changed dramatically in 1998, however, when Long-Term Capital Management, one of the most successful hedge funds in the United States, lost more than $4.5 billion in a single economic quarter. The heavy losses caused serious concern within the Federal Reserve (the nation's central bank, also known as the Fed), which organized a bailout (in business, the practice of providing financial assistance to a company on the verge of collapse) of the company. In spite of the bailout, Long-Term Capital Management was unable to regain its former success, and by 2000 it was out of business.

The downfall of Long-Term Capital Management resulted in numerous investigations, as well as demands for stricter regulation of hedge fund activities. In spite of this increased concern, by 2007 the number of hedge funds had grown to approximately 9,000, which collectively managed around $2 trillion. Many economic leaders were, accordingly, becoming increasingly worried about what might happen to the world economy in the event that the hedge-fund industry fell upon hard times.

One reason that unregulated hedge funds pose a danger to the world economy is that they make many of their investments using money borrowed from banks and other lenders. If several large hedge funds (some of the larger hedge funds manage more than $20 billion apiece) were to make bad investments, they would end up owing their lenders more money than they would be able to pay. The fact that so many hedge funds were borrowing so much money meant that a string of failed hedge funds could destabilize major international banks, triggering wider damage across the economy.

At a meeting of international economic leaders in 2007, U.S. Treasury Secretary Henry Paulson said of hedge funds (as reported by the *International Herald Tribune*), "I can't imagine we could be doing our jobs, those of us responsible for financial regulation, without talking about this topic." What the future of hedge fund regulation might be was unclear at that time, but most financial experts agreed that a more heavily regulated industry was likely.

---

techniques: taking a long position on some stocks and paying for these stocks with borrowed money, while simultaneously selling other stocks short. Prior to this time, both of these techniques were considered too risky to be commonly used, but Jones found that in combination they could be employed, paradoxically, for the purpose of protecting an investor from risk.

In 1948 Jones and four friends started what he called a "hedged fund," a way of investing that appeared to offer something unimaginable: the possibility to make money without any risk of losing it. While Jones's approach successfully protected investors from risk, it required foregoing the huge gains to be made during economic booms. The tradeoff for financial safety was a modest, but consistent, level of growth.

More Detailed Information

Unlike Jones's *hedged* fund, today's *hedge* funds generally have a different purpose. Like Jones's clients, the people who trust hedge funds with their money today expect to profit even when the economy as a whole is struggling, but hedging against the risk of loss is not the primary purpose of today's funds. Instead, hedge funds attempt to outpace the gains of all other forms of investment. Whereas traditional investment firms and mutual funds (a more highly regulated and more conservative way of pooling money to invest in financial markets) often hope to keep pace with the gains made by the stock market as a whole, hedge funds openly attempt to outperform the market.

Hedge funds are able to offer this possibility because they take more risks than mutual funds and traditional investors, and they are able to take these risks with the money of others because they are not subject to substantial government regulation. They have avoided regulation primarily because they do not allow just anyone to give them money; they manage the money, generally, of only very wealthy people who are experienced investors. Whereas anyone can contribute money to a mutual fund, and whereas mutual funds are generally not even allowed to sell short, hedge funds collect money privately from the very rich and are allowed to use virtually any investment techniques they want.

To outperform the economy as a whole, an investor must find investment opportunities that others have overlooked. Because of their freedom from regulation, hedge funds can find imbalances in financial markets and exploit them, making large amounts of money in a matter of hours or days, before other investors catch on to the opportunity.

Most of the investing techniques employed by hedge fund managers are complex and difficult for nonexperts to grasp. One common feature of most hedge-fund investments, however, is that they rely on borrowed money. The reason hedge funds borrow money is that this allows them to multiply the effects of a small opportunity, such as a slight change in a stock's, bond's, or currency's value. The risk of this approach is that bad investments mean funds (and their individual clients) could end up owing lenders more money than they possess. Another feature common to hedge-fund investing is that the freedom from oversight allows them to take advantage of time-sensitive investment opportunities to which other investment firms cannot, because of regulatory constraints, react quickly enough.

Because of their relative freedom from regulation, hedge funds are also able to operate in secrecy. They typically do not provide their investors or the general public with detailed information about their strategies, their actions, or the amount of money they have. Hedge funds have therefore developed an aura of mystery in the popular imagination. People who work in the hedge-fund industry generally do not talk to the press, and few ordinary people understand what a hedge fund is.

What many people do know about hedge funds is that they pay their employees enormous sums of money. One reason that those in the hedge-fund industry make so much money is that the funds charge the highest fees of any form of investment. The typical hedge-fund fee structure is known as 2-20: the fund collects two percent of a client's investment total for managing his or her money, no matter what happens, and then the fund collects 20 percent of all gains made by the fund's investments. Some hedge funds charge significantly more than this. As of 2007, for example, Renaissance Technologies Corporation, a hedge fund run by James Simons, had a 5-44 fee structure. To encourage managers to invest responsibly, the managers of hedge funds are expected to place their own money in the fund. Thus, in a single year the managers of the largest and most lucrative hedge funds can make hundreds of millions of dollars in fees in addition to increasing their own invested sums by hundreds of millions of dollars. Single-year incomes of $1 billion are not unheard of in the industry.

Recent Trends

The number of hedge funds, and the amount of money under their management, increased dramatically in the early years of the twenty-first century. The number of hedge funds was in the hundreds through the end of the 1990s; by 2007 there were an estimated 9,000 hedge funds. Likewise, the amount of money managed by hedge funds grew from around $2 billion in 1999 to around $2 trillion by 2007.

There were several basic reasons for this explosive growth. One reason was that investors in general had become increasingly comfortable with taking big risks in the financial markets. Whereas high-risk investing in the mid-to-late twentieth century was typically seen as fool-

ish, it was commonplace for investors to put some of their money into riskier forms of investment by the beginning of the twenty-first century. Another reason for the growth of hedge funds was that when the U.S. stock market crashed in 2000 and lost 40 percent of its value by 2002, many hedge funds lost no money, and some even prospered during this time. In the years following this economic downturn, more and more investors looked to hedge funds as though they had a magic formula for wealth creation.

Finally, the growth of hedge funds was a product of the growing participation of institutional investors: organizations such as banks, insurance companies, and retirement funds that invest huge pools of money on behalf of numerous individuals. Only in the early years of the twenty-first century did hedge funds begin to be perceived as legitimate investment opportunities for the most reputable of institutions. Institutions, obviously, are in possession of far larger sums of money than even the very wealthy individuals who were the main investors in early hedge funds. With access to these new pools of money in the twenty-first century, hedge funds were poised to continue growing and gaining influence over world affairs for some time to come.

$ Capital Gains and Losses

What It Means

Capital assets is a financial term that refers to everything a person owns for both personal use and investment, such

A safe-deposit box is a fire-resistant box where bank customers can store valuables like jewels, documents, and family heirlooms. Safe-deposit boxes are stored on shelves in a special vault. *AP Images.*

BAREFOOT PILGRIM

One of the most interesting things about the world of finance is its slang, especially the language associated with heavy losses. For example, a person who refuses to do proper research and therefore consistently loses large sums of money because he makes unwise investments is called a "barefoot pilgrim." A barefoot pilgrim is liable to get stuck with a "falling knife," which is a stock that has dropped in value significantly in a short period of time. These unsophisticated investors are also prone to buying "turkeys." This refers to any business deal that turns out a lot worse than expected. In the first few years of the twenty-first century, for example, many investors who put money into start-up technology firms soon discovered that they had turkeys on their hands.

as homes, cars, jewelry, computers, household furnishings, and stocks and bonds. When the value of a capital asset increases from its original purchase price, the owner is said to have experienced a capital gain. If the value of a capital asset decreases after the purchase, then the owner suffers a capital loss.

For example, if a person bought a house for $120,000 and five years later sold it for $150,000, that person would have a capital gain of $30,000. On the other hand, if the house sold for only $100,000, the person would realize a capital loss of $20,000. To use an example involving the stock market, if an investor purchased 10 shares of stock in the ABC Corporation for $100 per share (an investment of $1,000) and later sold those 10 shares for $110 per share (for a total of $1,100), that person would realize a capital gain of $100.

Both capital gains and capital losses are measured at the point of sale of the asset. This means that if a house purchased at $150,000 were later estimated to be worth $180,000, that additional $30,000 would only be regarded as a capital gain if the house were actually sold for $180,000. If the owner decides to keep the house, then no capital gain has been realized. The potential profits from unsold assets are called unrealized capital gains.

When Did It Begin

When a person sells a capital asset for more than he or she originally paid for it, he or she makes a profit called a capital gain. But although profit and capital gain and both refer to making money, there is an important distinction to be made between the two terms. *Profit* is a word that refers to money made on any sale; the concept has existed for many centuries. *Capital gain* is a more recently coined term that is used in the context of filing taxes.

The U.S. government first imposed income taxes (taxes on what people earn through their jobs and investments) during the Civil War (1861–65). At the time capital gains were counted as regular income and taxed at the same rate. It was not until 1913 that Americans were taxed separately for capital gains. Initially this was a simple 7 percent tax on all capital gains. Since 1922, however, capital gains tax laws in the United States have changed frequently and become complicated. By the start of the twenty-first century, tax rates on capital gains had come to depend on a number of factors, including the investor's overall income level and the amount of time an investor owned an asset before selling it.

More Detailed Information

When setting income tax rates, the United States Internal Revenue Service (IRS) makes a distinction between long-term and short-term capital assets. Assets that the investor has owned for more than a year are long-term assets; assets that have been held for less than a year are short-term assets. For any capital gains on long-term assets, the tax rate is lower than the rate for short-term assets and regular income. Capital losses, which can be deducted from ordinary income, can reduce the amount of taxes an individual owes. For example, if capital losses are greater than capital gains, a taxpayer can deduct up to $3,000 in capital losses from his ordinary income. This means that if a person declared $70,000 in salaries, tips, and wages but also recorded a net capital loss of $5,000 after selling stocks during the year, that person would subtract $3,000 (the maximum amount allowed) from his yearly total and report earnings of $67,000 instead of $70,000.

Calculating taxes on capital gains and capital losses is an involved process. First the investor must separate long-term capital gains and losses from short-term capital gains and losses. Short-term gains are taxed as ordinary income, which means that, depending on his or her tax bracket (the category that determines what percentage a person must pay as tax; it increases as income increases), an investor can pay as much as 38 percent tax on a short-term capital gain. Long-term capital gains, on the other hand, can be taxed at rates varying from 8 percent to 28 percent, depending on the investor's tax bracket and on the type of asset that was sold. Most long-term capital gains are taxed at or around 15 percent. The higher rates for long-term capital gains apply to the sale of some collectibles and small-business stock. The lower rates on long-term capital gains (those tax rates in the 8 to 10 percent range) apply to investments that have been held more than five years.

After distinguishing between short- and long-term capital gains and losses, the investor must calculate the net (overall) capital gain or loss. This figure indicates whether the investor had a net profit or a net loss from his or her sale of all capital holdings that year. To determine this number, short-term capital losses are subtracted from short-term capital gains, and long-term capital losses are subtracted from long-term capital gains. Following a formula determined by the IRS, the short-term capital losses or gains are then calculated against the long-term losses or gains to arrive at a net figure. Although no investor wants to lose money, capital losses are not always bad for taxpayers. For example, a person who has earned a large profit in short-term capital gains can reduce the final amount owed in taxes by selling some capital assets at a loss. This is called loss harvesting or tax gain.

If homeowners earn a profit on the sale of their home, they do not necessarily have to worry about paying high capital gains taxes. According to 1997 tax laws, a homeowner does not have to pay capital gains taxes if he purchases a more expensive house within two years of the sale of his previous home. In addition, homeowners are able to subtract the cost of improvements to the home from their capital gains. This law applies only to the sale of a homeowner's principal residence and does not include vacation homes or time-shares (vacation homes co-owned by a group of people who take turns staying there).

Recent Trends

Starting in 1997 people who had invested in housing realized tremendous capital gains. From 1997 to 2005, housing prices in the United States rose 73 percent. During that span many other countries experienced a similar boom in their housing markets. For example, prices rose 244 percent in South Africa, 192 percent in Ireland, and 145 percent in Spain. Economists attribute this surge to two factors. First, low interest rates encouraged people to borrow money for homes. Second, in general most middle-class investors view real estate as a safer venture than the stock market.

After 2005, however, housing prices leveled and even dropped in some countries. For example, although prices in Great Britain rose 154 percent from 1997 to 2004, they declined by 20 percent from 2004 to 2006. In the United States interest rates began to rise steadily, and Americans therefore bought fewer second homes and rental properties. Despite this downturn, economists predicted that the housing market would flatten rather than collapse, as the stock market probably would if stock prices were to drop dramatically. Statistics show that an investor is far less likely to sell a house for a loss than a stock. Also, regardless of market conditions, economists reason that people will stay in the real estate market because a home is a necessity.

$ Safe-Deposit Box

What It Means

A safe-deposit box is a fire-resistant metal box housed in a bank vault that is used to store valuables safely. Safe-deposit boxes are available to individuals, families, and organizations; they come in a variety of sizes and may be rented for a period of time ranging from months to years.

PLOT DEVICE!

Safe-deposit boxes (fire-resistant metal boxes held in bank vaults that are designed for the safe storage of customers' property) carry a certain aura of mystery about them because only the person or persons who rent the box know what is inside. Because of this, the safe-deposit box has long been used as a plot device in novels and films, where the guarded box must be accessed in order to discover someone's secret identity, find evidence of a murder, or steal a fortune in diamonds. In the 1956 movie *Man in the Vault,* for example, the plot centers on the efforts of a mobster, Willis Trent, to steal $200,000 that is in a Los Angeles safe-deposit box. Produced 50 years later, the 2006 movie *Inside Man* revolves around another bank heist situation, but there turns out to be more at stake than money when it emerges that the safe-deposit box in question contains evidence that the bank's founder was in league with the Nazis.

The principle behind using a safe-deposit box in a bank is that it is a more secure place to keep certain items than in your own home, where they are more vulnerable to being destroyed by fire or flood, stolen by burglars, or even simply misplaced.

People use safe-deposit boxes to store a variety of important possessions, including family heirlooms, such as jewelry; rare coins, works of art, and other collectibles; negatives of irreplaceable photographs; and important documents, such as birth certificates, military records, and deeds of property (documents showing proof of ownership of the property). Many people also keep a video record of the contents of their home for insurance purposes (in case of damage or theft) in their safe-deposit box.

Whatever you choose to keep in your safe-deposit box, its contents are strictly confidential: only you, and any other parties you authorize, will have access to it; not even bank representatives know what is inside. This high level of security and privacy may be desirable; one of the drawbacks of keeping things in a safe-deposit box, however, is that you may only access your belongings during bank hours.

When Did It Begin

African-American inventor Henry Brown is credited with developing one of the earliest prototypes of the safe-deposit box in the United States in the late nineteenth century. Brown saw the need for a safe and convenient way to store valuable items and documents. At that time, though banks already offered a safe place to store jewelry and other material valuables, the storage was not private, and there was nothing to prevent nosy bank employees from looking through customers' personal papers. Thus most people kept their important documents tucked away in cardboard or wooden boxes at home, unprotected from destruction and theft.

Patented on November 2, 1886, and described by its inventor as a "receptacle for storing and preserving papers," Brown's box was made of forged metal and could be sealed with a lock and key. In the decades that followed, safe-deposit boxes became a standard offering in most banks.

More Detailed Information

Procedures for renting a safe-deposit box may vary from one bank to the next, but in general you must present valid identification (such as a driver's license or passport) and complete the necessary paperwork, including a rental agreement with the bank that stipulates the monthly or annual fee, as well as various rules and regulations. When the paperwork has been signed and authorized, the bank will provide you with two keys to your safe-deposit box and will recommend that you keep them in separate locations. These are the only keys to the lock on your individual safe-deposit box. The bank does not keep its own copies, so if the keys are lost, the safe-deposit box must be drilled and the lock replaced at your expense.

In order to access the box, you must fill out an admission request form. When the form has been approved, a bank attendant will escort you into the vault where your safe-deposit box is held. The lock on the box has two sets of tumblers requiring two keys to open it: your key and one that is held by the attendant. Neither key alone can open the box. Once the box has been unlocked, the attendant will leave you alone in a viewing room until you have finished your business and are ready to return the box to the vault.

You may authorize another person or persons (such as a spouse or a lawyer) to access your safe-deposit box, but there are strict procedures for doing so. Merely giving someone else a key will not be sufficient to grant them access.

Although rare, theft and damage to safe-deposit boxes can occur. Be advised that items kept in a safe-deposit box are not considered actual deposits to the bank (a safe-deposit box is only a storage facility provided by the bank) and are therefore not insured by the FDIC (Federal Deposit Insurance Corporation, the U.S. government agency that guarantees bank deposits). It is the responsibility of each individual safe-deposit-box holder to buy insurance for the contents of his or her box and to keep an accurate inventory of these contents at all times.

Also, it is unlawful to keep some things in a safe-deposit box, including drugs, weapons, stolen goods, and toxic, radioactive, or explosive substances. If local, state, or federal law enforcement authorities suspect that you are keeping any illegal substances in your safe-deposit box, they may obtain a warrant from the appropriate court to search and seize the contents of the box.

Recent Trends

In 2000 banks and other companies began to use technology to open up a new frontier in safe-deposit storage, offering customers electronic, or "virtual" safe-deposit boxes. This service allows customers to pay for an account in which to store their important documents (everything from legal, medical, and tax records to family photos and architectural blueprints) electronically. In order to access their account, customers must enter a user identification name or number, a PIN (personal identification number), and a password.

The benefit of electronic document storage is that customers can access their important personal information from any computer day or night, without having to visit a safe-deposit box in a bank. The service is also considered a convenient and reliable way to back up a computer hard drive. The disadvantage of such digital storage, however, is that despite extensive security measures, electronic data may still be vulnerable to certain kinds of security breaches.

Protecting Yourself from Risk

$ Overview: Insurance

What It Means

Insurance is an agreement that guarantees an individual, company, or other entity against the loss of money. Insurance agreements, sold by insurance companies, are called policies. An insurance policy stipulates that the company agrees to compensate the insured individual (or other entity) for potential future losses of such things as health, home, or car, in exchange for the regular payment of fees called premiums.

The purpose of insurance is to protect the financial well-being of an individual, company, or other entity in the case of an unexpected loss, such as damage to a building or the loss of health because of illness or injury. State and federal governments can mandate that some kinds of insurance, such as automobile insurance, be held; other types are optional.

Any risk that can be quantified in some manner most likely has a type of insurance to protect it. The most common kinds of insurance are medical, automobile, home, and life insurance. Once the insured policyholder pays the required premiums, medical insurance will provide the policyholder with financial support (usually the full or partial coverage of doctor, hospital, and pharmaceutical charges related to medical care) if medical treatment for an illness or injury is required. Automobile insurance provides financial support in the event of an automobile accident that damages the vehicle of the policyholder or of someone else. Life insurance guarantees payment to the beneficiaries if the insured person dies.

When an insured individual or company suffers a loss, they file a report, called a claim, to the insurer for the amount of the loss. When the insurance company reimburses the insured (or directly pays for the charges) the reimbursement comes out of a fund to which many policyholders have contributed premiums. That way, when the insurance company needs to pay for an indi-vidual loss, the burden of paying it is divided among many insurance holders and does not fall heavily on the individual or entity who has incurred a loss. The challenge for insurance companies is to set aside enough

Insurance protects individuals and companies against financial loss resulting from illness, damaged property, and other unexpected events. The benefits of an insurance policy are outlined in the insurance policy. © *Rob Casey/Brand X/Corbis.*

SHOPPING FOR AN INSURANCE POLICY

When shopping for an insurance policy, it is wise to consider several factors in addition to the cost of the insurance. There are several things to do before actually purchasing a policy, including the following:

- Decide what type of policy is needed.
- Determine how much insurance is needed.
- Assess how much the insured person can afford to pay or is willing to pay for the insurance.
- Find out how much insurance the insured already has.
- Find out what insurance may be available through an employer, a spouse, a professional-association membership, or credit card companies.
- Gain familiarity with insurance terminology.

Companies may charge different premium rates for similar coverage. Customers should compare the prices of several insurance companies' policies before actually purchasing a policy. They should also consider the quality and level of service as well as the specific coverage provided.

money for anticipated losses so that they have profits resulting from whatever is left over, called the margin.

Different insurance policies establish different terms of agreement. Typically a policy will state the prices of the insured person's premiums, how frequently they need to be paid, who should receive payment in case the insured dies, what types of loss events are covered and the time period of coverage, and how much the company will reimburse. Policies typically state that the policyholder is responsible for paying a part of the loss, known as a deductible, and that the insurer will pay what remains.

When Did It Begin

The essential concepts of insurance have been in existence for thousands of years. Whenever people have helped one another in the event of a loss, the idea of insurance has essentially been enacted. For example, if a house is damaged in a storm, the neighbors of the owner might step in to help rebuild. If they did, the owner would then have an incentive to help his neighbor, or potentially face not having his neighbor's assistance in a future loss.

Early agreements to share or distribute the risk for certain types of losses were used by Chinese and Babylonian traders as far back as 3000 BC. Chinese merchants would divide the wares they were shipping among many boats in order to limit the amount of loss they would suffer if one or two ships capsized or could not complete the journey. In ancient Babylon merchants could pay fees to take out special loans stipulating that, if the ship or cargo

was lost at sea, the merchant did not have to repay the loan; this protected the merchant from going into debt.

The ancient Greeks and Romans organized guilds called benevolent societies, which paid funeral expenses and cared for the families of its members when they died. These guilds, along with those in the Middle Ages (the period from about the fifth to the fifteenth century) that functioned in similar ways, were the foundation of modern health and life insurance.

In the fifteenth and sixteenth centuries, when ships from Europe began sailing for the Americas, marine insurance, which protected cargo and vessels in case they capsized, became useful and popular. After the Great Fire of London in 1666, in which thousands of buildings were destroyed, fire insurance was developed. The first fire-insurance company in the United States was founded in 1752 by Benjamin Franklin (1706–90). Franklin also helped establish the first life insurance company in 1759.

More Detailed Information

Insurance companies must carefully screen potential customers in order to make sure that the risks of certain customers are not too great. For instance, automobile insurers check a person's driving record before issuing them a policy. Insurance companies rely on several criteria that help them determine whether or not it is in their best interest to insure specific events. Mainly, they must have confirmation that enough similar instances of potential loss exist; knowing that they do guarantees that the company can predict what it will have to cover. Companies must have assurance of predictability before they can risk the promise of protection.

Additionally, insurance companies must know that the amount of loss they will cover has a limit (meaning it must be "noncatastrophic"), even if it is very high, because they cannot afford to be jeopardized by unpredictable losses of massive proportions. Insurers typically seek to avoid drastic losses of their own financial reserves by purchasing reinsurance (insurance for insurance companies).

Insurance companies also require the loss events of their customers to be definite, measurable in financial terms, and located at a specific time and place. For instance, if an apartment renter is robbed and seeks reimbursement from the insurance company that sold him his rental insurance, he must be able to document such things as the date of the robbery, the report filed with police, and the value of the stolen property. Insurance companies must be sure that the loss of property was not intentional.

Insurers select the risks they will insure and determine the costs of the premiums that will cover them through a process known as underwriting. Underwriters draw on enormous files of data to research adverse events and develop predictions of the chances that claims will be filed against them. Attempting to maintain a balance between low-risk and high-risk individuals in the pool of insured candidates, underwriters carefully consider such things as each applicant's potential for physical or psychological risk. The tasks of underwriting are complex, challenging, and crucial to the process of creating reliable insurance policies.

Another type of professional critical to the business of insuring people is an actuary. Actuaries are trained to use mathematical and statistical methods to assess various risks, and insurance companies employ them to help to determine potential risks and losses. For example, in determining the prices for life insurance policies, an actuary would analyze mortality models, which illustrate, for persons of each age, what the probability is that they die before their next birthday. In determining the prices for health insurance policies, an actuary would focus on statistical models showing rates of disability, morbidity (illness), mortality, and fertility.

One of the most commonly held types of insurance is life insurance. It was originally created to protect an individual's family when his or her death left the surviving family without income. Over time, various life insurance policy plans have evolved. With a "whole life" policy, the insured person pays premiums of a fixed amount throughout his or her lifetime, and the money deposited accumulates interest (fees paid to the customer by the company; interest is usually calculated as a percentage of the amount in the account). At the time of the insured's death, the insurance company pays the amount that has accumulated, in addition to the interest it has earned, to someone previously designated as the beneficiary (recipient of benefits). Even if the insured had ended the policy while alive, the benefit is still paid.

In a "universal life" policy, the insured individual can vary the amount and the timing of the premiums he or she pays to the company; the funds accumulate over time to create what is called the death benefit. A "variable life" policy allows fixed premiums to be invested in a portfolio (a selected group) of investments. As the premiums earn interest, the interest payments are put back into the portfolio, which increases the total amount that is invested; the death benefit is based on the performance of the investment. In a "term life" policy, the insurance coverage is for a specified time period, such as 10 to 15 years. In this type of plan, the value of the policy does not build up over its term.

Another type of insurance that many people, businesses, schools, and other organizations hold is fire insurance. Fire insurance usually protects against accidentally caused fires in the home that are damaging to property, as well as damage from lightning. Other types of insurance against natural elements are flood, tornado, hail, and drought insurance.

Recent Trends

Several developments in the twentieth century affected the insurance industry. In 1944 Congress took over the regulation of insurance companies, which had until that time been managed by the individual states. For the first half of the century, most U.S. insurance companies were only allowed to provide one type of insurance, but in the 1950s Congress passed legislation that allowed fire and casualty insurance companies to underwrite other types of insurance as well. As a result, many insurance companies expanded or merged to create enormous insurance corporations. Companies that provide multiple types of insurance—from auto, life, fire, and flood insurance to marine insurance (which protects boats) and credit insurance (which protects businesses against loss when customers fail to pay the amounts they owe)—are standard. Additionally, federal law had prohibited banks from entering into the insurance business, but in 1999 Congress repealed those laws. As a result, major banks have expanded into the insurance industry.

TYPES OF INSURANCE

$ Home Insurance

What It Means

A home insurance policy is a contract between an insurance company and a homeowner that protects the homeowner from financial losses that can result from damages to the structure of his dwelling and to the possessions stored in that dwelling. There are many different types of home insurance policies. A typical policy covers a wide variety of potentially costly damages to the house, the garage, and other structures on the property, such as storage units. Personal possessions covered in most insurance policies include furniture, appliances, clothing, and items stored in the garage (such as bicycles and power tools). Home insurance policies also cover injuries suffered by visitors to the property. For example, if a guest cut herself on the host's chain-link fence and required stitches, the medical expenses would be covered by the host's home insurance policy (assuming it was established that the injury was not caused by negligence on the part of the host or the guest).

The extent of the perils covered by a home insurance policy depends on the type of policy, but a typical policy will protect against windstorms, fire, and theft. Most people purchase "all-risk" (also called "open-peril") homeowner's insurance, which protects against all perils except those specifically excluded in the policy. All-risk policies often exclude damages caused by floods and earthquakes; protection from these natural disasters can be purchased separately. Most homeowner's policies do cover damages resulting from volcanic eruptions and hurricanes, but the deductible for hurricane damage is usually quite high. (A deductible is a previously agreed-upon amount of money that the homeowner has to pay toward the repairs before the insurance company makes

A home insurance policy provides homeowners with financial protection in the event their house is damaged or destroyed. Home damage resulting from unforeseen natural disasters—such as a sinkhole, or hole in the ground—is not always covered. *AP Images.*

its contribution.) The deductibles for hurricane and storm-related damage are larger in high-risk areas such as the Gulf Coast states, which include Texas, Louisiana, Mississippi, Alabama, and Florida. Damages caused by war are excluded from all policies.

When Did It Begin

Homeowner's insurance developed in the United States during the 1950s. Prior to that, American homeowners had to purchase separate insurance policies to cover losses from theft, damage to personal property, fire, and other perils that could affect a person's home. Although it became possible in the 1950s to buy a single policy that insured against most types of damage to a home, these policies varied from company to company and were often difficult to understand. A crisis soon emerged for both insurance companies and consumers. On the one hand, insurers had limited access to data that allowed them to screen potential customers and to determine accurately

the risk they were assuming by insuring homes in certain areas. Customers, on the other hand, had trouble comparing policies among companies because the language was incomprehensible to anyone not trained in the field of homeowner's insurance.

To alleviate these problems, in 1971 Insurance Services Organization (ISO) was established as a nonprofit agency in Jersey City, New Jersey. ISO developed a comprehensive database that provided insurance companies with records on millions of insurance policies and on insurance fraud. This helped the companies limit fraud by screening both potential clients and employees. ISO also sought to help insurance customers by provided standardized language for insurance policies. As of 2007 there were seven standardized home insurance policies, numbered H0-1 through H0-7. The most commonly purchased homeowner's policy is H0-3, also known as an all-risk policy. It protects against damage to all aspects of the home's structure and contents and against injuries suffered by visitors to the property.

More Detailed Information

A home insurance policy is effective for a fixed period of time, which is called the term of the policy. After the term expires, the provider maintains the right to cancel the policy. Many providers will choose to do so if the insured party makes too many costly claims against the policy (a claim is a report of loss and a request for reimbursement). The price of the policy is called the premium. Insurance providers base premium amounts on the risks they assume when underwriting (granting) a policy. For example, if a person buys a home in a location where natural disasters are rare, her premiums will be relatively low compared to the premiums for a policy on a house along a waterfront. A house with a burglar alarm and a smoke-activated sprinkler system lodged above the kitchen stove will cost less to insure than a home without these precautionary devices. If they choose not to cancel a policy at the end of term, most providers will at least raise the premiums of those who make numerous claims on the policy.

Homeowner's insurance is not required by law in the United States. The overwhelming majority of Americans who buy homes, however, do so with a home loan (also called a mortgage), and mortgage lenders require borrowers to purchase homeowner's insurance as a precondition of granting the loan. Lenders do this to protect their own interests, because until the loan is paid off, the lender owns part of the home, so if the house were to be destroyed, it would be a loss for the lender. With insurance, in the event that the home is destroyed, the insurance company would be required to pay off the rest of the loan, and the lender would recoup its loss. In most cases, the premium for the home insurance policy is included in the borrower's monthly payments to the mortgage lender.

A mortgage lender may not require homeowner's insurance if the value of the land on which the house is built is equal to or greater than the balance (the amount remaining) on the borrower's loan. For example, if a borrower had only $40,000 left to pay on his mortgage, and the plot of land on which his house was constructed was appraised at $50,000, then the lender may not require him to continue maintaining a home insurance policy. In such a case, if the uninsured home were destroyed and the borrower could not pay the balance owed on the loan, the bank would foreclose the loan, or repossess the property, and thereby immediately recoup the value of the outstanding balance on the loan.

Although home insurance policies exclude some notable disasters, they do cover a wide range of costly damages. For example, most policies include protection against water damage (other than that caused by floods or homeowner negligence). For example, if an early frost hit, causing a homeowner's water pipes to freeze and burst, the insurance company would pay for repairs. If a policyholder had tile damage resulting from a chronically leaking hot water heater, however, the insurance company likely would not pay for repairs. If there were ice damage from hail or from the weight of ice gathered atop the house, most policies would cover the necessary repairs. Policies also protect against violence and vandalism. This means that if a teenager threw a rock through an expensive picture window or drove across a homeowner's lawn, expenses for repairs would be covered by the insurance policy. Most home insurance policies also include a provision called "loss of use," according to which the owner of the policy is reimbursed for the expense of having to live in another residence while his home is being restored following a disaster.

Many homeowners seek additional coverage such as extended replacement cost coverage. Such coverage pays a certain amount above the policy limit, usually 120 to 125 percent, to repair or rebuild a home that has been destroyed by a peril covered in the policy. Most policies account for inflation (the overall rising of prices throughout the economy), which means that the company agrees to pay a higher amount for repairs later in the policy as such costs rise. Some events, however, cause repair prices to rise well beyond the rate of inflation, in which cases extended replacement cost coverage is a great benefit. For example, if a hailstorm caused significant damage to 1,000 roofs in a given neighborhood, roofers in the neighborhood might conspire to charge exorbitant rates for repairs because the demand was so high. While an insurance agency might properly assess damages at $5,000, a roofer may ask for $6,500. In such a case, extended replacement cost coverage would make up the difference.

Recent Trends

At the start of the twenty-first century, premiums for homeowner's insurance were rising significantly

CITIZENS PROPERTY INSURANCE CORPORATION

The Citizens Property Insurance Corporation, or "Citizens," as it is often called, is a government-owned insurance company in Florida. Citizens was created in 2002 in response to the fact that many private insurance companies were refusing to offer homeowner's insurance because of an increase in claims for damages caused by tropical storms, flooding, and sinkholes (holes in the ground, ranging from one foot to several hundred yards in diameter and depth, formed when large amounts of water displace soil). Citizens became an insurer of last resort for Floridians in high-risk areas (those areas especially susceptible to hurricanes and floods) and for people who could not obtain coverage in the open market. To avoid competition with the state's private firms, Citizens charged the highest legal rate for homeowner's insurance. In 2003 Citizens began selling policies to private insurance companies in Florida willing to assume the risk. The crisis worsened in 2004 and 2005, when there were record levels of damage during the hurricane seasons. Many residents of Florida considered the insurance crisis the most important issue in the 2006 gubernatorial elections.

throughout the United States because of an increase of claims for damages caused by severe weather conditions such as hurricanes, hailstorms, droughts, floods, and wildfires. Whereas in the early 1970s insurance companies paid between $2 billion and $3 billion annually for property damages, from 1995 to 2005, companies paid an average of $15 billion per year in property damages. Three times in that span annual damages totaled more than $25 billion, including a record high of more than $45 billion in 2004. That year $30 billion was paid out for hurricane damages alone. After the catastrophic losses in 2004, the National Association of Insurance Commissioners scheduled a meeting in New Orleans for September 2005 to discuss the effects of global climate change on insurance premiums. That meeting was canceled because of Hurricane Katrina, which flooded and severely damaged the city.

No state has been hit harder by severe weather than Florida, where insurers paid $25.1 billion in 2004 and another $10.8 billion in 2005. According to some reports, the storms of 2004 completely exhausted the claims-paying capacity that Allstate Floridian Insurance Company, one of the leading issuers of homeowner's insurance in the state, had built (by collecting premiums from customers) over the previous 10 years. Following the two successive years of crisis, hundreds of thousands of homeowner's policies were canceled in Florida. In the wake of the disasters, many companies refused to write new homeowner's policies, leaving Floridians to purchase insurance from the state-owned Citizens Property Insurance Corporation.

$ Renter's Insurance

What It Means

A person buys property insurance as a way of transferring the financial risk of losing his or her property, either through theft or damage. The company that sells the insurance assumes the risk of the property being lost and promises to reimburse the property owner for damaged or stolen items. Renter's insurance is a form of property insurance for people who rent, rather than own, their homes.

When you rent an apartment, the landlord (or owner) of the building you live in is required to carry insurance on the building itself, but the landlord's insurance does not cover the contents of your apartment, such as clothing, furniture, stereos, cameras, bicycles, and televisions. If you cannot afford to replace these personal belongings if they are ruined in a fire or stolen by a burglar, buying renter's insurance will help protect you financially.

In addition to paying for your damaged or lost property, renter's insurance will cover your additional living expenses (such as a hotel bill and restaurant meals) if your apartment is temporarily uninhabitable in the aftermath of a fire, explosion, windstorm, or other peril that is covered by your policy (an insurance contract is called a policy; in insurance terms, "peril" is defined as that which can cause loss).

Renter's insurance also contains liability coverage, or protection against third-party claims. This means that if someone decides to sue you after tripping on your rug and breaking an arm, getting bitten by your dog, or otherwise being injured on your premises, renter's insurance will pay for your legal bills and any payments to the injured party that are stipulated by the court.

U.S. statistics suggest that people who rent their homes are more likely to be victims of vandalism and theft than people who own their homes. Renters are also are also at risk for substantial losses caused by fire and other such perils. Renter's insurance is inexpensive compared to homeowner's insurance, because it covers only the contents of the home and not the home itself. The average cost of a renter's insurance policy is about $20 per month (or $240 per year) for coverage of $20,000 in property and $500,000 in liability.

When Did It Begin

Property insurance as we know it today traces its roots to seventeenth-century London. Following the Great Fire of 1666, which destroyed more than 13,000 houses, fire insurance emerged as a vital business. Although some fire insurance was issued to individuals by private companies, it was more common for people seeking insurance to form a mutual company, a group of people in which each individual owned a share of the collective risk.

The first mutual insurance company in the United States, the Friendly Society of Mutual Insuring of Homes Against Fire, was established in Charleston, South Carolina, in 1732. Twenty years later Benjamin Franklin (1706–90) organized the Philadelphia Contributionship for the Insurance of Houses from Loss by Fire. As demand for fire insurance continued to grow, mutual societies multiplied across the eastern United States, and many companies that once had offered marine (shipping) insurance exclusively began to sell fire insurance as well. Whereas the mutual companies only insured real estate against fire, however, the private companies now began to insure the contents of the buildings, too.

In the nineteenth century the broadening scope and specialization of the types of insurance available in the United States ran parallel to the marked expansion of Americans' personal economic prosperity. In addition to fire and other natural perils, for example, people began to seek financial protection from burglary and related crimes. Renter's insurance was likely introduced toward the end of the century, as apartment living became fashionable among the wealthy in urban areas, especially New York City.

More Detailed Information

Before you buy renter's insurance, it is a good idea to take an inventory. Make a list of all of the items you want to insure, including price estimates and dates of purchase (to the extent that this is possible). It is also wise to photograph each item, as this visual evidence will make it easier if you ever need to file a claim (to file a claim with the insurance company is to report that something has been

People who live in rented properties often take out renter's insurance to insure their possessions against potential damage or theft. This photo shows the remains of an apartment complex in Florida after a tornado. *AP Images.*

lost or damaged and to request reimbursement). Once you have an idea of what your belongings are worth, it will be easier to decide how much coverage you need. Also, make sure to keep a copy of your inventory somewhere outside your apartment, such as with a friend or relative or in a safe-deposit box (a private locked box inside a bank that an individual can rent).

When shopping for a renter's insurance policy, there are a few key variables to consider: the kind of policy, the deductible, and additional coverage for expensive items.

Renter's insurance covers your possessions in one of two ways: actual cash value or replacement cost. A policy that covers actual cash value will determine the amount of reimbursement for any given item by considering the item's original purchase price and then reducing this value according to the age and condition of the item at the time it was stolen or damaged. Simply put, a cash-value policy will only cover what your property is actually worth, not what you originally paid for it or what it would cost to buy a comparable item today. So, for example, if you paid $250 for a pair of designer boots three years ago, and you wore those boots every day of the winter for three years until they were burned in your apartment fire, the insurance company might determine that the actual cash value of those boots was only $20. A policy that covers replacement cost does just the opposite, by reimbursing you for the amount it would cost you to buy the same or a comparable pair of boots three years later. The replacement-value policy seems preferable, but it also costs more.

The deductible is the amount of loss you, the policyholder, are responsible for before the insurance kicks in. So, for example, if you have a $500 deductible, and someone breaks into your apartment and steals your $700 bike, the insurance will only reimburse you for the $200 that is over and above your deductible. Here again, the policy that offers the most coverage is also the most expensive (that is, the lower the deductible, the higher the cost of the policy).

A third important variable is additional coverage. Basic renter's insurance policies have coverage limits on certain kinds of valuables, such as jewelry, silverware, and computers. For example, most policies cover only about $2,000 in stolen jewelry. Find out what these limits are and how they apply to your own belongings. If you need additional coverage for a certain category of valuable, it is possible to buy what is called a floater, an addendum to your policy that will cover the full value of the valuables in question.

When comparing different renter's insurance options, it is also smart to ask about discounts. Oftentimes, for example, your auto-insurance company will give you a discounted rate if you buy your renter's insurance from them, too. Insurance companies also offer discounts to renters who reduce their risk of peril, such as nonsmokers, and those who install dead-bolt locks and smoke detectors.

RENTER'S INSURANCE: A MUST FOR DOG OWNERS

Renter's insurance provides financial protection to people who rent their homes. In case of fire, theft, or other peril (an event that causes property loss or destruction), the insurance company will reimburse the insured renter (called the policyholder) for the property he or she has lost. A lesser-known benefit of renter's insurance is that, like homeowner's insurance, it covers the policyholder against liability (financial responsibility) if someone is injured in the policyholder's home or is bitten by the policyholder's dog (even outside the home).

Statistics show that about 4.5 million people in the United States are victims of dog bites every year, and that more than 300,000 of these victims are admitted to hospitals for treatment for dog-bite wounds. The cost of treating these injuries is estimated at $1 billion per year. If your dog bites or injures someone, and you get sued, you could be required to pay extensive damages. In order to avoid such an eventuality, experts in dog-bite law urge dog owners who rent to buy a renter's insurance policy that includes dog-bite coverage.

When you have found a policy that suits your needs and your budget, make sure to read it carefully, and ask the insurance agent to clarify anything you do not understand before you sign the papers.

Recent Trends

According to a national survey conducted by Trusted Choice, an alliance of independently owned insurance agencies in the United States, 25 million families who rented their homes in 2006 did not have renter's insurance. Indeed, the survey found that, even while 89 percent of families that rented owned at least one valuable electronic device, only one in three carried rental insurance coverage.

The survey addressed the question of why so many Americans were going without rental insurance even though the overwhelming majority of financial advisers, realtors, and other industry professionals advised getting it. According to the survey 26 percent of those without coverage felt that it was too expensive, 17 percent did not know they needed it, and 8 percent had never even heard of renter's insurance.

$ Car Insurance

What It Means

A car insurance policy is a contract between an insurance company and the owner of a vehicle that protects the vehicle's owner (or the person who leases the vehicle) from financial losses that result from car accidents. While many different types of car insurance policies are available, these policies in general cover the policyholder, the policyholder's vehicle, and third parties. Third parties may include other drivers, pedestrians, or cyclists who suffer injuries from a collision with the policyholder or whose property is damaged in a collision caused by the policyholder. All vehicle owners and lessees in the United States must have car insurance. Specific requirements vary from state to state, but all U.S. drivers are required to have insurance against damages inflicted upon third parties.

An insurance policy can save a driver a considerable amount of money. For example, if an insured driver causes a collision that results in damage to another driver's vehicle, the first driver's insurance policy would pay a significant portion of the cost to repair or replace the other driver's car. If the driver of the hit car also suffers bodily injury, the first driver's insurance company would pay a significant portion of the injured driver's medical fees.

Most car insurance policies in the United States last for six months. The person taking out the policy (the policyholder) pays the insurance company a fee called a premium, which is due every six months. If the policyholder is not involved in any collisions and does not cause damage with his or her vehicle, then most insurance companies will renew the insurance policy automatically at the end of each six-month term. In 2007 drivers paid on average $774 a year to insure a car in the United States. This means that U.S. drivers paid an average premium of $387 every six months for car insurance policies.

When Did It Begin

The first car insurance policy on record in the United States was issued by the Travelers Insurance Company to Dr. Truman Martin of Buffalo, New York, in February 1898. Dr. Martin paid $12.25 for the policy, which gave him $5,000 worth of coverage. The Travelers Insurance Company wrote its first car insurance policy on forms it normally used for covering damages caused by horses and mules. In fact, Martin's primary concern was to obtain a policy that would cover damages caused by horses. He was not worried about damage caused by other cars; at the end of the nineteenth century, an estimated 20 million horses and only 4,000 cars were used for travel in the United States. Other drivers soon followed Martin's lead. By 1899 car insurance policies were common in the United States.

Collisions became more common in the United States during the early part of the twentieth century as more cars were produced and roads became more congested. The first measure taken to reduce damage caused by collisions was the installation of bumpers, which first appeared on U.S. cars in 1915. These bumpers were not included with the car but sold by car dealers as an additional feature. They were mounted on spring-and-steel brackets at the front of the car. It was not until 1973 that the U.S. government set standards for the placement and quality of bumpers.

More Detailed Information

Insurance rates (the cost for insurance premiums) vary widely and depend on a number of factors. One of the primary factors is the profile of the driver. Before entering into an agreement with a new client, an insurance company will assess the likelihood that the new client will make a claim against the policy (in other words, formally request that the insurance company pay for damages to the driver, to his or her vehicle, or to a third party). If the company determines that a client is likely to make a claim, the company will charge more money for the policy. If the person appears to be too great a risk, the company will not sell him or her a policy. The chief factor in assessing the risks associated with insuring a prospective client is the client's past driving record. If the person has been in a number of accidents or received a number of traffic tickets, the insurance company will regard him or her as a greater risk than a person without any prior accidents or tickets.

Aside from the client's driving record, insurance companies base their determination of risk on several other factors. Insurance companies make these determinations based on close analysis of statistics from traffic accidents and past claims made on insurance policies. For example, young drivers aged 18 to 25 are a greater risk than older drivers, and they are therefore charged higher rates. In the 18-to-25 age range, male drivers are a greater risk than female drivers. Single drivers are a greater risk than married drivers. Where the car will be most frequently driven also affects the premium. For example, it costs more to insure a car that will be driven in a densely populated urban center than it costs to insure a car that will be driven in a rural area.

There are many different types of car insurance. Liability insurance covers bodily injury to others and damages to other drivers' vehicles. The extent of liability insurance is usually listed as a series of three numbers that show how much money, in thousands of dollars, an insurance company will pay if it is determined that a policyholder is at fault in an automobile accident. For example, in the event of an accident a 100/300/50 liability insurance policy will pay up to $300,000 of bodily injury coverage to the injured parties (other than the policyholder) not exceeding $100,000 to any individual and $50,000 for property damages to third parties. Although laws in most states require substantially less liability coverage (15/30/5 in California, for example), most experts recommend that a driver purchase 100/300/50 worth of liability insurance.

Since injuries and damages caused by car accidents can be extremely costly, victims of accidents often sue the people they believe to be responsible for the damages. These lawsuits can cost millions of dollars. To limit the number of lawsuits, 12 states in the United States have adopted what is called "no-fault insurance." No-fault insurance policies require drivers to purchase personal injury insurance (PIP) for their own protection and limit policyholders' ability to sue other drivers for damages. In a no-fault system, a policyholder's insurance company will cover injuries to the policyholder regardless of who is at fault. Meanwhile, the other driver's insurance will cover his own injuries. Only one party in the accident will be permitted to sue if an arbiter determines that the personal injuries were excessively severe and that the fault lay with the other driver.

Other types of insurance include collision insurance and comprehensive insurance. Collision insurance covers the policyholder's vehicle in the event of an accident in which the policyholder is determined to be at fault. This sort of insurance includes a deductible, or an amount of money that the policyholder must pay before the insurance company will begin to cover expenses. For example, if a driver holding $10,000 worth of collision insurance with a $500 deductible is at fault in an accident that causes $3,000 worth of damage to his vehicle, the policyholder will pay $500 for the repairs to his vehicle and the insurance company will pay the remaining $2,500. Comprehensive insurance covers damages to the policyholder's vehicle caused by incidents that are not considered to be collisions. Such incidents may include theft, fire, hurricane damage, or vandalism.

Recent Trends

Since the early years of the twenty-first century, Americans have been turning to the Internet in increasing numbers for car insurance information. From 2004 to 2006 an estimated 70 million prospective insurance customers received quotes for car insurance prices online. However, in 2004 and 2005 most of these people did not actually purchase car insurance online. That began to change in 2006, when online car insurance purchases increased by 58 percent. Through January and February 2007 online car insurance purchases were 45 percent higher than they were at the same time the previous year.

Market analysts attribute this trend to three factors. First, insurance companies have made a concerted effort to direct potential clients to the Internet. Most commercials for car insurance encourage customers to visit the company website, and some companies offer discounted rates for web clients. Second, insurance companies have invested large sums of money in upgrading their websites, which now typically display complex sets of information in a clear, easy-to-read format. Most of these websites have a "Frequently Asked Questions" (FAQ) section that covers the issues that most people discuss with insurance agents. Third, Americans have gradually become more comfortable sharing such confidential information as social security and credit card numbers on-

ROADSIDE ASSISTANCE

In the past most car insurance policies only covered the cost of towing a vehicle if that vehicle had been damaged in an accident. Many drivers require towing, however, because of mechanical problems or breakdowns that occur on the road. To insure themselves against the cost of such damages, many U.S. drivers purchase membership in the American Automobile Association (AAA or "Triple A"). In exchange for yearly dues, members of AAA receive roadside assistance in the event of a breakdown. When called, a representative of AAA visits the scene of the breakdown and repairs or jump-starts the car or, if necessary, tows the vehicle to a location where it can be repaired. Since the first years of the twenty-first century, many insurance companies have begun offering roadside-assistance coverage. These policies often include coverage for towing, battery jump starts, fuel delivery (for drivers who run out of gas while on the road), and locksmiths (for drivers who lock their keys in their cars).

line. Information of this sort is required for online car insurance application forms.

$ Warranty

What It Means

In legal terminology, a warranty is a promise or assurance made by one party to another concerning the truth or integrity of a certain statement of fact. In other words, a warranty is a kind of guarantee that governs the terms of a transaction between two parties. Warranties are used in a variety of business contexts. The three most common situations in which a warranty is used are the sale of goods and services, the sale of real estate, and the sale of insurance.

In the sale or lease of goods and services, the seller or manufacturer of a product (for example, a dishwasher) provides the consumer with a warranty, which certifies that the product is truthfully represented (meaning that it will work as promised). This warranty is a form of contract that also specifies the conditions under which the seller will grant a refund, provide an exchange, or repair the product at no extra charge to the consumer. The warranty also specifies various restrictions, including how long the terms of the warranty will remain in effect and under what circumstances they will be void. This type of warranty usually accompanies the sale of cars, appliances, and electronic goods such as computers.

In real estate, the most common form of warranty is a general warranty deed. Provided by the seller of a house, apartment, land parcel, or other property, it certifies that the title to the property (a certificate of proof of ownership), which will be transferred to the buyer at the

The New Vehicle Limited Warranty provides 36-month/36,000-mile comprehensive coverage, 5-year/60,000-mile powertrain coverage, plus 5-year body panel corrosion perforation warranty. See Owner's Warranty Information booklet for details. An extended service contract may be available for the vehicle. Ask dealer for details.
Manufacturer's suggested retail price includes manufacturer's recommended pre-delivery service. Gasoline, license and title fees, applicable federal, state and local taxes and dealer and distributor installed options and accessories are not included in the manufacturer's suggested retail price.

A product warranty states that if a product does not function as it should, at least for a designated period of time after its sale, the manufacturer will fix, replace, or refund it. The new vehicle warranty shown here specifies the terms and limits of its coverage. *Photograph by Kelly A. Quin. Cengage Learning, Gale.*

time of sale, is free from encumbrances. This means that no one else, such as a bank, construction company, or judgment debtor (someone who is awarded a claim to the house in a court settlement), has a preexisting claim to the house.

In insurance, the validity of an insurance policy (or contract) is often contingent upon certain warranties provided by the insured party at the time the policy is written. Insurance companies require these warranties as a way to limit and control the amount of risk they assume in extending insurance to the party in question. So, for example, a health insurance company might require that the insured person provide a warranty certifying that he or she has not been diagnosed with cancer or some other potentially fatal disease. If this warranty is found to be untrue, it is considered a breach of contract, and the insurer has the right to refuse coverage and terminate the policy.

In each of these scenarios, the purpose of the warranty is to limit the risk associated with the transaction: the risk that the dishwasher will stop running after one month, the risk that the property title is encumbered by hidden claims, and the risk of insuring someone whose illnesses will be costly to treat.

When Did It Begin

The word *warranty* has been used for various kinds of guarantees and assurances since the fourteenth century. Under feudal law in England at that time, for example, the grantor of a freehold estate provided a warranty to the grantee (the relationship between grantor and grantee was similar to that between landlord and tenant), promising that if the grantee were to be evicted from that particular piece of land, the grantor would provide him with another, equally valuable piece of land somewhere else. The earliest known usage of the word *warranty* in relation to the sale of consumer goods has been traced to

1543; in relation to insurance, the earliest known usage of the word dates to 1817.

In the United States consumer warranties are governed by the Magnuson-Moss Warranty Act, which was passed by Congress in 1975, largely as a result of the consumer-protection movement that began in the 1960s. The first federal statute to address the issue of warranties, the act was intended to eradicate the widespread problem of merchants issuing false or misleading warranties with their products. Magnuson-Moss does not require manufacturers or sellers to provide written warranties with their products; it does, however, stipulate that any warranties that are provided must disclose their terms and restrictions in clear, easy-to-understand language. The act also states that written warranties must be clearly identified as either "full" or "limited." A full warranty states that defects, malfunctions, or other problems with the product must be repaired or otherwise remedied by the responsible party in a timely way at no extra charge to the consumer. A limited warranty may include reasonable restrictions that limit the responsibility of the manufacturer or seller for the repair or replacement of the product. Magnuson-Moss is enforced by the Federal Trade Commission (FTC), an independent agency of the federal government whose responsibilities include protecting American consumers from various kinds of fraud and deception.

More Detailed Information

A consumer warranty is either express or implied. An express warranty is one in which the manufacturer or seller explicitly guarantees the quality or performance of the product and specifies the circumstances under which the product can be returned, exchanged, or repaired. This kind of warranty is usually, but not necessarily, given in the form of a written document that assures the quality of the product, its workmanship, and its materials. An express warranty might also apply to services rendered: for example, a house painter might guarantee his paint job to last for two years and promise to repaint at no charge any spots that should peel before that time. An advertisement describing a product (for instance, stating that a table is "solid oak" or that a necklace is "22-karat gold") may also be considered an express warranty, such that the consumer is entitled to a refund if the terms of the advertisement turn out to be untrue. An express warranty can even be delivered orally by a salesperson—for example, if she states, "These shoes are ergonomically designed; they are recommended for people with back problems by the National Association of Orthopedic Medicine." Still, however, many promises made by salespeople are recognized as "puffery" (a term for un-verifiable exaggerations), which does not constitute an express warranty. An example of puffery is "These shoes will make you feel like you're walking on air."

An implied warranty is one that is not explicitly stated by the seller but rather can be understood (or expected) by the buyer as a basic fact of the sales trans-action. Implied warranties are based on the common-law principle that a consumer should expect to receive "fair value for money spent." The two main forms of implied warranty are the "warranty of merchantability" and the "warranty of fitness for a particular purpose."

A warranty of merchantability refers to the basic as-sumption that a given product is in good working con-dition and can be used in the intended way. For example, a water heater can be expected to provide hot water; a lawn mower can be expected to cut grass; and a coffee-maker can be expected to brew coffee. A warranty of fitness for a particular purpose relates to the consumer's stated purpose in purchasing a product and his right to assume that the salesperson will sell him a product that is appropriate for that purpose. For example, if you go to a camping store and tell the salesperson you need a sleeping bag for snow camping, you should be able to rely upon his judgment to sell you a sleeping bag that is designed for sub-zero temperatures. If, in fact, the salesperson sells you a sleeping bag that is only good down to 50 degrees, he can be said to have breached (or broken) the implied warranty of fitness for a particular purpose.

Recent Trends

Retailers often encourage customers to buy "extended warranties" in addition to the manufacturer's express warranty that normally comes with home appliances, electronic equipment, power tools, and many other consumer goods. An extended warranty (sometimes called a service contract) is a form of product insurance that is sold separately from the product itself; it promises to protect the consumer if something goes wrong with the product after the manufacturer's warranty has expired.

EXTENDED WARRANTIES: GOOD FOR RETAILERS, NOT CONSUMERS

If you have purchased any electronic equipment in the last de-cade or so, you have probably been urged by the salesperson to consider buying the "extended warranty." A warranty is a form of contract in which the manufacturer or seller promises to re-place or repair a defective product for a certain period of time after the product is purchased. An extended warranty, then, is one that extends the period of time for which the product is guaranteed. On average, an extended warranty can add be-tween 10 to 30 percent to the price of the product. This is a nice bonus for the retailer, but consumer groups warn that it is rarely worth it for the consumer, particularly because extended war-ranties often contain fine print that makes it impossible for consumers to get the repairs to which they thought they were entitled.

Say, for example, you go to an electronics store and, after much deliberation, decide to purchase a new laptop computer for $999. The computer comes with a one-year warranty from the manufacturer, but the salesperson strongly urges you to buy an extended three-year war-ranty for an additional $300. This seems like a hefty price increase on the original $999, but what if your computer breaks just a month after the manufacturer's warranty expires? The $300 for the extended warranty is a lot less than the cost of a whole new laptop. Indeed, under considerable pressure from salespeople, many consumers agree to buy the extended warranty because it seems to offer some sense of security about the investment they are making in a given product.

Extended warranties were first introduced in the 1980s and have since become big business. According to *Stores* magazine, a retail-trade journal, extended warran-ties accounted for more than $5 billion worth of sales in North America in 2002. Yet *Consumer Reports* and many other consumer-protection groups routinely advise con-sumers against buying these extended warranties, citing evidence that they are usually not worth the cost.

$ Medical Insurance

What It Means

Medical, or health, insurance is a contract under which a private medical insurance company or a government agency promises to pay for or provide health-care ser-vices. In most cases the people who are insured pay a set monthly amount, called a premium, for medical insur-ance. The insurance company compensates customers (called the insured) for qualifying medical expenses or sometimes pays the health-care provider directly. The insurance contract often must be renewed every year, at which time the premiums may go up. Medical insurance is a form of financial protection for the insured, who, though they must pay monthly premiums, will be guaranteed against significant monetary loss in case of illness or injury.

Medical insurance exists in every country in the world, though the form it takes varies. The United States is the only developed, industrial nation without a universal health-care system (one in which all residents have access to health care regardless of their ability to pay or of their medical condition), though 27 percent of the population is insured by tax-financed government programs, such as Medicare and Medicaid. Under a fully public medical insurance system, the national government serves as an insurance company, collecting health-care fees (in taxes and government subsidies) and paying out costs. In contrast, private medical insurance companies are generally for-profit businesses that work with providers (physicians, hospitals, and others who supply health-care services) to offer several options in insurance plans. The financial goal of private-sector insurance is to end up with a profit after customers' claims (requests for payment of medical expenses) are paid out of the premiums the company takes in.

The United States has a market-based system in which the private sector rather than the government provides most of the health care and insurance and in which costs are determined by market forces, such as supply (what providers are willing to provide and at what price) and demand (what consumers want and are willing to pay for). The federal government allows individual states to regulate the health-insurance system, including the insurance companies' conduct in marketing (advertising and selling their services), underwriting (selecting who and what they will cover and, conversely, which policyholders and risks they will deny for coverage), and rate setting.

About 60 percent of Americans obtain medical insurance through their workplace, which subscribes to and partially funds a group plan for employees. Insured employees pay a small part of the premium and, for a higher amount, can also cover spouses and children up to the age of 21, if the children are still in school. Federal law does not require workplaces to provide medical insurance packages to employees, though many states require employers to buy workers' compensation insurance, which pays for care related to injuries suffered when a worker is on the job. Part-time workers and those who work for businesses with few employees often cannot get medical insurance through their workplace. State teachers associations, bar associations (for lawyers), and other work-related support groups sometimes provide insurance for members who qualify. Nine percent of Americans subscribe to individual medical insurance plans, which are costly and offer more limited options. Other people qualify for government-sponsored insurance (Medicare or Medicaid). Approximately 16 percent of Americans (more than 45 million people) are uninsured.

When Did It Begin

Injury and illness have always posed financial risks to people, and the idea of moderating the risks by spreading them out over time and over groups of people has been around since the days of the Roman Empire, when artisans organized rudimentary forms of medical insurance. The craft guilds in medieval England (the medieval period lasted from about 500 to about 1500) also insured members against losses due to illness and injury, and the practice eventually led in the nineteenth century to English mutual aid societies (voluntary organizations that collected dues and assisted members in need). The idea of mutual aid spread through Europe alongside industrialization, though participation was low and the organizations were not able to pay adequate benefits. Germany passed the first national compulsory medical insurance law (under which the government was required to make health care accessible to everyone) in 1883. By 1920 many European countries had nationalized medical insurance (governments used taxes to run hospitals and pay doctors) in place. Today more than 60 countries have compulsory governmental medical insurance programs.

In the United States the first mutual protection association was established in San Francisco in 1851. In the 1870s railroad and mining industries began hiring company doctors to treat workers. The department store chain Montgomery Ward developed one of the first group medical insurance plans (in 1910). Before 1920 most Americans spent relatively little on medical treatment. A household's main illness-related expense was lost wages from missed work. Private companies did not offer medical insurance. Proposals for universal health care were defeated by physicians and pharmacists, who feared their businesses would suffer, and by a lack of perceived need on the part of the population.

An increased demand for medical care in the United States in the 1920s coincided with advances in medical science and higher standards for physician licensing; medical costs began to rise. In 1929 Blue Cross established the first prepaid hospital care plan for Dallas public school teachers, who paid 50 cents a month for a guarantee of 21 days of hospital services. These plans became more common during the Great Depression (which lasted from 1929 to about 1939), when patients and hospitals both had less income. The first prepaid plan that covered physicians' services was established in 1939 by physicians hoping to fight both hospital control of insurance and those who promoted compulsory insurance. The American Medical Association lobbied to defeat nationalized medical insurance proposals, including one

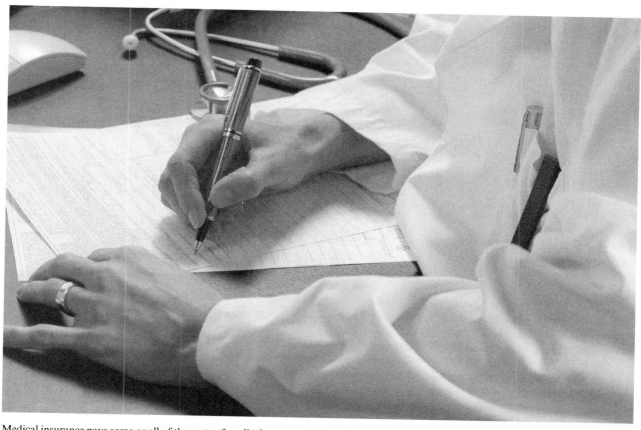

Medical insurance pays some or all of the costs of medical care, usually in exchange for a monthly fee. Both patients and physicians typically file claims, or requests for payment, with the insurance provider © *Larry William/Corbis.*

made by President Harry S. Truman (1884–1972), in 1935 and 1949.

During World War II (1939–45) the U.S. government began providing tax benefits to employers and workers who participated in private medical insurance plans. The number of employers offering medical insurance through the workplace grew, and through these plans insurance companies targeted a relatively young, healthy population that would be profitable to work with. The number of people with medical insurance rose from fewer than 20,000 in 1940 to more than 120,000 in 1960. By 1959 more than 75 percent of Americans had medical insurance. In his 1960 presidential campaign John F. Kennedy (1917–63) supported the Medicare program, which, along with Medicaid, was signed into law by President Lyndon B. Johnson (1908–73) in 1965. Former president Truman was the first to enroll in Medicare.

More Detailed Information

Four distinct kinds of medical insurance are available in the United States: indemnity plans, two types of managed-care plans, and government-provided insurance. Many insurance plans combine features of the different types.

Indemnity (or traditional) insurance plans pay for some expenses, though usually at a set percentage of the cost (for instance, the insurance company pays 80 percent and the insured pays 20 percent; the 20 percent is called a coinsurance payment) up to a certain limit per year (the out-of-pocket maximum), beyond which the company pays 100 percent of qualifying expenses. The insured can choose any standard health-care provider or hospital and must pay for whatever services are not covered by the plan. In addition to premiums and coinsurance, the insured must pay a deductible each year. A deductible is a fixed initial sum, ranging from a few hundred to several thousand dollars, in qualified medical costs that the insured pays before insurance coverage takes over its part. Many insurance plans allow the insured to choose among deductible amounts: a higher deductible means a lower premium and vice versa. Plans that have very high deductibles and that are designed to cover only long-term or catastrophic illness or injury are called major-medical plans. Indemnity plans are the most flexible medical insurance coverage in terms of choice, but they often cost more than managed-care plans.

Both health maintenance organizations (HMOs) and preferred provider organizations (PPOs) are types of managed care, a concept that began to influence health-care policy in the 1980s. Managed care was designed to reduce medical costs in several ways, including by encouraging doctors and patients to choose less expensive forms of care, by reviewing services patients or doctors request to determine whether they are medically necessary, and by controlling admissions to hospitals and lengths of hospital stays. HMOs provide the actual health services to their clients rather than reimbursing patients for medical expenses. They require that the insured's health care be coordinated through a primary care physician (PCP), who must be consulted first and who can then write out a referral for any specialist care. The insured must choose providers and hospitals from a list of those associated with the HMO and must pay a co-payment (a standard fee, usually $10 or $20) at the time of service. HMOs provide insurance coverage through employers and are usually the least expensive type of private insurance.

PPOs are insurance companies that work with networks of physicians and hospitals who agree to provide medical services and supervision at reduced fees to people insured under their plan. Most PPO plans require payment of a deductible and coinsurance. The insured may choose to receive services from a doctor or an institution not on the plan (these are called out-of-network providers), but the insured will have to pay a larger portion of the bill and in some cases the whole bill.

The U.S. government provides some insurance programs that are free or inexpensive for qualified users and that are funded by federal income taxes and some premiums. These include Medicare, which covers U.S. citizens who are 65 or older, people with disabilities, and others with specific illnesses; Medicaid (this program is cofunded by the states, which administer the program), for people who live on very low incomes or who have a disability not covered by Medicare; the State Children's Health Insurance Program, which covers children of low-income families; and the U.S. Department of Veterans Affairs, which covers injured veterans (former members of the armed services) and currently active servicemen and women.

People usually need to begin thinking about medical insurance when they turn 21 or graduate from college; they may be covered under family insurance plans or children's health-care programs until they are 21, and most universities provide students with medical insurance. It is commonly considered risky to forgo insurance altogether, because an accident or illness can use up savings and lead to large debts. Also many insurers refuse to cover any condition that develops during a gap in coverage. There are benefits to going directly from one group medical insurance plan to another, such as that preexisting conditions (these may include bunions, asthma, depression, cancer, and so forth) may continue to be covered if the lapse in coverage is 30 days or less. Full-time jobs often come with medical insurance benefits (even if there has been a gap in coverage), but sometimes employees cannot enroll in a plan until they have been on the job for several months, and any health care related to preexisting conditions may not be covered for a certain period of time after the policy does become effective.

There are many things to keep in mind when selecting medical insurance. Even work-related insurance often involves choosing among several plans. Good questions to ask include the following: How much are the premium, deductible, and co-pay or coinsurance amounts? What medical services does the policy cover and exclude? Are preexisting conditions covered? Does the policy cover enrollees right away, or is there a waiting period? Does the plan limit the choice of providers? Does it require preapproval for certain services? What are the out-of-pocket and lifetime maximum expenses that the insured may be responsible for?

When a person goes to a health-care provider's office, he or she usually has to show proof of insurance or sign an agreement to pay in part or in full. Uninsured people may have to pay up front, and a person on an HMO plan may need to pay a co-payment. The health-care provider most often bills the insurance company and receives payment from the company directly and then bills the patient for any remaining amount. The insurance company usually has a schedule of fees it considers reasonable for each service or procedure. The provider must discount the rest of the bill for those on HMO or PPO plans; in some cases the insured must pay the difference. Prescription drugs are often covered under a separate plan with the same insurance company. Pharmacies usually bill the insurance company directly; they have the insurance schedule in their computers and charge only the uncovered portion of the charges.

Recent Trends

Medical costs in the United States are rising quickly, partly because of costly advanced technology (which American health-care providers use earlier and more often than do doctors in other countries) and partly because people are living longer. The baby-boom generation (those born during an era of high birth rates after the end of World War II) is beginning to reach retirement age and can expect to live another two decades, with associated medical costs. In 2004, however, life expectancy in the United States (77 years) was lower than in 22 other nations, including Japan, Australia, New Zealand, Canada, and nearly all the western European countries.

Associated costs that are rising include hospital stays and specialist charges. The price of a day in the hospital rose from less than $200 in 1965 to more than $1,200 in 2004. Patients are seeing specialists more often, and charges for their services are nearly twice as high as for more general practitioners. Americans do not go to the doctor or hospital more than people in other countries,

UNIVERSAL MEDICAL INSURANCE

Universal medical insurance means that all the residents of a nation, regardless of their medical condition or their financial state, are entitled to health care through a national insurance program. The idea has been debated in the United States since the 1920s, when many European countries instituted national health-care plans, but it has never been implemented.

Those who oppose the idea of universal health care in the United States see health-care insurance as a product or service like any other, including those offered in such similar industries as car and home insurance. They urge that it should remain a free-market offering, citing the facts that universal medical insurance would have to be paid for with higher taxes and that nonprofits and government-run hospitals already care for the uninsured (no one can be refused medical service because of lack of insurance). Many also believe that government-run agencies are inefficient; that the free market has always benefited the consumer financially; that patients might overuse a free system so that total costs would rise; that possible reductions in provider pay and greater government control might lead to poor patient care and might discourage people from becoming doctors; that healthy people would end up paying for the care of the unhealthy, including smokers and the obese; that the transition to universal care would cause job losses and business closures; and that the program might be impossible to remove once established, even if costs get out of control.

Those in favor of universal coverage for U.S. residents believe health care has special characteristics that call for government involvement, either in mandating or providing health care for residents or in regulating those who do provide health care. These people see health care as a basic human right. They argue that unlike providers of other services or products, those in the field of health care are bound by law and by the oaths of service they take in their profession to give treatment that will save lives. They cite the facts that 40 million Americans are uninsured, that health care has become increasingly expensive, and that the health-care insurance industry is very complex for people to understand and generates massive amounts of paperwork. Many Americans also believe that under a more nationalized program, medical professionals could concentrate on healing rather than on insurance procedures; that a centralized national database could facilitate diagnosis and treatment; and that while people currently avoid preventive measures, such as annual exams, because of the cost, under universal health care they would be encouraged to look into health problems early, when treatment would be briefer and more successful.

but the treatment they get is more intensive and the costs are higher. Insurance premiums are also skyrocketing. In 2006 a single person who had insurance through work paid approximately $627 a year in insurance premiums, while the employer paid an additional $3,615 for that worker; a family of four paid $2,973, with the employer contributing another $8,508. To make matters worse, fewer employers are offering health benefits to their employees: 69 percent in 2000, as compared to 60 percent in 2005.

Americans spend more on health care than do people in any other country: in 2005 the United States spent $5,267 per person, compared with $2,931 in both Great Britain and Canada; 14.6 percent of the U.S. gross domestic product (the total financial value of all goods and services produced in the country in a given time period) goes to medical costs, as opposed to 9.6 percent in Great Britain and Canada. Also in 2005, 7.3 percent of U.S. national health spending went to administration and insurance costs, compared to only 1.9 percent in France. Many agree that the situation is not sustainable.

In 1976 some states began providing medical insurance plans for people unable to get medical insurance in other ways (because of preexisting conditions or self-employment), usually at a higher cost. In 2006 Massachusetts was the first state to pass a universal health-insurance coverage plan, and California, Maine, and Vermont are working on similar plans, with at least 15 other states considering this option.

At the federal level efforts to reform medical insurance practices have largely failed. President Bill Clinton (b. 1946) set up the Task Force on National Health Care Reform in 1992, charging it to come up with a plan that would provide universal health care for all Americans. Hillary Rodham Clinton (b. 1947) headed the committee, whose bill was finally defeated by Republican opposition and competing Democratic plans in 1994. A decade later President George W. Bush (b. 1946) signed the Medicare Prescription Drug, Improvement, and Modernization Act into law in 2003; it was to help senior citizens pay for their prescription drug costs. Opponents criticized the bill for its complexity and cost, and when the plan went into effect on January 1, 2006, some seniors were confused by its options and regulations and were concerned that the promised discounts would not materialize.

HEALTH MAINTENANCE ORGANIZATION

What It Means

A health maintenance organization, commonly referred to as an HMO, is an organization in the United States that provides a specialized form of health insurance for a prepaid monthly fee. With a typical health insurance policy, the insurer is required to pay for medical coverage according to the terms set forth in the insurance plan (called a policy). An HMO, however, not only pays for health care but also provides avenues for patients to

In the United States a health maintenance organization, or HMO, is a type of health insurance provider that tries to lower costs by limiting patients to certain procedures and doctors. Pictured here in 1999, President Bill Clinton urges Congress to pass health care reforms, including new rules for HMOs. *AP Images.*

receive that care. In fact, in order for a member of an HMO to receive coverage for medical expenses, he or she must use doctors, hospitals, clinics, and other facilities and providers approved by the HMO. In addition, to receive nonemergency medical coverage, that person may only submit to medical procedures that have been pre-authorized by the HMO. This means that if a member were to break her leg in a skiing accident and require emergency medical attention, she would not have to first seek approval from her HMO. But if that member wanted to have surgery on her inner ears to improve a non-life-threatening ailment, she would have to have the operation preapproved by her HMO.

This manner of providing medical services is one of several examples of what is called managed care. In any managed-care arrangement, the insurance company establishes guidelines according to which care must be provided if it is to be covered by the policy. In order to manage the care that they give to members, HMOs contract with a set of doctors, hospitals, and clinics who agree to receive more patients in exchange for charging a smaller fee. In this way, the HMO cuts costs on the money it has to pay out for members' medical care. HMOs also try to save money by eliminating what they deem to be unnecessary procedures. To accomplish

this, they require that each member select a primary care physician (PCP), who must give assent to all specialized treatment in order for those treatments to be covered. In other words, if a member of an HMO has a chronic earache, he must first see his PCP, who then chooses whether or not to refer him to an ear specialist. If the PCP does not make the referral and the patient consults the specialist regardless, that care will not be covered.

When Did It Begin

Although it was not called an HMO, the first example of prepaid, organized health care is believed by some to have occurred in Tacoma, Washington, in 1910, when the doctors at the Western Clinic provided service to lumber-mill owners and their employees for a monthly fee of 50 cents per member. Many others consider the Ross-Loss Medical Group of Los Angeles to be the first HMO. Established in 1929, that group initially offered health care to 500 employees at the Los Angeles Department of Water and Power for $1.50 per month. Shortly thereafter many other employees of Los Angeles County enrolled, and by 1951 the group had more than 35,000 members.

During the early 1930s other grassroots organizations formed agencies that resemble modern HMOs. The most notable of these was begun by the industrialist Henry Kaiser (1882–1967), who responded favorably when physician Sidney R. Garfield (1906–84) offered to treat Kaiser's construction workers in exchange for a prepaid fee. The arrangement worked so well that Kaiser deployed it throughout his business empire. Another notable event was the founding of Blue Cross, which originally provided prepaid insurance for physicians' services to 150 teachers at Baylor University in 1933.

It is believed that the term *health maintenance organization* was coined in the 1970s by physician Paul Ellwood, an adviser to the federal government on medical care. At that time, the original appeal of HMOs was dwindling, and there were fewer than 40 such organizations remaining in the United States. Ellwood was a leading figure in the push to revive this system of health care, which culminated in the passage of the Health Maintenance Organization Act of 1973, at which point the term *HMO* became a fixture of American medical parlance.

More Detailed Information

The Health Maintenance Organization Act of 1973 had three main provisions. First, it stated that the federal government would provide funds, in particular grants and loans (grants do not have to be repaid; loans do), to start or expand an HMO. Second, state-imposed restrictions on HMOs were to be eliminated if the federal government certified an HMO. Third, the act required all businesses with at least 25 employees to offer (upon request from the staff) an HMO option alongside standard health insurance. This final provision, which is called the dual-choice provision, allowed for the rapid growth of HMOs because it allowed them to offer more group plans to a wider range of employers, who up to this point had tended to offer more-expensive models that covered costs but did not manage care.

At the time, HMOs appeared to be a better alternative to such arrangements because they were cheaper and provided a connection to a network of health-care providers. For instance, if a person working for a technology firm were part of a group plan sponsored by an HMO, that person would pay for coverage by having a flat fee (which would be smaller than the fee for standard health insurance) deducted from each paycheck. The employer would also make some contribution to the group policy. In addition to the flat fee, the insured person might be required to pay a small fee called a co-payment for each doctor visit and prescription. In exchange, he or she would have access to all of the physicians, specialists, hospitals, and clinics approved by the HMO. Over time, however, HMOs received criticism for denying treatment to members as primary care physicians became less likely to refer HMO members to specialists. Also, as HMOs acquired more members and more pro-

IS MICHAEL MOORE RIGHT?

Sicko, a documentary by the controversial American filmmaker Michael Moore, was released in 2007. It examines the private health-care system in the United States and argues that a publicly funded system would better serve Americans. In the film Moore notes that, according to an international ranking system, the United States provides only the 37th-best health care in the world. In one scene, Linda Peeno, a physician who had served as a medical reviewer for the health maintenance organization Humana, admitted before Congress that her job was to save the HMO money. She confessed to refusing a heart transplant to a patient she knew needed the operation. Another HMO, Kaiser Permanente, is criticized for endorsing the transportation of homeless patients to shelters after the patients had received inadequate health care. Some still had IVs in their arms when they were left at the shelters.

Reaction to *Sicko* was mixed. Some viewed the film as exposing the weaknesses of the U.S. health system, which, despite its highly trained physicians and well-financed hospitals, did not give Americans equal access to medical care and was plagued by rising costs. Others found the movie politically motivated and believed Moore oversimplified health-care problems and distorted important facts. Even detractors, however, admitted the American medical system needed reform.

viders, administrative costs skyrocketed, and these expenses were passed on to members.

There are several types of HMO, each of which offers access to a different range of providers. According to the staff model, physicians are salaried employees of the HMO itself. These doctors hold offices in HMO buildings. There is also a group model, according to which the HMO contracts with a physician group, and that group disburses funds among the physicians as it sees fit. Both the staff and the group models are regarded as closed-panel HMOs because the providers may only see patients belonging to an HMO. According to a third model, independent practice organizations (IPOs) match HMOs with independent physicians. This is called an open-panel model because the physicians maintain the freedom to serve both HMO and non-HMO patients. Since 1990 most HMOs have operated according to a network model, in which they contract with physician groups, IPOs, and independent physicians to provide care for their members.

In addition to having a primary care physician who oversees the member's medical needs and makes referrals to specialists as needed, HMO members receive several levels of care. Most HMOs cover prescriptions, although they typically require a co-payment for this service. If a person requires overnight or extended hospital care, the HMO will usually cover room and board, laboratory tests, radiation treatment, and operating-room expenses (including the fees for the procedures, materials associated with the procedure, and the fees to the surgeons, anesthesiologists, and medical staff required to perform the procedure). Surgical fees typically require no co-payment. The HMO will not cover nonmedical expenses associated with hospital stays, such as fees for the use of televisions and telephones.

Physical therapy, both inpatient (that is, administered to patients staying in the hospital or health-care facility) and outpatient (administered to patients not required to stay at the hospital), is covered by most HMOs without co-payment. Other outpatient services that are covered by HMOs (contingent upon a referral by a PCP) include mental-health services, alcohol- and drug-abuse services, preventive health services such as checkups and physicals, and diagnoses and treatments administered by specialists. Most HMOs do not cover experimental procedures such as laser surgery for eyes and cosmetic care such as plastic surgery, unless it is required following a traumatic accident.

Recent Trends

Rising medical costs have been a concern in the United States since the early 1970s, and the passage of the HMO Act of 1973 has done little to defray these costs, as it was intended to do. In 1980 medical costs constituted 8.8 percent of the nation's GDP (gross domestic product; the market value of all the goods and services produced within a country during a specified period). By 1993 that number had risen to 13.4 percent. Meanwhile, membership in HMOs had increased dramatically, from 6 million people in the mid-1970s to 37 million people in 1993. Membership continued to rise throughout the rest of the 1990s, peaking at more than 81 million in 1999. In 2000 membership was holding steady at more than 80 million.

After stabilizing at about 13 percent of the GDP for a few years, in 2000 medical costs continued to rise, reaching as much as 16 percent of the GDP by 2006. At the same time, HMO membership began to decrease, dropping from 80 million members in 2000 to 69.5 million in 2005. Analysts generally agree that the reason HMOs have become less popular is that most Americans want more choices available to them in their health plans. By requiring referrals from primary care physicians and preauthorization for many procedures, HMOs limit patient freedom.

PREFERRED PROVIDER ORGANIZATION

What It Means

A preferred provider organization (PPO) is a network of health-care providers in the United States that contracts with an insurer (usually an insurance company) to offer medical care at discounted rates in exchange for an in-

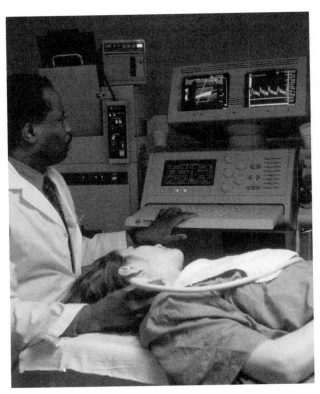

In the United States preferred provider organizations, or PPOs, are associations of medical professionals who work with insurance companies to offer discounted health care to a large number of patients. Here a physician working for a PPO performs an ultrasound on a patient. *Publiphoto/Photo Researchers Inc.*

creased volume of patients. Medical procedures can be very expensive, especially for serious conditions, and the need for them is unpredictable. As with all insurance plans, a PPO is designed to make medical expenses manageable for patients and ultimately to protect people from financial hardship in the event of illness or injury.

A PPO provides a kind of health insurance known as managed care; the other main form of managed care in the United States is the health maintenance organization (HMO). The two work according to a similar approach. With both, members pay an annual fee called a premium. In exchange they receive medical care at reduced rates from a preapproved list of doctors, hospitals, and other providers.

There are significant differences between PPOs and HMOs. A PPO offers members more freedom in choosing a health-care provider; whereas HMO members are only covered for seeing doctors in the HMO network, PPO members may see doctors outside the network (at a reduced rate of coverage). Further, with an HMO a primary-care physician manages the patient's care and must provide a referral to a specialist provider, but with a PPO the member may go directly to a specialist. The trade-off for having more choice is that PPOs cost more than HMOs.

When Did It Begin

After World War II (1939–45) it became common for U.S. companies to provide their employees with health insurance. These plans usually operated on a fee-for-service basis, with the insurance company simply paying for the insured person's medical expenses. As insured patients became accustomed to having their expenses fully covered, they sought out more frequent and extensive medical care. And as health-care providers became accustomed to full and unquestioned reimbursement from insurance companies, they developed more advanced (and more expensive) treatment methods. By the 1960s this had resulted in a dramatic rise in the cost of medical care. To control these costs, many employers and insurers in the 1970s turned to managed-care plans, in which both patients and providers are given incentives to keep costs down. One type of managed care, the HMO, became especially popular during the 1970s. With an HMO a patient chooses a primary-care physician, who manages the patient's treatment options, serving as a sort of gatekeeper to specialized care.

PPOs as they are known today emerged in the 1980s, largely in response to patients' frustrations with the limitations of HMOs. The idea of having access to a broader range of providers appealed to consumers. Many employers, meanwhile, found that because they had more flexibility in designing PPO contracts, they could find more ways to cut costs.

More Detailed Information

A PPO essentially offers a discount plan for medical expenses; providers who join the network agree to accept fees that are lower than the market rate. The insurance company will have contracted with a range of health-care providers and facilities, including doctors, hospitals, laboratories, mental-health professionals (such as psychologists), and physical therapists. Members will also usually be given a list of pharmacies affiliated with the PPO.

As with HMOs, most people enroll in PPO plans through their employers, with the employer covering part of the cost. The employee pays the rest of the annual fee, called a premium, in installments; this is typically done by having payments subtracted directly from each paycheck. Because they cover a broader range of providers, PPOs cost more than HMOs. The premiums are higher and usually have a deductible, an amount that the member must pay before the insurer will take over payment (for instance, the member might be responsible for the first $600 of a hospital stay, and then the insurer will pay for the rest of it). They may also require a higher co-payment (a portion of each expense for which the patient is responsible).

The main feature that sets PPOs apart from HMOs—and that makes them a more attractive option to many consumers—is that PPO contracts allow members to see any health-care provider, even those that do not

EXCLUSIVE PROVIDER ORGANIZATIONS

In addition to HMOs (health maintenance organizations) and PPOs (preferred provider organizations), managed-care health plans include EPOs (exclusive provider organizations). They resemble PPOs in that both are networks of health-care providers that have contracted with an insurer to charge patients discounted fees. But there is an important difference. Whereas PPOs are designed to give patients the option to pay more to see doctors outside the network, EPOs will not cover out-of-network doctors; in this they are similar to HMOs. Structurally, however, they are very different from HMOs, which must be licensed and accredited and are subject to government regulations. Because EPOs do not have to meet any such requirements, they are more simple and inexpensive to run; this allows them to offer lower prices than either HMOs or PPOs.

belong to the PPO. The member will pay more to do so, usually by having to meet a higher deductible or having a smaller percentage of the expense covered (for instance, the insurer might cover 80 percent for providers in the PPO but only 60 percent for out-of-network providers). In addition some plans require the patient to obtain authorization (also called precertification) from the insurer before seeing an out-of-network provider, unless it is a medical emergency. These increased charges and authorization requirements are intended to encourage members to seek care from providers who are in the network. Most plans have a similar rule for hospital stays (both network and out-of-network), requiring that the patient's doctor request authorization from the insurer. This is another cost-cutting measure; because hospital care is so expensive, the insurer wants to make sure that it is absolutely necessary. Likewise insurers try to minimize their customers' use of emergency rooms, which are extremely expensive; although they acknowledge that it is not always possible, insurers usually suggest that their PPO subscribers consult with their doctor before going to an emergency room.

PPO plans vary widely in terms of what treatments are covered and to what extent. Every contract has a summary of benefits that sets out its rules; these outline the specific coverage for each possible medical circumstance (these might include, for instance, annual checkups, emergency-room visits, organ transplants, speech therapy, prescription drugs, mental-health treatment, newborn care, and hearing aids). The summary of benefits also lists what the coverage will be for out-of-network providers of each of these services. In addition the contract details what treatments are not covered (common examples are cosmetic procedures that are not medically necessary, dental procedures, and alternative treatments such as acupuncture).

Recent Trends

In 1990 PPO enrollment overtook HMO enrollment in the United States and grew steadily over the decade that followed. In 2000 HMO membership began declining. By 2006 the majority (60 percent) of Americans with health insurance were enrolled in PPOs, while only 20 percent were enrolled in HMOs.

The growing preference for PPOs over HMOs was usually attributed to people's assumption that having more choice would provide a more satisfactory health-care experience. Some studies, however, concluded that this assumption was unwarranted. For instance, in 2001 *Consumer Reports* released survey results indicating that HMO customers were just as satisfied with their overall health-care experience as were PPO customers, in terms of both choice and the quality of care.

Industry observers reported that HMOs and PPOs were actually becoming more similar to each other. In response to waning customer interest, HMOs had begun expanding patients' options; for instance, some eliminated the requirement for referrals to specialists. Meanwhile PPOs sought to control costs for employers by developing plans with more restricted benefits.

COBRA

What It Means

COBRA (Consolidated Omnibus Budget Reconciliation Act) is a U.S. federal law requiring group health-insurance plans sponsored by employers with 20 or more employees to offer continued health-insurance coverage to workers after they leave their jobs. The law also states that a worker's dependents have a right to continue receiving health-insurance coverage under the conditions of the company's health-care plan after a worker has discontinued his or her employment. COBRA allows departing employees to extend their coverage for up to 18 months. Their dependents are permitted to extend their insurance coverage for as many as 36 months. COBRA is available to employees and their dependents and spouses whether or not the employee leaves the job voluntarily. This means that employees who are fired are eligible for COBRA benefits. Only those employees who can be shown to have caused destruction willfully to the business may be denied COBRA benefits.

Under COBRA the departing employee is required to pay the entire premium (the fee for insurance coverage) plus a 2 percent service charge in order to continue receiving health benefits for himself and his dependents. Insurance premiums are usually paid on a monthly basis. The terms of an insurance plan may require the sponsoring company to pay $500 a month to insure one employee. The employee may be asked to contribute an additional $60 per month, which is deducted from his paycheck. According to COBRA a departing employee would be required to pay $560 per month plus another $11.20 (the 2 percent service fee) to continue receiving health benefits. Although costly, the COBRA fee is substantially less than what the individual would pay if he were to purchase his own health-insurance policy.

When Did It Begin

The COBRA bill became a law in the United States on April 7, 1986; however, its official name is the Consolidated Omnibus Reconciliation Act of 1985. Because it was not passed until the following year, the law is sometimes identified in print as the Consolidated Omnibus Reconciliation Act of 1986. To avoid confusion and because it is easier to say, most people refer to the legislation simply as COBRA. In the years after the legislation was passed, many employers complained that COBRA's rules were difficult to understand. Many companies with 50 or more employees hired outside firms to interpret COBRA and to make sure that the employer was abiding by the law in its dealings with employees. Many employers were irritated by this added expense. As a result of the complexity of the law and the expenses associated with managing employee health insurance, many employees were denied the opportunity of taking advantage of COBRA in the years immediately following the legislation.

Congress revised COBRA legislation in 1999 in an attempt to reduce confusion and to ensure that continued health-insurance coverage was provided for deserving employees. The new guidelines clarified employers' responsibilities to their employees and limited some of the employees' options for continued coverage. According to the first version of the act, a COBRA recipient could choose the amount of coverage he or she wanted to continue receiving. For example, the recipient could choose to continue with major medical coverage but to discontinue coverage for prescription drugs and dental care. According to the new plan, however, the recipient may be asked either to continue with all of the coverage available in a health plan or to discontinue the insurance policy.

More Detailed Information

Several different events at a workplace can make an employee eligible for COBRA. These events are called qualifying events. They include voluntary or involuntary termination of employment, an employee's failure or inability to return to work after a medical leave, the bankruptcy of the business, and a reduction of an employee's hours from full- to part-time. Many employers who offer health insurance allow only full-time employees (those who work 40 or more hours per week) to receive this benefit. During slow periods of business when profits are down, employers often reduce their workers' weekly

COBRA Coverage Periods

Qualifying event	Person(s) eligible for COBRA	Duration of coverage
Loss of job for any reason other than gross misconduct	Employee Spouse Dependent child(ren)	18 months
Quit voluntarily	Employee Spouse Dependent child(ren)	18 months
Working hours are reduced	Employee Spouse Dependent child(ren)	18 months
Employee is eligible for Medicare	Spouse Dependent child(ren)	36 months
Employee becomes divorced or legal separated	Spouse Dependent child(ren)	36 months
Employee dies	Spouse Dependent child(ren)	36 months
Loss of dependent-child status	Dependent child(ren)	36 months

Established in the mid-1980s, COBRA is a law that entitles employees who participate in group health insurance plans provided by their employers to maintain their coverage for a period of time after they leave their jobs. This table outlines the various eligibility requirements and extent of coverage under COBRA. *Illustration by GGS Information Services. Cengage Learning, Gale.*

hours to save money on payroll expenses. When this happens, a worker not only loses weekly income, he or she may also lose health insurance and other benefits. If this person is able to pay the premiums, COBRA allows him or her to continue receiving the same level of health insurance that the company provided before cutting his or her hours.

Provided they are part of the employee's insurance plan at the time of the qualifying event, an employee's spouse and dependents are eligible for COBRA upon the employee's death, on the occasion of a separation or divorce, or if there is a change in the status of one of the dependents included on the policy. Most insurance policies cover spouses and children up to age 21 or 22, provided those children are still in school. By the time most students graduated from college, they are no longer covered on working parents' health-insurance policies. Many of these graduates leave school without jobs that provide health insurance. Under COBRA these recently graduated students can extend the insurance coverage they had for another 18 months. This gives them a year and a half to find a job that offers health-insurance benefits.

COBRA legislation assigns several important responsibilities to the employer. First, the employer is required to make any new employee who qualifies for the company's health-insurance plan aware of his or her right to continue health-insurance benefits at the time that the employee begins working. If an employee formerly ineligible for health insurance becomes eligible, the employer must discuss COBRA when reviewing the company's health-care plan with the newly eligible employee. The company has 30 days after a qualifying event (the

termination of an employee, for example) to notify the insurance company about the employee's change in status. Upon receiving the update, the insurance company then has 14 days to contact the former employee and review the costs and benefits included in continued coverage. The former employee has 60 days to decide whether or not he or she wishes to continue receiving coverage.

If the employee wishes to extend coverage, the insurance coverage is retroactive to the day that the qualifying event occurred. For example, if an employee was fired on May 15, 2007, the insurance company may not receive notice until as late as June 14, 2007. The insurance company, in turn, may not contact the former employee until June 28, and the former employee may not decide to accept coverage until August 28. However, if that person does accept the coverage, his COBRA insurance would be effective as of May 15, 2007, and would last until November 15 of the following year. The employer would have the right to terminate the COBRA policy if the recipient was more than 30 days late with a payment or if the recipient accepted a new job that provided health insurance. The company would also be permitted to terminate coverage if the recipient became eligible for Medicare (a publicly funded health-insurance program for the disabled and people aged 65 and over).

Recent Trends

In the 1940s and 1950s many businesses offered continued health-insurance coverage to retirees. They were

FAMILY AND MEDICAL LEAVE ACT OF 1993

The Family and Medical Leave Act of 1993 permits an employee to take unpaid leave to care for a sick family member or to look after a newborn or newly adopted child. According to the legislation, any company employing 50 or more workers must extend this benefit to full-time employees. In order to be eligible for the benefit, an employee must have worked at a company for at least 12 months and must have worked a minimum of 1,250 hours in that time. Qualifying employees are entitled to 12 workweeks of leave for every 12 months they have worked at the company. This means that an employee who has worked with a company for two full years would be entitled to 24 weeks of unpaid leave. Upon returning, the employee would resume the same job at the same rate of pay. If the same position were not available, the employee would be entitled to a position that offered similar responsibilities and paid at the wage he or she earned on the date that the leave began.

able to do this because the U.S. economy was thriving after World War II and because there were relatively few retirees seeking coverage. With the introduction of Medicare, employers' responsibilities for their retirees' health insurance were reduced. Over the years, companies have been less willing to offer health benefits to retirees at affordable rates. Beginning in the early 1990s changes in accounting and tax laws made retiree health-insurance plans substantially more expensive for employers. As a result, most employers who continued offering this coverage required their retirees to pay for a larger portion of the insurance.

The rising cost of health insurance for the elderly has been a pressing concern in the United States since the changes in retirement health benefits in the 1990s. Many retirees take advantage of their rights under COBRA to continue receiving health-insurance benefits for the first 18 months after retirement. While maintaining coverage through COBRA keeps a retiree insured, it is extremely costly for many retired people because the retiree must pay 102 percent of the cost his employer paid per month to continue his insurance. If the 18 months expires before the retiree turns 65, then that person must seek other insurance options before he becomes eligible for Medicare.

$ Dental Insurance

What It Means

Dental insurance is a plan designed to make dental care more affordable. As with health insurance, most people with dental insurance enroll in a plan through their employer. Plans vary widely in covered procedures, which can range from routine maintenance to more complicated treatments, such as surgery. The three main types of dental insurance plans are indemnity, PPO, and HMO.

Indemnity plans were once the standard model for dental insurance. Today they tend to be the most expensive option. The patient can go to any dentist, and the insurer will cover either a set dollar amount or a certain percentage of the fee (typically 50 to 80 percent). In addition, the patient usually has to meet a deductible before the insurer will take over payments.

A form of insurance that is more popular is the dental PPO (preferred provider organization). By enrolling in this kind of plan, a person gains access to a network of approved providers. These are dentists and other dental-health professionals who have a contract with the insurer stating that they agree to give discounted rates to plan members; in return these providers receive a larger volume of patients. PPO members may also see providers who are not in the network, but patients who do this will be responsible for a larger portion of the fee.

Dental HMOs (health maintenance organizations), also called DHMOs, resemble the health insurance plans known as HMOs in that the member designates a primary-care dentist, who will then manage the patient's access to specialists. DHMOs are usually the least expensive option, offering the lowest annual fees (called premiums) and the lowest out-of-pocket costs. With DHMOs patients will only be covered for treatments received from providers who are in the network.

When Did It Begin

Dental insurance emerged in the 1950s as a result of efforts on the part of longshoremen who worked the docks in California, Oregon, and Washington. Through union bargaining with management, these workers won coverage for hospital and surgical expenses. Wanting also to secure affordable dental care for the members' children, the union in 1954 asked the Oregon Dental Association to come up with a program for such care. In response the association in the following year founded the Oregon Dental Service, which would administer prepaid dental programs for the union and other groups. The American Dental Association endorsed dental service corporations in 1957 and created an agency to oversee such corporations in 1965. In 1969 this agency was named the Delta Dental Plans Association. By 1978 it was supervising 44 dental service corporations nationwide.

In 1959 the Continental Casualty Company became the first commercial insurer to offer dental insurance. Over the following two decades membership in private dental insurance plans increased dramatically. One million Americans (0.5 percent of the population)

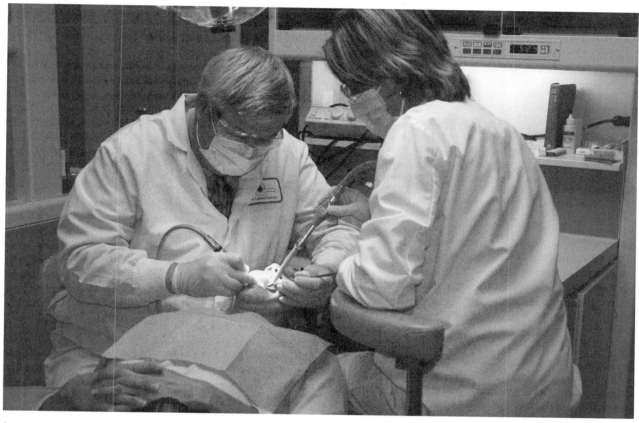

Some companies offer their employees dental insurance in order to help defray the costs of dental care. Most dental plans cover both routine and major procedures. *Photograph by Kelly A. Quin. Cengage Learning, Gale.*

had such dental insurance in 1962; by 1978 that number had increased to 60 million (27.3 percent of the population).

More Detailed Information

Dental insurance resembles health insurance in many ways, but it is fundamentally different in its emphasis on preventive care. Unlike most other kinds of illness and injury, dental-health problems are largely preventable. Preventive care (regular cleanings and checkups) ultimately keeps the cost of dental care low by reducing the need for more serious and expensive procedures. DHMOs thus encourage their subscribers to seek preventive care, usually by covering 100 percent of such procedures; some also cover sealants and fluoride treatments. As treatments become more complicated, the insurer covers a smaller percentage of the cost. For instance, it may only reimburse the patient for 50 percent of the cost of restorative procedures.

Nearly all dental insurance plans cover basic care, which includes cleanings and checkups (twice a year), X-rays to detect cavities (once a year), a complete X-ray survey (every three years), and cavity-preventing sealants for patients under the age of 18. More involved treatments, such as fillings, crowns, root canals, and dentures, may be partially covered or not covered at all. Some policies offer optional coverage for orthodontia (correcting tooth alignment with mechanisms such as braces). Dental insurance almost never covers cosmetic procedures, such as tooth whitening or porcelain veneers.

Dental insurance is usually completely separate from health insurance; often a person's dental and health plans will be provided by two different companies. Sometimes (for instance, when surgery is required) it is not clear whether a situation is a medical emergency or a dental emergency. For this reason many health insurance contracts stipulate that they will not pay for any treatment associated with the teeth or gums.

Recent Trends

In 2000 the U.S. surgeon general released a report titled "Oral Health in America" that drew national attention to the issue of dental care as a public-health concern. The report argued that dental care should not be viewed as something separate from health care. For instance, it stated, dentists play an important role in early detection of disease (including HIV, cancer, and diabetes), and untreated dental problems can lead to serious health

DENTAL TOURISM

In the first decade of the twenty-first century, a new trend in dental care, dental tourism, was gaining popularity. Americans needing expensive dental procedures were having the work done by dentists in Eastern Europe, Mexico, and India, among other locations, and combining the trip with a vacation. Because the overall wages in developing countries were low by American standards, dentists there charged less, enabling patients to save thousands of dollars, even after factoring in travel expenses. The rising cost of dental care in the United States, combined with reductions in dental insurance benefits, made dental tourism an attractive option for many people, mostly those in need of substantial procedures, such as root canals and crowns (artificial replacements for portions of teeth). Crossing borders for dental care had been an established practice among Europeans for decades. With the rise of the Internet, Americans were finding it easier to gain information on foreign dentists, and those dentists also began to use websites to drum up business from American and British patients.

The American Dental Association (ADA) expressed concern about the phenomenon. While acknowledging that there are skilled dentists in less-developed countries, the ADA pointed out that lack of regulations in such countries made dental care there much more risky than in the United States. U.S. dentists must meet rigorous standards, including being licensed by both national and state dental boards and following numerous regulations for infection control, radiation safety, and waste disposal. Another issue that the ADA addressed was whether the patient would be able to complain, get a refund, or sue should something go wrong. It also emphasized the importance of follow-up visits, which would not be possible when seeing a dentist abroad.

problems, such as heart infections, oral cancer, and pregnancy complications.

The report also included evidence that poor Americans have less access to dental care and as a result have more problems with oral disease. For instance, studies showed that more than 30 percent of poor children ages two through nine had cavities, but only 17.3 percent of children who were not poor did. The surgeon general also concluded that dental insurance was a significant factor in whether people received dental care. Studies showed that children from families without dental insurance were two and a half times less likely to see a dentist than were insured children, and uninsured children were three times more likely to have dental problems than were insured children.

The surgeon general's recommendations for improving the situation included establishing outreach programs in communities with insufficient access to dental care, making dental insurance available to more Americans, and getting more dentists to participate in

public health-insurance programs (such as Medicare) by offering them more competitive rates of reimbursement.

$ Disability Insurance

What It Means

When a person cannot work because of an accident or illness, disability insurance (sometimes called disability income insurance) replaces a portion of that person's income. For example, if a painter had disability insurance and one day, while working on the outside of a house, slipped off his ladder and broke his leg, he would receive monthly checks to pay for his living expenses. He would continue to receive money until his leg healed and he was able to go back to work.

In many countries some form of disability insurance is provided by the government. In the United States the national government provides several types of assistance for the disabled. Social Security Disability Insurance (SSDI), available to workers under the age of 65, covers people who cannot do any "substantial gainful activity"— that is, people who cannot do any job, regardless of their profession before the disability. In the example of the painter, if he were still able to do another job, such as telemarketing or working in a tollbooth, he would not be eligible for SSDI. Some disabled people with very low incomes, including those 65 years or older, might also be eligible for additional money called Supplemental Security Income. The U.S. Department of Veterans Affairs provides money and other forms of assistance to disabled soldiers.

Private disability insurance also exists. In the United States, because government assistance is available for some disabled people, private disability insurance is directed toward people who want to protect themselves against the possibility of being disabled but not qualifying for SSDI or for people who, in the case of a disability, would like a higher income than SSDI would provide. A lawyer, for instance, could purchase private disability insurance that would provide income if he had an accident or illness that prevented him from working in his existing profession, the law. In order to receive SSDI, the accident or illness would need to keep him from doing any work at all.

Private disability insurance is sometimes provided by companies for their employees. Individuals can also purchase it.

When Did It Begin

The idea of disability insurance, providing income to ill or injured people who cannot work, is not new. Some early examples were for soldiers. The ancient Greeks cared for their ill soldiers until they recovered, and in the seventeenth century soldiers in Holland were insured against the loss of hands or feet and other physical problems. In

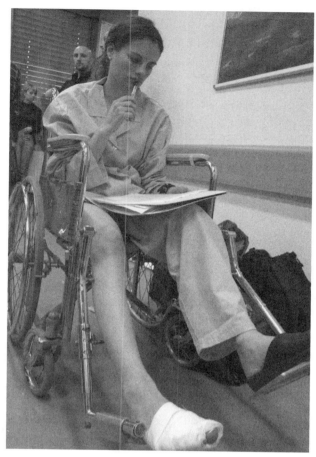

Disability insurance provides a measure of financial security to people who cannot work because of an accident or illness. In the United States the national government began providing a type of disability insurance in the mid-1950s. *AP Images.*

1757 the British government provided assistance to dock workers who were sick or injured.

Private disability insurance in the United States began to be popular in the early twentieth century. Insurance companies, unlike in previous times, started offering disability insurance that could not be canceled by the company and for which premiums (the payment for the insurance) could not increase.

During the Great Depression (the worldwide economic downturn that began in 1929 and lasted until about 1939) the U.S. government took a greater role in protecting Americans from economic risk. In 1935 it passed the Social Security Act, which provided income assistance to retired workers aged 65 or older. In the mid-1950s the act was amended to assist younger Americans who were involuntarily retired, or disabled, because of an accident or illness.

As the government became more involved in protecting Americans from complete poverty, insurance companies increasingly sold disability insurance

to wealthier consumers and professionals, including physicians.

More Detailed Information

Private disability insurance can be divided into two categories, short term and long term. Short-term disability insurance covers a worker for a period of a few weeks to a couple years. Companies often provide short-term disability insurance to their employees. Long-term disability insurance might last five years or longer, sometimes until the worker is 65 years old, when he or she would qualify for income payments from Social Security.

Important in any disability insurance is how it defines disability. Some insurance will cover a person who can no longer work in his or her chosen profession, such as teaching. According to other insurance, however, a person is disabled only when he or she cannot find work consistent with his or her training or experience. A doctor who suffered brain damage from a fall, for example, would not need to look for work that required little education, such as a job at a fast-food restaurant.

Disability insurance generally covers only a portion of the person's previous income. Sixty percent of the former monthly salary is common, though with more expensive insurance, one can receive a higher percentage. Some insurance will provide a monthly payment, though reduced, to disabled people who can return to work part-time.

People buy disability insurance with the hope they will never be disabled and thus will never have to use it. One has to make a choice between making lower payments now and possibly receiving less income later or making higher payments now and possibly receiving more income in the future. As with any insurance, it is a risk.

Recent Trends

In the 1980s U.S. insurance companies competed aggressively to sell disability insurance to professionals, especially physicians. Doctors made a lot of money and could afford insurance, and they also tended to be dedicated to their work even when they developed physical problems.

In the 1990s—a decade that saw a dramatic increase in health-care costs and in the popularity of managed-care companies, such as HMOs and PPOs (health maintenance organizations and preferred provider organizations, respectively, which both attempted to limit health-care costs, including physicians' fees)—doctors began to make less money, and many were frustrated with the new working conditions of managed care. As a result, an increasing number of physicians with physical ailments chose to stop working and to collect disability payments. Companies selling disability insurance, which

WRITER—A DANGEROUS PROFESSION?

A serious illness or accident can leave someone without the ability to work. Disability insurance, intended for such events, replaces a portion of the person's income. Insurance companies divide occupations into several classes depending on the risk the occupations pose to workers. In general, the higher the risk of injury, the more expensive the disability insurance is. Among jobs considered safe are biologist, pharmacist, and librarian. There are few things in a library, for example, that are potentially harmful. Jobs more likely to lead to injury and thus insurance claims are roofer and furniture mover. A roofer could fall off a house, and a furniture mover could hurt his back.

Some jobs, such as pilot and soldier, are considered too risky and are not eligible at all for private disability insurance. Many writers, too, are not eligible for disability insurance. Insurance companies, however, are not afraid that writers will be harmed at work, that they will stab themselves with a pencil or staple a finger. Instead, like many self-employed workers, writers often have unstable incomes, and many insurance companies fear that writers, once they are receiving disability checks, will not be motivated to return to their jobs.

once viewed physicians as attractive clients, suffered huge losses.

$ Life Insurance

What It Means

A life insurance policy is a legal agreement between an insurance agency and the policyholder, according to which the insurance agency agrees to pay a predetermined amount of money to a person or to a group of people, such as the insured's family, upon the death of the policyholder. Those who receive this money are called the beneficiaries of the life insurance policy. Most policies also state that the insured person, rather than the beneficiaries, becomes eligible to receive these funds if he or she lives to be a certain age, often 90, 95, or 100. In return for these benefits, the policyholder pays a fee called an insurance premium. Most policyholders pay this fee annually. Many people receive life insurance as part of the benefit package (the terms of employment contract including insurance coverage and other benefits) associated with their jobs.

For example, a life insurance policy identifies the policyholder's wife as the beneficiary scheduled to receive $200,000 in the event of the policyholder's death. The policyholder is required to pay a $90 premium annually. If the policyholder dies three years after buying the policy (having paid only $270), the insurance company will pay his wife $200,000. Assuming this is one of the most basic types of policies, the insurance company would be required to pay the same fee of $200,000 if the policyholder died 20 years after buying the policy, having paid a total of $18,000 in premiums to the insurance company. The policy also states that if the policyholder lives to be 95 years old, he will collect the $200,000. Over the life of the policy, the policyholder is free to change beneficiaries or to add beneficiaries to the policy. If the policyholder's wife were to die before he did, he would be able to name one of his children as the new beneficiary. If the policyholder wishes to add a child to the policy, he is required to stipulate how the $200,000 should be divided among the beneficiaries.

When Did It Begin

Life insurance dates back to ancient Rome, when groups of men formed burial clubs. Members pooled their money together, establishing a common fund. When one of the members died, the living members used the funds to pay the deceased's funeral expenses and to provide financial support for the surviving members of his family. Life insurance more closely resembling the policies available today first appeared in sixteenth-century London. This life insurance was originally available only to merchants and shipowners who met with policy sellers at a place called Lloyd's Coffee House to draft the terms of the policies. Out of these meetings grew Lloyd's of London, one of the world's best-known insurance firms.

In the United States life insurance was initially sold to plantation owners in the South who bought the policies for their slaves. According to some records, an insurance company called Nautilus sold more than 450 policies to slaveholders during a two-year period in the 1840s. Life insurance first appeared in the northern United States in the early 1760s, when Presbyterian churches in New York City and Philadelphia established the Corporation for Relief of Poor and Distressed Widows and Children of Presbyterian Ministers. Churches of other Protestant denominations followed suit later in the decade, and shortly thereafter many more life insurance companies appeared. From 1787 to 1837 nearly 30 new life insurance companies opened, but only a small fraction survived.

More Detailed Information

At first glance, it might seem insurance companies take an unwise financial risk when selling an insurance policy. There is a chance that any given client could die shortly after purchasing the policy, in which case the insurance company has to make a large payout to a beneficiary without having received much money from the policyholder. To minimize this risk and to maximize the probability that they will profit from the sale of the policy, insurance companies use a complex statistical system to establish premiums for each of their clients. The

CHICAGO CONTAINS A FRACTION MORE THAN 1% OF THE NEGRO POPULATION OF AMERICA, AND ABOUT 4½% OF AMERICAN NEGRO WEALTH, ESTIMATING THE WEALTH OF THE NEGRO IN THE UNITED STATES AT TWO BILLION DOLLARS.

HOME OF "LIBERTY LIFE"

Home of Liberty Life Insurance Company, first Old Line Legal Reserve Insurance Company to be operated by Negroes in the North. Organized by Frank L. Gillespie; incorporated June 30th, 1919, under the laws of the State of Illinois; capital, $200,000.00; resources, $360,000.00. Branch offices are maintained in Illinois, Michigan, Kentucky, Missouri and Washington, D. C. "Liberty Life" owns its present home at 35th Street and Grand Blvd. and is contemplating a skyscraper improvement on the same site at a cost of $5,000,000.00.

A life insurance policy provides an individual's family members or other beneficiaries with a monetary payment when the individual dies. This photo shows the headquarters for the Supreme Liberty Life Insurance Company in Chicago, the first African American-owned insurance company in the northern United States. *General Research and Reference Division, Schomburg Center for Research in Black Culture, The New York Public Library, Astor, Lenox and Tilden Foundations.*

professionals who analyze mortality (death) rate statistics to determine the cost of a policy are called actuaries, whose practice is called actuarial science.

When establishing premiums actuaries consider a number of important variables, such as the age and gender of the client, the type of policy being purchased, and the number of dangerous lifestyle obligations, habits, or hobbies that the client maintains. Holding a life-threatening job, such as firefighting, or having a dangerous habit, such as smoking tobacco, or having a risky hobby, such as skydiving, increases the likelihood of an early death. Therefore clients who participate in such endeavors are required to pay higher premiums for their life insurance policies. Insurance companies also review the health history of a client's family to determine the cost of the policy. If, for example, there is a history of cancer in his family, the client will be required to pay a higher premium. Evaluating risk and determining price through

these exhaustive background checks, which include questioning both the client and his or her physician, is called "underwriting." An insurance company pools the premiums it receives from individual clients and makes investments to cover losses incurred when a client dies.

Different types of life insurance are available; the most common are term insurance, whole life insurance, and universal life insurance. Term life insurance is the most basic and least expensive type of policy. It offers a predetermined payoff only in the event of the policyholder's death. According to most term life insurance policies, the client begins by paying a small annual premium and gradually pays a higher rate as he or she gets older. Experts recommend term life insurance for young people in their early to mid-20s who do not receive some form of life insurance from their employers. Experts also recommend that these people obtain what is called a "guaranteed renewable policy," since many life insurance

DOUBLE INDEMNITY

When purchasing life insurance many policyholders attach what is called a rider to the policy. A rider is an additional feature that offers a substantial benefit to customers for a small to moderate increase in price. One of the most frequently purchased riders attached to life insurance policies is called accidental death, or double indemnity, insurance. With a double indemnity rider, a life insurance policy will pay twice the amount of the policy's original face value if the insured person dies of accidental causes. *Double Indemnity* is also the name of a famous 1944 movie starring Fred MacMurray and Barbara Stanwyck about a life insurance scam. The movie is based on a novel of the same name written by James M. Cain, a well-known U.S. writer of crime fiction. In this film thriller MacMurray plays an insurance agent named Walter Neff who conspires with Stanwyck's Phyllis Dietrichson to murder Dietrichson's husband and flee with the settlement on the life insurance policy.

companies retain the right to terminate the agreement if the condition of a policyholder's life changes.

As with term life insurance, whole life insurance policies usually pay beneficiaries at the end of the insured's life. However, with these policies the insured usually pays the same high premium throughout the policy. According to these policies, a specified portion of every premium is invested on the insured's behalf in an interest-bearing account. The interest earned on the funds in this account increases the value of the payoff to the beneficiary upon the death of the client. There are many different types of whole life policies, each of which offer clients various options. According to some policies, clients can control the amount they invest and how the money is invested over the course of the policy. Clients can often borrow money against whole life policies. Despite these options, it has been shown that whole life insurance policies tend on average to yield relatively small returns. Universal life insurance policies were established in the 1980s to offer potentially higher returns than whole life policies. Such policies offer a wider range of investment choices and often guarantee fixed interest rates on investments for a year at a time.

Recent Trends

Reports from the first years of the twenty-first century indicated that more people worldwide purchase life insurance than any other form of insurance. In 2005 a total of $1.45 trillion was paid in life insurance premiums across the globe, while the combined premiums paid for all other types of insurance that year totaled $1.97 trillion. The ratio of life insurance premiums to all other nonlife premiums was nearly the same in the United States, where $517 billion in life premiums and $626 billion in

nonlife premiums were collected in 2005. These figures made the United States the largest life insurance market in the world. Japan was the second largest market with $376 billion in life insurance premiums collected, and the United Kingdom was third with $101 billion.

Other data from 2005 indicate that excluding Japan, the rest of Asia was the largest growing life insurance market. The total in premiums collected in this geographic region increased 10.5 percent from the previous year. The growth, especially in China and India, has been attributed to three closely related factors. First, improvements in technology, namely the development of the Internet and data-management technologies, have allowed the world's leading insurance firms to perform more sophisticated actuarial studies in emerging markets in the developing world. In other words, insurers now have the capacity to analyze a much broader customer base in more parts of the world. Second, rapidly developing economies in these areas have created a larger base of people able to afford life insurance policies. Third, governments in these markets have passed laws allowing major international firms to open branch offices there in order to compete with local insurance underwriters.

GOVERNMENT PROTECTION

$ Medicare

What It Means

Medicare is a national health-insurance program in the United States that provides coverage to people age 65 and older as well as people under age 65 with certain disabilities and anyone with end-stage renal disease (permanent kidney failure requiring a kidney transplant or dialysis).

The program gives health-care benefits to more than 41 million Americans, among whom more than 6 million have disabilities and more than 5 million are over the age of 85. More than half of Medicare recipients have annual incomes of less than $20,000, and over 90 percent live with at least one chronic health problem. Based on their financial limitations and health status, these people generally can neither afford nor qualify for private health-insurance plans (most private health-insurance companies refuse coverage to people with known "preexisting conditions" because the cost of their health care is too expensive). Thus, Medicare provides a much-needed safety net for some of the country's most vulnerable citizens.

Medicare is designated as an "entitlement" program, which means that coverage is guaranteed to anyone who meets eligibility requirements. Like Social Security (the federal program that provides retirement income, disability income, and other payments to workers and their dependents), coverage is not based on financial need. All

Medicare is a U.S. government program designed to help the elderly pay for medical care. In this photo Medicare recipients in New York City protest efforts in 1995 to scale back the program, which is one of the largest government expenses in the United States. © *Vivian Moos/ Corbis.*

Americans (or their spouses) must pay Social Security tax (a payroll tax on employee earnings that is taken out of every paycheck and matched by the employer) during their working years. These taxes go into the Social Security and Medicare Trust Fund, the primary source of funding for both programs. When workers reach retirement age (65), they are automatically eligible for both Social Security and Medicare benefits.

The federal government funds and administers Medicare through the Centers for Medicare and Medicaid Services, a division of the Department of Health and Human Services. Medicare should not be confused with Medicaid, a U.S. program that provides health-care benefits to low-income individuals and families. And yet, while the programs are distinct from one another, many low-income elderly Americans are "dual eligibles," meaning they can receive benefits from both programs.

When Did It Begin

Before Medicare existed, nearly 35 percent of American senior citizens lived in poverty, and about 50 percent had no health insurance. President Harry S. Truman (in office 1945–53) introduced the first legislation for a national medical-care program for the aged in 1952, but the American Medical Association fiercely opposed the bill and exerted enough political pressure to defeat it. The debate over Medicare continued for more than a decade before a compromise was reached.

In 1965, during the presidency of Lyndon Johnson (in office 1963–69), Medicare was finally enacted as part of the Social Security Act Amendment. (The original Social Security Act was passed in 1935 under President Franklin D. Roosevelt, who was in office from 1933 to 1945.) A cornerstone of Johnson's "Great Society" (a program of social reform, the goal of which was to eliminate poverty and racial injustice in the United States), Medicare went into effect in 1966. By the end of that year it had enrolled some 3.9 million individuals.

The Medicare program was originally designed to cover only people age 65 and over, but in 1973 it was expanded to include people with permanent kidney failure and those with specific types of disabilities.

Medicare was overseen by the Social Security Administration until 1977, when the program was transferred to the Health Care Financing Administration (HCFA), a division of the U.S. Department of Health

MEDPAC TO THE RESCUE

According to most experts, Medicare, the U.S. health-insurance program for people age 65 and older, is in dire straits. The cost of the federally funded program has been growing at an unsustainable rate: Medicare accounted for 5.6 percent of the federal budget in 1979; by 1999 this figure had swelled to 12.4 percent. Moreover, many predicted that, unless costs were drastically contained, the Medicare Trust Fund (the program's primary source of funding) would be exhausted by the year 2018.

Established in 1997, the Medicare Payment Advisory Commission (MedPAC) is a 17-member panel of analysts specializing in economics, health policy, public health, and medicine whose job it is to advise Congress on ways to avert this national health-care disaster.

and Human Services. The HCFA was later renamed the Centers for Medicare and Medicaid Services.

More Detailed Information

Eligibility Medicare coverage is available to the following populations:

- People over the age of 65 who have been U.S. citizens or permanent legal residents for at least five years

- People who are legally disabled and have collected Social Security benefits for at least two years

- People who are undergoing dialysis for kidney failure or are in need of a kidney transplant

- People with amyotrophic lateral sclerosis (also called Lou Gehrig's disease)

Workers are not required to retire at age 65 in order to receive Medicare. Also, those people who are 65 or older but have not worked long enough (that is, have not paid enough Social Security taxes) to receive Medicare as a retirement benefit are able to enroll in the program by paying a monthly premium (payment). Individuals whose income is too low to afford the Medicare premium are usually eligible for Medicaid.

Coverage Medicare coverage is divided into two major parts. Part A is the hospital-insurance program. It covers inpatient hospital care, nursing-home care following a hospital stay (up to 100 days), and some hospice and home health care. It does not cover custodial or long-term care in a nursing home. Most people (those who have paid Social Security taxes for at least 10 years) are automatically enrolled in Part A when they turn 65. There is no premium for this coverage.

Part B is a supplementary medical-insurance program. It helps pay for outpatient medical services that are delivered by Medicare-approved doctors and facilities. These include nursing and physician services, outpatient hospital procedures, X-rays and lab tests, other diagnostic tests, short-term medication for pain relief and symptom management, prosthetic devices (such as artificial limbs), flu and pneumonia shots, blood transfusions, services provided by a home health aide, medical equipment (such as oxygen for home use and wheelchairs), counseling services, kidney dialysis, and limited ambulance transportation. Part B does not cover routine checkups, routine foot care, orthopedic shoes, hearing aids, eyeglasses, most dental care, or dentures. Part B is optional and requires enrollees to pay a monthly premium (in 2006 the standard premium was $88.50 per month). Still, the majority of the funding for Part B comes from the federal government.

Additional Coverage Options In 1997 the government introduced a new option for Medicare beneficiaries: instead of receiving Medicare benefits through the traditional Medicare (Parts A and B) plan, they could elect to receive them through a private health-insurance plan. Originally called the MedicareChoice, or Part C, plan, this option later became known as the Medicare Advantage (MA) plan. MA plans generally provide comparable coverage to that offered by Medicare Part A and Part B, along with some prescription-drug benefits.

Medicare recipients may also enroll in a Part D plan for prescription-drug coverage. Although Medicare benefits cover a broad range of medical services, neither Part A nor Part B covers the cost of prescription drugs. This was a major shortcoming of Medicare until 2003, when Congress passed the Medicare Prescription Drug, Improvement, and Modernization Act. In order to receive the prescription-drug benefit, an individual must enroll in a Medicare Advantage plan with prescription-drug coverage or a private insurance company's prescription-drug plan. These insurers administer the plans and are reimbursed by Medicare. There is a wide variety of plans available so that beneficiaries can choose one that best fits their needs. Part D also requires enrollees to pay a small monthly premium ($20 or less in 2006).

Cost to the Beneficiary Even with Medicare coverage, most beneficiaries have to pay some out-of-pocket expenses for medical services. In addition to monthly premiums (which may apply to all but Part A), beneficiaries pay what is called a deductible. All forms of insurance carry some deductible, a base amount that the insured person must pay before insurance takes over. In 2006 the deductible for Medicare Part A was $952 per benefit period (a benefit period begins when the patient first checks into a hospital and ends when there has been a break of at least 60 consecutive days since the beneficiary last received inpatient hospital or nursing care). So, for instance, a Medicare beneficiary who was hospitalized was required to pay the first $952 of his or her hospital bill before Medicare assumed the burden of payments. For low-income beneficiaries (who qualify for both Medicare and Medicaid), these costs may be covered by Medicaid.

Medicare beneficiaries are also required to pay a coinsurance fee (a fixed percentage of the total cost) for the services they receive. For example, in 2006 beneficiaries were required to pay 20 percent of their Part B medical costs after they met their deductible.

Recent Trends

The cost of Medicare has risen dramatically in recent decades. This is partly the result of an increase in the number of beneficiaries (because a greater proportion of the population is 65 or older and because the average life expectancy is longer, meaning that the duration of Medicare benefits is likely to be longer for each beneficiary). Other reasons for the increase are the skyrocketing cost of medical care overall and the fact that advances in medical technology have led to more expensive specialized treatments and procedures.

Federal government expenditures for Medicare were $256.8 billion in 2002; they were expected to reach $450.1 billion by 2011, the year that the baby boom generation begins to retire (the baby boom was an increase in the U.S. birthrate that occurred in the decade or so after World War II ended in 1945). In 2006 the Medicare Board of Trustees (a six-member panel in charge of overseeing the Medicare Trust Fund) reported to Congress that if costs continued to escalate, the Medicare Trust Fund would be completely depleted by 2018.

The question of how to reform the Medicare program to avoid this disastrous eventuality was a subject of heated public and political debate during the first decade of the twenty-first century.

$ Medicaid

What It Means

Medicaid is a government-assistance program in the United States that provides health-care benefits to individuals and families with low income and limited resources. Medicaid recipients include children, parents, the elderly, and people with disabilities. Medicaid does not provide health care to its clients directly; rather, it is an insurance program, which pays (or reimburses) hospitals, doctors, nursing homes, and other health-care providers who treat eligible patients.

Indeed, Medicare is the largest health insurer in the United States. In 2006 it provided health coverage to nearly 60 million low-income Americans, including 28 million children, 16 million adults (mainly low-income working parents), 10 million persons with disabilities, and 6 million senior citizens.

Medicaid is jointly funded by the federal government and state governments; it is administered at the state level and monitored at the federal level by the Centers for Medicare and Medicaid Services, a division of the De-

partment of Health and Human Services. Medicaid should not be confused with Medicare, a federally administered health-insurance program that focuses specifically on citizens age 65 and older and persons with certain disabilities or end-stage kidney disease. Millions of low-income senior citizens are "dual eligibles," meaning that they receive benefits from both programs.

State participation in Medicaid is voluntary, but all 50 states choose to participate. Medicaid benefits vary considerably from one state to the next, however, because each state is free to design its own benefits package as long as it meets federal minimum requirements. Also, the level of federal funding varies from state to state, according to that state's poverty level. (The poverty level is determined by the proportion of people in that state who live at or below the poverty line, which is the level of household income beneath which an individual is determined to be living in poverty.) Thus, the wealthiest states receive only 50 percent matching funds (one federal dollar to match every state dollar) from the federal government, while the poorest states receive as much as 77 percent of their Medicaid funding from the federal government (a little more than $1.50 in federal funds for every state dollar).

When Did It Begin

Before Medicaid was established, the federal government and the states did little to ensure that the poor had access to health care. Low-income Americans typically lacked health-insurance coverage and were less likely than their more affluent counterparts to go to the doctor for treatment of illnesses (even while they experienced illness more frequently). Those who did seek out traditional medical care were often saddled with overwhelming bills, which further undermined their economic stability. Others relied upon charitable care from public and non-profit hospitals and clinics as well as certain altruistic doctors. In general, low-income households had markedly higher infant-mortality rates and shorter life expectancies than middle- and upper-class households.

Thus, in 1964, when President Lyndon Johnson (1908–73) began to outline his plan for a "Great Society" (a series of domestic programs aimed at eradicating poverty and racial injustice in America), the need to provide health care for low-income Americans became a cornerstone of his vision.

Medicaid was established in 1965 under Title XIX of the Social Security Act Amendment. (The Social Security Act was originally passed under President Franklin D. Roosevelt in 1935.) Johnson signed the amendment into law at the Truman Presidential Library in Independence, Missouri, in the presence of Harry S. Truman (1884–1972) himself, who had championed the idea of both Medicare and Medicaid during his own presidency 20 years earlier.

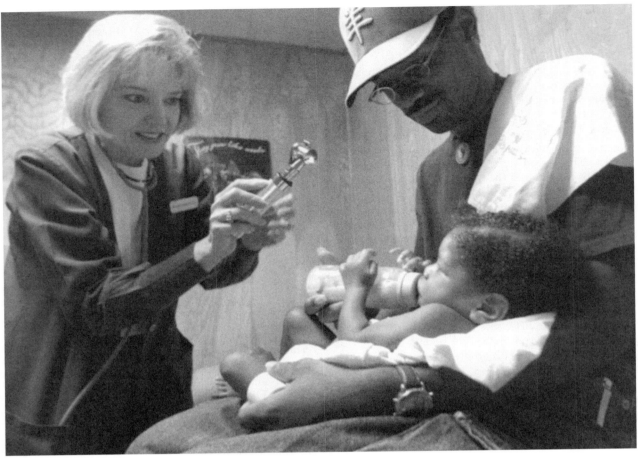

Medicaid is a federal program that provides subsidized health care to needy individuals and families. Under Medicaid, children and infants from low-income households can receive free medical examinations. *AP Images.*

By the early 1970s every state except Arizona had adopted its own Medicaid program; in 1982 Arizona became the 50th state to do so. Since that time Medicaid has been continuously available in every state in the country.

More Detailed Information

Eligibility Medicaid is classified as an "entitlement" program, meaning that coverage is guaranteed to anyone who fulfills federal and state eligibility requirements and that states are assured of receiving enough federal funding to cover at least 50 percent of their Medicaid costs.

Federal and state eligibility requirements have been revised repeatedly over the years. As of 2006 federal requirements (upon which funding is contingent), specified that the following populations must be covered under Medicaid programs:

- Parents whose income is low enough to qualify them for Temporary Assistance for Needy Families, a cash-assistance program

- Children between the ages of 6 and 18 who live in households with an annual income below the federal poverty line (in 2006 the poverty line was $16,600 for a family of three)

- Children younger than 6 who live in households with an income below 133 percent of the federal poverty line ($22,078 in 2006)

- Pregnant women with a household income below 133 percent of the poverty line

- Most elderly persons and persons with disabilities who already qualify for Supplemental Security Income, another cash-assistance program

At its own discretion, each state may also choose to extend Medicaid coverage to certain "optional" populations, such as those whose incomes exceed the eligibility requirement but whose medical expenses are sufficiently high to drive them below the poverty line.

Significantly, many low-income Americans are not eligible for Medicaid, especially those adults who do not have children and are not pregnant, disabled, or elderly.

Usually a person must be a U.S. citizen to be eligible for Medicaid; legal immigrants may qualify in some cases if they have lived in the United States for a certain length of time. Illegal aliens do not qualify for Medicaid, except for emergency care.

Covered Services The federal government also stipulates that state Medicaid programs must cover certain mandatory services, including inpatient and outpatient hospital care; physician, midwife, and nurse-practitioner services; early and periodic screening, diagnosis, and treatment (referred to as EPSDT) for children under 21 years of age; family-planning services and supplies; laboratory and X-ray services; and nursing-home care and home health care.

States have the option to receive federal matching funds for other services, including prescription-drug coverage, hearing aids, eye care, dental care, and personal-care services (assistance with everyday activities) for elderly and other people who need long-term care. While the federal government determines which services are mandatory, however, the states retain broad flexibility in deciding the amount, length, and scope of their Medicaid services. So, for example, while every state must provide Medicaid coverage of in-patient hospital care, each state is free to decide how many hospital days are covered. Given this flexibility, Medicaid coverage varies widely from state to state. Individual hospitals, doctors, and health-care providers are not required to participate in Medicaid, and many of them choose not to participate.

Costs vs. Benefits Medicaid is far and away the most expensive U.S. government-assistance program. Together, the federal government and the states were expected to spend about $300 billion (about 20 cents of every tax dollar) on Medicaid in 2006. And even while federal funding covers an average of 57 percent of Medicaid costs per state, each state still spends about 25 percent of its annual budget on the program.

Although such figures might seem alarmingly high, they are perhaps put in perspective when one considers the magnitude of Medicaid's role in the American health-care system. In 2006 it was estimated that Medicaid covered health-care costs for one in every three births per year in the United States, one in every four American children, three in every five nursing-home residents, one in every five low-income adults, and more than half of the people living with HIV and AIDS in the United States.

Recent Trends

In the early 1990s the cost of Medicaid rose dramatically, at an average of 30 percent annually. These increases tapered off in the latter half of the decade, but in 2006 it was estimated that Medicaid costs would continue to grow at an annual rate of 7 percent over the next decade. There were a number of reasons for these escalating costs:

THE STATE CHILDREN'S HEALTH INSURANCE PROGRAM (SCHIP): A COMPLEMENT TO MEDICAID

Medicaid is a government-assistance program in the United States that provides health-insurance coverage to low-income individuals and families. Although Medicaid benefits are available to millions of Americans (including one in four children), there is still a huge segment of the population whose income is slightly too high to qualify for Medicaid but who still cannot afford the high cost of private health insurance. Established in 1997, SCHIP is a companion program to Medicaid that aims to prevent the children in these households from being uninsured. In its early years the program seemed to be enormously effective: indeed, between 1998 and 2004, the percentage of uninsured children in the United States fell from 15.4 to 10.8 percent (a change that could be attributed to increased enrollment in SCHIP and Medicaid, because during the same period the percentage of children with private health coverage declined). In spite of SCHIP's success in providing health-care coverage to a vulnerable population of children, the program was slated to expire at the end of 2007, unless Congress voted to reauthorize it.

- The increased number of eligible low-income individuals

- The rise in the number of eligible senior citizens, a result of the general increase in life expectancy and also of the aging of the large generation known as the baby boomers (those Americans who were born in the decade after World War II, which ended in 1945)

- The rising price of medical care, including hospital care, diagnostic testing, prescription drugs, and long-term care

- The expansion of coverage in many states to include not just the minimum benefits package but also optional populations and services

Thus, in the first decade of the twenty-first century, the question of how to contain Medicaid costs became an increasingly urgent national issue and a subject of intensive public and political debate.

$ Food Stamp

What It Means

A food stamp is a coupon that can be redeemed for food at a grocery store. Food stamps are provided by a federal program on a monthly basis to individuals in the United States who do not have the means to buy enough food themselves or their families. The stamps can be used to buy almost any food or to buy seeds or plants to grow food for the household. They cannot be redeemed for alcohol, tobacco products, household supplies such as soap and paper products, medicines, or vitamins. In the past, food stamp benefits were issued as paper vouchers enclosed in a book, but today most are distributed using Electronic Benefit Transfer (EBT) cards, which are similar to ATM (automated teller machine) cards.

People only qualify for food stamps if their total household income is less than a certain amount set by the federal government. A household is defined as individuals who live together and buy and prepare food together. Single individuals may also qualify. In 2003 the average gross (total) monthly income per food stamp household was $640. The income limit is higher for elderly or disabled persons. People seeking food stamps generally apply for them at their local Department of Social Services.

The Food Stamp Program, administered by the U.S. Department of Agriculture, is the federal assistance program that provides food stamps. Its mission is to raise the level of nutrition of low-income households. Food stamps are most commonly provided to support needy households as well as those who are moving off of receiving welfare and into working. The program is funded by the federal government, but it is administered at the state level, by local offices of public-assistance agencies. In

In the United States a food stamp is a government-issued coupon that is used to buy food at grocery stores. Food stamps are granted to disadvantaged individuals who lack the economic means to pay for groceries on their own. *Michael Spafford/Photodisc Green/Getty Images.*

2000 the program provided food stamps to 17.2 million individuals in 7.3 million U.S. households.

When Did It Begin

When the Great Depression of the 1930s halted the growth of the American economy, the Department of Agriculture developed a food assistance program with two goals: to support farmers who needed help distributing their surplus (excess) agricultural goods and to provide food for Americans who were out of work. In 1939 the first Food Stamp Program was started in Rochester, New York. By 1943 it had spread to hundreds of counties across the nation, at its peak feeding millions of people simultaneously. When the U.S. economy recovered in the early 1940s, allaying concerns about hunger, the Food Stamp Program ended.

In the early 1960s President John F. Kennedy (1917–63) led an effort to revive the food assistance program. Inspired to address poverty in the United States because his 1960 campaign had brought him in touch with some of the nation's poorest citizens, he pushed his new administration to develop a relief program. Administrators first put pilot (trial) programs into place. The success of these supported the passage of the Food Stamp Act of 1964, which established a permanent federal food-relief program for farmers and needy Americans. The program allowed eligible people to buy stamps at an amount that was determined by their level of income. It also distributed bonus coupons that could be exchanged for surplus food (food that farmers had overproduced and could not sell; the government helped farmers by purchasing these products). In these ways, the Food Stamp Program served both the needs of the poor and the needs of American farmers who had the serious problem of unmarketable products.

More Detailed Information

For years after the Food Stamp Act was passed, the Food Stamp Program grew steadily. In 1965 the number of recipients was just over half a million; by 1974 it had grown to 15 million. Although the program satisfied millions of food stamp recipients, there were many who challenged its expense to the federal government as well as its efficiency (because of delays in the certification process, it was difficult to provide benefits in a timely way). In 1971 Congress passed new legislation that established work requirements for those receiving benefits and imposed national standards for determining who was eligible to participate. The program was expanded to include recipients in Puerto Rico, Guam, and the U.S. Virgin Islands as well as drug addicts and alcoholics attending treatment centers. The U.S. government allotted $1.75 billion to the program in 1971.

Similar to all massive federal programs, the Food Stamp Program has required the continual attention of lawmakers and policymakers. One of the complaints about the program throughout the 1970s was about the rule that recipients had to purchase their food stamps. Many critics of the program believed that the fact that recipients had to pay for stamps discouraged many from using the program. When Congress passed the Food Stamp Act of 1977, it removed the purchase requirement. The change was put into place in January 1979, and in one month participation in the program increased by 1.5 million people.

The Food Stamp Program continued to increase in size, and in 1985 it benefited an average of 19 million people per month and cost almost $20 billion for the year. The enormous expense caused the program to come under the scrutiny of legislators, who voted to cut its funding in 1981 and 1982. The effects of these cutbacks included eliminating outreach programs and setting new income requirements to determine whether an individual or household was eligible for benefits.

In 2005 the Department of Agriculture conducted a study about participants in the Food Stamp Program; it revealed that 51 percent of all participants were children, 65 percent of whom lived in single-parent households. In addition, the study indicated that 9 percent of participants were elderly and that the average gross monthly income per food stamp household was $640. The department also stated that 46 percent of participants were white, 31 percent were African-American, 13 percent were Hispanic, 2 percent were Asian, 1 percent were Native American, and 7 percent were of unknown ethnicity.

Recent Trends

The hunger problem in the United States increased in the 1980s, and to address it, certain changes were made to the Food Stamp Program. Congress removed the sales tax on food purchases for recipients, gave homeless people eligibility for the program, and provided funds for nutrition education. New legislation also established the Electronic Benefits Transfer (EBT) system, which gave food stamp recipients an alternative way to access their benefits. The program continued to improve and expand throughout the 1980s. By 1994 participation had increased to a record 28 million recipients.

Employment levels in the United States directly affect the levels of participation in the Food Stamp Program. When unemployment levels declined in the late 1990s, food stamp participation also fell, because more workers were able to find jobs. In 2001 unemployment began to increase again, and in 2005 nearly 25.8 million people participated in the program.

Some critics of the Food Stamp Program make the argument that individuals who participate in the program for long periods of time can grow dependent on it. Another criticism is that the food provided through the program is not nutritious and results in health problems for participants.

TAX DEDUCTIONS FOR FOOD STAMP PARTICIPANTS

Once a person qualifies to receive benefits from the Food Stamp Program, he or she may legally subtract certain expenses and portions of their income from the taxes they owe the government. These allowances are designed to help participants' food stamp benefits go further by letting them keep more of the money they earn.

In 48 states (that is, not including Alaska and Hawaii), the following tax deductions were allowed as of 2004:

- Standard deduction: This deduction is adjusted once a year to reflect changes in the cost of living.
- Earned income deduction: Members of the household who are working are able to subtract 20 percent of their gross earned income from their earnings. In other words, they are not taxed on that 20 percent.
- Dependent care deduction: Households receive a deduction for the cost of child or incapacitated adult care when the cost is necessary to enable a household member to have a job.
- Excess shelter costs: Households can also subtract monthly expenses such as rent and utilities (for instance, electricity, household gas, and water).

Others have pointed out that the program does not actually achieve its specific goal of increasing the quantity of nutritional food that people buy. Rather, its real effect is to increase recipients' incomes: most buy the same food they normally would and use the money they would have spent on food to pay for their housing expenses. Therefore, these critics argue, the program is ineffective, because it is often no different from giving people money to supplement their income.

$ Social Security

What It Means

Social Security commonly refers to a U.S. government program designed to help the elderly, the surviving family members of deceased breadwinners, and the disabled. The program, administered by the Social Security Administration (SSA), provides monthly payments to those Americans who have reached retirement age or who otherwise qualify for Social Security benefits. The SSA also oversees the payment of health care benefits under a system called Medicare.

Social Security payments are primarily funded through payroll taxes (a percentage of an employee's salary that is withheld by his or her employer each payday), together with a matching amount paid by the employer. The employer sends these monies to the government. The logic behind the program is that people pay into the Social Security system over the course of their career and are then entitled to be paid back in monthly installments upon retirement or disability. The benefit extends to the spouses and dependents of qualifying workers who die before retirement age.

Anyone in the United States who has worked the minimum amount specified by the SSA and who files for old-age benefits can currently retire at age 62 and receive some amount of Social Security payments. To receive full benefits (the largest amount to which a person is entitled based on his or her work history), however, those born before 1950 can only file for benefits upon reaching age 65. Those born between 1950 and 1960 can retire with full benefits at age 66, and those born after 1960 must continue working until they are 67. The maximum amount that the benefit pays usually does not rise far above the poverty level (the amount of income that the government says is required to purchase the most basic necessities).

When Did It Begin

Social security in its broader sense refers to any government attempt to provide its citizens with a safety net should they become unable to work. Among modern nations Germany was the first to create a nationwide system of such protections when it provided workers and their dependents with sickness and old-age insurance in the 1880s. Other industrialized countries in Europe and elsewhere followed suit in the next decades, but the U.S. government generally stuck to a policy of not involving itself in citizens' economic affairs. It was not until 1935, as a response to the ongoing Great Depression (from 1929 to about 1939) that had impoverished large numbers of U.S. citizens through no fault of their own, that President Franklin D. Roosevelt introduced the Social Security Act. The centerpiece of Roosevelt's New Deal (a sweeping system of laws meant to counteract the effects of the Depression), the Social Security Act created the Social Security Administration.

More Detailed Information

The Social Security Act of 1935 was not especially progressive by European standards, which tended to redistribute wealth (taxing the wealthy and using that money to pay for social benefits that would bring poorer people up to a reasonable level of comfort) rather than requiring employees to pay part of their own social security benefits. The European systems also covered a wider proportion of the population. The U.S. program initially covered primarily industrial workers, excluding those in such fields as education, farm work, and domestic services and those in family businesses, as well as all people who were self-employed. Nevertheless, the new Social Security system represented a dramatic departure from the existing U.S. government approach to the public welfare. Prior to

Social Security is a U.S. government assistance program that delivers monthly payments to Americans who have reached retirement age. Pictured here is Ida May Fuller of Ludlow, Vermont, who in 1940 was the first American to receive a monthly Social Security check. *AP Images.*

the establishment of Social Security and other New Deal programs, government in the United States took little or no active role in ensuring all citizens a degree of financial stability, regardless of their individual circumstances. At the time of the Social Security Act, conservative critics argued that social security contradicted the basic American philosophy of self-determination (the belief that each individual is entirely responsible for his or her own well-being). Meanwhile, progressive critics argued that the program did not go far enough to protect U.S. citizens from circumstances beyond their control.

The principle features of the U.S. Social Security system (that it collects payroll taxes from employers and makes payments to those in old-age and their survivors, as well as the disabled) have remained in place during the decades since the program was established; the largest change to its structure was the addition of industries that had been excluded and the expansion of the program to include Medicare. Although it is still funded in the same way as Social Security, Medicare has gone on to function as a separate program, both in practice and in the minds of most Americans. Together, these two government programs represent the largest-ever U.S. government effort to provide for the economic welfare of its population. They are not, however, what is commonly referred to as welfare. This term is applied to programs that exclusively target the poor. Because Social Security and Medicare serve all retirees regardless of their poverty or wealth, these programs typically do not come under attack as directly or as fiercely as so-called welfare programs, which are often faulted (as the Social Security program once was) for contradicting the self-reliance that some believe is essential to the American character.

As a program that primarily benefits the elderly, however, the Social Security system has a key vulnerability. In the United States the baby boomer generation (those born in the two decades after World War II, which ended in 1945) represents a much larger group of potential retirees than the country has ever seen before (78 million by some estimates). To compound the challenges faced by the Social Security program because of this generation's size, life expectancy has increased greatly in the United States in the years since World War II. This means that an unprecedented number of people are poised to enter the ranks of Social Security beneficiaries (those who claim benefits) and that they can be expected to collect benefits for much longer, on average, than any other generation has so far done.

Recent Trends

The U.S. Social Security program is funded by payroll taxes, but these taxes have usually generated a surplus. In other words, more money has been collected in any given moment than has been distributed to beneficiaries at that same moment; the leftover money is called the surplus. This surplus is placed in a trust fund (an arrangement allowing one person, in this case the government, to hold the property of another person, in this case all citizens who contribute payroll taxes), and the trust fund is invested in government bonds (a form of risk-free investment that pays a low but steady rate of interest. Many economists and politicians predict, however, that when the full force of baby boomer retirement is felt, the Social Security trust fund will be exhausted, and payroll taxes alone will not allow the system to pay back what workers retiring in the future will have put into it. In 2007 the program's trustees predicted that the amount paid out in benefits would begin to exceed the amount collected as taxes in 2017 and that the program would run out of money in 2041, when Americans born in 1974 would be ready to retire. The program would still be taking in taxes but only enough to pay 75 percent of the promised benefits.

The issue of how to deal with this predicted shortage of funds has been hotly debated. One idea is to raise the retirement age, which for those born after 1960 was 67 years old. This would serve to reduce the total amount of money paid to retirees. Reducing benefits would have a similar effect. Cutting benefits, however, is never a popular option, and many politicians are hesitant to support this idea lest they alienate voters. Another suggestion is to

IN THE BEGINNING

The Social Security Act, which guaranteed monthly payments to retirees, disabled people, and the dependents of workers who had died, was enacted in 1935. The U.S. government began collecting payroll taxes and preparing to make payments to beneficiaries in 1937. Those who retired between 1937 and 1940 were entitled to a one-time, lump-sum payment; the government was not ready to begin making recurrent monthly payments until January 1, 1940. The first American to receive a monthly Social Security check was Ludlow, Vermont, resident Ida May Fuller, an unmarried former legal secretary (and a onetime classmate of President Calvin Coolidge). Her check was for $22.54, and it was dated January 31, 1940. Fuller had made three years' worth of payroll-tax payments (an amount estimated at about $25) before becoming eligible for benefits, but she ultimately collected Social Security for 35 years after retiring. Fuller died in 1975 at age 100, having received in excess of $20,000 from the Social Security Administration. The total most Americans receive in Social Security in their old age is much closer to the amount they have paid in over the course of their lifetime's work.

increase the Social Security tax. As of 2007 the Social Security payroll tax was 12.4 percent (with 6.2 percent paid by the employee and 6.2 percent paid by the employer); the trustees estimated that, in order for the program to remain solvent for the following 75 years, the payroll tax would need to be increased to 14.35 percent. Opponents of this idea say that it would put a greater financial burden on many workers. They also argue that it would make it more expensive for employers, who have to pay matching amounts for employee contributions to Social Security, to hire people, which would lead to the loss of jobs.

Some politicians proposed increasing the Social Security tax on high-income workers. As of 2007 there was a Social Security tax cap: only the first $97,500 of a person's annual earnings was subject to the 12.4 percent payroll tax. Raising the cap would enable the program to collect more revenue; for instance, raising it to $150,000 would mean that for each person earning this amount or more, the government would collect $18,600 a year for Social Security, as opposed to $12,090. Similar proposals included imposing a surtax (additional tax) on earnings over the $97,500 cap.

Many conservatives advocate allowing part of the Social Security trust fund to be invested on the stock market (where people can buy and sell stocks, or shares of ownership in private companies), which is capable of larger returns than government bonds. Money invested in the stock market can be lost at any moment, however; neither the government nor any other force can guarantee funds that are invested in this way. Critics of this approach worry that ordinary people would be exposed, in such a situation, to the very economic insecurity against which Social Security was designed to protect them. The issue of how to fund the Social Security system in the future remains one of the central political debates of the early twenty-first century.

$ Temporary Assistance to Needy Families

What It Means

The program Temporary Assistance to Needy Families (TANF) is a form of government assistance in the United States designed to help parents provide their children with food, shelter, and other necessities (such as clothes and school supplies) during periods of financial difficulty. The type of federally funded aid provided by TANF is more commonly known as welfare. Welfare comes in many different forms, including money payments, the allocation of food stamps (coupons with monetary value that can be used to purchase groceries), subsidized (that

is, government funded) health care, and other benefits. TANF was created in 1996 as part of the Personal Responsibility and Work Opportunity Reconciliation Act (PRWORA), a law designed to overhaul the existing U.S. welfare system.

The primary goal of TANF is to create employment opportunities for parents of needy children, so that these individuals will no longer be dependent on federal assistance. TANF helps promote job opportunities through skills assessment procedures, employment training programs, and assistance with job placement. At the same time, TANF also offers guidance to program recipients on such issues as marriage and pregnancy planning, as well as other matters relating to maintaining a secure family life. One of the most significant aspects of the TANF program is that it establishes firm limits on the amount of government assistance a particular individual or family can receive. Indeed TANF was specifically created to replace earlier government welfare programs, which imposed almost no limits on benefits. Under TANF regulations aid recipients are required to find paid employment as soon as possible. If a TANF recipient has not found a job within two years of first qualifying for assistance, their

The Temporary Assistance to Needy Families program provides government aid to families during times of economic trouble. This photo shows students applying for government assistance at the New Futures School, an educational institute for teenage mothers in Albuquerque, New Mexico. *Stephen Ferry/Getty Images.*

benefits are terminated. That said, TANF recipients are eligible to receive additional assistance in the event they become unemployed again, although the maximum lifetime duration of benefits is five years per family.

The TANF program is administered by the Office of Family Assistance (OFA), a division of the U.S. Department of Health and Human Services.

When Did It Begin

Signed into law by President Bill Clinton on August 22, 1996, Temporary Assistance to Needy Families was designed to replace earlier welfare programs, in particular Aid to Families with Dependent Children, which was intended to provide financial assistance to needy children living in low-income families. Originally known as Aid to Dependent Children (ADC), the program was a key component of President Franklin Delano Roosevelt's New Deal, a series of laws and social assistance programs enacted in the 1930s to stimulate economic recovery during the Great Depression (a period of severe economic hardship, both in the United States and worldwide, that lasted from 1929 until about 1939).

ADC originated as a provision of the Social Security Act, a law passed by the U.S. Congress in 1935 that required the federal government to provide financial assistance to retirees, the unemployed, the disabled, and other needy Americans. Prior to passage of the Social Security Act, responsibility for providing social welfare fell on state governments, and programs and benefits were financed primarily through local property taxes. With its formation in 1935, ADC became the first federal program to guarantee financial assistance for dependent children living in poverty.

Under the provisions of the original law, ADC provided financial benefits only for dependent children living with a parent or another relative. In 1962 ADC was amended to provide additional financial assistance to unemployed, disabled, or otherwise incapacitated parents of needy children, at which point it became known as Aid to Families with Dependent Children (AFDC). The ADC and AFDC programs, more commonly known as welfare, represented the first federally mandated financial assistance program in U.S. history.

One unique feature of ADC, and later ADFC, was its promise of an open-ended commitment of federal assistance for needy children and families. In other words, the federal government imposed no limits on either the number of recipients eligible for the program or the length of time recipients were allowed to receive federal aid. During the 1980s AFDC began to receive a great deal of criticism, predominantly from Republicans but also from conservative Democrats, who argued that the program's open-ended benefits policy provided little incentive for recipients to seek means of providing for their own financial security. These concerns led to the passing of the Personal Responsibility and Work Opportunity

WELFARE TO WORK

Created in 1996, Temporary Assistance to Needy Families (TANF) is a program designed to provide government assistance (or welfare) to families suffering economic hardship. Although individuals qualify for TANF benefits based on financial need, the program is primarily focused on helping recipients to become financially self-sufficient in order to eliminate their dependence on government assistance. This concept, popularly known as welfare to work, originated during the 1960s, when Congress launched a series of programs designed to promote employment opportunities for parents and adults receiving welfare. In 1962 the federal government established funding for Community Work and Training (CWT) programs. The CWT programs were designed to provide employment opportunities for adults receiving welfare benefits at wages comparable to those earned in similar jobs in the community. In 1968 the Work Incentive (WIN) program required all states to fund employment-training programs for welfare recipients. In 1988 WIN was replaced by the Job Opportunities and Basic Skills (JOBS) program, which greatly expanded federal funding for state welfare-to-work programs nationwide. While these programs were designed to help welfare recipients achieve financial security, it was not until the creation of TANF in 1996 that the federal government became more aggressive in putting welfare recipients to work by setting a maximum time limit of five years for an individual's benefits eligibility.

Reconciliation Act (or PRWORA; commonly referred to as the Welfare Reform Act) on August 22, 1996. The new law eliminated ADFC, replacing it with Temporary Assistance for Needy Families. Unlike earlier welfare programs, TANF established strict limits on the amount of time a program recipient would be allowed to receive benefits, in addition to imposing restrictions on the total amount of money beneficiaries would be able to receive. This shift in the way that the federal government administered financial assistance to needy families was commonly known as welfare reform.

More Detailed Information

TANF provides money to states in the form of a block grant. A block grant is a form of funding that a central government (such as the federal government) provides to smaller regional governments (for example, state governments). By administering TANF funds as a block grant, the federal government enables individual states to budget and manage their own social assistance programs. In addition to providing block grants to individual states, the government also offers TANF grants to Native American tribes; these grants are used to establish and manage welfare programs on reservations.

While the federal government allows state governments a fair amount of latitude when administering

TANF programs, there are still a number of basic requirements a state must fulfill in order to continue receiving funding. For example, states are required to comply with federal guidelines concerning time limits on individual welfare benefits, submit periodic reports on the status of the program, and work vigilantly to ensure that all adult welfare recipients actively pursue employment while receiving assistance.

Recent Trends

In 2005 the U.S. Congress enacted the Deficit Reduction Act, a law designed to reduce the federal deficit (or debt) by reducing funding for various social welfare programs. One target of the law was the Temporary Assistance to Needy Families program. Although the program was reauthorized in 2006, it was revised to include stricter guidelines concerning the management of welfare programs in the states, with an emphasis on creating a wider range of job opportunities for TANF recipients.

$ Special Supplemental Nutrition Program for Women, Infants, and Children

What It Means

The Special Supplemental Nutrition Program for Women, Infants, and Children, popularly known as WIC, is a national program in the United States whose mission is to improve the nutrition of low-income women, infants, and children under the age of five who are deemed to be at nutritional risk. The premise of the program is that early intervention in the health and nutrition of children during critical periods of growth and development can help prevent future medical and developmental problems.

Funded primarily by the United States Department of Agriculture (USDA), WIC is administered at the federal level by FNS (Food and Nutrition Service), an office within the USDA, and at the state level by designated WIC agencies. WIC is available throughout the United States, with specific agencies dedicated to 34 Indian Tribal Organizations (ITOs). It is also available in U.S. territories, such as American Samoa, Guam, Puerto Rico, the Virgin Islands, and the Northern Mariana Islands. In all there are 90 state agencies that administer the WIC program through 2,200 local agencies and 9,000 clinic sites.

WIC attempts to supplement the diets of low-income women and children by providing foods that are rich in the nutrients they most often lack, such as protein, iron, calcium, and vitamins A and C. Commonly provided WIC foods include infant formula, infant and adult cereal, milk, cheese, eggs, peanut butter, juice, and dried beans or peas. Breast-feeding mothers also receive carrots and canned tuna.

In most states WIC participants are given food vouchers or checks with which to purchase specific WIC-approved foods at participating supermarkets and small grocery stores. Retailers submit the vouchers to their bank, and the bank then submits them to the WIC state agency to receive reimbursement for the retail or shelf price of the WIC items. In 2004 the average monthly retail cost of a WIC food package was about $55 per individual.

Nutrition counseling is another significant component of the WIC program. Individual and group sessions focus on educating pregnant and postpartum (those who have already given birth) women about the basic food groups, the elements of a healthy diet for pregnancy, important nutrients for mother and baby, nutrients contained in WIC foods, and how to shop for and prepare healthy meals. WIC also provides its clients with referrals for health care and social services that are critical for childhood and family well-being, such as immunizations, support programs for quitting smoking and substance abuse, parenting classes, child support enforcement resources, and others.

WIC's services are free of charge to participating clients. In 2007 WIC provided benefits to more than 8.1 million women and children each month.

When Did It Begin

Before WIC was established, low-income mothers often had to take drastic measures, such as diluting baby formula, to make food supplies last for their children. As a result many infants and young children developed malnutrition-related health problems, such as compromised development, anemia (a deficiency of red blood cells in the bloodstream), and tooth decay. Inadequate nutrition in pregnancy led to more premature births and babies born with low birth weight.

With the Child Nutrition Act of 1966, the government instituted a free-breakfast program in public schools and authorized other measures to improve the nutrition of school-age children. Still, the act did not address the needs of pregnant, breast-feeding, and postpartum mothers or of infants and young children.

In response to a national survey that found anemia and substandard growth to be common problems among young children in low-income families, WIC was established in 1972 as an amendment to the Child Nutrition Act. The program was designed to counteract the negative effects of poor nutrition on the health of low-income individuals during pregnancy, after birth, and in the early childhood years. Originally conceived as a two-year pilot program, WIC was permanently authorized in 1974. When it began, WIC served 88,000 people. By 1985 the program was assisting 3.1 million.

In 2004 average monthly participation in WIC had grown to about 7.9 million women and children, and the program's annual budget was $5 billion. That year nearly 50 percent of all infants in the United States, 25 percent

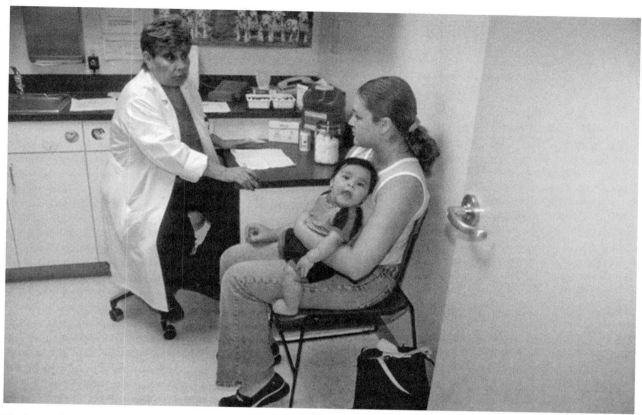

The Special Supplemental Nutrition Program for Women, Infants, and Children, commonly known as WIC, is a government program that provides food to women and children from low-income households. In this photo a Virginia woman discusses her WIC benefits with a program administrator. © *USDA Photography Center.*

of all children between the ages of one and four, and 25 percent of all pregnant women participated in the WIC program.

More Detailed Information

As with many other government assistance programs, applicants must meet certain requirements in order to receive WIC benefits. Women interested in applying for WIC are advised to schedule an appointment with their state or local agency to find out if they are eligible.

To qualify for WIC benefits, a woman must be pregnant or she must be postpartum (up to six months after the birth or the end of the pregnancy) or breast-feeding (up to the infant's first birthday) or both. A baby qualifies as an infant until its first birthday, and children are eligible up to their fifth birthday. Also, applicants must live in the state where they apply for benefits. Applicants must meet the income requirement (earning a wage that is at or below a certain level) determined by each state agency. Finally, applicants must be at nutritional risk. A nutritional risk is defined as any medical or dietary problem that is caused by or associated with the food a person eats (or doesn't eat). To determine whether or to what degree an applicant is at risk, WIC

provides free health screenings to measure height and weight, conducts a simple blood analysis, and reviews each participant's medical history and dietary intake.

If the applicant meets all of these criteria, then she or he is eligible for WIC benefits. WIC is a short-term program. An eligible individual usually receives WIC benefits for between six months and a year, after which time she or he must reapply.

In addition to providing actual nutritional supplements (food), WIC strives to improve women's knowledge of nutritional issues through education and counseling. Perhaps WIC's biggest and most long-standing priority in this area is raising awareness about the benefits of breast-feeding (which are not only nutritional but also economical and emotional) for both mother and baby. Scientific research has overwhelmingly concluded that there is no better food than breast milk during an infant's first year of life. WIC seeks to educate women about the importance of breast-feeding and provides counseling and support to help them become comfortable and proficient with breast-feeding methods. WIC also provides incentives to encourage mothers to breast-feed, including higher priority for certification and longer access to WIC services than nonnursing mothers,

FARMERS' MARKET NUTRITION PROGRAM

In 1992, 20 years after the inception of WIC (a supplemental nutrition program set up by the U.S. government for low-income women, infants, and children), Congress established the WIC Farmers' Market Nutrition Program (FMNP). The program has a dual purpose. First, it provides fresh, unprepared, locally grown fruits and vegetables to WIC participants. Second, it supports the local farm economy by enhancing the public awareness and economic vitality of farmers' markets. Like participants in the regular WIC program, FMNP participants are given coupons or vouchers that they can redeem at authorized farmers' markets for various kinds of produce. FMNP not only encourages participants to improve and expand their diets by including fresh fruits and vegetables; the program also educates them on how to select, store, and prepare the produce they buy with their FMNP coupons.

FMNP experienced notable success over the course of its first decade. In 2002, 2.1 million WIC participants received farmers' market benefits, purchasing more than $20.8 million worth of fresh fruits and vegetables from more than 13,000 local farmers at 2,800 market outlets.

enhanced food packages (which include butter, as well as extra milk, eggs, cheese, and meat), and free breast pumps and other nursing equipment to support the initiation and continuation of breast-feeding.

In its efforts to connect mothers and children with other valuable resources for health and well-being, WIC also provides immunization screenings and referrals for immunization services. Immunization against diseases (such as diphtheria, whooping cough, tetanus, hepatitis B, polio, meningitis, measles, mumps, and rubella) is an important aspect of children's health, but immunization rates for children in low-income households have persistently lagged behind the rates for children in middle- and high-income households. To improve these rates, in 2000 WIC implemented a new policy of reviewing the immunization records of all infants and children under the age of two at WIC certification visits. Although WIC seeks to raise parents' awareness about immunizations their child might be lacking and serve as a conduit between clients and health-care providers, the receipt of WIC benefits is in no way contingent upon immunization records or an infant or child's immunization status.

Recent Trends

One of WIC's fundamental goals is to encourage mothers to breast-feed their infants. For women who choose not to breast-feed, however, WIC provides infant formula at no cost. In the mid-1980s infant formula accounted for nearly 40 percent of WIC's total food expenses. At that time state WIC agencies looking for ways to contain costs devised the infant formula rebate program, first implemented in Tennessee. Under this system, formula manufacturers bid against one another for the exclusive rights to supply infant formula to WIC in a given state. In return for access to a huge number of consumers in that state, the manufacturer that wins the bid agrees to give WIC a rebate (a partial refund) for each can of formula purchased with vouchers by WIC participants.

The infant formula rebate program proved hugely effective for reducing WIC's food costs, which enabled the program to provide services to more women and children than ever before. According to a 2003 report before Congress by the Weston A. Price Foundation (a nonprofit that focuses on nutrition and health), infant formula rebates provided WIC with $32 million in additional funding in 1988. By 2001 the amount of additional funding from formula rebates had reached $1.5 billion, and WIC was able to add 2.1 million new participants to its program that year.

Unfortunately, however, the unintended result of the rebate program has been to greatly increase the amount of formula consumed by WIC participants, and critics charge that WIC has inadvertently provided a disincentive, or deterrent, to breast-feeding by supplying free infant formula. While the percentage of breast-feeding WIC mothers made slow but steady increases during the 1990s, breast-feeding in the WIC program continued to lag well behind national averages. In the first years of the new century WIC began seeking new ways to promote breast-feeding among its participants. In 2002, for example, based on research that showed that fathers have a significant influence on mothers' decisions about breast-feeding, WIC launched the Peer Dad Program, an initiative to educate fathers about the benefits and methods of breast-feeding so that they would be better equipped to support their babies' mothers in their decisions.

$ Worker's Compensation

What It Means

Worker's compensation is a type of insurance that employers must have to protect employees who experience work-related illnesses or injuries. The insurance typically covers a fixed amount of the costs of medical coverage and the replacement of a portion of lost income owed to the employee if he or she does not work during the injury or illness. For example, if an employee of a house-painting company falls off a ladder while at work and injures his back, the company's worker's compensation insurance pays for a percentage of the employee's medical bills and replaces some of his lost income while he takes a month off work to recover from the injury.

Worker's compensation also provides benefits for dependents of workers who die in work-related accidents or because of work-related illness. In some cases worker's compensation covers what is known as "occupational diseases," or chronic illnesses that occur as a result from work. For example, many workers whose jobs necessitate working on a computer or operating machinery for long periods of time find that the strength and function of their arms or hands deteriorates (a condition known as carpal tunnel syndrome). Some worker's compensation plans may cover carpal tunnel disease.

Employers are required by law to carry worker's compensation insurance. The insurance protects employers as well as employees, since it shields the employer from the risk of having to pay hefty medical fees out of the company's own resources. Worker's compensation is designed to protect companies from being sued by employees for workplace conditions that caused the injury or illness, and in many states, but not all, the insurance does provide that coverage. The benefits from worker's compensation programs are managed at the state level, usually by the state department of labor. Each state has the power to define the benefit level for the employers in that state; that is, the extent of compensation available to injured or ill workers varies by state.

When Did It Begin

In the eighteenth and nineteenth centuries increased industrialization meant that greater numbers of workers suffered injuries on the job. Workers began to blame employers for injuries that were the direct result of dangerous work environments. Without the protection of worker's compensation laws, injured workers had to individually file lawsuits for damages against their employers and carried the burden of proving that their injury was the fault of the employer. Workers who did file suits risked losing their jobs as well as wages. Successful lawsuits sometimes resulted in unpredictable and devastating financial losses to employers.

In 1884 Germany became the first country to legislate a compensation program for workers and employers mandating that employers share in the cost of paying benefits to injured workers. In 1897 Britain also passed a similar law protecting workers and employers. Maryland became the first state to pass a worker's compensation law in 1902. All 50 states had passed a worker's compensation law by 1949. The first programs reimbursed workers for medical, rehabilitation, and lost-time costs. They also limited the costs of the insurance to employers.

In the United States employers are required to have worker's compensation, a form of insurance that pays for the work-related illnesses and injuries of their employees. This photo shows an office worker wearing wrist braces for repetitive stress syndrome, a common source of worker's compensation claims. *Photograph by Kelly A. Quin. Cengage Learning, Gale.*

OCCUPATIONAL SAFETY AND HEALTH ADMINISTRATION

The Occupational Safety and Health Administration (OSHA) was created by Congress in 1971 to create safer work environments in U.S. companies. Many industrial-safety regulations currently in place in the United States are the result of OSHA enforcement, including expanded guards on all moving parts of machinery to prevent accidental contact with the machine; limits on permissible exposures to certain chemicals and dust; mandated use of gloves, ear protection, goggles, respirators, and other protective equipment; and requirements for workers to use a partnership system when working in manholes, pits, and other confined spaces. OSHA regulations have helped lower workplace fatalities by more than 60 percent and work-related injury and illness rates by 40 percent since the agency was formed. During this time the employment level in the United States rose from 58 million workers at 3.5 million work sites to over 115 million workers at 7.2 million work sites.

More Detailed Information

Worker's compensation benefits are generally provided to workers who experience an isolated injury while working. For example, a delivery-truck driver is hit by another vehicle and is injured, or a malfunctioning machine in a textile factory damages a worker's thumb. Worker's compensation may also cover occupational diseases in which workers have develop illnesses from exposure to asbestos or other toxic chemicals while on the job. Worker's compensation can even cover mental illness as a result of work-related incidents. If a worker can demonstrate that a specific incident at work contributed to his or her mental illness, treatment for the illness will typically be compensated.

In general, there are two types of worker's compensation benefits: indemnity benefits and medical benefits. Indemnity benefits cover the worker's loss of income or loss of his or her capacity to earn income because of a work-related illness or injury. The worker may claim different levels of benefits depending on his or her medical status and ability to work after the injury. For example, an injury must prevent a worker from carrying out his or her job in order for the worker to collect any indemnity benefits, but a worker who is disabled permanently may be able to claim permanent total disability benefits. Permanent total disability benefits differ from other categories of disability benefits, including temporary total disability, temporary partial disability, and permanent partial disability. The second type of worker's compensation benefit is medical benefits. These benefits pay for medical treatments (such as medications, surgery, or care services) related to the injury or illness of the worker. Some states also provide vocational rehabilitation to workers with injuries or illnesses. This benefit provides the worker with training for a different type of job if the injury or illness prevents him or her from returning to the original job.

Although some state laws provide exemptions to very small companies and independent contractors, in most states worker's compensation represents a huge cost to employers. Small businesses are especially burdened by the costs of meeting state requirements for worker's compensation coverage. For most companies worker's compensation payments are the largest business expense after payroll. As a result business advocacy groups try to reduce the costs of worker's compensation coverage to businesses, while labor advocacy groups try to increase the worker's compensation benefits paid to workers.

Employers may choose from three different methods of obtaining worker's compensation insurance. State insurance funds are operated by a dozen states; these insure state employees. (Individuals who work for the federal government get compensation from funds that are set aside for the insurance.) In most states private insurance companies provide worker's compensation benefits to employees in both the public and private sectors. Finally, self-insurance allows employers to tag funds in anticipation of claims filed for worker's compensation. This is a way of keeping business costs down, particularly if the business has a strong safety record.

Recent Trends

Worker's compensation must continually evolve as a social program in order to respond to the changing nature of work and its hazards. For instance, newer health risks to workers include exposure to radioactive and toxic materials. Although worker's compensation was created in part to set a limit on employers' obligations to their employees who suffer work-related injuries, since the 1970s an increasing number of workers have filed lawsuits against employers for money in excess of what worker's compensation provides. Many businesses criticize worker's compensation because it is expensive and covering injured individuals can cause the business's premiums (fees paid for insurance coverage) to go up. An additional concern is that some employees falsify injuries in order to receive benefits.

$ Consumer Bill of Rights

What It Means

The Consumer Bill of Rights is a set of U.S. regulations that protect consumers from hazards in the products they purchase and from misleading information about products. These regulations also provide support for consumers in instances when a product fails, breaks, or is faulty.

When consumers purchase products that are defective or flawed, or when they have been misled by

The Consumer Bill of Rights is a set of federal laws designed to protect consumers against unsafe or defective products, as well as false or misleading labeling, packaging, and advertising. According to the Consumer Bill of Rights, the women pictured here should be able to rely upon the accuracy of the fabric content labels of the clothes they buy. © *2007/Jupiterimages.*

advertising, the Consumer Bill of Rights gives them a framework for taking action to correct the situation. For example, if a customer responds to advertising that indicates that a particular washing machine will operate using 10 gallons of water, and after purchasing it finds that it actually needs 20 gallons of water to operate, the Consumer Bill of Rights will support the customer when he complains to the store or seeks to return the washing machine for a refund.

Consumer-protection laws are important because they address a basic inequality between the legal power of consumers and businesses. In the event that a customer has a complaint, a business generally has more resources and power than the individual consumer does.

The original code of consumer laws was developed in the early 1960s. They have been expanded, but the four tenets established at that time—the right to be informed, the right to safety, the right to choose, and the right to be heard—remain the most widely recognized.

When Did It Begin

Today it is commonly understood that consumers have rights and are a powerful element in any economy. Consumers were not viewed this way until the twentieth century. By that time, countries that had industrialized rapidly (such as the United States and European nations) had built substantial populations of consumers. Businesses in these countries had grown very powerful, and when they treated consumers unfairly, there was often little that consumers could do about it.

In the 1950s consumers started to devise ways to protect themselves from harmful business practices. Advocates for consumers helped to pass laws that held manufacturers liable (legally responsible) when they put a product up for sale knowing that it had not been inspected for defects that could cause harm or injury. These laws are known as product liability laws, and they made manufacturers responsible for ensuring that their products were safe for consumers.

Product liability laws paved the way for a broader system of laws to protect consumers. In 1962 President John F. Kennedy presented the four basic rights of consumers in a speech to Congress. These consumer rights—to choose freely, to be heard, to be informed, and to be safe—formed the foundation of federal protection for U.S. consumers and became what is known as the Consumer Bill of Rights. In the years that followed, numerous laws were passed to expand support for the interests

BETTER BUSINESS BUREAU

The Better Business Bureau (or BBB), a national organization unaffiliated with state or federal government, is equipped to provide political support and action on behalf of consumers. Established in 1916, the BBB operates as a system of local offices that are supported by the local business community, usually retailers, manufacturers, and advertising agencies. Its membership is made up of more than 100,000 companies.

When consumers have complaints about products, the first place they can turn is their local Better Business Bureau. The agency investigates consumer complaints and helps protect consumers from deceptive business practices. One of its primary roles is to provide crucial oversight on truth and accuracy in advertising.

of consumers in issues concerning the advertising, financing, labeling, and packaging of products. The United Nations, an organization of countries that fosters international peace and cooperation, adopted and expanded the Consumer Bill of Rights in 1985.

More Detailed Information

Each of the consumer rights presupposes that people will exercise responsibility when purchasing products. For instance, consumers have the responsibility to use products for the purposes they are intended. They also have the responsibility to dispose of merchandise appropriately. Because of the Consumer Bill of Rights, people can expect businesses to offer a range of goods and services at prices that are competitive. It is the consumer's responsibility, however, to choose products at affordable prices and to bring their concerns or complaints, when they have them, to business or government authorities.

The first right, the right to be informed, requires that businesses give consumers the information they need to make choices about products. The information a business provides about a product must always be truthful and complete. More than the other consumer rights, the right to be informed has been enhanced by many acts of legislation since it was first established.

In 1975, for instance, Congress passed the Magnuson-Moss Warranty Act, which required manufacturers and sellers of consumer products to give customers detailed information about what coverage a warranty provides. A warranty is a written guarantee specifying that, for a given period of time, the manufacturer will make repairs or replace defective parts for no charge. The passage of this law meant that businesses would compete for customers by improving their warranties; it also made it possible for customers to use warranty information in comparison shopping.

Consumers' right to be informed was further supported by new laws that required money lenders to provide detailed information about the true costs of credit transactions. Several laws were also passed to set standards for product packaging, such as requiring accurate descriptions of contents and information about the potential dangers associated with a product. For example, the Cigarette Labeling Act (1965) forced cigarette manufacturers to put warning labels on their products' packages.

A second consumer right, the right to safety, allows people to expect to be protected from products (other than automobiles) that pose a fire, electrical, chemical, or mechanical hazard. Examples of these products are toys, power tools, cribs, cigarette lighters, and chemicals used for household purposes. A federal agency called the Consumer Product Safety Commission (CPSC) supports consumer safety by setting the requirements for warning labels and product testing and also by establishing performance standards for products.

The right of consumers to know that they will have, within reason, a range of quality products available to them at competitive prices is protected by the right to choose. One of the ways the government upholds this right is by limiting the ownership of product concepts. It does this by putting time limits on patents (a patent is the governmentally granted right to be the exclusive manufacturer or seller of an invention).

The fourth point of the original Consumer Bill of Rights, the right to be heard, allows consumers to voice complaints and to be responded to by business and government authorities. State and federal attorney generals are required to help consumers when they have a complaint against a business that may have broken consumer-protection laws. At the federal level, the Office of Consumer Affairs publishes a consumer-resource handbook listing agencies that defend consumer rights. The Better Business Bureau is a lobbying and action group that supports consumers.

Recent Trends

In addition to the four basic rights developed from President Kennedy's declaration, in 1985 the United Nations General Assembly endorsed four more consumer rights. These four tenets, when added to the original four, became the UN Guidelines for Consumer Protection.

The right to redress or remedy gives consumers the opportunity to have a hearing or complain about a product so that the complaint is legally settled to their satisfaction. Settlement can include compensating consumers for the misrepresentation of product information or for unsatisfactory services or goods.

The right to environmental health protects consumers from harmful effects of pollution that may be caused by businesses.

The right to service gives consumers the right to be treated with respect and assures them that their needs and problems concerning products they purchase will be responded to appropriately. Service, in this case, also means access to basic needs such as food, clothing, shelter, health care, education, public utilities, water, and sanitation.

Finally, the right to consumer education encourages people to gain knowledge that will help them make informed decisions in the marketplace. This includes information about consumer rights and responsibilities, the benefits and costs of consumption, and the environmental impact of consumer behavior.

$ Consumer Credit Protection Act

What It Means

The Consumer Credit Protection Act (CCPA) is one of the central consumer protection laws in the United States. Such laws are designed to safeguard American consumers against fraud, deception, and other unfair business practices. Whereas some consumer protection laws regulate the advertising, quality, and safety of the goods and services consumers buy, the Consumer Credit Protection Act is specifically aimed at regulating the consumer credit industry.

Credit is a kind of loan that makes it possible for consumers to buy things without paying for them outright, or all at once, at the time of the purchase. When a financial institution extends a line of credit or credit financing to a consumer, it means that the consumer is given permission to spend up to a predetermined amount of money and pay it back over time. Home mortgages, student financial aid, and credit cards are all examples of consumer credit. Financial institutions do not lend out this money for free; rather, they charge interest (a percentage of the money borrowed) and other fees for their services. Also, financial institutions do not lend money to every consumer who asks for it; there is always a risk that the borrower will not be able to repay it. Thus, credit

Passed into law in 1968, the Consumer Credit Protection Act, or CCPA, is designed to protect consumers against unfair practices in the consumer credit industry. While the CCPA provides certain safeguards against fraud, it is still important for consumers to monitor their credit activity closely. *Photograph by Kelly A. Quin. Cengage Learning, Gale.*

TRUTH IN LENDING

The Truth in Lending Act (TILA) is the central provision of the Consumer Credit Protection Act, a U.S. law that was passed in 1968 to protect consumers against unscrupulous lenders, who try to obscure the various finance charges associated with the credit (or loan) they offer. By requiring lenders to disclose fully all of the terms and charges associated with a credit offer, TILA is intended to help consumers compare their credit options with various financial institutions and make informed financial decisions.

Even with the protections offered by the TILA, however, some credit card issuers, mortgage (home loan) lenders, and other credit providers still manage to lure unsuspecting consumers into accepting credit under unfavorable or even untenable conditions by inserting contingencies into the fine print of the loan terms.

lenders routinely conduct background checks on people who apply for credit, in order to verify that the applicant has a good history of paying his or her bills on time, can afford to repay the amount of money he or she has requested, and is generally a financially reliable person. A person's credit report is a record of his or her financial history. If this report is deemed unfavorable by the lender, the applicant may be denied credit.

Consumer protection legislation is implemented both at the state and the federal level. The CCPA is a federal law that was passed by Congress in order to shield consumers from unfair lending practices. Contained within the CCPA are the Truth in Lending Act, the Fair Credit Reporting Act, the Equal Credit Opportunity Act, and other subchapters, each addressing specific credit-lending issues.

The CCPA is enforced by the Federal Trace Commission (FTC; a government agency whose mission it is to protect consumers from various kinds of abuses) and state consumer protection agencies.

When Did It Begin

Consumer credit was not widely available in the United States during the first half of the twentieth century. In the aftermath of World War II (1939–45), however, the nation experienced an unprecedented boom in population growth, home construction, and consumer spending. The 1950s also marked the birth of the consumer credit industry. The industry grew quickly, as more and more people began to rely on credit as a way to finance their lives. Without any existing regulations or government oversight, however, some lenders took advantage of borrowers by charging exorbitant interest rates or extending credit without fully disclosing the terms of the loan. It was not long before consumer advocates began to

call for the government to establish guidelines to specify the difference between fair and unfair lending practices.

In 1968 Congress passed the Consumer Credit Protection Act, the umbrella term for what has become a series of laws governing consumer credit transactions.

More Detailed Information

The foundational provisions of the Consumer Credit Protection Act are contained within the Truth in Lending Act (TILA), which requires the lending institution to state fully the terms of the loan it is offering. The lender must provide a written disclosure in plain, easy-to-understand language, specifying the following details:

- The amount of the loan or line of credit

- The interest rate, or APR (annual percentage rate), as an expression of the full cost of borrowing the money (meaning that there must not be hidden costs compensating for an artificially low interest rate)

- The method used to compute the monthly finance charge (the interest payment)

- The total cost of all payments (this applies to loans of a specific amount, not to credit)

- Any other conditions or terms of the loan, including the payment due date, any late fees, and early repayment penalties

In addition to requiring transparency from lenders about the terms of their loans, the CCPA also places important restrictions on wage garnishment. Wage garnishment is a legal procedure whereby a portion of a person's earnings is withheld from his or her paycheck in order to pay off a debt. Wage garnishment can be ordered by a court when a person has defaulted on (failed to repay) a loan. The CCPA stipulates that an employer cannot fire an employee because his or her wages are being garnished for a single debt (the employer can fire the employee if his or her wages are garnished for more than one debt). It also sets a legal limit on how much (what portion) of a person's wages can be withheld from any one paycheck. Usually, no more than 25 percent of a person's wages can be garnished.

The Fair Credit Reporting Act (FCRA) was added to the CCPA in 1971. It was the first federal regulation to address the credit-reporting industry. (Credit-reporting agencies, also called consumer-reporting agencies or credit bureaus, are companies that collect and compile consumers' credit-history information. The three major nationwide credit bureaus are Equifax, Experian, and TransUnion). The FCRA is intended to insure the accuracy, privacy, and fairness of consumer credit files. Protections contained in the FCRA also apply to consumer-reporting agencies that sell information about people's medical histories (often used by insurance companies to decide whether or not to extend medical insurance coverage to individuals) and rental histories (used by prospective landlords). According to its provisions:

- The consumer has a right to see the information contained in his or her credit report. Traditionally there was a charge for accessing the report, but recent changes allow people to request a free credit report once a year from each of the major nationwide credit bureaus.

- The consumer must be notified if information in his or her credit report has been used to deny him or her credit.

- The consumer has a right to dispute any inaccurate information contained in his or her report, and the reporting agency is required to investigate any such claims unless they are deemed frivolous or baseless.

- Credit-reporting agencies are required to correct or delete any information about a consumer that is inaccurate, incomplete, or unverifiable.

- Credit-reporting agencies are not allowed to report negative information that is outdated (more than seven years old).

- Credit-reporting agencies may only give out an individual's credit report to people with a valid need for seeing it, such as a prospective lender, landlord, insurer, or employer. Additionally, an individual must give the reporting agency written consent to disclose his or her credit report to an employer or prospective employer.

Another amendment to the CCPA, the Equal Credit Opportunity Act, which was added in 1976, prohibits credit lenders from discriminating against applicants on the basis of sex, race, age, marital status, religion, or national origin. Implemented in 1978, the Fair Debt Collection Practices Act (FDCPA) prohibits abusive, deceptive, and unfair debt-collection tactics, such as threats, persistent and intrusive phone calls, and other kinds of harassment.

The CCPA is designed to protect individual consumers. Its larger purpose, however, is to maintain consumer confidence in the financial system and thereby promote a robust economy. If consumers fear that they will be cheated by credit lenders, or that they have no access to, or control over, the information that is contained in their credit histories, their loss of confidence could cause them to avoid lending institutions altogether. A widespread loss of consumer confidence could lead to a major upset in the economy, something that the government, financial institutions, businesses, and consumers all have an interest in avoiding.

Recent Trends

The Consumer Credit Protection Act has been amended and updated several times since its inception. Among the most recent additions to the law is the Fair and Accurate Credit Transactions Act (FACTA), an amendment to the Fair Credit Reporting Act. Enacted by Congress in 2003, FACTA is aimed at protecting consumers against identity theft (the illegal act of stealing a person's financial identity and using their credit to make purchases or otherwise profit). With the rapid growth of the Internet and electronic banking, identity theft has become an increasingly widespread criminal activity, which can cause serious damage to a person's credit report. In order to help consumers monitor their own credit histories to make sure no one is impersonating them, FACTA stipulates that individuals must be able to obtain a free copy of their credit report from each of the major credit bureaus annually. The act also makes it possible for an individual to place a fraud alert on his or her credit history if he or she suspects that someone has stolen his or her identity.

$ Usury Laws

What It Means

Usury laws in the United States limit the fees, called interest, that lenders can charge those who borrow money. Usury laws vary from state to state, and they consist of a maximum rate (a percentage of the total loan amount) that lenders can charge.

Though usury today is defined as charging more interest than the law allows, many civilizations in history defined usury as charging any interest at all and either looked down on the practice, made it illegal, or limited its use. The distaste for interest generally stemmed from a belief that one should not be able to collect money from someone without doing anything to earn it, and religious societies in particular tended to believe that interest was incompatible with morality. Gradually interest came to be considered a necessary part of ordinary business, and lenders were seen as providing a useful and valuable service. Prejudices against the practice are minimal in the modern world, but many people still worry about the ability of large lenders such as banks and credit card companies to take advantage of consumers.

Today's usury laws, therefore, are meant to prevent abuses by lenders. If a business that charges interest violates a state's laws, it may be fined, prevented from collecting any interest from the consumer, or both.

When Did It Begin

Whether or not the charging of interest is legitimate is a question that dates back to the dawn of Western civilization. The Greek philosopher Aristotle (384–322 BC) offered the definitive argument against the collection of interest in the ancient world. In his work *Politics* he wrote that money was intended to be exchanged for other goods, not used to create more money; interest was, in his view, the most unnatural of all ways of acquiring wealth. The legal codes in ancient Rome did not

Usury laws are designed to limit the interest, or fees, that a bank or other lender can charge on a loan. In some countries lending institutions, such as this Saudi Arabian bank, are forbidden to charge interest altogether. © *Thomas Hartwell/Corbis.*

strictly prohibit interest, though they did strictly limit the forms of interest that could be charged, and a maximum interest rate of 12 percent was established in 88 BC. This cap on interest rates remained in place until 533 AD, when the Emperor Justinian established a variety of different maximum interest rates depending on the form of the loan.

In the Christian-dominated world of medieval Europe, interest was considered usury and was outlawed, though it was legal to profit from a loan as long as the lender shared the borrower's risk (that is, stood to lose the money if the borrower's venture failed). By the 1500s, however, increasing business activity led to an increased demand for borrowed money, and some theologians began arguing for the loosening of the restrictions on interest. Gradually, the attitudes toward usury of most Christian thinkers and secular lawmakers shifted, so that the main criteria became not simply the existence of interest, but the intentions of the lender. Usury laws in the sixteenth and seventeenth century outlawed only excessive amounts of interest, which were deemed immoral.

U.S. usury laws followed this approach. Basing their usury laws on existing English laws, the early colonies and states outlawed excessive levels of interest as violations of moral standards.

More Detailed Information

Usury remains a matter defined mainly by the states rather than the federal government. The federal government requires, as part of the Truth in Lending Act (1968), that lenders disclose the interest rates that they charge borrowers prior to making a loan, but it does not set any limits on rates. Different states set different rates, and these rates have been subject to substantial revision over the course of history, often as a result of evolving local economic conditions.

Most states also tend to establish different rates for different kinds of loans. Loans for the purchase of consumer products (such as cars or appliances), for instance, are generally allowed to carry higher interest rates than mortgage loans (loans for the purchase of homes). Some states do not regulate the interest rates that lenders can charge large companies, since companies have the leverage necessary to negotiate with lenders.

Usury laws apply to any business that makes loans. Examples include banks, mortgage companies, rent-to-own stores, and credit card companies. Individuals who make informal loans to one another are also subject to usury laws. If you loan a friend $1,000 and try to charge him an interest rate of 75 percent, you would likely be in violation of your state's usury laws. The practice of setting illegally high interest rates and using the threat of force to collect payments is called loan sharking. Loan sharks often work for organized crime syndicates (also known as the mob), providing loans to people who cannot obtain them from legal businesses. When loan sharks get caught, they are often prosecuted for violation of usury laws, fined, and imprisoned.

Legal businesses in violation of usury laws are generally fined and/or prevented from collecting the illegal interest that they are seeking to collect. Sometimes courts alter lending agreements found to be usurious, making borrowers liable only for the principal (the original amount of the loan) plus payments that equal a legal interest rate.

Economists often dismiss the effectiveness of usury laws, pointing out that most such laws have origins in religious rather than economic theories and that they prevent the efficient functioning of credit markets (the system bringing together lenders and borrowers). In economic theory, markets driven by self-interested sellers (lenders, in this case) and self-interested buyers (borrowers) are generally considered more effective regulators of economic affairs than the government. Even extremely high interest rates are sometimes justified by economists as a fair compensation for the high level of risk that some borrowers represent.

Consumer advocates, on the other hand, claim that usury laws are needed to protect individual borrowers, who have little or no leverage over lenders (often large corporations such as international banks). Other proponents of strong usury laws claim that high rates of interest are unethical because those people who must borrow money at extremely high rates often do so out of necessity, because of financial hardships that make them unqualified for more attractive loans.

In general, usury laws in the United States rarely interfere with the interest rates businesses want to set. This is because individual states typically make allowances for companies and do not aggressively seek to control credit markets. Consumers themselves are largely responsible for guarding against the negative effects of high interest rates.

Recent Trends

In the late twentieth and early twenty-first century, credit card companies charged rates of interest that many people considered usurious. It was possible, at this time, for

---

DANTE'S VIEW OF USURY

Today, few people in the developed world frown on the practice of loaning money and charging interest (fees for the use of borrowed money). Interest is considered necessary to the functioning of any complex economy. For most of history, however, this has not been the case. The collection of interest was considered usury, a sin according to most religions, and it was illegal in much of the world until the sixteenth or seventeenth century. To get a sense of how people in medieval Europe viewed usury, consider the depiction of usurers in the poet Dante Alighieri's *Inferno* (an imaginative depiction of hell and of those who occupied it, which served as the first volume of his three-volume *Divine Comedy,* written between 1308 and 1321). Dante, as the poet is commonly called, placed usurers in the seventh of his nine circles of hell, the first circle housing those who committed the mildest sins, such as being born before the birth of Jesus, and the ninth housing Satan himself. Dante envisaged usurers' punishment as being forced to sit in a desert of flaming sand while flakes of flame rained continually down on them.

---

someone who had fallen behind on credit card payments to be charged interest of 30 percent or more per year.

Credit card companies' ability to charge such high rates was connected to the absence of any national standards for usury. Fewer than half of all U.S. states limited the interest rates that credit card companies could charge, so credit card companies were able to seek out those states lacking usury laws and establish their headquarters there. Even if a credit card holder was based in a state with strict usury laws (Arkansas, for example), those laws did not apply if that person owed money to a credit card company based in a state that did not cap interest rates. Only the law in the lender's home state applied.

The credit card division of the New York-based Citibank, for example, moved its headquarters to South Dakota in 1981 in order to take advantage of that state's lax usury laws. Likewise, the following year, four other credit card companies moved their operations away from traditional financial centers and into Delaware, where similarly liberal restrictions applied. In response, other states began raising or eliminating their interest-rate caps, hoping to make themselves more attractive to credit card companies.

Entrepreneurship

The World of Business

Introduction: Entrepreneurship

$ What It Means

Entrepreneurship is the practice of forming a new business or commercial enterprise, usually in an industry or sector of the economy with a large capacity for growth. Entrepreneurship is generally synonymous with resourcefulness, ingenuity, and the ability to take calculated risks in order to introduce a new, untested product or service into the marketplace. These traits are often referred to collectively as the "entrepreneurial spirit."

Entrepreneurship is driven by the entrepreneur, a person who launches and oversees the operations of a new business venture. The entrepreneur is generally self-employed, self-motivated, and ambitious and is willing to take chances to meet his or her goals. Unlike the capitalist, a businessperson who generally limits his or her role to financing commercial ventures, the entrepreneur is the driving force behind the formation of a new business and asserts a great deal of control over the key management decisions. Many entrepreneurs also assume responsibility for hiring and managing employees. Successful entrepreneurs tend to be highly skilled at organizing and motivating their employees.

In some cases the entrepreneur invents or develops a new product or service, which then forms the core of his or her new business. In other cases, however, the entrepreneur simply discovers a new way to market and sell an existing product or service. The risks undertaken by the entrepreneur are often considerable. Some entrepreneurs invest everything they own into their new enterprise, with no guarantee that the business will succeed. Other times a successful businessman will risk his reputation on a new idea, the failure of which could potentially jeopardize his entire career. Because of the high level of risk involved in entrepreneurial endeavors, the entrepreneur generally hopes to earn a high rate of return in the venture.

According to many twentieth-century economists, entrepreneurship is an indispensable aspect of capitalism. Capitalism is an economic system characterized by free markets (situations in which goods and services are bought and sold, with competition determining the prices), private or corporate ownership of the means of producing and distributing goods and services, and minimal government regulation of business practices. In a capitalist economy prosperity is driven by economic growth. Entrepreneurship helps promote such growth by continually providing the economy with new ideas that ultimately lead to more efficient and profitable business models.

$ When Did It Begin

While qualities of entrepreneurship have undoubtedly played an important role in business innovation since the earliest days of commerce, the concept of entrepreneurship is relatively new. According to economic historian Fritz Redlich (1892–1978), entrepreneurship first emerged in the sixteenth century, when German military officers regularly recruited mercenaries for armed expeditions throughout Europe. In Redlich's view, these recruiters exhibited many of the qualities of the modern business entrepreneur, demonstrating a willingness to take great risks in traveling into hostile territories and embarking on dangerous military campaigns.

The word *entrepreneur* was first introduced by the Franco-Irish economist Richard Cantillon (1680–1734), who coined the term in his landmark work *Essay on the Nature of Commerce in General*. Although Cantillon wrote the book just before his death in 1734, it was not published until 1755. In the early nineteenth century French political economist Jean-Baptiste Say (1767–1832) was among the first to argue that the entrepreneur played an indispensable role in promoting economic growth.

The writings of British political economist and philosopher John Stuart Mill (1806–73) brought the word *entrepreneur* into popular use. Like Jean-Baptiste Say, Mill viewed the entrepreneur as a dynamic force in business innovation. Mill's contemporaries, however, felt

The term entrepreneurship refers to the act of creating a new business. Andrew Carnegie (1835–1919), pictured here, was founder of the Carnegie Steel Company and is widely regarded as one of the great American entrepreneurs of the late nineteenth century. *AP Images.*

that the concept of entrepreneurship was at odds with classical economics (a theory asserting that economies were driven by markets rather than individuals). As a result, the importance of entrepreneurship was downplayed by most mainstream economic thinkers of Mill's time.

$ More Detailed Information

In modern capitalism, entrepreneurship found its most fertile breeding ground in nineteenth-century America. A number of significant factors contributed to the emergence of the entrepreneur in the early decades of the United States. For one, the American sense of national identity, rooted in qualities of personal freedom, independence, and a strong work ethic, proved highly conducive to the rise of the entrepreneurial individual. At the same time, the ready availability of raw materials in the United States, combined with the nation's large geographical size and rapidly expanding population, provided the resources and the potential markets for long-term economic growth. Furthermore, the federal government imposed few regulations on private business and allowed liberal access to the nation's natural resources. All of these circumstances led to the rise of enterprising, ambitious

entrepreneurs who, rather than feeling overwhelmed by the challenges of building a new national economy, viewed the seemingly limitless potential for growth as an unprecedented opportunity.

One of the most important American entrepreneurs of the late nineteenth century was the Scottish-born steel magnate Andrew Carnegie (1835–1919). The epitome of the "self-made man," Carnegie rose from humble origins to become one of the wealthiest and most powerful businessmen in America. He embodied many of the essential characteristics of the entrepreneur. Hardworking and friendly, Carnegie impressed his early employers with his dedication, intelligence, and ambition, qualities that earned him rapid advancement at an early age. He was also fiercely dedicated to self-improvement, and throughout his life he strove to educate himself on a range of subjects, from economics and business to literature and art.

In many ways, the story of Carnegie's success is representative of the entrepreneurial ideal. At age 16 he began working as a messenger for a telegraph office and quickly earned a series of promotions, becoming superintendent of the Pittsburgh branch of the Pennsylvania Railroad Company before he was 20. Although his pay was modest, Carnegie soon began making shrewd investments, eventually earning enough capital to begin investing in larger, more lucrative businesses, such as oil and steel. By the 1870s he had purchased his first steel mill in Braddock, Pennsylvania; numerous other steel mill purchases followed, and in 1892 he formed the Carnegie Steel Company, which soon became the most profitable corporate entity in the world. In 1901 he sold his steel holdings and devoted the rest of his life to philanthropic pursuits.

By the early twentieth century economists had begun to develop more sophisticated theories of entrepreneurship. In his book *The Theory of Economic Development* (1912), Austrian economist Joseph Schumpeter argued that creativity, initiative, and risk taking, all key characteristics of the entrepreneurial enterprise, were essential to technological innovation and economic growth. Schumpeter's writings proved influential, and as a result the entrepreneur took on far greater significance in twentieth-century economic theory. In his early work Schumpeter emphasized the role of the individual who possessed *unternehmergeist* ("entrepreneurial spirit") in driving innovation. Later he focused on the entrepreneurial aspects of the corporation, arguing that the solitary entrepreneur was being replaced by corporate research and development departments, in which groups of individuals collaborated to develop new business ideas.

Later in the twentieth century a number of economists, notably American Frank H. Knight (1885–1972) and Austrian-born Peter Drucker (1909–2005), tried to quantify the role of innovation and risk in defining the modern entrepreneur. In Knight's view the risk associated with entrepreneurship was primarily calculated and controlled, and the entrepreneur's decision-making process was greatly informed both by his or her own past business experience and by close analysis of diverse business models. Knight argued that the successful entrepreneur paid careful attention to the laws of probability (the likelihood of a particular event occurring) in assessing the risk of a particular business decision. In his book *Innovation and Entrepreneurship* (1985), Drucker examined forms of entrepreneurship that focused less on technological advances and more on discovering new ways to market existing products and services. In Drucker's view the quintessential entrepreneur was Ray Kroc (1902–84), the founder of McDonald's, who transformed a single hamburger restaurant into an internationally branded chain. Drucker also asserted that the characteristics of the successful entrepreneur were not innate to the unique individual but rather were traits that most people could study and learn to adopt.

$ Recent Trends

In the late twentieth century the rise of the corporation resulted, to some degree, in the diminished importance of the individual entrepreneur. Joseph Schumpeter had foreseen this shift almost a century earlier. He had predicted that the advancement of entrepreneurship, particularly its role in making corporations more systematized and efficient, would ultimately diminish the power of the individual to act with the decisiveness and boldness characteristic of the entrepreneur. Schumpeter argued that the eventual result would be corporatism, a bureaucratic system composed of diverse, politically organized groups that would assume responsibility for the management of certain sectors of the economy, while the traditional figure of the entrepreneur would be replaced by the corporate manager or director.

In the 1980s institutionalized, corporate entrepreneurship became known as "intrapreneurship." The

ENTREPRENEURSHIP AND PHILANTHROPY

Entrepreneurship, the practice of forming a new business or product, is generally associated with economics. The characteristics that distinguish the entrepreneur (such as ingenuity, resourcefulness, and risk taking) also have important applications outside of the business world. For example, the founding of the modern university system was the result of entrepreneurial innovation, while a number of important political organizations throughout history were spearheaded by strong-willed, entrepreneurial individuals.

Many of the great business entrepreneurs of the nineteenth and twentieth centuries also used their entrepreneurial skills to create philanthropic institutions (organizations dedicated to helping people instead of making money). One notable example was Andrew Carnegie (1835–1919), the Scottish-born founder of the Carnegie Steel Company, which in the late nineteenth century became the largest, most profitable corporation in the world. After selling his company in 1901, Carnegie turned his attention to humanitarian concerns. His numerous philanthropic endeavors included forming the Carnegie Institute of Technology in Pittsburgh, Pennsylvania; creating the Carnegie Hero Fund, a grant intended to recognize acts of heroism worldwide; and building public libraries throughout the United States.

word was coined by Stanford economics professor Robert A. Burgelman in 1983, and it was later popularized by author Gifford Pinchot in his book *Intrapreneuring: Why You Don't Have to Leave the Corporation to Become an Entrepreneur* (1985). In Pinchot's view, successful intrapreneurship relies on the collective efforts of creative individuals working within a corporate setting.

How Businesses Are Run

$ Overview: Business Organization

What It Means

The term *business organization* describes how businesses are structured and how their structure helps them meet their goals. In general, businesses are designed to focus on either generating profit or improving society. When a business focuses on generating profits, it is known as a for-profit organization. When an organization focuses on improving the social good through the arts, education, health care, or some other area, it is known as a nonprofit (or not-for-profit) organization and is not typically referred to as a business.

There are different categories of business organizations that relate to how the business is established, owned, and operated. The basic categories of business organization are sole proprietorship, partnership, and corporation. Each type of business organization has benefits as well as disadvantages. For example, a sole proprietor of a small business is able to operate independently of much of the government regulation that affects larger businesses, but he or she is liable (responsible) for all financial risks of the business. Therefore, the owner of a small grocery store is able to keep all the profits for herself, but she is also liable for all of her business debts, even if she must repay a debt with her personal finances.

No matter how a business is organized, it takes on certain risks as it operates. One way to minimize risk is for a business to use its assets and investments wisely, whether these are equipment, knowledge, property, or relationships. The more efficiently a business uses its assets, the greater the chance that it will make a monetary profit.

Business organization affects how a business is treated under the law. State and federal governments provide incentives and rules for every type of business organization. Profitability in industry helps a country's economy grow, so governments generally support corporations by passing laws that protect investors from liability for the debts of the business.

When Did It Begin

Contemporary forms of business organization have their roots in the Industrial Revolution. During the Industrial Revolution, manual labor was largely replaced by machine-based labor. Industry developed around factories in which machines, not people, were the primary tools of production. Many individuals, artisans, and family groups ceased working in homes, in small workshops, and on farms and took factory jobs offering pay for unskilled labor. As organizations became more focused around machines, they divided up responsibilities among workers and developed chains of command to organize workers and managers in order of authority. Individual worker's jobs became more specialized and more routine.

In 1776 Scottish economist Adam Smith (1723–90) published *An Inquiry into the Nature and Causes of the Wealth of Nations*, which highlighted the division of labor in production. Manufacturers understood that they increased a business's efficiency and productivity by assigning workers simple, machine-based tasks. Workers were trained to be disciplined and to support the routines of factory production.

English mathematician and inventor Charles Babbage (1791–1871) also studied the division of labor in production. He applied the methods of science and mathematics to his analysis of organization, management, planning, and labor in factories. In the early twentieth century Babbage's ideas were gathered into a theory of organization and management called scientific management, which profoundly affected how businesses operate.

The theories of scientific management were further developed by American engineer Frederick Taylor (1856–1915), who organized the theory into five essential principals. The first principle called for the shifting of responsibility within a business organization from the worker to the manager. Managers, Taylor believed, needed to plan and design all of the work, and workers needed to carry out assigned tasks. The second principle called for using scientific methods to gain maximum efficiency in the

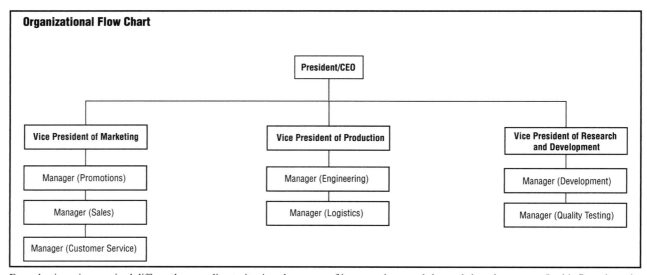

Organizational Flow Chart

President/CEO

Vice President of Marketing

Vice President of Production

Vice President of Research and Development

Manager (Promotions)

Manager (Sales)

Manager (Customer Service)

Manager (Engineering)

Manager (Logistics)

Manager (Development)

Manager (Quality Testing)

Every business is organized differently according to its size, the nature of its operations, and the goals it seeks to meet. In this flow chart the three vice presidents report directly to the president/CEO, while the managers all report to the vice president in their branch of the company. *Illustration by GGS Information Services. Cengage Learning, Gale.*

production of goods. This meant that workers needed to complete their tasks in a cost- and time-saving way. The third principle called for the necessity of choosing the best and most qualified person to perform each job so that the skill level of the worker and the demands of the task would be matched. The fourth principle stated that the worker must be trained efficiently. The fifth stated that worker performance had to be monitored so that procedures could be followed and the desired financial results achieved. Taylor's principles can still be seen at work in such modern businesses as fast-food restaurants.

More Detailed Information

The three main categories of business organization are sole proprietorship, partnership, and corporation. Ownership is one of the most important features of business organization. A sole proprietorship is a business with a single proprietor, or owner. It is the most basic type of for-profit organization and the least regulated by government. The owner of a sole proprietorship makes all the decisions about the business and is free to keep all the profits he or she makes from the business. However, the owner is also solely liable (responsible) for the debts of the business, meaning that his or her personal assets are at risk if the business cannot repay its debts.

When two or more people choose to own and operate a business together, the business is known as a partnership. In a general partnership, all the owners share in the financial profits and losses, and they share the liability for all of the debts. In a limited partnership, one or more of the owners (called the general partners) run the business and have unlimited liability, or are held entirely responsible for the business's debts. But there may also be limited partners in the business who invest in the business

and have only limited personal liability for the business's debts.

Sole proprietorships and partnerships are popular types of businesses. In fact, there are more sole proprietorships than any other type of business. However, most large businesses in the United States are corporations. Corporations are organized very differently from proprietorships and partnerships. The ownership of a corporation is not connected to one individual or a small group of individuals; ownership of a corporation is represented by shares of stock that can be transferred between owners, or stockholders. A corporation is a legal entity in the same sense that an individual person is, meaning that the corporation has designated rights, responsibilities, and privileges. When a corporation borrows money, it does so in its own name (instead of in the name of its original founders or any other persons). As a result, the liability for the company's debts is limited; the most a stockholder can lose is the amount he or she has invested. A large corporation can have millions of owners, or stockholders.

To start a corporation, a charter (or articles of incorporation) must be drawn up in the state where the corporation intends to do business. The charter includes the corporation's name, the forecasted length of its life, its business purpose, and the number of shares of stock that can be distributed or sold. Another requirement for starting a corporation is the creation of bylaws, which are rules that govern the actions of the business. For example, bylaws will state how the business's directors are to be selected. In large corporations, the stockholders elect a board of directors. The board of directors then elects the company's managers, who oversee the operations of the corporation in the interest of the stockholders. The result of this arrangement is that stockholders, because they have control over the directors, have control of the corporation.

The managers of a corporation have a responsibility to report to the board of directors of a corporation. The management of a company must ensure that the company is meeting short-term and long-term goals and that it is making a profit. A management team of a small to mid-size corporation might include a chief executive officer (CEO), a president, a chief financial officer (CFO), and a human resources director. Each of these individuals might lead a team of managers who in turn oversee smaller groups of employees. This cascading organization of leadership and authority is known as a hierarchy.

When a person of higher authority passes the responsibility of a task, project, or other work-related assignment to a person working below him or her in the hierarchy, it is known as delegating. The practice of delegating is important because it allows a manager or head of a department to share his or her workload with those working for him or her. It also allows those in lower positions to take on new responsibilities and to learn about the duties and responsibilities required of higher-up positions. *Labor management* is the term used to describe the processes of planning which workers will take on which tasks, how workers will be organized, and who will supervise and direct them. Even in small businesses, the complex work of managing individuals, tasks, finances, and schedules demands highly skilled leadership.

Recent Trends

For many decades large corporations have been owned by their stockholders and run by managers who organize and oversee workers to meet the financial and operational goals of the business. In recent years, however, companies have focused on yet another key group that must support the business if it is to succeed: the customer. A rapidly growing global economy means that there is no limit to businesses' competition for customers. In many industries products and services are similar from manufacturer to manufacturer, and prices do not differ enough to boost the consumption of one manufacturer's product over another's. Customer service has grown to be one of the key ways in which a business can differentiate itself from its competitors.

Customer service is the term for building a relationship with customers and making this relationship a high priority for the business. In order to develop a strong customer focus, businesses often conduct market research to find out what their customers want and need. Once they determine customer priorities, these are integrated into the company mission, communicated to all managers and employees, and reinforced on a regular basis.

Many hospitals, airlines, retailers, manufacturers, and other organizations have developed business practices that enhance the purchase, use, and ownership of the products the business develops. Customer-service strategies may include lowering prices on products at certain times of the year, offering free bonus products, extending

---

THE SUCCESS OF FEDEX

FedEx is a U.S. courier company that delivers freight, packages, and mail. With one of the world's largest cargo airlines and tens of thousands of delivery trucks, FedEx moves millions of packages and letters a day to and from countries all over the world. The company was founded in 1971 by former U.S. Marine Fred Smith, who implemented many concepts of scientific management into the business organization and operations. The company devotes extensive time to training new employees. When FedEx trains its workers, it mandates utmost precision in completing tasks, even those as simple as delivering a package.

FedEx also uses another business strategy known as supply-chain management. A supply chain is all of the elements in a process that result in the delivery of a product or service to a customer, beginning with the raw material and ending with the sale of a finished product or service. Supply-chain management analyzes how companies plan and control the supply chain, which helps companies increase efficiency and profits. To improve its own supply chain, FedEx has business practices that are uniform throughout its worldwide sorting operations, an intricate information technology system that provides data to workers and customers, and highly detailed plans of how products move through its system. The company also offers supply-chain management services to other companies.

---

unlimited or unconditional guarantees on products, and providing free shipping. In the first years of the twenty-first century, Dell Computers, one of the top manufacturers and direct suppliers of personal computers in the world, opened stores in shopping malls throughout the United States. These stores gave customers the chance to ask questions about their computers or to have them serviced in person without having to telephone the company or use its website.

TYPES OF BUSINESSES

$ Corporation

What It Means

People often think of corporations as large businesses, such as Barnes & Noble and Wal-Mart, but they can be of any size, from one person to thousands of employees. What makes a corporation different from other companies is that it has a legal identity independent from the people who own or manage it. Thus, Wal-Mart is simply Wal-Mart, regardless of its current owners or directors. Like other types of businesses, corporations might perform any number of activities, including making clothes, building computers, and selling insurance.

Corporations are also defined by how they are owned and managed. A corporation sells stocks (also known as

MICROSOFT CORPORATION

The world's largest software developer, Microsoft Corporation, began in 1975 as an unofficial partnership between 19-year-old Bill Gates and 21-year-old Paul Allen after they saw a mock-up of the Altair, the first personal computer, on the cover of *Popular Electronics* magazine. Together they wrote a computer language called BASIC and flew to Albuquerque, New Mexico, to demonstrate their work to MITS (Micro Instrumentation and Telemetry Systems), the company that designed the Altair. The program was a success, and in 1976 Gates had four programmers working for him out of a small office in Albuquerque. Microsoft became a corporation in 1981.

Throughout the 1980s profits grew steadily into the billions and by the mid-1990s, when individuals began using e-mail and the Internet, Microsoft had grown to nearly 18,000 employees. Among its most successful products were the Windows operating system and the Internet Explorer web browser.

shares), which are certificates that represent ownership in the business. By purchasing stock a person becomes part owner of a corporation. For example, if a corporation had a total of 500,000 shares and a person bought 100,000 shares, that person would own one-fifth of the company. Anyone who owns stock is called a stockholder or shareholder. Shareholders, in turn, elect a board of directors, who oversee the corporation on their behalf. The board then chooses the corporate officers who manage the daily affairs of the corporation. These might include a chief executive officer (CEO), a president, and a treasurer. In the United States corporations must be registered with the state in which they are headquartered.

Corporations enjoy many of the same rights and obligations as individuals. For example, corporations can buy property and sign contracts, and like most individuals, corporations have to pay taxes. Stockholders, moreover, have "limited liability," meaning they cannot lose more money than they spent to purchase their stock. Even if the corporation goes out of business and cannot pay its bills, a stockholder generally will not lose any personal assets or property, such as a house. Likewise, if a customer were injured at a Kinko's branch location and decided to sue Kinko's, that person would not be able to seek damages from any single shareholder in the Kinko's corporation. Shareholders buy stock with the hope of making money, either from an increase in the value of the stock or from dividends, which are a share of the corporation's profits.

Other types of corporations include nonprofit corporations, which are often formed for political, religious, or charitable purposes; municipal corporations, which are created by local governments; and government-owned corporations, which sponsor and manage government programs. Organizations such as these, considered non-

stock corporations, consist not of shareholders seeking to make profits off of investments but rather of members who vote on policy and procedures.

When Did It Begin

The existence of corporations dates back to ancient India and Rome. Though these early institutions were structured differently from modern corporations, they consisted of individuals who invested money for a specific purpose. In the Middle Ages the Catholic Church was regarded as a corporate structure; everyone understood that the Church was more than the sum of its individual members and that the institution would continue to exist after its current members died. In this sense, the world's oldest surviving corporation is the Benedictine Order of the Catholic Church, which was founded in 529 AD.

The oldest corporation that most resembles a twenty-first-century business corporation is the Stora Kopparberg mining community in Falun, Sweden. This group received its charter (a document allowing it to do business) from King Magnus Eriksson (1316-74) in 1347. In the early history of the United States, the American government granted only a limited number of corporate charters each year through acts of Congress. To win a charter, a group would have to prove that their corporation would serve the public good, for example, by building roads and canals. Because laws were so strict, many of the largest enterprises in the United States were not corporations. In 1882 John D. Rockefeller (1839-1937) organized Standard Oil as a trust (a collection of companies overseen by a board of directors, or trustees). In 1889 Andrew Carnegie (1835-1919) established his steel empire as a limited partnership (a company in which two or more people, or partners, manage a business together and are personally responsible for the company's debts). New Jersey and Delaware were among the first states to write laws that were friendly to the development of corporations. Today many corporations are still chartered as "Delaware corporations" because this state has the most corporate-friendly laws.

More Detailed Information

At one time corporations could receive a charter only through an act of legislation, but today corporations typically submit documents called articles of incorporation and pay a yearly filing fee, which ranges from $100 to $800 depending on the state in which the group is seeking to incorporate. The articles of incorporation include information about the nature of the corporation, the amount of stock available to shareholders, and the names and addresses of its directors. After a charter has been granted, a corporation's board of directors meets to draft the organization's bylaws, which state the corporation's internal operating procedures. In the past, corporate charters were issued for a specific, finite period of time, after which corporations were often dissolved and their assets distributed among shareholders. Today corporations can enjoy an unlimited lifespan, provided that they obey all laws and pay their yearly filing fee.

In the United States most corporations are registered with a state government rather than with the federal government. Corporations are subject to laws of the state in which they are registered. Because laws pertaining to corporations vary from state to state, many corporations register in one state but conduct operations from another. For example, many corporations seek registration in Delaware because this state does not charge tax on activities outside the state. Corporations seeking privacy and increased protection of assets often register in Nevada because it does not mandate disclosure of share ownership. In such cases corporations are also subject to the laws of their host state in matters pertaining to employment, civil actions, crimes, and contracts.

A traditional for-profit corporation is called a C Corporation because it is taxed under Subchapter C of the United States tax code. It could be said that a C Corporation is taxed twice. First, the corporation, as a single entity, is taxed for its profits. Next, individual stockholders are taxed on the dividends, or payments, they receive. Another type of corporation is called an S Corporation, which is taxed under Subchapter S of the U.S. tax code. An S Corporation is taxed as if it were a partnership. In a partnership all profit is passed directly to each partner, who in turn pays taxes as an individual. In order to be eligible for S Corporation status, a corporation must be based in the United States and have 100 shareholders or less. All shareholders must be U.S. citizens. In addition, this group must have only one class of stock (with only one kind of voting and dividend arrangement), and profits and losses must be allocated in direct proportion to each stockholder's financial share of the corporation.

In the case of what are known as public or publicly traded corporations, investors buy and sell corporate stocks through a stock market, such as the New York Stock Exchange or the Nasdaq. The largest U.S. businesses, such as Google and Nike, are publicly traded corporations. The majority of corporations, however, are not. These enterprises are called privately held or close corporations and are managed by small groups of businesspeople. Publicly traded and privately held corporations do business in similar ways, but publicly traded corporations are subject to stricter laws and more intense scrutiny, especially with regard to mergers with other corporations and elections of directors. Many of the largest corporations, such as Coca-Cola, Wal-Mart, Starbucks, and Microsoft, have grown beyond the national level and have established a presence throughout the world. These are called multinational corporations.

Recent Trends

Since the 1990s centers of corporate activity have shifted from the United States and Western Europe to Asia, particularly China. By 2005 Asia, excluding Japan, accounted for 13 percent of the world's economy, while Western Europe accounted for 30 percent. It was estimated that by 2025 those figures would be nearly equal. That shift was expected to be even more dramatic in the technology industries, affecting where corporations would hire their workers. In the past large American and Western European corporations established factories in developing (poorer and less industrialized) countries, including India and China, so that they could pay low wages to an unskilled labor force. While that practice has continued, corporations have increasingly sought skilled labor, such as computer programmers, from these same developing countries, also at lower wages. In 2005 33 million of the world's young professionals came from developing countries, which was more than twice the number of those in developed (wealthy and more industrialized) countries.

BOARD OF DIRECTORS

What It Means

A board of directors (usually simply called a board) is a group of individuals who determine the general policies

A board of directors is a group of people, led by a chairperson, charged with creating the policies and guiding principles of a public company. Sometimes the board of directors is chaired by the company's chief executive officer, as was the case with Kenneth Lay (1942–2006) of Enron Corporation. *AP Images.*

THE BOARD AND THE CHAIR

The words *board* and *chair,* as used to describe, respectively, the group of individuals who determine the policies of a corporation and the leader of that group, originated in colonial America. According to Ralph D. Ward, author of the 1997 book *Twenty-First Century Corporate Board,* the directors of these colonial companies traditionally gathered around a table consisting of a board laid across two barrels whenever they met to discuss business. Chairs were in short supply during colonial times, but if a chair was available, it was customary to give it to the largest board member, making him, by default, the company "chairman."

of a public company (a company owned by people, typically referred to as investors or stockholders, who have purchased shares in the company's ownership). The members of a board are elected by the stockholders to represent their interests in shaping the company's policies. Duties of a board include hiring and firing executive officers (individuals who oversee the operational management of the company), determining executive salaries, setting policies on dividends (money paid on a regular basis to stockholders; the amount depends on the performance of the company), and deciding on other policies regarding stocks (shares of ownership in a company). Typically a board of directors elects or appoints a chairperson to oversee board meetings.

When Did It Begin

The origin of the modern board of directors goes back to the early nineteenth century. As international trade (trade between different nations) expanded, public companies grew larger and attracted a larger and more diverse group of investors. As more investors became involved in the ownership of a corporation, it became impossible for all stockholders to play a direct role in the company's governance. In order to allow the company to run efficiently, investors began electing boards of directors, who were entrusted with representing the investors' interests in deciding corporate policy.

More Detailed Information

Although the board of directors of a corporation wields substantial power in determining corporate policy, they play almost no role in the company's day-to-day operations. In choosing a company's executive officers, the board delegates the management of the company to this team of officers. In this respect the board plays a predominantly advisory role in the overall management of a company's affairs.

The chief executive officer, or CEO, is the highest-ranking member of a company's management team and serves as the principal liaison between the company and the board. The second most critical member of the company's executive team is the chief financial officer, or CFO. The CFO of a corporation is primarily responsible for managing the various financial operations of the company, including financial planning, overseeing accounting procedures, and generating reports on a company's past performance and future prospects. At the same time the CFO is the executive officer responsible for assessing the financial risks involved with a company's specific projects or goals. In most cases a CFO reports directly to the company's CEO.

Boards monitor the affairs of a company by holding regular meetings, during which they discuss company affairs with the CEO and other executives. Ideally a company CEO will speak honestly with the board about company operations so that the board can make informed decisions about corporate policy. Although candor between the CEO and the board is a critical component in formulating sound policy, it also makes the CEO subject to greater scrutiny and allows him less independence in overseeing the company's daily operations. In some companies the CEO also serves as the chair of the board, and the CFO may also be on the board.

Recent Trends

The late 1990s witnessed a general breakdown in the relationship between CEOs and their boards of directors. CEOs of a number of major corporations lied habitually to their boards, leading to a lack of oversight and to mismanagement and corruption. In the case of Enron Corporation (an energy company that traded on the stock market in fuels, electricity, and other forms of energy), fraudulent accounting practices (the recording and disclosure of a company's financial dealings) resulted in the company's bankruptcy in 2001. The bankruptcy shocked the business community because Enron's CEO and board chairman Kenneth Lay (1942–2006) had previously asserted that the company's health was strong. In the wake of this scandal and others, boards throughout the United States have become subject to intense scrutiny, with investors demanding that their directors exercise more rigorous oversight and control over corporate operations.

LIMITED AND UNLIMITED LIABILITY

What It Means

In business, liabilities are debts that companies take on as they conduct business. It is common for businesses in the normal course of growth and activity to accumulate debts as they borrow money for new operations or expansions, purchase supplies and raw materials using credit, or take out mortgages on property or equipment. There are two general categories of liabilities: current liabilities, which are paid off within one year, and long-term liabilities, which are paid off in time frames greater than one year.

The term *limited liability* is used to describe a situation in which those responsible for paying back a debt are limited in the amount of money they owe in repayments. In terms of business ownership, limited liability describes a legal arrangement in which business owners are financially responsible for only the amount of money they have put into the business. For example, if the owner of a small business sets up his company with limited liability, and later the business loses so much money that it must file for bankruptcy, the owner will owe only the amount of money that he initially put into the business.

The term *unlimited liability* describes a situation in which those obligated for paying back a debt have unlimited responsibility to pay it back. This means that a business owner is held personally responsible for the debts of his business if the business runs out of money to pay its debts. If the business accumulates debts and then closes down or is successfully sued for a large amount of money, the owner of the business will usually have to pay out of his personal finances.

When Did It Begin

The concept of limited and unlimited liability has developed apace with modern accounting, the growth of business, and the evolution of the modern stock market. Before the nineteenth century, incorporation (or the formation of a legal corporation) for businesses was uncommon; many businesses did not incorporate but operated as loosely organized associations. Legal issues, such as issues of debt, were often difficult to resolve because laws did not govern unincorporated businesses.

Limited partnerships were types of business organizations formed in Europe and the United States in the eighteenth and early nineteenth centuries. The liability of the owners of the business was limited to a certain extent. One partner, or owner, in a limited partnership was held entirely liable for any losses the business suffered, and other partners, or member-owners, were held liable only to the extent that they had contributed to the business.

In England two laws were passed in the middle of the nineteenth century that affected liability regulations for businesses. The Joint Stock Companies Act of 1844 permitted businesses to incorporate legally using the investment contributions of a group of individuals who became the shareholders of the company. However, the law did not limit the liability of investors. The Limited Liability Act of 1855 established the legal ability of companies to limit liability if it had more than 25 owners. Over the next several years, similar laws were passed in France and the United States. These laws played an important role in the development of large, well-funded businesses.

Limited and unlimited liability refer to the level of responsibility an individual or group has in repaying debts when a company fails. In the United States corporations, such as General Motors, have only limited liability for business losses, meaning their owners would owe no more than they have invested in the business. *AP Images.*

More Detailed Information

Liability laws play a significant role in how businesses are established and run. More than 25 million businesses operate in the United States, but there are essentially only a few different types of legal categories of businesses. These legal definitions are based on the conditions of ownership. In a sole proprietorship, a single owner possesses the business, is entitled to all of the after-tax profits, and is responsible for all of the obligations of the firm, meaning he or she has unlimited liability. Most businesses are sole proprietorships, partly because they are the easiest form of business to start.

In a partnership, the responsibilities of the firm are shared between co-owners, called general partners, of which there may be more than two. The general partners share the investment of financial and other resources as well as any profits the business generates. They also share unlimited liability for debts and obligations. This type of business arrangement is common for doctors, lawyers, and architects.

The risks of unlimited liability can be daunting to some people since it means that they stand the chance of

UNLIMITED LIABILITY AT LLOYD'S

One of the world's most famous insurance companies, Lloyd's of London was founded in the seventeenth century with a unique structure that allowed some of its members, individuals called "names," to underwrite (or take on financial responsibility for) insurance policies on the basis of unlimited liability, and thereby put their total assets at risk. These members typically had great amounts of wealth and, by backing insurance policies written by Lloyd's, stood to gain even more wealth. What distinguished Lloyd's in the insurance market was that money invested in the firm could also be used to pay for an insurance policy. If, for example, an insurance policy was backed by an individual's collection of stocks and bonds, the investor maintained ownership and collected any interests and dividends. Although risk was involved in this practice, those who took on great risk were generally able to profit. By the 1990s, however, large numbers of prestigious members of Lloyd's, after losing money to asbestos and other environmentally related insurance claims, declared bankruptcy, and in 2002 the firm ended its practice of allowing unlimited liability amongst its members.

having to use their personal resources as payment if they are sued or if their business shuts down. This compels some people to form their business as a corporation, which divides the ownership among those who buy shares of stock. The stock represents the power of the shareholder to vote for members of a board of directors of the corporation. The board of directors hires the managers of the business. One of the primary advantages of forming a corporation is the fact that the liability of the owners is limited to the amount each has paid for his or her share or shares of stock. Even if the company faces financial setbacks or goes bankrupt, the owners' personal wealth is not vulnerable to loss.

Although unlimited liability is a feature of sole proprietorships and partnerships, it is also the primary legal feature of a company that forms as an unlimited liability company. Although this type of company is uncommon, it is an appropriate arrangement for a company that is formed only to hold land or other investments and not trade in goods or property.

The owners of a company are one source of money for businesses; businesses are also able to borrow money from banks and other financial institutions or from individual lenders. The individual who loans financial resources to a business or organization is called a creditor. Creditors loan money to organizations to earn a return on their investments. They usually loan money for a specific period of time and are promised a specific rate of return on their investments, usually a fixed rate such as 10 percent. Owners, on the other hand, typically invest their

money for an unspecified amount of time (which generally lasts until they decide to sell their investments), and they receive a return that depends on the profits earned by the business.

Recent Trends

Another category of business organization, the limited liability company (LLC), has become popular in the United States since the mid-1970s. The LLC combines aspects of partnerships and corporations in an effort to maximize the advantageous aspects and minimize the disadvantageous aspects of both types of businesses. As in a partnership, the members of an LLC may be unlimited in number and are not shareholders. Instead of being required to split their profits equally between members, they may distribute their profits according to their own arrangements. The primary characteristic of the limited liability company is that, like a corporation, it is a legally separate entity from its owners, and the company's owners cannot be held personally responsible for the business's debts should the business not meet them. Another advantage of the limited liability company is that the Internal Revenue Service (IRS) recognizes the LLC as a separate business entity and establishes well-defined tax rules for it. The LLC does not have a charter in the same way a corporation does, and it is not required to fulfill many of the obligations of corporations. For example, an LLC does not have to have meetings or keep written records of meeting details (called minutes) or resolutions. In general, it is simpler to operate an LLC than it is a corporation.

MULTINATIONAL CORPORATION

What It Means

A multinational corporation (MNC) is a company that operates in more than one country. Generally, multinational corporations consist of separate companies (called subsidiaries) in different countries, all of which answer to a central office located in the firm's home country. Most MNCs today are headquartered in the United States, Japan, or Western Europe. Examples include General Motors, Coca-Cola, Microsoft, Exxon Mobil, Sony, Honda, Royal Dutch Shell, and British Petroleum.

Companies choose to operate across national borders primarily in order to cut costs and increase profits. By expanding into multiple countries, firms gain various advantages, including increasing their customer bases and their access to lower labor and production costs. Since the 1950s MNCs have proliferated rapidly and are unquestionably one of the dominant forces in global life. The largest of the multinational corporations spend and bring in more money in a year than some small countries.

When multinational corporations move operations overseas to find cheaper labor, they eliminate jobs in their home countries. They are also able to exert enormous

Multinational corporations are companies that conduct business in more than one nation. Hong Kong, pictured here, attracts many multinational corporations because of its pro-business economic policies. © *Gareth Brown/Corbis.*

influence on the economies and politics of the developing countries in which they often seek to locate new facilities. Perhaps inevitably, then, many people distrust MNCs, and such companies are subjected to a wide range of criticisms.

When Did It Begin

The British East India Company, founded in 1600, and the Dutch East India Company, founded in 1602, are often called the first multinational corporations. Headquartered in England and the Netherlands, respectively, these firms were set up to trade goods such as cotton and spices over a large portion of South and Southeast Asia, then called the East Indies. These and other similar European trading companies that emerged in the following centuries gained great political power and often played a direct role in the European colonization of Asia and Africa.

During the seventeenth, eighteenth, and early nineteenth centuries, difficulties involving communications and transportation limited a firm's ability to do business efficiently beyond the local or regional level. That began to change in the mid-nineteenth century, however, with improvements in steamship speed and the expansion of railroads and telegraph cables. These and other inventions broadened business possibilities and paved the way for the emergence of a wide range of multinational corporations. The first American multinational corporation was I.M. Singer and Company (later called Singer Manufacturing Company), which made sewing machines. Founded in 1851, Singer initially sold its machines abroad through independent agents, but in the succeeding decades the company itself gradually took over global sales, and by the end of the century it had established several foreign branches.

Multinational corporations, especially those based in the United States, began to proliferate after World War II (1939–45). Government leaders in the United States believed that future international stability depended on economic growth worldwide, not only in Europe but also in unindustrialized countries. U.S. presidents Harry Truman (in office 1945–53) and Dwight Eisenhower (in office 1953–61) saw increased business investment

THE OIL INDUSTRY

While people around the world are generally suspicious of multinational corporations (MNCs), the increasingly large international firms that dominate the world economy today, no group of MNCs is more suspect, in the eyes of ordinary people, than the oil industry. Perhaps nothing in modern history did so much to create consumers' negative impressions of the oil industry than the 1973 oil crisis.

The crisis began when the Organization of the Petroleum Exporting Countries (OPEC), an alliance of oil-producing Arab nations, cut off oil supplies to the United States in retaliation for U.S. support of Israel (which was at war with neighboring Arab countries). Predictably, gas prices in the United States soared, and people had to wait in long lines to get gas for their cars.

Many U.S. citizens believed that the oil industry, which wielded an unusual amount of power over the countries in which it operated, had engineered this sequence of events to drive up profits. These suspicions seemed confirmed by the fact that profits for all of the major oil companies increased sharply in 1974: Exxon's profits grew 28.6 percent, Gulf's 33 percent, and Mobil's 23.3 percent. These profits came at the same time that the U.S. economy was experiencing its most severe crisis since the Great Depression of the 1930s.

abroad as a way of fighting the influence of the Soviet Union, whose socialist goals were at odds with American interests at the time (in the Soviet Union socialism entailed having the government control all economic activity).

Additionally, the plans for recovering from the war included creating the international organizations the International Monetary Fund and the World Bank, which were designed to facilitate international commerce. These helped to increase the amount of foreign investment first in Europe and then in poorer countries.

By the mid-1950s economic conditions worldwide had stabilized enough that U.S. corporations became strongly inclined to invest abroad. They built factories in other countries and established new markets for their products at a vigorous rate. Since then the growth of MNCs and of their overseas operations has increased steadily.

More Detailed Information

From the perspective of a corporation, there are a variety of motives for expanding into foreign countries.

First, there is the basic desire for growth. A company that has grown as much as possible in its home country, reaching all or most of its prospective consumers and maximizing its opportunities for profit, might be able to extend its growth and profits by setting up a subsidiary (a company that is controlled by the main company) in another country. This would enable it to develop a new pool of potential customers. Similarly, a company might decide to grow by buying up its competitors in other countries. This has the added benefit, from the company's perspective, of reducing present and future competition.

Another motive for becoming a multinational corporation is the ability to avoid trade restrictions. When a company based in one country exports its products to another country, it often must pay tariffs (special taxes levied on imports) to the receiving (importing) country. Tariffs are meant to protect the importing country's industries from foreign competition by increasing the retail price of foreign goods (this happens because the producer of the goods will pass its tariff costs along to the consumer). By setting up a subsidiary in the country that imposes the tariff, however, a corporation can avoid this added cost and thus price its goods more competitively.

Yet another powerful motive for setting up foreign subsidiaries is the company's ability to take advantage of cheaper labor than may be available in its home country. For instance, in the late twentieth century many U.S. corporations moved their manufacturing facilities to Latin America, Asia, and other parts of the world where workers demanded lower wages than their U.S. counterparts.

Multinational corporations are also able to create what economists call economies of scale. An economy of scale refers to the advantages that companies obtain by expanding their operations. In general, the more units of a product a company makes, the lower the average cost of making one unit becomes. A company that expands its operations across borders mobilizes a larger supply of labor and raw materials and can increase production to levels that allow it to cut costs significantly and price its goods lower than those of competitors.

In their pursuit of economies of scale, MNCs are aided by the increased flexibility that comes from operating in many different countries. Depending on the price of labor in the various countries in which it operates, and on the nature of the products it makes, a MNC may choose one of two basic models for producing and distributing its products. It may have factories in a few locations that make its products from start to finish, or it may have factories in many locations, each of which makes separate components of the final products. A company with global reach can seek out whatever locations in the world offer it a business advantage.

Recent Trends

As multinational corporations have become one of the dominant forces in the modern world, they have sparked a wide range of controversies.

In the late twentieth and early twenty-first centuries, the trend toward moving operations to foreign countries where labor was cheaper aroused widespread resentment toward MNCs in their home countries. In the United States the number of manufacturing jobs declined drastically as MNCs sought to cut costs and increase profits by locating their factories overseas. Many economists argued that the economic efficiency gained when companies cut costs would eventually balance out these job losses and produce greater wealth for the home country in the long run, but the effect on communities and regions that depended on manufacturing jobs was devastating.

In their host countries MNCs were often criticized for exerting too much control over local economies and politicians. Poor countries had to compete to attract corporations by easing regulations and eliminating taxes, and local politicians were often seen as catering to MNCs at the expense of their constituents. Many developing countries had weak economies centering on one or a few natural resources that multinational corporations wanted. MNCs were sometimes seen as exploiting these resources without regard for local customs, the environment, or human rights issues.

Many people also believe that MNCs wield an inordinate amount of influence in global politics. MNCs are among the largest donors to politicians in developed countries such as the United States (where many of the largest multinational corporations are based). They have enormous financial resources available for political donations, and they naturally use these resources with the intent of persuading politicians to pass legislation favorable to their business interests. For example, an oil company might urge the U.S. government to avoid imposing high fuel-economy standards on automobiles, because cars that use less gas, while they benefit the environment, would cut into oil-industry profits.

Defenders sometimes point out that, although multinational corporations do have influence over politicians, this is counterbalanced by governments' abilities to regulate MNCs. Governments have the power to set the terms according to which corporations may operate. Relations between MNCs and governments, then, are not as one-sided as they are made to seem. Defenders also argue that MNCs create economic opportunities for workers in poor countries and that they pay better wages and have better environmental records than do the existing companies in most of these countries.

$ Partnership

What It Means

When two or more people combine resources to form a profit-seeking business, that arrangement is called a partnership. In this sort of organization all profits and debts are shared proportionately according to the resources that each partner put in at the beginning. Partners are also personally liable (responsible) for all losses and damages suffered by the business. For example, if two college students each invested $250 to begin a painting business, and they made $4,000 by the end of the first summer, each would receive $2,000. On the other hand, if on the first day of the job one of the painters broke a large window that cost $3,000 to replace, both partners would have to draw $1,500 from personal funds to cover the damages. In this way a partnership is different from a corporation, a kind of business in which the owners cannot be asked to draw from personal accounts to cover damages.

There are two basic types of partnership: general and limited. In a general partnership, such as the arrangement described above, partners own and manage the business together. In a limited partnership one or more general partners manage the business and assume personal liability for losses, while limited partners contribute money, work space, or other resources but are not involved in the management of the enterprise. This is why they are sometimes referred to as silent partners. Limited partners are only liable for the amount they invested in the business.

When Did It Begin

Business partnerships have existed since early civilization; the oldest known reference to such an arrangement dates back to the eighteenth century BC, with a law code of the

References to business partnerships, in which two or more people share ownership in a company, can be found in the Hammurabi Code, a set of laws established more than 3,500 years ago. In this image King Hammurabi of Mesopotamia receives his legal code from the sun god Shamash. *Mansell/Time Life Pictures/Getty Images.*

THE SILENT PARTNER

A limited partner, or silent partner, is someone who offers money or some other resource but is otherwise not involved in the day-to-day running of a business. This arrangement, which is common in business today (especially in real-estate enterprises), dates back to the eleventh century, with sea exploration in Italy. At that time sea merchants enlisted the support of stay-at-home investors, who would fund the merchants' trips in exchange for a percentage of the profits. If the investor supplied all the money for the voyage, he was entitled to 75 percent of the profits upon the ship's return to harbor. In this relationship the investor was known as the commendator, and the merchant was known as the tractator.

ancient empire of Babylonia (in present-day Iraq). This evidence suggests that, for as long as there have been people willing to pool resources to make more money, there has also been a need for rules and written documents to settle disputes between partners.

In Europe partnerships (which were then called *commendas*) first arose in the eleventh century, when trade relations between Italy and the eastern Mediterranean began to grow. These business partners created agreements based on a combination of Roman commercial law and Islamic religious law. Borrowing from this original model, the English business community of the 1600s had partnerships called *societas*. More modern versions of these businesses spread widely in England throughout the 1800s, and in order to regulate their activities, the country formally ratified the Partnership Act in 1890. The United States in 1914 passed its Uniform Partnership Act, which was adopted by all the states except Louisiana. The act underwent a series of modifications between 1994 and 1997. By the start of the twenty-first century most states had adopted the Revised Uniform Partnership Act of 1997.

More Detailed Information

A partnership is much easier to create than a corporation, which usually requires official authorization from a state government and a yearly licensing fee. To create a business partnership, no formal papers need to be filed with any state or federal agency, and there is no licensing fee. Two or more individuals just need to reach a verbal agreement and begin business.

Most partnerships, however, are formed through a written agreement called the articles of partnership, which outlines each party's rights and obligations. In the absence of a written agreement, partnerships in the United States are governed by either the Uniform Partnership Act or the Revised Uniform Partnership Act, depending on the state that the partnership is in. The main

provisions of both acts are the same. They say that partners must share profits, losses, and obligations and that the partnership must be a for-profit business. Charitable organizations and nonprofit groups can not legally be considered partnerships.

There are many advantages to structuring a business as a partnership rather than as a corporation. The primary advantage is flexibility: the partners themselves manage the business and need only consult each other to change daily operations. That is not often the case with traditional corporations, which consist of stockholders (people who have invested money in the company and therefore own it), a board of directors (elected by the stockholders to represent them), and officers (who run the daily operations). Each of these has a say in the company's major decisions, so changes to corporations often involve layers of bureaucracy. Partnerships also offer an important tax advantage over corporations, which are, in effect, taxed twice: the corporation itself is taxed for all profits, and individual stockholders also pay taxes on their shares of the profits. With a partnership, however, all profits go directly to the partners, who only pay individual income tax on what they earn from the business.

There are some disadvantages to maintaining a partnership instead of a corporation. Most of these have to do with liability. To be liable means that each of the partners is personally responsible for covering any money the partnership owes. Furthermore, a decision made by one partner is binding to all partners, whether they know about the decision or not. For example, if three partners set up a small computer-merchandise shop and one of them agrees to pay a distributor $20,000 for equipment, then all partners are liable for that $20,000. If the three partners cannot pay the bill, the distributor can sue them for the money. If the partner who signed the agreement has no personal savings, the distributor can recover funds from either or both of the other partners.

Recent Trends

Because corporations experience what is called double taxation by the federal government (the corporation is taxed as an entity for its profits, and then individual shareholders are taxed), many entrepreneurs prefer to pay fewer taxes by running their businesses as partnerships or S corporations. The latter is a type of business entity that consists of 100 or fewer shareholders and receives the benefits of incorporation while being taxed as a partnership. Between 2000 and 2004 the number of partnerships in the United States grew by 23 percent, and the number of S corporations increased by 21 percent. Many states reacted by rewriting their business tax laws in an effort to raise revenues. States such as New Hampshire, Ohio, and Tennessee, for instance, began to impose what have been called franchise taxes or commercial activities taxes on some partnerships and S corporations.

$ Franchise

What It Means

A franchise is a license allowing one party, the franchisee, to use the brand name and business processes already developed by a parent company, the franchisor. Acquiring a franchise usually involves paying a start-up fee and agreeing to pay a regular percentage of sales to the parent company. Franchises are an extremely popular way of starting a business in the United States, especially for those who want to compete in the fast-food, automotive sales and rentals, lodging, real-estate, and other retail industries. Specific corporations that engage in franchising include McDonald's, Subway, Baskin-Robbins, Coca-Cola, Ford, Chevrolet, Toyota, Hertz, Avis, Thrifty, Holiday Inn, Howard Johnson, Days Inn, Century 21, and RE/MAX.

Franchises offer advantages and disadvantages for the entrepreneur. The use of an established brand name and/or a proven business model can significantly simplify the launching and operation of a business. This and other advantages may be outweighed, in some cases, by the sometimes-steep franchise fees that must be paid each month or year. Additionally, depending on the type of franchise and the particular company, a franchisee may have very little leeway in his or her decision-making.

When Did It Begin

Sewing-machine maker I. M. Singer and Company (later called Singer Manufacturing Company), which was started by Isaac Singer in 1851, is generally considered the first company to engage in franchising in the United States. Singer enlisted independent dealers to sell his sewing machines in the early stages of his company's development. Though the company ultimately abandoned the franchise model for a more centralized corporate structure, other companies adapted the original franchising strategy with better results. The Coca-Cola Company, which began operating on a franchise basis in the late nineteenth century, was one of the most successful early examples, and its operations today still technically follow the franchise model. (The parent company sells the condensed syrup that is the basis of the drink to franchisee bottlers, who mix it with water and sell it to retailers.) Franchising began to assume its modern form in the early 1900s, when A&W Root Beer began establishing fast-food restaurants on a franchise basis. The Howard Johnson's hotel chain began selling

A franchise is a license issued by a corporation, such as a fast food chain, allowing someone to operate a business in the corporation's name. This photo shows a Kentucky Fried Chicken, or KFC, franchise in Damascus, Syria. *AP Images.*

MCDONALD'S

The franchise, a business arrangement whereby an entrepreneur (a franchisee) buys the right to use an already established brand name or business model from a company (a franchisor), came to prominence in the late twentieth century. No company played a larger role in the rise of franchising than the fast-food giant McDonald's, which in the opinion of many experts is the world's most successful franchise-based business in the world.

McDonald's started out as a drive-through hamburger restaurant in San Bernardino, California, owned by a pair of brothers, Richard and Maurice McDonald. When a Chicago-based milkshake-machine salesman named Ray Kroc saw how popular the original McDonald's was, he understood that the restaurant had great potential for expansion. The McDonald brothers were not interested in expanding the restaurant themselves, so they reached an agreement whereby Kroc would oversee the expansion, giving them a portion of the fees he would charge franchisees. Ultimately Kroc bought out the McDonald brothers, and he is known as the true founder of the McDonald's chain.

Kroc did not invent the concept of fast-food franchising, but his innovation was to exert a high level of control over individual franchises, ensuring that all branches of McDonald's lived up to the same quality standards. From one drive-through burger restaurant, McDonald's grew to more than 6,000 franchises in its first 25 years. As of its fiftieth anniversary in 2004, McDonald's boasted more than 31,000 restaurants in 119 countries.

franchises in the 1930s, bringing the trend to that industry. The popularity of franchises increased with the construction of the interstate highway system in the United States in the 1950s. Travelers were likely to trust a brand-name hotel or restaurant over unknown local competitors. The expansion in franchising that led to the proliferation of chain stores seen all over the United States today occurred mainly after 1965.

More Detailed Information

There are two common models for franchises in the United States today. One type, called product franchising, is less restrictive for the franchisee than the other type, business-model franchising.

In product franchising relationships a parent company gives a franchisee the right to sell its products and use its brand name and trademarks, but it does not tell the franchisee how to run his or her business. Such arrangements are common in the automotive sales industry, in which car dealerships are franchises with the rights to sell certain brands but do not have to do so according to specific directions from the manufacturers of those brands. The arrangement between Coca-Cola and

its regional bottlers is also an example of product franchising. Bottlers have the right to bottle and sell Coke, but they run their business affairs largely on their own. Product franchising generates about two-thirds of all the money brought in by franchises in the United States.

Business-model franchising comes with more specific guidance from the parent company. In this type of franchising the franchisee purchases more than the rights to a brand name. The franchisor often provides assistance with the launch and the operation of the business; the parent company may decide where the franchise should be located, what the physical layout will look like, what equipment should be used, and how employees should be trained, among other features of the business. In the fast-food industry business-model franchising is the norm, and it explains why each branch of most national chains (such as McDonald's, Wendy's, Burger King, Subway, and KFC) looks virtually identical to all others and conducts business in such a way that you can expect the same experience from franchises whether you are in Walla Walla, Washington, Tampa, Florida, or anywhere in between. Though business-model franchises are more widespread than product franchises, accounting for three-quarters of all franchised businesses, they bring in only one-third of the revenue generated by all U.S. franchises.

Entrepreneurs gain significant advantages when they choose to buy a franchise rather than start a business from scratch. Foremost among these advantages is the head start provided by an established brand name. Whereas a new business may spend years and huge amounts of money building its brand through advertising and customer interactions, a franchisee has the privilege of selling a brand consumers already recognize and seek out. Franchisees also commonly benefit from national advertising campaigns and other promotional efforts conducted by the franchisor. Highly visible marketing of this type is not otherwise available to small business owners, who generally operate on a limited budget. Most franchise agreements also include a provision giving the franchisee rights to be the only seller of the franchisor's brand within a certain territory. This represents an important competitive advantage in many cases.

There are potential downsides to consider before deciding to purchase a franchise, however. One of the most serious of these negative aspects is the financial arrangement between the franchisor and the franchisee. In addition to paying the start-up expenses related to opening any business (such as rent, construction, labor, and product costs), a McDonald's franchisee as of 2007 was required to pay a fee of $45,000 for the right to operate under the brand name for a period of 20 years. Beyond this initial investment a franchisee is further obligated to pay fees amounting to 12.5 percent of all sales to the franchisor. Burger King charges a higher start-up fee ($50,000) but requires a lower percentage of sales (4.5 percent). Other franchisors may offer lower fees, but this is typically because the brand is less established. McDonald's can charge high fees because of its enormous consumer base. In any case, a franchisee should plan on handing over a substantial portion of whatever money he or she makes to the parent company.

Additionally, the success of franchises is based on conforming to a single business model. For the entrepreneur who wants to make his or her own decisions, this might not be a fulfilling environment. While the advantages of a proven business model are significant, they may undercut the personal satisfaction some entrepreneurs seek when they go into business for themselves. Further, the obligation to conform can become a liability if the parent company does not hold up its end of the bargain. If the advertising on behalf of the brand is ineffective or if the parent company otherwise fails to maintain high standards for the brand, the individual franchisee may be locked into a struggling business model at a time when individual creativity could help avert losses.

For established companies franchising offers a way to expand a brand without undertaking all of the costs of doing so in a more centralized fashion. A company intent on owning all of its own outlets must use its own money to buy equipment and hire workers with each new branch opening. This may mean putting off profitability for several years. By contrast, a franchisor's expenses are minimal; willing franchisees undertake much of the financial burden of expanding the brand's reach. The result is the possibility for extremely rapid expansion. For example, it took the real-estate franchisor Century 21 only eight years (1972–80) to establish 7,400 branches. The fast-food giant McDonald's grew to 6,200 franchises and one of the world's most recognized brands within 25 years (1955–77), and at its fiftieth anniversary in 2004, it had more than 31,000 outlets in 119 countries.

One of the risks of being a franchisor is that a handful of inept franchisees can cause serious damage to the overall brand. For example, the standardization of fast-food restaurants leads many consumers to consider the various branches interchangeable. Health-code violations or other scandals at a few franchises can affect consumer perceptions nationwide, cutting into profits at the corporate level.

Recent Trends

Franchises spread rapidly across the United States at the end of the twentieth century. During the 1960s and 1970s franchises reached most areas of the country, and a further boom in franchises occurred in the 1980s and 1990s as a result of increased wealth, the massive marketing campaigns of franchisors, and the widespread American belief in the value of entrepreneurship. By the early twenty-first century there were more than 2,000 franchisors in the United States and more than 500,000 franchisees. The 600,000 franchises owned by these

franchisees generated roughly one-third of all retail sales in the country.

There were numerous critics of franchises and their place in American culture at this time. Some critics pointed to the fact that franchises generally paid low wages, employed most workers on a part-time basis, and almost never offered benefits such as health insurance. Since franchises were such a dominant force in the economy, many believed that their labor practices harmed the employment conditions for workers in general. At the same time, the poor pay and lack of benefits meant that franchisees often found it difficult to keep good employees.

An additional criticism of franchises was that they drained money away from local economies, since such a large portion of any franchisees' profits went to the parent company. The ability of franchises to use their established brands to fight off local competitors meant, further, that it was harder and harder for strictly local businesses to compete, increasing the amount of money leaving individual communities over time.

Finally, many ordinary citizens disliked the fact that the growing presence of franchises nationwide made American towns and cities increasingly indistinguishable from one another. During the early twenty-first century an increasing number of towns began passing regulations meant to keep out franchises and other chain stores, in an attempt to preserve community values and provide opportunities for local businesses.

$ Sole Proprietorship

What It Means

A sole proprietorship is a business that has only one owner. It is the simplest and most common form of commercial enterprise in the United States. A sole proprietor with a license may hire employees and run any sort of lawful business. The most common sole proprietorships are in the areas of food service, home maintenance and improvement (roofers, electricians, and cabinet makers, for example), auto repair, and child care. The greatest advantage of running a sole proprietorship is the autonomy, or self-direction. Unlike in a corporation or a partnership, a sole proprietor need not consult with anyone else before making important decisions about running a business. Of course, the sole proprietor also bears the full burden of the consequences of those decisions.

The greatest disadvantage to operating a business as a sole proprietorship is the extent of liability (financial responsibility). A sole proprietor is completely liable for all debts incurred and damages caused in the process of doing business. For example, if one of the employees of a sole proprietor injures a client or damages property while on the job, the sole proprietor must pay for all monetary losses. If the proprietor's insurance does not cover the

MOMTREPRENEURS

Angelina Musik founded MOMtrepreneurs with her husband Daniel Comp in the spring of 2003 in San Antonio, Texas. The organization offered networking opportunities (chances to exchange information or services and establish productive relationships with others in similar businesses) and other types of support to women, with or without children, who were looking for new ways to promote and market their businesses. Membership consisted of businesswomen from the United States, Canada, the United Kingdom, and Australia. Musik launched a successful motivational radio and television show through this organization. Inspired by Oprah Winfrey, Musik overcame several personal crises, including domestic violence and a failed marriage, before starting numerous small businesses. Aside from MOMtrepreneurs, her most successful venture was Intelligent Netware, a software applications and technological marketing firm that she also ran with Comp.

damages, the courts may demand that the sole proprietor liquidate (sell or convert into cash) personal assets to pay for the losses or the harm done. If there are still outstanding damages, the sole proprietor will then be forced to file for bankruptcy (financial ruin).

When Did It Begin

Running a sole proprietorship is one of the oldest ways of doing business in the world. It is also the riskiest form of business venture. At least as far back as ancient Greece, individual entrepreneurs (people who start businesses) have recognized the need to combine resources with others in order to minimize risk and maximize profit. Many modern businesses trace their roots to the joint stock companies that formed in the early 1600s when European countries expanded their overseas trading and colonizing efforts. A joint stock company consisted of a group of members, each of whom contributed money to the business. Members were given certificates of ownership, or stocks, in exchange for their contributions. These commercial organizations searched for legal ways to limit the liability of individual members. The problem remained largely unsolved for nearly three centuries, however, until a court handed down the *Salomon v. Salomon and Company* verdict in England in 1896. Deciding on a seemingly small case involving a leather merchant, the House of Lords voted unanimously to recognize a company as a separate legal identity, distinct from its owner(s). This ruling gave a significant advantage to people doing business as a corporation rather than as a sole proprietorship, in which there is no legal distinction between the business and the owner of the business. In the following century a series of corporation-friendly laws

were passed in many other nations, including the United States.

More Detailed Information

The majority of businesses begin as sole proprietorships. One reason for this is that starting a sole proprietorship involves few steps. In fact, after getting the appropriate licensing for a given task (an electrician, for example needs to be licensed and certified in order to open an electrical repair shop), a business is automatically considered a sole proprietorship unless the owner takes specific steps to classify it some other way (for instance, as a partnership or a corporation). Most sole proprietors follow the easiest course and do business under their own names. A mechanic running his own garage may call his business Bill Jones Auto Repair without further paperwork. If an owner wishes to use a trade name, or what is often referred to as a fictitious name, he or she must file a trade name certificate in the city, county, or state in which the establishment is based. Going back to the above example, if Bill Jones wished to call his business Superstar Auto Repair or even Bill's Auto Repair, he would have to file such a certificate. Bill Jones would only be permitted to use one of these trade names if no other businesses had been previously registered under these names.

A sole proprietorship terminates with the death of the sole proprietor. If a spouse or relative continues operating the business after the death of the proprietor, the business is legally considered a different establishment. Sole proprietorships are also terminated when they are sold or when the owner goes bankrupt.

Aside from autonomy, owners of sole proprietorships enjoy two key benefits at tax time. First, the owner can use a personal 1040 tax form (the form all individuals and families use) to pay taxes or file for a tax refund. This form is much simpler than the ones required of a partnership or corporation. Second and more important, the owner is only taxed once on all profits. This is not the case in a corporation, where the business is first taxed as a single entity, and then shareholders (people who invested money in the business) are personally taxed on all dividends (shares of the profits). This possible financial benefit must be weighed against other limitations and challenges. Sole proprietors, for example, frequently have a more difficult time raising money to start or expand their business and securing loans than corporations do.

The flexibility and autonomy of running a sole proprietorship come with some other negatives. Chief among them is the fact that the sole proprietor must be skilled in all aspects of the business. In the example above Bill Jones probably started his auto repair shop because he is a talented mechanic. In order to succeed, however, he must also be able to market (find customers for) his business and organize his account books (recording payments made to him, expenses, and so forth). If he does not have the time or the inclination to look after these things carefully, he will have to hire someone else to manage these tasks. A sole proprietor may have a harder time than a corporation in finding good, long-term help, because corporations can often afford to offer many more benefits (such as health care and vacation pay) to employees.

Recent Trends

Woman-owned sole proprietorships are one of the fastest growing forms of business in the United States. In terms of number of businesses and profit totals, female-owned sole proprietorships have been growing faster than their male-run counterparts for more than two decades.

According to the U.S. Small Business Administration nearly 85 percent of all the businesses run by women operate as sole proprietorships. These businesses tend to make moderate rather than large profits. Data from the mid-1990s through 2006 indicate that approximately 87 percent of woman-run sole proprietorships earned $50,000 per year or less, while about 2.7 percent of female-run sole proprietorships earned $200,000 or more.

Nearly 75 percent of the women's businesses are based in the service industries, such as day care and catering, and another 18 percent are in finance and insurance. More than half of the female sole proprietors in the United States run their businesses in one of the country's top 10 urban centers. By contrast less than one-third of the male-run sole proprietorships are based in urban centers.

$ Independent Contractor

What It Means

An independent contractor is a person or company that works for another person or company without being a regular employee. Independent contractors usually enter into short-term contracts for specific projects, and they often work for more than one client at the same time.

Independent contractors work in a variety of fields. For instance, housecleaners, roofers, website designers, farmworkers, writers, cabdrivers, and business consultants all commonly work as independent contractors.

An independent contractor is someone who works for a company, often on a short-term, per project basis, without being a regular employee. Many independent contractors work from home and make their own hours. *Photograph by Kelly A. Quin. Cengage Learning, Gale.*

MICROSOFT'S PERMATEMPS

In the 1980s and 1990s it became common for corporations to cut costs by classifying workers as independent contractors rather than employees. When a company pays independent contractors, it does not need to pay taxes to the state and federal government, and it does not have to provide the worker with benefits such as health care, retirement planning, or stock options (shares of ownership in the company that gain value as the company grows and prospers). Independent contractors generally work on a specific project instead of on an ongoing basis. One form of independent contracting occurs when temporary staffing agencies (commonly called temp agencies) place workers with a company. In these situations the temp agency itself is an independent contractor for the company, and the individual worker is considered an employee of the temp agency.

Microsoft, the giant computer-software corporation based in Seattle, Washington, relied heavily on temp workers in its early years. This allowed it to cut costs at a time when it did not have enormous amounts of cash on hand. As the company grew, however, it tended to maintain long-term relationships with workers without ever classifying them as employees. This meant that these workers did not enjoy the handsome benefits packages available to Microsoft employees, most notably stock options (the right to purchase shares in the company at discounted price), which gained value by leaps and bounds in the company's early years. In 1992 Microsoft's "permatemps," as they had come to be called, filed a class-action lawsuit (a lawsuit that represents a large number of plaintiffs) asking to be reimbursed for the benefits they had been denied.

The case, together with a second permatemp class-action suit, made its way through the courts through much of the 1990s. Microsoft finally came to a settlement with its permatemps in 1999, agreeing to pay a total of $97 million to account for the unpaid benefits to these workers. When the permatemps were finally paid in 2005, however, their lawyers claimed $27 million of the total. At the end of the case, each permatemp got slightly less than $8,500.

Distinguishing an independent contractor from an employee, however, is not as simple as identifying a person's profession. There may be room for misinterpretation, especially when the work is being done by an individual rather than a business. From a legal standpoint the determining factor is the nature of the worker's relationship with the employer. If the employing company has control over the final product of someone's work but not the means by which that person accomplishes the work, then the individual probably qualifies, under U.S. law, as an independent contractor rather than an employee.

This distinction is important for both the worker and the employer. For the worker the distinction matters because employees are entitled to benefits and job security that are not available to independent contractors. On the other hand, employees have less autonomy and personal flexibility than independent contractors, who possess the freedom that comes with being one's own boss. Also, independent contractors have different responsibilities and advantages regarding the payment of state and federal income taxes. When an employer hires an employee, he or she must withhold a portion of the employee's paycheck for taxes and send it to the state and federal governments; an employer, however, is not involved in paying the taxes of an independent contractor. Although hiring an independent contractor is often cheaper and easier than hiring an employee, an employer can get into trouble with the Internal Revenue Service (also known as the IRS, the U.S. agency that collects taxes from all American individuals and businesses) if he or she hires someone on an independent-contractor basis when that person falls under the legal definition of an employee.

When Did It Begin

Independent contractors have always been a feature of the American economy. In the 1960s, however, the IRS began actively investigating employers suspected of avoiding their tax responsibilities. A common problem, for instance, was people employing domestic workers on a cash basis without reporting payments to the agency (by law, all income must be reported to the IRS). These investigations led to an increased focus on employer-worker relationships in general.

The IRS's attention to the way that employers classified those who worked for them (as independent contractors versus employees) intensified greatly in the 1980s and 1990s, when it became common practice for corporations to cut costs (related to paying taxes, paying for paperwork and other administrative affairs, and paying for employee benefits) by hiring independent contractors rather than new employees. Since then the IRS has spent a great deal of time and energy on getting improperly classified independent contractors reclassified as employees. When the IRS succeeds in doing this, the employer guilty of the misclassification must pay back taxes (the taxes that would have originally been contributed to the government when the employee was given his or her paycheck) as well as fines. This process can be costly for companies that rely on independent contractors, and it has become a major source of revenue for the government.

More Detailed Information

In making its decisions about whether to classify a worker as an independent contractor or an employee, the IRS refers to what is called common law, the body of laws that have arisen through customs and the rulings of courts rather than having been explicitly written by government legislators. The agency asks a number of questions about the employer-worker relationship, all of which relate to the amount of control the employer has over the work process. When an employer exercises control over not just the final product but also the process by which a worker arrives at that final product, the employer usually must classify that worker as an employee, not an independent contractor.

For example, the IRS considers the instructions given to the worker. Has the employer specified where or when certain parts of the work must be done, or in what sequence different parts of a job must be performed? Has the employer required that the worker use certain materials or equipment? Has the employer provided the worker with specific training in how to achieve the desired final result? An affirmative answer to such questions suggests an employer-employee relationship rather than an employer–independent contractor relationship.

Additionally, the IRS considers how much financial control the employer has over the worker. Has the employer provided him or her with tools and equipment, or has the worker invested independently in the necessary materials for practicing his or her trade? Does the employer pay expenses that the worker incurs on the job, or does the worker pay these out of his or her own pocket? Is the employer the worker's main or only employer, or does the worker maintain an independent business presence and advertise his or her services within the industry? Is the worker paid by the hour or week (as employees generally are), or is he or she paid a flat fee as a job is completed (as independent contractors generally are)?

Finally, the IRS considers evidence of the nature of the employer-worker relationship. If contracts have been signed, these should provide evidence of the amount of control the employer seeks to have over the job. If the worker's job represents a crucial part of the overall business, rather than an occasional or periodic need, or if the relationship is meant to be ongoing, rather than strictly limited to the time period of a specific project, then the worker may need to be considered an employee.

Recent Trends

Since the IRS began increasing its attempts to reclassify more workers as employees at the end of the twentieth century, many business owners have voiced their disapproval. Some have complained that the classification guidelines are interpreted inconsistently by individual IRS employees. They have also argued that standards for independent contractors and employees differ from industry to industry because different forms of work require different kinds of employer-worker relationships. The IRS claims that its actions are in the best interest of workers who might be taken advantage of by employers, but some business owners believe that reclassification is popular simply because it provides the government with a sizeable source of revenue.

＄ Nonprofit Organization

What It Means

A nonprofit organization is an institution that conducts business for reasons other than the desire to make a profit. Schools, churches, homeless shelters, museums, conservation groups, sports leagues, arts foundations, research institutes, private universities, social clubs, political groups, and some hospitals function as nonprofit organizations in the United States today, among many other groups.

Nonprofits combine the diversity of the business world with the public-service mission of the government, but they are distinct from both of these other main sectors of the economy. There are endless varieties of nonprofit organizations, and they collectively play a larger role in American life than they do in the lives of those who live in other wealthy countries. This is partly a result of the extreme wealth in the United States, which results in greater sources of funds that can be used to do good works, but it is also a result of the U.S. government's general reluctance to spend taxpayers' money on social programs. The U.S. government encourages nonprofit groups to fulfill society's needs by exempting qualifying organizations from paying taxes and by allowing people who donate money to many of these organizations to reduce their own tax payments in proportion to their donations.

When Did It Begin

Many different kinds of institutions are classified as nonprofit organizations in the United States today, and some of these, such as churches, hospitals, and museums, have roots stretching back hundreds or thousands of years. Major world religions have been particularly instrumental throughout history in encouraging works done on behalf of the public, rather than for financial gain.

The large and varied nonprofit sector of today's economy also owes a great deal to the attitudes brought to the United States by settlers and immigrants. Whereas works of charity were typically carried out by churches and the nobility in the old world countries of Europe, those who first settled the United States had no choice but to band together to create the public services that they needed. For example, an early American settlement would have gone without such institutions as churches, hospitals, and schools if not for volunteer activity, since there were no nobles or religious institutions to pay for them. The U.S. government has also traditionally been less willing to take on the burden of caring for the unfortunate or for promoting social well-being than have similarly developed European governments. While European countries are more active in using tax revenues to provide public services to their citizens, the United States

A nonprofit organization performs a service—education, health care, community guidance, or some other activity designed to promote public welfare—without concern for earning a profit. This photo shows John R. Bryant, founder of Operation Hope, a Los Angeles-based nonprofit group dedicated to providing education about finances and economics to underprivileged children. *AP Images.*

has historically been more reliant on private nonprofit groups.

The ideas and actions of wealthy industrialists such as Andrew Carnegie and John D. Rockefeller were instrumental in shaping today's nonprofit sector. After making his fortune in the steel industry, Carnegie in 1889 wrote an essay called "Wealth" (also called the "Gospel of Wealth"), in which he put forward the idea that the rich should use their money to benefit the public rather than leaving it to their families. Carnegie put his ideas into practice, giving away most of his riches to establish libraries and educational institutions in the United States, Scotland (where he was born), and elsewhere around the world. Similarly, John D. Rockefeller (whose company, Standard Oil, dominated the American oil industry) gave away an estimated $500 million in the late nineteenth and early twentieth centuries, focusing his gifts on universities and medical institutions. Changes to the U.S. tax code in 1921 created further incentives for individuals to make

donations to nonprofit groups, and additional changes in 1935 made it more attractive for corporations to give away money. Donating to nonprofit organizations has become ingrained among people of moderate as well as great wealth, and the number of nonprofit organizations in the United States has grown steadily and rapidly since that time.

More Detailed Information

Nonprofit organizations play an important role in everyday life across the United States. They attempt to improve communities and the world at large by tackling issues important to the public. This may involve taking direct action to cause changes, providing services to people, or pushing for government involvement in their area of concern. Nonprofits are not limited to any particular portion of the political spectrum; some are overtly political while others have little or no involvement in politics. There are nonprofits focused on virtually all areas of human activity. Because their operations differ from both the public sector (government) and the private sector (business), nonprofits are said to constitute a third sector of the economy.

Nonprofits differ from businesses in that their goal is not to produce wealth. Many nonprofits do, however, sell products or charge fees for services, and they often bring in more money through sales or donations than they spend on their operating costs. This excess income is not profit, however, because it is used to further the group's social or other goals, rather than being distributed to owners or investors. Nonprofits differ from the government in that they do not accomplish their goals by making or enforcing laws. They promote the public welfare, instead, by mobilizing the money of donors and the effort of paid or volunteer workers to address the issues that they seek to change.

Nonprofit organizations in the United States can be broken down into various segments. First and most numerous, there are churches and religious organizations, which account for roughly a third of all nonprofits. Because they occupy such a distinct position in society, churches are often considered as a separate segment of the nonprofit sector, not sharing many of the common traits of other nonprofits.

Another prominent segment of the nonprofit sector encompasses associations that work to advance the interests of businesses, professionals, workers, and political groups. For example, the local chamber of commerce in any town does not attempt to make a profit for itself; instead, its goal is to increase the economic well-being of community businesses. The American Medical Association similarly attempts to further the interests of doctors and medical students, and labor unions such as the AFL-CIO work on behalf of a variety of workers. Political groups that raise money for candidates in local, state, and national elections fall into this category of nonprofits, as do political action committees such as Moveon.org, which attempts to advance the interests of progressive political candidates and issues across the United States.

Within the nonprofit sector there are also numerous organizations designed to promote the social and civic interests of their members. Examples of this kind of nonprofit organization are college fraternities and sororities, benevolent groups such as Elks lodges (officially known as the Benevolent and Protective Order of Elks), parent-teacher associations, organizations uniting people of a particular ethnic group in a community, and a wide range of other social clubs.

Another important class of nonprofits consists of social advocacy organizations. These are groups that are dedicated to a specific social or political goal. The goal might be one that benefits a broad range of humanity, such as voter education, the protection of human rights, or the preservation of the natural environment. Non-

profits of this type might also address issues that benefit a specific group of people, such as children, the disabled, or the elderly.

Finally, there are grant-making organizations, also known as charitable trusts. These nonprofits give money directly to people or institutions for a wide range of reasons. Grant-making organizations fight diseases, promote educational goals, alleviate poverty, and endow museums and universities, among many other activities. These nonprofit organizations fall into two subcategories: private foundations and public foundations. Private foundations are generally funded by one or a few sources, such as an individual or group of individuals, a family, or a corporation. The largest of all foundations, such as the Bill and Melinda Gates Foundation, the Ford Foundation, and the J. Paul Getty Trust, are private foundations. Public foundations receive money from a variety of sources, which may include the government, individuals, corporations, private foundations, and fees charged for goods and services. Community foundations, which are set up to benefit a specific geographic area, are the most common type of public foundation.

Because they promote social well-being and do not attempt to enrich those who work for them, nonprofits are not required to pay taxes on the money they bring in through donations or through their business operations. Depending on the legal classification of a particular nonprofit organization, the people and businesses that donate money to them are often allowed to deduct money from their own government tax bills in proportion to their donations. In general, donations made to groups that attempt to influence political elections or the legislative process are not tax deductible.

Recent Trends

During the late twentieth and early twenty-first centuries, the nonprofit sector of the U.S. economy expanded dramatically. This was primarily a result of growth in the U.S. economy, which outpaced economic growth in the rest of the world, creating unprecedented wealth for individuals and companies and, therefore, more potential donations to nonprofits. Whereas other wealthy countries channeled their wealth through the government, which in turn provided many social services, the U.S. government during the 1980s and 1990s was moving away from large public-spending programs, leaving nonprofit organizations to fill the gap.

The nonprofit sector employed around 6 million Americans in 1977; by 2004 that number had climbed to 12 million, not counting volunteer service. Nonprofit spending amounted to $1.4 trillion, or about half of what the U.S. government spends each year on non-defense goods and services. These numbers were, moreover, conservative estimates of the nonprofit sector's size, since they do not account for the size and spending of churches

FOR-PROFIT CHARITY

At the beginning of the twenty-first century, a new trend in philanthropy was emerging. A number of successful entrepreneurs, having concluded that nonprofit organizations had not achieved success in ending poverty and other problems around the world, began experimenting with ways of using profit-making businesses to solve the world's problems. Whereas successful businesspeople who wanted to improve the world had traditionally donated their money to good causes, the new "philanthropreneurs," as they were sometimes called, believed that more progress could be made if the profit motive could be applied to charitable causes.

The founder of eBay, Pierre Omidyar, was one of the leading philanthropreneurs. His goal was to use so-called microloans, rather than gifts of money, to help people in the third-world start small businesses. Thus, investors could contribute money to help the poor make investments that, while small by U.S. standards, make a life-or-death difference to those who receive them. For example, a microloan might enable a villager in South America to buy a few farm animals, and the farmer would, like any businessperson, pay a fee for the use of the borrowed money, allowing the investors to profit while also helping the farmer make a living.

and religious organizations, which are not required to report extensively on their activities.

Perhaps the most visible evidence of the growing influence of nonprofits was the increasing size of the private and public foundations that used donations to advance charitable causes. In 2005 these grant-making organizations were in possession of assets amounting to $525 billion, up from $30 billion in 1975 (this figure is stated in 2005 dollars, adjusted to account for inflation, which causes a consistent decline in the value of a dollar over time). U.S. foundations gave away $33.6 billion to charitable causes in 2005, more than double the amount given by foundations a decade earlier (again, the comparison is adjusted to account for inflation).

This time was also noteworthy for the emergence of a foundation of unprecedented size and scope: the Bill and Melinda Gates Foundation. Established in 1994 by Microsoft founder Bill Gates and his wife Melinda, the foundation had $29 billion in assets in 2006 when another of the world's richest people, Warren Buffett (founder of the investment company Berkshire Hathaway), pledged the bulk of his own wealth to the foundation over time, an amount that was eventually predicted to exceed $30 billion. The foundation, which focused on reducing inequality in the United States and around the world, was thus capable of helping the world's poor people on a scale rivaled only by national governments.

CHARITY

What It Means

A charity is an organization that is established with the sole purpose of providing help or relief to people in need. A charity may be an institution, such as a hospital, that provides care for the sick or injured free of charge. It can also be a fund that provides financial resources for those who need them or an organization that provides such things as shelter, clothing, or education.

Charities have roots in ancient cultures, and they have always been focused on addressing the needs of the poor. In many countries charities are the primary organizations helping the poor survive and thus allowing the societies in which they exist to sustain themselves and move forward. Societies with well-respected and active charities are regarded by some as the healthiest societies.

In most countries charities are supervised by the federal government. Whether they are public or private, charities must register with the government and report on their financial and operational activities on a regular basis. Charities rely primarily on donations from private citizens and organizations for their funding and resources. Donations are typically made in the form of cash, but donors can also give real estate, clothing, computers or other electronic equipment, motor vehicles, or securities, such as stocks or bonds (stocks are shares of ownership in a company, and bonds are shares of governmental and other types of debt; both can earn profits or interest). Usually when individuals or corporations make a donation, they may then deduct a certain amount from their income taxes related to the value of the donation.

When Did It Begin

The belief that charity is a virtue has its roots in ancient times and is associated with religious traditions around the world. In Islam, for example, aid to the poor is not only encouraged but is seen as a duty, traditionally requiring Muslims to give away 2.5 percent of their total wealth each year. The Torah, a Jewish holy book, commands Jews to give to the poor every year as well; charity, repentance, and prayer are believed to overcome evil edicts, bring redemption, and save those who practice them from a meaningless death. Christians received their understanding about the importance of giving to the poor from the Bible's New Testament, which names the three great virtues as faith, hope, and charity. It is considered a Christian duty for the rich to help the poor in the form of alms-giving (any voluntary contribution to aid the poor). Over time these various religious beliefs have been combined with the idea that philanthropic activity on the part of the wealthier classes made a difference in the lives of the poor.

The earliest institutional charities started forming centuries ago. The Hospital of St. Cross in Winchester,

Charities are organizations dedicated to providing assistance to people in need. Founded in London in 1865, the Salvation Army provides meals and shelter to disadvantaged individuals throughout the world. *The Library of Congress.*

England, formed in 1136, is the oldest charitable institution in Britain. Known as an almshouse, it continues to care for old people and even provides what is known as the "Wayfarer's Dole" (traditionally bread and ale) to passing travelers. Until the nineteenth century charities were typically established by rich merchants or other wealthy people who left a portion of their wealth in their will to create a charitable fund or institution.

Until the mid-1900s charities carried the bulk of the responsibility of caring for hundreds of thousands of poor people in the United States. After the war the government created welfare policies, and many of the obligations that formerly fell to charities were absorbed by the state.

More Detailed Information

Over the centuries the mission of charitable institutions has evolved along with the needs of societies. Today, charities focus on wide array of different needs, from hunger relief to veterinary care to disease eradication.

Charities are nonprofit organizations. This means that their primary objective is to support an issue of private interest or public concern for noncommercial purposes. In many countries nonprofits may apply to the federal government for tax-exempt status. If they receive this status, they do not have to pay taxes on income or other activities. In some cases exempt status also means that financial donors can deduct the amount of their charitable donation from the taxes they owe to state and federal governments.

Charities are sometimes referred to as foundations. A foundation is a type of humanitarian or charitable organization set up by individuals or institutions as a legal entity (a corporation or trust). Foundations support causes in keeping with their goals by distributing sums of money, called grants, to these causes. The Bill and Melinda Gates Foundation, for example, is a philanthropic organization that has a strong focus on world health, so it funds projects that address disease and education, such as immunizing children in developing countries and running mobile boat libraries in Bangladesh.

Charitable donations are not just given in the form of cash or other assets. Individuals may also contribute to charities in their final financial arrangements, known as wills or final bequests. Donors giving to charity in this way are called grantors. One way a grantor can contribute to a charity is by establishing a charitable lead trust. This is an arrangement in which income (for instance, rental or

THE SALVATION ARMY

One of the most famous and widely recognized charities anywhere is the Salvation Army, a nonmilitary, international religious and charitable organization. William Booth (1829–1912), a former Methodist minister, founded the Salvation Army in London in 1865. Booth's mission was to bring salvation to the poor, the homeless, and the hungry. In 1880 a branch was established in New York City, and the organization has since spread to 111 other countries. It is now one of the largest providers of social aid in the world. The charity operates adult rehabilitation centers for homeless people, children's camps, general hospitals, maternity homes and hospitals, children's homes and foster-care centers, residences for senior citizens and young working women, senior citizen's centers, and centers for alcoholics. In the United States it gives aid to more than 30 million people.

interest income) from property or investments is given to a charity while the grantor is living; at the grantor's death the ownership of the property or investment passes to the grantor's heirs (those specified in the will to inherit), and the charity no longer benefits.

A grantor may also establish a charitable remainder trust. This is an arrangement in which assets (property or money) are put into a trust (a property interest held by one person for the benefit of another) in the name of a charity, but the grantor continues to use the property or receive income from it until he or she dies (or sometimes until the grantor and the grantor's spouse both die). After that point the charity receives the total income from the property as well. Charitable remainder trusts are attractive to many wealthy grantors because they can avoid some of the income taxes on the donated assets during their lifetime. Also, the grantor may reduce the taxes on his or her estate (the assets left at death) since, once donated, the asset is removed from the estate.

Recent Trends

Within Christianity two trends have grown out of the broad concept of charity as the church first promoted it many centuries ago. One, the Catholic Church has encouraged members to donate alms, or to act charitably, as a way for individuals to find spiritual redemption. Many organizations serving local, state, and national communities act under the auspices of the Catholic Church. In contrast, Protestants developed the belief that individuals find justification by faith alone, and that where faith exists, charity will also exist. Protestant churches are less involved in organizing and operating charities than Catholic churches.

In the early part of the twentieth century, many large charitable organizations were established in the United States. The emphasis on compassion was replaced by an emphasis on effectiveness. For example, in 1919 a program called the Cleveland Community Chest was established that used business practices to raise money for the poor. This effort supported the idea of charity as a community responsibility, not simply an obligation of the wealthy. It became part of the United Way, today one of the nation's largest charities.

BASIC BUSINESS CONCERNS

$ Starting a Business

What It Means

Starting a business involves many activities related to organizing the organization. The process includes generating of an idea for the enterprise (called concept development), researching the idea's potential for success, and writing a business plan. Someone who is starting a new business is called an entrepreneur. This person takes on the financial risks of the initiation, operation, and management of the business. An entrepreneur may want to establish a small, local business organized as a sole proprietorship (a business owned and operated by a single person), or he or she may hope to one day grow his or her business into a large, multinational business organized as a corporation.

Starting a business of any size requires an investment. Entrepreneurs who want to build large companies or corporations often look to investors, called venture capitalists, to finance the start-up costs in exchange for a share of ownership, called equity. Once the business is established, the entrepreneur may decide to raise more money, or capital, by selling shares to the public through an initial public offering (IPO), which is the company's first sale of stock.

Regardless of the size of a business, it must be unique in order to succeed. Many large, successful corporations began as small organizations with a business idea that was significantly different from anything else on the market. An entrepreneur must be assured that his or her business idea offers a unique good or service to customers. The entrepreneur must also have a sense of who his or her potential customers are and what products they might choose. Finally, the new business owner must have a plan for running and growing the company through its first year and beyond. The business plan may cover short-term goals, ranging from 6 to 12 months, and long-term goals, ranging from two to five years.

When Did It Begin

Entrepreneurship and small businesses in the United States have their roots in the trading practices and pioneering spirit of early American settlers. Many early business enterprises in the United States were agricultural. These agricultural enterprises were supported by a federal law passed in 1862 called the Homestead Act, which granted undeveloped land to individuals for farming if the landholder agreed to meet certain requirements, such as building a structure on the property and farming the land for a minimum of five years.

During the nineteenth century the Industrial Revolution introduced mass production into U.S. business. Companies in the mining, railroad, and other industries grew into corporate giants, dominating certain areas of the economy and reaping huge shares of the country's industrial output. Small businesses, including many sales and service firms, continued to prosper throughout the nineteenth and twentieth centuries.

The U.S. government has taken action on numerous occasions to support the formation of small businesses. During World War II the federal government created the Smaller War Plants Corporation, which provided loans to private business owners and gave corporations incentives for extending credit to small businesses. The Small Business Administration was formed in 1953 with the passage of the Small Business Act. It was not only designed to provide assistance and protection to small businesses but also required that a portion of government contracts be offered to small business contractors.

More Detailed Information

The preliminary stages of planning a new business idea can be challenging, but they are important to other aspects of building the business. A business owner must answer several key questions about the business: What does the owner want to achieve with the business? What is the business's product or service? How large or small will the business be? How many employees will the business have, if any, and how will they be managed? Who will be the business's customers?

Potential customers can provide helpful information to the business owner during the research phase of business planning. Many new business owners conduct customer surveys during the preliminary phases of starting a business to find out more about customers' habits, needs, and behaviors. The business owner should determine what unmet needs customers have and how the new business will answer those needs. Customers' perceptions, both positive and negative, of competitors and of the new business can be very helpful in planning sales and marketing efforts. Customers and their level of satisfaction with a business's goods and services are a critical aspect of a business. The business owner should have a firm grasp on how the business will make an impact on customers

Starting a business, no matter how big or how small, requires a great deal of planning. Everyone involved in the project must work together, as the group pictured here is doing, to define the prospective company's vision, as well as its financial plan. © *2007/Jupiterimages.*

FREE RESOURCES AND ADVICE FOR NEW BUSINESS OWNERS

One of the most popular resources new business owners use is an affiliation of thousands of retired executives who offer free and confidential advice to entrepreneurs. The Service Corps of Retired Executives (SCORE) provides workshops, chapter offices where individuals may consult one-on-one with an adviser, an e-mail advice center, and an online library of how-to articles and business-related forms. SCORE advisers can provide guidance in any area of business, including market research, local regulations, business financing, and taxation.

The U.S. Small Business Administration (SBA) also provides advice and resources to entrepreneurs wishing to start, build, and grow their businesses. The agency provides financial assistance, including information about loans and loan programs. It has resources on business contracts and how to register or certify a small business. It also provides disaster assistance for businesses of all sizes. Its loans are the primary form of federal assistance for repair and rebuilding of businesses following a disaster, such as a flood or a fire. Numerous minority and special-audience business groups, including women entrepreneurs, veterans, Native Americans, and Spanish-speaking entrepreneurs, find special resources at the SBA. One of the most popular services the agency offers is a series of online courses. The Small Business Primer helps people determine their readiness to start a business and learn about the planning, legal, and financial aspects of the process. Other courses help with writing business plans and contracts.

and how customers' satisfaction with the company will be measured.

The competition, or other businesses operating within the same industry as the new business, is an excellent source of information. Competitors and their products can provide information about what is missing in the market and how the new company can fill a niche. The entrepreneur should carefully analyze the competition's approach to and place within the market to determine how the new business can improve on what the competition offers.

Planning for costs and obtaining the money needed to start a new business are major challenges that the entrepreneur faces. How the business will make money, how much it will spend, and how much potential it has to earn money are all part of a segment of business research called financial projections. Other elements of the financial projections for a new business include the amount and source of start-up money, sales forecasts, and the amount the business will spend every month on rent, insurance, salaries, and other operating costs. A business owner also needs to be aware of how the company will

pay the suppliers who sell it the raw materials it needs and how payment will be collected from customers. The business owner must plan how these accounts will work together to keep the company operating profitably.

A company's market research and financial information is included in a master plan for the business called a business plan. This written document describes the business, its marketing, finances, and management. The plan specifically outlines the strategies the business will use to accomplish its financial goals, usually planning for several years into the future. The financial section of the plan may include information about the business's applications for loans, lists of its equipment and supplies, detailed financial projections of profits and losses, and other documents.

Before a business can be legally recognized, the owner must decide what type of business he or she will establish. This decision will determine two important things: which income tax return the owner will have to file and who will be liable for the business. Sole proprietorship, partnership, and corporation are the most common types of businesses. In a sole proprietorship and a partnership, the owner or owners are financially liable (responsible) for the debts of the business, and they control any profits that the business makes. In a corporation, individuals called shareholders invest money in the business and receive partial ownership of the company. The shareholders are not held financially liable for all the debts of the business. If the business does not succeed, the company's shareholders lose only the investment they put into it. If the business makes a profit, the shareholders gain a percentage of that profit based on their share of ownership.

Every business, no matter its size, is subject to state and federal laws. In general, businesses are required by the government to have an Employer Identification Number (EIN; also known as a Federal Tax Identification Number), which is used to identify a business the way a social security number identifies an individual. If a business is small, simple in structure, has no employees other than the owner, and fulfills other basic requirements, it does not need an EIN. The EIN is used on tax forms and other documents exchanged with the Internal Revenue Service (IRS). Some types of business are required by the state in which they operate to obtain a license in order to legally conduct business. Examples of businesses that need licenses to operate are barbers and hairstylists, attorneys, doctors and health practitioners, dentists, insurance brokers, opticians, and veterinarians.

Recent Trends

Technological advances have fundamentally changed the ways in which new businesses are established and operated. By the late twentieth century, businesses were able to use e-mail and the Internet to speed communications with suppliers and customers, conduct market research, manage taxes, and complete many other tasks. Other technology, such as the personal digital assistant (PDA) and the mobile phone, permitted businesspeople to send and receive e-mail, place telephone calls, and browse the Internet from their home, from the office, or in transit at any time of the day.

The high-tech tools that were once available only to large corporations are now available to small businesses. For example, a small business can now easily set up its own Intranet (a restricted-access network that enables a business to share resources, such as organization policies, announcements, or information about new products, with its employees without making confidential information available to those outside the company). Small businesses use the global, online marketplace to tap into relationships far beyond their local environment. A business's website has become an extremely important marketing tool. The Internet allows limitless opportunities for customers to conduct research, and customers increasingly expect a high level of information, convenience, and specialized treatment on a business's website.

$ Business Plan

What It Means

A business plan is a document that describes what a business is, what strategies it will use to accomplish its financial goals, and how it expects to do business as it grows, usually planning for several years into the future. Business plans are usually created when companies are just starting. A small business that is simply organized may develop a very basic business plan. A large company that produces many different products usually has an extensive business plan. Every business plan addresses four essential categories: the business itself (what products or services it will produce), the market for the product or service, the financial profile of the business, and the person or persons who will manage production of the product or service.

There are many purposes for a business plan. One purpose is to help those who are starting or running a business to have a clear, detailed account of the most important aspects and goals of the business. After a business plan is drawn up, a business can use it as a measurement of its progress and performance. Entrepreneurs often rely on their business plan to help them attract potential investors. Some businesses use their business plan to try to recruit potential employees or to develop relationships with suppliers of raw materials that the business needs.

A business plan may be changed, updated, or completely revised when significant changes occur in the company. Sometimes businesses need to generate a new business plan because an existing plan is no longer useful. If a business operates within a rapidly changing industry, then its business plan may be updated at the start of a new financial period (annually, quarterly, or even monthly). If a business needs to borrow money, lenders will need an up-to-date plan to help them determine how much they should loan the business. If changes in customer needs or new regulations have affected the market, then an updated plan will show how the business intends to respond to those changes. If the business is about to develop a new product or service, an updated plan will detail the market, financing, and production of the new product. When a business reaches an important growth point, such as moving to a larger facility or office or meeting a significant sales goal, it usually updates its business plan to reflect this growth.

When Did It Begin

Business plans as they are known today originated during the period of rapid economic growth following World War II. During that time a method of rehabilitating large companies that had run into financial trouble known as long-term (or long-range) planning emerged. Long-term planning addressed the major aspects of a business, including its finances, products, management, and sales and marketing strategies. Business planning advanced in the 1970s and 1980s. Businesses began detailing more complex business activities in their plans, including operational activities, forecasts of consumer demand for products, and strategic approaches to new markets.

In 1984 University of Texas Business School students developed a competition in which Masters of Business Administration (MBA) students worked in teams to create an idea for a new business, develop a business plan, and present the plan to a panel of judges. By 1989 the program had expanded to include teams from other prestigious U.S. schools, and in 1990 the competition was opened to participants from Europe, Latin American, and Asia. Other U.S. universities launched their own business plan competitions, and many entrepreneurs who won these competitions were able to turn their plans into successful business ventures.

More Detailed Information

In a new business the person who is promoting the business will sometimes consult with finance or marketing experts while creating a business plan. In an existing business, a group of people from different areas of the company, such as finance, marketing, and product development, will come together to revise the business plan. While each business plan is different because it is written to address the unique needs of a particular business, every business plan follows roughly the same format.

The first section of the business plan is called the executive summary. This section outlines the entire plan and presents a strong, succinct case for the creation and funding of the business. Generally, the executive summary describes the reason why the plan is being written or rewritten, the background of the company, the product

A company uses a business plan in order to outline its financial goals, strategies for future growth, and other important aspects of its business operations. In this photo a corporate executive employs charts to illustrate features of his company's business plan. *Joerg Koch/ AFP/Getty Images.*

or service and why it is unique or necessary in the market, the market for the product, the financial projections in terms of how much money the product will cost to make and how much the product will sell for, the management team's qualifications, and the plan for spending the money raised.

The next section of the plan is called the business profile. It describes the market for the product or service and shows how the business is unique and why it will succeed in the industry. This section also provides a description of the product's development as it currently stands. For example, the product may be partially or fully developed, or it may still be in the planning stages. Finally, this section states the objectives of the business. For example, a business may strive to become a high-ranking business in a particular industry. Or, it may aim to make a certain amount of profit by its fifth year.

The market section of the plan draws together data to give a profile of the current market for the new product or service, including the market's size and its growth. The number of potential users for the product or service is a critical piece of information here. If the market for a product is seasonal (as it is for many types of agricultural and tourism products), this information is conveyed in this section. If there are outside factors, such as government regulations, which affect the market, these are also covered in this section. Most products are developed with a targeted group of consumers in mind. The

market section of the plan describes these consumers as well as how the business will differ from the existing competition for the same consumers in the industry.

The next section of the plan addresses how the company will reach its business goals. For example, if one of the business's goals is to reach a certain volume of sales to a particular audience, this section explains how the business will reach that goal. Generally, this section states the strategy the company will use to reach each goal of the plan. It may even set milestones for reaching the goal and describe how these milestones will be achieved. For example, if one of the company's goals is to sell the product to 10 percent of the market within the first three years of operation, then a sales strategy might include an unconditional guarantee on the product to consumers. The plan would outline how to present the information about the guarantee to consumers and how to survey customers to find out how the guarantee affected their purchasing decisions.

A marketing strategy is another key component of the business plan. It is an explanation of how a product will be defined in relation to its competitors and how customer perceptions about the product will be shaped. For instance, a perfume may be marketed as an elite, luxury product for high-end consumers or as an affordable, everyday product for middle-market consumers. Finding a position in the market is known as finding a "niche." Other essential parts of the marketing strategy are pricing a product and showing the amount of sales projected over certain time frames. This may also involve describing the organization of the sales department and incentives for sales employees.

The section of the business plan that describes the business's management structure shows that the firm has the necessary resources to plan, organize, control, and lead the business. The management section summarizes the backgrounds and qualifications of key leaders in the company and external persons, such as CPAs, bankers, and attorneys, who may make contributions to the business. This section of the plan also describes the organizational structure of the business, the costs for staffing, and the facilities that the business uses.

The final section of the business plan addresses the financial aspects of the business, which many people consider to be the heart of the business plan. The section first summarizes financial needs, which shows how much cash a business needs to begin operations or to begin a new phase of business. Depending on the business, this section also covers a revenue model, which shows how the company will generate money. If the business aims to generate revenue through selling its product, this section shows how the pricing of the product will affect revenue. A profit-and-loss statement (also called an income statement) is also included here and lists the business's profits and losses over a period of time. Other documents that may be included here include the cash-flow statement, which shows the amounts of cash needed over a period of time as well as cash coming in, and the balance sheet, which states the value of the business's assets and debts.

Recent Trends

The growth of personal computing and the Internet has given people ready access to financial and business tools and information. Entrepreneurs use the Internet to conduct market research for their product or to find information on how to price products, how to create a sales strategy, and how to write their business plan. Spreadsheet software helps business owners create the financial documents, such as cash-flow predictions and forecasting models, they need in their business plans. Other types of software help users create entire business plans. In addition to using these resources, many people faced with the daunting task of writing a business plan work with a consultant who can provide broad-based expertise in a particular industry.

Electronic-based business plans can be easily customized to fit specific situations and audiences. For example, a business plan may be formatted specially as a graphic presentation to a group of investors. Or, if the business plan is presented to a supplier, the information in the plan most relevant to the supplier can be highlighted. When a business plan is used internally in a business, it may not need to present specific information on the backgrounds of company management. Customization of

BUSINESS PLAN COMPETITIONS

Since the first business plan competitions took place in the 1980s, many similar competitions have sprouted up all over the world. Schools of business and management within universities typically organize the competitions. Some competitions require that entrants be members of a certain academic community. For example, a group of Arab universities sponsors a business plan contest in which each team must include Arab nationals and students at an Arab university. One competition focuses only on plans for businesses that support poverty reduction in the developing world. Another competition centers on security technology, requiring that the proposed products prevent or analyze terrorist incidents. Some competitions offer not only cash incentives but also the opportunity for students to have their business plans reviewed by venture capitalists (people who provide start-up funding to new businesses) in the industry. Other competitions award new businesses with funding and mentoring opportunities.

a business plan has become increasingly important as businesses strive to differentiate themselves in a competitive global economy.

$ Management

What It Means

Management is a broad term referring to the process of running a business smoothly and effectively. The managers of a business lead the organization to achieve its goals. In a small organization there may be only one or two managers, and in larger organizations there may be many. Managers may include the president of a company, the chief executive officer, and the chief financial officer. These individuals supervise employees as well as make decisions about the direction the company takes.

Many different tasks and activities are involved in managing an organization. In a restaurant, for example, there are the people who buy food products and ingredients for the meals, those who cook the food, those who serve the food, those who advertise or promote the restaurant, those who handle the accounting and bookkeeping work, those who hire and train the employees, and even others. There might be one manager for the whole restaurant, or multiple managers overseeing groups of employees.

In general, businesses are organized in a hierarchy, meaning that there is a ladderlike organization of employees. Lower-level managers report to mid-level managers, and mid-level managers report to higher-level

WHAT DOES IT TAKE TO BE AN EFFECTIVE MANAGER?

Many business managers have received graduate degrees from management programs, such as a master of business administration (MBA) degree. A management degree typically includes the study of economics, finance, accounting, business ethics, and marketing. Some of the other skills managers need to be effective in their jobs are:

- Communication Skills. Managers must be able to explain the goals of the organization and the tasks that they expect workers to carry out. They must be able to give directions and offer support, conduct meetings, and present talks. They must be able to listen and to write clearly and convincingly.
- Interpersonal Skills. Managers must be able to understand and relate to different personality types and cultures in order to supervise employees of different backgrounds and guide them to work well together.
- Computer Skills. Managers must be familiar with and knowledgeable of the computer technology used in their offices, factories, plants, warehouses, and other work environments.
- Time-Management Skills. Managers must be able to juggle many projects and assignments at once, effectively deal with interruptions, oversee workers schedules effectively, and suggest ways to improve efficiency within the operation.
- Technical Skills. Managers must be familiar with the technical aspects of the work employees carry out in their jobs and be able to provide them training, support, and assistance with their work when necessary.

managers. Those managers highest in the organization typically report to the owners of the business.

When Did It Begin

The theories and practices surrounding business management changed significantly during the twentieth century, when large businesses became a prevalent feature of industrialized economies. As industry changed, managers responded with new methods of managing inventories of goods, overseeing production, and organizing, scheduling, and controlling the tasks of employees. When they encountered problems in the workplace, managers began to develop systematic ways of dealing with these problems.

Two distinct approaches to management have evolved over time. The first approach to emerge, the classical school of management, was born out of the experiences of industrial organizations during the late 1800s and early 1900s. Many managers during this time

had backgrounds in engineering, and their attitudes about management reflected a rational and logical approach to decision-making. As a result, the classical school of management is extremely systematic, hierarchical, and predictable. Another approach, called behavioral management, also emerged in the late 1800s and early 1900s. It focused on the social elements of management, the human experience, and psychology. In contrast to the classical school, behavioral management theories urge managers to focus on the individuality of workers as humans rather than as simply fulfillers of tasks.

More Detailed Information

Effective managers in any organization must be able to draw on a range of skills as they lead the organization. Whether they run a business, a church, or a city government, managers are generally involved in four main leadership activities: planning, organizing, directing, and controlling.

Managers must be able to create effective plans that can be understood and completed by those they manage. Long-range, or strategic, planning is normally the work of top-level managers in an organization. Decisions about what types of products or services are produced or sold, how these products or services should be marketed, and where they should be sold are examples of the decisions involved in strategic planning. Short-range, or tactical, planning involves developing detailed methods for completing a task and determining who should perform the task. For example, when a new type of sports car is being manufactured, short-range plans must be made to determine how the car will move through the manufacturing plant so that each worker can complete his or her assigned task. These plans can be made by managers who oversee the assembly process rather than by those managers who oversee overall company operations and who are responsible for the strategic planning of how the car will be marketed, for example.

All organizations must determine which employees will be responsible for each task that the business must carry out. Managers assign tasks to individual employees or teams of people and determine how to accomplish the established goals. This matching up of workers, tasks, and resources creates the organizational structure of the business. Depending on the products and the objectives of the business, managers determine the best organizational structure for the business.

One of the most challenging aspects of management is directing, or leading, workers to accomplish the goals of the organization. Managers must be able to assign tasks to workers, communicate goals, support workers, and evaluate workers and their performance on the job. Managers have different styles or methods of directing their employees. Some prefer to assign all tasks to workers, while some managers give workers more independence to make their own decisions and direct their own work.

Another challenging element of management is controlling the flow of work and ensuring that processes, timelines, and products mesh with the broader goals of the organization. For example, if the production goals of a publishing company are not met in the first quarter of the year, the manager needs to analyze the organization to see where the delays are taking place. Whenever a manager communicates the standards of performance and establishes the plan for meeting goals, it is his or her responsibility to manage performance to make sure these goals are met.

Recent Trends

In the late twentieth and early twenty-first centuries the field of management has come to encompass a wide range of elements. Managers are typically involved in many different aspects of management at one time, including human resources, operations, strategic planning, marketing, financial management, and information technology. Many managers have moved away from the expectation that workers are to be given commands and are more open to developing a collaboration with workers. As the tasks of workers in many industries have become less rigidly defined, managers have come to support the individuality of employees and view the workplace as a more of a democracy in which employees have certain rights as well as responsibilities. The role of the manager is perceived less as a "boss" function and more as a facilitator function. This tends to be true whether the organization is a for-profit business, a nonprofit entity, a school, or a governmental entity.

$ Risk Taking

What It Means

Risk taking is the part of business strategy that involves assessing how a business's decisions will harm or benefit the company. Every business encounters risks, which may or may not be anticipated or controlled by the company. A risk is defined as the possibility of loss, injury, disadvantage, or destruction. A business takes certain risks when it decides to expand into a new territory, for example, since it cannot know at the outset whether it will make enough of a profit in the new territory to cover the cost of expanding the business.

The field of risk management deals with risk taking. It involves identifying and analyzing risks and creating plans to reduce the losses that an organization faces as it conducts business. Risk management involves two main elements: (1) identifying and assessing the risk and (2) finding the right solution to manage the risk. Managers of businesses must first assess the market in their industry and understand its growth patterns when making decisions about new business ventures or expenses. Once a manager understands what the risks are, then he or she creates a plan to reduce the negative effects of risk tasking.

Risk taking is a very different concern for large and medium-sized firms than it is for small firms. Losses can disable and even destroy a small business. For example, a fire, a flood, or theft can destroy the business's physical property. The injury, disability, or death of an owner can take away one of the business's most important resources. A lawsuit can destroy the financial assets of the firm. These types of loss can impact profits, negatively affect the daily operations of the firm, impose financial challenges, and ultimately destroy a business. Usually, large firms hire risk managers to oversee their risks, whereas small firms may integrate the tasks of assessing and responding to risks into the many responsibilities of the owner.

When Did It Begin

Historically, managing business risk was the work of insurance companies, which help businesses protect themselves in case of loss. The field of risk management focused on helping businesses preserve their assets (including finances, physical property, and investments) and secure their earning power within their markets by avoiding costly risks. Risk management did not assess business operations, product development, sales, and business strategy.

In the 1980s the management approach known as total quality management was introduced into U.S. business. This philosophy assessed and monitored all activities of an organization, including product development, finance, marketing, and sales, in order to support the continuous improvements of products. The emphasis of total quality management was using measuring tools and statistical techniques to assess production and quality and to create the data managers needed to make improvements. One of the many results of total quality management was the understanding that the management of risk was an inherent part of total business and product quality. Businesses began to assess their overall mission within the context of risks. Specialists in risk management, called risk strategists, began to combine various approaches to risk management, including thorough investigations of a business's divisions, education of employees, and models that predicted the risk level of individual projects within the overall framework of the business. Numerous standards and methods of risk management were proposed in the 1980s, giving companies all over the world guidelines for managing their risks to positively affect business outcomes.

More Detailed Information

There are many ways a business can respond when it has identified a risk. One of the most common ways to respond to risk is to take out an insurance policy. An

PERSONAL RISK MANAGEMENT

Businesses are not the only entities that need to understand the risks they are taking and how to respond to them. Individuals and families are also exposed to risks, whether they are threats to personal assets, such as investments and property, or threats to their ability to earn a living. Personal risk management involves developing a plan for managing the financial risks of an individual or a family.

It is important to identify the events that may pose a financial risk to an individual or a family. If an individual takes part in risky hobbies, such as paragliding, he or she is prone to experience injury or even the loss of life. After assessing and analyzing the risks, the individual can make the same types of decisions businesses do: he or she can decide to assume the risk, transfer the risk to such a resource as an insurance policy, reduce or control the risk by taking safety precautions, or remove the risk entirely. For example, a person may identify that her old, unsafe car is a risk. In order to manage the risk, she may decide to get the car repaired to reduce the risks or even remove the risk entirely by getting rid of the car and using public transportation instead.

insurance policy requires the insured party to pay a premium (a fee) usually on a monthly basis, which guarantees financial reimbursement in case of loss or damage. For example, a business that operates in an area prone to earthquakes or floods may take out an insurance policy to protect itself financially in the event an earthquake or flood causes damage to the business's property. Most businesses have theft insurance to help them restore any lost property in case of a burglary. Some companies choose not to employ insurance agencies but instead establish their own accounts, which are drawn on only when there is a loss to the company.

A company can take active steps to avoid or reduce many risks, especially safety risks. Most employees are given safety training as a regular part of business practice. For example, workers in a chemical company who use toxic or harmful chemicals are carefully trained in the handling of dangerous chemicals and emergency procedures. Companies can also avoid safety risks by deciding not to produce certain goods because of safety issues. For example, a toy manufacturer may have the ability to produce a certain toy but decides not to do so because the toy contains a liquid that if swallowed, could be dangerous to a child's health.

When a business recognizes that a loss may occur as a result of a business decision and still goes forward with the decision, the firm is said to be "assuming" the risk. For example, a pharmaceutical company might know that one of its new drugs might have negative side effects for

some people who use it. But after carefully weighing the potential risks of side effects against the overall health benefits the drug may provide, the company may decide to assume the risks and launch the product.

Other aspects of managing risks arise out of planning and prevention strategies. A business may have a plan, for example, to shut down part of its operations or a certain business function for a designated period of time in order to avoid financial hardship to the company. To do this the company must know which functions are critical to the business's operations and which are not. For example, payroll is a critical business function in most businesses, since employees need to be paid on a regular basis. In contrast, training is a business function that can be suspended for several months without having a negative effect on the company's financial state. In large firms, each business division prioritizes its individual functions.

The field of risk management has developed strategies for assessing risks in many different types of business situations. In the financial world, corporate mergers and acquisitions involve enormous financial risks and require close management. Many businesses assess the risks of working within certain environments and the types of hazards to which workers and customers may be exposed. Security issues present challenges to businesses, especially since many business activities rely on secure online systems and transactions. In all of these situations, risk management establishes the priorities of the organization and determines which risks are potentially most damaging and most likely to occur.

Recent Trends

The introduction of websites and e-mail into daily business life has introduced new levels of risk into all types of businesses. It is common for the most important and sensitive company information, including financial and product information, to be discussed and shared in company e-mails. The potential risks a business takes on by using e-mail are numerous. For example, e-mail provides increased chances that written statements will be published publicly in order to defame or expose someone.

New technological developments have also resulted in security risks that range from hackers who might steal important company information to viruses that can destroy files and computer functionality. Access to advanced designing software allows people to copy the components and design of products easily. If a business's property is legally protected by a trademark, a copyright, or a patent and another business or group is able to copy pictures, logos, articles or other property, it is a crime known as infringement. For example, a small business that produces a patented household good in the United States many discover that pirated (illegal) copies of the product are being manufactured in China. If customers are able to purchase the pirated product for a cheaper price than the original product, the U.S. business may lose significant revenue. The risks to large businesses of copyright infringements on their products are significant and costly.

$ Venture Capital

What It Means

Venture capital is money that serves as financial backing for new, generally unproven business enterprises, typically known as start-up companies, or start-ups. Because venture capital is used to fund companies that have little to no history of success, it is also known as risk capital. Venture capital is usually invested in companies seeking to launch innovative new products or services. In the late twentieth century venture capital was often used to finance emerging technology companies.

Individuals or groups who provide venture capital for new businesses are known as venture capitalists. Venture capitalists can be wealthy individuals, corporations, subsidiaries (companies owned by other companies), or other business entities.

In exchange for giving unproven entrepreneurs (self-employed individuals who own and manage their own businesses) the opportunity to start their own businesses, venture capitalists often demand a high level of return once the business has become established. Venture capitalists generally expect to earn a return of between three and five times the amount of their initial investment. They also expect to see this return in a relatively short period of time, typically between five and seven years after funding the venture. Venture capitalists can also be involved in shaping the policies of new companies, and they often assume the role of partial owner of the company.

When Did It Begin

Throughout history, up-and-coming entrepreneurs have depended on some form of venture capital to finance a growing business. Traditionally, early venture capitalists were wealthy individuals or families. The modern venture capital industry emerged in the United States during the 1930s, when the federal government imposed tighter restrictions on the ways that banks lent money to corporations. In response to these regulations, business leaders began to develop new systems of investing in emerging companies.

In 1946 American businessman Georges Doriot (1899–1987) founded American Research and Development Corporation (ARD), the first publicly owned company dedicated to providing venture capital to new businesses (a company is said to be publicly owned when

Venture capital is a type of investment money used to finance new, usually innovative business opportunities. In this photo from 1984, the cofounders of Apple show off one of the first computers designed for the average consumer. *AP Images.*

THE DOT-COM BOOM

During the 1990s major advances in the fields of information technology and medical technology provided venture capital firms (companies that invest money in financing new businesses) with a host of new investment opportunities, many involving the Internet. This led to the dot-com boom, a frenzy of venture capital speculation in the technology industry. Investors scrambled to invest in companies that seemed to have almost limitless potential for growth. On the whole, however, this vast potential was far from realized. In early 2000 the NASDAQ, a stock exchange (a market where investors buy and sell shares in companies) where a high number of technology stocks are traded, crashed. Numerous start-up companies went bankrupt, leaving many venture capitalists with nothing to show for their investments.

the public is invited to buy shares in it). One of its most significant venture capital investments came in 1957, when it financed the founding of the Digital Equipment Corporation, or DEC, the first company in the world to manufacture minicomputers (the prototypes for the personal computer). ARD's initial investment totaled $70,000; by the time DEC went public (selling shares in the company on the stock market) in 1968, ARD's investment had grown to $37 million.

More Detailed Information

In order to acquire venture capital, start-up companies will usually submit a detailed business proposal to a venture capital firm or entity. This proposal typically includes a description of the start-up company's products or services; an overview of the company's goals (along with a timetable for achieving those goals); an outline of possible financing arrangements (including the amount of money needed, a schedule for repayment of the investment capital, and the projected gains on the venture capitalist's returns); and a marketing strategy (a plan describing how the company intends to build consumer awareness about its product or service). If a venture capital firm accepts the prospective company's proposal, it will usually submit a counterproposal outlining its own set of terms and timelines.

There are several potential sources of venture capital. In some cases, venture capitalists are wealthy individuals looking for an investment opportunity with a potentially high rate of return. These individuals can be enterprising investors, successful business entrepreneurs, or heirs to private fortunes. Because individual investors generally have less venture capital than larger investment firms, their investments are often used to finance relatively small companies.

Professional investment funds are entities that pool resources from various interests in order to raise large amounts of investment capital. Because they have more extensive financial resources, investment funds have a greater capacity for risk than individual investors, and so are able to finance more ambitious venture capital enterprises. On the other hand, securing venture capital from an investment fund tends to be highly competitive, because investment funds have a more formal and rigorous application process than other venture capitalists and invest a great deal of time and money in analyzing the new company's prospects for success.

The U.S. government supports the founding of small businesses with the Small Business Investment Company (SBIC) program. SBICs are government-sponsored private firms that assist entrepreneurs with the financing and management of their emerging companies. SBICs are licensed and financed by the Small Business Administration (SBA), a federal agency founded in 1958 to provide financial, legal, and administrative support to small businesses.

Other potential sources of venture capital include large corporations, investment-banking companies, and insurance companies.

Recent Trends

Although the venture capital industry has always been most prevalent in the United States, the practice increasingly became an international phenomenon toward the end of the twentieth century. At the start of the twenty-first century venture capitalism in Europe was growing rapidly: in 2005 more than 12.6 billion euros were devoted to venture capital enterprises throughout Europe, an increase of 44 percent over the previous year.

With the emergence of powerful economies in Asia in the late 1990s and early twenty-first century, venture capitalism began to acquire a truly global reach. Venture capital investments in China more than doubled between 2002 and 2003, from $420 million to $1 billion, while in 2005 venture capital levels in India approached $9 billion.

$ Small Business Administration

What It Means

The Small Business Administration (SBA) is an independent agency of the United States government whose stated mission is "to aid, counsel, assist and protect the interests of small business concerns, to preserve free competitive enterprise and to maintain and strengthen the overall economy of our nation."

Starting a small business is an act of entrepreneurship; that is, the practice of taking initiative and assuming financial risk in order to start a new business or business venture. According to the basic theory of a market economy (an economy, such as that of the United States, based on the buying and selling of goods and services

The Small Business Administration, or SBA, assists small businesses in a variety of ways, from helping them apply for loans to providing them with training and counseling services. In this 2003 photo SBA administrator Hector V. Barreto speaks about the agency's role in promoting the interests of small businesses. *AP Images.*

whose prices are affected by supply and demand), businesses should be able to compete against one another in a free and fair environment. In such a business climate, those who have the best ideas, work the hardest, and adopt the most efficient management practices will be most successful. For more than two centuries, American small businesses have embraced this spirit of competition and have been a major source of innovation and economic growth. Nevertheless, even the most promising small businesses must weather a variety of difficulties in their early stages, not least being stiff competition from larger, more established businesses. Thus, the thinking goes, promoting the entrepreneurial spirit by helping people to launch, build, and grow small businesses is not only good for individuals, but it is also good for the country.

The SBA serves as a source of support to these fledgling businesses in a number of ways. Foremost, it helps small businesses get the financing they need by acting as a guarantor (a financial backup) on loans issued by banks and other lenders. In addition, the SBA offers technical training and counseling services; helps small businesses procure government contracts; conducts special outreach programs to encourage business initiatives from women, minorities, and armed forces veterans; offers assistance to those whose businesses are damaged

by floods, earthquakes, or other disasters; and provides legal representation and advocacy services to businesses in matters of legislation, regulation, and disputes. The SBA delivers these services to small business owners (and prospective owners) throughout the United States, as well as in Puerto Rico, the U.S. Virgin Islands, and Guam. It operates through a broad network of field offices and in cooperation with various public and private organizations.

When Did It Begin

The SBA was established by the United States Congress under the Small Business Act of July 30, 1953. The agency's roots go back further, however, to 1932, when President Herbert Hoover chartered the Reconstruction Finance Corporation (RFC), a federal lending program for banks, railroads, farm mortgage associations, and other businesses that were threatened by the financial crisis of the Great Depression (1929 to about 1939). Franklin Delano Roosevelt embraced the agency when he took over as president the following year, and the RFC served as a major resource in implementing the programs of the New Deal, Roosevelt's program for national economic recovery. From 1932 to 1941 the RFC dispersed nearly $9.5 billion.

THE SBA IN THE GULF COAST

The Small Business Administration (SBA) is an independent agency of the United States government devoted to advancing the interests of American small businesses. In addition to guaranteeing small business loans, the agency provides disaster-relief financing to businesses of all sizes, homeowners, and renters who are the victims of floods, earthquakes, or other natural disasters. As such, the SBA faced one of its greatest challenges in September 2005 when the city of New Orleans, Louisiana, and the surrounding Gulf Coast region were devastated by Hurricane Katrina. In the six months following the hurricane, the agency processed 251,000 loan applications and approved more than 76,200 loans totaling $5.4 billion to victims in the disaster area. The following year the SBA co-sponsored a conference in New Orleans titled "Entrepreneurship: The Foundation for Economic Renewal in the Gulf Coast Region." The gathering's overarching theme was that small businesses would have a major role to play in restoring the social and economic vitality of the region.

Another predecessor of the SBA, the Smaller War Plants Corporation (SWPC), was created in 1942 to make it possible for small businesses to gain a share in the massive World War II production effort. The SWPC was dissolved when the war ended in 1945, and the RFC took over its lending and contract powers. About the same time the Office of Small Business (OSB), a division of the Department of Commerce (the Cabinet department whose mission is to promote national economic growth) began to offer educational resources for small businesses, the idea being that acquisition of knowledge and skills were critical for any business to succeed.

Following the onset of the Korean War in 1950, the Small Defense Plants Administration (SDPA) was formed to review and recommend small businesses that were qualified to receive government war contracts. Finally, when President Dwight Eisenhower signed the Small Business Act in 1953, the important functions of various existing agencies were consolidated into the SBA. Since its inception the SBA has served more than 20 million small businesses.

More Detailed Information

Although poor management is probably the number one reason why new businesses fail, insufficient or ill-considered financing can also be detrimental. Very few entrepreneurs have enough money to start a new business or expand an existing one without gathering other sources of financing. For most, this means taking out a loan. The SBA helps small business people acquire sound and prudent financing not by extending loans directly but by facilitating loan agreements with outside lenders, such as banks, community development organizations, and microlending institutions (private organizations that extend very small loans).

The SBA's primary loan program is called the 7(a) Loan Guaranty Program. This program alleviates much of a lender's risk associated with lending money to unproven businesses, thereby encouraging lenders to extend loans to small business people whose applications they would otherwise likely turn down.

Here is an example of how it works. Hector graduated from cooking school and now wants to borrow $90,000 to open his own restaurant. He submits a loan application to a bank. The application includes Hector's prospective business plan and many details about his financial situation. As the bank reviews the application, it considers whether it wants to take the risk of loaning money to Hector. If Hector's situation appears too risky (for example, he already has a substantial student loan debt) for him to merit the loan on his own, the bank will likely ask the SBA to guarantee it. If Hector's business plan meets SBA criteria, the SBA will guarantee the loan, meaning that if Hector defaults on the loan (if the business fails and he cannot repay it), the SBA will reimburse the bank for the bulk of the money it lent. Usually, the SBA guarantees as much as 80 percent on loans of up to $100,000 and 75 percent on loans of more than $100,000. In most cases the maximum loan the SBA guarantees is $1 million.

The SBA plays another major role by helping small businesses secure a reasonable portion of United States government contracts. Like other organizations, the federal government needs and must buy all kinds of goods and services in order to run, from office supplies, industrial machinery, and weapons to plumbing, architectural services, training courses, and specialized research. Thus many companies bid against one another for the opportunity to their certain goods or services to the government. The winner of the bid is awarded the contract. By maintaining close ties with those in the government who review and select the bids and referring qualified businesses to them, the SBA helps to ensure that smaller businesses do not get squeezed out of the bidding process by larger companies that can usually offer more product at less cost.

Yet another important job for the SBA is to foster the success of small businesses by acting as a central resource for business information, education, guidance, and training. The agency offers extensive information on the Internet as well as free online training courses on a variety of topics, including writing a business plan, identifying target markets, basic accounting, e-mail marketing, and small business taxes. In partnership with nongovernmental organizations such as the Service Corps of Retired Executives (SCORE), it offers mentorship and hands-on advice to new and prospective business owners.

Recent Trends

With the rapid growth of the global economy (the term refers to the way new technology has made it increasingly easy for businesses to sell their goods and services all over the world) that began in the 1990s, the SBA has placed new emphasis on international issues through its Office of International Trade (OIT). To help small American businesses export their products (sell them to other countries), the SBA offers special loan guaranty programs, such as Export Express, a pilot program introduced in 1998. In addition, since the passage in 1994 of the North American Free Trade Agreement (NAFTA; a treaty that eased regulations for doing business across the borders of Canada, the United States, and Mexico), the SBA has offered loans under the Community Adjustment And Investment Program (CAIP) to businesses that NAFTA has adversely affected (for example, by the loss of local jobs).

CREATING PRODUCTS AND SERVICES

$ Product Development

What It Means

Product development is the process of bringing a new good or service to market. It includes generating ideas for a new product (the good or service), gathering information about the needs and wants of the target market (the segment of consumers to whom the product is intended to appeal), designing and engineering the product, and testing it in typical situations where it will be used. A product may be considered new whether it is entirely novel, new to the company that is developing it, or a modification of an existing product. Changing any aspect of a product can be considered product development. This can be, for example, replacing the engines in a jetliner with an improved design, adding a new flavor to a line of familiar soft drinks, or even changing the color of the package of a brand of chewing gum.

The product itself, including its development, traditionally is considered one of the four primary elements of product marketing. The other three are pricing, which is the process of determining the appropriate price for the product; promotion, for example, advertising and publicity; and distribution, or how the product gets to the consumer. Together these four elements are called the "marketing mix."

In a growing economy, the range of available products tends to expand and the products themselves evolve as consumers typically seek to purchase the most updated and competitive version of a product they can find. In this kind of economic climate, ongoing product development is essential to a company's long-term success. The most successful companies may generate nearly half of their

Product development is the process by which business and engineering firms conceive of, design, produce, and market new products. In this picture representatives of Casio, a major electronics company, display some of their new products, including a watch with a built-in GPS, or global positioning system, and a miniature TV. *AP Images.*

sales from new products, compared with less successful companies, which generate only about 10 percent of their sales from new products.

When Did It Begin

In a general sense, product development has existed as long as have goods, services, and the marketplace (the world of trade and economic activity). Historically, products commonly consisted of agricultural produce and tools or implements made for use in the home or on the farm. Product development for many centuries simply involved fashioning the product to fit the purpose. Once goods such as textiles came to be crafted in sufficient quantity to be traded, people began to specialize in producing them in particular ways that made them appeal to the consumer. Even without formal structures for evaluating the market, farmers and artisans essentially were carrying out a kind of market analysis and improving their goods with an eye to competitors.

During the Industrial Revolution in the late eighteenth and early nineteenth centuries, the manufacture and distribution of goods was developed on a large scale. Relying mainly on machines for mass production, the industrialization of manufacturing allowed productivity

THE HISTORIC LAUNCH OF THE IPHONE

Many marketing specialists consider the publicizing of a new product in conjunction with its introduction to be a critical last step in product development. A case in point is the product awareness campaign launched in 2007 by Apple Computer, widely regarded as one the most innovative technology companies in the world, around its new cellular phone, the iPhone. The effort, which started six months before the phone was introduced, created such an advertising and media buzz that the iPhone became arguably the most anticipated gadget of all time.

One important advantage that the campaign exploited was brand recognition (the extent to which consumers recognize a company's brand among the competitors.) Apple already had a very loyal audience devoted to the principles of simple design and intuitive technology that had been incorporated in the company's earlier products such as the iBook computer and the iPod MP3 player. This segment of consumers had long been waiting for Apple to break into the cellular phone market, certain they would buy and appreciate whatever cell phone product the company developed. In many ways the imagination of the consumer was the most powerful marketing tool that the company had.

Apple also relied on the twenty-first-century communication tool of the blog (an online journal for recording activities, thoughts, and personal expressions) and the technologically savvy nature of its followers to spread the company's message about the iPhone. Apple passed information about its product to trusted bloggers (people who contribute to and maintain blogs) who posted it on the Internet and whipped up excitement about the iPhone in the early months of 2007. When the device went on the market at the end of June, lines of consumers in the United States were waiting for retailers to open their doors on the first day of sales. The iPhone became the fastest-selling Apple product in history.

to increase dramatically. Companies grew in size, products became more standardized, and production runs were longer, resulting in huge volumes of products.

Producers were able to turn out goods in greater quantity than the local economy could absorb. As distribution of these goods spread over greater geographical areas, the producers had less and less direct contact with their markets. Business operations gradually became market-oriented rather than product-oriented, meaning that producers had to concentrate on identifying the demands of their many varied and distant consumers and to develop products that would meet those demands. As the resources of business aligned itself with the needs and wants of the market, the process of product development grew more formalized and became an essential part of business activity.

More Detailed Information

Because most new products do not survive in the marketplace, developing a product that will be successful is a formidable task. Usually firms approach product development in a linear way, moving through a series of steps. The first step typically is an analysis of the market to be entered in order to understand it thoroughly. For example, if a company with a successful line of basic tooth-cleaning products wants to enter the market for toothpaste that fights the germs causing gum disease (part of the therapeutic toothpaste market), it first has to determine if there is a need for their product in that market.

A particularly challenging aspect of market analysis is sales forecasting. A company planning to introduce a new product needs to know the competition and to project a model for the growth of sales of its product in that competitive environment. Because real sales data is lacking, a company use surveys that attempt to read consumers' intentions about purchasing products. The ability to sell a new product under a familiar and trusted brand name can boost a sales forecast. A brand symbolizes to the consumer all of what he or she knows about the company and its products. Seeing the brand on a new product, called brand recognition, serves to create a set of associations and expectations about the product that can have a powerful influence on the consumer's decision to try it.

After a company decides to enter a market, it searches for new product ideas. These can come from a variety of sources such as users and sellers of existing products, inventors, company employees, and the general public. Some products are easier than others to develop. For example, if a company has chosen to develop a product similar to those already made by a number of competitors, it may use those existing products as reference points for its own.

Few new product concepts make it all the way to the marketplace. After product ideas are generated, they are screened to determine if they are feasible to make, affordable to invest in, and a good match with the company's overall goals. In addition, new ideas must fit with the company's understanding of consumer needs. Once a product concept has successfully survived the screening process, the product is designed. Consumers usually play an important role in the development of early models, called prototypes, of the product. Consumers are given prototypes to test under normal conditions of use and are asked to provide feedback. Any design changes that result from this consumer input may lead to additional rounds of prototype testing.

In the next step, called test marketing, the company promotes, distributes, and sells the product in a limited market, usually contained within a specific geographic area, to simulate the product's introduction in the broader marketplace. This step allows the company to evaluate the reaction of consumers to pricing, advertising, packaging, and other aspects of the product and make final refinements. The drawback of test marketing is that it gives competitors an early opportunity to learn about a company's new products.

Once the product is ready to be introduced to a national or international market, much of its success depends on whether consumers can be quickly persuaded to try it. For this reason, a company may offer a special introductory trial in which consumers receive the product free or at a discounted price.

In modern industrialized societies essentially all goods and services require ongoing product development. Consumer demands and the pressure of competition compel a business continually to reconsider the appropriateness of a product's price, the effectiveness of the advertising and distribution system, and other factors. The "life cycle" of many products is very short. Automobile models, for example, are regularly redesigned and reengineered by manufacturers, and many consumer electronics constantly change in order to keep up with technological advances.

Recent Trends

Today's global market has become more and more crowded with new goods and services, driven by consumers who can shop and compare values and prices with increasing efficiency (aided by the Internet) and who use their purchases for ever shorter periods of time. The faster a company can develop, test, advertise, and launch a new product, the more it can keep pace with its competition and the more it stands to profit.

Advances in communications and distribution methods have helped companies get their products through development and into the market more quickly than ever before. In addition, new technologies have played a significant role in speeding up product development. For example, computer-aided design (CAD) software allows engineers to create simulations of complex products (graphic computer models that can be tested for functioning and behavior under certain conditions) that previously might have taken weeks or months to develop. These simulations can serve as the blueprint for the product and can be useful for testing and refining of the product. Another process called rapid prototyping (RP) lets companies use CAD designs as directions for building three-dimensional physical models or prototypes of products with the use of computer-controlled equipment. Car manufacturers, for example, have used RP technology to create prototype components such as dashboards and transmission gears.

$ Brand

What It Means

A brand is a symbol that represents a product or service and that distinguishes the product or service from others in the marketplace. A brand may be an image, a logo, or a name showing who made the product. In addition to having visible characteristics, a brand also communicates a concept, a personality, and a set of expectations in the mind of the customer. For example, the brand logo of the Nike Corporation, a shoe company, is the "swoosh," or curvy stripe. The logo also represents status, fashion, and high performance in the minds of many consumers. When a brand is able to positively influence the customer's perception of a product or service, it becomes much more than just an image or logo.

The purpose of a brand is to create a relationship between the consumer and the product or service. A successful brand produces positive feelings in consumers, driving them to spend their money on the advertised product. The job of "branding" a product, or providing an image for a product that attracts consumers, is extremely complex. The global marketplace presents consumers with such a variety of products that companies competing for consumers' attention must create symbols, signs, and words that make their product immediately recognizable and compelling.

Because a brand can be the vehicle through which a company appeals to consumers, makes a profit, and becomes successful, the brand can become the most valuable thing a company owns, even more valuable than the products or services it produces. Such corporations as the Walt Disney Company (a children's entertainment and media company), Intel (a computer-product manufacturer), Ford (a car manufacturer), and McDonald's (a fast-food company) have brands worth billions of dollars. Once a company registers its brand with the government and obtains legal protection of it, the brand is known as a trademark, and it is illegal for another company to use the trademark.

The Microsoft Corporation has one of the most recognizable and valuable brands in the world. Within the overall Microsoft brand there are numerous brands for individual products, known as product brands. Microsoft started out making only computer software but went on to manufacture other products, including interactive toys, video games, and books. Microsoft has sought the legal protection of the names and logos for each of its product brands so that its brands may not be copied by a competitor.

When Did It Begin

Modern branding has its origins in the centuries-old practice of using heated tools to permanently mark the hides of livestock. Because cattle, sheep, and other livestock belonging to different owners often grazed together on open land, it was difficult to distinguish which animals belonged to whom. Owners developed their own special symbols, called brands, which they would mark on their animals using a heated metal tool called a branding iron.

Using a symbol called a brand to identify a product became prevalent in the nineteenth century, when industry developed the capability to mass-produce and mass-market goods that had previously been made locally. For example, goods for farms and households, such as rakes, brooms, and cleansers, once made in village shops or homes were increasingly made in factories during the nineteenth century. Manufacturers began to put their name or logo on their products, such as bars of soap, or on the containers in which the product was shipped to identify the product to consumers.

Companies learned that they needed to build the public's trust in their products so that consumers would choose their products over those of a competitor. Some brands that were developed in the nineteenth century and early twentieth century and that are still successful today include the Campbell Soup Company and the Quaker Oats Company. These brands' images and associations of reliability and quality have endured. In the early twentieth century companies began to develop advertising slogans, characters, and musical tunes called jingles, which appeared in print media and on the radio and further

Almost all companies use a brand—in the form of a logo, image, word, or phrase—to make their product stand out in a competitive marketplace. The distinctive Nike "swoosh" design is one of the most recognizable logos in the world. *AP Images.*

enhanced the relationship between consumer and product. The introduction of television and the Internet also contributed to consumers' awareness of brands.

More Detailed Information

While it is difficult to understand all of the reasons why a consumer chooses to purchase one product over another, generally a customer has an expectation of quality when he or she purchases a certain brand. A brand also might convince the consumer that he or she is lowering his or her level of risk in buying the product. If a certain brand of jeans is advertised as being better made or more durable, the consumer may feel he or she is spending his or her money wisely in purchasing the jeans. One reason many consumers choose a certain brand is because the brand conveys a sense of prestige. Different brands are prestigious in different ways to different groups of consumers.

There are many different types of brands. A corporate brand identifies a corporation, such as Clorox, Cable News Network (CNN), and Google. A corporate parent brand is a brand name in which the corporate brand is identified with individual product names. The Toyota 4Runner, for example, is a small truck made and sold by Toyota that is branded as a Toyota. Disneyland and Walt Disney World are individual products identified with the corporate parent brand Disney. A distinct product brand is a brand name separate from a corporate brand and unique to an individual product. Gleem toothpaste, for example, is a product brand that is not marketed with the Proctor & Gamble name, even if it is owned and produced by that company. A brand extension is a situation in which a well-recognized brand name is attached to a product in a different category. Arm & Hammer Baking Soda has a well-developed identity as a cleaning and deodorizing product, so the company created laundry detergents, toothpaste, and other products with the Arm & Hammer name. Co-brands are developed when two independent companies cooperate to have both of their brands highlighted in a product. For example, Ben & Jerry's ice cream developed a flavor called Coffee Heath Bar Crunch, which promotes the ice-cream maker along with the Heath candy bar.

A generic brand is a consumer product that does not associate with a brand name and that usually costs less than a brand name. Supermarket goods and prescription drugs are the most common types of generic products. Often, generic brand products can compete with branded products in quality. A store brand is the term for a product that can only be purchased from a specific retailer and that identifies the store's name. For example, Safeway grocery stores carry goods, such as pasta, coffee, and frozen vegetables, which are identified with the Safeway name. Usually store brands are less expensive than products manufactured and sold under a national brand name.

The value of a brand is affected by consumers' responses to the brand. When the brand satisfies customers or surpasses their expectations, the brand will gain value. The value of a brand to a company's owners is called brand equity. Strictly speaking, brand equity is a set of assets (usually a monetary value) associated with a brand name that either adds to or subtracts from the value the product or service provides.

Different measurements of a brand help determine its positive or negative value. Brand loyalty is the strongest measure of value. When customers are loyal to a brand, they buy the product repeatedly and endorse the product to friends and family. Brand awareness is the simplest form of brand equity. A brand a customer is aware of and familiar with will give the customer a feeling of confidence. That confidence will make the consumer more willing to choose the familiar brand over another brand. A brand's value does not rest solely on customers' awareness of the brand. Perceived quality is another measure of brand equity. Often a brand carries with it an aura of quality, either negative or positive. Brand associations, often subjective and emotional, differ from quality associations but are important to brand equity. Customers have personal and emotional associations with brands, whether these associations come from the media, from entertainment, or from personal history or experience. Other assets such as patents and trademarks are another measure of brand equity. Total brand equity is calculated by taking all of these measurements into account. Ultimately, brand equity helps determine the price of the product.

Recent Trends

Although the initial purpose of branding was simply to identify a product, branding has become crucial to modern advertising and business. For many companies, their brands are their most valuable assets. The success of a brand allows a company to charge higher prices (especially over generic brands) and reduces the company's risks when it introduces new products.

While televised, print, and online media allow companies to reach large numbers of customers (called aggregations), companies are also beginning to recognize the importance of engaging with customers on a more personal level. Companies use such methods as publications, e-mail, and call centers to respond to consumer needs. Customers are invited to play a role in shaping products to meet their specific needs. When companies market to unique sets of customer needs, it is known as disaggregated marketing.

The packaged-foods company Kraft Foods, Inc. has hundreds of successful product brands, including Oreo, Jell-O, and Miracle Whip. In 2001 Kraft launched a disaggregated marketing campaign centered on a free, customized magazine called *food&family*, which delivers online food-related articles, recipes, and advertising

BRAND EXTENSIONS

Companies spend millions of dollars on building brands. When they do create a successful brand, companies often attempt to extend the value of that brand into new categories of products. This is called brand extension. For example, the French company Michelin is a successful manufacturer of tires for automobiles, trucks, and other vehicles. It built its brand in part through its cartoon-character mascot known as the Michelin Man. The Michelin brand represented quality, reliability, and value to customers. In 2004 the company announced that it would launch a line of footwear based on its popular tire treads, and the Michelin brand of steel-toed work boots became a successful extension of the Michelin brand.

When a company decides to extend its brand into other products, it can spend less money on the extension than it would have to spend if it created an entirely new brand of product. The key question for a company researching a brand extension is whether or not the new product associated with the existing brand could damage the existing brand if the new product were unsuccessful. In fact, many brand extensions have failed. For example, the jean company Levi Strauss & Co. unsuccessfully extended its business into making men's suits in the 1980s. The failure of this brand extension, however, did not cause long-lasting damage to the brand.

geared toward the individual customer. This initiative shows how important it is for companies to reach and retain customers using new technologies.

$ Manufacturing

What It Means

Manufacturing involves transforming raw materials into new products using mechanical, physical, and chemical processes. Generally, manufactured goods are made in large quantities by machinery or by manual labor using mass-production techniques. This results in goods that are identical to one another and that are relatively inexpensive to produce. Many goods that modern consumers purchase, from plastic products to tools to mattresses to jelly beans, are manufactured using these methods.

The production, sale, and consumption of manufactured goods form the basis of modern economies. An industrialized country manufactures goods in order to build and maintain the nation's infrastructure (its roads, bridges, airports, and other public works) and to develop advanced areas of industry, such as information technology and national defense. In order to industrialize, a developing country must first establish manufacturing industries to provide the products it needs to build an infrastructure.

Manufacturing employs many workers. In the United States, manufacturing jobs represent over 10 percent of all employment. In 2006 approximately 14 million U.S. workers had manufacturing jobs. Among the largest manufacturing industries are those that produce iron and steel, textiles, automobiles, aircraft, lumber, and chemicals.

Manufacturing techniques involve a variety of mechanical processes, including machining, forging, casting, and injection molding. Machining is the most important manufacturing process. It involves using a machine tool to remove material from an object (by drilling, turning, milling, or grinding, for example) to create a final product. Machined parts, such as pins and fasteners, are used in many other manufacturing industries. Forging is a process in which heated metal is hammered, rolled, and shaped. Forging produces strong iron and steel parts that are used to make cars, trains, and other manufactured goods. In casting (also called founding), metal is shaped by being poured into a mold made out of sand or other materials. The casting process is used to make a variety of materials, including wheels and jewelry. Injection molding is a process used to shape heated plastic by pouring it into a mold. It is used to make a variety of plastic products, such as computer parts, toys, and containers.

When Did It Begin

Before the American Revolution the economy of colonial America was based largely on agriculture. Some types of commercial manufacturing, such as iron forges, existed and even prospered, but in general the colonies imported manufactured goods from England in exchange for such goods as tobacco, wheat, and fish.

After the American Revolution many Americans began their own manufacturing businesses as they sought economic independence from England. In New York, Massachusetts, and Pennsylvania, artisan-manufacturers pressured the state governments to pass legislation protecting manufacturing. Organizations such as manufacturing societies helped support and fund large-scale textile factories. In 1791 U.S. Treasury Secretary Alexander Hamilton called for greater investment in factory production in his *Report on Manufactures.* One of the results of the report was the creation of a multifactory corporation in Paterson, New Jersey, which attracted many wealthy investors.

The Industrial Revolution transformed the production of goods, especially the production of textiles, iron, steel, and transportation, in eighteenth-century England, and much of the knowledge about factory technologies was brought to the United States by skilled European immigrants. For example, British industrialist Samuel Slater (1768–1835) came to the United States in 1789 and helped establish the manufacturing technology for the nation's modern production of textiles, which involved the use of water-powered mills.

Manufacturing is the business of making products out of raw materials. Steel manufacturing has been concentrated in the eastern United States, where iron ore, coal, and the other natural resources required for steel are found. *AP Images.*

What eventually came to be known as the American system of manufacturing started in the 1790s with the technological innovations developed by U.S. inventor Eli Whitney (1765–1825). Whitney discovered the benefits of using "interchangeable parts" to make guns for the U.S. government. Until then guns had been made by hand, and each was unique. Whitney designed a new gun and the machines to make it. His machines produced many identical (or interchangeable) parts. The parts were put together by workers on an assembly line, a concept also developed by Whitney. Each finished gun was exactly identical. Whitney's manufacturing methods made it possible to produce better goods quickly and more cheaply.

More Detailed Information

The manufacture of iron and steel in the United States is located primarily in the northeastern and midwestern states. Ohio has the largest number of iron and steel forging employees. The aerospace, national defense, and automotive industries are the primary purchasers of iron and steel. Agriculture, construction, mining, and industrial-equipment manufacturers also use large quantities of forged steel. Many consumer products are forged, including hardware tools and bicycles.

The manufacturing process of forging heats iron and then presses, hammers, and shapes it. There are several different types of forging processes. Closed die forging, or impression die forging, uses metal blocks called dies to create a specified form. Open die forging hammers metal as it moves between flat dies. Seamless rolled ring forging punches a hole in a thick, round piece of metal and then rolls and squeezes it into a thin ring. Different types of metal can be forged; carbon steel and alloy steel are the most commonly produced metals.

Textile manufacturing plays an important role in U.S. manufacturing because it was of central importance to the Industrial Revolution in the United States. In its early years, textile manufacturing was simple enough to be conducted under the roof of one factory. Since then textile manufacturing has developed into a large industry encompassing several smaller industries, including those that produce fibers, those that produce cloth and dye, and those that spin yarn and print goods. Approximately one-third of the cloth manufactured in the United States is produced for use in clothing. Textiles are also used to make floor coverings, home furnishings, and cloth goods used in agriculture, construction, and medical supply.

At one time all textiles came from plant or animal sources and were made by hand, but modern textile manufacturing is a complicated process. The production of most textiles involves multiple processes, including the formation of the yarns or threads, formation of the fabric by weaving or by another method, processing the fabric using dyes or other chemicals, and fabrication (the assembly of a garment). Many different mechanized processes in textile production have replaced the manual production methods that were used for centuries. For example, cotton used to be picked by hand, a slow and labor-intensive task. Today machines called cotton gins quickly remove seeds from the cotton fiber.

Chemical manufacturing is an important part of modern industry because chemicals are essential to the production of motor vehicles, paper, electronics, pharmaceuticals, cosmetics, and other products. Chemical manufacturers make synthetic materials (such as polyester), agricultural chemicals (such as fertilizers), paints and adhesives (such as glue), cleaning chemicals (such as soap and cleansers), and pharmaceutical chemicals (such as aspirin). Based on the type of product they make, different chemical manufacturers use differently designed and operated factories. Companies that produce synthetic materials typically have large plants, while those that manufacture paints and adhesives tend to operate smaller plants. Chemical plants are usually located near other kinds of manufacturing. There are many chemical plants located in the Great Lakes region near automotive manufacturers, on the West Coast near centers of electronic production, and on the Gulf Coast near petroleum and natural gas manufacturers.

CHOCOLATE MANUFACTURE

The seeds of the cocoa tree, which grows in equatorial climates, is the basis of chocolate, but these seeds go through a number of steps to become the sweet, rich treat nearly everyone appreciates. After the cocoa seeds, or "beans," are harvested they are allowed to ferment for several days. This allows them to develop the chemical properties required of chocolate. The fermented beans are taken to a factory where they are sorted, inspected for quality, and roasted in large rotating cylinders. Roasting makes the shells of the beans crackle and brings forth the distinct flavors and aroma of chocolate. After the beans, now called nibs, are roasted, their outer shells are removed in a process called winnowing. Then the nibs are ground into a thick brown liquid. This liquid, called chocolate liquor, is made up of mostly cocoa butter, much of which is removed from the liquor using giant hydraulic presses. The substance that remains after the cocoa butter is removed is crushed into a powder, called cocoa powder, used for making drinking chocolate. Bakers and candy manufacturers also use cocoa for flavoring their sweet treats. Chocolate bars are made by mixing cocoa butter, chocolate liquor, sugar, and often, milk.

The U.S. manufacturing sector has been an important player in the development of the labor movement. Labor unions and trade unions are organizations of employees who unite to improve working conditions, benefits, and pay. In 1938 the Congress of Industrial Organizations (CIO) was formed to represent the basic manufacturing industries, including iron and steel, automobile, rubber, electric and radio, and shipping. Workers and union leaders in the CIO organized strikes, or work stoppages. The most effective work stoppage was the "sit-down strike," during which workers took over the plants in which they worked until their requests were met. The result was that many of the country's largest manufacturing firms were forced to negotiate collective bargaining agreements, which set out the terms of employment for members of a labor union and describe such aspects as wages, working hours, health insurance benefits, and vacation time. One of the greatest achievements of labor unions came in 1955, when U.S. auto manufacturers accepted a union-sponsored plan that guaranteed that workers would receive pay during unemployment.

Recent Trends

In the latter decades of the twentieth century, the number of U.S. manufacturing jobs declined because of outsourcing, or the practice of sending production activities that were previously done in the firm's plant to remote plants. For example, many manufacturers have outsourced the assembly of their products, recognizing that they do not need to build or purchase plants or equipment if they can have their products assembled at so-called contract manufacturers. In the 1970s contract manufacturers were typically smaller operations that offered a single service, such as the assembly of circuit boards, to a larger firm. Since then they have grown into multiservice specialists that can not only assemble and manufacture products but also design and distribute them. The main reason that manufacturers outsource aspects of production is so that they can save on materials, labor, and expenses.

Although it has many advantages, contract manufacturing has disadvantages as well. Since 2001 the United States has outsourced millions of manufacturing jobs to contract manufacturers located in other parts of the world, often to countries where workers have lower wages and fewer protections, such as negotiated wages, safe working conditions, and health benefits. This is a major concern of international human-rights and labor-issues groups. Also, when a firm employs a contract manufacturer it gives up a certain element of control that can make it hard to make extensive changes to engineering. Contract manufacturing is best for firms that have a steady demand for their products and that do not depend on assembly processes or equipment that is very complicated.

$ Mass Production

What It Means

Mass production is the term used to describe the manufacture, usually by machines, of products in large quantities. When a type of product, such as a toy, is mass-produced, each example of the product is made exactly

Mass production is a manufacturing process designed to produce a large quantity of a specific good in a short amount of time. In this photo a bakery moves a high volume of English muffins along a conveyor belt. *Kim Steele/Photodisc Green/Getty Images.*

the same, with the same parts and materials, using the same methods. Automobiles, household appliances, clothing, and shoes are just a few examples of mass-produced goods.

Mass production of a good often involves the use of many different automated machines, which carry out a series of short, repetitive tasks. In the mass production of athletic shoes, for example, one machine stitches together the pieces that form the upper part of the shoe. Another machine punches out the holes for laces. Then a different machine molds the upper part of the shoe and attaches it to the sole.

The development of mass production meant that manufacturers were able to produce more products than ever before, both quickly and inexpensively. This translated into a lower cost to the consumer. Mass-produced goods are not only cheaper to the consumer, they are also consistent in quality and more plentiful than non-mass produced goods. The mass production of food, clothing, computers, and other goods has played a vital role in improving the standard of living worldwide.

When Did It Begin

The first machines that allowed for mass production, called machine tools, were developed in Britain in the mid-eighteenth century. Precision lathes, measuring instruments, and planers were examples of these tools. They allowed workers to make many examples of one product, such as a piece of furniture, to the same size and material specifications.

In 1776 Scottish economist Adam Smith (1723–90) developed the concept of division of labor, which is crucial to mass production. With division of labor, machines or laborers work on different parts of the product, instead of one machine or laborer making the entire product. The concepts of mass production quickly took root in the United States, where U.S. inventor Eli Whitney (1765–1825) developed the concept of interchangeable parts to make guns for the U.S. government. Until then guns had been made by hand, and each one was unique. Whitney designed a new gun and the machines to make it. His machines produced many identical (or interchangeable) parts, and the parts were then put together by workers on an assembly line, a concept also developed by Whitney. Each finished gun was exactly identical.

In the early twentieth century, U.S. industrialist Henry Ford (1863–1947) introduced the assembly-line method into the factories of his Ford Motor Company. Auto parts were delivered to workers by moving hooks and overhead chains. Each worker was given only one task. Ford sold more than 15 million of his Model T automobiles in the United States. His success in mass-producing automobiles foretold how much the production method would change the manufacture of products.

More Detailed Information

Mass production has brought many benefits to manufacturing. Mass production minimizes what is known as nonproductive effort. For example, a furniture maker who makes tables in his small workshop must use many different tools many separate times to finish a single table. In a factory that mass-produces tables, each worker repeats one or two tasks using the same tool to perform the same or similar operations on a steady flow of products moving past him on the assembly line. Workers do not waste time on nonproductive effort, such as moving to different parts of the factory to locate or prepare materials and tools. Thus, the time it takes to mass-produce the furniture is much less than if a worker were making the table by hand on his own.

Mass production also limits human error to some extent. Since most operations in mass production are carried out by automated machinery or robots, the chances of workers making errors are reduced. And because humans take on much less of the work in a plant using mass production, the company spends less money paying wages.

Although it may seem like most all products can be mass produced, there are several criteria which help producers understand whether it is economical to mass-produce a particular product. Most importantly, there must be a large enough number of prospective consumers to warrant the investment involved in mass production, since the machinery used in mass production is costly. There must also be a long-term demand for the product, as mass-production methods are most economical with long production runs. The product must also be able to be constructed using standardized equipment and machinery, and the construction must be able to be broken down into relatively simple steps. If any of these conditions cannot be met, then the production of the good is not well suited to mass-production methods. Moreover, many consumers seek custom-made or one-of-a-kind goods, such as handmade furniture or clothing, and they constitute a significant market whose needs cannot be answered by mass-produced goods.

Recent Trends

During the twentieth century and early years of the twenty-first century in the United States, the middle class and its wages have grown dramatically. More than ever before, many Americans have significant discretionary income, or money that can be spent on goods and services they want, not need. Modern lifestyles and consumerism, or the emphasis on buying material goods as a way to become happy or fulfilled, have increased the demand for mass-produced products. Megastores, such as Wal-Mart and Costco, offer consumers an abundance of inexpensive mass-produced products.

Even as the demand for mass-produced products increases, more concern is being raised over assembly-line

MASS-PRODUCED FRENCH FRIES

In 1948 McDonald's became the first company to introduce mass production into the fast-food world. Founders Richard and Maurice McDonald established the principles of the fast-food restaurant with their "Speedee Service System." The restaurant decided to offer a relatively simple menu of hamburgers, cheeseburgers, french fries, milkshakes, soft drinks, and apple pie. Each worker's tasks were specifically determined in order to streamline the process of taking a customer's order, preparing food, and bringing it to the customer. This method of assembly-line production allowed the McDonald brothers to lower the price of their hamburger from $.30 to $.15. Today almost every fast-food franchise uses the concepts behind the Speedee Service System and mass production to offer quick, inexpensive food and make a tasty profit.

workers who feel frustrated and dehumanized by repetitive and monotonous work. In fact, studies have shown that workers who perform the same jobs repetitively become bored and are more likely to make errors in their work. Another concern is that many manufacturing facilities in newly industrialized countries have few or nonexistent protections for workers. This has brought about a greater international awareness of the experience of factory workers who are exploited or manipulated.

$ Outsourcing

What It Means

Outsourcing occurs when one business firm hires another business firm to perform one or more jobs on its behalf. For instance, a software company, rather than hire its own accountants to work in-house, might hire an accounting firm to keep its financial affairs in order; the software company is outsourcing its accounting work.

Increasingly, the term *outsourcing* has taken on the meaning of the word *offshoring*. Offshoring is outsourcing to a foreign country where labor is cheaper. It has become extremely common for U.S. corporations to move portions of their operations to countries like Mexico, India, China, or the Philippines, where workers typically make only a fraction of the wage that Americans would make doing comparable work. Offshoring has moved millions of American jobs to other countries. For this reason outsourcing has become a very controversial topic and a major issue in the political arena.

When Did It Begin

In the middle and latter part of the twentieth century, corporations wanted to expand and vary their business

THE ECONOMISTS VERSUS THE PEOPLE

Many U.S. economists argue that American workers need not be alarmed at the business trend of outsourcing (hiring other business firms to perform work on their behalf) jobs overseas. These economists view the freedom of American companies to have their manufacturing work done in other countries as a positive development in the world economy. They see overseas outsourcing, or offshoring, as a form of international trade. Free international trade and free markets in general, they say, lead to higher levels of competition among businesses, which theoretically results in the more efficient use of resources like labor (workers) and capital (money and equipment needed to run a business). When, for example, a U.S. computer company outsources its hardware manufacturing to Taiwan, where hardware can be made more cheaply, it can focus its American labor force and equipment on increasing the quality and decreasing the price of software, which American companies are particularly good and efficient at producing and distributing (American software dominates the world market). The benefits to the consumer are doubled: cheaper and better computers and cheaper and better software, neither of which would have been available without outsourcing. The benefit to the computer company is higher profits. Theoretically, most people are better off than they were before the outsourcing occurred.

Americans in general (more than 70 percent, according to polls conducted prior to the 2004 presidential election) fiercely oppose the practice of outsourcing, however. And, although economists believe that improved efficiency leads to more jobs overall in the country that originally outsourced its manufacturing, there is not yet a great deal of data showing that this is the case. Those who advocate free trade and unrestricted outsourcing are thus in a difficult position: that of trying to convince Americans upset about very visible, tangible job losses to put their faith in economic theories that seem abstract and remote from their everyday concerns.

holdings. A maker of processed foods, for instance, might try to grow by buying a business firm that manufactured lightbulbs, a firm that made movies, and a firm that provided life insurance. Among other benefits, these acquisitions would position the overall corporation to remain profitable in a wide variety of economic circumstances (if the processed-food business was in a slump, another sector could make up for those losses). Beginning in the mid-1980s, however, corporations increasingly found that running such diverse operations resulted in a lack of focus, and many corporations sold off subsidiaries (businesses they controlled), returning to a core group of businesses that took best advantage of their particular strengths. This idea of core competence (the centering of a business around the strengths that could

give it an advantage over its competitors) became one of the driving concepts in the corporate world. Part of the streamlining that corporations undertook to establish a core competency led to the outsourcing of basic operations that could be more efficiently handled by an outside company.

The offshore outsourcing trend started in the 1960s, when U.S. companies began to move manufacturing facilities to Mexico and, later, to other global sites offering cheap labor. Even taking into account foreign trade restrictions and the added expense of transporting goods back to the United States, companies typically found that they could reduce costs by 30 to 50 percent by moving the physical production of their goods to less-developed countries. Some items commonly manufactured abroad at the time included clothing, household furnishings, and electronics. Increasingly since this time, U.S. companies that have offshored their production work have focused more on managing the company and on sales and other service components of their businesses: those aspects requiring more human judgment and contact with consumers.

More Detailed Information

Outsourcing offers many advantages. For instance, the software company that outsources its accounting duties might find that the accounting firm can get the work done more efficiently because that is their specialty; the accounting firm would probably also charge less money than the software company would have to pay to maintain its own accounting department. Outsourcing can also make a company more adaptable by allowing for staff reductions and a stable staff size. If the software company's accounting workload suddenly doubles because new tax laws were passed, it can simply pay its partner accounting firm more money to take care of the extra work rather than undertake the cumbersome work of hiring several new in-house accountants and then firing them if, down the road, the accounting workload eased up.

Outsourcing enables companies to devote their energies to what they do best. This can be particularly important in the early stages of getting a business off the ground. A fledgling business is usually short-staffed, so delegating tedious, noncore tasks to other firms makes sense. Another advantage to outsourcing is that it can increase the level of accountability related to certain tasks. Because the accounting firm is being paid a fee, the software company can clearly demand excellence. If the accounting firm does not deliver an adequate level of service, the software company can terminate the contract and find another firm. The same issues are less clear-cut when working with in-house employees.

But the risks of outsourcing are real. The company that delegates its operations to another firm loses control over the end result. Though the company can fire the firm it hired to do the work, the firm might have done the

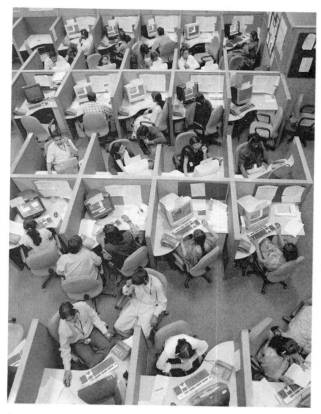

Outsourcing occurs when a business hires an outside company, sometimes in a different country where labor costs are cheaper, to perform aspects of its day-to-day operations. Outsourcing companies can be quite extensive with large numbers of employees. © *Sherwin Crasto/Reuters/Corbis.*

work so badly as to cause irreparable harm before the problem is even discovered. While this may become less of a risk over time, as a company develops solid working relationships with its partner firms, the risk at the outset of an outsourcing relationship is substantial.

Offshoring is one type of outsourcing that has brought American companies clear gains, but it has raised the opposition of American workers, many of whom have lost jobs because of the practice. When a U.S. shoemaker moves its manufacturing facilities to the Philippines, the motive behind outsourcing is unmistakable: the shoemaker can pay much lower wages in the Philippines than it paid American workers. The outsourcing allows the shoemaker to cut a large chunk out of its operating costs and to make substantially more in profits.

When a company chooses to offshore its production facilities, it can have a domino effect on the industry: once a single shoemaker has made such a business move, competing firms have to do the same if they want to stay in business. With its operating costs dramatically lowered, the first shoemaker can set its prices as far below those of its competitors as it wants. It can easily drive its compe-

titors out of business if they keep their manufacturing facilities in the United States. This model explains the inevitable nature of the most controversial types of outsourcing today. Without government intervention restricting such business practices, the market seems to make it impossible for companies to do otherwise than move American jobs to other countries.

Recent Trends

Although most people currently associate outsourcing with the movement of manufacturing jobs overseas, professional jobs, too, are increasingly being outsourced to countries where salaries are lower. Most notably, large numbers of high-tech jobs, such as computer programming, have been moved to India, which has a very educated but much lower-paid labor force than the United States. Some estimates predict that more than 3 million white-collar jobs will be moved overseas by 2015, representing a loss to American workers of roughly $135 billion. Accordingly, there is a great deal of popular opposition to the concept of outsourcing, and the issue has become increasingly central to national politics since the beginning of the twenty-first century.

Many economists and free-trade advocates argue, however, that opposition to the phenomenon of overseas outsourcing is short-sighted. According to economic theory, the world economy grows more efficient when high quality goods and services can be produced more cheaply. Additionally, some economists assert, the rise in income of workers in impoverished countries ultimately represents new markets for American products. From an economic point of view, to oppose outsourcing is to oppose the inevitable changes that capitalism brings, some of which have substantial benefits.

$ Quality Control

What It Means

Quality control is a system by which products or services are inspected and evaluated to determine whether they meet expected levels of overall quality. Manufacturers monitor the quality of what they produce in order to ensure customer satisfaction, which subsequently helps a company reach its sales targets. Quality control standards are also used to determine whether or not a product is safe for consumers to use.

In manufacturing, the quality control process involves either analyzing a small, random sampling of a specific product or analyzing the process by which the product is made. In some cases inspectors conclude that certain improvements need to be made to a product before it achieves an acceptable level of quality or safety. All products, from automobiles to toys, are subject to quality control standards.

In manufacturing, engineering, and other industries, companies try to ensure that products consistently meet predetermined standards of quality. At this beverage plant, inspectors randomly select bottles on the conveyor belt in order to evaluate the overall quality of the product. *Roger Ressmeyer/Science Faction/Getty Images.*

Although quality control is primarily used to evaluate quality in the manufacturing and engineering industries, quality control measures have also been implemented in other fields, notably education, health care, and the service industry. The service industry is a sector of the economy that includes restaurant service, retail sales, the distribution and delivery of goods, and other jobs that require interaction between employees and customers and therefore demand a high level of employee performance.

When Did It Begin

The concept of using a system to enforce quality levels dates to the Middle Ages, a historical era in Europe spanning from the fifth to the fifteenth century. During this period craftsmen formed guilds (associations of workers involved with the same trade), which created specific rules pertaining to issues of quality in the construction of tools, textiles, and other products. Craftsmen who did not observe the standards required by the guild (for example, by building a product of poor quality) faced fines or, in extreme cases, expulsion from the guild.

In the nineteenth century the manufacturing industry widely adopted the system of division of labor, in which individual workers are assigned responsibility for one specific aspect of the production process. With this system the responsibility for quality control shifted from the individual craftsmen to the foreman, a supervisor who oversees certain aspects of manufacturing operations. Another important development in quality control was statistical process control, a system that analyzes the process of production rather than the actual finished product. It was pioneered by Walter A. Shewhart (1891–1967), a prominent American engineer and statistician. During World War II (1939–45) statistical process control became the predominant form of quality control.

More Detailed Information

To gauge quality levels in a given product or service, modern systems of quality control rely predominantly on statistical analysis (the collection, evaluation, and interpretation of data). For this reason quality control is also known as statistical quality control. There are two principal forms of statistical quality control. The first form, usually referred to as acceptance sampling, focuses on an evaluation of the finished product. In acceptance sampling, an inspector determines the quality of a given batch of products by closely examining a small, random selection of products from that batch. If a certain percentage of the sample products fail to meet quality standards, then the entire batch of products is rejected.

For example, an inspector might be in charge of determining the quality of a new model of electric fan. Using the acceptance sampling method, the inspector chooses 10 fans out of 1,000 that have just been produced. He plugs in each of the fans to ensure that the fan's electrical system is working (in other words, that the fan will turn on). If the fan has speed settings, he will test the settings to ensure that each is functioning at its proper speed. The inspector will also test the product's safety. For example, he might measure the temperature on the surface of the fan to see whether or not it remains at a temperature that is safe for consumers.

The second principal form of quality control is known as statistical process control. Whereas acceptance sampling determines the quality of a batch of products by inspecting a select portion of those products, statistical process control focuses on the process by which the product is made. By using statistical analysis, or the analysis of specific product data, to determine the patterns by which certain problems occur, statistical process control can identify which aspects of the production process might need to be improved in order to ensure that the finished product meets quality control standards. With this method the fan inspector makes note of specific problems in a batch of products. If certain problems

---

AMERICAN SOCIETY FOR QUALITY

One of the most influential organizations dedicated to maintaining high quality control standards in the United States is the American Society for Quality (ASQ). It was founded in 1946 as the American Society for Quality Control (the word *control* was dropped in 1997) in order to ensure that the high quality control standards established during World War II (1939–45) would be maintained after the war. Today its members are quality control experts from around the world. Over the years the ASQ has been instrumental in expanding quality control practices into such fields as health care, education, and the government. By the early twenty-first century the ASQ had established branches in more than 100 hundred countries worldwide and had more than 100,000 members.

---

recur, the inspector submits his or her data to an analyst, who then studies the data to determine what aspect of the production process might be causing the problem. For example, if inspectors find a recurring problem with the stability of the fan blades, an analyst might determine that there is a problem with the stage of production that involves attaching the blades.

Recent Trends

After World War II there emerged a new focus in quality control as more and more companies began to evaluate the performance of management (people such as employers, managers, and directors). These new methods evaluated the performance of the individual manager, measuring such criteria as job experience, knowledge, and skill. In addition, this new quality control model also examined the personality of the individual manager, paying particular attention to qualities of motivation, self-confidence, and the ability to work cooperatively with coworkers. This new focus on management performance is an integral part of a strategy called Total Quality Management, which is intended to monitor quality in all aspects of a company's operations.

TOTAL QUALITY MANAGEMENT

What It Means

Total quality management (TQM) is a philosophy of business management that seeks excellence and maximum efficiency in all areas of the production of goods and services. The careful and reliable design of products is the most basic priority of total quality management. The philosophy also emphasizes reliable operational strategies that ensure that the firm can produce the good or service on a consistent basis.

The word *total* in total quality management is important. The emphasis of this management approach is that both good product design and proven, high-quality production methods must exist together for a company to achieve a competitive presence in the market. For many businesses a focus on these two areas relates efficiency and quality to other business areas, such as systematic measurement (involving statistical measurement), team-based organization, and attention to customer satisfaction. A focus on customer service includes using effective methods to collect customer feedback. Most businesses that apply TQM also use it to develop processes that ensure ongoing improvement and self-evaluation. One way a company might implement this is to involve lower-level employees in evaluations of those managing and running the company.

Businesses apply TQM in many ways. In fact, there is no single method of putting the philosophy into practice. One company may focus on creating and sustaining excellence in a collaborative workplace environment by building team-based efforts and approaches. Another company may emphasize state-of-the-art manufacturing by investing in the newest machinery and creating careful measurements of produced goods.

Total quality management's focus on product quality comes not only from the belief that customer satisfaction will drive sales of products but also from the fact that more efficient production processes will lower a company's costs. If systems are running as efficiently as possible, fewer raw materials will be wasted and fewer finished products will require repair. Additionally, employees value working for a safe and efficient business.

When Did It Begin

Total quality management has its roots in the work of U.S. inventor and engineer Frederick Taylor (1856–1915), who organized a theory of business management that became known as scientific management. Taylor viewed organizations essentially as machines and relied on fixed principles to organize a business so that it produced high volumes of goods with maximum efficiency. Part of Taylor's approach was an emphasis on the efficient training and close monitoring of well-qualified workers and precise guidelines for worker productivity. The innovations that Taylor popularized were adapted in the 1930s, when other management theorists developed statistical methods for measuring work tasks that improved manufacturing practices. These methods enabled managers to measure such things as the number of errors in the manufacturing run of a car engine, for example. They also provided managers with ways to locate glitches or problems in the production process that could result in faulty or defective products.

One of the leading statisticians of the early twentieth century, William Edwards Deming (1900–93) advocated the application of statistical methods to business. His

Total quality management is a business strategy that focuses on creating maximum efficiency in all aspects of the production process. American statistician William Edwards Deming (1900–93), pictured here, played a key role in transforming the Japanese manufacturing industry after World War II, making it one of the most efficient in the world. *AP Images.*

ideas were especially popular in Japan, whose economy had been devastated by World War II. Japanese manufacturers applied Deming's measurement techniques to production and operations, and by the middle of the twentieth century Japan had become a leading economic power on the world stage. The Japanese particularly surpassed U.S. companies in the production of automobiles and other durable goods, such as room air conditioners. In the 1980s and 1990s improving the quality of production became a priority in the United States, and the government launched incentives to help companies develop quality-measurement programs.

More Detailed Information

Essential to any company's quality program is how it determines the specifications of its product designs and the costs of achieving the level of quality it has targeted. Total quality management's focus on quality relies on a company's ability to systematically apply quality standards to production.

The term *design quality* refers to the inherent value of a product in the marketplace. The quality specifications of a product are the measurements that relate to the quality of the design and how well the product conforms to an established design. There are several so-called dimensions of quality, and they all go into measurements of product quality:

- The performance dimension is the primary characteristics of the product or service. For example, a fax machine might be designed to send a certain number of pages per minute.

- Features of the design are dimensions dealing with secondary characteristics, or anything that is added to the design as an "extra." Added features to the fax machine might be its capacity to be used as a copier.

- Reliability or durability dimensions have to do with how consistently the product will perform over time, the chances that it will fail, and how long it will last. The company producing the fax machine might measure this dimension by calculating an average time between failed transmissions or determining the "life expectancy" of each of the machine's components.

- Serviceability dimensions have to do with how easy the product is to repair. The availability of repair centers and the number of copies per print cartridge are measurements of serviceability.

- Aesthetic dimensions are a product's sensory characteristics, such as its sound, feel, and look. The fax machine's case color, button size, and display screen are examples of its aesthetic dimension.

- Perceived quality dimension has to do with customer perceptions and the product's past performance and reputation. The reputation of the fax machine's brand name and its rating in a consumer magazine are measurements of its perceived quality dimension.

Total quality management stresses systematic measurement to ensure that quality standards are defined and met. It also stresses a continuous effort on the part of manufacturers to put systems in place to keep product output at this maximum level. The most stringent applications of TQM impose sophisticated statistical analysis that aims to reduce the incidence of errors. Part of this ongoing analysis is collecting data on workflow, products, workers, and tasks and using the data to maintain a constant awareness of how production lines and the overall company production system are functioning. TQM proposes that if quality production is sustained, then mass inspections of goods are not necessary, since quality is ingrained in the product from its origin.

One of the ways in which companies apply TQM to design and production is to carefully analyze the costs of what they make. Quality costs are defined as the costs of

CONSUMER REPORTS

One of the most common ways for U.S. consumers to check the quality of products on the market is through *Consumer Reports* magazine. It is published by the Consumers Union, which uses a testing laboratory to assess products and then reports its findings in the monthly magazine as well as on its website. The quality of practically all consumer products is covered, including appliances, electronics and computers, home and garden products, health and fitness products, personal finance, baby and child goods, travel, and food. The Consumers Union asserts that it presents an objective, unbiased assessment of the quality of consumer products because the products it tests are purchased at the retail price and the Consumers Union does not accept any gifts or discounted goods from manufacturers. Although some companies have taken issue with reports in the magazine, the vast majority of companies acknowledge that it is an essential quality-assessment tool used by millions of consumers. Many consumers rely on the annual *Consumer Reports* car issue, which publicizes the Consumers Union's findings on owner satisfaction, predicted reliability, features, price, comfort, and other factors related to buying a car.

not creating a quality product or service. Every time work has to be redone, the cost of quality increases because, for example, a manufactured good needs to be reworked, a bank statement needs to be corrected, or a food order in a restaurant needs to be remade. Therefore a cost that would not have been incurred if quality were flawless becomes part of the cost of quality.

Businesses take on different types of quality costs. Prevention costs are those meant to prevent poor quality. Appraisal costs are those spent on any measurements, evaluations, or audits that help ensure quality standards are met. Failure costs result from products failing to meet requirements.

Recent Trends

In the late 1980s total quality management was used to advance a related philosophy known as Six Sigma. Bill Smith (1929–93), a vice president at the electronics manufacturer Motorola, took several different quality control methods, including TQM, and combined elements of each to create a new method to reduce the number of defects in manufactured goods and improve the effectiveness of production.

Like TQM, Six Sigma focuses on improving quality by giving businesses the tools to produce products and services faster, more cheaply, and of higher quality. However, Six Sigma differs from TQM in that it focuses on prevention of defects and elimination of the costs incurred because of waste. Companies that currently utilize

Six Sigma include financial management firm Merrill Lynch and technology company General Electric.

Quality management has come under scrutiny as global trade has increased and products manufactured in newly industrialized countries have been found to be defective or, in some cases, even dangerous. In 2006 and 2007 goods such as pet food, cough syrup, toothpaste, and tires imported into the United States and other countries from China were found to be defective and resulted in injuries and deaths. China is the largest exporter of consumer products in the world, but it does not have an established quality-management system to guarantee its products. In the age of the global marketplace, the challenge to the field of quality management is the adoption of international regulations for quality assurance.

$ Product Liability

What It Means

"Product liability" refers to a group of laws and legal rulings that apply to anyone involved in the manufacturing or sale of a product. Though product liability laws in the United States are established at the state rather than the federal level, all states enforce the basic notion that if you are responsible for any part of the manufacturing or sale of a defective product, you may have to pay damages to anyone injured because of the defect(s) in that product.

This was not always the case. Prior to the twentieth century the burden was on the consumer to exercise caution about the products he or she purchased. Increasingly the burden has shifted to all people and organizations along the manufacturing, distribution, and sales chain of any product.

When Did It Begin

In the nineteenth century the doctrine of privity generally applied to situations in which a person was injured by some manufactured good. The doctrine of privity said that an injured party had the right to sue the responsible party only if the two of them had signed a contract. Practically speaking, this meant that if a consumer bought a defective product from a retail store, he or she had no right to sue the manufacturer, because the manufacturer and consumer had not entered into any contract with one another. Likewise, product defects were not the fault of the retailer, so the consumer could not sue the retailer.

Product liability laws hold manufacturers accountable for any serious defects, particularly those that pose health or safety risks, in the goods they sell to consumers. Sometimes manufacturers are required by law to recall products that have been proven unsafe, as was the case with tires produced by the Firestone Tire and Rubber Company in 2000. *AP Images.*

Exceptions began to be made to the privity doctrine on a state by state basis. The first examples of these exceptions applied to situations where a manufacturer concealed dangerous defects about which it was aware before selling a product to a retailer. Later, some states expanded this form of exception to include all dangerous defects, whether or not the manufacturer had knowingly concealed them. A 1916 court case in New York (*MacPherson v. Buick Motor Co.*) essentially broadened the exceptions to the privity requirement so much that courts began ignoring the requirement. These and other precedents, coupled with increasing public sympathy for the victims of negligent companies, set the stage for modern product liability laws.

More Detailed Information

Those parties who might be held accountable for a product's defect include the manufacturers of individual parts of the product, the manufacturer who puts all the parts together, the wholesaler of the product, and the retailer of the product. If an individual sues any or all of these people and organizations, he or she must be prepared to prove that the product has a defect. A defect is usually defined as any imperfection that makes the product unreasonably dangerous. Unreasonably dangerous is different from simply dangerous. For example, automobiles by their very nature are dangerous. Car companies are not responsible, however, for the damage inflicted by ordinary car accidents. If, on the other hand, a car accident occurs because of a defect in an automobile, that automobile might be considered, by law, unreasonably dangerous.

There are three basic kinds of product defects: design defects, manufacturing defects, and marketing defects. Design defects are problems in the initial conception of the product. These predate the manufacturing and therefore usually occur in most or all versions of the product sold. A car whose design places the gas tank in a position that makes it likely to explode in the event of an accident might be found to have a design defect. In this case every car of that model may well be affected.

Manufacturing defects, meanwhile, stem from improper construction or assembly. These defects are usually much more limited in scope, occurring in only isolated examples of the product. If a light fixture is, because of a worker's carelessness, wired differently than its designer intended, causing a fire in the residence of a single family unlucky enough to have purchased that fixture, the homeowners might claim damages resulting from a manufacturing defect.

Marketing defects are those having to do with faulty instructions or misinformation about a product. When companies fail to warn consumers about possible dangers of products, either through packaging or advertising of any kind, they might be held liable for injuries that result from those unmentioned dangers. In order to avoid this type of lawsuit, for example, drug companies list all

HOT COFFEE

Product liability refers to laws and legal rulings that allow individuals to seek compensation from parties involved in the manufacturing or sale of a product. One of the most well-known product liability cases in recent years involved a woman who sued the restaurant chain McDonald's after being burned by the coffee she had purchased there. In 1992, 79-year-old Stella Liebeck of Albuquerque, New Mexico, spilled a 49-cent cup of McDonald's coffee in her lap, suffering third-degree burns over 6 percent of her body and ultimately requiring skin grafts and two years of medical treatment.

When Liebeck asked McDonald's to reimburse her for her medical bills, the company refused. As she continued to demand higher amounts of compensation through her attorney, McDonald's repeatedly refused to settle, based on previous court rulings stating that the dangers of hot coffee were obvious and not subject to product liability claims.

But Liebeck's attorney eventually persuaded an Albuquerque jury that McDonald's coffee was, in fact, hot to an unreasonably dangerous degree, and Liebeck was awarded $160,000 in damages, plus $2.7 million in punitive damages (damages awarded to plaintiffs with the intent of punishing the defendant). The judge in the trial later reduced the punitive damage award to $480,000, for a total award of $640,000. Liebeck and McDonald's both appealed this decision, and they eventually settled the lawsuit out of court for an amount estimated to be under $600,000.

possible side effects of their products in their packaging and marketing, even if the effects are only experienced in rare cases.

Product liability cases today are often judged according to the standards of strict liability. This means that if the product is judged defective by the court, it does not matter how careful the defendant was in trying to make the product safe. Strict liability benefits consumers, who often have no way of knowing what companies did or did not do at the various stages from manufacturing to selling a product. Strict liability is an alternative to proving that a company was negligent. A claim of negligence requires being more detailed about what the defendant did and did not do to render the product dangerous.

Under the standards of strict liability, plaintiffs who have been injured or lost property due to a product defect generally have to prove that the product was defective, that the defect caused the injury or damage specified, and that the defect made the product dangerous to an unreasonable degree.

Recent Trends

Since the 1960s those involved with making and selling products have frequently been held to the standards of strict liability in the United States, meaning that they are responsible for compensating victims of defective problems no matter how much care is taken to warn consumers and no matter how careless the victims are in their use of the products. This has made strict liability and related issues a topic of debate.

Those in favor of strict liability argue, among other things, that by placing the burden on manufacturers, distributors, and sellers of products, society forces those parties to be aware of the risks of their products before bringing them to market. If a product's potential to harm people is so great that a company will not be able to profit from it (because the company will have to pay out excessive amounts of money to people who are injured by it), then that product perhaps should not be sold. Strict liability thus becomes a way of promoting the good of society.

People who oppose strict liability often blame the policy for needlessly higher prices resulting from frivolous lawsuits. Critics also point to the wasted energy used to defend against potential lawsuits. For instance, we have strict liability standards to thank for shampoo bottles instructing people on the proper use of shampoo and for coffee cups warning the consumer that the coffee therein is hot. The time, money, and energy expended to warn people about such minor dangers suggests, to some, that product liability laws are a drag on the economy.

$ Customer Satisfaction

What It Means

In business the term *customer satisfaction* refers to how well a customer's expectations have been met by the product or service provided by a particular company. Customers experience satisfaction (or dissatisfaction) in response to not only the quality of a product but also the quality of service they receive, the atmosphere of the business in which they make the purchase, and various other intangible factors.

Business owners are increasingly aware that the success of their companies may depend to a significant extent upon whether they are able to attract and retain loyal customers. According to one estimate, the cost of attracting a new customer is five to seven times greater than the cost of retaining an established customer. Customer satisfaction is a key factor—some experts even argue that it is more important than price—in determining whether a customer will return to a business after his or her initial experience and whether the customer will be inclined to recommend the business to others.

Customer satisfaction is an abstract concept, and it is difficult to track. It is hard to know when a customer's expectations have been met after he or she has walked out the door of your business, and it is also difficult to know when he or she has been disappointed. Research indicates that less than 5 percent of customers express their dissatisfaction directly to the company, but that the average

dissatisfied customer does express his or her dissatisfaction to approximately nine other people, such as friends, family, and coworkers. In contrast, customers do not broadcast their satisfaction as widely as their complaints: it is estimated that satisfied customers tell approximately five other people about the excellent service they received or the terrific product they purchased. A business must give serious consideration to the way such word-of-mouth recommendations and criticisms will affect its financial performance. In general, it is widely believed that a company must figure out how to achieve a high level of customer satisfaction in order to be competitive in the marketplace.

When Did It Begin

The history of customer satisfaction has paralleled changes in the way goods are produced and changes in the relationship between the business and the customer. Before the Industrial Revolution introduced large-scale factories to Europe and America in the eighteenth and nineteenth centuries, goods and services were most often provided by small, independent shop owners and highly skilled craftspeople, who maintained direct personal contact with their customers. Although customers enjoyed having their individual needs catered to by these businesses, the cost of production was high, and many goods and services remained unavailable to anyone but the rich.

This dynamic was radically changed by the rise of factory manufacturing and particularly by the techniques of mass production that were pioneered by Henry Ford (1863–1947) in the American automobile industry in the early twentieth century. Mass production (which quickly spread to many other industries) brought a dramatic decrease in production costs (and therefore in sales prices), but it also lessened the importance of the individual customer. Even so, consumer demand for goods and services was high during the 1910s and 1920s, and the severe supply shortages brought on by the Great Depression (a period of worldwide financial decline that lasted throughout the 1930s) and World War II (1939–45) contributed to a widespread willingness among consumers to take whatever they could get.

Manufacturers and sellers in the United States maintained the upper hand over their customers until the 1980s, when an onslaught of foreign competition (especially from Japan) exposed the poor quality of American goods and services. With a plethora of new choices about how to spend their money, U.S. consumers gained a significant measure of power in the marketplace. American companies were suddenly forced to swallow the new wisdom: that quality matters and each and every customer is important.

More Detailed Information

Many companies are concerned about measuring the level of customer satisfaction they achieve and identifying

Customer satisfaction refers to the extent to which a customer is satisfied with a particular product or service. In this photo a passenger talks with customer service representatives at U.S. Airways. *AP Images.*

the areas where they need improvement. The problem of how to measure and evaluate this psychological state has been the subject of extensive research since the mid-1990s. The primary tool used for measuring customer satisfaction is the survey, or questionnaire. Satisfaction surveys are conducted through the mail, telemarketing, the Internet, and other media. Customers are asked to fill out surveys in movie theaters, dentist's offices, hotels, and many other businesses.

The questions in these surveys revolve around a number of components that make up a customer's overall level of satisfaction with a purchasing experience. These include the following:

- Quality (the customer's sense of how well a product is made, how well it will meet his or her needs, and how knowledgeable a salesperson was in recommending the product)

- Time issues (whether the desired product was available, the salesperson devoted enough time to answering questions and to other aspects of service, and the customer was able to make the purchases with a minimum of waiting in line)

- Atmosphere (how clean, organized, and pleasant the store was)

- Service personnel (whether store representatives generally made a good impression and were appropriately dressed, polite, attentive, and helpful)

- Convenience (the store's accessibility in terms of its location, parking, and hours of operation)

Customer-satisfaction surveys can help businesses meet a variety of objectives, such as understanding more precisely what customers need and expect; determining how well the business is performing to meet these expectations; setting priorities according to what is most important to customers; taking new initiatives to improve products or services according to customer feedback; and gauging customer response to a new product, service, or policy.

Consider the hypothetical example of Freddo's Sandwich Shop. Freddo opened his shop a year ago, but business is still slow, and he does not know why. Are his prices too high? Are his sandwiches too ordinary? Are his employees unprofessional? Should he offer more desserts and specialty sodas? Freddo places a stack of satisfaction questionnaires at the cash register and promises 10 percent off the next sandwich to every customer who deposits a completed questionnaire in the suggestion box. Over the course of two weeks, he receives 100

AIRLINES LESS POPULAR THAN THE IRS

The American Customer Satisfaction Index (ACSI) is an indicator that measures how well American businesses meet the expectations of their customers. Since the index was established in 1994, ACSI researchers have collected data via telephone interviews and used that data to allocate customer-satisfaction scores annually to individual businesses, economic industries, and government agencies. The ACSI score is considered a measure of a business or industry's economic performance. After more than a decade of research, certain industries have consistently fared better than others in their ability to satisfy customers. These successful industries include breweries, consumer electronics, e-commerce, and household appliances. Among the industries that have been least successful in satisfying their customers are telecommunications, cable-television providers, and airlines. Indeed, in 2007 the airline industry received an ACSI score of just 63 out of a possible 100 points. This was 2 points lower than the ACSI score for the IRS (Internal Revenue Service), the much-hated federal agency responsible for collecting income taxes.

not important enough to include. But now, based on the questionnaires, Freddo knew that he needed to make phone orders a top priority in order to increase his business: he reorganized the employee schedule so that he could allocate an extra sandwich maker specifically for phone orders between the hours of 12 and 2; he bought a second cash register to be dedicated for phone-order pickups; and he put up a big sign and bought a radio advertisement that announced, "Now taking phone orders!" Soon phone orders began pouring in. Within a month Freddo had doubled his weekday business and more than paid off the investments in advertising and a second register.

Recent Trends

In 1994 the National Quality Research Center (NQRC) at the University of Michigan's Ross School of Business established the American Customer Satisfaction Index (ACSI). The ACSI was the first national measure of quality in goods and services from the perspective of the customer.

To produce the index, the NQRC conducts nationwide telephone interviews with more than 80,000 consumers, asking questions about specific companies that are broadly representative of the spectrum of businesses that serve American households. It then processes the data it collects using a sophisticated analysis technique called "econometric modeling." Based on the results of this analysis, the each company receives an overall customer-satisfaction score between 0 and 100, which reflects its place on the index.

The ACSI measures customer satisfaction on an annual basis for more than 200 companies in 43 industries (including airlines, banks, hotels, hospitals, apparel manufacturing, Internet search engines, wireless telephone service, and supermarkets), which are categorized among 10 economic sectors (such as Retail Trade, E-Commerce, Finance and Insurance, Public Administration, and Utilities).

ACSI scores serve as a tool for individual businesses to evaluate their performance relative to that of their competitors and develop strategies to improve their business strength. The NQRC contends that the ACSI can also be used to gauge the growth of the national economy, because customer satisfaction is linked to consumer spending trends (the more satisfied customers are with the overall quality of products and services, the more likely they are to spend, and vice versa).

questionnaires. In response to questions about the quality and price of his sandwiches, customers are overwhelmingly satisfied: they love the fresh ingredients and the variety of condiments available, and they believe the sandwiches are fairly priced, considering their hefty size. Most customers are too stuffed after the sandwich to think of dessert, and few say they would pay an extra dollar for a gourmet soda. Customers agree that the decor of the shop is charming, there are plenty of napkins available, they like the jazz music, and the bathrooms are well maintained. Four out of five customers also found the employees friendly, efficient, and helpful. So what was the problem? The reason customers named Freddo's competitor, Sandwich Heaven, as their number one sandwich shop had to do with time. Most customers were trying to get a sandwich on a one-hour lunch break and were afraid of having to wait in a long line during the lunch rush. Sandwich Heaven took phone orders for sandwiches to go, but Freddo's did not.

Eureka! In the past Freddo had feared that phone orders would confuse and slow down the sandwich-production system, so he had decided that the service was

Attracting Customers

$ Overview: Marketing Mix: Product, Price, Place, Promotion

What It Means

Marketing mix is a term used by marketing professionals to describe the different factors that affect a company's attempt to reach customers. To sell a product successfully, a company must do many things in addition to developing the product. Chief among these tasks is determining a target market (the segment of the population likely to buy the product under consideration) and understanding that target market's needs and wants. Based on this understanding, a company must determine the appropriate marketing tactics for the product. The details about how to encourage people to buy a product can be broken down into decisions regarding the four factors that together make up the marketing mix. These factors, often referred to as the "four Ps of marketing," are product, price, place, and promotion.

A product is any good, service, or mixture of goods and services that is being offered to consumers. Price is, of course, the amount of money that the company asks consumers to pay for its product. Place refers to the location where the product will be available to consumers, relative to its channel of distribution (the path the product follows between manufacturing and final purchase). Promotion, finally, is the term used to describe all the methods a company has of communicating with its customers.

A company must consider each decision regarding the four Ps as it relates to the target market. If the company accurately understands the needs and wants of the target market and mixes its decisions regarding each of the four Ps accordingly, it has a solid chance of connecting with customers.

When Did It Begin

The Harvard Business School professor Neil H. Borden first devised the concept of the marketing mix in the late 1940s. Borden, however, conceived of a mix of 12 or more factors that companies needed to blend together successfully in order to satisfy the needs and wants of consumers. It was another marketing academic, E. Jerome McCarthy of Michigan State University, who refined the idea of the marketing mix by breaking it down into the four basic elements that he called the four Ps. The concept became well known as a result of McCarthy's 1960 textbook *Basic Marketing: A Global Management Approach*. Since its initial publication, when it was the first textbook to outline the four Ps, *Basic Marketing* has been updated more than a dozen times (with the help of coauthor William D. Perrault), and it remains one of the most popular marketing texts in the world.

More Detailed Information

When devising a marketing strategy, a company has four basic variables, the four Ps, to work with. When making decisions in each category, the company should keep the target market's needs and wants in mind. The resulting blend of decisions regarding the four Ps results in the marketing mix: the overall set of actions that the company

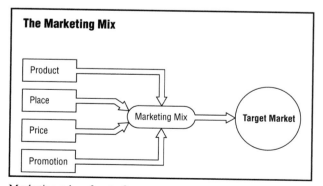

Marketing mix refers to four components— product, price, place, and promotion—involved in marketing a product and trying to attract potential customers. It is also referred to as "the four Ps of marketing." *Illustration by GGS Information Services. Cengage Learning, Gale.*

STUBBORN PS

Marketing professionals advise companies to adjust their decisions about the four Ps—product, price, place, and promotion—each time they introduce a new product or offer an existing product to a new segment of the population. In reality, however, it can sometimes be difficult to modify decisions about some Ps. Product and place represent much more stubborn variables than do price and promotion.

While marketers should ideally be able to influence the decisions to be made about the product, such as what it will look like, what safety features it will have, and what sort of packaging it will have, this is not always the case. Marketers are frequently in the position of marketing preexisting products whose basic qualities cannot be changed.

Similarly, place is a variable that cannot always be easily changed. Place refers not only to retail locations where the product will be encountered by customers but also to the manufacturing facilities, storage warehouses, and wholesaling businesses through which the product will pass on its way to the retail locations. Since it is difficult to integrate these various elements in the path a product follows to reach customers, the elements cannot be changed at will.

Decisions about product and place, then, usually can only be implemented over the long term. In the short term companies really only have access to two of the four variables that affect the success of their marketing efforts. The price of a product, like the form of promotions that will be used to communicate with customers, can be changed easily.

will pursue as it tries to reach the target market effectively. Generally, a company crafts a different marketing mix for each of its products. Likewise, if one product appeals to different target markets, a company will likely devise a separate marketing mix for each market.

The first element of the marketing mix is the product. A product can be a physical object or group of objects, such as a tennis racquet or a home theater system. A product can also be something that cannot be held or touched, such as a haircut or janitorial services. In the past products were created prior to any marketing efforts, and marketers simply worked with what they were given. In recent decades the marketing process has become integrated into the production process. For instance, automotive engineers base their designs on company research that tells them what consumers are looking for in a new car. Other decisions that marketers make prior to manufacturing include those having to do with styling, safety, packaging, and naming of the product. Each of these decisions will have a significant effect on who might want to buy the product.

Price is the second major factor marketers must consider when launching a product. The basic way that a company determines a price is by taking into account the quality of its product and determining how much people are generally willing to pay for a product of its type and quality. But the pricing of a good or service sends numerous messages to consumers, and marketers must make sure that they have tailored these messages to the target market. For instance, some goods, such as high-quality Swiss watches, send a message of status because of their exorbitant prices. One of the reasons Rolex watches appeal to their target market is that the high prices they command appear to be evidence of their quality. If Rolexes were to become cheaper, the target market might not want them anymore. In other cases, a company might intentionally price a product lower than people might expect it to be priced. This so-called market-penetration style of pricing allows the product to find an immediate niche, but it costs the company profits. Alternately, a company might price an item high when introducing it in order to recoup the costs it incurred while researching and developing the product. This is called a price-skimming strategy, and its downside is that the company risks lower sales in the attempt to recoup its investment.

The third P, place, refers to the location(s) at which the product will be sold to consumers. No matter how good the company's other strategy elements are, the product must be in the right place at the right time to capitalize on its target market's attention. This involves making numerous decisions about how and where the product will be manufactured, how and where the product will be stored after it is made, how and where wholesalers will obtain the product, and how and where retailers will obtain the product from wholesalers. All elements of this interdependent channel of distribution must function effectively together, minimizing conflict and allowing the product to be ready for purchase when members of the target market are ready to buy it. In some cases marketers might decide to avoid the limitations of normal channels of distribution by going directly to consumers through direct mail (offers to buy products sent directly to consumers via the mail system), factory outlets (retail stores owned by the company that produces the product), or television shopping networks.

The fourth P that marketers must manage is promotion. Promotion refers to all the methods a company has of communicating with consumers. Typically, promotion centers on four different methods of communication. One of these is a company sales force. Salespeople are often the most effective form of promotion, since they can tailor their sales pitches to individual consumers. Salespeople are an expensive way to reach consumers, however, so companies cannot rely on them exclusively.

Another chief way of communicating with customers is advertising. By using the various media (television, radio, newspapers and magazines, the Internet), a company can build desire for its products among the target market through emotional and intellectual appeals. Advertising has disadvantages, too, however. One is that it is very difficult to tell when an advertisement is effective or not. Another is that the lack of personal contact with the consumer means that the company sometimes has no way of closing a sale, even when it has created a desire for the product.

Sales promotion is another form of promotion. Sales promotion simply consists of the lowering of prices and the publicizing of these lowered prices through the same media as advertisements (for example, 30-second television commercials and Internet pop-up ads). The difference between advertising and sales promotion is that advertising tries to give people reasons to buy a product, whereas sales promotion simply uses the lure of low prices, independent of the product's quality or image, to convince people to buy. Sales promotion can be very effective, but its effects are not usually long-lasting, since it provides no reason other than price to buy a product.

The last form of promotion is public relations, which involves maintaining good relations with the media and with influential groups. Public relations does not always result directly in sales or consumer interest, but it can be used effectively in combination with other aspects of the marketing process.

Recent Trends

Some people claim that the four Ps approach to marketing worked best in earlier eras, when the economy was simpler and more exclusively devoted to tangible products, as opposed to intangible services. In recent decades marketing professionals have proposed numerous additional Ps, such as people, physical evidence, and process, but none of the additional Ps has achieved the wide acceptance of the first four.

Others criticize the marketing mix approach for promoting inefficiency, since it leads to companies that have specialized departments for various elements of the marketing mix. For instance, companies frequently have separate departments for new product development, advertising, public relations, and sales. If these different tasks were more integrated, according to these critics of the marketing-mix approach, companies would save time and money.

In spite of these additions and criticisms, the prevailing approach to the marketing mix remains the one based on the four Ps.

MARKETING AND ADVERTISING

$ Market Research

What It Means

Market research is the gathering and analyzing of data about the best ways to advertise, sell, or distribute a particular product or service: finding customers and po-

tential customers, researching competitor's offerings that may be similar, and looking into other characteristics of the market. An entrepreneur (someone starting a business) thinking of launching a new line of briefcases might use market research to determine whether or not there is a potentially profitable market for (that is, enough buyers to make a profit selling) such items. An existing business dealing in double-paned windows might use market research to determine whether or not its current advertising campaign is working and to decide what forms of marketing (product promotion) to use in the future. Prior to redesigning its minivan model, a carmaker might use market research to determine what qualities that model's target market (people who have bought or are thinking of buying the model) might be looking for in a new vehicle.

Market research is a complex and inexact field. There are numerous different ways of gathering and analyzing data about consumers and the marketplace, and it often costs a great deal of money to conduct the research process successfully. The price paid for making bad business decisions based on ignorance of the market, however, is generally much higher.

When Did It Begin

Market research was a natural outgrowth of the advertising industry in the early twentieth century. Advertising dates to ancient times, but the twentieth century saw the field grow in size and sophistication along with the rapid expansion of the American economy. One of the most prominent advertising professionals of the early part of that century was Daniel Starch (1883–1979); in the 1920s his company were pioneers in developing techniques of what we now call market research. Starch's employees would stop people on the street, ask if they were readers of certain magazines, and then determine whether or not they remembered particular ads from those magazines. By balancing the number of times specific ads were remembered against the circulation size of the magazines in which they appeared, Starch and his colleagues were able to gain insights into what made some ads more effective than others and to use these insights when making future decisions about how to design future advertising campaigns.

In the following decades countless advertisers and businesspeople adapted and improved on Starch's techniques. Today, virtually all advertising professionals and most businesspeople engage in some form of market research.

More Detailed Information

Some of the most common forms of market research are:

1. *Audience research.* Companies that advertise their products on television, on the radio, and the Internet, and in printed magazines and newspapers rely on research to determine who watches which programs, who

Businesses conduct market research for a variety of reasons, from finding new customers to learning more about the products that are being sold by its competitors. A company might use a call center to conduct surveys of potential customers and to learn about their buying habits. *AP Images.*

listens to which radio stations, who logs onto particular websites, or who reads certain publications. Advertisers craft ads with a specific audience, or target market (for example, urban teenagers, middle class professional women, or male sports fans aged 18–25), in mind, and companies buy ad space on those programs, stations and websites and in those publications that most clearly cater to the desired target audience. Of course the media, who rely on advertising for most of their revenues, are also very interested in finding out as much as possible about their audiences. If they can show they are more effectively catering to their audiences, they can charge higher advertising rates.

2. *Product research.* Product research involves soliciting consumer reactions to existing or planned products. A company engages in product research when it tests a prototype for a new product, gathers consumer responses to proposed changes in a product, or tries to identify new markets for an existing product. There are numerous other forms of product research, as well.

3. *Brand research.* A brand is a clear identity that a company carves out in the marketplace. For instance, Volvo is a car brand about which consumers have

specific feelings and opinions. Volvo might survey its loyal customers to find out what comes to mind when they think of Volvos, why they have a strong attachment to Volvos, and whether something about the brand's identity could be added to or improved upon. These and other investigations of a brand's identity and role in the marketplace constitute brand research.

4. *Psychological research.* Psychological research attempts to group people according to their past purchases, cultural identity, or other personal characteristics in order to predict what kinds of products they might buy in the future and why.

5. *Scanner research.* The scanners used at the checkout counter in most stores transmit information directly to researchers. Companies and their advertising agencies can find out what consumers are buying at any given hour, which allows them to fine-tune advertising and other business strategies from moment to moment.

6. *Database research.* Your name and the names of everyone you know will at some point show up on various databases (large collections of information) in the possession of companies and their marketers, whether you want it to or not. Marketers combine

different databases to make a wide array of business decisions. A company specializing in upscale fashions, for example, can easily obtain information about the relative wealth of people living in a certain zip-code area, and it can buy lists of subscribers to certain magazines catering to wealthy people (many magazines make money by selling their subscriber lists to other companies). Neither of these alone would be enough to identify which people are actually wealthy, because neighborhoods are mixed, and anyone can buy a magazine subscription. By cross-referencing the two databases, however, the company can generate a list of households that are likely to be wealthy; then it can more effectively target specific potential customers through direct mailings of catalogs or sale announcements.

7. *Customer satisfaction research.* After you buy a product, you may fill out a survey included in the product's packaging about your level of satisfaction with the product, or you may get a phone call from the manufacturer of the product that attempts to determine your feelings about the purchase you have made. Companies use such information to make future decisions about the product and their business operations.

Recent Trends

The above types of market research do not represent an exhaustive list of the forms the process can take. Market research varies widely from business to business, and new technologies and innovations are constantly altering both how data is collected and how it is analyzed by researchers. Every type of business demands its own particular mode of market research, and new methods for predicting the behavior of consumers and markets are always being tested. Some businesses (especially large corporations) do much of their own market research through their marketing departments, while many other businesses rely on market research firms or advertising agencies to gather and interpret data for them.

Yet, even as the sophistication of market research grows and as increasing numbers of market-research firms specialize in particular techniques of data collection and analysis, some of the most common forms of market research today are as low-tech as they were in the days of Daniel Starch. For instance, the consumer surveys to which many of us have been subjected over the phone (usually right around dinnertime) are not very different from the surveys Starch's company conducted on U.S. streets in the 1920s. Another constant in the world of business and advertising since then, one that no amount of technology or skillful data-mining can change, is that consumers are fickle. We buy goods and services for reasons that are not always clear even to ourselves, and we change our minds often. No matter how sophisticated market research becomes in the future, this fact of human

---

COOLHUNTING

One of the most difficult groups of consumers to attract is young people between the ages of 12 and 24. Teens and young adults often pride themselves on being resistant to traditional advertising and business ploys, and they are the most fickle of all consumers, highly sensitive to quick-moving fashion shifts and pop-culture trends. Companies in the fashion, music, movie, video-game, and mobile-phone industries in particular have turned to a special form of market research (the collection and analysis of information about how best to sell a certain product or service) called coolhunting.

Coolhunting is what its name implies: the attempt to interpret the tastes and desires of young people who have been deemed "cool" by their peers. Coolhunting techniques can vary from focus groups, which are gatherings of small groups of the target market (in this case teens or young adults) who agree to answer marketers' questions in exchange for money or merchandise, conducted by a coolhunting firm (a specialized form of advertising agency), to undercover coolhunting, which is when company pays a cool young person to observe his or her peers and report back to marketers. Undercover coolhunting also happens online: marketers sometimes pose as young people in chat rooms and on message boards in order to gather information about the cool kids.

---

nature will always, no doubt, limit the usefulness of the process.

$ Advertising

What It Means

The term *advertising* refers to all the methods that organizations use to communicate a message to potential customers. In most cases the message informs people about a product or service that the organization sells and then urges those people to purchase that product or service. For example, Progressive Auto Insurance has many television commercials that first state the benefits of the company' insurance policies and then try to persuade consumers to buy such a policy. Not all advertisements, however, ask customers to purchase an item for sale. Campaigning politicians may advertise their candidacy for office and request that people vote for them. A nonprofit organization (a group whose goal is to support an issue of public or private concern rather than to make money) may post an advertisement warning people about the dangers of alcohol or drugs.

Advertisers broadcast their messages in a number of ways, including through television and radio commercials, on billboards, along the sides of city buses, in magazines and newspapers, on the Internet, on movie theater screens, and through mass e-mails (spam).

Another advertising technique is called product placement: a company can arrange to have their product used in a movie or a television show. Many of the characters in the program, especially the most appealing ones, may wear Nike footwear, thus encouraging viewers to purchase their own Nikes. The organization promoting the product or service must pay for any of these types of advertising. Television commercials are the most expensive form of advertising, but they are also considered the most effective because they reach the widest audience.

When Did It Begin

As far back as 3100 BC, Egyptians used ink on papyrus to create sales messages and political arguments. Some historians regard these artifacts as the first examples of print advertising. Ancient Greeks and Romans also used papyrus to promote sales. After the invention of the printing press in 1445, advertisements for books and medicine began appearing on handbills or flyers. In the seventeenth century these products were also regularly advertised in London's newspapers.

In the United States classified ads became popular in newspapers during the eighteenth century. The classified section of a newspaper consists of a series of messages, usually appearing in small print, advertising merchandise for sale, available jobs and housing, garage sales, and so forth. In today's newspapers classified ads are normally posted by individuals selling their own cars or renting out living space, but in the eighteenth century larger corporations advertised their goods and services in this format. The success of classified ads led such major corporations as Sears to attempt to reach customers more directly, usually by mailing them catalogs that contained a complete list of their available products.

More Detailed Information

Most organizations follow a similar set of steps to craft an advertisement and broadcast it to potential customers. The first step is to identify a target market, which is the group of consumers most likely to purchase the product or service. The word *demographic* is also used to mean a target market. An advertising demographic is a specific segment or portion of the population determined by age, gender, and social class. One demographic, or target market, that advertisers have identified is urban professional males, ages 25–49; market research (data that charts consumer buying patterns) indicates that people in this group tend to buy similar products.

The second step in preparing an advertisement is to create a message that is likely to appeal to the target market. For instance, SUV (sport utility vehicle) advertisements tend to appeal to professional people who have families, enjoy outdoor activities, or both. Automakers create images to convey the message that these vehicles have enough space to accommodate the entire family and that the vehicles are ideal for trips to the countryside.

Advertisements for soft drinks, on the other hand, tend to appeal to younger males; these ads often depict kids engaging in such activities as skateboarding and skiing.

The third step in the process is to place the advertisement in a location where members of the target market are likely to see or hear it. For example, home improvement commercials often run during the breaks in televised sporting events because most people watching these programs are men who use home improvement products, such as power tools. Likewise, commercials for shampoo and cosmetics typically run during television shows that are known to have mostly female viewers.

Two of the most important aspects of advertising are brand names and value propositions. A brand is a complex term that refers to the identity or reputation of a product or service. Among many things a brand can include a logo (a graphic image that denotes a product or company), a slogan (a memorable phrase associated with a product or service), and a distinguished set of customers

In order to attract customers, advertisers create a brand identity for a product. Among the most famous examples is the Marlboro Man, shown on this billboard, which tries to link Marlboro cigarettes to an image of masculinity, individualism, and the American West. *Serge Attal/Time and Life Pictures/Getty Images.*

recruited to advertise the product. Taken together, these features connect a product with a set of ideas and a standard of excellence. For instance, the Nike brand identifies itself with the "swoosh" logo, a slogan that reads "Just Do It," and a series of famous athletes, such as Michael Jordan and Tiger Woods, who testify about the quality of Nike apparel. The slogan ("Just Do It,") links Nike products to the idea of adventurousness. The message is that, instead of procrastinating or wallowing in self-doubt, people who wear Nikes go out and do exciting things. Using famous athletes to present the products associates Nike with a high level of accomplishment. The implication is that the average consumer will also achieve athletic success by using Nike products.

A value proposition is the statement in an advertisement that explains the benefit of purchasing a product or service. For example, one technology firm may emphasize the statement "Service at Affordable Prices," while another technology firm claims that they are "Always Available to Help with Computer Problems." Saving money is the value proposition in the first case, and having reliable technical support is the value proposition in the second case. Because most consumers examine advertisements for less than 30 seconds, advertisers believe that it is important to clearly state only one value proposition per advertisement.

Conducting market research to discover the behaviors of a target audience and branding a product or service so that it appeals to that target audience increase the demand for the product or service. The logic is straightforward. Advertisers identify the needs of their target audience and then demonstrate how the product or service they are advertising fulfills that need. This increases the demand for that product or service. For example, in the early spring advertisers for lawn products will write ads that show middle-class homeowners that they need a well-groomed and healthy green lawn that is free of weeds. Next, advertisers will show how a given lawn product will provide consumers with grass that will make their neighbors envious. The goal is to distinguish this lawn-care product from rival lawn-care products.

In addition to branding the product for a specific target audience, the frequency of the advertisement (the number of times the advertisement appears) also has a significant impact on the demand for it. Some market analysts (professionals who study buying trends) even argue that the frequency of an advertisement promotes demand more than the content of the advertisement. This means that the companies with money to buy a lot of advertising time on the television and the radio and advertising space in newspapers and billboards are more likely to create demand than companies with smaller advertising budgets. Creating brand awareness through frequency requires creativity as well as cash, however. For instance, logos should be designed so that they promote immediate recognition of the product. For this to happen

THE SUPER BOWL

The Super Bowl, the game that decides the championship of the National Football League, is the most-watched single-day television program in the world. In fact, the 13 most-watched television programs in history have all been Super Bowls. A total of 141.3 million viewers watched Super Bowl XL (the roman numeral 40) in February 2006. The game was aired in 234 countries and territories and broadcast in 32 languages. Because there are so many viewers, advertisers are willing to pay high prices to market their goods during commercial breaks in the Super Bowl. For the 2006 game a 30-second commercial cost $2.5 million. The price went up to $2.6 million in 2007.

the logo has to be recognizable against any background and at any size. These qualities allow the manufacturer to display the logo most frequently.

In addition to their having a massive advertising budget, Nike shoes are in great demand because their logo is the most recognizable and visible of all the athletic-shoe logos. The Nike swoosh looks exactly the same whether it is displayed on the side of a sneaker, on the breast of a shirt, or across a billboard. What is more, the Nike logo seems to look presentable no matter how many times it appears on an athlete's clothing. Thus, viewers will spot the logo on the sides of an athlete's shoes, on the tongue of the shoe, on the back near the Achilles tendon. The logo will appear again on the breast of an athlete's shirt, in the back along the base of his shirt, as well as in two or three places on his athletic gloves. Furthermore the audience is likely to see the Nike logo displayed in several places at the auditorium.

Recent Trends

E-mail spamming is one of the most common and, many people find, bothersome forms of electronic advertising. This technique involves sending identical messages via e-mail to millions of recipients. Spam has been widely deployed since 1995, when e-mail and the Internet first became available to a large number of consumers. Some of the products and services most commonly advertised via e-mail spam messages include prescription drugs, mortgage offers, and computer ink cartridges. Frequently, goods of questionable value are advertised in spam e-mails, including counterfeit brand-name items, counterfeit software, and stocks (shares of ownership in corporations) offered at inflated prices for shares in dubious businesses.

A huge number of spam e-mails are sent in the United States, and the rate at which they are sent has increased alarmingly. In June 2005, 30 billion spam e-mails were sent each day. One year later the number had jumped to 55 billion per day, and by December 2006, 85 billion spam e-mails were being sent every day. According to some estimates, as much as 85 percent of incoming e-mail is spam. Most consumers have a spam-filtering device on their computers that scans all incoming e-mails for words that might indicate that the message is spam.

$ Mass Marketing

What It Means

Mass marketing is the practice by which a company tries to communicate with the largest possible number of consumers, with the aim of selling the highest possible volume of a particular product or service. Broadly speaking, marketing refers to a company's efforts to sell goods and services by establishing and maintaining a relationship with consumers. For the company, one of the most important aspects of marketing is conveying specific information about its products. Information that a company will try to share with consumers may include basic information about what the product does, where the product is available for purchase, the price of the product, and the desirability of the product.

As the name suggests, mass marketing is a form of marketing that attempts to create the largest possible market for a good or service. The underlying principle of mass marketing, then, is volume; the more people who receive information about a product, the greater number of potential customers the company will have. Effective forms of mass marketing include print, radio, and television advertising, mail-order catalogs, catchy slogans and songs, and flyers.

Companies use mass marketing to sell products with a potential appeal or use for all consumers. For example, mass-marketing campaigns are effective in selling products such as toothpaste, laundry detergent, and soft drinks because of the widespread use of these products. In contrast, items such as luxury cars and golf clubs are attainable only by a small percentage of consumers. To sell these products a company would be better served by using niche marketing, a strategy designed to communicate with a smaller, more specific group of customers.

When Did It Begin

Mass marketing arose in Europe and the United States as a consequence of the Industrial Revolution, a period of rapid economic expansion during the late eighteenth and early nineteenth centuries. Technological advances that emerged during the Industrial Revolution (for example, the increasing use of machinery in the manufacturing process) resulted in the rise of mass production, or the manufacturing of large quantities of goods in a short amount of time. As companies developed the capacity to produce large quantities of goods, it became imperative to establish a more expansive market for these goods.

In response to this need, companies began to look for new ways of marketing their products to a wider range of consumers. The second half of the nineteenth century saw vital improvements in communication technology (for example, the invention the telegraph, which allowed people to communicate rapidly over great distances). Occurring at the same time was the rise of newspapers and magazines with national readerships. American companies quickly took advantage of these new developments to market their products to consumers nationwide.

Two early pioneers of mass marketing were American businessman Asa Griggs Candler (1851–1929), who used mass marketing to transform the soft drink Coca-Cola into a nationally recognized brand; and American automobile manufacturer Henry Ford (1863–1947), who advertised the appeal and affordability of his Model T car to a large segment of the population.

More Detailed Information

The earliest form of mass marketing was advertising in national newspapers and magazines. In the 1890s Sears, Roebuck and Company pioneered the use of mail-order catalogs. This form of mass marketing enabled Sears to communicate with customers throughout the United States and proved especially useful for reaching people in rural areas, who had limited access to retail stores.

Early methods of mass marketing were often accompanied by advances in the ways that companies manufactured and delivered their products. Improvements in the mass-production process made it possible for Henry Ford to produce large quantities of inexpensive, reliable cars, which he in turn marketed to the general public. In the case of Coca-Cola, Asa Candler established a network of regional bottling plants, which enabled him to distribute his product to a greater number of customers in a short amount of time.

Mass marketing continued to evolve rapidly in the twentieth century. Radio was highly popular in the 1920s and 1930s, and the development of radio advertising enabled companies to broadcast their message to large numbers of people all at once. Mass marketing experienced another major surge in the years following World War II (1939–45). American families had accumulated wealth during the war by cutting back on spending, so when the war ended, there was a great demand for new products. This created a much larger market for consumer goods. At the same time, significant advances in mass media (forms of communication designed to reach a large audience) made it possible for companies to deliver information about their products to more people than ever before.

The most significant breakthrough in the history of mass marketing was the advent of network television (which provides the same programming for many television stations) in the late 1940s and the 1950s. Television

A company uses mass marketing techniques, such as advertisements in national newspapers and magazines, with the aim of reaching the widest possible audience for its potential customers. Sears, Roebuck and Company introduced a new practice in mass marketing when it created the first mail order catalog in the 1890s. *The Quin Family. Reproduced by permission.*

TELEVISION AND MASS MARKETING

Because of its ability to reach a large and diverse body of consumers all at one time, television has traditionally played a central role in mass marketing. In the 1960s, when there were only three network television stations, companies could rely on television advertising to market their products to a mass audience. The rise of cable television, however, caused a shift in the way that companies approached mass-marketing campaigns. In 1994 the average consumer had access to 27 television channels; by 2004 the average number of channels had risen to 100. As a result of this proliferation of television options, it was no longer possible to target as many consumers with the same 30-second advertisement. This shift had a major impact on the way that corporations allocated their marketing resources. For example, in 1999 the McDonald's restaurant chain devoted two-thirds of its marketing budget to television advertising; by 2004 that portion had shrunk to one-third.

quickly became the most popular form of communication in history, enabling companies to broadcast creative, memorable advertisements to huge numbers of people.

Recent Trends

Late-twentieth-century advances in communication technology, notably the Internet, have continued to play an important role in the development of mass-marketing techniques and practices. In the 1990s, however, companies began to move away from traditional mass marketing in favor of more specialized, targeted forms of marketing. A major reason for this shift has been the diversification of media outlets, or sources of information, available to consumers. The explosion of new media (for example, the increasing number of channels available on cable and satellite television and the rise of information sources on the Internet) has led to a fragmentation of the traditional audience for mass marketing. In the 1960s a single television advertisement had the potential to reach 80 percent of a particular group of consumers; by the twenty-first century the same advertisement would need to run on a hundred channels to have anywhere near the same impact.

At the same time consumers have used media technology to become more informed about available products. This increase in consumer education has forced companies to pay closer attention to the specific desires of the customer. By the early twenty-first century, then, more and more companies had begun to shift away from mass-marketing techniques in order to focus on marketing their products directly to those consumers most likely to be interested in them.

$ Niche Marketing

What It Means

Marketing refers to all of the activities that a company engages in to attract and build relationships with customers. Niche marketing is marketing that is focused entirely on one small segment of the population.

Imagine that you are intent on starting a women's clothing store in your midsize town. At first you think you will try and appeal to all women between 22 and 60 by offering a sampling of national mainstream brands in a wide variety of styles. But you realize that this might put you into direct competition with several existing stores, and you are afraid that to attract customers you would have to price your clothes lower than the competition. Customers would be ready to buy clothes at any of your competitors' stores the moment you raise your prices.

You decide to change tactics after reflecting on a trend you have noticed: because of good home prices and the vibrant arts scene in your town, a large number of people in their twenties and early thirties have been moving in from big cities recently. You decide, accordingly, to focus your store strictly on women in their late-twenties and thirties who have left the city to live in your town. To attract this specific group of customers you enter into contracts with a handful of small, up-and-coming designers whose work is not generally carried by stores outside of New York City, and you advertise in the arts section of the local alternative weekly newspaper. Your store develops a distinct image that makes it stand out from all others, and your customers are extremely loyal to you.

This is an example of niche marketing. Often, business success is dependent not on targeting the largest number of customers but on accurately targeting the right group and satisfying their desires.

When Did It Begin

A range of different marketing strategies, including niche marketing, has no doubt existed for as long as entrepreneurs and businesses have existed, and niche marketing comes naturally to small businesses, owing to the difficulty of reaching all portions of the population on a limited budget. The early twenty-first century, however, saw an overall rise in niche marketing across all segments of the U.S. economy. Technologies such as the Internet made it possible for companies to satisfy the desires of small subgroups of people scattered across a nation or the globe in much the same way that a clothing store could satisfy a small subgroup of a local population. This greatly expanded the possibilities for niche marketing. For example, whereas a physical clothing store for ex-urbanites might be able to survive if 2,000 out of the town's 30,000 women fit into the target niche, an online women's clothing business might be able to survive by appealing to one out of every 30,000 women, since it could draw

Niche marketing involves advertising and other strategies designed to attract customers that have similar occupational or lifestyle characteristics. Examples of niche markets include new parents, cattle ranchers, collectors of World War II memorabilia, and pop music festivalgoers. *AP Images.*

customers from across the globe until they collectively amounted to a sizeable customer base. Likewise, an ever-expanding U.S. economy and an increasingly unified global economy meant that consumers had more choice than ever before when it came to choosing what to buy. To stand out in this environment, it was more important than ever that a business, no matter its geographical range, have a distinct image of its customer base and of how to satisfy that group's desires.

More Detailed Information

Many entrepreneurs mistakenly assume that a business that appeals to the widest possible audience offers the best chance of generating high levels of profit and that any marketing efforts that appeal too specifically to one group in society will alienate potential customers that do not belong to that group. In fact, businesses that offer a wide range of products to a wide range of customers are generally more expensive to operate and less profitable than businesses that market to a specific niche.

Likewise, in today's crowded business environment, appealing to a wide range of the population means competing with many existing businesses. If your pro-

ducts are similar to those of your competitors, you will likely have to attract customers by pricing your products lower than the competition. It is difficult to stand out and create loyal customers in this way. Through successful niche marketing—zeroing in on one small group of consumers who are currently being underserved by the competition and fulfilling their needs—a company can avoid many of these problems, building customer loyalty and a distinct brand image in the process.

To isolate a fruitful market niche, an entrepreneur should be aware of some basic guidelines. First, the members of the selected niche must have identifiable needs in common that make them stand apart from the mass market. For example, if you are starting an online T-shirt business, targeting fans of 1970s rock music may not be fruitful; this group is so large that their needs may not be similar or very different from the needs of the average rock music listener. On the other hand, fans of 1970s German psychedelic rock bands might have more similar tastes and identifiable needs when it comes to T-shirts.

A group with identifiable and unique needs is not enough, though. There must be enough members of a market niche to support a business. This may never be

NICHE MARKETS AND POPULATION

It is often easier and more cost effective for a business to focus on a niche market—a small group of potential customers with clearly defined needs—than to try and appeal to a wide cross-section of any population. For small businesses it is particularly necessary to do this, since small budgets do not make it possible to stock products or offer services meeting a wide variety of needs, nor to advertise in mass-media outlets that will reach the largest number of consumers.

The reality of life for many entrepreneurs is that there often are not enough local customers in the niches they have identified to support a business. This means that small-town clothing stores, for instance, are often by necessity less specific in their offerings and their customer base than they would like to be. This also explains why the most highly specialized stores catering to the narrowest niches are often found in large cities, where they can draw from a larger total group of people.

true of the fans of 1970s German psychedelic rock, even if you add up all of them around the world. In the example of the clothing store, on the other hand, whereas in 1990 your town may not have supported such a store, the migration patterns of young people later in the decade and the early twenty-first century may have changed this situation.

Your product should also be unique in its ability to meet the niche market's needs. If other competitors offer products similarly capable of satisfying the niche, then you may not have discovered a fruitful niche. The clothing store for ex-urbanites would satisfy this condition, since there is no other store in town able to meet the needs of its niche market. But it is not strictly necessary for the uniqueness to be a feature of the products themselves. For example, if a large department store tried to compete with the smaller store by stocking the same clothes at comparable prices, the smaller store could distinguish itself through superior customer service or other attributes.

Even given unique products and a sizable, well-defined niche market, though, the business owner must be able to locate and communicate with that group in a way that is economically feasible. Possibilities for the clothing store might include advertising in a local newspaper, direct mailings using subscription lists of urban-themed magazines (these lists can often be purchased from magazines), and simple word of mouth.

Recent Trends

In the early twenty-first century Internet commerce was changing the ground rules according to which many industries and companies had long done business. Perhaps no industry was more affected than the entertainment industry, which was being reshaped by companies such as Amazon.com (an online bookseller), Netflix (an online DVD-rental company), and Apple's iTunes (an online music store). Technology writer Chris Anderson described the changing nature of the digital entertainment marketplace in his 2006 book *The Long Tail*.

Prior to the Internet age bookstores, video stores, and music stores had to allot their limited shelf space to the books, videos, and compact discs most likely to sell or rent in the greatest numbers. The limited physical capacity to sell these products encouraged the publishing, movie, and music industries to devote most of their money to marketing blockbuster entertainment products that would appeal to the largest possible number of Americans. If a store could only sell or rent a limited number of books, videos, or CDs, then it made sense for the companies behind those products to try to build up as much consumer demand as possible for those relatively few offerings.

By contrast, Amazon, Netflix, and iTunes could stock an unlimited number of books, videos, and albums (or songs) without increasing their operating costs substantially. As consumers' choices in entertainment stopped being limited by the scarcity of physical space, the sales of lesser-known books, videos, and songs became as important, if not more important, than sales of big hits.

Imagine an obscure novel that is of interest to only one reader in a town of 50,000 people. It makes no sense for local bookstores to carry this book, since that one reader's desires are not going to produce much of a profit. But one person out of every 50,000 in the United States amounts to a sizeable niche market (and sizeable profits) for Amazon. Additionally, there are far more books that appeal to only a few people than there are books that appeal to millions. Therefore, most of Amazon's book profits come from these books that appeal only to a niche market. Whereas the largest of the physical, bricks-and-mortar chain bookstores (such as Barnes & Noble) carry around 130,000 book titles, most of Amazon's profits come from books that do not place among its top 130,000 sellers. The company's profits can be thought of as stemming from a core group of best-sellers, combined with a "long tail" of books that sell only a few copies a piece.

In the digital economy, Anderson predicted, profitability would not longer be driven by "hits"; instead, the "misses" that appealed to only a handful of people would be more important to a business's success. The future, he argued, belonged not to the mass market but to a dizzying array of niche markets.

$ Direct Mailing

What It Means

Direct mailing is a form of what is called direct marketing. Marketing is a multifaceted strategy for selling goods, services, and other products; it entails research,

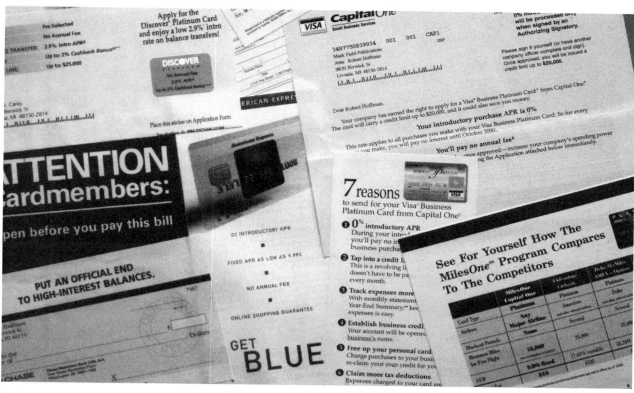

Businesses use direct mailing to promote their products, sending promotional postcards, catalogs, and coupon packets. Direct mailing is especially common in the credit card industry. *Photograph by Robert J. Huffman/Field Mark Publications. Reproduced by permission.*

advertising, pricing, promotion, placement (or distribution), and other activities designed to connect the product with the segment of people who will be most likely to buy it. When successful, marketing activities enable a company to perceive, understand, and satisfy consumer wants and needs.

Direct marketing, also known as direct-response marketing, is a specialized form of marketing in which promotional messages are delivered to a target population of people who have been identified as potential customers. Direct marketing's focus on attaining measurable results that can be tracked over time is what distinguishes it from other forms of marketing, wherein the effects of certain strategies can be difficult to verify. For example, Tangles, a new hair salon catering to young people, might use a direct-marketing campaign to hand out hundreds of leaflets on a college campus. The leaflet contains a coupon for $5 off a haircut; Tangles can therefore measure the success of its campaign—the number of customers it has attracted—according to how many students bring the coupon into the salon for a haircut. Similarly, Tangles could buy an advertisement on the college radio station KZAP; if the ad concludes with a line such as "Say you heard about us on KZAP and receive $5 off of a haircut," the salon can also measure the results of this ad by counting how many customers mention it. Indeed, any advertisement that asks the audience to respond with

some direct action (such as returning a postcard, calling a toll-free number, entering a free raffle, or visiting a website) may be categorized as direct marketing.

Direct marketers deliver their messages via television, the Internet, e-mail, billboards, magazine inserts, and other media. Still, the most prevalent form of direct marketing is direct mail, in which marketing messages are delivered through the postal service. The marketing pieces used in direct mail can take a number of forms, from a simple postcard with the customer's address on one side and a promotional message on the other, to a "value pack" envelope stuffed with coupons for a variety of local businesses, to a magazine-style catalog containing dozens of items for sale. In the United States and other industrialized countries, the volume of direct mail represents such a significant portion of the total mail circulation that a special rate class (called bulk mail) has been established to handle it.

When Did It Begin

The practice of advertising by mail can be traced to the invention of the printing press by Johannes Gutenberg (c. 1390–1468) in Germany in the mid-fifteenth century. It did not become widespread, however, until the late nineteenth century. In 1872 American salesman Aaron Montgomery Ward (1844–1913) launched the first mail-order

TONS OF MAIL

Direct mailing is a form of marketing in which companies attempt to gain the attention and business of a targeted segment of the population by sending advertisements and other solicitations through the mail. Many marketers swear by the effectiveness of direct-mail campaigns, but environmental groups object to it on the grounds that it constitutes an enormous waste of paper. While marketers call these marketing pieces "direct mail," millions of people call it "junk mail."

According the Consumer Research Institute, whose Stop the Junk Mail program is one of the most widely known such programs in the United States, 44 percent of direct mail is thrown in the trash, unopened and unread. The environmental impact of this mail, the institute says, is four million tons of unnecessary waste per year. Not only are millions of trees cut down for this mail, but billions of gallons of water are used to process the paper.

business by sending out a one-sheet catalog that consisted of a list of goods for sale, along with prices and ordering instructions. Three decades later Ward had expanded his catalog to a four-pound volume, which was mailed to three million customers. Ward's success led many other businesses to adopt direct-mail advertising techniques, and the industry grew rapidly: in 1917 a trade organization called the Direct Mail Advertising Association was established, and in 1928 the U.S. Postal Service introduced third-class bulk-mail postage rates to accommodate the large volume of direct-mail advertisements.

Direct mail as we know it today, however, was not introduced until the early 1960s, when Lester Wunderman (b. 1920), now hailed as one of the great marketing visionaries of the twentieth century, conceived of direct marketing as an interactive process between business and customer. Wunderman observed that people's desires and tastes were becoming increasingly individualized and that shopping was developing into a form of personal expression. Seeking to address the needs of the individual customer, he defined direct mail as a "system of interactive transactions that would restore a measure of dialogue and human scale to the way we made, sold, and bought things." One of Wunderman's legendary direct-mail success stories was his creation of the Columbia Record Club, which offered customers a free record when they joined the club and enabled members to buy records from a mail-order catalog. The public response to the record club was overwhelmingly positive and suggested the enormous potential of direct mail.

More Detailed Information

In order to use direct mail effectively (that is, to attain the largest number of responses from the marketing pieces

that are distributed), marketers conduct demographic research to determine their target audience. Population demographics include a wide range of statistical data about the people that make up a society, including age, race, sex, education level, occupation, income, marital status, number of children, and other information. A marketing agency that is preparing a direct-mailing campaign collects this information so that it can target a specific group of people, such as "single African-American women under 30 with college degrees" or "divorced dads over 40 with blue-collar jobs."

Marketing agencies collect demographical information from a number of sources, including the national census (a government survey of the population). Although the census itself is anonymous and marketers cannot get names or private information directly from it, it does help marketers to derive information about people. For example, using information contained in the census, marketers can infer things about a person's income level and lifestyle based on his or her zip code. Also, many companies are in the business of compiling and selling specialized mailing lists, so a business that wants to launch a direct-mail campaign can select the particular demographics it is looking for and buy a list of all the addresses in a certain area that fit those criteria. For instance, if a high-end day-care business is trying to boost its enrollment, it might buy a list of addresses for families in the area with children under the age of 10 and both parents working professional jobs.

How do mailing-list companies get this kind of information in the first place? Information about the purchases a person makes is often retained by the businesses, sold to the direct-mail organizations that compile the lists, and then resold to other businesses that are seeking to target similar consumers for their direct-mail campaigns. Say, for example, that you buy a new camera. In the box with the camera is a postcard that offers you a two-year warranty; all you have to do is complete the product-registration information that is requested and send the postcard in. A few weeks after you do this, you start receiving promotional flyers in your mailbox for Photosaurus, a new photo-printing business only a few miles from where you live. The flyer promises a free roll of film with your first set of prints at Photosaurus, if you bring in the postcard. But how did the Photosaurus know that you might be looking for a place to print your pictures? In all likelihood, the camera company sold your name to a direct-mail organization, which, in turn, sold it to Photosaurus. Product-registration cards are just one of many ways that companies can track what people buy and predict what they might buy in the future. If a person belongs to a professional organization, fills out a survey, signs a petition, or donates to a charity, it is likely that the information he or she gives will make its way to a mailing list. Also, any time someone registers a change of address with the post office, that information is sold to direct-marketing companies.

Recent Trends

Instead of simply broadcasting advertisements out into the world and hoping for good results, businesses can use direct mail to customize their marketing initiatives and aim them directly at the segment of the population that is most likely to respond. Still, using direct mail as a marketing strategy is not without its downsides. First, many consumers resent getting unsolicited mail, regarding it as both an invasion of their privacy and a waste of paper. In some cases, then, a business that uses direct mail might actually alienate a potential customer who would have been more receptive to some other form of marketing. Also, even after such careful targeting of its audience, a business has no guarantee that a mail recipient will open, or even look at, this advertising mail. Indeed, studies show that huge volumes of direct mail are thrown into the trash unread.

Since the 1990s privacy advocates have become increasingly active in the effort to help people avoid having their personal information sold to direct-mail organizations and their mailboxes flooded with unwanted marketing materials. In the United States one of the first steps to halting the influx of direct mail is to register with the Direct Marketing Association's Mail Preference Service. Once someone registers, his or her name and address are added to a "do not mail" file, which is updated monthly and distributed to direct marketers several times per year.

BRINGING THE PRODUCT TO THE CUSTOMER

$ Distribution

What It Means

Distribution is the movement of products from manufacturers to sales outlets to customers. Products and services usually pass through several different agents as they move from the manufacturer to the customer. For example, a sneaker manufacturer in the Philippines may ship its shoes to a distributor in Phoenix, Arizona, who in turn sells the shoes to a buyer employed by a sporting goods retailer in a Phoenix suburb, which then sells the shoes to customers in its local stores.

The path a product takes as it moves from producer to end user (the consumer) is called a channel of distribution. A channel of distribution provides a manufacturer with an efficient way to get its products to customers. All companies use channels of distribution, whether they have a sales force within their company that sells directly to consumers or whether they use other means, such as distributors, wholesalers, or retailers, to get their product

ONLINE MUSIC

Only a few decades ago recorded music was limited to vinyl records and cassette tapes and was sold in neighborhood music stores. Then came the compact disc (CD) and music megastores. These technologies and distribution methods were largely eclipsed by the introduction of digitally recorded music. Consumers are able to download music directly to their computers, digital music players, or mobile phones. Many experts predict that the digital music distribution channel will replace the traditional models of distribution.

There are many benefits to digital music distribution. Consumers can easily listen to samples of music before they make a purchase. They can purchase and download music through the Internet at any time of the day or night. Customers can buy single tracks instead of whole CDs. However, the growing problem of illegally downloading, copying, and sharing copyrighted music online concerns many people in the music industry. But some music publishers prefer online music since it provides them with advanced copyright protection that limits the chance that digital music will be pirated, or illegally copied.

to the consumer. Although many channels of distribution involve the physical movement of goods (this is sometimes called "logistics"), manufacturers of services also rely on distribution channels to reach customers. For instance, an airline uses its own telephone system and website as well as travel agents to provide customers with different ways to make airline reservations.

One of the most important decisions a business must make is determining how to distribute its goods or services at a low cost. Often this boils down to a choice between using a wholesaler or a retailer. A wholesaler (sometimes called a middleman or distributor) sells goods and services in large quantities and at lower prices to retail businesses, merchants, industrial firms, and other businesses. Traditionally the manufacturer pays less to distribute its goods through a wholesaler. A retailer, on the other hand, sells individual items directly to the consumer, usually in a store. Generally it costs manufacturers more to distribute goods through retailers.

When Did It Begin

The economic history of the United States has shaped the way goods and services have been distributed over time. The goods produced in colonial America were mostly from agriculture, mining, and other industries that removed material from the land or sea. Typically the people who had farmed, mined, logged, and collected these goods also played the role of distributor and merchant. In general, the person who produced a product also sold it to a customer. Later, the general store provided a way for some producers of such items as soap, food staples, and

Distribution refers to the process by which goods are transported from producers to consumers. Major companies, like Amazon.com, shown here, typically have large distribution departments to deal with high volumes of shipments. *AP Images.*

tools to sell their products in one place. Unlike today, many households did not purchase such goods, but made their own. Merchants distributed goods mainly to those well-to-do households who could afford to purchase essential goods, rather than make them.

The Industrial Revolution had a profound effect on the distribution of goods. The development of steamships, trains, and, later, automobiles changed the way goods were transported. Technological developments made it possible to produce and distribute goods on a much larger scale and to reach merchants and customers in far-off places. The general store that sold many different goods was gradually replaced by more specialized merchants who focused on selling textiles, drugs, or hardware, for example.

By the early twentieth century manufacturers were selling their products either to consumers or to industrial operations for use in production of other goods. Distribution of goods through wholesalers became more common, and wholesalers often resold products to retailers. Another event that drastically affected distribution was the beginning of chain stores and mass-retail stores. Such large department stores as Sears, Roebuck and Company; J.C. Penney Company; and Woolworth Company typically purchase the goods they offer to consumers directly from manufacturers. The local, independent merchant selling a range of products to consumers became increasingly obsolete.

More Detailed Information

Distribution channels can be very simple. When manufacturers sell directly to a customer, it is called direct distribution. This is usually the simplest and cheapest way to reach customers. Because of the development of the Internet and e-commerce (electronic commerce) many companies sell directly to customers without using an intermediary such as a retailer or distributor. For example, some financial companies developed websites where customers could directly trade stocks without using an intermediary called a broker.

Whereas a direct distribution channel is referred to as a zero-level channel, a situation in which a manufacturer sells goods to a retailer, who in turn sells them to customers is called a one-level channel. A two-level channel is when the manufacturer sells to a wholesaler, who sells an agent middleman, who usually receives a portion of the goods' value when he or she sells them to a wholesaler. The wholesaler in turn sells to a retailer, who sells to customers.

Whenever a distribution channel is more complex than the manufacturer selling directly to the customer, it is said to be indirect. Indirect channels of distribution are essential when "one-stop shopping" is important to customers. A department store, for example, provides different types of goods from different manufacturers to customers, who appreciate the convenience of having to go to only one store for all their shopping needs. Indirect channels of distribution may also allow the customer access to after-sales service or repair on such goods as electronics and appliances.

When a manufacturer determines whether to use direct or indirect channels of distribution, it weighs several important factors. First, the manufacturer determines if it would benefit financially from having a distributor or retailer work with customers and provide efficient access to products. If the manufacturer uses an intermediary of any kind, it must determine how much time, money, and effort will go into that relationship. Also, the manufacturer must analyze how its customers' loyalty to the product will be affected by using an indirect channel of distribution. When a customer buys an airplane ticket directly from an airline company, for example, the customer feels loyal to that airline company since no other agent has mediated the transaction. Manufacturers must also consider that a distributor, wholesaler, or retailer offers other products besides its own, which compete with the manufacturers' product.

No matter the type of distribution channel, many different functions are involved in getting a product from manufacturer to customer. They include selling, buying, sorting, storing, transporting, and working with customers. Even if a manufacturer that once used a distributor decides to eliminate that step in its distribution chain, the functions that the distributor performed still need to take place. For example, if the distributor had sorted and stored merchandise until customers bought it, the manufacturer will need to perform these tasks itself if it no longer uses the distributor.

Even after a manufacturer establishes a distribution channel, it must be willing to change it when necessary. Many companies that once used traditional channels of distribution involving salespeople and wholesalers have created websites that give customers additional ways to purchase the company's goods, interact with company representatives, and learn about the products.

Recent Trends

Many aspects of distribution have changed in recent years because of technological developments, including the personal computer (PC) and the Internet. In the early years of the personal-computer industry in the 1970s, a computer company's sales force distributed computers directly to consumers. Then computer retailers changed that distribution pattern and performed additional functions, such as selling computer hardware and software,

selling to individuals as well as businesses, and providing service and repair.

As consumer knowledge of PCs grew during the 1980s, the price and availability of personal computers became their most valued attributes. The growth of the market changed the way the industry handled distribution. Mass resellers purchased large quantities of PCs at a discount and sold them corporate customers willing to place large orders. The Internet became a critical channel for some manufacturers, who sold directly to customers through websites. Computer superstores grew into yet another popular distribution channel.

Other industries, such as hardware, electronics, and office equipment, have also undergone major shifts in their methods of distribution. Consumers today often research products before they buy. Educated consumers may not need personalized service but want a low price and a good product. The Internet, discount stores, and superstores answer these consumers' needs by foregoing a personalized service experience while offering low prices and a wide array of products.

$ Pricing

What It Means

Pricing is the process of determining and applying prices to goods and services. The price is the monetary cost of the product (the good or service) that is bought or sold, and the pricing process fixes the amount that a consumer pays for the product.

Pricing one of the four primary elements of product marketing. The other three are the product itself, which includes product development as well as packaging and branding; promotion, for example, advertising and publicity; and distribution, or how the product gets to the consumer. Together with pricing, these elements are called the marketing mix. Pricing is considered the most important element of the marketing mix, because it is one that directly affects a company's profits. A product's price also affects how that product is positioned, or located in relation to similar products, in the market. For example, an automobile that is priced high to appeal to consumers with money will position it in competition with other automobiles in the same price range.

Costs and the target market (the consumers the company hopes to attract) are crucial considerations in choosing the price of a product. A snowmobile, for instance, is fairly expensive to make, appeals only to certain kinds of consumers, and is in demand only in certain geographic regions. The price needs to be set high enough to offset the costs involved in the product, promotion, and distribution the snowmobile, and it needs to be appropriate for the people who might be interested in buying it.

More generally, prices have to take into account consumer reaction, or the willingness of consumers to pay

Pricing refers to the process of establishing the prices of goods and services. This photo features Jacqueline Woods, vice president of global marketing and pricing at software maker Oracle Corporation. *AP Images.*

the set price. In a market where consumers choose among competing products, prices are ultimately determined by the balance between supply (how much of a product a company is willing to produce over a range or prices) and demand (how much of a product consumers are willing to buy over a range of prices). A price must be set with a certain degree of confidence that consumers will pay it.

When Did It Begin

As American markets expanded in the early nineteenth century, companies generally were free from government intervention and regulation. Partly as a result of this freedom, some of these companies combined in ways that gave them the power to reduce or even eliminate competition in the marketplace. One ability of these consolidated companies, called trusts, was to set the price for the products in an industry. The prices were often set so low that other firms were driven out of business, and new firms could not enter the competition for consumers. The trust, if it so chose, could then raise prices for its products to increase its profits. The most famous example of this type of arrangement was the Standard Oil Trust, a conglomeration of companies that in the late 1800s

controlled the production, distribution, and sale of petroleum in the United States.

In a reaction to Standard Oil and other large trusts, the United States Congress passed the Sherman Antitrust Act in 1890. The law's purpose was the elimination of monopolies and their suppressive tactics. Individual states also passed their own antitrust laws, which in some cases were even stricter than the federal law. Another federal law, the Clayton Antitrust Act of 1914, specifically outlawed price fixing, a practice in which competing companies in a specific market secretly agreed to charge identical prices for the same product, thereby avoiding competitive pricing.

More Detailed Information

Although companies go about setting prices in a variety of ways, they generally begin by developing a marketing strategy for the product. In this step an analysis of the market in which the product will be sold is conducted. The state of the existing market plays an important part in determining where the price should be set most effectively. For example, a novel product that has the market all to itself (called a new entrant) can probably carry a higher price. On the other hand, a product entering a market in which many similar products are vying for consumers must have its price set to be competitive.

The next step in the pricing process is usually a careful analysis of the entire marketing mix in order to understand how the price interacts with the product, its promotion, and its distribution. For instance, because the price of a product is often directly related to its quality, setting a price influences the product's design and manufacture. If a furniture ensemble is to be targeted at consumers who wish to spend relatively little money for it, production of the furniture will need to be inexpensive, which probably will result in a lower-quality product.

Not part of the marketing mix but still essential to pricing is a consideration of any legal issues connected with the price of the product. For example, there are occasionally government-imposed price controls that set a limit on the price of goods in order to prevent inflation. In addition, antitrust laws make it illegal to conduct so-called predatory pricing, in which a firm prices a product so low that competitor producers of similar products cannot survive. Another outside factor to consider is the pricing strategy of competitors. If, for example, one firm sets an extremely low price for its product, the result may be a price war with a competitor that damages consumer perception of both firms.

Another step in the pricing process involves anticipating the level of consumer demand for the product so that the product's distribution can keep up with the demand. Still another step is calculation of the cost to the company of making the product. This production cost includes both fixed costs such as the rental of the factories in which the product is made and variable costs such as the salaries of the specialists who help design the product. The total production cost is used to find the unit cost to the company of each product unit. The unit cost establishes the lower limit on the price that the company might charge. It also allows the company to project the profit it might make from future product sales when the price is set at various levels. The amount that the price of an item is raised above the unit cost is called the price markup. The price markup can be represented either as a percentage or as a fixed amount.

Each time a company prices a product, it has a specific objective in mind for choosing that price. In some cases it may be to maximize the number of product units sold or the number of consumers served. In other cases the objective may be to use price as an indicator of quality so that stands out as the leader among its competitors. If the market for a product is saturated with competitors, a company may choose a price to cover its costs and simply allow it to survive in the market.

Recent Trends

Among the various aspects of marketing, pricing is probably the one most dramatically affected by the in-

DISCOUNTS

The basic price of a product as published or listed and before any price reductions, or discounts, are taken is called the list price. Consumers may find a product selling at the list price in some places and at discounted prices in others. There are several different types of discounts. A cash discount is the price given to consumers who pay their bill before a specified date. A promotional discount is a price set for a short time period and intended to stimulate sales of the product. A quantity discount is the price offered to consumers who purchase the product in relatively large amounts. Stores such as Costco have been successful in giving lower prices to consumers who are willing to buy certain kinds of goods in bulk.

A seasonal discount is a price based on the time of year that the purchase is made and chosen to avoid or reduce a drop in sales associated with that season. For example, the travel and vacation industries experience seasonal rhythms related to the changing climates where travelers live and where they wish to go. Thus, the off-season for one travel destination can be different from another. Generally, lower prices are offered for airfares, lodging, and activities in the off-season. Similarly, discount prices applied to long-distance and wireless telephone services encourage consumers to make their calls at times of the day or week when call volumes are relatively low.

troduction of the Internet into the world of the consumer. The Internet allows a consumer to search easily for information about the price of products and share that information with others. Without leaving home an online consumer can spot-check the prices of different competitors' products within a certain market. The Internet also has become an avenue for some companies, for example, consumer electronics businesses, to offer lower prices to buyers who choose to make their purchases online rather then in traditional ("brick and mortar") stores. Travel websites such as Travelocity and Orbitz have been successful because they have offered lower prices on airfares than travel agencies and reservation offices.

At Internet auctions, run by online businesses such as eBay, buyers rather than sellers set the final prices for products. Similar to the operation of traditional auctions, online bidders offer to pay ever higher prices for a given product until a time limit expires. The supply and demand for the product at a particular time determines the price of that product. A great advantage of the Internet auction is that the size of the bidding audience can greatly exceed what it would at a physical auction. Although the sellers at Internet auctions are typically individuals, some manufacturers have used these sites as places to sell their goods.

$ Selling

What It Means

When a good is exchanged for a sum of money, it is said to have been sold. Selling includes all of the activities involved in making sales of goods and services to buyers. These activities include contacting potential customers, presenting and demonstrating products, taking orders for products, delivering products, and collecting payment. Many activities are involved in selling a new textbook, for example, to a school district. The textbook publisher may send out information about the book, arrange meetings with curriculum directors at the school district, give presentations to demonstrate how the product will improve teaching and student learning, and answer questions about the textbook. If the buyer agrees to purchase the textbook, the seller then takes orders for the school district, makes sure that the books are delivered by a specified date, and ensures that payment for the books is received.

Sales management is the administration of a company's sales program. Sales managers are responsible for planning, executing, and controlling sales programs. The personnel who are employed to conduct sales activities are called the sales force. Large and mid-size companies typically have a sales force. Small companies may rely on the owner or another individual to oversee product sales.

A person who is employed to represent a business and to sell its products is a sales representative. In a larger company, once a sale has been completed, it becomes what is called a key account. The manager or executive of a key account is responsible for knowing all there is to know about the account, including its history, growth, major representatives, and future strategies.

Sales representatives are compensated either by a commission or by a salary. If a sales representative is paid on a commission, the compensation for closing (completing) a sale is directly tied to the value of the sale. Therefore, if a sales representative has a commission of 10 percent on every sale and he or she closes a sale valued at $10,000, he will be paid $1,000 by the company. If a representative is compensated with a salary, he or she is paid a fixed compensation periodically by the company.

When Did It Begin

The art and science of selling is thousands of years old. Merchants have always induced buyers to purchase their goods. In general, each merchant took care of all of the

Selling includes all of the activities involved in completing the sale of a product or service to a buyer. By the late twentieth century a great deal of selling was done over the telephone by sales representatives. © *Tom and Dee Ann McCarthy/Corbis.*

aspects of his or her enterprise, including creating the product, marketing, selling, and accounting.

The Industrial Revolution changed business in fundamental ways. As factories developed, industries were able to produce many different products in mass quantities. Businesses began to market and sell their products to consumers who lived far away. As a result, businesses needed dedicated salespeople to cover large areas and increase the number of customers. Most of these early sales representatives were paid on a commission basis and, in general, had little allegiance to the firm where they worked. Businesses tended to focus on sales quotas and whether the correct quantity of products was shipped rather than on customers' needs and how to increase customer satisfaction.

Beginning in the 1970s the sales environment shifted significantly. Greater competition forced companies to view selling as the way to gain the trust of prospective customers and build a relationship with existing customers. Developing and maintaining customer loyalty and satisfaction became one of the central imperatives of the sales force.

More Detailed Information

Personal selling is the term for selling that relies on an interpersonal, or person to person, influence between a sales representative and a customer. It often involves the seller's promotion of the product for sale, meaning that the seller emphasizes the benefits and strengths of the product in order to increase sales. Personal selling occurs through many types of sales channels, or ways that customers may access products. Each sales channel has unique aspects that suit it to particular sales situations:

- Over-the-counter selling involves customers coming to the place where the seller is conducting business. This type of selling is appropriate for moving goods and services, such as groceries, hardware, and household appliances, that meet typical, routine needs.

- Field selling is the term for sales presentations that the seller makes face to face with customers, usually traveling to customers' homes or businesses. Field selling is common in situations in which customers need solutions to complex problems and in which there will be many phases of the sale, such as setting up a computer system for a new business.

- With inside selling, an individual salesperson also makes sales presentations directly to customers. However, inside selling avoids the expenses of travel by relying on the telephone, mail, and e-commerce (commerce conducted via the Internet) to make sales and provide product service to customers. Inside selling is appropriate for situations in which customers need to ask questions

on an ongoing basis about the product they have bought.

- Telemarketing is the term for selling that generally relies on the telephone, though it may also involve sales representatives traveling to meet customers or customers initiating calls themselves in order to obtain information and place orders. Usually telemarketing is conducted by sellers who want to reach new customers or the customers of their competition.

- With online selling, all elements of the sale are conducted via the Internet. Customers use the Internet to access product information, check prices, and place their own orders without input from an actual salesperson.

There are numerous other types of selling. A trade salesperson has a position with a manufacturer and is in charge of representing the manufacturer's products to wholesalers or retailers. The job entails visiting wholesalers or retailers, presenting information about new products, closing sales, and following through on the order delivery. Technical selling is similar to trade selling, but it differs in that the products are more technical in nature, such as chemicals as electronic equipment. The customers are other businesses that use the product. Missionary sales is a type of sales role in which a specialized salesperson promotes a company's products to potential customers. For example, a missionary salesperson working for a food manufacturer might visit grocery stores, discuss products with retailers, and help display products, without actually being responsible for the sale to consumers.

The sales process begins with identifying potential customers, called prospecting. This also involves an activity called qualifying, or finding out if a sales prospect has the need and the income to become a customer. The information collected during the prospecting and qualifying stages of the sales process is important to the next step of the sales process: the approach, or the salesperson's initial contact with a prospective customer. The information gathered during the prospecting and qualifying stages is used to customize the approach to meet the customer's needs. The seller gives a presentation describing a product's main features and benefits and relates these to the customer's need or problem.

After the seller has delivered a presentation that has expressed how the product will satisfy the buyer's needs, the buyer has an opportunity to respond with any expressions of resistance to the sale. The buyer may resist the price of the product, for example, or the seller's assessment of the buyer's needs. After the buyer and seller have satisfactorily addressed issues surrounding the sale, the communication usually ends with the salesperson asking the customer to make a decision about the purchase. If the customer does purchase the item and the

SALES QUOTA

When companies plan their growth for a period of time, such as a year, two years, or five years, they set sales goals known as sales quotas. A sales quota is a numeric goal that is assigned to a selling or marketing unit, such as a sales representative, a sales territory, a regional office, or a distributor. A sales quota helps ensure that the company's financial goals are met. Most all companies require the sale of a certain amount of goods or services over a certain period of time in order to meet the costs of making the goods or services.

A sales quota can take many forms. Among the most common sales quotas are quotas for sales activity. This type of quota measures such things as the number of sales calls in a designated span of time, such as per day or per week. Another type of sales quota is one for a dollar volume of sales, meaning that the salesperson or division must bring in a certain amount of money to meet the quota. The quota also might take the form of a unit volume, meaning that a certain number of units of product must be sold in a given time. Companies often establish some kind of monetary incentive or bonus for salespeople who meet or exceed their sale quotas.

product is delivered, the seller follows up with the customer to see if he or she will become a repeat customer. The goal of the follow-up activities is to build long-term relationships with customers.

Recent Trends

As personal selling has become more prevalent, an arrangement known as relationship selling has evolved. Relationship selling involves establishing a relationship between the seller and buyer through regular contacts over an extended time period. Another type of personal selling that has evolved in recent decades is one that promotes a product by teaming up salespeople with specialists from other areas in a business, such as technology, design, or product development. This type of sales strategy is useful in situations that require detailed knowledge of new, complex, and rapidly evolving technologies.

Another recent trend in selling is the use of computer applications to make sales functions more efficient and competitive. Sales force automation (SFA) and sales force management (SFM) are terms for computer systems that support a company's sales functions, including developing contact lists, sales proposals, and the stages of strategic sales efforts. The benefits of these systems include easy access to information about a company's inventory and its sales prospects. They also provide sellers with up-to-date information about products and help sales managers share market-research information.

These systems not only help improve the effectiveness of a sales force, they also enable a sales team to communicate with other parts of the business crucial to their work, such as finance and product development. In the most developed versions of sales force software, customers can customize their product. This kind of customization is popular within many industries, including the athletic shoe industry and the automobile industry.

$ Retailing

What It Means

Retailing is the activity of selling goods to consumers. Everything that is sold directly to customers who will use or consume a product (not resell it) is a retail good. Retailing encompasses an enormous range of retail goods, including food, gasoline, clothing, and electronics. A retailer is a merchant who sells products to customers, who will then use or consume the product. While retailing usually takes place in a shop, it can also take place in other forums, including websites.

Retailing plays a crucial role in the supply chain, the network of entities that manufacture, assemble, deliver, and sell a product. Retailing is significant because it establishes a link between the producers of the good and the consumers of the good. A retailer can provide producers with first-hand information about the success of products and the concerns and habits of consumers. For example, a supermarket is a retailer of many types of goods. Supermarket customers' purchases and returns of unsatisfactory goods allow the supermarket to gather information about goods and its customers that it can, in turn, pass on to the producers who supply the store.

Retailers play an essential role in the sale of products because they choose how to promote goods to customers. For example, a retailer may cut prices on a particular product or even offer it for free for a limited time. The retailer may also issue coupons to customers that give discounts on products. In many stores it is possible to see how the retailer is driving the sale of products by displaying them in a certain way. One popular way to promote a product is to use an end-of-aisle display (also called an endcap), which usually highlights a price cut. Another way to promote a product is to hang a sign called a "talker" on the store shelf with information about the product and its price. These retailer promotions can persuade customers to switch brands or purchase greater quantities of goods.

When Did It Begin

For many centuries, town markets, fairs, and bazaars were the main ways in which producers brought their goods to consumers. Throughout the fourteenth, fifteenth, and sixteenth centuries, many producers sold their goods directly to buyers. During this time there were established buildings where frequent markets and bazaars took place. In later centuries, fixed shops in which retailers would sell goods were established.

Retailing refers to the selling of goods and services to consumers, whether in stores, through mail-order catalogs, or over the Internet. In the modern retail market, new products sold in the United States are identified with an electronic bar code. *Photograph by Kelly A. Quin. Cengage Learning, Gale.*

The growth of retailing was closely tied to the growth in consumption in early modern societies. In China throughout the sixteenth century and most of the seventeenth century, only rulers and other elite members of society were consumers of nonessential goods, such as art or antiques. But in the seventeenth century another class of society began to emerge: merchants who lived in cities and had money to purchase nonessential items. In response, retailers not only provided essential goods (such as food) to consumers, but also cultivated shopping as a recreational activity for society's wealthy consumers.

In colonial America consumers were almost exclusively dependent on imported goods from England and Europe. Customers typically shopped in a small general store, which carried many different kinds of goods. Over time, competition increased and different types of retailers emerged. The first large-scale retailing operations, including the first department stores, appeared in the nineteenth century, when mechanized production allowed producers to create great quantities of different goods.

More Detailed Information

There are three basic types of retailers. One type, the market, is when buyers and sellers come to a common site (such as a designated street, town park, or arena) at a designated time. An example of a market retail operation is the holiday fair that operates in the month of December in many cities and towns. Craftspeople and artisans set up booths and sell their goods at this type of fair.

Shops and stores operating on an on-going basis within designated hours offer a second type of retail ex-perience. Shops and stores may be owned independently by the retailer or owned by a larger entity, such as a corporation. The retailer may produce the goods for sale, or the retailer may sell goods manufactured by another entity. In most shops and stores, customers may touch the goods for sale or try them on, as in the case of apparel (clothing) retail.

Another type of retail experience is when customers purchase goods through the mail or a website or by telephone. In this case customers forego the chance to handle or try on goods for the convenience of ordering them from wherever they are. This type of retail works better for some goods, such as music and books, than it does for other goods, such as shoes or cars.

Regardless of the type of retailing establishment, retailers must have a retailing strategy in place before doing business. The main component of the retail strategy is the product and a clear reason for marketing it. The retailer also must have a clear idea of the quantity of the product he or she wants to sell. For example, if a large department store wants to market bed linens to consumers, it will likely order a much larger amount of bedding from its suppliers than the amount a retailer of a small, boutique housewares store will order. Store location is another important part of strategy. Often retailers of high-end products vie for space in exclusive shopping districts. When a retailer chooses to sell products online, there are advantages and disadvantages to not having an actual store. Pricing and marketing appeal are other important components of the retail strategy. The price of a good may be the most important element of the product for many consumers. Marketing appeal is how the retailer appeals to customers, whether through convenience, shopping atmosphere, customer service, or other means.

There are several different types of retail establishments. A specialty store sells only one or a few kinds of merchandise. Specialty stores are often owned independently. A pet store that specializes in rare birds, a gardening store that specializes in roses, and a clothing store that specializes in Italian apparel are all examples of specialty stores.

A department store is a large store that is organized into different departments, such as home furnishings, men's clothing, and kitchen appliances. Department stores are usually owned by a corporation. Compared with a smaller retailer, a department store can efficiently promote a wider range of products and services to customers.

A discount store offers goods at discounted prices. A retailer can discount prices by providing coupons or by reducing the price of goods. A discount store may carry name brands (or brands from known manufacturers) or generic brands.

A chain store is an organized group of retail outlets that are owned and managed by a central entity. Usually chain stores are able to offer lower costs on goods

SHOPPING MALLS

The traditional bazaar or market, in which many merchants and traders offered a variety of wares in one location, has a modern equivalent: the shopping mall. In today's society, the shopping mall supports retailers of many different types, from clothing to entertainment to housewares to food. The first shopping malls developed in the mid-1950s and were known as shopping centers. Typically a large retailer, such a grocery store or a variety store, was the center of the shopping center, and there were smaller stores in a row of storefronts. The first shopping center had two department stores on either end of a large, two-story mall (an open passageway) that enclosed a court. Built in 1956 outside of Minneapolis, Minnesota, the Southland Mall was the first shopping mall to create an enclosed space for shoppers. This physically secured type of mall was such a success that it inspired hundreds of others like it to be built in the following decades, both in suburban areas as well as in revitalized urban areas. In addition to shopping, the mall became a place for socializing, going to the movies, and dining out, especially for young people. In recent years, however, shopping malls have suffered a decline because of the growing popularity of large discount stores and the increasing preference of customers to shop online.

because the purchasing and marketing are done on a large scale, which reduces the cost to each outlet. Chain stores include many fast-food restaurants and large booksellers.

Recent Trends

In recent years consumers have been presented with many new ways to buy goods and services. The biggest innovation in retailing was the introduction of online retailing. "Dot-com" retailers (companies that market their products or services through a website) made great profits with this new approach to reaching consumers.

Successful online retailers, such as Amazon.com, do not simply put up websites, they strategically work to improve their customers' shopping experience. Online companies carefully track their customers' online experiences to provide easier navigation and more relevant information. They create sophisticated customer databases and use them to customize e-mail messages to send to consumers.

One of the biggest challenges in online retailing is maintaining customers. Successful online retailers use various strategies to keep their customers from shopping elsewhere. For example, they might design special services and promotional offerings, such as giving valued customers discounts, providing phone representatives to answer questions about products, or sending customers advance notice of new products, sales, and store events.

$ E-Commerce

What It Means

E-commerce, or electronic commerce, is the conducting of business through electronic means (typically computer systems and the Internet) rather than through traditional face-to-face, mail-order, or telephone transactions. There are two major categories of e-commerce transactions: business-to-business and business-to-consumer. A business-to-business transaction occurs when one business makes a purchase from another business, for example, when a store manager orders merchandise from a supplier. A person who runs a landscaping business would likely purchase more peat moss by going to his supplier's website and entering a code to access his online account (the record of his purchases and payments to the supplier). The landscaper would request more supplies by clicking on the proper links and icons, the fees would be automatically deducted from his business's bank account, and the supplier would ship the peat moss to him.

An electronic business-to-consumer transaction occurs when a customer goes to a business's website to purchase goods or services. For example, many people buy books and DVDs at Amazon.com rather than going to a traditional store to purchase these items. Most business-to-consumer transactions require the consumer to visit the company's website and place items in an online "shopping cart" (by clicking on computer images or links that signal a request to purchase an item). The customer "checks out" by providing credit-card and mailing information in the appropriate boxes. There are, however, other types of business-to-consumer e-commerce. For instance, people can arrange to pay bills electronically. If a customer were to set up a bill payment plan with his or her telephone company, the phone company would automatically deduct the amount of the phone bill from the customer's checking account at the end of each month.

When Did It Begin

Charting the beginnings of electronic commerce depends on how one defines the term *electronic*. In the broadest sense of the definition, electronic commerce was first made possible in 1844 when Samuel Morse (1791–1872) invented the telegraph. By 1858 stock brokers (agents who negotiate purchases and sales of stock) in Europe were telegraphing orders to buy and sell stock (shares of ownership in corporations) to brokers in North America. Almost 20 years later, in 1877, Western Union, the world's largest telegraph company, arranged for a total of $2.5 million in electronic financial transactions.

What contemporary American consumers normally consider e-commerce (the buying and selling of goods over the Internet) was made possible in 1994, when the World Wide Web became available to large numbers of

E-commerce is the nickname for electronic commerce, which refers to the practice of buying and selling over the Internet. Meg Whitman, CEO of eBay, is pictured here in 2001 with Steve Ballmer, CEO of Microsoft, after the two companies announced a new strategic alliance. *AP Images.*

people. Amazon.com and eBay, two of the largest e-commerce websites, were both created in 1995. Amazon.com originally sold books online but has since expanded; it sells a wide range of merchandise that includes clothes, appliances, auto parts, computer software, and home appliances. eBay is an auction website, which means that sellers put products up for sale and potential buyers bid against each other for the products. When a transaction is complete, the buyer and seller make arrangements for shipping the merchandise. eBay makes money by charging the seller in the transaction a fee for facilitating the sale.

More Detailed Information

Most market analysts (people who analyze trends in the economy) agree that the success of e-commerce depends primarily on consumers' faith in the technology that conducts the transaction. This was true even before before the Internet was first used to sell products. In the 1980s automated teller machines (ATMs), which offer another form of e-commerce, became commonplace in the United States. These machines had taken a long time to catch on in this country, however. The first ATM was installed in 1939 in New York City but was removed after just six months because the customers of the City Bank of New York were reluctant to use it. The next ATM is believed to have been installed in the late 1960s in London. This time bank clients gradually came to trust the technology and by the mid-1970s ATMs, sponsored mostly by Lloyd's Bank, were being installed throughout the United Kingdom.

By comparison, the general population developed faith in web-based technology and online purchasing quickly, taking approximately five years to grow comfortable with Internet transactions. Several factors restricted the early growth of online markets, however. First, many customers were not comfortable entering their credit-card numbers onto a website to be transported to the company via the Internet. These consumers worried that hackers (people who gain illegal access to other people's and businesses' computer systems) could use the Internet to break into a company's computer files and steal all of the credit-card numbers stored in a database there. This problem was largely resolved by 1998 with the development of a secure encryption system, which is a very complex method of scrambling, or

EBAY

eBay Inc., an online shopping and auction website, was founded by Pierre Omidyar on September 3, 1995, in San Jose, California. Omidyar originally launched the business as AuctionWeb. The first item sold on AuctionWeb was Omidyar's broken laser pointer, which was purchased for $14.83 by a man who claimed to collect broken laser pointers. AuctionWeb became eBay in September 1997. Omidyar had hoped to change the company name to Echo Bay, which was also the name of his technology consulting business, but the domain name (the part of the website address after "http://www") echobay.com had already been taken by a gold-mining company. There are a multitude of items available on eBay, merchandise ranging from seemingly useless gadgets to expensive cars. Anything that is not illegal or listed by eBay as a restricted item may be advertised and sold on the website.

encoding, credit-card information so that only the vendor's computer system can read it.

Though encryption is a highly technical process that is difficult for the average consumer to understand, it is relatively easy for a consumer to know whether or not his credit-card information will be encrypted. Normally, the initial portion of a website's address reads "http://." When a customer begins the check-out portion of online shopping, however, the initial part of the web address should read "https://." The added "s" indicates that all data entered onto that web page will be encrypted. Even though this secure technology existed in 1998, consumer purchasing statistics indicate that the average consumer did not become comfortable with online transactions until 2001-02.

Another factor that slowed the growth of online shopping was that the average consumer did not have access to web technology in the 1990s. According to most reports, about 40 million people across the globe were connected to the Internet by the end of 1996. That number grew to 605 million people in 2002. Customers were also reluctant to give up the social aspects of shopping, such as gathering in a common area (a mall or large store) with large numbers of people and speaking with check-out clerks. Perhaps the most important obstacle to online shopping was the fact that consumers generally want to have their products or services immediately after they make a purchase, which is frequently impossible when buying online.

Recent Trends

By 1996 Internet use was doubling every 100 days, and business people viewed the World Wide Web as a remarkable new opportunity to reach more customers. At that time some economists predicted that business-to-consumer e-commerce would be a $300 billion dollar industry by the early 2000s. Thus between 1998 and 2000, the number of dotcom companies (businesses that sell goods and services exclusively on the Internet rather than in traditional brick-and-mortar, or actual, stores) increased drastically. Two examples of online-only or dotcom enterprises were Pets.com, which sold pet food, and Webvan, which sold groceries. In the spring of 2000, the e-commerce boom ended, primarily because many of the companies attempted to grow too large too quickly, and a general recession followed, lasting through 2001 followed. Many of the dotcoms, including Pets.com and Webvan, went out of business.

Since 2002 e-commerce has gradually increased, but the market has changed. Whereas before the recession there were numerous businesses like Pets.com and Webvan, there are now fewer enterprises that sell merchandise exclusively on the Internet. Most large brick-and-mortar businesses, however, such as Barnes & Noble (a bookstore) and Macy's (a department store) offer online shopping. In addition many medium-sized and small local businesses conduct sales online as well as offering a traditional in-store shopping experience.

WEB MANAGEMENT

What It Means

Web management refers to all of the activities included in the process of posting and maintaining a website on the World Wide Web. Though many individuals and businesses create and manage their own sites, the majority of websites are professionally designed and maintained by technology firms; this is because every phase of website development requires technical expertise.

The web management process begins with the design phase. At this point in a business relationship between a client and a technology firm, the client meets with the graphic designer to present his or her company's logo and colors and to discuss the image the company hopes to portray on its new website. In addition to creating a site that properly represents the company, the graphic designer has to build a navigation system that makes the site easy to use for all web visitors. The navigation system refers to the series of links that gives users access to the subpages (the pages other than the main page, or home page, on a website; users bring subpages up on the computer screen by clicking on certain words and images on the site) containing the information they need. On an ideally designed website, users are only one or two clicks away from the information they need at any given point during the visit to the website.

After designing a visually appropriate, easy-to-navigate site, the graphic designer gives a mock-up (a visual model or picture of the new site) to a programmer, who writes the code that will present this material on the Internet. After the website has been designed and the code has been written, the site needs to be hosted on a web server and maintained. The web server is the computer that holds the website and transmits the code that displays the website on the end user's computer screen. Maintenance involves posting new words and images on the website whenever the company needs to update the information on the site.

When Did It Begin

The origin of the World Wide Web can be traced back to 1980, when London native Tim Berners-Lee (b. 1955) created the first version of hypertext (the words and images that change appearance by becoming bold, changing color, and sometimes appearing underlined when users move the cursor over them, a feature that indicates to users that they can access more information by clicking on these words). At the time Berners-Lee was working in a physics laboratory, and he drafted the code for this clickable computer language so that the physicists in his research group could share information more easily. Berners-Lee's code, though it was only used in this small community, was the basis for HTML (hypertext markup language), the computer language that is most commonly used to present text and pictures on the World Wide Web.

When the Internet first became widely available to the public in 1995, website development and management became one of the fastest growing industries in the world. Because of the early success of such online stores as Amazon.com and eBay, thousands of other businesses wanted to use the Internet to market and sell their goods and services. In 1995 there were approximately 1,000 companies in the United States that designed and hosted websites for clients. Within only 10 years there were 30,000 such firms; by that time most businesses considered a website a necessary part of their operations.

More Detailed Information

A number of technical terms associated with web management are easier to understand than they may sound. People hoping to do more than just surf the web (visit websites to examine the information there) need to master this vocabulary in order to follow the conversations among people who work in the field of computer technology. To begin, a web browser is a software application (a program that enables a computer to perform specific tasks) that allows a user to view websites on a computer. Many people who use the Internet access the World Wide Web with a web browser called Internet

Web management refers to the various tasks involved with creating, maintaining, and updating an Internet web site, often done by an outside firm. Here the founders of www.800hosting.com, a Dallas-based web management company, review their own web page. *AP Images.*

PRICELINE.COM

Priceline.com was one of the most popular e-commerce websites in the late 1990s and early 2000s. The site sells airline tickets and performs other services, such as making rental car and hotel reservations, for travelers looking for discount rates.

Priceline.com's former methodology was unique and captivating. It was called the Name Your Own Price system. Users who accessed the website were asked to submit their e-mail address, credit card information, travel dates, and the price they wanted to pay for their airline tickets, car rental, hotel, or some combination of those. After accepting the information, Priceline.com consulted its database for vendors willing to sell at those prices during that time period and sent an e-mail notifying customers of whether their request had been satisfied. If Priceline.com could satisfy the request, the client was required to make the purchase, with no option to cancel. In its early days Priceline.com often found irresistibly cheap airfares for clients, which made their customers quite happy and made the company quite popular. There was a hitch, however: customers had to use the companies Priceline.com found for them and travel according to the itinerary Priceline.com set for them. Airline customers, for example, often had to fly at inconvenient times and endure long layovers in exchange for the discount prices.

Priceline.com still offers the Name Your Own Price option, but relatively few customers use it, and it is no longer the only way they do business. The website now offers a more traditional web interface in which customers enter their travel schedules and select from a range of vendors and prices. Airline customers, for example, can enter their departure and return dates, then see a list of airlines and price options. Those customers can select the flight they wish to take rather than being forced to accept the flight that Priceline.com finds for them.

Explorer. All users have to do to get online is to click the Internet Explorer icon on their computer screen.

Connectivity (the ability to communicate with other computers) is a term used to talk about the technology that transmits or carries the data from the web server to the user's computer screen. When a user clicks the Internet Explorer icon to open the web browser, the computer sends a signal, often through a telephone line, to a web server that transmits the HTML (coded instructions) for displaying the web page on the user's computer. After opening the browser, the user will see a website, such as Google. The user can then access another website by entering the appropriate web address in the field at the top of the page. The length of time it takes for the user's computer to present the new site depends on the quality of the user's connectivity. The science involved in transmitting the website's programming code from the web server to the user's computer screen is quite complicated. Average users, when choosing an internet service provider (such as AOL or EarthLink), only want to know how fast the connection will allow them to load a website and how much they will have to pay per month to be able to connect to the Internet. Many individual users today have a DSL (digital subscriber line) connection to the Internet, which posts information within seconds after the user enters a web address in the field at the top of his screen or clicks a link on a website.

In general there are two types of websites a user can visit. The first is called a static site. A static site displays information when a user clicks a link, and it additionally allows the user to e-mail the organization sponsoring the site. Other than this, however, the user cannot interact with the company through the website. A dynamic site, on the other hand, offers the user an opportunity to conduct business with or interact with the company via the Internet. For example, on some dynamic websites users can purchase merchandise. Such a website is called an e-commerce site. Other dynamic websites allow visitors to post their opinions in writing and to read the opinions of others. This type of site is called a blog, which is short for web log.

Recent Trends

Though the web development industry remains quite large and profitable, more and more individuals are learning how to manage their own websites. Such software programs as Microsoft FrontPage and Adobe Dreamweaver allow computer users to build websites without knowing how to write HTML code. With Dreamweaver, for example, users need only browse through their files for the picture they want to display on their website and click the appropriate icon on the Dreamweaver command menu; the software will automatically write the code that presents the picture on the website. Given the ease of developing and maintaining a website with these software programs, many small businesses now design their own sites. Medium and large businesses often use web development firms, but they also usually purchase what is called content management software, which allows them to change the content of the site (the text and pictures) without consulting the web development firm. Since the year 2000, web development has become less costly. Prices for design software and hosting fees have gone down, and more intricate applications such as e-commerce and e-newsletter software are also less expensive.

❖ Public Relations

What It Means

Public relations involves building relationships with the public. For-profit businesses and nonprofit groups rely on public relations to communicate with their customers, investors, suppliers, local communities, and employees. Public relations (PR) helps an organization let the public know who the organization is, what it does and why, and what is important about it.

The goal of public relations is to build support for the organization by giving its audience ways to respond and interact with it. All organizations have reputations to protect and a public image to maintain. For example, when an oil company's tanker runs ashore and causes damage to the environment, the company will then rely on its public relations department to improve its image in the public eye. Public relations is both a science and an art: it involves delivering accurate, consistent, and timely messages as well as conveying the right message to the right audience.

Whether they are major multinational corporations or small businesses, organizations of all sizes rely on public relations. Most large and midsize companies have their own public relations departments. Smaller businesses may employ their own public relations director, integrate public relations activities into the roles of managers, or hire public relations firms or consultants to handle public relations activities.

Public relations is a multifaceted field, involving several different areas of focus. Media relations involves working with the news outlets that cover the organization or industry. Community relations involves participating in the local business community and creating positive attitudes about the organization in the community. This may involve sponsoring local events, such as concerts or athletic events, or supporting public projects, such as park improvements or the construction of a new sports stadium. Government affairs involves communicating with legislators and government groups on behalf of the organization. The financial relations aspect of public relations involves maintaining relationships with regulatory agencies, industry analysts, investors, and shareholders. Internal communications develops the relationship between the organization and its own employees. Trade relations deals with the relationships between the organization and other firms in the industry.

When Did It Begin

Business and its role in public life developed rapidly in the eighteenth century, and by the early nineteenth century U.S. businesses needed formalized public relations campaigns to help communicate their objectives to the public. Big business was often controversial in the eyes of some groups, and public relations attempted to show business practices in a positive light. Many journalists, skilled at communicating targeted messages to specific audiences, were hired in the new field of public relations.

A public relations department provides information about a company or other organization to the public. An important goal of a public relations employee is to protect the organization's reputation and public image. © *Martha Tabor/Working Images Photographs.*

WHAT IS A PUBLIC RELATIONS PLAN?

A public relations plan is the first step in starting a public relations campaign. Whether the goal is to inform customers about a new product or to improve a company's public image after its president is convicted of a crime, the public relations campaign can only be successful if it has a clear plan from the outset. The public relations plan must clearly identify the goals of the campaign. For example, the goal of a public relations campaign may be to increase sales to a certain amount or to introduce a new product to retailers and customers.

The public relations campaign also must identify how the business will be perceived by the public as a result of the campaign. For example, an accounting firm might want to be seen as the most convenient and friendly accounting firm in town. Once this goal is determined, the public relations materials can better express the message of the campaign.

A public relations plan also defines the specific strategies of the campaign. The campaign may rely on the media, its employees, or an event to help communicate its message. The company's public relations team may schedule a press conference to provide representatives from television, radio, and print media with the chance to ask questions.

The first public relations firm was opened in 1904 by Ivy Ledbetter Lee (1877–1934), a former newspaper journalist. Lee began to recognize the power of public relations when he represented coal miners and later a Pennsylvania railroad. He understood how alerting the press of important business events could help the public better understand organizations and their goals.

Edward L. Bernays (1891–1995), the nephew of psychoanalyst Sigmund Freud, also played an important role in shaping early public relations through his work with a wide range of organizations. In the early 1900s Bernays was a publicist (someone who handles public relations for an organization) for theater productions in New York City and later helped the U.S. government build public support for World War I. Bernays also developed public relations strategies for such large businesses as soap manufacturer Proctor & Gamble and cigarette manufacturer Lucky Strike. Bernays helped these companies reach the public with special events, customer contests, gallery exhibits, and department-store window displays.

More Detailed Information

Public relations can help an organization meet a range of different goals. It can help a young organization build a presence and establish credibility in its community. It can help an established organization remain aware of what is important to its customers and stakeholders through customer surveys or shareholder meetings. Public rela-

tions can also provide the public with educational materials that explain complex products and services. If an organization goes through a significant transition and changes its products, services, or mission, the organization may use a public relations firm to communicate these changes to those who will be affected.

In general, a corporation relies on public relations to help increase its sales through such activities as media events that focus on the development or launch of a new product. Many nonprofit organizations, such as schools, social service agencies, hospitals, and environmental and arts groups, use public relations to develop and convey a certain image of the organization. All nonprofit organizations need to raise money on a regular basis, and their public relations campaigns can help them communicate the organization's mission and raise funds. Politicians rely heavily on public relations to help them run election campaigns and present their term in office in a positive light. Many public figures in contemporary life, from star athletes to prominent entertainers, rely on public relations to shape the public's perception of them.

Probably the most important aspect of public relations is interacting with the media. Businesses often put together public relations materials for the media in an organized format called a press kit. A typical press kit provides information on the organization's history and background; information on its products and services, including such information as technical information and specifications; biographical sketches of the organization's important leaders or executives; and contact information for those employees at the organization in charge of media communications.

A "media contact" is a person within an organization's public relations team who takes all initial calls from reporters, writers, and editors. The media contact may set up an interview between the press person and someone within the organization, such as the company president or the developer of a new product. In a large company, the company spokesperson may speak to the media. This person is responsible for speaking intelligently and simply about an organization or a product, what it is, and why it is significant.

When working with the media, public relations professionals may target specific reporters or media outlets. For example, if an organization is developing software for doctors in Detroit, Michigan, the organization's publicists would contact Detroit newspaper reporters who cover technology and medicine. The organization's publicists would also contact television and radio stations that have programs on medicine or technology and send press kits to trade magazines and websites related to medicine and technology.

If an organization has specific news to announce, it sends out what is called a press release to the media covering the organization or industry. A written document that is usually no more than two pages long, a press release contains the newsworthy information about the organization, its people, its products, and a specific newsworthy event. The goal of the press release is to present the media with opportunities to write about the organization. Press releases may be created to announce new products, new hires, new partnerships with other firms, funding or awards received, or major sales or results from a finished project.

Businesses often use public relations to tie their product or service to something else that is happening in the news, the community, or the society at large. For example, if a city opens a new park with public tennis courts, a local sports store may contact the city's newspaper to describe how its tennis equipment can be used at the park's facilities. Or an education company that creates standardized tests for students may set up a booth at an educational trade fair to communicate with educators about its product.

Recent Trends

An important trend in public relations is presenting information to the public and specific audiences through the Internet and other new technologies, such as satellite feeds. Many companies post their press kits and other public relations material on their websites. Press releases are sent by mass e-mail and may include links to related stories and sound and video clips.

In recent years the public relations industry has relied heavily on opinion polling and focus groups. Opinion polls are surveys conducted by telephone and in-person interviews in which people are asked their opinions about a product, a service, or even a person. Large-scale public campaigns, such as campaigns for the U.S. presidency, rely heavily on such opinion polls. Focus groups help organizations conduct research by presenting small groups of people with a new product or service and asking them questions about it. Generally, focus groups show public relations professionals what their customers' attitudes and habits are and how their customers react to a product or service. This information can help companies shape their communications about the product or service to their audience.

Money Management

$ Overview: Accounting

What It Means

All businesses and organizations must keep accurate and current accounts of their financial information so they can make sound business decisions. The process of analyzing and interpreting financial information is called accounting. Accounting work is conducted by professional accountants, who are trained in statistics, economics, accounting law, and other disciplines. Accounting includes bookkeeping, which involves the creation of records and documents that show financial activity. An accountant may also prepare the information that is needed to file a federal income tax return (a report that shows the U.S. government the income a person or business has received over the course of a year so that the person or business can pay taxes to the government).

Accounting provides an organization with the information it needs so that the organization's managers can responsibly decide how to use resources and set realistic goals. Accountants analyze records, estimates, and other information and communicate specific information to different audiences. For example, an accountant may give a manager information that helps the manager decide which ventures will be affordable for the business. Accounting done for the internal use of an organization is called managerial accounting. Accounting also serves the purpose of informing external parties, such as government groups, shareholders (people who own part of the company), and the public, about the financial health of an organization. Accounting done for external parties is called financial reporting.

For-profit businesses as well as government and nonprofit organizations use accountants. Accounting within governmental and nonprofit organizations, called nonbusiness accounting, covers the financial record-keeping and analysis for such organizations as independent schools or camps, hospitals, universities and colleges, and trade and government organizations.

Accountants also help individuals review their personal finances for various purposes. For example, an individual who inherits money or land might hire an accountant to review how the executor (the person assigned the duty of carrying out the instructions of the deceased person) has managed the finances of the deceased person. Individuals involved in a financial partnership, such as a small business, may hire an accountant to analyze each individual's financial responsibilities within the partnership.

When Did It Begin

The practice of bookkeeping dates back thousands of years to when ancient traders and merchants began keeping records of their financial transactions. The earliest examples of what is known as double-entry bookkeeping date from fourteenth-century Italy. In double-entry bookkeeping, which is an important part of modern accounting, each transaction is shown as a transfer from a source account (as a debit) to a destination account (as a credit).

During the Industrial Revolution, new accounting techniques were developed to address the mass production of goods and factory-based operations. Business practices grew increasingly more sophisticated during the nineteenth century, and the profession of accounting evolved to respond to the complexities of industry and corporate practice. The first public accounting agencies were opened in the late nineteenth century, and licensing requirements for accountants were established in the early twentieth century.

In the late twentieth century computer-based accounting grew prevalent. With the use of sophisticated data-processing software, accountants can present useful financial information to a wide range of parties who need this information to make business decisions, including managers, business owners, employees, customers, and government authorities.

More Detailed Information

The field of accounting includes several divisions: auditing, taxation, financial-statement analysis, and managerial accounting. An inspection of the accuracy and validity of financial statements is called an audit. An audit is usually conducted by an auditor who is trained in accounting. Large organizations sometimes employ full-time auditors to maintain the ongoing accuracy of the firm's accounting information. Accountants are often responsible for providing a firm's income tax returns, which can involve extensive work with the firm's financial data as well as sufficient knowledge of corporate tax laws. Accountants who specialize in taxation are often employed by businesses to file annual tax returns. Financial-statement analysis is the process of using financial information to analyze the performance of a firm. Accountants who specialize in financial-statement analysis develop measures of a firm's performance as it relates to other firms in the same industry. Accountants involved in managerial accounting compile the data that firms need to plan and make decisions. They examine the various costs of operating the firm, ensure the firm is operating within certain standards or rules, and create reports for the managers of the firm to use.

Accountants use two important financial tools: the balance sheet and the income statement. Sometimes known as the statement of condition, the balance sheet shows a company's total assets (everything that the company owns), its liabilities (the amount of money the company is obligated to pay; its debts), and the value of shareholders' equity (the amount of assets owned by a company's shareholders). It is known as a balance sheet because the total assets must equal the liabilities combined with the shareholders' equity. Stated another way, assets minus liabilities equals the shareholders' equity.

Whereas the balance sheet shows a picture of a company's condition at a given point in time, the income statement illustrates financial activity over the course of a specified time period, such as a quarter of a year or a full year. Sometimes an income statement is referred to as a profit-and-loss statement because the statement shows sales transactions or other revenue-generating activities as well as expenses or costs to the company for producing goods, such as costs for raw materials, facilities costs, and labor costs. Essentially, the income statement reviews the revenues and expenses for the company over a designated time frame. It also reflects any gains and losses from assets sold or acquired.

Accounting refers to the process of keeping track of financial activities. Most businesses use computers to make the accounting process faster and more efficient. *Photograph by Kelly A. Quin. Cengage Learning, Gale.*

The balance sheet and the income statement play important roles in bookkeeping. Bookkeeping involves recording transactions in a journal. Most organizations use a double-entry system, in which both the debit and the credit side of the transaction are recorded. All of the information entered in the journal is also put into a book known as a ledger. When the bookkeeper transfers information from the journal to the ledger, this is known as posting. The ledger thoroughly illustrates the organization's finances, and subsidiary ledgers illustrate specific accounts. For example, all the wages a company pays its employees may be shown in the ledger, and a subsidiary ledger may record each employee's wages.

The information in ledgers forms the basis for the financial analysis that accountants perform. An accountant will take the information bookkeepers provide and prepare what are called adjustments. For example, an adjustment might show the cost of a piece of machinery as an expense spread out over the time it will be used by the company. An accountant makes adjustments before he or she prepares the balance sheet, the income statement, and other financial statements. These statements review the balances in the various accounts of the company.

Because accountants play a large role in managing and communicating the health of businesses, they are often relied on as decision makers. All accountants adhere to a general set of assumptions and principals that affect the decisions they make. For example, the disclosure principle requires that the financial statement an accountant creates provides the most useful amount of information relating to the firm at the time, meaning that no information is excluded in order to mislead the statements' readers.

When accountants provide financial information to those inside a firm, they do not have to adhere to any regulations other than their responsibility to provide guidance to the firm and to rely on fundamental accounting concepts. However, numerous regulatory bodies set rules for accountants whose work is reported to the public. State governments are responsible for licensing certified public accountants (CPAs), who operate by a set of standardized principals of accounting. The U.S. government agency known as the Securities and Exchange Commission (SEC) regulates the public trading of stocks and bonds. The Internal Revenue Service (IRS) regulates taxation and collects taxes from businesses, nonprofits, and other organizations.

Recent Trends

In the early part of the twenty-first century the accounting profession came under intense scrutiny because of financial scandals within large corporations resulting from accounting fraud. Arthur Anderson LLP was the accounting firm responsible for auditing the financial records of the Enron Corporation, a Texas energy company. Through its accounting firm Enron led its investors and the public

CERTIFIED PUBLIC ACCOUNTANTS (CPAS)

Individuals who wish to make their careers in accounting must go through a rigorous process of preparation and training in order to be granted the title of Certified Public Accountant (CPA) by the American Institute of Certified Public Accountants. The designation of CPA shows that there are professional standards, licensing requirements, and a code of professional ethics in place in the accounting industry. Generally, a CPA must be licensed to be allowed to review and give opinions about financial statements. As a result of their extensive training and depth of expertise, many CPAs are sought after not only for their accounting skills but also for their general knowledge of business.

In order to become a CPA, an accountant must meet the requirements of the state in which he or she wants to work. This means that he or she must successfully complete accounting courses, pass the Uniform CPA Examination, and work for a specified amount of time before he or she can become a CPA. Although the specific requirements vary by state, basic requirements for taking the CPA exam include a completed undergraduate degree in accounting and a certain number of advanced courses in the field. The CPA exam is a two-day exam covering the topics of auditing; financial accounting and reporting; accounting and reporting: taxation, managerial, and governmental and not-for-profit organizations; and business law and professional responsibilities.

to believe that it had achieved record profits, when it had actually lost hundreds of millions of dollars from 1997 to 2001. Employees at Arthur Anderson LLP were caught shredding (destroying) documents relating to the Enron case and charged with obstructing justice in 2002.

Another corporate scandal involving the telecommunications corporation WorldCom shed further light on the crucial role of accounting in business. WorldCom's accountants created false financial reports that excluded reports of billions of dollars in expenses and showed that the company had been extremely profitable. In fact, the company had lost $1 billion over 15 months.

The result of these scandals was the passage of the Public Company Accounting Reform and Investor Protection Act of 2002, which created a board authorized to punish accounting firms that report on companies' finances in misleading ways. The law also gave the board the legal ability to perform annual audits of accounting firms who work for large companies.

As a result of large corporate scandals and the growing interdependence of corporations in a global economy, many analysts and accounting industry leaders have called for the adoption of a set of global accounting rules. Such a set of rules would make it easier to evaluate financial information about different companies, no matter where they were located. Established in 1973, the nonprofit International Accounting Standards Committee (IASC) developed a set of international accounting standards, which many companies worldwide now voluntarily use.

$ Cash Flow

What It Means

Cash flow is the movement of ready money, or cash, into and out of a company over a specified time. Cash flow can be calculated for a company as a whole or for a particular project within the company. A statement of cash flow is a document that is issued periodically by a company and that identifies the important business activities that generate inflows and outflows of cash for the company. The document helps to reveal how the company is using the financial resources it has available and how well it is able to pay its bills. In other words, the cash flow statement can provide a short-term picture of the company's overall financial health.

When a company receives more money than it spends during a specified time period, the company is said to be cash flow positive. When the company spends more than it receives, it is said to be cash flow negative. A company that keeps its cash flow positive over time shows that its employees and lenders can be reliably paid. A company that has negative cash flow is in danger of losing the ability to keep up its day-to-day operations; if the negative cash flow is sustained, the company risks going bankrupt (being declared legally unable to pay its debts).

The cash flow statement is the standard financial accounting document for reporting a company's cash flow. It reveals the sources and uses of the company's cash by putting each cash receipt or cash payment under one

Cash flow refers to the amount of cash going into or out of a business during a given time period. It is an important measure of a company's overall financial health. *Photograph by Kelly A. Quin. Cengage Learning, Gale.*

of three main sections: operating activities, investing activities, and financing activities. Operations refer to the company's core business activities such as the marketing, sales, and production of its goods or services. Investments refer to such activities as the purchase or sale of an asset such as a building or manufacturing equipment. Financing refers to such activities as the receipt or payment of loans or the issuing of company stock.

The cash flow statement is one of three major documents that a company prepares to reveal the state of its financial situation. The other two are the balance sheet and the income statement. The balance sheet describes the company's assets (for example, cash, inventory, land and buildings, and long-term investments) and liabilities (for example, bills, wages, and taxes to be paid) on a specified date and indicates where they have come from. The income statement, calculated for a particular time period, shows the sources of a company's net income (the difference between the income derived from its goods and services and the expenses it had while that income was being generated).

When Did It Begin

Contemporary cash flow statements trace their origin to statements prepared by American companies in the 1950s and 1960s. These documents, which listed the sources of any uses of the company's funds, were basically records of the different increases and reductions of the company's balance sheet items. In 1961 an accounting research study conducted by the Accounting Principals Board (APB), then the authoritative body for accounting principles in the United States, recommended that accountants develop a funds statement for recording cash flow that would be required from every company as part of its annual financial reporting. The name of this cash flow statement became the Statement of Source and Application of Funds, and most businesses adopted the standard form of it. In 1984 the Financial Accounting Standards Board (FASB), the successor to the APB, recommended that a statement of cash flow become a part of the primary financial statements for every company and that the statement show cash receipts categorized by their sources and cash payments categorized by their major uses.

More Detailed Information

As mentioned, the cash flow statement is an indicator of the performance of a company or of one of its projects over a certain time period. In addition, the statement shows if a company is liquid; that is, whether it can quickly and easily convert (liquidate) assets to cash. Although a company may be generating a profit through strong sales of its products, it still may have trouble liquidating assets when a demand for cash arises, such as when its bills are due. A factory, for example, is an asset that is hard to convert into cash because it is usually time-consuming to sell. On the other hand, stock certificates are more easily and quickly convertible to cash because they can be sold within hours if necessary.

The cash flow statement presents each major source and use of cash, listing the transactions that directly affect the cash account over a certain time period. It answers the questions "Where did cash come from?" and "Where did cash go?" Therefore, it explains the business activities that resulted in an increase or decrease in cash. In a company's first year of operation, the beginning cash balance is $0. At the end of its first year, its net increase or decrease in cash is its net cash flow (cash receipts minus cash payments) from operating, investing, and financing activities.

The operating section of the cash flow statement includes those transactions that relate to wages, purchases of merchandise, and other operating activities including the company's sale of goods and services. This section also identifies cash paid for the resources that are used to make goods and services. For instance, if a dairy farmer purchases 10 dairy cows one year, the expense for the cows falls under the operating section. Having a positive cash flow in the operations section of the statement is important, because a negative cash flow is an indication that the company has not made a profit for the time period of the statement. Generally, if a company remains unprofitable for an extended time, it goes out of business.

The investing section of the cash flow statement includes cash transactions associated with the purchase of long-term assets and financial investments. This section shows the cash flow involved when fixed assets (which are tangible pieces of property, such as buildings or equipment, that a business keeps for a fairly long time) are purchased or sold. Investing cash flow is simply the difference between the amount the company paid for long-term assets and the amount it received from selling such assets.

The finance section of the cash flow statement includes cash transactions between a company and its shareholders (individuals or firms that have invested money in the business) or its creditors (individuals or firms to which the company owes money). These transactions relate to the borrowing or repaying of debt and investments, such as stock. If the company pays dividends (shares of the company's profits) or makes other cash distributions to shareholders, these activities fall into the finance section. Cash flow in this section is affected positively when, for instance, the company either borrows cash by taking on more debt or sells stock to shareholders. It is affected negatively when the company pays off some of its debt or pays dividends to shareholders.

Recent Trends

In the past several decades one strategy available to a company to improve the public's perception of its cash flow has been to purchase some of its own stock shares from the marketplace. This is sometimes called a share buyback or a stock repurchase. By using its own cash to

---

CASH FLOW AND NET INCOME

There are crucial distinctions between cash flow and net income, also known as bottom-line earnings, which is the profit or the loss that a company shows after all the costs and expenses are subtracted from the total receipts, or revenue. A company includes on its income statement the revenue that it earns when it delivers the good or service to its customer, which is not necessarily when the company is actually paid in cash. The customer, for example, may have promised to pay at a later time. Therefore, even if the net income statement shows a profit and the business has technically made money, "cash is king," as the saying goes, because only when the money has been collected can it be spent. A company that cannot take care of its bills runs the risk of going bankrupt (being legally declared unable to pay its debts).

The state of a company's cash flow is also important to those outside of company operations. Investors care more about cash than about revenue (that is, more about the company's ability to pay its bills than about its income), and stock prices on the market are set as result of the amount of cash the company has or can easily get when needed.

---

buy shares, the company is, in a sense, investing in itself. Because there now are fewer shares (claims on the company's profits) in the marketplace, the value of the remaining shares (known as the "earnings per share") increases because the profits are distributed over a smaller number of shares.

When a company buys its shares on the open market in the same way as an individual investor, it generally is viewed by the investing public as a confident move by the company. It is interpreted as a sign that the company has an excess of cash to spend and that an investment in its own stock is the best investment possible, even better than other major investments such as purchases of facilities. This signal of confidence, in turn, can enhance the price of the shares remaining on the market. However, after a company buys back its own stock, its financial performance needs to live up to the confidence that it has signaled.

$ Costs of Production

What It Means

The costs of production are the expenses to which a company is subject as it goes through the process of generating, selling, and delivering goods and services to consumers. The various resources on which the company relies to produce a product (the good or service) are known as factors of production. These factors, which all represent costs to the company, can include labor, equipment, real estate, machinery, technology, insurance, and other resources.

A company is concerned with the costs of production because, in general, it seeks to make a financial profit on the sale of its products. The profit a company makes on its products is calculated by subtracting the total cost of production from the total revenue the company brings in (which is largely through sales of its products). If the company chooses not to raise prices for its products, it can maintain (or increase) its level of profit only if it can keep steady (or decrease) the costs of production. The more a company can lower its costs of production while at the same time increasing its revenue (through increased numbers of sales), the more profitable the company will be. For example, if a candle manufacturer produces and sells 1,000 candles a month and if the total costs of production are $3 per candle, the business can make a profit only if it charges more than $3 per candle to consumers. To increase its profit, the business must find a way to lower the costs of production per candle, to sell more than 1,000 candles per month, to get a higher price for the candles, or some combination of the three.

Determining the costs of production per product and understanding the sources of those costs are important for several reasons. Foremost, a company can set a profit-making price on a product if it knows how much the product costs to produce. Understanding the production costs also makes it possible to determine what part of the total costs of a manufacturing process or a building lease is associated with a particular product. Furthermore, understanding the production costs makes it possible to identify costs that are too high and to make comparisons between the costs of different activities in the company.

When Did It Begin

The Scottish philosopher Adam Smith (1723–90) was the first person to develop the concept of costs of production as an economic theory. Smith analyzed the role of the production of goods in a market economy. In his most noted book, *The Wealth of Nations* (1776), he argued that, although the free market (an economic market operating by free competition) appears unrestrained, in actuality an "invisible hand" guides the market to produce the optimal amount that will be consumed. For example, if there is a shortage of an essential good, its price increases because its producers understand that consumers are willing to pay more to acquire it. This encourages other producers to enter the market, which ultimately eliminates the shortage. If there are more than enough producers of a certain good, the competition for the consumer brings the price of the product down to what Smith called its "natural price," which is the cost of producing it. Even though a company makes no profit when a good is sold at the price it costs to produce it, there is still an incentive to produce it because the selling

Costs of production are expenses involved in manufacturing consumer goods and services, such as equipment purchases, real estate costs, and employee wages. This cartoon reflects the loss of American jobs associated with offshoring, a trend beginning in the twentieth century in which American companies began to establish operations in foreign countries to take advantage of cheaper labor costs. © 2003 by Mike Lane and Cagle Cartoons.com. All rights reserved.

price also pays the company owner's salary, which is included in the costs of production.

More Detailed Information

Because the costs of production are intimately tied to the ability of a company to generate a profit, they are the subject of detailed analysis. In economics, cost is considered to be a measure of the opportunities that are passed up when a company chooses one product or activity over others. Consequently, the costs of production of any good or service can be considered opportunity costs. For instance, by choosing any given production venture, a company always foregoes the chance to choose another venture and, therefore, foregoes the value of that alternative. The earnings that would have been made on taking another product to market or making another investment are the opportunity costs.

A company's opportunity costs of production can be divided into two main categories: explicit costs and implicit costs. The implicit costs are essentially costs that are not transacted directly in money, even though they are measured in money. For example, if the owner of a company foregoes a salary that he could have made by working for someone else and, instead, works at the company he owns for a lower salary, he never sees the amount of money he did not make, but he knows what it is.

The explicit costs are more easily valued in money. They include direct payments for factors of production such as wages, rent, and utilities. Economists usually take both implicit and explicit costs into consideration, whereas companies and their accountants focus only on explicit costs. To a business, the term *costs of production* refers to costs of producing and supplying goods for which it is liable in the short term. Two different types of costs make up the explicit costs that a firm incurs: fixed costs and variable costs.

Fixed costs are associated with the factors of production that remain unchanged no matter how many units of the product are produced. Generally, they are all the costs of setting up a business. Among the many different fixed costs are the rent paid for office or factory space, the costs of salaries for full-time employees who work on the product, the costs paid for insurance premiums that the business carries, and the property taxes on the land the business sits on. Fixed costs also include the depreciation (the decline in value due to age and wear and tear over time) of such things as plants and equipment.

The total amount of a fixed cost does not change as the level of production activity varies. For example, if a company raises the number of units of a product it makes by 20 percent, the total fixed cost of production remains the same.

The variable costs of production are subject to change according to the number of units of a product made or with the scale of the company's operation. Examples of variable costs include the materials used to make the product and the wages paid to workers who are hired specifically for the production of that good. For instance, the cost to an automaker for the sheet metal that goes into its cars generally will increase in proportion to the number of cars it produces; if it makes 10 percent more cars in a certain time period, its cost for sheet metal will also increase by 10 percent. Likewise, if it costs the carmaker $10,000 to make one car, and manufacturing activity doubles from a production rate of 100 cars a month to a rate of 200 cars a month, then the total variable costs double from $1 million to $2 million. On the other hand, the variable cost of making each car (the carmaker's cost per unit) stays the same no matter how much the activity increases. It costs the carmaker $10,000 to make each car, whether the car is the first one manufactured in a given month, the 50th, or the 200th.

To better understand its costs of production, a company needs to trace as many costs as possible directly to the activities that cause them to be incurred. Consequently, an important distinction to be made is the difference between direct and indirect costs. A cost that can be associated with a particular department or other specific segment of a company is called a direct cost of that segment. For example, a salary of a television repair person is a direct cost of the service department at a consumer electronics store. An indirect cost is one that cannot be directly attributed to a particular segment. The costs of advertising for a large multinational corporation are as-

SUNK COSTS

A cost of production that has been incurred by a company in the past, that does not affect future costs, and that cannot be changed by any current or future actions or decisions is called a sunk cost. For example, manufacturing equipment that a company bought ten years ago may or may not be useful today, but its cost cannot be changed by anything the company does now or later. The cost is therefore not relevant to future decisions about whether the equipment should be replaced or disposed of. Sunk costs can be contrasted with variable costs, which are costs of production (such as wages and raw materials) that can vary in the future depending on what actions the company takes. Sunk costs also can be contrasted with fixed costs, which are costs of production (such as rent on factory space) that do not change in relation to a relevant time period or scale of production activity, although fixed costs are not absolutely unchanging (factory rent, for example, will rise eventually).

Often company management believes that it needs to hold onto old equipment or other assets because a certain amount of money was paid for them, even if the equipment is not working properly or is causing the company to incur other costs. A company may allow sunk costs to affect future decisions, usually at the expense of greater profitability, even if it knows that future decisions should be based on future costs.

sociated with all its divisions and departments. Similarly, the salary of a company's president or its chief financial officer is an indirect cost of the company as a whole.

Recent Trends

Beginning in the last decades of the twentieth century, globalization (a process involving the merging of economies, governmental policies, political movements, and cultures around the world) has encouraged the opening up of information and communication channels and enhanced the sense of a global market. As one consequence of globalization, many companies based in the United States have transferred the tasks that once were done by American engineers to countries, such as India and the Philippines, where the costs of engineering production are significantly lower than in the United States. This activity is known as offshoring. Some companies have saved as much as 70 percent in their total costs of production by sending work to other countries, where in some instances the wages are as little as 10 percent of those paid to American engineers. Large multinational technology firms such as Microsoft, General Electric, and Google are among those who not only have offshored engineering jobs but also have built research and development centers in countries where labor is relatively cheap. Many start-up companies (fledgling businesses) also have made offshoring a part of the plans they have presented to venture capital firms (companies with funds available to invest in fresh enterprises).

As a result of this trend, an industry of offshoring companies has grown up and has become successful and important quite quickly. These businesses, of which many are Indian (although some are American with offices in India, the Philippines, and elsewhere), provide American companies with workers as well as human resources services, recruitment services, information technology, and even physical offices in low-cost countries.

$ Cost-Benefit Analysis

What It Means

Cost-benefit analysis is a method of comparing the positive and negative effects of a project, a decision, or another business venture that an organization is considering. A cost-benefit analysis is a forecast; that is, it is done in advance of starting a project to show whether the project's negative effects (the costs) will outweigh its positive effects (the benefits). In general, the only business projects that are justified are those in which the benefits exceed the costs. Cost-benefit analysis evaluates

such factors as how much the project will cost, how long it will take to create, and how it will affect current and future employees.

Businesses, nonprofit organizations, and governmental agencies use cost-benefit analysis to identify how best to expend their money, effort, and materials. Money and time are finite resources for every organization. Cost-benefit analysis can help organizations avoid taking on projects that could ultimately waste money, time, and human energy. For example, a business might use cost-benefit analysis to determine whether it should include gym membership in its employee benefit plan. A nonprofit educational organization that is considering starting a new tutoring program might use cost-benefit analysis to determine if the program is financially feasible.

When Did It Begin

Cost-benefit analysis was first used by government agencies to understand if the benefits of certain programs, laws, and projects would outweigh their costs. Cost-benefit analysis was applied in the U.S. Flood Control Act of 1936. This legislation required that the U.S. Army Corps of Engineers evaluate the costs and benefits of

Cost benefit analysis is a tool used by people in business and other professions to weigh the potential advantages and disadvantages, or gains and losses, that might result from a particular course of action. The woman pictured here is using a flow chart to map out her cost-benefit analysis. © *2007/Jupiterimages.*

flood-control and water-resource projects. The objective of the law was to show that flood control, in such forms as levees and canals, impacted human lives. After this law was passed, other government agencies in the United States began using cost-benefit analysis to study how public-works projects affected social welfare.

In England in the 1950s and 1960s, the government used cost-benefit analysis in its improvements of the nation's transportation system. A cost-benefit analysis showed that a new subway line, called the Victoria Line, would improve the quality of life and mobility for those passengers who lived and worked along its proposed route, running from the southwest to the northeast of London. When it was ultimately built, the Victoria Line was the world's first automatic railway line.

More Detailed Information

There are many different scenarios in which cost-benefit analysis is a useful tool. A business might use cost-benefit analysis to determine whether to open an office in another country or invest in new computer equipment. A nonprofit organization that provides programs for young parents might use cost-benefit analysis to determine which programs would provide the most services to its customers for the specified amount of money the organization has to spend. Cost-benefit analysis is also used to evaluate major investments of public funds in the building of bridges, roads, transit systems, convention centers, and dams. Before approving projects, experts study the project's impacts and rewards. The costs and benefits of a project may be tangible, such as money spent and earned, or intangible, such as improvements in quality of life.

In general, benefits are those things that increase the prosperity of the organization. The sale of a certain product will bring cash into a company; this is an example of a monetary benefit. Another project might save the company money. Other benefits may be indirect and harder to measure. The benefits to the public of a new city park are clear, but they can be difficult to measure.

In general, a cost is any spending or payment that an organization makes in order to reap some form of benefit, even if the benefit may not be measurable until a future date. The costs of a project or decision can be direct or indirect. The costs of buying new manufacturing equipment and hiring more employees, for example, are measurable in terms of dollars. It is harder to estimate indirect costs in such areas as quality of life, job satisfaction, reputation, or company morale, though, in some cases, these factors are assigned monetary values.

A cost-benefit analysis is a fairly straightforward process when all costs and benefits can be measured in monetary terms. Assume, for example, that a snow-clearing business must decide whether to purchase a new snowplow that costs $15,000. The business owner estimates that the new plow will bring in additional revenue of $20,000. The benefit of this additional revenue

exceeds the cost of the plow, so the owner decides to purchase the new plow.

Recent Trends

Businesses and organizations have become more complex over the last few decades, and the methods of cost-benefit analysis also have become more complex. At the government level, experts have developed cost-benefit analysis methods to distribute funds to projects that will have the most positive impact on the public. For example, program directors use cost-benefit analysis to set environmental standards and establish air-quality rules. In these cases, experts must often put a monetary value on human life or the environment, which often makes their decisions controversial.

Most areas of government have used cost-benefit analysis since the 1960s to plan and develop budgets. Some governmental projects, such as building roads and constructing water systems, can be analyzed with a high degree of accuracy. Other types of projects can be harder to estimate accurately, such as the costs and benefits of engaging in military conflict.

$ Inventory Control

What It Means

Every company that produces physical goods must maintain levels of inventory, which include its raw materials, unfinished products, and finished products that have not yet been shipped out of the company. All of the tasks and activities related to this maintenance are known as inventory control. This includes keeping detailed records on the amount and value of a company's

A company has to maintain and keep track of its inventory, such as merchandise, supplies, and raw materials for production. Here a sales associate at a home improvement store makes sure there is an adequate inventory of space heaters during the cold weather months. *Tim Boyle/Getty Images.*

inventory and ensuring that materials and products are appropriately stored, accessible when needed, and not in oversupply. Inventory control also sometimes includes the final assessments and protection of the finished goods within the company before purchasers take possession; these activities involve recording the receipt of goods from production, inspecting them, and handling them in storage.

The purpose of inventory control is to ensure that the company has sufficient amounts of finished goods to meet consumer demand in a timely way without creating an oversupply of products, which are costly to store. Companies with inventory strive to maintain a smooth flow of acquiring the necessary materials, making products, selling products, moving the products out of the company, and collecting on the sale of the products. Inventory is linked to all other aspects of production and sales, since changes in sales strategies can affect the levels of inventory on hand.

The primary challenge of inventory control is to balance a company's inventory ordering costs against its inventory carrying costs in an effort to keep down total costs. Ordering costs are all of the expenses that are incurred by a company in purchasing materials and supplies for its inventory. They can include expenses for postage, telephone service, order-processing software, and the salary of employees who handle purchase orders. Carrying costs (also called holding costs) are those spent on "carrying" the inventory, meaning protecting and storing it. These costs can include expenses for property insurance, rent or storage, and any monetary losses if the materials or products deteriorate in value or are stolen. Generally, the more inventory a company has, the higher its carrying costs will be.

When Did It Begin

Inventory is regarded and managed very differently today than it was hundreds of years ago. The basis for individual enterprise for many centuries was land and land ownership. For example, an individual who had a successful farming operation could store his harvest on his land, and the more bountiful the harvest was, the wealthier he was considered. Likewise, a sheep farmer with a large, healthy herd could store his wealth, in the form of his sheep, on his land. Because commerce and trade did not move very quickly, it was not necessary to keep careful tabs on inventory.

The Industrial Revolution of the late eighteenth and early nineteenth centuries marks the time when machines were first used to mass-produce goods. The vast increase in the number of goods that a manufacturer could turn out also increased the volumes of raw materials and finished goods that it needed to control and maintain. Since that time, global trade and electronic commerce have stimulated competition around the world. This, in turn, has pushed down prices and put pressure on a company's inventory control to guard stringently against excess stock so that the flow of products, and thus collections on the sales of the products, remain high.

More Detailed Information

The specific inventory control activities and tasks required of a manufacturing company depend on the types of inventory it needs to manage. For most manufacturers, inventory generally falls into one of three categories. One category is raw materials; that is, whatever materials the company uses at the starting point or elsewhere in the production process. For example, iron ore is used by steelmakers, and silicon chips are used by computer makers. A second category of inventory is work in progress, which is any kind of unfinished product the company has on hand. As the production process grows more complex and the number of components in the product rises, the amount of this inventory increases. For example, a tractor manufacturer would have a much larger work-in-progress inventory than a tire manufacturer. The third category of inventory is composed of finished goods, which are the products ready for shipment to customers.

Which category of inventory a particular material or good falls into depends on the business of the manufacturing company, because the finished product for one company can be a raw material for another. For example, the finished products of the silicon chip manufacturer are the chips themselves, which serve as a raw material for the computer maker.

In today's business environment, computers handle most purchase orders for a company and keep track of goods as they are taken out of its inventory. Generally, when a computer processes an order, it also manages a variety of data about the product, including how its purchase affects the overall supply of inventory. The company uses such information about inventory to help shape its sales and production operations.

In addition to managing the flow of materials and products, inventory control manages the physical space in which goods are stored and protected. Many goods require specialized environmental conditions, such as controlled temperature or moisture, or sufficient space so that, for example, they are not stacked so high as to risk being damaged. It is common for manufacturers to check their computerized ledgers of inventory movement periodically against a human check of the physical inventory that is stored. This practice not only verifies financial records. but it also catches inaccuracies or mistakes in the system of processing inventory.

Recent Trends

Just as manufacturers employ inventory control to maintain a timely flow of goods and minimize the costs of inventory storage, so also do retailers in managing the movement of goods from producers to consumers. Beginning in the last decades of the twentieth century, retailers have worked to cut significant portions of inventory costs in innovative ways and with the help of advances in communications and information technology. In the United States the discount chains Costco and Sam's Club and some home-improvement chains such as Home Depot and Lowe's operate large warehouse-like retail establishments. There, customers make their purchases where the products are stored, which reduces the need of the businesses for renting or buying additional inventory space, one of the largest carrying costs. In large

JUST-IN-TIME INVENTORY

One of the most significant innovations in inventory control was first put into practice by the American industrialist Henry Ford (1863–1947), who saved millions of dollars by purchasing the suppliers of many of the raw materials he needed to manufacture his cars. Mines and smelting operations came under the direct control of the Ford business empire, which helped Ford reduce the amount of inventory in his automobile factories waiting to be used in production. When in the 1950s the Japanese automaker Toyota adopted the underlying principle to reduce inventories in its own operations, the strategy was dubbed just-in-time inventory.

The objective of the just-in-time approach is to avoid excess on-hand inventory by ensuring that materials and supplies arrive at a manufacturer just when they are needed, and it is most commonly used by companies with high inventory costs. To implement it, companies must determine how small an amount of each of the materials it purchases (usually raw materials) is needed for the smooth flow of production. An analysis of time is crucial to the process, since the company must understand how long it takes to carry out every step of the manufacturing process, both from the supply side as well as from the production side.

part because of their efficient handling of inventory, these "warehouse stores" are able to provide discounted products to consumers.

The American retailing giant Wal-Mart keeps its carrying costs low by using information supplied by the company's suppliers about the availability of goods. Integrating that information with information about the rates of product sales in Wal-Mart stores allows the chain to keep only minimum amounts of inventory on hand. Additionally, Wal-Mart uses radio-frequency identification (RFID) technology to track items from the manufacturers' factories to its distribution centers and then to stores. RFID is an automatic identification method that uses an information-encoded electronic tag attached to each item to be tracked and a scanner that can remotely detect the tag as much as several feet away. All the items in a sealed box, for example, can be identified by scanning the box at each location in the journey from producer to retailer to consumer. Using RFID in this way, a company can add a whole shipment of goods to its inventory system at one time without having to unpack the boxes and identify each item separately.

$ Investment Management

What It Means

Investment management is the activity of overseeing and making decisions regarding the investments of an individual, company, or other institution. Individuals having personal investments in the form of either physical assets (such as real estate) or paper assets (such as bonds and stock shares) may take on the tasks of managing their investments on their own, or they may use an investment manager to make decisions about their investments. Usually companies and other large organizations employ investment managers to guide and oversee all aspects of the company's investments. In addition to corporations, institutions such as insurance companies and pension funds may rely on professionals to handle their investments. The investment manager may be an individual or a firm.

One reason companies regard investment management as important is that they often rely on investments to help expand their business. For example, if an airline desires to expand operations into a new market, it will need a large amount of ready cash to pay for building a new customer base, advertising, and other requirements. In this situation, the airline's investment manager will examine the company's investment portfolio (the collection of investments held by the company) to determine which investments, when converted to cash, could provide the funding the firm needs for the new operation. The company may own stocks or bonds and may have invested in certain funds such as mutual funds.

Investment management goes by a variety of names that can depend on the type of investors and investments involved. Private individuals with investments of large value usually refer to the investment management services they use as wealth management or portfolio management. When financial firms such as banks and insurance companies manage investments, it is usually called fund management. Asset management is the name for the management of mutual funds, managed funds, and other funds that allow large numbers of shareholders (investors) to participate in a range of investment opportunities. As an industry, investment management is a crucial part of the global corporate culture.

When Did It Begin

Investment management in the United States has developed rapidly in the few decades it has existed. Until the 1970s, most wealth in the United States was managed by money managers in Europe or by private trust companies. Families in possession of wealth that required management typically employed private portfolio managers.

The Employee Retirement Income Security Act of 1974 required a new process for the statistical measurement of retirement portfolios, which resulted in the emergence of investment management firms to oversee such corporate investments as employee-benefit-fund assets. In the late 1980s these management firms, which until then had served only institutions, started providing services to individual investors. In 1985 the Investment Management Consultants Association (IMCA) was

Investment management allows individuals and companies to make informed decisions about how to invest their money. In order to do that, investment managers need to know the individual's or company's financial goals. *AP Images.*

established, which advocated high standards for the education of professional investment managers.

More Detailed Information

Growth in the amount and value of assets is important to the overall worth of a company and the wealth of its stockholders. Among the various types of assets a company may possess, most require investment management. Fixed assets (also known as long-term assets) are generally forms of physical property that are held for a long time (for instance, buildings, equipment, and heavy machinery) and that are used to generate revenue. Most fixed assets lose their value over time due to wear and tear, a process called depreciation. Bonds are another kind of fixed asset. A bond is a long-term loan an investor makes to the entity that issues the bond, for example, the United States government. Current assets (also called liquid assets) are held by an investor for relatively short time spans, typically less than 12 months, and they can be easily converted to cash, sold, or consumed. Examples of a company's current assets are cash, tradable stock, and inventory.

When a group of assets have similar characteristics, generally perform similarly when invested in, and are regulated in the same way by laws, they are said to be in the same asset class. Equities, which are public stocks, are in one such asset class. Fixed-income bonds are in another, and cash equivalents such as bank certificates of deposit are in yet another.

Investment portfolios are typically managed through decisions about purchases and sales of assets. Investment managers must be able to analyze the finances of investors, understand how to select different types of assets, set realistic investment goals, and know how to monitor investments and make adjustments when changing economic situations require them.

When an investment manager is first engaged by an investor, the manager generally begins by analyzing the investor's current financial situation to create a profile. This activity involves assessing the net worth of the investor, which is the value of all property owned (assets), less any debts or obligations (liabilities). It also involves determining the cash flow of the investor, which is the amount of cash earned in a certain time period after paying all expenses and taxes.

After the investment manager has established the investor's financial profile, the manager and the investor work together to identify and define investment goals. Goals depend on many factors, including the percentage of wealth the investor wants to commit, the level of investment risk appropriate to the investor, the desired rate of return (the earnings expected from an investment over a specific time period), and the relative percentages of the total investment that should be put into long-term and short-term assets.

MODERN PORTFOLIO THEORY

An investment strategy used by many investment managers, called modern portfolio theory, was developed by the American economist and Nobel laureate Harry Markowitz (b. 1927) in 1952. Modern portfolio theory identifies the connection between risk (the chance of losing money in an investment) and reward (the gain from an investment) and the tendency for investors to be rewarded by taking risks over time. Those managers who apply the theory seek to create investment portfolios (the investment collection held by the investor) that have the lowest possible volatility for an investment (the frequency and size of the price fluctuation of the investment). They also aim for the highest return (the earnings derived from the investment) within an established level of risk.

Using mathematical relationships between risk level and return level, Markowitz's portfolio theory shows investors how they can evaluate the future performance of an investment portfolio. The investment manager must determine the risk tolerance of the investor, which is the extent at which the investor can risk his investments to achieve a desired rate of return (the earnings of an investment over a specific time period).

Next, the investment manager employs financial models that assess the likelihood of achieving the investment goals. These models, which are run on a computer, use statistics, mathematics, logic, economic information, and other resources to construct a representation of a particular investment strategy over time. Results from the models give the investor and the manager an idea of how realistic the investment goals are. If they have concerns about realizing these goals, they can adjust their overall strategy.

Recent Trends

The field of investment management has become increasingly complex beginning in the last decades of the twentieth century due to such factors as the development of new kinds of investments, advances in communications networks, and the ability of individuals and companies to access financial information quickly through the use of the Internet. Also over that time, investment management has become so established that many business schools incorporate investment management in their course outlines for students, while some offer masters' degrees in the field.

Within investment management several subcategories of tasks and activities have developed. Professional fund managers, for example, are individuals or firms governmentally licensed to manage a fund, most commonly a mutual fund, pension fund, or insurance fund. In general the manager of the fund invests money on behalf of the fund owners. Mutual fund managers oversee funds that have been given to an investment company by shareholders, and they invest the funds in a range of assets that can include stocks, bonds, options, commodities, and money market securities. The investments, which are made on the basis of the investment company's objectives, give shareholders ways to put money into a diverse set of investment opportunities.

Increasing numbers of investors have turned to relatively new investment products such as separate accounts. A separate account uses money collected from numerous sources to buy individual assets. The investor then owns the assets (such as stocks and bonds) instead of a portion of a larger pool of assets, as would be the case for a mutual fund. Most separate accounts have a minimum investment level of $100,000.

$ Business Financing

What It Means

Business financing is just it what it sounds like: the activity of funding the many aspects of a business, whether the funding be for starting a business, running it, or expanding it. Regardless of the size or type of business, there are fundamental questions involving financing that must be addressed.

For example, most businesses purchase a variety of items, such as buildings, machinery, or office furniture and equipment, that are intended to be useful for a long time. Such items are called long-term investments. Any business making long-term investments must carefully consider what those investments will be, how much they will cost, and how much they will hold their value over time. Just as important is the question of where to get the money needed to pay for them.

When a business is just starting, it typically borrows money from banks or other financial institutions, or it brings in additional individuals or institutions (that is, investors) to share ownership in the business in order to procure the initial capital it needs to cover the costs of building a new business. Capital is the term given to the money or other things of worth that are needed to produce goods or services. Capital can take the form of human beings, physical goods, or some means of financial exchange. Examples of capital are skilled labor, factories, office space, tools, machinery, and money.

When a businesses is up and running and managing the everyday financial operations, it may likewise turn to banks and investors for financing, but it typically relies on its customers for generating the money needed to finance the business. If the business is profitable and the company saves some of the money it makes from commercial activity, it may use that money to make new investments that will further expand its business. There are many different methods businesses use to acquire the financing

Business Financing Options

	Nature of Funding	Considerations	Payoff Terms
Banks	Banks offer a wide variety of funding options—from short and long term loans to business credit card accounts—with dollar values ranging from a few thousand to several million dollars.	These lenders maintain strict terms and usually only lend to established companies.	The loan must be paid off in installments over a designated period of time.
Private "Angel" Investors	Angel investments are most often made by wealthy individuals (or groups of individuals) who are willing to help fund a project in its earliest stages, before other financing options are available.	Each deal with an Angel investor is unique. Most Angels make investments close to home, so they can oversee the company's progress directly.	Angels often expect fo see a profit when the company is established enough to attract its first major investor. Sometimes the Angel is willing to defer this profit until the company reaches a later milestone, such as its second round of financing.
Venture Capital Firms	There are thousands of venture capital firms, offering a wide range of financing options. The amount of financing usually begins at $1 million and may be as much as several million dollars.	Few venture capital firms work with new, unproven companies. Venture capital firms expect a high return on their investment in a relatively short period of time. For example, many firms expect to *at least* triple their money in 3–5 years.	There are a many different scenarios. Venture capital firms often seek to invest in companies that are likely to be bought out by larger companies or "go public" by selling shares of the company in the stock market.
Government Programs	The Small Business Association and hundreds of other local, state, and national programs offer business grants, loans, investments, and tax incentives.	Although there are a wide variety of programs to choose from, it can be difficult to find one that is suited to your needs and offers a real financial benefit.	Varies widely. Some types of funding must be repaid, but others are considered outright donations.

When businesses do not have enough money to fund their operations, they seek outside financing. As the chart indicates, each financing option carries its own considerations and payoff terms, so it is important for every business to figure out which option is best suited to its needs. *Illustration by GGS Information Services. Cengage Learning, Gale.*

they need to fund large projects and to improve their profitability.

When Did It Begin

Recorded instances of business financing date back to ancient times when wealthy Greeks arranged loans to shipping concerns that needed financing to transport freight. Greek lenders also funded miners and erectors of public buildings. In the Middle Ages Jewish merchants living in Italy loaned money to Christian Italian farmers. This practice established merchants in Europe as the main source of loans for farms and businesses and originated the concept of the "merchant bank."

In 1781 the first commercial bank was established in the United States. Named the Bank of North America, it extended short-term loans to merchants who then passed them on to wholesalers of imported goods. The wholesalers, in turn, extended loans to retailers, often country stores and independent peddlers.

Another step in the development of business financing in the United States was taken in 1904, when the American banker A.P. Giannini (1870–1949; later to be nicknamed "America's banker,") opened the Bank of Italy in San Francisco in 1904. Immigrants who sought to borrow money to start businesses but had been turned down because they had no established wealth were supported by the Bank of Italy, which became the Bank of America in 1930. California industry and agriculture and Hollywood filmmaking were among the many interests supported by Giannini's financing enterprise.

The Small Business Investment Act of 1958 established ways to make venture capital (funds from investors seeking to share ownership in new businesses) and long-term loans available to small, independent businesses in the United States. This program was the first to give small American businesses the financing they needed to start, maintain, and expand their operations.

More Detailed Information

As businesses grow, their financing needs evolve and typically become more complex. In the case of a small business, the owner generally makes the financial decisions for the firm. In the case of a large company, the owner or owners (who in some cases are the stockholders) do not get involved in financial decisions. Instead, they hire managers who take on the financial responsibilities. In large companies, this person is known as the chief financial officer (CFO) or vice-president of finance.

The process of planning and managing the long-term investments of a business is known as capital budgeting. Usually this process involves seeking those business opportunities that will earn the company more than they will cost the company. For each type of business, these opportunities are distinct. For example, for a commercial airline the decision about whether to begin regular service to a new city would be an important capital budgeting decision. For a large discount retailer the decision about whether to introduce a new line of gardening products would be one. Other types of capital

INITIAL PUBLIC OFFERING

A common way for a private company to raise money for new projects is through a process called an initial public offering (IPO), in which the public is given its first opportunity to purchase ownership in the company. When a company is privately owned, its stock is available only to privately selected investors. If the company decides to "go public,", it makes shares of its stock available on the public market. Organizing an IPO is a costly and time-consuming process for a company, but the capital it raises does not need to be repaid, as would a loan. On the other hand, if the company generates profits after the IPO, it must share them with its new investors.

Companies who organize IPOs typically are young and relatively small, but sometimes larger companies also turn to them for financing. The IPO was a frequent topic of news and conversation in the late 1990s when many new, small Internet-technology companies, dubbed dot-com companies, organized IPOs quickly to take advantage of investors eager to make money on the new wave of Internet-based enterprise. Although many companies staged successful IPOs at that time, many others fizzled. The difficulty involved in completing an IPO means that companies need to have distinct plans for long-term growth before they embark on the process.

budgeting opportunities (for example, investments in computer systems or human labor) are common to almost all businesses.

When a company's financial manager reviews a proposed capital budgeting decision, he or she must respond to several issues concerning the flow of cash associated with an investment. Primary considerations are the amount of cash the company is likely to make from an investment, when the company can collect the cash, and how high is the risk of the investment (that is, the chance of losing money in it). Basically, all capital investments must be evaluated for their size, timing, and risk. In the example of the airline's beginning a new route, mentioned above, the financial manager must estimate how much money the company will make once the route is established, when it will earn the money, and how reliable the new market will be.

When a company makes a long-term investment, as it does when it decides to develop a new product or open a new division, it must know from where the needed money will come: from outside the company, from within the company, or some combination of the two. Long-term investments require what is called long-term financing. The financial structure (sometimes called the capital structure) of a company is the particular mix of long-term borrowing and the equity that it can use to pay for its operations and new investments. The company, for example, may have a certain amount of long-term debt

incurred from borrowing money for its startup or to make new investments. The equity is the market value of the business's property held by the owners and shareholders. Financial managers constantly weigh the levels of debt and equity. Equity allows a company to keep growing and gives it its value. Debts must be kept under control because they represent the level of financial risk a company takes upon itself; the greater its debts, the greater it risks financial instability.

The term *working capital* refers to the short-term investments a business can draw upon. A business's short-term investments may be the inventory of goods it has produced. A business also may have short-term debts in the form of money it owes to the suppliers who provide materials to the business. The owners or the financial manager of the business must manage these short-term investments and debts of the firm on a daily basis so that the firm does not lose track of its costs, run out of ready cash, or interrupt its operations.

Recent Trends

An area of business finance that has grown steadily in the late twentieth and early twenty-first centuries is the practice of extending small loans to poor entrepreneurs who live in developing countries. The practice is known as microlending, and the loan is often called microcredit. The purpose of microlending is to assist individuals in creating income for themselves (for instance, by farming, weaving, or making crafts) and therefore to improve their living standards. Usually the individuals borrowing money have no existing property to use as collateral and no credit history and so would not qualify for a traditional bank loan.

Microcredit is generally issued for a short time period (one year or less), and the terms mandate that it be paid back on a weekly basis. Interest rates on the loans generally are high (in some places 40-50 percent) because costs of running the programs are high. The loan programs also generally seek to improve the education and health care of those enrolled. Microcredit is extended to women more often than men, and usually it is arranged as a community program, which cultivates responsibility to repay the loans because the whole community takes on the risk involved in improving the financial situation of its constituents.

$ Financial Statements

What It Means

Financial statements are documents that provide details about a company's performance and well-being over a given period of time. They are the equivalent of scorecards that break down a business's financial wins and losses during the specified period. Companies usually release financial statements for each quarter (each three-month period of a year) and for each year.

MacAllister Rafting Company
Balance Sheet
December 31, 2006

Assets			Liabilities and Capital		
Current Assets			*Current Liabilities*		
Cash	$12,500		Accounts payable	$ 9,100	
Accounts receivable	23,100		Wages payable	11,725	
Inventory	32,290		**Total Current Liabilities**		**$20,825**
Prepaid Insurance	2,700				
Total Current Assets		**$70,590**	*Long-Term Liabilities*		
Fixed Assets			Bank Loan Payable	17,700	
Equipment	100,400		**Total Long-Term Liability**		**17,700**
Less: Accum. Deprec.	(78,421)		**Total Liabilities**		**38,525**
Total Fixed Assets		**$21,979**	*Capital*		
Total Assets		**$92,569**	Sarah MacAllister, Capital		54,044
			Total Liabilites/Capital		**$92,569**

Financial statements offer a snapshot of a company's performance during a certain time period. Balance sheets, such as the one here for MacAllister Rafting Company, show the financial value of a business's assets and its liabilities, as well as the difference between these two, which is called capital. *Illustration by GGS Information Services. Cengage Learning, Gale.*

Within a company employees use the information presented in financial statements to make decisions about future operations. Outside a company investors use this information to determine whether it might be wise to invest in the company (by buying shares of company ownership called stock, which may gain value if the company prospers, or by loaning the company money through the purchase of bonds, which pay the investor a fee called interest). Banks and other lenders likewise use financial statements to judge the wisdom of loaning money to companies, and the government uses them to keep track of business activity for taxing and regulatory purposes.

There are three main types of financial statements, each of which offers a useful perspective on a company's health. These are the balance sheet, the income statement, and the cash flow statement. The balance sheet details a company's possessions and debts, the income statement details a company's earnings and expenses, and the cash flow statement details the movement of money into and out of a company. Together these three documents are meant to provide a thorough and accurate picture of a company's current financial status.

When Did It Begin

Businesses have no doubt always kept records to track their profitability and performance. Records from ancient civilizations in Mesopotamia and elsewhere provide evidence of the kind of financial record-keeping that eventually grew into the present-day concept of the financial statement.

Despite the ancient roots of this form of business accounting, the need for reliable public information about companies did not become pressing until the nineteenth century. This was a result of the increasing size of companies during this time. Prior to the nineteenth century, most companies could raise all the money they needed for their operations through their earnings or by borrowing from banks or other lenders. With increasingly large companies needing increasingly large sums of money to fuel their projects, however, financial markets moved to the center of the economic stage, since a company can raise far more money by selling stocks or bonds than any bank or other lender would be able to provide. To attract investors companies had to offer some proof that their stocks and bonds were likely to be good investments. It became common by the mid-nineteenth century for companies to provide investors with financial statements such as balance sheets and, more rarely, income statements.

Though balance sheets and other financial statements were widely used in the United States by the early twentieth century, the accountants who prepared these records answered to the companies that employed them rather than to the government or the public. The U.S. stock market boomed in the 1920s, but stock prices were not always related to company performance (frequently stock prices were valued much higher than they should have been, given the underlying value of companies), in part because there was a lack of reliable financial reporting. After the stock market crashed in 1929, triggering the Great Depression (the severe economic crisis that lasted for most of the 1930s), the need for more reliable accounting and financial reporting became apparent. Under President Franklin D. Roosevelt, the Securities and Exchange Commission (SEC) was established in 1934 to oversee the financial markets. The SEC began

ANNUAL REPORTS

Financial statements are documents detailing a company's financial well-being. Most companies release their financial statements quarterly (once every three months) and then provide a financial statement covering the entire year. These yearly financial statements are included in what is known to shareholders as an annual report, an attractively printed publication meant to entice investors to purchase shares of stock (portions of company ownership). In addition to the company's financial statements, many other documents are included, such as messages from top executives, mission statements, and other information meant to give a full sense of the company's culture and status.

requiring companies to disclose information more fully and reliably, accounting standards became more rigorous, and the modern system of regular financial reporting began to emerge.

More Detailed Information

No accurate estimate of a company's financial status can be obtained without studying its balance sheet, its income statement, and its cash flow statement. Though these financial statements vary in format and complexity from company to company, the basic information is consistent regardless of the company.

A balance sheet discloses the details of a company's assets, liabilities, and shareholders' equity. Assets are possessions that have value. This includes money and investments as well as property such as office equipment, factories, machinery, and inventory. This also includes intangible forms of property such as copyrights, patents, and trademarks (legal protections that assert the right of an individual or company to be the only business to profit from original ideas). Liabilities are sums of money that the company owes to others. These may take the form of bank loans, rent, wages due to employees, taxes, fines, or customer orders that have been paid for but not yet filled. Shareholders' equity is the value held by the company's owners. In the case of a public company, people who own stock are the company's owners; a private company is one that does not sell stock and that is owned by private citizens. Shareholders' equity accumulates as a result of company earnings over time. It equals the amount of money that would remain if a company were to sell its assets and pay off its liabilities. The remaining assets would rightfully belong to the shareholders.

A company's assets, accordingly, must equal its liabilities plus shareholders' equity. A balance sheet lists a company's assets on the left side of the page and its liabilities and shareholders' equity on the right side of the

page; the two total amounts "balance" one another. By breaking these balanced amounts down into their component parts, the balance sheet provides an important glimpse into the financial workings of the company.

Income statements supplement the information provided by balance sheets. An income statement breaks down a company's revenues (the total amount of money brought in through its business activities) and costs, and shows how much profit the company made or how big the company's losses were during the time period under consideration. Profit is the amount of revenue left over after costs have been paid, and losses result when costs exceed revenue. People commonly refer to a company's profits or losses as its "bottom line" because this figure is the last one listed on an income statement. A company in good condition will show growth both on the top line, revenue, and on the bottom line, profit.

Another important piece of information on income statements is a company's earnings per share. This figure represents the hypothetical amount that would be paid out for each share of stock if the company were to distribute all of its earnings. To calculate this figure a company simply divides its profits by the number of its shares that are owned by investors. In reality, companies keep all or most of their earnings and use them to fuel further growth, but earnings per share provides a standard for measuring the worth of a share of stock.

The cash flow statement draws on the information used in both the balance sheet and the income statement, but this information is used to show a different facet of company performance: the movement of cash into and out of a company. A balance sheet shows the value of a company's assets, liabilities, and shareholders' equity, but it does not track the amounts by which cash on hand has increased or decreased. Likewise, an income statement shows how much money a company brought in and how much it paid out, but it does not reflect the changes in cash balances that resulted from this activity. Cash flow statements indicate the amount by which the cash a company possesses has increased or decreased in the time period under consideration, and they break down these movements of cash according to the type of company activities that produced them. The amount of money a company has on hand is important because companies must be able to meet their expenses and purchase assets.

Recent Trends

In 2001 and 2002 the high-profile collapses of several major U.S. corporations led to the most serious reform of the standards for accounting and financial reporting since the Great Depression. The most prominent of the collapses were those of Enron, a Houston-based energy company, and WorldCom, a Mississippi-based telecommunications company. Both companies grew tremendously in the 1990s, and their stocks were among the fastest-growing and most valuable of all those traded on the U.S. stock market. During the global economic downturn of 2001–02, however, when the stock market crashed and the two companies began to struggle, it became apparent that neither was as healthy as their stock prices had led investors to believe. Enron and WorldCom both went bankrupt, and their stock became almost worthless, causing shareholders, including many Enron and WorldCom employees whose retirement funds consisted of company stock, to lose billions of dollars virtually overnight.

Investigations into these events revealed that both companies had intentionally misled investors through fraudulent accounting methods on their financial statements. In response, Congress passed the Sarbanes-Oxley Act of 2002. Among many other provisions intended to improve the accuracy of financial reporting and protect investors, the act established a new regulatory body charged with overseeing company accounting practices, and it made the top executives of corporations legally accountable for the information contained in financial statements.

$ Depreciation

What It Means

Depreciation is the decline in the value of an asset (an item someone owns) over time. For example, it is said that a new car begins depreciating (losing value) the moment the buyer drives it off the dealer's lot. This means that if an owner who paid $18,000 for a car tries to sell the vehicle one month later, that same car may only be worth $16,000.

Assets lose their value for a number of reasons, including use, age, exposure to weather, and obsolescence. An object has obsolesced (or become obsolete) if no one uses it anymore. For instance, a businessperson may own 15 functional typewriters, but even though these items work, they are of little value because the staff requires up-to-date computers to do their jobs. It is important to note that the concept of depreciation does not apply to one-time damage or destruction. An asset is not said to have depreciated if it is destroyed in a fire, a flood, or an accident.

Because objects such as computers and machinery depreciate, businesses lose money on equipment each year. If, for example, a shipping company needs to maintain a fleet of trucks to operate its business, and it purchases a truck for $120,000, that truck may only be worth $110,000 the following year. This means that the company has lost $10,000 on the value of the truck. After 10 years the truck may no longer be serviceable. To help businesses compensate for this loss, the government allows them to claim depreciation as a business expense on tax forms. Because businesses pay taxes on their net profits (the amount of money they have made after subtracting all expenses), claiming depreciation as an

HOSTILE TAKEOVER

One of the side effects of corporation-friendly depreciation tax laws (laws that allow a company to subtract larger sums for the aging of its equipment, or assets, from the amount it owes the government in taxes) is an increase in hostile takeovers. A hostile takeover occurs when a bidder (an individual or corporation) takes control of a corporation against the wishes of the target corporation's management. If a bidder wants to acquire a controlling interest in a corporation, that bidder must buy at least 33 percent or more of the voting shares of the corporation's stock. Stock, which is sold in individual shares, denotes partial ownership in a corporation. Shareholders are paid a percentage of the corporation's profits according to how many shares they own. Voting shares, a specific type of shares, give their shareholders the right to vote on corporate policy. Normally, a bidder will discuss his or her interest with the target corporation's board of directors before making an offer. In a hostile takeover the bidder either purchases the target corporation's stock without consulting the board or continues to attempt to make the purchase after the board has rejected the offer.

One way to persist with a rejected offer is to impose what is called a bear hug on the target corporation. This slang term refers to the act of offering a purchase price for the shares of the corporation that far exceeds their recognized value. Even if the corporation's management wants to keep control by retaining the majority of shares in the corporation, they may be legally obligated to sell those shares because the law requires that management look out for the financial interests of the rest of the shareholders, who stand to make more money if the company is sold at a high price.

expense reduces the net profit and therefore reduces the tax that a business must pay.

When Did It Begin

The first tax law in the United States that allowed businesses to deduct (subtract) an amount for the depreciation of their assets from the taxes they owed the government was the Tariff Act of 1909. Since 1909, tax laws regarding depreciation have changed at least once every decade. These changes often reflect the government's attitude about the purpose of depreciation. In 1909 Congress voted to institute the new tax law because big business, in order to determine net profit accurately, needed to measure the value of their assets at the end of each year. At that time most corporations did not measure the depreciation of assets in their accounting records. Because of this their yearly net profit measurements were overstated: they were not counting the declining value of their equipment as a financial loss and thus, a business expense. The 1909 tax law was designed to help businesses by reducing their taxes so they would have more

Depreciation refers to the gradual loss in value in a company's assets. Manufacturing equipment, such as a cement truck, undergoes a steady decline in value over time. © *Joseph Sohm/Visions of America/Corbis.*

money available to maintain their assets and/or to purchase more assets.

From the 1950s through the middle of the 1960s, changes to depreciation tax laws were introduced for another reason: to encourage businesses to reinvest their profits (that is, to put money back into their own company). During this time tax laws permitted corporations to deduct large amounts of money for the depreciation of their assets; they could thus pay less in taxes and then use the money they saved to maintain assets and to expand their businesses. The thinking was that this reinvestment would create more jobs and help the nation's economy grow.

More Detailed Information

Depreciation is not a cash cost (an amount of money that a business pays out to someone); it is an expense that is logged in company books for a given tax period. Figuring depreciation for tax purposes can become complicated and confusing very quickly. For this reason most business owners hire an accountant to balance their books and calculate the depreciation of business assets. Accountants can use several different methods to chart the declining value of assets. One of the simplest methods is called straight-line depreciation.

To compute the straight-line depreciation of an asset, a business must first determine the asset's life span and salvage value (the value of what remains when its life span is over). Returning to the example of the shipping company, assume that the new $120,000 truck will last for 10 years. This is the truck's life span. Next, assume that after 10 years the company will be able to sell the truck for $20,000 to another company that will recycle the vehicle's parts. This means that the salvage value of the truck is $20,000. Subtracting the salvage value from the original cost shows that in its 10-year life span the truck will depreciate by $100,000. The straight-line method calculates depreciation evenly over those 10 years. In the case of the truck, this would be a depreciation of $10,000 per year, which means that every year the company can deduct $10,000 from its profits. The company can reduce its taxes in this way and keep more money to buy new equipment.

Another option for calculating declining values of assets is called accelerated depreciation. Though computing accelerated depreciation is more complicated, most businesspeople and accountants prefer this method to straight-line depreciation because it allows for larger tax deductions in the early years of owning the new asset. Among the many ways of figuring accelerated depreciation, the declining-balance method is the most common. This method allows a company to deduct as much as twice the amount of the straight-line value in the first year of owning a new asset. The company is permitted to deduct slightly less each succeeding year.

Using the straight-line method, the shipping company deducted $10,000 (or 10 percent of the truck's total depreciation) from its taxes each year. The declining-balance method allows the company to deduct 20 percent ($20,000) each year in the early part of the life span of the vehicle. The company would not deduct that 20 percent from the fixed figure of $100,000 in those years, however; it would deduct the 20 percent from the depreciated value of the truck. The second year it owned the truck, then, the company would deduct 20 percent of $80,000 ($100,000 minus the $20,000 deducted the previous year), which is $16,000. The third year the company would deduct 20 percent of $64,000, or $12,800. When the deduction for the declining-balance depreciation is less than the straight-line figure ($10,000 in the case of the truck), the company can use the straight-line method for the rest of the life span of the truck.

Recent Trends

Since the 1980s depreciation tax laws in the United States have sought either to increase corporate investment or to reduce the national debt, which includes money that the federal government owes to other countries and to lenders within the United States. Favorable depreciation laws (those permitting businesses to claim high values for depreciation) tend to stimulate corporate investment, while more strict depreciation laws (those that let corporations keep less money for depreciation) raise tax dollars that the government can use to reduce the national debt. In 1981, in an effort to come out of a recession, the U.S. Congress passed the Economic Recovery Tax Act. This law treated depreciation in a new way. Until 1981, laws had kept allowable deductions for depreciation reasonably consistent with the declining value of the product over its useful life. The 1981 law, however, let companies use depreciation as a way to quickly recover the money spent on assets. Corporations were allowed to fully depreciate some assets in as few as three years, regardless of how long the assets were useful. This greatly reduced corporate taxes, thus increasing the amount of money corporations had and could use to expand their businesses. Corporations bought more assets, hired more employees, and requested more loans for long-term projects, such as building new offices and factories. All of this improved the economy. Although the Revenue Reconciliation Act of 1993 required that depreciation deductions accurately reflect the value of assets, in 2000 the government returned to a policy of extending tax benefits to corporations.

$ Trade Credit

What It Means

Trade credit is a contractual agreement in which one business receives goods or services from another business without having to pay immediately for those goods and services. The business that has received the goods or services will pay the lending business at a later date, which is specified in the agreement. For example, a hot dog business that gets trade credit from a supplier receives hot dogs from that supplier at the start of the month and does not have to pay for the inventory for two months. Such an agreement is called a "Net 60 agreement," which means that the supplier would expect the invoice (the bill) for the hot dogs to be paid in full after 60 days.

In most Net 60 agreements, a discount is offered if the bill is paid early. In this case the owner of the hot dog stand might receive a 20 percent discount for paying the bill within 10 days and a 10 percent discount for paying the bill within 30 days. For example, if the owner of the hot dog stand was billed $1,000 on a Net 60 agreement, he would have to pay only $800 if he paid the invoice within 10 days of receiving the shipment. He would have to pay $900 if he paid the invoice within 30 days of receiving the shipment. A Net 30 agreement is another common arrangement, according to which full payment is due 30 days after receiving the goods or services. Most Net 30 arrangements offer a 2 percent discount if payment is received within 10 days.

When Did It Begin

In a sense, trade credit has existed since the beginning of commerce because people have always had to borrow from one another in order to survive. When a person provided goods in exchange for other goods that would be received at a later date, that person was extending a form of trade credit. A person might trade wood to a neighbor, for example, in exchange for a crop that would be harvested later in the year.

Trade credit resembling the exchanges that take place today first began in the nineteenth century at the end of the Industrial Revolution in Europe. At this time, manufacturers often needed large amounts of raw materials to run their machines before they had the money to pay for those materials. For example, the coal that was required to run textile mills (which produced such items as clothing and carpeting) was often purchased on credit and paid for with the proceeds from the sale of the textiles.

More Detailed Information

Trade credit offers the company receiving the goods or services a significant benefit: the invoice for the goods or services need not be paid until after a profit has been made. For example, assume that the hot dog vendor receives 1,000 hot dogs on the first of the month for

B2B

The term *business-to-business*, or B2B for short, refers to the marketing or advertising of transactions that occur between two businesses. B2B transactions are distinct from B2C (business-to-consumer) transactions, which include all sales of goods and services from a company to an individual. When a person buys athletic shoes or groceries, he or she has engaged in a B2C transaction. When a technology firm purchases office supplies, that firm has engaged in a B2B transaction. The amount of money spent in B2B transactions far exceeds that spent in B2C transactions. For example, the U.S. government, the largest buyer of products in the United States, spends more than $300 billion a year on products and services. For those persons considering starting a business, there is greater potential to earn money by selling goods and services to businesses rather than selling to individual customers.

$1,000. The vendor sells the hot dogs at a markup, or higher price, to his customers. He charges $3 for a hot dog. After a good weekend at the start of the month, the vendor sells 334 hot dogs for a total cash intake of $1,002. He is able to pay his invoice within 10 days, and, because he is paying early, he will owe only $800. So, he has already made a profit of $202, and he still has 666 more hot dogs to sell. In another scenario, the weather is bad in the early part of the month, and the vendor sells very few hot dogs. But he need not worry about paying his bill immediately because he has 60 days to earn the $1,000 needed to pay the invoice.

Although the terms of the trade credit agreement seem to favor the hot dog vendor in this case, it is possible to look at the agreement in another less favorable way. The trade credit agreement could be regarded as a high-interest, short-term loan. According to the terms of a Net 60 agreement, the hot dog vendor has just 10 days to pay an $800 bill. If he cannot make that $800 payment, then he could pay as much as 20 percent interest on that loan.

Regardless of how one views this type of financial relationship, both parties can benefit from trade credit. The receiving company, which is often smaller than the lending company, can maintain a steady level of inventory and thus have product available to its customers. Trade credit also gives the receiving company an opportunity to manage its inventory and to understand the spending habits of its customers. By keeping accurate records the receiving company can anticipate how many supplies it will need and order the appropriate amount so that it can pay its bill within 10 days and receive its discount.

The lending company can also use trade credit to help increase its profits. Suppliers are always looking for businesses that need their goods. By offering favorable terms of trade credit, a supplier can find new businesses to

purchase its supplies. The supplier may offer a start-up company trade credit if the supplier thinks that the start-up company has a good chance to become a successful business. If the start-up company flourishes it will require more inventory, and the supplier's profits will therefore increase along with the start-up's. A supplier may use favorable terms of trade credit to lure an established business away from its current supplier. Suppliers monitor the paying habits of all businesses that receive their supplies. These suppliers often reward their best customers with improved terms of trade credit.

Recent Trends

The risks associated with extending trade credit vary, depending largely on the economy in the part of the world to which a company is extending trade credit. Many countries in Latin America, for example, are reducing their national debt, which in turn makes the business environment in these countries more stable. This stability has made it possible for businesses to receive more trade credit because they are not as likely to default on, or fail to pay, their bills. Latin America has also experienced increased political stability in the last decade, and this political stability indicates that recent economic growth might be long lasting.

Economies in other parts of the world are growing, too, but a lack of political stability has increased the risk associated with extending trade credit to businesses in these countries. For example, the Commonwealth of Independent States (CIS), a coalition of 11 former Soviet Republics including Russia, is thriving economically, but the threat of political upheaval looms throughout the region. Therefore, high risk is associated with lending to businesses in the CIS. The same is true in Central Europe, Turkey, the Near and Middle East, and North Africa.

$ Dividends

What It Means

Dividends are the part of a business's profit that is distributed to shareholders, individuals who own shares of stock in the company. The size of the dividend payment a business, or firm, owes to a shareholder is calculated by taking the accumulated earnings they choose to distribute and dividing that amount by the number of shares held by the shareholder.

Assume that in July 2003 Corporation A had 200 million shares of stock outstanding, meaning that 200 million shares had been issued (sold) and were owned by members of the public. If one individual owned 4,000 shares of Corporation A's stock, then he or she owned 4,000 out of 200 million, which, calculated as a percentage, equals 0.002 percent of Corporation A. This means that this individual is, in essence, entitled to 0.002 percent of Corporation A's profit.

Dividends are portions of a company's profits that are paid to its investors. The amount of a dividend is usually listed in a stock report. © *Bob Jacobson/Corbis.*

Dividends are usually distributed to shareholders on a quarterly basis (every three months). In the United States companies generally pay their dividends in cash, but sometimes they pay them in stocks or bonds (additional shares in the company). A company's ability to pay out dividends on a regular basis is often a strong signal to investors that the company is financially secure and likely to prosper in the future.

When Did It Begin

When a company is profitable and hence able to pay dividends to its shareholders on a regular basis, it can show both shareholders and the public how healthy and financially stable it is. In fact, in the early years of the twentieth century, when corporate practices were just developing, the ability of a company to pay dividends to its shareholders was one of the few ways it had to indicate how healthy it was.

After the stock market crash of 1929, Congress passed the Securities and Exchange Act (1934). As a result of this law, corporations were required to issue financial statements that explicitly showed their profits, debts, and other information. These statements allowed investors to make informed decisions about when,

whether, and how much to invest in the company. Even with the development of this more transparent way of reporting company information, the dividend payment remains a reliable indicator for those who want to learn about and predict a company's financial performance.

More Detailed Information

Most companies do not use their entire profit to pay out dividends to shareholders. A portion of the profit is typically kept in the category of retained earnings, to be used to strengthen the business with the purchase of property, hiring of personnel, or other investment. Technically, any shareholder of a profitable company is a part owner of these retained earnings as well, even if there is no immediate benefit to owning them.

When a company does not make a profit in a given quarter or year, it may choose to suspend (refrain from paying out) the dividend to its shareholders. It also may choose to continue paying them, but to do so it must use the retained earnings from previous quarters or years for the payments.

The board of directors of a company (a group of people that the shareholders have elected to represent them in company matters) is typically responsible for

EXTRA DIVIDENDS

A company will sometimes pay two cash dividends to its shareholders: a regular cash dividend and what is known as an extra cash dividend (sometimes called a special dividend). By labeling a part of the payout "extra," the board of directors of the company indicates to shareholders that it is a one-time payment with no guarantees of being repeated in the future. If a company has an exceptionally strong quarter or year financially and does not want to keep the cash on hand for its own purposes, it might issue an extra dividend. A company might also issue an extra dividend if it is changing the way it is financially organized. Usually extra dividends are large in size. They may be issued on a different date than the normal dividends.

deciding how much and how often to issue dividends to shareholders. Sometimes the board will decide to pay no dividends because it believes that reinvesting all profits back into the company is the best way to serve the shareholders. If all profits are reinvested in the company, it is likely that future profits will be even higher.

When a corporation reinvests its profits, it has the chance to develop new products or even buy other companies. If the company spends its money well, it can increase its profits and, as a result, increase its dividends. For example, the computer giant Microsoft Corporation, a company that grew rapidly during the 1990s, only occasionally paid dividends to shareholders during those years. It was able to sustain its expansion partly because of this practice of reinvesting profits into the company. This decision to reinvest is typical of companies during their high-growth phases. After a company matures out of the time during which it would substantially benefit from reinvesting profits, it begins to pay dividends to shareholders.

Companies can issue different types of stock. The type of stock a shareholder owns has an influence on the type of dividends he or she can expect. Preferred stock is stock with what is called "dividend priority" over another type of stock known as common stock. Preferred stock typically has a dividend rate that is a fixed percentage of the profit (as opposed to common stock, which has dividend rates that are determined each quarter by the company's board of directors). Preferred stock has preference over common stock, and therefore its dividends are issued to shareholders before the remaining amount may be divided among the common shares.

Recent Trends

Over the last century investors have found that corporate stocks have generally been good places to invest money. On average, corporate stocks sustained an annual return rate of 15 percent. This means that the average $100 invested in the stock market on January 1, 1990, would have increased in value to $404.56 by the beginning of 2000. Over shorter periods of time, however, one cannot assume that stock prices will necessarily rise at all.

Microsoft is a good example of what a company can achieve by reinvesting its profits. Those investors who purchased shares of Microsoft stock in the 1990s were especially able to benefit from the company's rapid expansion and its practice of reinvesting profits back into research and development for new products. By the middle of 2003 Microsoft's shares had reached a total value of almost $300 billion, which gave its shareholders confidence that they would eventually profit from their investment; the company paid its first dividend in March 2003.

Working with Employees

$ Overview: Hiring and Managing Employees

What It Means

The task of hiring and managing employees plays a crucial role in the day-to-day operations of a company or business. By definition employees are people who work for a company, an individual, or another entity in exchange for some form of compensation, typically a money payment. In broad terms the first step toward becoming an employee of a company is referred to as the hiring process. When a company hires an employee, it agrees to offer him or her compensation in exchange for his or her labor. Employees can be hired on a temporary or permanent basis. Once a company has hired an employee, it proceeds to manage that employee for the duration of his or her service to the company. There are numerous aspects of employee management, including overseeing the process through which employees are compensated and evaluating employee job performance.

In larger companies the responsibility for hiring and managing employees generally belongs to a specific department. This department is commonly known as the human resource department, or simply human resources. Human resource departments oversee numerous aspects of an employee's service with a company and are responsible for establishing and maintaining employee rules. Human resources is responsible for hiring employees and for making sure they adhere to an agreed-upon work schedule and also get paid. Human resources is responsible for ensuring that the company's employment needs are addressed, by keeping track of employment openings at the company (in other words knowing when specific job positions become available) and seeing that these openings are filled in a timely manner. Human resources also deals with issues relating to employee performance and is responsible for making sure that all employees are working to the satisfaction of the company's managers, supervisors, and executive officers.

In most companies the human resource department is also responsible for addressing employee grievances (specific complaints made by employees or groups of employees). Most employee grievances are minor; for example, employees may complain that a snack machine in the employee lunchroom lacks an adequate range of healthy food options, or an employee may request that he no longer be required to work overtime because he wants to spend more time with his family. Other employee grievances (for example, if a particular employee habitually uses abusive or offensive language or if a supervisor makes sexual advances toward his or her assistant) are more serious and will generally be brought to the attention of the company's owner or executive officers.

When Did It Begin

In the United States the modern practice of hiring and managing employees traces its origins to the industrial revolution. The industrial revolution was a period of profound economic change that took place in Europe and the United States during the late eighteenth and early nineteenth centuries. In broad terms the industrial revolution represented the transition from an agrarian (farming) economy to an industrial (large-scale manufacturing) economy and was characterized by a number of technological innovations (in particular the use of complex machinery rather than traditional tools in the production of goods). By using machines companies were able to manufacture a far greater quantity of products, in a much shorter amount of time, than was previously possible. This process of large-scale manufacturing is commonly referred to as mass production.

In order to operate these machines, many of which were quite large, manufacturers built factories, or mills. The first modern factory in America was built in 1814 in Lowell, Massachusetts, by the Boston Manufacturing Company, a maker of textiles. A number of other companies followed shortly thereafter, and soon there were several factories operating in Lowell and in other New

APPLYING FOR A JOB

Several steps are involved with applying for a job. First, a prospective employee must decide what sort of job he or she is interested in pursuing. A person can look at job listings (perhaps in a newspaper or on the bulletin board of a college campus), or they may learn about job openings from friends, family members, or former coworkers (a process commonly known as word of mouth). After deciding on a job position to pursue, an applicant will submit an application (a written document that lists basic information about the applicant, such as age, work and education experience, and so on), as well as a résumé (a formal document listing the applicant's experience and qualifications). When an applicant is currently unemployed (for example, if he or she has recently graduated from college or quit another job) it is generally a good idea to submit applications for several job positions at once; because multiple applicants usually apply for a particular job, the job-application process is very competitive, and so applying for more than one job at a time increases an applicant's chances of getting a job. If the applicant's application interests a potential employer, the applicant will be contacted for an interview. The interview involves meeting a representative of the company (usually the person for whom the applicant will work in the event he or she is hired) and answering questions about his or her qualifications and career goals. If the interview is successful the company representative might offer the job to the applicant at the end of the interview or call him or her later that day or week. Typically an applicant has the privilege of asking for time (usually a day or a few days) to make a decision about whether to accept the job.

England cities. These early factories were designed to accommodate diverse aspects of the textile production process, from making the thread to weaving the thread into cloth.

With this shift to factory-based labor, the concept of hiring and managing employees changed radically. These early factories recruited young women from throughout the region to operate the textile machines. These women (who were commonly known as mill girls) lived in boarding houses that were owned and supervised by the various companies. The mill girls were expected to adhere to very strict moral codes, both at work and in the boardinghouses. In the factory the mill girls were supervised by foremen (men responsible for supervising employees). The size of these new workforces was unprecedented; for example, the Boston Manufacturing Company employed more than 300 young women in its Lowell factory.

As the nineteenth century progressed a number of other manufacturers (makers of furniture, shoes, or other goods) began to adopt the model of mass production created by the textile factories. As demand for new products increased, so did demand for employees. As a consequence recruiting and managing labor became a vital aspect of the manufacturing industry.

More Detailed Information

When a company hires an employee it agrees to compensate that person in exchange for his or her labor. The hiring process is often complex and can sometimes take several weeks to complete. A number of stages are involved with hiring employees. First companies will post a job listing, either as a classified advertisement in a newspaper or another publication, on a job board (a bulletin board, often found on college campuses), on an Internet employment website, or at an employment agency (an organization that helps companies find employees, in exchange for a fee). The job listing will generally include the job title, a description of the duties the potential employee will need to perform, the amount of money the job pays, and a description of other forms of compensation, such as benefits (usually health insurance) and paid vacation time (in the United States this is typically two weeks for new employees). The job listing will also include information on how to apply for the job. Most companies ask that prospective employees begin by submitting a résumé (a document providing a detailed description of previous work experience, educational background, and relevant job skills; also known as a curriculum vitae, or C.V.).

After reviewing the résumés of various applicants a company will contact the most qualified potential employees to arrange interviews. When trying to fill a particular position companies generally consider several candidates at once, with the aim of finding the best possible fit for their needs. Although they do not actually interact with each other, these prospective employees are all in competition with each other and must therefore present themselves in the best possible light to increase their chance of getting the job. During the interview the representative of the company (either a member of the human resource department, the specific supervisor or manager for whom the job applicant will potentially work, or even the owner of the company) will ask questions concerning the applicant's past work experience, as well as his or her career goals. The company representative will also ask the applicant the reasons why he or she feels qualified for the job in question. Generally the company representative will have a copy of the applicant's résumé at the time of the interview, so that he or she can ask specific questions relating to the applicant's experience. In considering the applicant's answers to these questions, the company representative will pay attention not only to the clarity of the applicant's ideas (in other words whether the applicant has a clear idea of what his or her responsibilities would be or whether the applicant has clear, specific goals concerning his or her future) but also to the manner in which the applicant replies. Applicants who appear focused and attentive, who are articulate, and

$ Job Applications

What It Means

Consultants to employers and job seekers alike frequently emphasize the importance of making a "good fit" between the business and the employee. A mismatch (or personalities or job skills), they warn, can prove to be a major waste of time, energy, and money for everyone involved. For the employer, it is important to screen applicants carefully in order to determine who is the best candidate to fill a particular position. This screening process begins with the job application.

A job application is a type of questionnaire provided by the employer, which every applicant for a given position must complete. Depending on the level of skill and experience required for the position, job applications can vary widely in terms of what information they require from an applicant. For example, an application for a job flipping burgers will probably be less rigorous and detailed in the questions it asks than an application for a job as a computer programmer or a paramedic.

Still, as a general rule, all job applications are designed to create a basic profile of a job candidate, including his or her contact information, level of education, previous employment history, and relevant skills. Most job applications also require the applicant to indicate whether he or she has ever been arrested or convicted of a crime and whether he or she is a citizen of (or otherwise able to work legally in) the country where he or she is applying for the job. Many jobs require candidates to submit a résumé in addition to, or instead of, an application form. A résumé is a more formal, polished summary of one's education, employment history, and skills. It is also known as a curriculum vitae, or C.V.

A job seeker may fill out a job application in response to a simple "Help Wanted" sign in a storefront window, or perhaps after reading a detailed job description in a trade magazine or on an employment website. In either case, the purpose of the application, from the applicant's perspective, is to capture the employer's interest enough so that the applicant may advance to the next stage of the screening process, such as an interview. From the employer's perspective, the application is a useful tool for separating qualified candidates from unqualified ones. Once the employer has selected a handful of the most promising applications, he or she can arrange one-on-one interviews with each of these candidates in order to ascertain the more subtle differences between them.

When Did It Begin

Job applications have been in use at least since the Industrial Revolution, an era of sweeping economic change in Europe and the United States during the late eighteenth and early nineteenth centuries. During this period the introduction of large-scale manufacturing processes brought a massive influx of job seekers to urban centers. It was historically common practice for employers to use discriminatory standards in their hiring practices. Job candidates could be required to include with their application information about their ethnic or religious identity, and employers routinely used these applications as a tool for excluding certain groups of people from consideration

who shape their responses intelligently will impress the company representative more than applicants who mumble or who seem bored.

Recent Trends

Since the emergence of the Internet in the late 1990s, typical practices associated with hiring and managing employees have changed dramatically. On the one hand the hiring process has been transformed by the development of online employment resources, as more and more human resource specialists place job listings on websites or else recruit prospective employees who have posted their résumés online. At the same time, the Internet has transformed the ways that companies communicate with their existing employees. Electronic mail (commonly known as e-mail) has made it possible for company managers or human resource directors to pass along important information to employees more quickly and easily and accounts for a large proportion of interoffice communication in the early twenty-first century.

Typically the number of employees working for a company is in constant flux. Larger companies must contend with continual changes to personnel, as employees retire, quit, are laid off or asked to resign, or take an extended leave of absence (for example, when an employee takes a leave of absence to take care of a new-born baby, also known as maternity leave). These changes to company personnel are commonly known as employee turnover. In managing its employees a company must often confront difficult decisions concerning a specific employee's future with the company. Because of the effort and costs involved with hiring an employee, companies are generally reluctant to fire an employee unless his or her performance falls significantly below company expectations. In some cases (for example, when profits are lower than expected) a company is compelled to lay off a certain number of employees; this process is often referred to as downsizing. In other instances a company will want to replace an older employee with a younger employee, even when the older employee has continually met the company's expectations over the course of a long career, in the belief that a new employee will bring more energy and a fresher perspective to a particular job. Sometimes a company will try to persuade the older employee to leave, usually through financial incentives like pensions (annual payments made to retired employees) or early-retirement bonuses. The *golden boot* is a term often used to describe the incentives a company offers an older employee to persuade him or her to accept an early retirement.

for a job. In the United States in the nineteenth and early twentieth centuries, such discrimination was most often applied to certain immigrant groups.

Preliminary prohibitions against employment discrimination in the United States were included in the Unemployment Relief Act of 1933, but they were virtually unenforceable. The Civil Rights Act of 1964 served to establish the Equal Employment Opportunity Commission (EEOC), a government agency whose mission is to "ensure equality of opportunity by vigorously enforcing federal legislation prohibiting discrimination in employment," especially discrimination on the basis of race, color, religion, sex, or national origin. Still, however, it was not until the passage of the Equal Employment Opportunity Act of 1972 that the EEOC gained the power to bring employment-discrimination cases to court. Similar protections were extended to job applicants with disabilities by the Americans with Disabilities Act of 1992. Preemployment inquiries about a person's race, color, religion, or national origin, or a requirement that a photo be submitted with an application, may now be subject to charges of discrimination.

More Detailed Information

The typical job application asks for the following information:

- The applicant's name, address, e-mail address, and telephone number
- The position (or positions) for which the applicant is applying
- The applicant's educational history, including the names of schools he or she attended and the degrees, diplomas, or certificates he or she completed
- The applicant's employment history (usually covering his or her last 3 to 5 jobs held), including the names and addresses of these employers, the positions or job titles held by the applicant, and the duties he or she performed
- The applicant's employment references (the names and contact information of former employers who can recommend the applicant as a qualified and reliable candidate)

A job application requests information about education, prior work experience, and other areas relevant to the position available. In most cases job seekers must fill out applications in order to be considered for employment.　　Photograph by Kelly A. Quin. Cengage Learning, Gale.

A job application is a written form containing information about a prospective employee's education, work history, and skills. Job applicants submit these forms, and employers review them looking for the most qualified and talented candidates.

- A summary of the applicant's skills as they apply to the position in question. For example, if the applicant is applying for an administrative position, he might list the computer programs with which he is proficient; or, if the applicant is applying for a customer-service position, he might list qualities such as "friendly and outgoing" and "excellent communication skills."

The application may also ask whether the applicant is seeking full-time or part-time work, when she is available to start, and what wage or salary she expects to earn.

Most job applications function as a preliminary fact sheet on the candidate without offering much insight into her character or personality. Usually it is not until the employer conducts an interview with the candidate that either party can gain a sense of whether or not the applicant is well suited for the position. Still, there are certain "red flags" an employer can look for in a completed job application that may eliminate a candidate from consideration. For example, if there are significant, unexplained gaps in her job history (gaps that are not attributable to a pursuit such as going back to school or having a baby), the employer may question whether the candidate is a consistent and reliable individual and whether she has a solid work ethic.

Other potential red flags include the following:

- A series of short-term positions (Was the candidate unmotivated? Unskilled? Unable to get along with coworkers?)
- A number of unrelated jobs (Is the candidate fickle? Does she lack clear goals?)
- A series of jobs that does not reflect any advancement of skills or responsibility (another possible indication that the candidate is not highly motivated)
- An application that contains numerous spelling or grammatical errors (If the candidate does not pay attention to detail when he is trying to impress a prospective employer, how can the employer expect that he will be conscientious on the job?)

In addition to advising employers to scan for such obvious red flags, hiring and management advisers recommend that employers begin the hiring process by writing a thorough and detailed job description (including concrete duties and more abstract qualities such as "patience," or "ability to multitask") as well as a profile of the key qualifications and experience that the ideal candidate should have.

Recent Trends

Since the mid-1990s the process of hiring employees, or finding a new job, has been dramatically transformed by e-mail and the Internet. Whereas job seekers once had to respond to each individual job listing posted in the newspaper or other print sources by sending a paper application and résumé by mail, the Internet enables them to reply to job listings instantaneously. Similarly, employers can post job listings electronically on job-search websites and know that their advertisements are accessible not just by readers of the local paper but by job seekers all over the globe.

Although employers have benefited from technological advances that give them a larger pool of applicants, there are also drawbacks to hiring in the electronic age. Perhaps the most notable downside is that, with the increased ease of sending out applications and résumés electronically, many job seekers simply flood employers with applications, without reading the job description carefully or giving real consideration to whether or not they have the skills or the experience for the position. As a result, many employers find their e-mail inboxes stuffed with hundreds of applications, the bulk of which are from candidates who are wholly unqualified for the job.

GOOGLE RECEIVES 1,300 JOB APPLICATIONS PER DAY

Some employers receive more job applications than others. Still, few, if any, employers receive as many job applications as Google, the wildly successful Internet-search-engine company based in Mountain View, California. In 2007 Google ranked number one on *Fortune* magazine's list of the 100 best companies to work for in the United States. Widely known for pampering its employees, the company offers free gourmet cafeteria food, free on-site laundry facilities, and permission to wear pajamas and bring pets to work.

Company officials claimed that the cost of such perks was justified because it helped to attract the most talented job candidates. Certainly, rumors of Google's utopian work environment drew a tremendous volume of applicants. In 2007 the company was reportedly receiving 1,300 job applications per day. True to its philosophy of valuing its workers, the company claimed that it read each and every application.

$ Human Resources

What It Means

In economics the term *human resources* has two distinct but interrelated meanings. In the most basic sense human resources are employees, or workers. An economist might refer to human resources in relation to a certain company, to a particular industry or field, or to a specific segment of

sponsible for managing a company's employees and for determining and maintaining company policy. Traditionally this department has also been known as personnel, although this term became less common toward the end of the twentieth century.

In corporate America human resources are widely regarded to be a company's most important asset. All companies must draw from a diverse range of resources to conduct business effectively. For example, some of the resources used by an automobile manufacturer will include the parts (such as axles, fenders, and tires) that go into a car's construction, the machinery (conveyor belts, welding equipment, and other tools) required to put the cars together, and the fuel and other energy resources (gas, oil, electricity) needed to run the factory. In addition the auto manufacturer will employ many of the same resources common to all companies, such as financial resources (money used to buy equipment and materials), office equipment (including phones and computers), and so on. While all of these resources are vital to the automaker's existence, their effectiveness depends on the human resources (the workers operating the machinery, the business personnel who oversee the company's accounts, the managers responsible for placing orders and tracking shipments, and so on) that the company employs. For this reason human resources represent the most critical aspect of a company's overall performance.

When Did It Begin

The modern concept of human resources traces its origins to the Efficiency Movement of the late nineteenth and early twentieth centuries. The Efficiency Movement was an American intellectual movement concerned with identifying, and subsequently eliminating, wasteful or inefficient aspects of economic production. One of the leading figures in the Efficiency Movement was Frederick Winslow Taylor (1856–1915), an American engineer. Taylor was particularly interested in discovering ways that managers and employees could work together to maximize productivity. Taylor's 1911 work *The Principles of Scientific Management* outlines a number of innovative approaches to the question of employee efficiency, with an emphasis on specialized training, highly detailed planning, and efficient and clear communication between management and the general labor force.

In the 1920s Australian sociologist George Elton Mayo (1880–1949) began to consider the question of worker productivity from a psychological perspective. Based on a series of experiments conducted during the 1920s and 1930s (commonly known as the Hawthorne Studies), Mayo argued that social factors (namely the quality of the interactions between managers and employees or between employee and other employees) played a key role in determining employee attitudes and behavior. According to Mayo's findings employees performed most effectively when they felt they had a

A company's human resources department is responsible for hiring new employees, managing employee compensation and benefits, and handling employee complaints. Common tasks include reviewing a job candidate's resume, explaining a company's health insurance plan, and planning a team building exercise. © *Terry Wild Studio.*

a population. In the context of a company human resources are sometimes referred to as personnel.

In the business world the term *human resources* also refers to the individual or department that is responsible for overseeing the hiring, management, and payment of a company's employees. All companies have established procedures for dealing with human resource matters. In smaller companies, where there is a relatively small number of employees to manage, the person responsible for handling human resource issues generally performs other work-related tasks, such as bookkeeping or general administration (for example, answering phones, filing documents, and other duties related to maintaining an office); in some small businesses the owner will take direct responsibility for human resource decisions. Larger companies generally have an entire human resource department or division, typically referred to as human resources, or HR. Human resource departments are re-

personal investment in the company for which they worked. In order to cultivate this sense of personal investment, Mayo concluded, companies were best served by instilling feelings of trust, loyalty, and camaraderie in their workers.

Mayo's ideas soon took firm root in American corporate culture. Hiring and maintaining a workforce no longer was considered to be a simple matter of assigning tasks and distributing paychecks but rather was a question of meeting the personal and professional needs of employees in order to increase productivity. As a result the human resource department, which was designed to address the increasing complexity of employee management in the workplace, became a fixture in most American companies by the mid-twentieth century.

More Detailed Information

In a corporate setting a human resource department assumes responsibility for a range of tasks relating to the management of a company's employees. One of the primary responsibilities of the human resource director involves the hiring of employees. In hiring employees human resource directors often place job listings in newspapers or other print publications, at government employment centers (bureaus responsible for helping unemployed members of a community find work), and on Internet job boards (for example, Monster, an extensive online employment database, or craigslist, a popular online classifieds directory). Employment listings will generally include information about the job title, skills the prospective employee should have to apply for the job, and the application process. This aspect of human resources is typically known as recruiting. In most companies potential employees will be asked to submit a résumé (a piece of paper offering a detailed outline of a person's past work experience and qualifications, also known as a curriculum vitae, or C.V.).

In addition to managing the hiring process, a company's human resource department also takes responsibility for employee compensation. The most important element of employee compensation is the payroll (the amount of money paid to a company's employees during a given pay period). Human resource directors must ensure that all employees receive their paychecks on the specified pay date (commonly known as payday). In addition to an employee's pay human resource departments must also manage other forms of employee compensation, such as health insurance (money that goes toward covering employee medical expenses) and stock options (the right to purchase shares in the company).

Human resource directors are also responsible for evaluating employee performance. In determining the level of quality in an employee's job performance, human resource directors will address such issues as whether an employee performs the tasks he or she was hired to do, whether the employee arrives at work on time, whether

---

CASUAL FRIDAY

In American business the term *human resources* typically refers to the division of a company that is responsible for hiring and managing the company's employees. Because employee satisfaction is generally considered to be a major factor in employee job performance, the human resource department plays an important role in monitoring and improving employee morale. Since the mid-twentieth century one of the most popular methods of boosting employee satisfaction in a corporate setting has been casual Friday. Originating in the 1950s, casual Friday is a policy that allows company employees to wear casual attire (for example, blue jeans) on Fridays, with the idea that employees will feel more relaxed, and therefore happier, while performing their jobs. During the 1990s a number of American companies even allowed workers to begin dressing casually every day, as traditional notions of formality in the business world became outdated.

---

the employee has positive personal relationships with other employees, and so on. Human resource directors also make certain key decisions related to an employee's continued role with a company. If an employee has an excellent performance record and makes a consistently positive contribution to the company, then the human resource director may decide to offer this employee a raise (an increase in pay) or a promotion (an elevation to a more prestigious position with the company, typically accompanied by a raise and additional responsibility). If an employee's performance has a significantly negative impact (if, for example, he or she is chronically late for work or exhibits a bad attitude toward his or her responsibilities) then a human resource director will take responsibility for discussing the problem with the employee. A human resource director is also responsible for firing employees in certain extreme cases.

Recent Trends

Questions of employee motivation and morale are central to evaluating levels of satisfaction in a workplace. Over the years human resource specialists have developed a number of innovative ways of fostering and improving the overall happiness of employees. One approach to employee motivation that began to gain popularity in the early twenty-first century was the concept of team building. Team building is a practice by which human resource directors attempt to improve qualities of cooperation, loyalty, and trust among a company's employees. Team building often involves having employees participate in organized activities. In some cases these activities are designed to help employees become more familiar with each other's personalities and work styles, through seminars, creative exercises, or other group projects.

Often team-building exercises are designed to provide employees with the opportunity to have fun and get to know each other in a relaxed environment, away from the stressful demands of work. Cookouts, camping retreats, and interdepartmental softball games are only a few of the activities a company uses to create a sense of enjoyment, as well as solidarity, among its workers.

$ Payroll

What It Means

Generally speaking the term *payroll* refers to the record (or set of records) a company uses to keep track of all the money it pays to its employees over a specific period of time. When an individual works for a company, he or she earns some form of monetary compensation, typically in the form of wages (a set amount of money, usually calculated on an hourly basis) or a salary (an amount of money calculated on an annual basis). In a less formal sense the term *payroll* is also synonymous with the total amount of money a company pays out to its employees, either during a regular pay period or over the course of an entire year.

In this latter sense payroll forms an integral part of a company's overall budget. A budget is a detailed outline of a company's total expenditures, including employee payroll, production costs (for example, equipment and other materials needed for manufacturing operations), administrative costs (office supplies, computers, and telephones), operational costs (energy bills and Internet service), and other expenses. In determining its payroll a company will calculate the overall cost of paying its employees over a certain period of time and measure this total against the total amount of revenue the company earns over the same period, minus other budgetary expenses. If the company is not satisfied with its final profit margin (in other words, the amount of money it retains after paying expenses), then it will consider various ways it can reduce costs or increase its revenues. In many cases a company will decide to make cuts to its payroll, either by terminating the jobs of employees it considers to be less effective or by implementing pay reductions.

A company's payroll record typically includes a list of paid employees, the number of hours each employee has worked during a set period of time (also known as a pay period), and the amount of money each employee has earned over the course of a pay period. Pay periods vary

A company's payroll record is an accounting of the hours worked and money earned by its employees. Here a payroll clerk is inputting information from handwritten logs of employee hours into an electronic payroll database. *Photograph by Kelly A. Quin. Cengage Learning, Gale.*

from company to company. Most large corporations pay their employees twice a month or in some cases every two weeks; some smaller companies pay their employees once a week. Although salaried workers have their income calculated on a yearly basis, they still receive a portion of this income during the company's established pay period. A company's payroll will also include an account of the sums of money deducted from each employee's earnings for tax purposes; collectively these deductions are known as a payroll tax.

When Did It Begin

Payrolls have existed, in one form or another, since people first began employing, and paying, other people. In ancient times monarchs and other rulers maintained what historians sometimes refer to as a royal payroll. A royal payroll was generally used to compensate thinkers, prophets, or other prominent personages whom the ruler considered worth paying, generally either because the ruler valued their ideas or because their presence lent prestige to his court. Emperors in ancient Greece and Rome regularly kept a payroll of philosophers, who often served as teachers to the emperor and his family. Scholars believe that Charlemagne (742 or 747–814), emperor of the Franks (a group of Germanic peoples inhabiting Western Europe between the sixth and tenth centuries), kept an entourage of priests on his payroll. During the Renaissance (a period of cultural rebirth in Europe beginning in the fourteenth century and continuing into the seventeenth century) the practice of paying great thinkers and artists to play a role in courtly life came to be known as royal patronage. A number of famous Renaissance artists and thinkers, notably Leonardo da Vinci (1452–1519), depended on this form of patronage for their livelihood.

Payroll in the modern sense first began to take shape during the Great Depression (a period of severe economic hardship, marked by high jobless rates, from 1929 to about 1939) with the passage of the Social Security Act of 1935. The Social Security Act was a law enacted by the U.S. Congress to help offset the financial difficulties suffered by retired and unemployed workers as a result of the Great Depression. Under the law all employers and employees were required to deduct a specific amount of money from their earnings, known as the social security tax, which was paid into a fund for retired and unemployed workers. With the implementation of these new taxes company payrolls became more complex, as they needed to divide the various deductions, which were paid to the government, from an employee's net earnings (the money an employee keeps after taxes), which were paid directly to the employee. This practice continued into the twenty-first century.

More Detailed Information

A payroll record is typically divided into rows and columns. Each row will usually be designated for the name of each employee, while each column will provide information relating to a particular aspect of the employee's work hours, compensation, and taxes. In addition to providing a list of employees, how much they work, and what they earn, a payroll record will usually contain additional subcategories. For example, next to the column indicating the number of hours an employee has worked, there might be a column dedicated to overtime hours. Overtime hours are the number of hours an employee works beyond the accepted number of hours in a standard workweek; in the United States the standard workweek is usually 40 hours. By law overtime hours entitle an employee to a higher hourly wage than a normal hourly wage, typically at least one and a half times the standard hourly amount (also referred to as time and a half).

Besides an employee's work hours, a payroll will generally also include a column relating to an employee's vacation time. With most full-time jobs employees are eligible for at least two weeks (or 80 hours) of paid vacation time. Sometimes an employee will take a full week of vacation at once, in which case the payroll record might indicate 40 hours of vacation and no work hours; in other cases an employee might take two days off, in which case the payroll might reflect 24 work hours and 16 vacation hours. Along with vacation hours employees are also entitled to a certain number of paid sick hours per year, which are also included on the payroll.

Following the columns relating to the various types of hours for which employees are paid will generally be several more columns, dedicated to various taxes. Each tax—for example, federal, state, and local (city or county)—will typically have its own column. In the United States all employees must pay a social security tax (also known as Federal Insurance Contributions Act taxes, or FICA for short), as well as Medicare tax (or MedFICA), which is a tax that goes toward medical care for retired employees; these two taxes generally appear in the same column, though they are broken down into two separate amounts. The payroll will also include a column for unemployment tax. There is also a column for garnished wages (a portion of wages that must be deducted from an employee's paycheck in the event they owe money to someone and a court of law has ordered the employee to pay it back).

There are many steps involved in the preparation of a company's regular payroll. In cases where employees earn an hourly wage, employers begin by accumulating a record of the total number of hours earned by each employee. These hours might be recorded by hand, on an employee timesheet or printed onto a time card by a time clock. A time clock is a time-keeping device used to keep track of the precise times that an employee is on the job. When an employee arrives at work, he or she places a time card into the time clock; the time clock then stamps the time onto the card. This process, commonly referred to as

EXORBITANT PAYROLLS

Payroll generally has two meanings. In the more exact sense payroll refers to the record a company maintains of the payments it makes to its employees over a specific period of time. In the broader sense payroll can also refer to the total amount of money a company pays its employees over the course of a given period, usually a year. All corporate entities, from shoe-manufacturing firms to professional sports teams, have payrolls. Indeed professional sports teams are famous for having some of the largest (and most high-profile) payrolls in the business world. Since the early 1990s the payrolls of professional sports teams have risen dramatically. For example, in 1990 the New York Yankees (a professional baseball team) had an annual payroll of $21 million, fourth highest in major league baseball (that same year the Kansas City Royals had the highest payroll, at $23.9 million). By 2007 the Yankees opened the season with a payroll of $189 million, by far the largest payroll of any professional sports team in history.

clocking or punching in, is typical of most manufacturing jobs.

Recent Trends

Since the late 1990s a number of specialized payroll management companies have emerged. Preparing company payroll is often a meticulous, time-consuming process, and payroll management companies are designed to spare businesses the trouble of preparing their own payroll records. Although these companies charge a fee for their services, by preparing payroll more efficiently than the company could do by itself, they can often save a business money (the money it would have to pay its own employees to manage payroll). The process by which businesses hire other companies to manage certain aspects of their operations is commonly known as outsourcing.

$ Cost-of-Living Adjustment

What It Means

The term *cost of living* refers to how much money is required to maintain a certain basic level of material comfort from one year to the next. In the United States the Cost-of-Living Adjustment (COLA) is an annual adjustment of wage contracts, retirement benefits, and other payments; it is intended to offset increases in the cost of living.

One of the main figures used to formulate the COLA is the Consumer Price Index (CPI), an index compiled by the Bureau of Labor Statistics (a division of the U.S. Department of Labor) that tracks the changing price of basic goods and services (such as milk, gasoline, bus fare,

and electricity) in the United States. Change in the CPI is a measure of inflation, the general increase in the prices of goods and services in the economy.

COLAs are applied to government-assistance benefits such as Social Security (which provides retirement, disability, and survivors' benefits to workers and their families and administers the Supplemental Security Income program for elderly, blind, and disabled persons with little or no income); federal-employee pension benefits; and military pension benefits. In general, the purpose of the COLA is to protect those people living on a fixed income from having the value of their income eroded by inflation over time. COLAs have also been used by labor unions as an important bargaining tool in negotiations of employee wages and pension plans. In many cases the term *cost-of-living adjustment* is used informally to mean a negotiated annual salary increase that is not tied to the CPI or other official indexes.

When Did It Begin

The Consumer Price Index was first instituted during World War I (1914–18), a period of rapidly increasing prices, as a way to calculate appropriate wage increases. Social Security retirement benefits were established in 1935. In the decades that followed, Congress periodically passed increases in Social Security benefits to compensate for gradual inflation, as measured by the CPI.

In the late 1960s and early 1970s, however, a considerable jump in inflation rates threatened to erode the real purchasing power of Social Security benefits and other fixed payments. During this period Congress approved four Cost-of-Living Adjustments in five years. Passed in 1972, the fourth of these increases included a provision that permanently calibrated COLAs to the CPI, making such adjustments an annual certainty for recipients of Social Security benefits. Automatic COLAs, no longer contingent upon Congressional approval, went into effect in 1975.

More Detailed Information

The rate of inflation is represented as a percentage increase. If annual inflation is estimated at 4 percent, for example, this would suggest that the price of a bus ride would increase from $1.00 to $1.04 over the course of a year. The COLA, which is also represented as a percentage increase, is usually about equal to the rate of inflation. For instance, the U.S. inflation rate for 2006 was estimated at 3.23 percent, and the COLA for that year was calculated at 3.3 percent. Suppose a retiree received a monthly Social Security benefit check of $1,011 throughout 2006; beginning in January 2007 that person would receive a monthly benefit check of $1,044 (an increase of $33, or 3.3 percent of $1,011).

COLAs are also applied to other kinds of payments. For example, the U.S. Department of Agriculture (USDA) applies COLAs to food stamp allotments (food

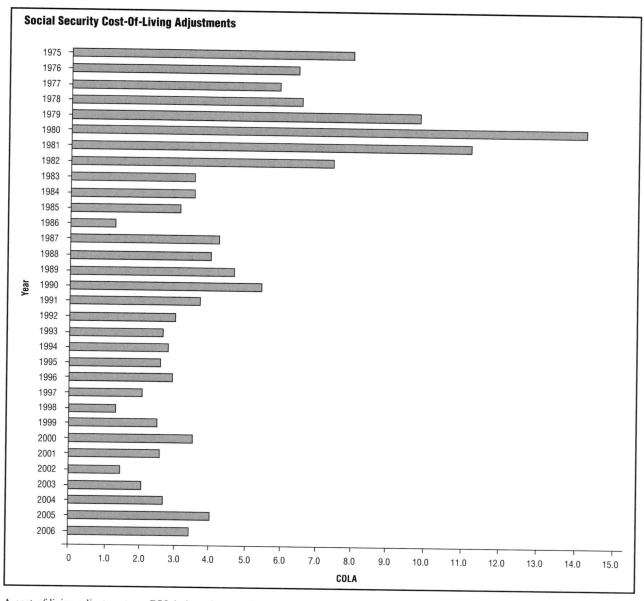

Social Security Cost-Of-Living Adjustments

A cost-of-living adjustment, or COLA, is an increase in wages or payments that is intended to offset increases in the cost of living due to inflation. This table, which charts COLAs that have been automatically applied to U.S. Social Security benefits between 1975 and 2006, shows a 1980 adjustment as a result of particularly high inflation. *Illustration by GGS Information Services. Cengage Learning, Gale.*

stamps are coupons that can be exchanged for groceries; the USDA distributes them to low-income households). The agency also makes cost-of-living adjustments to its standards of eligibility for the Food Stamp Program. For example, whereas a few years ago a person with a monthly income of $750 might have earned too much to qualify for food stamps, inflation means that $750 buys less than it used to (that is, the cost of living is higher). Therefore, in order to deliver the Food Stamp Program to the neediest population of Americans, the USDA must increase its maximum income level for eligibility.

The idea of a cost-of-living adjustment is that payments should be calibrated and recalibrated according to how much money the recipient needs to maintain a basic level of health and comfort. Thus, such adjustments are sometimes implemented to offset regional differences in the cost of living. For instance, the cost of renting a two-bedroom apartment in San Francisco, California, is significantly higher than it is in Vicksburg, Mississippi. For this reason, COLAs may be appropriate in cases where an employee relocates from a relatively inexpensive area of the country to a relatively expensive one. In addition to

COLAS DO NOT BENEFIT EVERYONE EQUALLY

The Cost-of-Living Adjustment (COLA) is an annual percentage increase in payments to retirees and other Americans who receive government-assistance benefits (regular payments to cover living expenses). It is designed to offset the impact of inflation (the ongoing increase in prices) so that benefits recipients will be able to maintain a certain standard of living on a fixed income, even in the face of rising prices. Nearly all Americans age 65 and older are eligible for retirement benefits through the national Social Security program, and all Social Security benefits are subject to COLAs. But whereas government employees also have COLAs applied to their pensions (benefits a retiree receives directly from his or her former employer), most private pension plans do not provide COLAs. In the early 1990s it was estimated that government retirees (both civilian and military) received an annual income that was twice as high as that of nongovernment retirees. Moreover, it was estimated that, because of COLAs, many government retirees were receiving pension payments higher than what they earned during their working years.

the national CPI, the Bureau of Labor Statistics also compiles region-specific CPIs and CPIs that correspond to 27 different metropolitan areas around the United States.

For servicemen and servicewomen who are stationed in certain areas of the country that are categorized as "high cost" (there were 63 such areas as of 2007), the U.S. military compensates for the increased cost of living. It pays what is called a CONUS (Continental United States) COLA; in this case the abbreviation stands for "cost-of-living allowance," because the adjustment is a stipend, or temporary extra payment, rather than a salary increase. These COLAs are calculated by the military, and they vary according to where the servicemember is stationed, whether he or she has any dependents (a spouse, children, elderly parent, or other person for whom the servicemember is financially responsible), and what his or her pay grade is. The standard, CPI-based COLA is also applied to military retirement benefits.

Recent Trends

In 2006 many senior citizens were worried that the Social Security COLA was not keeping pace with their needs, such that the real value of their Social Security benefits was dwindling. They argued that, while the COLA averaged slightly less than 2.6 percent from 2001 to 2006, the costs of home-energy bills, health care, and other expenses were growing at a much higher rate. Indeed, even though the COLA for 2007 was 3.3 percent, much of that was absorbed by the 5.6 percent increase in the

amount that seniors had to pay for Medicare (a national health-insurance program for Americans age 65 and older). These critics of the Social Security COLA maintained that the CPI (which was used to determine the COLA) was based on goods and services purchased by young, urban workers and did not accurately reflect the most important expenditures of seniors, such as medications, doctor visits, and other kinds of health care.

Seniors and senior-advocacy groups decried the unfairness, inaccuracy, and inadequacy of this methodology and began to call for the Social Security COLA to be calculated according to the CPI-E, or Consumer Price Index for Elderly Consumers. The CPI-E already existed; it had been compiled and calculated by the Bureau of Labor Statistics for many years. The number of seniors in the United States was rising and constituted a powerful voting block, one that hoped to exert its political influence to change the way the Social Security COLA was calculated.

$ Employee Benefits

What It Means

Employee benefits, also known as fringe benefits, are the compensation an employee receives in addition to an hourly wage or annual salary. Common forms of fringe benefits include health insurance (a fund designated to help employees pay for medical expenses in the event they become ill or injured), paid vacations, and retirement pensions (annual payments made to former employees after they retire).

Although their overall value is generally secondary to an employee's wages, fringe benefits do have a monetary value for employees. For example, businesses that offer health insurance benefits usually charge employees only a nominal amount to subscribe to the program. Employees who decline membership in their company's health insurance program would generally pay a great deal more for individual health insurance. In this sense fringe benefits serve as an indirect means of offering employees greater financial gain.

Employers often offer additional fringe benefits, also known as perquisites, or perks, to attract highly qualified employees. Typical perks for upper-level or senior employees include expense accounts (an additional allowance of funds allotted for business-related travel, dining, and entertainment), use of a company car, and personalized stationery.

When Did It Begin

The modern practice of offering employee benefits began during the Great Depression (a period of economic hardship that lasted from 1929 until about 1939). In 1929 Justin Ford Kimball, a former school superintendent in Dallas, Texas, accepted a job as an administrator

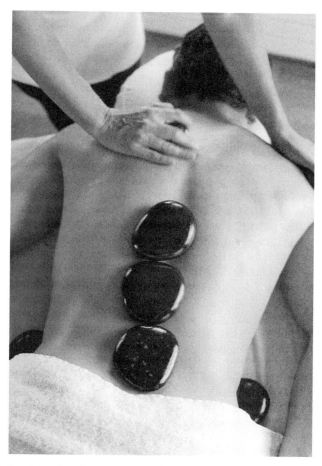

Employee benefits are compensation employees receive on top of their regular wages. Employee benefits typically refer to medical insurance and paid vacation, although some employees receive more luxurious benefits such as free meals, travel expense accounts, and massage therapy. © *Royalty-free/Corbis.*

at Baylor Hospital. In a short time Kimball began to notice that a lot of the hospital's unpaid bills belonged to teachers. Because he had been an educator, Kimball knew that teachers earned too little to pay the bills. To remedy the problem he created a fund that allowed teachers to pay a small portion of their salary (only 50 cents a month) toward mutual health coverage. As a result of Kimball's efforts, teachers in Dallas became the first American employees to receive a group health insurance plan as part of their contract. First known as the Baylor Plan, Kimball's group insurance later became known as the Blue Cross hospital insurance plan.

The term *fringe benefits* originated during World War II. At this time, in the midst of continued economic difficulties, the government imposed strict limits on wage increases as a means of controlling the flow of financial resources. To retain employment levels in the face of these limitations, the National War Labor Board (an organization dedicated to negotiating disputes between business and labor interests) created a system of fringe benefits to help offset the losses suffered by workers receiving low pay. After the war offering fringe benefits became standard practice in most industries.

More Detailed Information

Employee benefits are generally regarded to be an important incentive when people are deciding whether to accept a particular job. Most companies offer their full-time employees (those employees who work at least a standard number of hours per week, usually 40 hours, though perhaps fewer hours at certain companies) some form of health insurance, generally at a reduced cost to the employee. In some instances labor unions obtain employee benefits for their members by negotiating collective bargaining agreements, or contracts, with employees. For the most part these bargaining agreements will pertain to such issues as health insurance; paid sick leave, also known as sick days (an employee will continue to be paid if he or she becomes ill); or the creation of day-care facilities for employees with young children. In other situations employers offer prospective employees fringe benefits on their own initiative.

The main advantage of offering fringe benefits is that it allows employers to attract the most qualified candidates for certain jobs, particularly if several companies are interested in hiring a specific individual. Unique, specialized benefits for highly skilled or senior employees generally fall under this category. These benefits can range from the general, such as stock options (agreements through which employees have the right to purchase stock, or shares, in the company's ownership) and profit sharing (additional cash payments based on the company's profitability), to highly personal, often unusual perks. For example, contracts between professional sports teams and athletes often include provisions for travel allowances, additional game tickets for family members, personal chefs, and masseuses. One of the most extensive fringe benefits package in the history of professional sports was created in December 2006, when the Boston Red Sox (a professional baseball team) signed a young pitcher from Japan named Daisuke Matsuzaka. In addition to a yearly salary of $8.67 million, the team also provided Daisuke with housing, a translator, a personal assistant, a physical therapist, a massage therapist, and between 80 and 90 flights to Japan over the course of the six-year deal.

Recent Trends

Toward the end of the twentieth century, as the American labor force became more diversified, companies started devising innovative forms of fringe benefits tailored to meet the evolving needs of their employees. Examples include on-site day-care centers, which allow parents to return to work after having children, and

MUTUAL ADVANTAGES OF FRINGE BENEFITS

Employee benefits (also known as fringe benefits), or the compensation that an employee receives beyond his or her salary or wage, are generally financially advantageous for both the employer and employee. There are many types of fringe benefits; some of the most common include health insurance (money that is available to assist employees with medical costs), vacation pay (money an employee receives when he or she is not working, typically between two and four weeks a year for most jobs in the United States, depending on the amount of time an employee has worked for a company), and retirement pensions (a monthly salary an employee receives after he or she stops working). The primary advantage to the employee is that, although fringe benefits have a monetary value, they are not taxable. Employers, for their part, have the right to deduct the costs of offering fringe benefits on their tax returns.

tuition-reimbursement programs, as a way of encouraging employees to pursue higher education.

$ Equal Opportunity

What It Means

The United States and other countries officially aspire to provide every citizen with an equal chance of obtaining an education and a job and of being treated fairly on the job and in life generally. This aspiration is encapsulated in the term *equal opportunity*, which is most commonly used to refer to a company or organization's hiring and business practices. In the United States it is illegal for companies or organizations that employ more than 15 people to discriminate based on race, sex, religion, color, national origin, disability, or age. In all their dealings with employees (hiring, firing, promoting, setting wages, allotting vacation time, etc.), employers must enforce state and federal guidelines regarding equal opportunity.

Equal opportunity became a pressing national goal during the Civil Rights Movement of the 1950s and 1960s, prior to which African Americans were subject to widespread mistreatment and unfairness, particularly when it came to voting, education, and employment. The Civil Rights Act of 1964, passed at the urging of President Lyndon B. Johnson, gave the federal government the power to stop discrimination based on race, color, religion, or national origin. Title VII of the Civil Rights Act (the act consisted of different sections or "titles," each of which focused on a particular subject important to the larger goal of equality) dealt specifically with employment and established the Equal Employment Opportunity Commission (EEOC), the federal agency that investigates situations in which individuals claim they have been subject to discriminatory treatment.

Since the passage of the Civil Rights Act, Title VII has been supplemented by numerous state and federal laws that have updated the original protections and widened the scope of equal opportunity to defend the rights of such groups as disabled and older workers. Additionally, Title VII has been the basis of the practice known as affirmative action, according to which the government requires employers to diversify their workforce by giving preferential treatment, in the hiring process, to women and minority groups. While there have always been some critics of equal opportunity in general, affirmative action in particular has been by far the most controversial portion of the government's drive to promote fairness and equality.

When Did It Begin

While the Civil Rights Movement brought the issue of equal opportunity to the forefront of American politics and culture, the roots for the goals of the movement go back to 1868 when, following the abolition of slavery, the Fourteenth Amendment to the U.S. Constitution was passed. The Fourteenth Amendment promises "equal protection under the law": in other words, all citizens were to be treated fairly by the government. In practice, however, this did not happen. African Americans were systematically mistreated, often with the knowledge or direct cooperation of government. So-called Jim Crow laws in the southern United States mandated separate public facilities and educational systems for African Americans, and on a national level employers did not commonly make any effort to promote equality when it came to hiring employees. Though minority groups as well as groups concerned with justice continually tried to force societal change based on the promises of the Fourteenth Amendment, it was not until 1954 that a major victory came. In the court case *Brown v. Board of Education* of that year, the Supreme Court explicitly forbade the segregation of schools by race. This provided the spark that ignited the Civil Rights Movement.

Equal opportunity in employment became a key part of the broader Civil Rights Movement. In 1961 President John F. Kennedy signed an executive order establishing equal opportunity in competing for government jobs. The crowning achievement of the Civil Rights Movement was the Civil Rights Act of 1964. Signed into law by President Lyndon B. Johnson, the act outlawed discrimination based on race, color, religion, or national origin. Title VII of the act set guidelines for employers and established the EEOC, which was empowered to investigate claims of unfairness. The Civil Rights Act went into effect in 1965.

More Detailed Information

The concept of equal opportunity is closely connected to basic beliefs in what kind of country the United States

Equal Opportunity refers to the idea that all members of a society should be treated equally and have the same access to education and jobs. Supporters of the Equal Rights Amendment, which would place in the U.S. Constitution a ban on sex-based discrimination, are shown above at the 1980 Democratic National Convention. *Bill Pierce/Time Life Pictures/Getty Images.*

should be. U.S. citizens like to believe that their country is a meritocracy, a society in which those who succeed do so because of ability and hard work. This belief has always been a simplistic view of the reality of life in the United States, however. While there has never been a class of aristocrats (people whose ancestry entitles them to occupy a privileged place in society) in the United States, wealth can be handed down from one generation to the next. This means that equal opportunity has never been strictly possible, because inherited wealth necessarily tilts the scales in favor of certain people. Two children with identical abilities and work ethics, for instance, cannot be said to enjoy equal opportunity if one of them is born wealthy and the other poor.

But most Americans see a difference between this form of inequality, which does not occur because of active wrongdoing, and the racial and gender inequality that existed for roughly 200 years after the country's founding. The systems of slavery (in the eighteenth and nineteenth centuries) and segregation (in the late nineteenth through the late twentieth century) actively promoted discrimination against African Americans. Likewise, women at all levels of society were subject to a wide range of discriminatory laws and customs. When people of certain races, or when women, are prohibited from participating fully in society, then an obvious inequality of opportunity exists.

The system of equal-opportunity laws that grew out of the Civil Rights Movement seeks to correct these and other forms of inequality. The most accepted way in which these laws have functioned is by setting standards for employers. Those employing 15 or more employees must, if they want to stay in business, ensure that they do not display any biases against prospective or current employees because of factors such as race, religion, color, gender, national origin, age, or disability. In practice, however, identifying biases is not always a simple matter.

If, for example, someone born in another country is fired from his job as a computer programmer in the United States, he might believe he was fired because of his national origin, while his boss might argue that he was fired for poor performance. If this employee feels strongly about the matter, he might contact the EEOC and file a complaint about his employer. The EEOC would then investigate the matter to determine whether or not national origin played a role in the employee's firing. If the agency found that national origin did play a role in the firing, it might attempt to mediate between the employer

AFFIRMATIVE ACTION UNDER FIRE

Since the late 1970s there have been numerous legal rulings that have restricted affirmative action, the policy of giving preferential treatment to racial minorities in educational and employment matters. Prior to the late 1970s state universities commonly set aside a certain number of spots for minority groups. These "quotas" were outlawed by the U.S. Supreme Court in 1978, but public universities were allowed to continue to use race as a factor in admissions. Several rulings in the late 1980s saw the Supreme Court narrow the circumstances under which affirmative action could be used in college admissions. Then, 1996 saw both California (through a vote by citizens) and Texas (in state court) outlaw the use of race as a factor in the admissions process at public universities. The Supreme Court upheld these laws by declining to hear appeals to them. In 2003 the Supreme Court did hear an important appeal to a similar measure outlawing affirmative action in Michigan state schools. This time the Court ruled that affirmative action was constitutional but that race could not be the main factor in the admission of one student over another.

and the employee. In the event that no agreement could be reached between the two parties, the EEOC might file a lawsuit against the company.

Recent Trends

Companies, of course, want to avoid the potentially costly attentions of the EEOC. It is common today for large companies to have entire departments and substantial portions of their operating budgets devoted to making sure that the work environment is fair to employees regardless of their race, religion, color, gender, national origin, age, or disability. These so-called "race-blind" or "gender-blind" policies (policies that attempt to get people to look beyond categories such as race and gender) have been widely accepted by the American public despite the effort and expense they impose upon businesses.

Since the Civil Rights era, another major way in which the federal government and state governments have attempted to promote equal opportunity is through affirmative action. Affirmative action means giving preferential treatment to certain groups in matters of education and employment. Especially in the area of university admissions, racial minorities have benefited from affirmative action. But whether or not the increase in racial diversity at universities has promoted equal opportunity remained a subject of debate among experts as well as ordinary people at the beginning of the twentieth century, and the legal status of affirmative action was likewise coming under increased scrutiny.

$ Ergonomics

What It Means

Ergonomics is the science of designing simple tools, complex machines, and work environments that allow people to perform tasks productively and safely. For example, an ergonomically designed office chair will not only be comfortable, but its shape will help an employee maintain good posture. This will allow the worker to accomplish more and will minimize the number of days missed as a result of work-related injuries. Likewise, an ergonomically sound dashboard in a vehicle will permit a driver to view all the gauges easily and to adjust equipment, such as the lights, windshield wipers, and temperature controls, with a minimum amount of bodily movement.

According to the principles of ergonomics, the work environment should be adapted to suit the physical qualities and needs of the workers. Equipment should be adjustable so that people are not required to sit or stand in uncomfortable positions for long periods of time. An ergonomic scientist also studies other factors, such as how much light is required for a given task and the proper temperature settings for a work environment.

When Did It Begin

Polish biologist Wojciech Jastrzebowski (1799–1882) invented the term *ergonomics* in 1857. He combined two Greek words: *ergon,* meaning work, and *nomos,* or natural laws. Ergonomics, then, is the science of work. At the end of the nineteenth century, American business leaders began commissioning scientists to study ways of improving tools and maximizing worker production. This trend became known as the Efficiency Movement, which flourished in American industry from 1890–1930, with engineer Frederick Winslow Taylor (1856–1915) as its leading thinker. Also at this time a new field of research called motion studies, pioneered by Americans Frank (1868–1924) and Lillian Gilbreth (1868–1972), attempted to minimize the number of steps a worker used to complete a job. The field of ergonomics grew again during World War II (1939–45), when the most skilled American pilots were having difficulty handling planes. Scientists discovered that the operating panels were too confusing, and subsequent planes were designed with more pilot-friendly control systems.

More Detailed Information

Ergonomic research can be divided into two separate but related fields. The first is product design. Manufacturers of any item, from can openers and power tools to automobile seats and portable music devices, spend large sums of money finding the way to make a product that is the most comfortable to use for the widest range of consumers. Producing the particular goods listed above requires researching such topics as the ideal grip and weight for tools, the perfect alignment for seats, and the

The science of ergonomics is dedicated to developing healthier, more effective ways for employees to use their work environments. The woman pictured here has arranged her workstation in order to achieve maximum efficiency with minimum stress on her body. © *Martha Tabor/Working Images Photographs. Reproduced by permission.*

most convenient ways to store and retrieve digital music files on a portable player.

The other general field of ergonomic research studies ways to minimize work-related injuries. Scientists have discovered that the most costly and harmful occupational injuries occur slowly over a long period of time. These injuries include chronic back pain, carpal tunnel syndrome (the compression of nerves in the wrist), and tendonitis (the inflammation of a tendon). They result from tasks that require a worker to maintain an awkward posture and repeat the same activity for prolonged periods of time. Researchers call such injuries Cumulative Trauma Disorders, or CTDs. Those at greatest risk for CTDs include assembly-line employees, people who operate power tools, and office workers required to use computers for most of the day. In addition to designing equipment that is less likely to cause these troubles, ergonomic scientists have devised a series of preventative (or safety) measures for workers to follow. For example, workers are advised to rotate tasks and to take hourly 5- or 10-minute breaks to stretch muscles and joints.

By the mid-1990s ergonomic considerations had begun to enter into labor negotiations. The Occupational Safety and Health Administration (OSHA), a subgroup of the Department of Labor, responded to workers' mounting concerns by publishing in the late 1990s a catalog of basic ergonomic standards for businesses. President Clinton signed a law requiring businesses to pay as much as 90 percent of workers' wages if they missed work because of an ergonomics-based injury. In 2001 the Bush administration, working with a Republican Congress, reversed many of these safety rules. These measures were denounced by labor unions but were applauded by small business owners who had trouble paying to restructure the work environment.

Recent Trends

Since the technology boom of the 1990s, ergonomics has become an increasingly important science, for both commercial and medical reasons. Manufacturers use ergonomics commercially, in order to sell more products. Most companies can no longer build products that

CARPAL TUNNEL SYNDROME

Carpal tunnel syndrome occurs when the nerve running from the forearm to the hand is pinched at the wrist. Physicians believe that holding one's wrists over a keyboard at an uncomfortable angle for long periods of time increases the likelihood of suffering from this condition. Initial symptoms include numbness in the palms and fingers. As the condition worsens, a person may have trouble gripping small objects and distinguishing between hot and cold temperatures with his or her fingers. According to most reports, women (who usually have a smaller tunnel housing the nerve) are three times more likely to get carpal tunnel syndrome than men.

significantly outperform the products of their competitors. For example, all top-of the-line cell phones, regardless of their brand name, do essentially the same thing. Because the way the equipment functions is similar, manufacturers try to gain a competitive advantage by making their products more user-friendly.

Meanwhile, computer-related injuries have been costing employers large sums in medical expenses. By the mid-1990s it was estimated that more than 700,000 employees missed work each year as a result of tendonitis, carpal tunnel syndrome, and other injuries associated with office work. The cost to employers was estimated at $12 billion per year. To reduce this loss, most large businesses have included an ergonomics strategy in their operating budgets.

$ Stress Management

What It Means

In the workplace, stress management is a set of strategies or responses designed to reduce the causes and effects of stress on workers and the organization. Stress is a mental and physical response to the demands that are placed upon a person. Stress occurs in all facets of life, and a certain amount of it is normal. In the workplace, stress can help propel employees to meet deadlines, win new clients, solve problems, improve sales figures, and learn new skills. Stress on the job becomes a problem, however, when:

- the requirements of the job exceed the employee's capabilities,

- workplace pressures are more than the worker can deal with,

- job satisfaction is eroded by frustration and fatigue.

Long-term exposure to stress can trigger negative emotional and physiological responses, including depression, irritability, headaches, back pain, insomnia, stomach ulcers, a weakened immune system, and relationship problems with friends and family.

Stress can also have a profoundly negative effect on the health of a business or organization as a whole. Stress on workers often results in poor job performance; absenteeism (when workers do not show up to work); employee turnover (when workers leave the company); workplace accidents (or even violence); medical, legal, and insurance costs; and worker's compensation awards (financial compensation for employees who are unable to work because of they were injured or disabled on the job). In 2004 it was estimated that job stress cost U.S. companies more than $300 billion annually. To avoid overstressed employees, many employers are seeking new and innovative ways to manage stress in the workplace.

When Did It Begin

Stress existed in the workplace long before there was a word to describe it. The concept of stress as it applies to biology was "discovered" in the mid-1930s by a young Hungarian-born endocrinologist named Hans Selye (1907–82). While conducting research on rats at McGill University in Montreal, Canada, Selye inadvertently hit upon what he called the General Adaptation Syndrome (G.A.S.), a theory of how the body responds to "noxious agents," any number of external influences or events, which the scientist later called "stress." First published in the British journal *Nature* in 1936, Selye's findings paved the way for a new field of medical research focused on the biology of stress and its effects.

Stress was not recognized as a legitimate problem in the workplace, however, until 1960, when a Michigan court granted worker's compensation claims to an automotive factory worker who had suffered significant mental stress because of his inability to keep up with the pace of production on the assembly line. In an effort to keep from falling behind, the worker tried to assemble several pieces at once; this led to mistakes and harsh criticism from his supervisor. Finally, the worker had a mental breakdown. In the decades since that court decision, awareness of job stress as a social problem has grown. In 1992 a United Nations Report declared job stress "the twentieth-century disease." Four years later the World Health Organization said stress had become a "worldwide epidemic."

More Detailed Information

In order for employers to reduce stress levels in the workplace, the causes (called stressors) that most often lead to debilitating stress in the workplace must be understood. These include:

task-related factors, such as an excessive workload; performing tedious, repetitive, and seemingly meaningless tasks; working long shifts with few

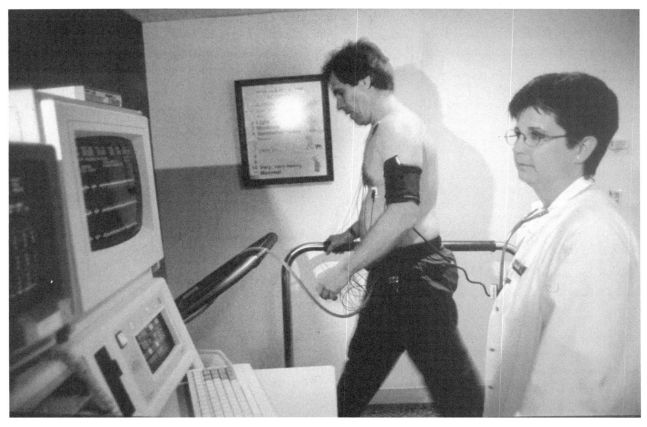

Although it is normal to feel stress from time to time, long-term job stress can lead to employee health problems and diminished job performance. Stress management includes various measures, such as physical exercise, that are designed to mitigate and diffuse job stress. *Michael L. Abramson/Time and Life Pictures/Getty Images.*

rest breaks; a lack of opportunity to take initiative or utilize skills;

issues of management style, such as unclear or conflicting expectations; lack of positive feedback; indirect communication; unwillingness to include employees in the decision-making process; failure to implement family-friendly policies;

inhospitable or unsafe workplace environments because of a lack of fresh air; noise; lack of windows; overcrowding; safety hazards, such as toxic chemicals, hot ovens, or heavy machinery; ergonomic problems related to repetitive tasks, such as sitting in the same position for continuous long hours, faulty computer keyboards, or an otherwise poorly designed work station;

difficult interpersonal relationships caused by unsupportive supervisors; uncooperative subordinates; a lack of teamwork; personality conflicts; office politics, gossip, or competition; sexual, racial, or other kinds of harassment;

issues of workplace change, such as the threat of layoff (losing one's job because of budgetary constraints or a company reorganization); constant employee turnover; sudden technological changes; lack of opportunity for promotion.

Combating these stressors is a two-step process. First, employers must give their employees the tools and resources to manage stress. Many companies now offer stress-management courses, which help raise employees' awareness about the sources of their stress. Employee assistance programs (EAPs) also provide a wealth of support to supervisors and employees in the form of counseling services, crisis intervention, management consultations, coaching for personal and professional development, health and wellness workshops, and other support services. Employers may also encourage employees to release stress by offering company gym memberships or onsite lunchtime yoga sessions.

While EAPs and other stress-management measures provide relief for the symptoms of stress, they do little to address the underlying causes of stress. Because stress-management initiatives focus on the worker who is experiencing the stress, rather than on the environment

STRESSED? LAUGH IT OFF

Job stress is brought on by the feeling of being overwhelmed and out of control in one's work life. As the problem of job stress has gained attention in recent years, many new strategies and practices have emerged for helping workers manage their stress. Many of these strategies emphasize the power of laughter. Clinical studies have shown that a few minutes of laughter, whether in response to something genuinely funny or even just simulated, can relieve muscle tension, bring an influx of oxygen to the body, lower blood pressure, alter brain chemistry, and stimulate the immune system. In order to promote the benefits of laughter as a natural anti-stress medicine, many employers have begun to offer laughter training, in which employees can learn laughter exercises and breathing techniques designed to induce laughter. Other businesses encourage their employees to attend laughter meetings and even join laughter clubs.

that is producing it, the benefits of these initiatives are likely to be superficial and short lived. If employers are serious about reducing stress in the workplace, experts agree that they must find ways to implement organizational change; that is, they must take steps to improve overall working conditions.

Research shows that common to almost all job stress is the feeling of having little control in one's work life: employees have no say in how they manage their time and workload, or they feel unable to approach their supervisor with ideas, or they feel isolated from coworkers. To answer this problem, organizational change should focus on ways to give employees "ownership" of their own jobs and a sense of active involvement with the company. Employees will feel more secure in their positions if:

- their roles and responsibilities are clearly defined, so they know exactly what is expected of them;

- managers encourage initiative taking and independent problem solving;

- managers share information that affects their job security.

Employees will feel more valued and respected if:

- managers ask them for input about decisions that directly affect their jobs;

- managers demonstrate some flexibility about scheduling in order to accommodate family needs;

- managers give credit for a job well done.

Employees will more purposeful and effective in their work if:

- they are not expected to meet unrealistic deadlines;

- they are given opportunities for professional growth and career advancement;

- managers promote social interaction, teamwork, and a sense of mutual interdependence among staff.

By fostering a working environment in which employees have a greater sense of agency, or control, in their work, managers not only reduce employee stress and its many negative consequences but also gain happier, more motivated, and more productive employees.

Recent Trends

Since the mid-1990s advances in technology have added many conveniences to the workplace. E-mail, instant messaging, and voicemail have quickened and increased the volume of communications. Cell phones have enabled employees to get a little bit of extra work done while sitting in traffic or at the airport. Laptop computers and PDAs, or handheld electronic planners, have made it possible for employees to take work home, on public transportation, on vacation, or anywhere.

These conveniences also have brought a significant increase in job stress for many workers, who report feeling pressure to be constantly available or "in touch" with the office and to respond immediately to memos, requests, and other work-related business. For many workers who feel compelled to take a business call in the middle of a family dinner or a child's soccer game, there is no longer a clear divide between work and home. With frustrated spouses and disappointed children at home and demanding supervisors and coworkers at the office, many workers struggle with technology-related stress more than ever.

Business Ethics and the Law

$ Overview: Business Ethics

What It Means

Business ethics are the moral values or principles that play a role in shaping the business practices of companies or individuals. The question of business ethics addresses a wide range of concerns, both within and outside a company. On one hand companies contend with ethical issues as they engage in their own day-to-day operations. Ethical concerns often guide the ways that company owners treat their employees, as well as the manner in which employees approach the performance of their jobs. At the same time, ethical concerns play a large role in the ways that companies interact with other companies, consumers, and society as a whole. The business practices of companies inevitably have some sort of impact, either positive or negative, on the world around them. If a company's actions have a negative impact on others (for example, when a company engages in unfair competitive practices to drive rival companies out of business or when a company creates a misleading marketing campaign to convince consumers to buy a product they do not need or that might actually be harmful), the business ethics of that company can be viewed as questionable.

At the center of most debates concerning business ethics are the dual, often conflicting issues of legality and fairness. In some cases a company that operates within the confines of the law is not necessarily acting in an ethical manner. For example, when a company decides to lay off a large sector of its workforce to increase shareholder profits, that decision can have a far-reaching, negative impact, not only on the company's unemployed workers but also on the workers' families, as well as on the community where they live. In other cases a company's manufacturing process might release pollution into the environment. While a company's pollution levels might conform to standards established by law, the pollution might still pose a health hazard to people living near its source. Technically a company has a right to make its own

personnel decisions or to produce acceptable levels of industrial pollution or waste, regardless of how those decisions affect the lives of its employees or the city or town where they do business. When companies engage in activities that ultimately destroy the economic health of a

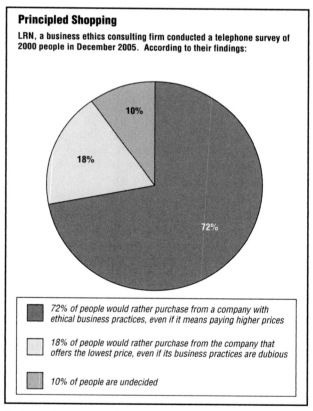

Principled Shopping

LRN, a business ethics consulting firm conducted a telephone survey of 2000 people in December 2005. According to their findings:

10%

18%

72%

72% of people would rather purchase from a company with ethical business practices, even if it means paying higher prices

18% of people would rather purchase from the company that offers the lowest price, even if its business practices are dubious

10% of people are undecided

Business ethics are all of the moral concerns that affect the decision-making processes of a company. As the graph illustrates, because the majority of consumers value ethical behavior over price, ethical businesses may gain a competitive advantage over less ethical competitors. *Illustration by GGS Information Services. Cengage Learning, Gale.*

BUSINESS ETHICS IN THE WORKPLACE

Breaches of business ethics (the application of moral considerations to business practices) frequently occur within the workplace. Employers will sometimes refuse to institute important safety measures into the work environment in order to avoid the additional cost or merely because they are morally unconcerned with the welfare of their employees. At the same time, employees might engage in activities that misrepresent the number of hours they have worked in a given period of time or take credit for tasks that someone else has completed. Although these ethical problems are generally minor when compared to some of the larger ethical violations that occur in the business world, they still have a negative impact on the company's ability to function effectively. To address these problems many companies create codes of ethical conduct, which define proper workplace behavior for both managers and employees.

community or create health problems for members of that community, however, the ethics behind their practices may be questioned.

When Did It Begin

The concept of business ethics is as old as business itself. Aristotle discussed the ethical ramifications of unfair business conduct in his writings, while the Bible contains numerous prohibitions on certain business practices, including interest, or fees, for lending money. In his *De Officiis* (44 BC) the Roman statesman Cicero (106–43 BC) asserted that, in the conducting of business, people should prioritize the welfare of the community over personal profit. Throughout the Middle Ages (c. 500–c. 1500) Christian societies were deeply concerned with questions of fairness in business dealings, particularly in the buying and selling of goods; Saint Thomas Aquinas (1225–74) argued in the *Summa Theologica* (1265–74) that selling goods for profit is immoral.

In the United States the emergence of modern business ethics traces its beginnings to the political activism of the 1960s. As large portions of the American public became more concerned with issues of social equality, they began to question the balance of power in the United States, both in the political and economic spheres. In the eyes of many people during this period, large corporations represented the interests of the wealthy and powerful, at the expense of the larger population. As companies came under more intense scrutiny, they began to reevaluate their business practices, trying to regain the public trust. At the same time, this shift toward more ethical business conduct was driven by legislation. The Civil Rights Act of 1964, which prohibited racial, reli-

gious, and other types of discrimination, forced companies to develop new hiring practices that offered equal opportunities to all job applicants. In 1969 the Environmental Protection Act mandated that corporations adhere to strict standards concerning industrial pollution and waste disposal; in 1970 the Occupational Safety and Health Act made companies responsible for safeguarding employee safety. The Council on Economic Priorities, an organization dedicated to evaluating the social and environmental impacts of corporate policies in the United States, was founded in 1969. Eventually the U.S. Congress began to pass laws that applied to corporations that conducted business overseas. One notable example was the Foreign Corrupt Practices Act of 1977, which prohibited U.S. companies from contributing money to foreign governments in exchange for favorable treatment.

More Detailed Information

All companies confront intense pressures to succeed in a competitive business world. In a capitalist economy the most fundamental indication of a company's success is its profitability. A company's net income, or the amount of money it has left over after deducting all operational expenses, is commonly known as its bottom line. If a company fails to meet its bottom line, it must consider making serious changes to its business strategy or else run the risk of going out of business. For example, if demand for a certain product the company manufactures suddenly decreases or if shortages in natural resources lead to a more widespread economic downturn (also known as a slump), a company might be forced to lay off part of its workforce or seek out cheaper materials to use in the manufacturing of their products. This is sometimes known as the cost of doing business.

In an extremely competitive economy, however, a company will sometimes seek out other ways to gain advantages over its rivals and possibly cross the line into unethical behavior in the process. For example, a pharmaceutical company might willingly mislead consumers regarding the safety of a medication it is trying to market. Such a practice is commonly known as misbranding. A well-publicized case of drug misbranding made headlines in May 2007, when Purdue Pharma, an American pharmaceutical company based in Stamford, Connecticut, pleaded guilty to lying about the addictive potential of one of its products, OxyContin, a powerful painkiller. The case revealed that, during its original marketing campaign for OxyContin, the company deliberately misled federal agencies, medical professionals, and consumers about the drug's potency. The company had powerful financial incentives to do so; soon after the drug's launching in 1996, annual sales of OxyContin exceeded $1 billion per year. While the medication generated high profits for Purdue Pharma, it also wreaked a heavy toll on patients who used the drug, and by the year 2000 widespread instances of addiction and abuse began to emerge. As a result of the guilty verdict in 2007, Purdue Pharma was required to pay more than $600 million in fines, while three former executives of the company were ordered to pay an additional $34.5 million.

In other instances a company might behave unethically by allowing its pollution levels to exceed those mandated by the Clean Air Act of 1990. Sometimes a company will ignore pollution requirements because it has determined that it is more profitable to pay the resulting fines than it is to invest in cleaner manufacturing technologies or to scale back its operations to comply with the law. In other cases a company will conceal the extent to which it pollutes the environment or the level of harm this pollution inflicts on the community. One of the most notorious corporate polluters of the late twentieth century was the General Electric Company, an American technology firm. From the 1970s into the twenty-first century, General Electric was ordered to pay more than a billion dollars in fines relating to the pollution or contamination of water, soil, and other violations of the Environmental Protection Act. Indeed General Electric's ethical breaches were not limited to environmental violations, and the company also incurred heavy fines related to defrauding government agencies, knowingly selling defective products, and other unethical actions.

In some cases corporate polluters avoid paying large fines through lobbying (the concerted effort to influence politicians to support, oppose, or modify certain legislation, according to the interests of the lobbying party) or by simply ignoring legal mandates they know will be costly and time consuming for officials to enforce. When a company's reputation becomes tarnished by a long history of repeated environmental violations, however, the company will sometimes try to distance itself from its past reputation by marketing a new image. In 2005, for example, General Electric launched its "ecomagination" campaign, a publicity strategy aimed to coincide with its decision to begin producing and marketing products that were environmentally friendly (products or processes that have little to no negative impact on the environment).

Economists differ widely on the subject of what constitutes ethical behavior in the business world. Some experts, notably American economist Milton Friedman (1912–2006), have argued that a corporation's sole ethical obligation is to its shareholders. In Friedman's view a company is entitled to take whatever actions are necessary to increase its profitability. Other experts, however, have contended that, while this "bottom-line" mentality might bring large dividends to shareholders in the short term, over the long term it can inflict a far greater negative impact on the company's future, by either undermining its public reputation, exhausting human and environmental resources necessary for future growth, or creating troublesome legal issues for the company.

Recent Trends

With the rise of multinational corporations during the 1990s, the question of business ethics began to extend across international borders. In response to the new challenges raised by a global economy, in 1996 the International Trade Administration, a branch of the U.S. Department of Commerce, created the Best Global Practices Program as a means of promoting a set of ethical guidelines for American companies conducting business overseas. These guidelines, which became known as the Model Business Principles, were intended to address such issues as fair labor practices, workplace safety, environmental impact, and fair competition as they related to businesses operating abroad.

$ Business Laws

What It Means

Business laws (also referred to as commercial laws) are the laws that determine, govern, and regulate business practices. They can be categorized as private laws (laws or statutes that regulate interactions between individuals or other private entities, such as companies) or public laws (statutes that govern relationships between private entities and the government). Business laws apply to a wide range of commercial activities, from the drafting of business contracts (written agreements concerning trade, labor, or some other aspect of a commercial transaction) to the disposal of industrial waste.

There are several types of business law, each designed to address a specific aspect of commercial activities. In the United States some business laws (such as the Federal Trade Commission Act of 1914) are designed to ensure that all companies comply with business practices that foster and promote competition. Other laws (for example, the Occupational Health and Safety Act of 1970, commonly known as OSHA) mandate that businesses maintain a safe working environment for their employees.

In the United States the passage and enforcement of business laws are the responsibility of both individual state governments and the U.S. Congress. State business laws typically establish guidelines for a range of issues, including consumer protection rights (for example, safeguarding consumers against business fraud), commercial contracts, and bank lending practices. On the federal level the U.S. Congress is primarily responsible for enacting and enforcing laws that apply to intrastate commerce (in other words business transactions that occur between two or more states). The Uniform Commercial Code (UCC) is a set of regulations designed to create uniform standards for business practices in all 50 U.S. states. The first state to enact the UCC was Pennsylvania, in 1954; by the early 1970s the UCC had become law in all 50 states. In cases where there is a discrepancy between a state and a federal law, the federal law will almost always take precedence.

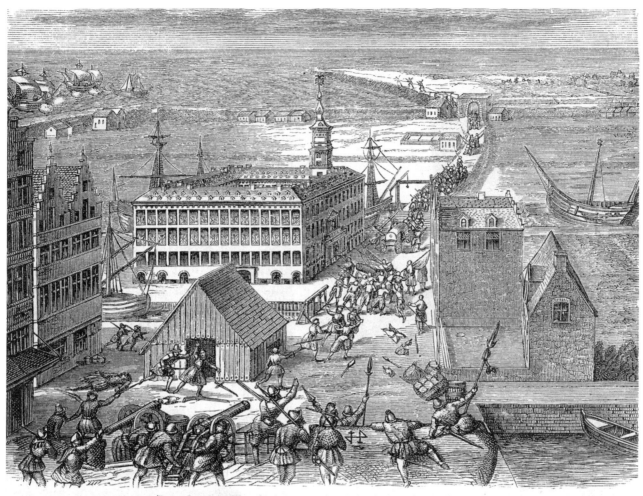

Der Hanſahof zu Antwerpen im ſechzehnten Jahrhundert.

Governments have long used laws to regulate business practices. Pictured here are the old headquarters in Belgium of the Hanseatic League, a former confederation of commercial towns that formed in the thirteenth century to protect the business interests of merchants. © *Mary Evans Picture Library/The Image Works.*

The Federal Trade Commission (FTC), a government agency founded in 1914 as a provision of the Federal Trade Commission Act, is also involved with ensuring that businesses comply with laws and regulations relating to competitive practices, consumer rights, and other issues relating to the promotion of fairness and honesty in business transactions.

When Did It Begin

Laws governing business transactions have been traced to the earliest human civilizations. Archaeological evidence has revealed that standardized codes of commercial conduct existed in ancient Egypt and Babylonia (a city-state located in what is now Iraq). The Hammurabi Code, a system of laws created by the Babylonian king Hammurabi in the eighteenth century BC, includes a number of regulations relating to business transactions,

including rules governing contracts between merchants and fair wages for manual laborers. The Bible contains numerous references to laws governing business practices, notably rules governing the charging of interest on loans. In most cases business regulations in the ancient world were enforced by merchants themselves and generally remained outside the jurisdiction of civil courts (the branch of government responsible for interpreting and enforcing laws). This practice changed in the Roman Empire, when business laws became incorporated into the broader legal system.

With the destruction of the Roman Empire by barbarian hordes during the fifth century AD, many of Europe's long-standing commercial networks were left in ruins, and business transactions fell into a state of near anarchy. Over the next several hundred years more and more established trade routes began to form between cities throughout Europe, and merchants once again began to draw up codes regulating business practices. In the early Renaissance (a period of cultural rebirth in Europe beginning in the fourteenth century and continuing into the seventeenth century) wealthy merchants in Italy and France enjoyed significant political power and often played a key role in drafting legislation relating to commerce. Throughout the Renaissance business laws in Europe were adjudicated by commercial (rather than civil) courts and were enacted and enforced according to rules established by the merchant class. This system of rules and procedures, created and overseen by merchants and lying outside the jurisdiction of the civil legal system, came to be known as the *Lex Mercatoria*, or "Law Merchant."

In the seventeenth century the royal court in England expanded its powers to include cases involving business disputes. By the late eighteenth century the Law Merchant had become incorporated into English common law (laws that emerge as a result of judicial decisions, and the precedents established by those decisions, rather than as a codified system of laws). This integration of business and civil law became the basis of the American legal system after the United States won its independence from Great Britain in 1781.

More Detailed Information

Throughout history business laws have been established to address specific issues or problems related to commercial activities. Traditionally business laws were created by the merchant class and were designed to ensure that commercial transactions took place under conditions that were fair and safe for the merchants involved. At the same time, special courts were established to mediate and resolve disputes. In medieval Europe (or the Middle Ages, from about 500 to about 1500) merchants and traders working in a particular region would frequently organize into groups, with the aim of securing their mutual financial interests against hostile forces, such as pirates or foreign armies. One of the most famous of these organizations was the Hanseatic League, a confederation of commercial towns in northern Germany and other parts of Europe. Formed in the mid-thirteenth century, the Hanseatic League emerged at a time when Germany lacked a central government; it was designed to protect the interests of German merchants in the absence of a unified legal system. At its height the Hanseatic League regulated trading practices over a wide swath of northern Europe, extending all the way from London, England, to Novgorod, Russia.

With the rise of democracy in the eighteenth and nineteenth centuries, the role of merchants in the formation of business laws diminished considerably, as elected governments assumed responsibility for regulating commercial activities. As governments became involved in enacting commercial legislation, the rights of

---

GOVERNMENT PROTECTION OF THE COMPETITIVE MARKETPLACE

Business laws are designed to regulate the activities of companies and other commercial enterprises. Two business laws with a far-reaching impact in the development of the modern American economy were the Sherman Antitrust Act of 1890 and the Clayton Antitrust Act of 1914. The Sherman Antitrust Act arose in response to the large number of business monopolies (a situation in which a single company or group of companies enjoys complete control over a certain business sector, thereby allowing them to determine prices, production levels, and so on; also known as trusts) that formed in the United States in the 1880s; some of the most prominent monopolies were Standard Oil, the Distiller and Cattle Feeders Trust, and the National Linseed Oil Trust. As these trusts gained a greater level of control over their respective industries, other companies experienced increasing difficulty competing in these industries, thereby threatening the continual growth of these industries. At the same time, these trusts brought a disproportionate amount of wealth to a relatively small number of companies. To address these problems Congress passed the Sherman Antitrust Act, which made it illegal for companies to engage in business practices that inhibited the ability of other companies to compete. In 1914 this act was bolstered by the Clayton Antitrust Act, which specifically outlawed the formation of business monopolies.

---

consumers became a more significant factor in the crafting of business laws. In the United States the federal government began to play an active role in determining economic regulations in the decades following the Civil War. A number of these laws, notably the Sherman Antitrust Act of 1890 and the Clayton Antitrust Act of 1914, were aimed at preventing corporations from engaging in monopolistic practices (business practices aimed at unfairly limiting or eliminating competition in certain sectors of the economy, allowing companies to maximize earnings at the expense of other companies as well as consumers). Other laws were aimed at protecting consumers from unfair or unsafe business policies. One of the earliest, and most important, consumer protection laws was the Pure Food and Drug Act of 1906. This act was the first law to require producers of foodstuffs and medications to provide consumers with complete and accurate information concerning the ingredients of their products. The law also gave the federal government the right to inspect food-production processes, notably those involving meat, to ensure that food products were being prepared under sanitary conditions. This trend toward increased government regulation of business activities in the United States would predominate throughout most of the twentieth century.

Recent Trends

In the 1970s many politicians and economic thinkers began to question the efficacy of government regulation. For one they believed that government involvement in business activities inhibited economic growth by burdening companies with the responsibility of abiding by excessive regulation. At the same time, these opponents of regulation believed that the government's dedication to regulatory activities was overly costly; in order to finance these activities, high taxes were imposed on American individuals and businesses, which further compounded the economic woes of many companies. By the late 1970s the U.S. Congress began to pass laws designed to deregulate (in other words remove regulations) certain industries. One of the first major acts of deregulation was the Airline Deregulation Act of 1978, which eliminated government involvement in determining airline activities and fare prices, thereby allowing the airlines to compete with each other more freely. Over the next two decades a number of other significant acts of deregulation followed. This general trend toward deregulation on the federal level paved the way for state governments to deregulate their energy utilities in the 1990s,

subsequently creating regional competition in the power generation industry.

$ Bait and Switch

What It Means

Bait and switch is a fraudulent or deceptive marketing tactic in which a retail business advertises a certain product at an irresistibly low price (the bait) in order to lure consumers into their store. When the consumer arrives at the retail establishment seeking to buy the advertised item, however, a sales representative reveals that the item is "no longer available", and then attempts to redirect the customer's attention to a substitute product at a higher price (the switch).

Notorious as one of the most commonly used false advertising scams, bait-and-switch tactics are unfair for two reasons. First and most obviously, it is unfair to put out advertisements that make false promises to customers; if customers cannot depend on advertisements to deliver truthful information, they will not able to make informed choices about how to spend their money. Bait-and-switch tactics are also unfair because such advertisements often

Bait and switch refers to a misleading business practice in which retailers advertise low prices on products they do not have in stock with the hope of selling customers different products at higher prices. An electronics retailer, for example, might use a bait-and-switch tactic in order to gain an edge on its competitors. *Justin Sullivan/Getty Images.*

lure customers away from other businesses that are playing by the rules (that is, advertising merchandise they actually have in stock at real prices). A tactic that gives one business an unfair advantage over another is described as anticompetitive. The right to free and fair competition in business is one of the foundational principles of the American economic system; therefore, anticompetitive business practices are generally illegal. Indeed, bait-and-switch tactics are outlawed by the Federal Trace Commission (FTC), a U.S. government agency devoted to protecting American consumers from fraud and deception and to preserving the integrity of free competition in the marketplace.

When Did It Begin

The American advertising industry grew and developed at a rapid rate between 1900 and the mid-1930s. Whereas advertisements had previously been generated directly by the manufacturer of a product, in the early twentieth century advertising agencies emerged as a sophisticated creative and strategic force in American business, using methods of applied psychology in their advertising campaigns. Bait-and-switch tactics were among the many strategies conceived during this era to entice consumers to spend their money in ways they had not planned to spend it.

Although the FTC was originally founded under the Federal Trade Commission Act of 1914 to address the primary problem of anticompetitive practices in business, during the decades that followed, the agency became increasingly involved in efforts to protect American consumers from deceptive and misleading advertising practices. To this end the Wheeler-Lea Act was passed in 1938 as an amendment to the FTC Act, stating that false or deceptive advertising practices (including bait-and-switch) are illegal and granting the FTC its first official authority to regulate false advertising. Under the amendment the FTC may investigate and potentially fine businesses believed to be perpetrating such fraud.

More Detailed Information

Bait-and-switch tactics use psychological tricks to prey upon a customer's emotions: by offering something that is of high value to the customer (say, a 50-inch plasma HDTV, or high-definition television, normally at least a $2,000 purchase, on sale for $399), the advertisement puts him or her in the mindset of making a purchase. The customer enters a state of anticipation or expectation. When the advertised television turns out to be "sold out" (although it is questionable whether there were ever any available at this price in the first place), the customer is disappointed; the desire for a new, high-tech television that was awakened by the advertisement remains, and the customer is now in a state of discomfort because his or her expectation of buying a new TV has not been fulfilled.

"WHILE SUPPLIES LAST"

Bait-and-switch tactics are commonly used by a wide range of retailers, including auto dealers, furniture stores, electronics stores, and others. Bait advertising is a deceptive way of luring consumers into a store with the promise of a great bargain. The promise is insincere, however, as the retailer never intends to honor the terms of the ad. When the customer arrives to purchase the item, the retailer simply says it is "sold out" or otherwise no longer available and commences to switch the customer's attention to some other merchandise. Bait-and-switch tactics are outlawed in the United States, along with other false advertising practices, and yet the scheme is still widely used. How do retailers get away with it? According to federal regulations, as long as the advertisement includes a clause indicating that supplies of the advertised item are limited, the ad is legal. With this simple loophole many businesses are able to draw customers into their stores with the promise of great savings, even though very few, if any, customers will be able to take advantage of the offer.

At this moment of disappointment, the customer is vulnerable to the suggestion of buying some other television or piece of home entertainment electronic equipment because making a purchase will help alleviate the discomfort of the unfulfilled expectation. "We do have some other great items on sale," the sales representative will say. "How about this 30-inch flatscreen TV? It comes with a built-in DVD player and VCR. What a great deal for only $309!" Usually the switch product holds a lesser value (or is less desirable) for the customer but is more profitable for the retailer to sell. In the television scenario, for example, the customer who walks out with the 30-inch flatscreen TV has spent less money than he or she would have spent on the advertised 50-inch plasma TV, but the price of the flatscreen is close to its normal retail price, whereas the advertised price of the plasma TV was well below even its wholesale cost (meaning that the retailer would have incurred a significant loss if he had sold the plasma TV for $399). The overall value of the flatscreen TV is considerably less than that of the plasma TV, but the retailer makes a greater percentage of profit on the sale of the flatscreen.

We have seen how bait-and-switch tactics may unfairly affect a customer's decision-making process. Now consider how this kind of false advertising affects the larger business environment. Mr. Palmero has been running his own electronics store for 20 years. He has built his reputation on selling quality products at fair prices, and business has always been steady. Suddenly, however, a new chain store called Crazy Larry's moves into town and starts flooding the newspapers and radio waves with advertisements for outrageous deals on electronics products. One week it is a clearance on the top brand camcorder; the next week it is a three-for-one offer on MP3 players. These deals are too good to pass up, and people flock to Crazy Larry's to take advantage of them. When they arrive, of course, Crazy Larry is "sold out" of the advertised item, but he encourages them to have a look around at some of his other great products. Some customers simply walk out, but a good many decide to purchase something because they have already made the trip to the electronics store. Every sale that Crazy Larry makes using bait-and-switch advertising is, in effect, unfairly taking business away from Mr. Palmero and other honest electronics stores like his. Taken to the extreme, Crazy Larry's advertising scams could put many other stores out of business, and then local customers would have no choice but to shop at Crazy Larry's. If Crazy Larry eliminates his competition, he will be free to charge whatever prices he likes, causing further detriment to consumers.

A market economy like the one in the United States depends on competition between businesses to keep quality and prices at optimum levels. Bait-and-switch tactics are listed among the false advertising practices outlawed by the FTC because they are both unfair to the customer and anticompetitive.

Recent Trends

Bait-and-switch tactics are used in a wide range of settings. With the housing boom that began in the late 1990s and lasted through 2006, many people reported being victimized by "the old bait-and-switch" when taking out a home loan. In this scenario the lender promises the borrower a certain set of terms for his or her loan. These terms (including the interest rate, loan fees, repayment schedule, and other details) are favorable enough to get the borrower committed to the loan (or, "off the street," as they say in the industry). When it comes time to finalize the loan however, the borrower discovers that the loan papers reflect very different and much less favorable terms, such as a higher interest rate, penalties for paying the loan off early, or higher fees associated with the loan.

Although it seems like the borrower would protest immediately and refuse to sign the loan papers under the new terms, many borrowers are harried by all of the details and procedures of buying a new house or are worried that any delay will cause the seller to become annoyed and back out of the agreement, so they sign off on the new terms, vowing to revisit the issue later. Unfortunately, once the loan is signed, the process of changing the terms is complicated and can be expensive, especially if lawyers are needed. Many borrowers end up stuck with a loan they never would have accepted in the beginning.

$ Pyramid Scheme

What It Means

A pyramid scheme is a fraudulent business practice that involves the building of a network, or "pyramid," of investors who pay money into the scheme with the hope of earning a high return on their investment. Hierarchical in structure, a pyramid scheme has a single individual or entity at the top of the pyramid, underneath which is an expanding base of investors. An investor pays to participate in the scheme and then recruits other investors to join the pyramid, who subsequently pay money to the investor who recruited them. Pyramid schemes rarely provide an actual product and rely solely on the willingness of recruits to invest money into the scheme. Pyramid schemes are considered a form of business fraud in most countries and are therefore illegal.

In most pyramid schemes, the person who originates the scheme sends a letter or other form of communication to a number of individuals. The letter typically describes a business opportunity that promises a high financial reward in a short time and that requires little effort. In some cases, the letter will purport to offer the recipient an actual product, such as a financial report, or, in the case of many Internet pyramid schemes, a computer code. These products generally contain no intrinsic value, however, and are used to persuade participants to pay money into the scheme. The recipient of the proposal is asked to send a relatively low sum of money, the

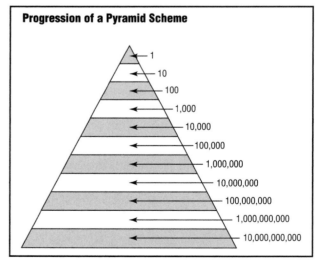

A pyramid scheme is a type of investment scam that requires each person to give money to the scheme and then recruit a certain number of people to do the same thing. This chart—which shows how many people would be involved if one person recruited 10 people who then recruited 10 more people—explains why only the first few investors could make money, as in just 10 steps the number of people required for the scheme would be 10 billion, more than the world's population. *Illustration by GGS Information Services. Cengage Learning, Gale.*

"investment," to the person who sent the communication. The recipient is also asked to send the same letter with the same instructions to a number of other people. The letter, which is sent to an increasing number of recipients, is called a chain letter.

The revenue, or income, of a pyramid scheme is generated through the recruiting of more and more participants who are willing to send money to the people who invited them to participate in the scheme. The success of a pyramid scheme depends on the number of people who are willing to become involved in the scheme. As the network of potential participants expands, the pyramid scheme begins to collapse as lower percentages of people are willing to send money to the people above them and the scheme ceases to generate income. The only people who profit from a pyramid scheme are those that join it near the beginning. Without exception, the people who form the bottom levels of the pyramid, those who join the scheme after it is well under way, lose their money.

When Did It Begin

Although the exact origins of the pyramid scheme are unknown, one of the earliest and most notorious pyramid schemes in modern history dates to the years immediately following World War I. The scheme was created by Italian-American Charles Ponzi (1882–1949). In December 1919 Ponzi founded the Securities Exchange Company, a firm that promised to double investors' money within 90 days of the initial investment. As Ponzi lured more and more people into his scheme, he began paying the scheme's earliest investors double the amount of their initial return. Word quickly circulated of the company's success, and soon Ponzi was taking in more than $1 million a week. By July 1920 newspaper reports began to expose some of the flaws in Ponzi's business model, and by the end of the summer it was revealed that he was bankrupt. Ponzi disappeared after a brief stint in prison, only to emerge a decade later in Florida, where he ran another lucrative pyramid scheme involving fraudulent land deals.

More Detailed Information

A legitimate business model involves a product or a service that creates wealth for the people who participate in the business. For example, a person invests $20 to buy supplies to build a birdhouse. After building the birdhouse, the person then sells it to a customer for $40. The person earns 100 percent profit ($20) on his initial investment, and the consumer receives a product he or she considers valuable.

Pyramid schemes, on the other hand, do not create wealth. No product or service is actually offered, other than the *idea* of wealth. The majority of people who pay into the scheme lose money. Pyramid schemes involve a redistribution of existing wealth from the hands of many

PYRAMID SCHEMES IN THE FORMER SOVIET UNION

Following the collapse of the Soviet Union, a number of fraudulent corporations began to emerge amid the chaos of the newly capitalist era in Russia. One such company, known as MMM (named after the company's three founders), perpetrated one of the most elaborate and devastating pyramid schemes in history. After failing at several businesses, MMM launched an investment opportunity in 1993 that promised investors 1,000 percent profit on their initial investments. MMM marketed its business aggressively, using television advertising and word of mouth to attract new investors. At its height, MMM earned more than U.S.$11 million each day by selling shares in the company to the Russian public. After the company was investigated for tax evasion in July 1994, it was revealed that the company owed investors anywhere from $50 million to $1.5 billion. After the scam was exposed, a number of MMM investors committed suicide.

into the hands of a few, without actually providing an actual product or service in exchange.

The unsustainable nature of a pyramid scheme becomes apparent when one considers how quickly the number of recruits grows. For example, say the originator of the pyramid scheme, a single individual, writes a letter to 10 people inviting them to participate in a "can't miss" business opportunity. The letter instructs the recipient to send the same letter to 10 additional people. In this way, the number of investors increases exponentially; that is, the number of investors continues to multiply at a constant rate, even as the number of investors grows higher and higher. Say that each of those 10 individuals contacts 10 more individuals, creating a total of 100 individuals. Those 100 individuals contact 1,000 individuals, the 1,000 individuals then contact 10,000 individuals, and so on. Theoretically, the pyramid scheme would encompass 1 billion participants by the 10th round of contacts.

Recent Trends

The Internet brought on a revolution in human communication, creating an electronic network for people to communicate with one another and to buy and sell goods. Along with new communication and business opportunities, the Internet also created a wealth of new opportunities for scam artists. The speed of Internet communications made it possible for pyramid schemes to grow at a rate that would have been impossible using traditional mail. Easy-money opportunities have become prevalent on the World Wide Web, as invitations to participate in various schemes, from marketing electronics to joining money-making online "games," flood people's e-mail accounts daily.

$ Identity Theft

What It Means

Identity theft is the act of stealing another person's identifying information, including his or her name, address, telephone number, Social Security number (SSN), bank account numbers, and credit card numbers. Having obtained some or all of this information about someone, the thief may pose as that person and attempt to carry out financial transactions, such as credit card purchases and bank account withdrawals, in the victim's name.

To understand identity theft, imagine that a person named Jim accidentally leaves his wallet on the counter at a store and that the wallet is discovered by a second person named Bob. Bob gets Jim's address from the driver's license in the wallet and steals some mail from Jim's mailbox. Bob then goes to a financial institution and presents Jim's driver's license, SSN, and the mail that

Identity thieves try to steal people's social security numbers, bank account numbers, and other personal financial data and to use the information to impersonate their victims, emptying funds from their accounts and making expensive purchases in their names. One way of avoiding identity theft is to put financial documents through a paper shredder before throwing them away. *Photograph by Kelly A. Quin. Cengage Learning, Gale.*

verifies Jim's current living address. (Assume for the sake of the example that Bob resembles Jim closely enough that the bank representative does not notice anything amiss when looking at the picture on the license.) Bob requests and obtains a loan in Jim's name. Bob subsequently fails to make the required payments on the loan, and creditors call Jim requesting the missing funds. Jim's credit rating has been badly damaged, and he must prove to his creditors that the loan was falsely attained. Meanwhile Bob has purchased an expensive new car with the money loaned to him by the bank and driven away without leaving a trace of evidence.

Identity thieves have a number of methods of acquiring information, but the most common involve stealing wallets, watching people enter personal identification numbers (PINs) when they make withdrawals from automated teller machines (ATMs), and using computer technology to obtain people's confidential personal and financial data. Identity theft often occurs in the workplace, where individuals have access to computer files with confidential employee information.

When Did It Begin

The term *identity theft* was first coined in around 1992, though such thefts had certainly occurred earlier in varying forms. It was during the 1990s that identity theft became the fastest-growing crime in the United States. In 1992 an average of 3,000 complaints of identity theft per month were registered with TransUnion, one of the three major American credit bureaus (for-profit companies that collect information about a person's or a business's financial stability and ability to pay future debts and sell it to such interested parties as banks and credit card companies). By 1997 TransUnion was receiving 47,000 complaints per month. According to U.S. Secret Service reports, nearly 95 percent of the arrests for financial crimes between 1995 and 1997 involved identity theft.

The huge increase in identity theft during the 1990s has been attributed to the development of the Internet and the growing popularity of online shopping (purchasing goods and services over the Internet by entering credit card data into company websites). Since 2000 online security technology has grown more sophisticated, and online shopping with credit cards has become considerably safer and more reliable. Before that time, however, hackers (people who illegally gain access to a person's or an organization's computer system) had considerably less difficulty accessing confidential information.

In response to this growing crisis, the United States Congress passed the Identity Theft and Assumption Deterrence Act on October 30, 1998. This act made identity theft a federal crime punishable by up to 15 years in prison, with fines of up to $250,000. Equally important, the act named the person whose identity had been stolen the true victim of the crime. Before this time the financial institutions that had been defrauded were named the victims of the identity theft.

More Detailed Information

Most legal experts agree that identity theft is easier to prevent than to resolve after it has happened. To prevent identity theft, people should avoid giving out personal information, such as birth dates, credit card numbers, and Social Security numbers, except when necessary. They should only share such information with known individuals and reputable institutions. It is recommended that people review monthly bank account and credit card statements double-checking that all transactions are authentic and shred any offers for pre-approved credit cards that arrive in the mail.

A Social Security number gives an identity thief the most access to a person's private records and offers the greatest opportunity to cause harm. An SSN is a nine-digit number issued to U.S. citizens and residents that allows the government to track individuals for taxation purposes and to allocate retirement payments; employers, creditors, insurance companies, and others often require employees and customers to give their SSN as an identification number. An SSN is very difficult to change or invalidate, whereas if a credit card is stolen, the victim need only call the credit card company and cancel the card to avoid having to pay for any further purchases made on that card. Additionally credit card companies will usually inform their clients if they notice any uncharacteristic purchases, which would include items that the person does not normally buy and purchases made at geographic locations from which the client has never previously bought anything. If someone steals an SSN, however, he or she can obtain a credit card in the victim's name, request a high credit limit (the amount of money that can be charged to the card), and do considerable financial damage before the victim even knows what has happened.

Furthermore a Social Security card comes with only two personal identifiers: the holder's name and the number. Because there is no picture on the card, nor any other personal information such as the holder's height, weight, or eye color, it is very difficult to tell whether or not a person using an SSN is the rightful holder of that SSN. Most institutions do not question that the person offering the number is the rightful holder of that information. Therefore, it is crucial that an individual never reveal an SSN over the phone or in an e-mail. In addition identity theft can result from putting an SSN on an official document, such as a license, a personal check, or a membership card to an institution. It is also unwise to carry an SSN in a wallet because wallets can be lost or stolen.

It is strongly advised that victims of identity theft call local police and keep records of all police reports. The victim should also call the following credit bureaus: Experian (http://www.experian.com), Equifax (http://www.equifax.com), and TransUnion (http://www.

MORE IDENTITY THEFT TERMINOLOGY

A number of interesting words have come into use in describing the methods people use to steal other people's important private information. The term *dumpster diving* has been adopted to refer to the act of sorting through another's garbage for private data. The phrase *shoulder surfing* means looking over someone's shoulder to obtain that information. A common electronic form of identity theft is perpetrated by a technique called *phishing*. Identity thieves who phish impersonate a representative of a trusted organization and send out e-mails requesting confidential financial data. For example, a victim might receive an e-mail requesting verification of account numbers from someone claiming to work at the bank where the victim holds an account. If the person provides the information, the thief will then attempt to withdraw money from the account or, worse, get a credit card in the victim's name.

---

transunion.com). Each of these agencies can take immediate steps to prevent the thief from continuing to cause damage. The final step is to cooperate with any of the agencies who have extended credit to the thief.

Recent Trends

Patterns in reported cases indicate that the instances of identity theft are decreasing but that the amount of money lost per stolen identity is rising. In other words thieves are stealing fewer identities but making more money. In 2003, 10.1 million adults reported that identity fraud crimes had been committed against them. This number dropped to 9.3 million in 2005 and to 8.9 million in 2006. In 2003, however, the reported amount of money lost in identity fraud cases was $52.3 billion. That number rose to $54.4 billion in 2005 and $56.6 billion in 2006. The average amount of money lost per victim of identity theft was $5,249 in 2003, $5,885 in 2005, and $6,383 in 2006.

Identity fraud cases are tending to take longer to resolve, though this pattern has fluctuated over the years. In 2003 the average resolution time was 33 hours per victim. In 2005 the average time was 28 hours, and in 2006 it was 40 hours. Resolution of identity theft does not mean that a suspect has been apprehended. Rather it means that fraudulent transactions have been identified and measures have been taken to discontinue future illegal transactions.

$ Insider Trading

What It Means

Insider trading refers to the buying or selling of a company's securities (financial holdings, such as stocks,

---

Insider trading occurs when a shareholder in a public company buys or sells stock in that company using information that is unavailable to the general public. In the early 2000s, lifestyle entrepreneur Martha Stewart, shown here, caused a scandal when she was accused of using inside information to sell her shares in the pharmaceutical company ImClone.   *AP Images.*

bonds, and mutual funds) by a company insider, which can be a company director, official, or any individual with a stake of 10 percent or more in the company. Insiders frequently buy and sell stock in their companies, but there are legal and illegal forms of insider trading. When someone buys or sells securities based on knowledge about the company unavailable to the general public, the trade is illegal. For example, the president of a technology company would be guilty of illegal insider trading if he sold thousands of shares of stock in his own company after learning that the company was going to lose one of its most important clients. The sale in this example is illegal because the president knew that the company was going to lose money before most other stockholders. He therefore had an unfair advantage over the other investors.

For insiders to trade legally in company stocks, they must base trades only on public information, and they must report their transactions to the Securities and Exchange Commission (SEC; a government agency that protects investors and maintains fair, orderly, and efficient markets) within two days of the purchase or sale. The SEC then posts this information on its website where any investor can find it.

When Did It Begin

The United States has been a world leader in establishing insider trading laws and in prosecuting cases against corrupt investors. The first U.S. laws against insider trading were not established by Congress and then tried in the nation's courts, in the normal way federal laws against an illegal activity are enacted; these laws were developed in the Supreme Court. The first known prosecution for insider trading occurred in 1909, 25 years before Congress passed a law dealing with the violation.

In 1909 the Supreme Court ruled that a corporate executive was guilty of fraud for buying a large number of shares of company stock when he knew that the stock was going to jump in price. Congress did not formally ban insider trading until 1934, when the first law on the topic was included in the Securities Exchange Act. Section 16 (b) of that act forbids insiders from both buying and selling corporate stock within the same six-month period. This provision helps ensure that insiders make long-term investments in their companies rather than using insider knowledge to gain short-term profits.

More Detailed Information

The SEC's official term for inside information is *material nonpublic information*. Though the majority of insider trading cases involve corporate insiders, anyone who buys or sells a stock based on material nonpublic information is guilty of insider trading. This means that family or friends of insiders can also be found guilty if investigators determine that they have traded stocks based on inside information. For instance, a finance journalist could be prosecuted for insider trading if he bought or sold stock in a company based on information he discovered in the process of reporting on the company. The journalist in this instance would be recognized as a temporary insider.

Gathering enough evidence to prove that someone is guilty of insider trading is one of the SEC's most difficult challenges. The SEC monitors all stock trades closely, looking for suspicious behavior. In addition, stock markets such as the New York Stock Exchange and NASDAQ (the National Association of Securities Dealers Automated Quotation System) also follow trading activity closely. Evidence used against those accused of insider trading often consists of phone and e-mail records and the testimony of informants. Penalties for insider trading vary, with the maximum sentence being 10 years in prison and a fine of $1 million for an individual. A corporation found guilty of insider trading may be fined up to $2.5 million.

Not everyone thinks that insider trading should be illegal. In fact, debate is vigorous on this matter. One of the arguments opponents of insider trading laws put forward is that while insider trading is illegal in the stock market, the same activities are legal in the real estate sector. For example, if a person happened to know that there were large deposits of precious metals, such as gold and silver, under someone's property, that person could make an offer to buy the property without telling the current homeowners about the gold underneath their home.

Many investors follow the patterns of legal insider trading when they buy and sell on the stock market. For instance, if an investor is thinking about buying stock in Google, that investor can consult the SEC website to see if insiders at Google are buying or selling their stock in the company. If insiders are selling their Google stock, the investor might decide to sell his or her stock as well.

MARTHA STEWART

Martha Stewart, a famous television personality who offered tips on cooking and homemaking, was accused of insider trading (the purchase or sale of stocks, bonds, or mutual funds based on knowledge about the company unavailable to the general public) by the Securities and Exchange Commission (SEC; a government agency that protects investors and maintains fair, orderly, and efficient markets) in 2002. It was suspected that Stewart acted illegally on insider information when she sold her shares of stock in ImClone, a pharmaceutical company, just days before the public announcement that the U.S. Food and Drug Administration had rejected ImClone's application to produce a new drug. Stewart was eventually convicted in March 2004 of four counts of obstructing justice and lying to investigators. Beginning in October 2004, she served five months in prison and six months of house arrest.

Though this is not a foolproof investment strategy, market reports indicate that when executives buy large amounts of stock in their own companies, those companies tend to outperform other companies on the market, which means that prices for those shares tend to rise, and investors make money.

Recent Trends

Between 2001 and 2006, the SEC brought 300 charges of insider trading against more than 600 individuals. During that time insider trading cases made up 7 to 12 percent of the SEC's caseload. Several of these cases received attention in the national news. In 2001 Oracle Corporation CEO (chief executive officer) Larry Ellison was accused of insider trading when he sold $900 million worth of stock before the value of the company's stock fell significantly. In 2005 Ellison paid $100 million to charity to settle the charges brought against him. Jeffrey Skilling, the former CEO of the Texas-based energy company Enron, was convicted of insider trading in 2006. Many economists argue that the numerous charges of fraud against Enron in 2001 brought about the SEC's increased vigilance. In 2002 the SEC initiated 598 enforcement actions, a 24 percent increase over the number of cases in 2001, and in 2005 there were more securities lawsuits than in the previous 10 years combined.

$ Better Business Bureau

What It Means

The Better Business Bureaus (BBB) system is a nonprofit organization (meaning that its primary goal is to benefit the public rather than achieve financial gain) in the United States whose mission is to promote fair and ethical business practices in sales and advertising. The organization achieves this mission by establishing standards for good business practices, receiving and investigating consumer complaints about unfair practices, evaluating and reporting on the practices of specific businesses, and alerting the public to deceitful or fraudulent tactics in sales and advertising. The BBB is not a government agency, nor does it have the power to take legal action or impose sanctions or penalties against businesses that engage in improper practices. It does, however, have considerable power to influence a company's public image (positively or negatively) by disseminating information about its business practices. Using this leverage, the BBB can compel most companies to regulate their own business practices voluntarily and to make good faith efforts to resolve disputes with customers in a timely way.

The Better Business Bureau is funded by membership dues paid by the companies who belong to the organization. Belonging to the BBB is like a badge of honor: a company that becomes a member enhances its reputation as an ethical business that is concerned with consumer rights and consumer satisfaction, and it benefits thereby from the increased trust (and patronage) of customers. Not all businesses qualify for BBB membership, however; applicants must be reviewed, approved, and invited by the BBB to join. In order to maintain its own reputation and integrity, the BBB maintains strict standards for its members and reserves the right to revoke the membership of any business that fails to meet these standards.

BBB membership is composed of a range of business interests, including retailers, manufacturers, advertising agencies, and media representatives; nearly 300 leading national corporations and more than 100,000 local, regional, and state companies belong to the BBB. The BBB system consists of more than 150 branches in the United States, Puerto Rico, Canada, and Israel. Individual BBBs are licensed and overseen by the Council of Better Business Bureaus (CBBB; founded in 1970), a parent organization with headquarters in Arlington, Virginia.

When Did It Begin

The Better Business Bureau traces its origins to the first decade of the twentieth century, when the issue of

The Better Business Bureau promotes fair and ethical business practices by establishing standards of conduct and publishing reports on the behavior of companies in the United States. Pictured here in the late 1990s is James L. Bast, then president of the Council of Better Business Bureaus, announcing the organization's new online service. *AP Images.*

fraudulent (or dishonest) advertising provoked a wave of public concern and activism. The need for truth in advertising was first promoted by the National Federation of Advertising Clubs of America (later renamed the Associated Advertising Clubs of America), a volunteer organization that formed in 1904 to "expose fraudulent schemes and their perpetrators." Shortly thereafter, Samuel C. Dobbs (1868–1950) emerged as a leading figure in the truth in advertising movement. A sales manager at the Coca-Cola company who went on to become its president and chairman from 1919 until 1922, Dobbs was shocked to hear a Coca-Cola attorney defend the company's advertising practices in court by proclaiming that all advertising was exaggerated. Dobbs began to investigate the advertising industry, and in 1909 he became president of the Associated Advertising Clubs of America (renamed again as the American Advertising Federation, or AAF). In 1911 he helped to establish one of the first codes of ethical advertising, known as the Ten Commandments of Advertising. The following year he oversaw the formation of local Vigilance Committees, which took it upon themselves to monitor the advertising practices of businesses in their areas, receive public complaints, and attempt to resolve hundreds of disputes between customers and businesses involving allegations of advertising abuse. These Vigilance Committees were the earliest incarnations of the Better Business Bureaus as we know them today.

More Detailed Information

Reliability Reports The Better Business Bureau is most widely used as a source of information about specific businesses. An individual bureau may receive as many as 1,000 inquiries per day from consumers seeking information about the reputation of a certain business before they make a purchase or otherwise patronize that business. In response to consumer inquiries or complaints, the BBB collects information on millions of individual businesses (both members and nonmembers) in a wide range of categories, including automotive, clothing and accessories, computers and electronics, construction and contractors, food and dining, home and garden, media and communications, real estate, shopping, travel and transportation, and others.

The BBB's findings are published in what are called Reliability Reports. Available on the BBB website, these reports include information about the ownership and management of the business; its products and services; its location, phone, and fax numbers; the date it was established, incorporated, or both; whom to contact with questions; the terms of its refund and exchange policy; and whether the business is a BBB member. The report also details the company's complaint history over a given reporting period (typically three years), including the nature of the complaints, whether the company made efforts to resolve the issues, and whether the customers accepted the resolutions. Depending on the size and

LEMON LAW COMPLAINTS

If your new or new used car has a defect that substantially impairs its use, value, or safety, and if the car has been repaired four or more times for the same defect within the warranty period and the defect has still not been fixed, your car probably qualifies as a lemon.

Every state in the United States has a lemon law: a set of standards defining when a car dealer or manufacturer should be required to repurchase (buy back) or replace a car it has sold because that car is a lemon.

One of the major functions of the Better Business Bureau (BBB, a national agency that protects consumers from unethical business practices) is to help consumers file complaints against lemon law infractions through its BBB Auto Line Program. Established in 1978, BBB Auto Line also provides a neutral arbitration program for the resolution of lemon law disputes.

nature of the business, the report may also divide complaint issues into subcategories. A Reliability Report on the Home Depot Corporation, for example, lists disputes in such categories as advertising, billing or collection, sales practices, delivery, repair, customer service, warranty, refund or exchange, and others. The BBB identifies a pattern of complaints if it perceives one, rates the company's business performance as satisfactory or unsatisfactory, and notes whether the company has been subject to any enforcement actions taken by a government agency, such as the Federal Trade Commission, the Food and Drug Administration, the U.S. Postal Inspection Service, or the state attorney general.

Dispute Resolution Another major function of the BBB is to facilitate dispute resolution through its arbitration program. Established in 1973, the arbitration program aims to settle disagreements between businesses and customers without the use of lawyers and courts. Maintaining its position as a "staunchly neutral" third party and upholding a core belief that voluntary self-regulation is ultimately in the self-interest of every business that depends on consumer trust, each BBB offers access to trained volunteer arbitrators (judges) from the local community whose services are available at no cost to the customer and usually at no cost to the business. A hearing is held during which the arbitrator or arbitrators listen to both sides of the dispute and deliver a decision within 10 days thereafter. Most informal arbitration cases are successfully settled within 40 days.

Charity Review In addition to collecting information on businesses, the BBB also evaluates local and national charities in order to help prospective donors make good decisions about where to give their money and to foster public confidence in the reliability of philanthropic organizations. The BBB's Philanthropic Advisory Service was established in 1971 under the umbrella of the Council of Better Business Bureaus' Foundation (CBBBF). In 2001 it merged with the National Charities Information Bureau to form the BBB Wise Giving Alliance (WGA). A self-described "charity watchdog," the organization uses its Standards for Charitable Accountability (developed in 2003) to review the governance, spending practices, truthfulness in representation, and willingness to disclose basic information of hundreds of philanthropic organizations.

Recent Trends

In response to the rapid rise of e-commerce in the mid-1990s, the CBBB established BBB*Online* in 1996, an agency devoted to promoting ethical relationships between businesses and consumers on the Internet. The agency seeks to identify websites that meet its standards for advertising, sales practices, information privacy and security, and customer satisfaction and complaint resolution, among other things. BBB*Online* recognizes that consumer confidence is more important than ever when shopping online. Just as BBB approval is desirable for regular businesses, BBB*Online* promotes its Reliability Seal and its Privacy Seal as important ways for online businesses to distinguish themselves among hundreds of thousands of online businesses and to establish trust with prospective customers. According to the BBB*Online* website, "Seventy-three percent of purchasers and 82 percent of nonpurchasers cite reliability of business as a major concern when shopping online"; and "almost 90 percent of online shoppers would feel more confident shopping on a site that displays the BBB*Online* Privacy Seal."

Further Reading

HOW THE ECONOMY WORKS

BOOKS

Bryce, Robert. *Pipe Dreams: Greed, Ego, and the Death of Enron*. Oxford: PublicAffairs, 2002.

Buchholz, Todd G. *New Ideas from Dead Economists: An Introduction to Modern Economic Thought*. 2nd rev. ed. New York: Plume, 2007.

Calavita, Kitty, Henry N. Pontell, and Robert Tillman. *Big Money Crime: Fraud and Politics in the Savings and Loan Crisis*. Berkeley: University of California Press, 1997.

Canterbery, E. Ray. *Alan Greenspan: The Oracle behind the Curtain*. Hackensack, N.J.: World Scientific, 2006.

Case, James H. *Competition: The Birth of a New Science*. New York: Hill & Wang, 2007.

Chancellor, Edward. *Devil Take the Hindmost: A History of Financial Speculation*. New York: Farrar, Straus, and Giroux, 1999.

Coyle, Diane. *The Soulful Science: What Economists Really Do and Why It Matters*. Princeton, N.J.: Princeton University Press, 2007.

D'Amato, Paul. *The Meaning of Marxism*. Chicago: Haymarket Books, 2006.

Ebenstein, Lanny. *Milton Friedman: A Biography*. New York: Palgrave Macmillan, 2007.

Fishman, Charles. *The Wal-Mart Effect: How the World's Most Powerful Company Really Works—and How It's Transforming the American Economy*. New York: Penguin Press, 2006.

Friedman, Benjamin M. *The Moral Consequences of Economic Growth*. New York: Knopf, 2005.

Friedman. Thomas L. *The World Is Flat: A Brief History of the Twenty-First Century*. New York: Farrar, Straus, and Giroux, 2005.

Green, James. *Death in the Haymarket: A Story of Chicago, the First Labor Movement, and the Bombing That Divided Gilded Age America*. New York: Pantheon Books, 2006.

Greenspan, Alan. *The Age of Turbulence: Adventures in a New World*. New York: Penguin Press, 2007.

Harford, Tim. *The Undercover Economist: Exposing Why the Rich Are Rich, the Poor Are Poor—and Why You Can Never Buy a Decent Used Car!* Oxford: Oxford University Press, 2006.

Horowitz, Daniel. *Anxieties of Affluence: Critiques of American Consumer Culture, 1939–1979*. Amherst: University of Massachusetts Press, 2004.

Kay, John Anderson. *Culture and Prosperity: The Truth about Markets—Why Some Nations Are Rich but Most Remain Poor*. New York: HarperBusiness, 2004.

Kynge, James. *China Shakes the World: A Titan's Rise and Troubled Future—and the Challenge for America*. Boston: Houghton Mifflin, 2006.

Levy, David M. *How the Dismal Science Got Its Name: Classical Economics and the Ur-Text of Racial Politics*. Ann Arbor: University of Michigan Press, 2001.

Lowenstein, Roger. *Origins of the Crash: The Great Bubble and Its Undoing*. New York: Penguin Books, 2004.

Maugeri, Leonardo. *The Age of Oil: The Mythology, History, and Future of the World's Most Controversial Resource*. Westport, Conn.: Praeger Publishers, 2006.

McMillan, John. *Reinventing the Bazaar: A Natural History of Markets.* New York: Norton, 2002.

Rivoli, Pietra. *The Travels of a T-Shirt in the Global Economy: An Economist Examines the Markets, Power, and Politics of World Trade.* Hoboken, N.J.: John Wiley & Sons, 2005.

Rose, Mike. *The Mind at Work: Valuing the Intelligence of the American Worker.* New York: Viking, 2004.

Sachs, Jeffrey D. *The End of Poverty: Economic Possibilities for Our Time.* New York: Penguin Books, 2006.

Samuelson, Paul A., and William A. Barnett, eds. *Inside the Economist's Mind: Conversations with Eminent Economists.* Oxford: Blackwell, 2007.

Scheidel, Walter, and Sitta Von Reden. *The Ancient Economy.* New York: Routledge, 2002.

Schlosser, Eric. *Reefer Madness: Sex, Drugs, and Cheap Labor in the American Black Market.* Boston: Houghton Mifflin, 2003.

Shlaes, Amity. *The Forgotten Man: A New History of the Great Depression.* New York: HarperCollins Publishers, 2007.

Skidelsky, Robert. *John Maynard Keynes, 1883–1946: Economist, Philosopher, Statesman.* New York: Penguin Books, 2003.

Skousen, Mark. *The Big Three in Economics: Adam Smith, Karl Marx, and John Maynard Keynes.* Armonk, N.Y.: M.E. Sharpe, 2007.

Stalcup, Brenda, ed. *Turning Points in World History— The Industrial Revolution.* San Diego: Greenhaven Press, 2002.

Watson, Bruce. *Bread and Roses: Mills, Migrants, and the Struggle for the American Dream.* New York: Viking, 2005.

Wheelan, Charles J. *Naked Economics: Undressing the Dismal Science.* New York: Norton, 2002.

PERIODICALS

Hardy, Quentin. "Hope and Profit in Africa." *Forbes* (June 18, 2007).

"India on Fire: India's Economy." *The Economist* (February 3, 2007).

"Outsourcing: Old Assumptions Are Being Challenged as the Outsourcing Industry Matures." *The Economist* (July 26, 2007).

Prestowitz, Clyde. "The World Is Tilted: The Popular Idea that America Is One Step Smarter and More Sophisticated than Its Rivals Is a Dangerous Myth, and a Threat to the Global Economy." *Newsweek* (November 28, 2005): p. 16.

"Secrets, Lies, and Sweatshops: American Importers Have Long Answered Criticism of Conditions at their Chinese Suppliers with Labor Rules and Inspections. But Many Factories Have Just Gotten Better at Concealing Abuses." *Business Week* (November 27, 2006).

WEBSITES

Economic Policy Institute. <http://www.epinet.org> (accessed November 9, 2007).

History of Economic Thought Website. <http://cepa.newschool.edu/het> (accessed November 9, 2007).

Peterson Institute for International Economics. <http://www.iie.com> (accessed November 9, 2007).

Public Citizen. <http://www.citizen.org> (accessed November 9, 2007).

World Economic Forum. <http://www.weforum.org/en/index.htm> (accessed November 9, 2007).

PERSONAL MONEY MANAGEMENT
BOOKS

Alford, Ron. *Car Insurance Secrets: The Stuff You Need to Keep You in the Driver's Seat.* Queens, N.Y.: The Plan, 2002.

Altman, Nancy J. *The Battle for Social Security: From FDR's Vision to Bush's Gamble.* Hoboken, N.J.: J. Wiley, 2005.

Davis, Kristin. *Financing College: How Much You'll Really Have to Pay and How to Get the Money.* 3rd ed. Washington, D.C.: Kiplinger Books, 2007.

Ehrenreich, Barbara. *Nickeled and Dimed: On (Not) Getting By in America.* New York: Metropolitan Books, 2001.

Ellenbogen, Michael. *The Insider's Guide to Saving Money.* Victoria, Canada: Trafford Publishing, 2005.

Fives, Theresa, and Holly Popowski. *Getting through College without Going Broke: A Crash Course on Finding Money for College and Making It Last.* New York: Prentice Hall Press, 2005.

Fowles, Debby. *1000 Best Smart Money Secrets for Students.* Naperville, Ill.: Sourcebooks, 2005.

Gary, Tracy. *Inspired Philanthropy: Your Step-by-Step Guide to Creating a Giving Plan and Leaving a Legacy.* 3rd ed. San Francisco: Jossey-Bass, 2008.

Harris, Nancy, and Helen Kothran, eds. *Does the United States Need a National Health Insurance Policy?* Detroit: Greenhaven Press, 2006.

Hock, Dee. *One from Many: Visa and the Rise of the Chaordic Organization.* San Francisco: Berrett-Koehler, 2005.

Jones, Brian T. *Getting Started: The Financial Guide for a Younger Generation.* Potomac, Md.: Larstan Publishing, 2006.

Karger, Howard Jacob. *Shortchanged: Life and Debt in the Fringe Economy.* San Francisco: Berrett-Koehler, 2005.

Modu, Emmanuel, and Andrea Walker. *Mad Cash: A First Timer's Guide to Investing $30 to $3,000.* New York: Penguin Books, 2003.

Newlin, Kate. *Shopportunity: How to Be a Retail Revolutionary.* New York: Collins, 2006.

Orman, Suze. *The Money Book for the Young, Fabulous & Broke.* New York: Riverhead Books, 2005.

Schor, Juliet B. *Born to Buy: The Commercialized Child and the New Consumer Culture.* New York: Scribner, 2005.

Shipler, David K. *The Working Poor: Forgotten in America.* New York: Vintage Books, 2005.

Silver, Don. *High School Money Book.* Los Angeles: Adams-Hall Publishing, 2007.

Weiner, Erik J. *What Goes Up: The Uncensored History of Modern Wall Street as Told by the Bankers, Brokers, CEOs, and Scoundrels Who Made It Happen.* New York: Little, Brown and Co., 2005.

Yancey, Richard. *Confessions of a Tax Collector: One Man's Tour of Duty Inside the IRS.* New York: HarperCollins, 2004.

PERIODICALS

Conlin, Michelle, with Jessi Hempel. "Unmarried America: Say Good-bye to the Traditional Family. Here's How the New Demographics Will Change Business and Society." *Business Week* (October 20, 2003): p. 106.

Der Hovanesian, Mara. "Nightmare Mortgages." *Business Week* (September 11, 2006): p. 70.

Grow, Brian, and Keith Epstein. "The Poverty Business: Inside U.S. Companies' Audacious Drive to Extract More Profits from the Nation's Working Poor." *Business Week* (May 21, 2007): p. 56.

Ordoñez, Jennifer. "Baby Needs a New Pair of Shoes." *Newsweek* (May 14, 2007): p. 50.

Walczak, Lee, and Richard S. Dunham. "'I Want My Safety Net.'" *Business Week* (May 16, 2005): p. 24.

WEBSITES

GoodPayer: Education for Financial Wellness. <http://www.goodpayer.com> (accessed November 9, 2007).

Practical Money Skills for Life. <http://www.practicalmoneyskills.com/english/index.php> (accessed November 9, 2007).

SmartMoney. <http://www.smartmoney.com> (accessed November 9, 2007).

360 Degrees of Financial Literacy. <http://www.360financialliteracy.org> (accessed November 9, 2007).

Young Money. "A leading national money, business and lifestyle magazine written primarily by student journalists." <http://www.youngmoney.com> (accessed November 9, 2007).

ENTREPRENEURSHIP
BOOKS

Adamson, Allen P. *BrandSimple: How the Best Brands Keep It Simple and Succeed.* New York: Palgrave Macmillan, 2006.

Battelle, John. *The Search: How Google and Its Rivals Rewrote the Rules of Business and Transformed Our Culture.* New York: Portfolio, 2005.

Baumol, William J., Robert E. Litan, and Carl J. Schramm. *Good Capitalism, Bad Capitalism, and the Economics of Growth and Prosperity.* New Haven, Conn.: Yale University Press, 2007.

Buchholz, Todd G. *New Ideas from Dead CEOs: Lasting Lessons from the Corner Office.* New York: Collins, 2007.

Cantando, Mary, with Laurie Zuckerman. *Nine Lives: Stories of Women Business Owners Landing on Their Feet.* Raleigh, N.C.: Cantando & Associates, 2003.

Capparell, Stephanie. *The Real Pepsi Challenge: The Inspirational Story of Breaking the Color Barrier in American Business.* New York: Free Press, 2007.

Cobbs, Price M., and Judith L. Turnock. *Cracking the Corporate Code: The Revealing Success Stories of 32 African-American Executives.* New York: American Management Association, 2003.

Conley, Chip, and Eric Friedenwald-Fishman. *Marketing That Matters: 10 Practices to Profit Your Business and Change the World.* San Francisco: Berrett-Koehler, 2006.

Drachman, Virginia G. *Enterprising Women: 250 Years of American Business.* Chapel Hill: University of North Carolina Press, 2002.

Esty, Daniel C., and Andrew S. Winston. *Green to Gold: How Smart Companies Use Environmental Strategy to Innovate, Create Value, and Build Competitive Advantage.* New Haven, Conn.: Yale University Press, 2006.

Evans, Harold, with Gail Buckland and David Lefer. *They Made America: From the Steam Engine to the Search Engine: Two Centuries of Innovators.* New York: Little, Brown and Co., 2004.

Gloor, Peter A., and Scott Cooper. *Coolhunting: Chasing Down the Next Big Thing.* New York: AMACOM, 2007.

Hughes, Mark. *Buzzmarketing: Get People to Talk About Your Stuff.* New York: Portfolio, 2005.

Koehn, Nancy F. *Brand New: How Entrepreneurs Earned Consumers' Trust from Wedgwood to Dell.* Boston: Harvard Business School Press, 2001.

Krass, Peter. *Carnegie.* New Jersey: John Wiley and Sons, 2003.

McCraw, Thomas H. *Prophet of Innovation: Joseph Schumpeter and Creative Destruction.* Cambridge, Mass.: Belknap Press of Harvard University Press, 2007.

Morris, Charles R. *The Tycoons: How Andrew Carnegie, John D. Rockefeller, Jay Gould, and J. P. Morgan Invented the American Supereconomy.* New York: H. Holt and Co., 2005.

Newton, Lisa H. *Permission to Steal: Revealing the Roots of Corporate Scandal.* Malden, Mass.; Oxford: Blackwell Publishing, 2006.

O'Loughlin, James. *The Real Warren Buffet: Managing Capital, Leading People.* London: Nicholas Brealey Publishing, 2003.

Parker, Ciarán. *The Thinkers 50: The World's Most Influential Business Writers and Leaders.* Westport, Conn.: Praeger Publishers, 2006.

Ridgway, Nicole. *The Running of the Bulls: Inside the Cutthroat Race from Wharton to Wall Street.* New York: Gotham Books, 2006.

Savitz, Andrew W., and Karl Weber. *The Triple Bottom Line: How Today's Best-Run Companies Are Achieving Economic, Social and Environmental Success—and How You Can Too.* San Francisco: Jossey-Bass, 2006.

Schiffman, Stephan. *The Young Entrepreneur's Guide to Business Terms.* New York: Franklin Watts, 2003.

Tapscott, Don, and Anthony D. Williams. *Wikinomics: How Mass Collaboration Changes Everything.* New York: Portfolio, 2006.

Watson, Joe. *Without Excuses: Unleash the Power of Diversity to Build Your Business.* New York: St. Martin's Press, 2006.

Zygmont, Jeffrey. *Microchip: An Idea, Its Genesis, and the Revolution It Created.* Cambridge, Mass.: Perseus, 2003.

PERIODICALS

"The Battle for Brainpower." *The Economist* (October 5, 2006).

Byrnes, Nanette. "Secrets of the Male Shopper." *Business Week* (September 4, 2006): p. 44.

Frauenheim, Ed. "Your Co-Worker, Your Teacher: Collaborative Technology Speeds Peer-Peer Learning." *Workforce Management* (January 29, 2007): p. 19.

Grow, Brian. "Hispanic Nation." *Business Week* (March 15, 2004): p. 58.

McGregor, Jena. "How Failure Breeds Success." *Business Week* (July 10, 2006).

WEBSITES

AllBusiness. <http://www.allbusiness.com> (accessed November 9, 2007).

Entrepreneur Magazine. <http://www.entrepreneur.com/> (accessed November 9, 2007).

Franchising.com. <http://www.franchising.com> (accessed November 9, 2007).

Idea Cafe. <http://www.businessownersideacafe.com> (accessed November 9, 2007).

Startup Journal. <http://www.startupjournal.com/> (accessed November 9, 2007).

Index

Italic type indicates volume numbers. Illustrations are marked by (ill.)

10/10